Code X8/10-99

Renault Owners Workshop Manual

Peter G Strasman

Models covered
Renault 5, L, TL, GTL, TS, TX, Gordini and
Gordini Turbo, including Automatic, Le Car 2 and
special edition models
845 cc, 956 cc, 1108 cc, 1289 cc and 1397 cc

Does not cover 'New 5' or mid-engined Turbo models

THE BOOK

(141-10U6)

ABCDE
FGH

2

Haynes Publishing
Sparkford Nr Yeovil
Somerset BA22 7JJ England

Haynes Publications, Inc
861 Lawrence Drive
Newbury Park
California 91320 USA

Acknowledgements

Thanks are due to Champion Spark Plug who supplied the illustrations showing spark plug conditions, to Holt Lloyd Limited who supplied the illustrations showing bodywork repair, and to Duckhams Oils who provided lubrication data. Thanks are also due to Regie Renault, particularly Renault Limited (UK) for their assistance with technical information and the provision of certain illustrations. Sykes-Pickavant provided some of the workshop tools. Lastly, thanks are due to all those people at Sparkford who assisted in the production of this manual.

© **Haynes Publishing Group 1992**

A book in the **Haynes Owners Workshop Manual Series**

Printed by **J. H. Haynes & Co. Ltd, Sparkford, Nr Yeovil, Somerset BA22 7JJ, England**

ISBN 1 85010 190 6

British Library Cataloguing in Publication Data
Strasman Peter G.
  Renault 5 ('72 to '85) owners workshop manual.
  –(Owners Workshop Manual)
  1. Renault automobile
  I. Title II. Series
  629.28'722   TL215.R4
  ISBN 1-85010-190-6

We take great pride in the accuracy of information given in this manual, but vehicle manufacturers make alterations and design changes during the production run of a particular vehicle of which they do not inform us. No liability can be accepted by the authors or publishers for loss, damage or injury caused by any errors in, or omissions from, the information given.

Restoring and Preserving our Motoring Heritage

Few people can have had the luck to realise their dreams to quite the same extent and in such a remarkable fashion as John Haynes, Founder and Chairman of the Haynes Publishing Group.

Since 1965 his unique approach to workshop manual publishing has proved so successful that millions of Haynes Manuals are now sold every year throughout the world, covering literally thousands of different makes and models of cars, vans and motorcycles.

A continuing passion for cars and motoring led to the founding in 1985 of a Charitable Trust dedicated to the restoration and preservation of our motoring heritage. To inaugurate the new Museum, John Haynes donated virtually his entire private collection of 52 cars.

Now with an unrivalled international collection of over 210 veteran, vintage and classic cars and motorcycles, the Haynes Motor Museum in Somerset is well on the way to becoming one of the most interesting Motor Museums in the world.

A 70 seat video cinema, a cafe and an extensive motoring bookshop, together with a specially constructed one kilometre motor circuit, make a visit to the Haynes Motor Museum a truly unforgettable experience.

Every vehicle in the museum is preserved in as near as possible mint condition and each car is run every six months on the motor circuit.

Enjoy the picnic area set amongst the rolling Somerset hills. Peer through the William Morris workshop windows at cars being restored, and browse through the extensive displays of fascinating motoring memorabilia.

From the 1903 Oldsmobile through such classics as an MG Midget to the mighty 'E' type Jaguar, Lamborghini, Ferrari Berlinetta Boxer, and Graham Hill's Lola Cosworth, there is something for everyone, young and old alike, at this Somerset Museum.

Haynes Motor Museum

Situated mid-way between London and Penzance, the Haynes Motor Museum is located just off the A303 at Sparkford, Somerset (home of the Haynes Manual) and is open to the public 7 days a week all year round, except Christmas Day and Boxing Day.

Telephone 01963 440804.

Contents

Spark plug condition and bodywork repair colour pages between pages 32 and 33

Renault 5 (UK model)

Renault 5 Gordini Turbo (UK model)

About this manual

Its aim

The aim of this manual is to help you get the best value from your vehicle. It can do so in several ways. It can help you decide what work must be done (even should you choose to get it done by a garage), provide information on routine maintenance and servicing, and give a logical course of action and diagnosis when random faults occur. However, it is hoped that you will use the manual by tackling the work yourself. On simpler jobs it may even be quicker than booking the car into a garage and going there twice, to leave and collect it. Perhaps most important, a lot of money can be saved by avoiding the costs a garage must charge to cover its labour and overheads.

The manual has drawings and descriptions to show the function of the various components so that their layout can be understood. Then the tasks are described and photographed in a step-by-step sequence so that even a novice can do the work.

Its arrangement

The manual is divided into thirteen Chapters, each covering a logical sub-division of the vehicle. The Chapters are each divided into Sections, numbered with single figures, eg 5; and the Sections into paragraphs (or sub-sections), with decimal numbers following on from the Section they are in, eg 5.1, 5.2, 5.3 etc.

It is freely illustrated, especially in those parts where there is a detailed sequence of operations to be carried out. There are two forms of illustration: figures and photographs. The figures are numbered in sequence with decimal numbers, according to their position in the Chapter – eg Fig. 6.4 is the fourth drawing/illustration in Chapter 6. Photographs carry the same number (either individually or in related groups) as the Section or sub-section to which they relate.

There is an alphabetical index at the back of the manual as well as a contents list at the front. Each Chapter is also preceded by its own individual contents list.

References to the 'left' or 'right' of the vehicle are in the sense of a person in the driver's seat facing forwards.

Unless otherwise stated, nuts and bolts are removed by turning anti-clockwise, and tightened by turning clockwise.

Vehicle manufacturers continually make changes to specifications and recommendations, and these, when notified, are incorporated into our manuals at the earliest opportunity.

We take great pride in the accuracy of information given in this manual, but vehicle manufacturers make alterations and design changes during the production run of a particular vehicle of which they do not inform us. No liability can be accepted by the authors or publishers for loss, damage or injury caused by any errors in, or omissions from, the information given.

Introduction to the Renault 5

The Renault 5 was introduced as a three-door hatchback in 1972 using an 845cc overhead valve engine. Since then the engine capacity has been progressively increased. Five-door and automatic versions have also become available.

The car is a conventional front wheel drive vehicle which should present few difficulties in servicing or overhaul. The length of its production run ensures ample availability of new pattern and secondhand spares.

All models in the range provide good performance, a comfortable ride and fuel economy whether powered by the smallest engine or the latest turbocharged unit.

Fault diagnosis

Introduction

The vehicle owner who does his or her own maintenance according to the recommended schedules should not have to use this section of the manual very often. Modern component reliability is such that, provided those items subject to wear or deterioration are inspected or renewed at the specified intervals, sudden failure is comparatively rare. Faults do not usually just happen as a result of sudden failure, but develop over a period of time. Major mechanical failures in particular are usually preceded by characteristic symptoms over hundreds or even thousands of miles. Those components which do occasionally fail without warning are often small and easily carried in the vehicle.

With any fault finding, the first step is to decide where to begin investigations. Sometimes this is obvious, but on other occasions a little detective work will be necessary. The owner who makes half a dozen haphazard adjustments or replacements may be successful in curing a fault (or its symptoms), but he will be none the wiser if the fault recurs and he may well have spent more time and money than was necessary. A calm and logical approach will be found to be more satisfactory in the long run. Always take into account any warning signs or abnormalities that may have been noticed in the period preceding the fault – power loss, high or low gauge readings, unusual noises or smells, etc – and remember that failure of components such as fuses or spark plugs may only be pointers to some underlying fault.

The pages which follow here are intended to help in cases of failure to start or breakdown on the road. There is also a Fault Diagnosis Section at the end of each Chapter which should be consulted if the preliminary checks prove unfruitful. Whatever the fault, certain basic principles apply. These are as follows:

Verify the fault. This is simply a matter of being sure that you know what the symptoms are before starting work. This is particularly important if you are investigating a fault for someone else who may not have described it very accurately.

Don't overlook the obvious. For example, if the vehicle won't start, is there petrol in the tank? (Don't take anyone else's word on this particular point, and don't trust the fuel gauge either!) If an electrical fault is indicated, look for loose or broken wires before digging out the test gear.

Cure the disease, not the symptom. Substituting a flat battery with a fully charged one will get you off the hard shoulder, but if the underlying cause is not attended to, the new battery will go the same way. Similarly, changing oil-fouled spark plugs for a new set will get you moving again, but remember that the reason for the fouling (if it wasn't simply an incorrect grade of plug) will have to be established and corrected.

Don't take anything for granted. Particularly, don't forget that a 'new' component may itself be defective (especially if it's been rattling round in the boot for months), and don't leave components out of a fault diagnosis sequence just because they are new or recently fitted. When you do finally diagnose a difficult fault, you'll probably realise that all the evidence was there from the start.

Electrical faults

Electrical faults can be more puzzling than straightforward mechanical failures, but they are no less susceptible to logical analysis if the basic principles of operation are understood. Vehicle electrical wiring exists in extremely unfavourable conditions – heat, vibration and chemical attack – and the first things to look for are loose or corroded connections and broken or chafed wires, especially where the wires pass through holes in the bodywork or are subject to vibration.

All metal-bodied vehicles in current production have one pole of the battery 'earthed', ie connected to the vehicle bodywork, and in nearly all modern vehicles it is the negative (–) terminal. The various electrical components – motors, bulb holders etc – are also connected to earth, either by means of a lead or directly by their mountings. Electric current flows through the component and then back to the battery via the bodywork. If the component mounting is loose or corroded, or if a good path back to the battery is not available, the circuit will be incomplete and malfunction will result. The engine and/or gearbox are also earthed by means of flexible metal straps to the body or subframe; if these straps are loose or missing, starter motor, generator and ignition trouble may result.

Assuming the earth return to be satisfactory, electrical faults will be due either to component malfunction or to defects in the current supply. Individual components are dealt with in Chapter 10. If supply wires are broken or cracked internally this results in an open-circuit, and the easiest way to check for this is to bypass the suspect wire temporarily with a length of wire having a crocodile clip or suitable connector at each end. Alternatively, a 12V test lamp can be used to verify the presence of supply voltage at various points along the wire and the break can be thus isolated.

If a bare portion of a live wire touches the bodywork or other earthed metal part, the electricity will take the low-resistance path thus formed back to the battery: this is known as a short-circuit. Hopefully a short-circuit will blow a fuse, but otherwise it may cause burning of the insulation (and possibly further short-circuits) or even a fire. This is why it is inadvisable to bypass persistently blowing fuses with silver foil or wire.

Spares and tool kit

Most vehicles are supplied only with sufficient tools for wheel changing; the *Maintenance and minor repair* tool kit detailed in *Tools and working facilities*, with the addition of a hammer, is probably sufficient for those repairs that most motorists would consider attempting at the roadside. In addition a few items which can be fitted without too much trouble in the event of a breakdown should be carried. Experience and available space will modify the list below, but the following may save having to call on professional assistance:

Spark plugs, clean and correctly gapped
HT lead and plug cap – long enough to reach the plug furthest from the distributor
Distributor rotor, condenser and contact breaker points
Drivebelt(s) – emergency type may suffice
Spare fuses
Set of principal light bulbs
Tin of radiator sealer and hose bandage
Exhaust bandage
Roll of insulating tape
Length of soft iron wire
Length of electrical flex
Torch or inspection lamp (can double as test lamp)
Battery jump leads
Tow-rope
Ignition water dispersant aerosol
Litre of engine oil
Sealed can of hydraulic fluid
Emergency windscreen
Worm drive hose clips

If spare fuel is carried, a can designed for the purpose should be used to minimise risks of leakage and collision damage. A first aid kit and a warning triangle, whilst not at present compulsory in the UK, are obviously sensible items to carry in addition to the above.

When touring abroad it may be advisable to carry additional spares which, even if you cannot fit them yourself, could save having to wait while parts are obtained. The items below may be worth considering:

Clutch and throttle cables
Cylinder head gasket
Dynamo or alternator brushes
Fuel pump repair kit
Tyre valve core

One of the motoring organisations will be able to advise on availability of fuel etc in foreign countries.

Engine will not start

Engine fails to turn when starter operated

Flat battery (recharge, use jump leads, or push start)
Battery terminals loose or corroded
Battery earth to body defective

Engine earth strap loose or broken
Starter motor (or solenoid) wiring loose or broken
Automatic transmission selector in wrong position, or inhibitor switch faulty
Ignition/starter switch faulty
Major mechanical failure (seizure)
Starter or solenoid internal fault (see Chapter 10)

Starter motor turns engine slowly
Partially discharged battery (recharge, use jump leads, or push start)
Battery terminals loose or corroded
Battery earth to body defective
Engine earth strap loose
Starter motor (or solenoid) wiring loose
Starter motor internal fault (see Chapter 10)

Starter motor spins without turning engine
Flat battery
Flywheel gear teeth damaged or worn
Starter motor mounting bolts loose

Engine turns normally but fails to start
Damp or dirty HT leads and distributor cap – crank engine and check for spark, or try a moisture dispersant such as Holts Wet Start.
Dirty or incorrectly gapped distributor points (if applicable)
No fuel in tank (check for delivery at carburettor)
Excessive choke (hot engine) or insufficient choke (cold engine)
Fouled or incorrectly gapped spark plugs (remove and regap, or renew)
Other ignition system fault (see Chapter 4)
Other fuel system fault (see Chapter 3)
Poor compression (see Chapter 1)
Major mechanical failure (eg camshaft drive)

Engine fires but will not run
Insufficient choke (cold engine)
Air leaks at carburettor or inlet manifold
Fuel starvation (see Chapter 3)
Ignition fault (see Chapter 4)

Engine cuts out and will not restart

Engine cuts out suddenly – ignition fault
Loose or disconnected LT wires
Wet HT leads or distributor cap (after traversing water splash)
Coil or condenser failure (check for spark)
Other ignition fault (see Chapter 4)

Engine misfires before cutting out – fuel fault
Fuel tank empty
Fuel pump defective or filter blocked (check for delivery)
Fuel tank filler vent blocked (suction will be evident on releasing cap)
Fuel inlet needle valve sticking
Carburettor jets blocked (fuel contaminated)
Other fuel system fault (see Chapter 3)

Engine cuts out – other causes
Serious overheating
Major mechanical failure (eg camshaft drive)

Engine overheats

Ignition (no-charge) warning light illuminated
Slack or broken drivebelt – retension or renew (Chapter 2)

Ignition warning light not illuminated
Coolant loss due to internal or external leakage (see Chapter 2)
Thermostat defective
Low oil level
Brakes binding
Radiator clogged externally or internally
Electric cooling fan not operating correctly
Engine waterways clogged
Ignition timing incorrect or automatic advance malfunctioning
Mixture too weak

Note: *Do not add cold water to an overheated engine or damage may result*

Low engine oil pressure

Gauge reads low or warning light illuminated with engine running
Oil level low or incorrect grade
Defective gauge or warning lamp sender unit
Wire to sender unit earthed
Engine overheating
Oil filter clogged or bypass valve defective
Oil pressure relief valve defective
Oil pick-up strainer clogged
Oil pump worn or mountings loose
Worn main or big-end bearings
Note: *Low oil pressure in a high-mileage engine at tickover is not necessarily a cause for concern. Sudden pressure loss at speed is far more significant. In any event, check the gauge or warning light sender before condemning the engine.*

Engine noises

Pre-ignition (pinking) on acceleration
Incorrect grade of fuel
Ignition timing incorrect
Distributor faulty or worn
Worn or maladjusted carburettor
Excessive carbon build-up in engine

Whistling or wheezing noises
Leaking vacuum hose
Leaking carburettor or manifold gasket
Blowing head gasket

Tapping or rattling
Incorrect valve clearances
Worn valve gear
Worn timing chain
Broken piston ring (ticking noise)

Knocking or thumping
Unintentional mechanical contact (eg fan blades)
Worn fanbelt
Peripheral component fault (generator, water pump etc)
Worn big-end bearings (regular heavy knocking, perhaps less under load)
Worn main bearings (rumbling and knocking, perhaps worsening under load)
Piston slap (most noticeable when cold)

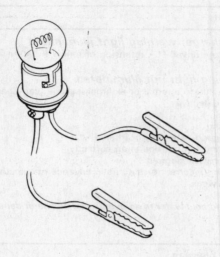

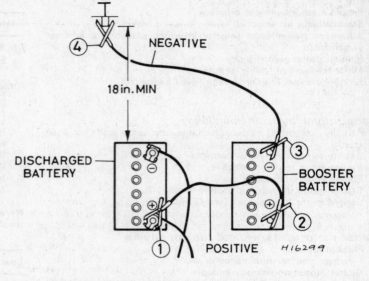

A simple test lamp is useful for checking electrical faults

Jump start lead connections for negative earth vehicles –
connect leads in order shown

NEGATIVE

18 in. MIN

DISCHARGED BATTERY

BOOSTER BATTERY

POSITIVE

H16299

Carrying a few spares can save you a long walk!

Safety first!

Professional motor mechanics are trained in safe working procedures. However enthusiastic you may be about getting on with the job in hand, do take the time to ensure that your safety is not put at risk. A moment's lack of attention can result in an accident, as can failure to observe certain elementary precautions.

There will always be new ways of having accidents, and the following points do not pretend to be a comprehensive list of all dangers; they are intended rather to make you aware of the risks and to encourage a safety-conscious approach to all work you carry out on your vehicle.

Essential DOs and DON'Ts

DON'T rely on a single jack when working underneath the vehicle. Always use reliable additional means of support, such as axle stands, securely placed under a part of the vehicle that you know will not give way.

DON'T attempt to loosen or tighten high-torque nuts (e.g. wheel hub nuts) while the vehicle is on a jack; it may be pulled off.

DON'T start the engine without first ascertaining that the transmission is in neutral (or 'Park' where applicable) and the parking brake applied.

DON'T suddenly remove the filler cap from a hot cooling system – cover it with a cloth and release the pressure gradually first, or you may get scalded by escaping coolant.

DON'T attempt to drain oil until you are sure it has cooled sufficiently to avoid scalding you.

DON'T grasp any part of the engine, exhaust or catalytic converter without first ascertaining that it is sufficiently cool to avoid burning you.

DON'T allow brake fluid or antifreeze to contact vehicle paintwork.

DON'T syphon toxic liquids such as fuel, brake fluid or antifreeze by mouth, or allow them to remain on your skin.

DON'T inhale dust – it may be injurious to health (see *Asbestos* below).

DON'T allow any spilt oil or grease to remain on the floor – wipe it up straight away, before someone slips on it.

DON'T use ill-fitting spanners or other tools which may slip and cause injury.

DON'T attempt to lift a heavy component which may be beyond your capability – get assistance.

DON'T rush to finish a job, or take unverified short cuts.

DON'T allow children or animals in or around an unattended vehicle.

DO wear eye protection when using power tools such as drill, sander, bench grinder etc, and when working under the vehicle.

DO use a barrier cream on your hands prior to undertaking dirty jobs – it will protect your skin from infection as well as making the dirt easier to remove afterwards; but make sure your hands aren't left slippery. Note that long-term contact with used engine oil can be a health hazard.

DO keep loose clothing (cuffs, tie etc) and long hair well out of the way of moving mechanical parts.

DO remove rings, wristwatch etc, before working on the vehicle – especially the electrical system.

DO ensure that any lifting tackle used has a safe working load rating adequate for the job.

DO keep your work area tidy – it is only too easy to fall over articles left lying around.

DO get someone to check periodically that all is well, when working alone on the vehicle.

DO carry out work in a logical sequence and check that everything is correctly assembled and tightened afterwards.

DO remember that your vehicle's safety affects that of yourself and others. If in doubt on any point, get specialist advice.

IF, in spite of following these precautions, you are unfortunate enough to injure yourself, seek medical attention as soon as possible.

Asbestos

Certain friction, insulating, sealing, and other products – such as brake linings, brake bands, clutch linings, torque converters, gaskets, etc – contain asbestos. *Extreme care must be taken to avoid inhalation of dust from such products since it is hazardous to health.* If in doubt, assume that they *do* contain asbestos.

Fire

Remember at all times that petrol (gasoline) is highly flammable. Never smoke, or have any kind of naked flame around, when working on the vehicle. But the risk does not end there – a spark caused by an electrical short-circuit, by two metal surfaces contacting each other, by careless use of tools, or even by static electricity built up in your body under certain conditions, can ignite petrol vapour, which in a confined space is highly explosive.

Always disconnect the battery earth (ground) terminal before working on any part of the fuel or electrical system, and never risk spilling fuel on to a hot engine or exhaust.

It is recommended that a fire extinguisher of a type suitable for fuel and electrical fires is kept handy in the garage or workplace at all times. Never try to extinguish a fuel or electrical fire with water.

Note: *Any reference to a 'torch' appearing in this manual should always be taken to mean a hand-held battery-operated electric lamp or flashlight. It does NOT mean a welding/gas torch or blowlamp.*

Fumes

Certain fumes are highly toxic and can quickly cause unconsciousness and even death if inhaled to any extent. Petrol (gasoline) vapour comes into this category, as do the vapours from certain solvents such as trichloroethylene. Any draining or pouring of such volatile fluids should be done in a well ventilated area.

When using cleaning fluids and solvents, read the instructions carefully. Never use materials from unmarked containers – they may give off poisonous vapours.

Never run the engine of a motor vehicle in an enclosed space such as a garage. Exhaust fumes contain carbon monoxide which is extremely poisonous; if you need to run the engine, always do so in the open air or at least have the rear of the vehicle outside the workplace.

If you are fortunate enough to have the use of an inspection pit, never drain or pour petrol, and never run the engine, while the vehicle is standing over it; the fumes, being heavier than air, will concentrate in the pit with possibly lethal results.

The battery

Never cause a spark, or allow a naked light, near the vehicle's battery. It will normally be giving off a certain amount of hydrogen gas, which is highly explosive.

Always disconnect the battery earth (ground) terminal before working on the fuel or electrical systems.

If possible, loosen the filler plugs or cover when charging the battery from an external source. Do not charge at an excessive rate or the battery may burst.

Take care when topping up and when carrying the battery. The acid electrolyte, even when diluted, is very corrosive and should not be allowed to contact the eyes or skin.

If you ever need to prepare electrolyte yourself, always add the acid slowly to the water, and never the other way round. Protect against splashes by wearing rubber gloves and goggles.

When jump starting a car using a booster battery, for negative earth (ground) vehicles, connect the jump leads in the following sequence: First connect one jump lead between the positive (+) terminals of the two batteries. Then connect the other jump lead first to the negative (–) terminal of the booster battery, and then to a good earthing (ground) point on the vehicle to be started, at least 18 in (45 cm) from the battery if possible. Ensure that hands and jump leads are clear of any moving parts, and that the two vehicles do not touch. Disconnect the leads in the reverse order.

Mains electricity and electrical equipment

When using an electric power tool, inspection light etc, always ensure that the appliance is correctly connected to its plug and that, where necessary, it is properly earthed (grounded). Do not use such appliances in damp conditions and, again, beware of creating a spark or applying excessive heat in the vicinity of fuel or fuel vapour. Also ensure that the appliances meet the relevant national safety standards.

Ignition HT voltage

A severe electric shock can result from touching certain parts of the ignition system, such as the HT leads, when the engine is running or being cranked, particularly if components are damp or the insulation is defective. Where an electronic ignition system is fitted, the HT voltage is much higher and could prove fatal.

General dimensions and weights

The following values are all typical

Dimensions
Overall length
N. American models	3617 mm (142.5 in)
R1223 and 122B	3555 mm (140.1 in)
All other models	3506 mm (138.1 in)

Overall width
N. American models	1525 mm (60.1 in)
R1225	1549 mm (61.0 in)
All other models	1525 mm (60.1 in)

Height (unladen)
N. American models	1400 mm (55.2 in)
R1223 and 122B	1395 mm (55.0 in)
All other models	1400 mm (55.2 in)

Wheelbase
N. American models:	
LH	2434 mm (95.9 in)
RH	2404 mm (94.7 in)
R1223 and 122B:	
LH	2442 mm (96.2 in)
RH	2412 mm (95.0 in)
All other models:	
LH	2434 mm (95.9 in)
RH	2404 mm (94.7 in)

Front track
N. American models	1288 mm (50.7 in)
R1223 and 122B	1294 mm (51.0 in)
All other models	1280 mm (50.4 in)

Rear track
N. American models	1244 mm (49.0 in)
R1223 and 122B	1254 mm (49.4 in)
All other models:	
Before Nov. 1975	1240 mm (48.9 in)
After Nov. 1975	1244 mm (49.0 in)

Ground clearance (laden)
All models	130 mm (5.12 in)

Weights
Kerb weight
North American models	825 kg (1819 lb)
R1223	850 kg (1874 lb)
122B	870 kg (1918 lb)
All other models	775 kg (1709 lb)

Towing weights
All models:	
Trailer without brakes	410 kg (904 lb)
Trailer with brakes	453 kg (999 lb)

Renault 5 La Cinq (USA model)

Buying spare parts and vehicle identification numbers

Buying spare parts

Spare parts are available from many sources, for example: Renault garages, other garages and accessory shops, and motor factors. Our advice regarding spare part sources is as follows:

Officially appointed Renault garages: These will be the best source of parts which are peculiar to your car and are otherwise not generally available (eg complete cylinder heads, internal gearbox components, badges, interior trim etc). It is also the only place at which you should buy parts if your car is still under warranty; non-Renault components may invalidate the warranty. To be sure of obtaining the correct parts it will always be necessary to give the storeman your car's vehicle identification number, and if possible, to take the 'old' part along for positive identification. Remember that many parts are available on a factory exchange scheme – any parts returned should always be clean! It obviously makes good sense to go straight to the specialists on your car for this type of part for they are best equipped to supply you.

Other garages and accessory shops: These are often very good places to buy materials and components needed for the maintenance of your car (eg oil filters, spark plugs, bulbs, fan belts, oils and greases, touch-up paint, filler paste etc). They also sell general accessories, usually have convenient opening hours, charge lower prices and can often be found not far from home.

Motor factors: Good factors will stock all of the more important components which wear out relatively quickly (eg clutch components, pistons, valves, exhaust systems, brake cylinders/-pipes/hoses/seals/shoes and pads etc). Motor factors will often provide new or reconditioned components on a part exchange basis – this can save a considerable amount of money.

Vehicle identification numbers

Modifications are a continuing and unpublished process in vehicle manufacture, quite apart from major model changes. Spare parts manuals and lists are compiled upon a numerical basis, the individual vehicle numbers being essential to correct identification of the component required.

All of the models in this manual are known as the Renault 5 – however, there are considerable specification differences. You should acquaint yourself with your car's model number (oval plate), as most model differences are indicated in this manual by reference to those numbers.

The storeman will also need to know the *oval plate number* (photo) under all circumstances. For engine and transmission parts he will need to know the *engine number* and the *gearbox number* respectively in addition. For certain chassis and body parts he may need to know the *diamond (or rectangular) plate number* (photo). The *paint code* may be required if the shade of the car is not easily described. This is given by means of an adhesive label, or on later models it is included on the oval plate. All these numbers are located in readily visible places.

Vehicle identification oval plate

Vehicle production detail plate

Tools and working facilities

Introduction

A selection of good tools is a fundamental requirement for anyone contemplating the maintenance and repair of a motor vehicle. For the owner who does not possess any, their purchase will prove a considerable expense, offsetting some of the savings made by doing-it-yourself. However, provided that the tools purchased meet the relevant national safety standards and are of good quality, they will last for many years and prove an extremely worthwhile investment.

To help the average owner to decide which tools are needed to carry out the various tasks detailed in this manual, we have compiled three lists of tools under the following headings: *Maintenance and minor repair, Repair and overhaul,* and *Special.* The newcomer to practical mechanics should start off with the *Maintenance and minor repair* tool kit and confine himself to the simpler jobs around the vehicle. Then, as his confidence and experience grow, he can undertake more difficult tasks, buying extra tools as, and when, they are needed. In this way, a *Maintenance and minor repair* tool kit can be built-up into a *Repair and overhaul* tool kit over a considerable period of time without any major cash outlays. The experienced do-it-yourselfer will have a tool kit good enough for most repair and overhaul procedures and will add tools from the *Special* category when he feels the expense is justified by the amount of use to which these tools will be put.

It is obviously not possible to cover the subject of tools fully here. For those who wish to learn more about tools and their use there is a book entitled *How to Choose and Use Car Tools* available from the publishers of this manual.

Maintenance and minor repair tool kit

The tools given in this list should be considered as a minimum requirement if routine maintenance, servicing and minor repair operations are to be undertaken. We recommend the purchase of combination spanners (ring one end, open-ended the other); although more expensive than open-ended ones, they do give the advantages of both types of spanner.

> Combination spanners - 10, 11, 12, 13, 14 & 17 mm
> Adjustable spanner - 9 inch
> Engine sump/gearbox/rear axle drain plug key
> Spark plug spanner (with rubber insert)
> Spark plug gap adjustment tool
> Set of feeler gauges
> Brake adjuster spanner
> Brake bleed nipple spanner
> Screwdriver - 4 in long x $\frac{1}{4}$ in dia (flat blade)
> Screwdriver - 4 in long x $\frac{1}{4}$ in dia (cross blade)
> Combination pliers - 6 inch
> Hacksaw (junior)
> Tyre pump
> Tyre pressure gauge
> Grease gun
> Oil can
> Fine emery cloth (1 sheet)
> Wire brush (small)
> Funnel (medium size)

Repair and overhaul tool kit

These tools are virtually essential for anyone undertaking any major repairs to a motor vehicle, and are additional to those given in the *Maintenance and minor repair* list. Included in this list is a comprehensive set of sockets. Although these are expensive they will be found invaluable as they are so versatile - particularly if various drives are included in the set. We recommend the $\frac{1}{2}$ in square-drive type, as this can be used with most proprietary torque wrenches. If you cannot afford a socket set, even bought piecemeal, then inexpensive tubular box spanners are a useful alternative.

The tools in this list will occasionally need to be supplemented by tools from the *Special* list.

> Sockets (or box spanners) to cover range in previous list
> Reversible ratchet drive (for use with sockets)
> Extension piece, 10 inch (for use with sockets)
> Universal joint (for use with sockets)
> Torque wrench (for use with sockets)
> 'Mole' wrench - 8 inch
> Ball pein hammer
> Soft-faced hammer, plastic or rubber
> Screwdriver - 6 in long x $\frac{5}{16}$ in dia (flat blade)
> Screwdriver - 2 in long x $\frac{5}{16}$ in square (flat blade)
> Screwdriver - 1$\frac{1}{2}$ in long x $\frac{1}{4}$ in dia (cross blade)
> Screwdriver - 3 in long x $\frac{1}{8}$ in dia (electricians)
> Pliers - electricians side cutters
> Pliers - needle nosed
> Pliers - circlip (internal and external)
> Cold chisel - $\frac{1}{2}$ inch
> Scriber
> Scraper
> Centre punch
> Pin punch
> Hacksaw
> Valve grinding tool
> Steel rule/straight-edge
> Allen keys
> Selection of files
> Wire brush (large)
> Axle-stands
> Jack (strong scissor or hydraulic type)

Special tools

The tools in this list are those which are not used regularly, are expensive to buy, or which need to be used in accordance with their manufacturers' instructions. Unless relatively difficult mechanical jobs are undertaken frequently, it will not be economic to buy many of these tools. Where this is the case, you could consider clubbing together with friends (or joining a motorists' club) to make a joint purchase, or borrowing the tools against a deposit from a local garage or tool hire specialist.

The following list contains only those tools and instruments freely available to the public, and not those special tools produced by the vehicle manufacturer specifically for its dealer network. You will find occasional references to these manufacturers' special tools in the text of this manual. Generally, an alternative method of doing the job without the vehicle manufacturers' special tool is given. However, sometimes, there is no alternative to using them. Where this is the case and the relevant tool cannot be bought or borrowed, you will have to entrust the work to a franchised garage.

> Valve spring compressor
> Piston ring compressor
> Balljoint separator
> Universal hub/bearing puller
> Impact screwdriver
> Micrometer and/or vernier gauge
> Dial gauge
> Stroboscopic timing light
> Dwell angle meter/tachometer
> Universal electrical multi-meter
> Cylinder compression gauge
> Lifting tackle
> Trolley jack
> Light with extension lead

Buying tools

For practically all tools, a tool factor is the best source since he will have a very comprehensive range compared with the average garage or accessory shop. Having said that, accessory shops often offer excellent quality tools at discount prices, so it pays to shop around.

There are plenty of good tools around at reasonable prices, but always aim to purchase items which meet the relevant national safety standards. If in doubt, ask the proprietor or manager of the shop for advice before making a purchase.

Care and maintenance of tools

Having purchased a reasonable tool kit, it is necessary to keep the tools in a clean serviceable condition. After use, always wipe off any dirt, grease and metal particles using a clean, dry cloth, before putting the tools away. Never leave them lying around after they have been used. A simple tool rack on the garage or workshop wall, for items such as screwdrivers and pliers is a good idea. Store all normal wrenches and sockets in a metal box. Any measuring instruments, gauges, meters, etc, must be carefully stored where they cannot be damaged or become rusty.

Take a little care when tools are used. Hammer heads inevitably become marked and screwdrivers lose the keen edge on their blades from time to time. A little timely attention with emery cloth or a file will soon restore items like this to a good serviceable finish.

Working facilities

Not to be forgotten when discussing tools, is the workshop itself. If anything more than routine maintenance is to be carried out, some form of suitable working area becomes essential.

It is appreciated that many an owner mechanic is forced by circumstances to remove an engine or similar item, without the benefit of a garage or workshop. Having done this, any repairs should always be done under the cover of a roof.

Wherever possible, any dismantling should be done on a clean, flat workbench or table at a suitable working height.

Any workbench needs a vice: one with a jaw opening of 4 in (100 mm) is suitable for most jobs. As mentioned previously, some clean dry storage space is also required for tools, as well as for lubricants, cleaning fluids, touch-up paints and so on, which become necessary.

Another item which may be required, and which has a much more general usage, is an electric drill with a chuck capacity of at least $\frac{5}{16}$ in (8 mm). This, together with a good range of twist drills, is virtually essential for fitting accessories such as mirrors and reversing lights.

Last, but not least, always keep a supply of old newspapers and clean, lint-free rags available, and try to keep any working area as clean as possible.

Spanner jaw gap comparison table

Jaw gap (in)	Spanner size
0.250	$\frac{1}{4}$ in AF
0.276	7 mm
0.313	$\frac{5}{16}$ in AF
0.315	8 mm
0.344	$\frac{11}{32}$ in AF; $\frac{1}{8}$ in Whitworth
0.354	9 mm
0.375	$\frac{3}{8}$ in AF

Jaw gap (in)	Spanner size
0.394	10 mm
0.433	11 mm
0.438	$\frac{7}{16}$ in AF
0.445	$\frac{3}{16}$ in Whitworth; $\frac{1}{4}$ in BSF
0.472	12 mm
0.500	$\frac{1}{2}$ in AF
0.512	13 mm
0.525	$\frac{1}{4}$ in Whitworth; $\frac{5}{16}$ in BSF
0.551	14 mm
0.563	$\frac{9}{16}$ in AF
0.591	15 mm
0.600	$\frac{5}{16}$ in Whitworth; $\frac{3}{8}$ in BSF
0.625	$\frac{5}{8}$ in AF
0.630	16 mm
0.669	17 mm
0.686	$\frac{11}{16}$ in AF
0.709	18 mm
0.710	$\frac{3}{8}$ in Whitworth; $\frac{7}{16}$ in BSF
0.748	19 mm
0.750	$\frac{3}{4}$ in AF
0.813	$\frac{13}{16}$ in AF
0.820	$\frac{7}{16}$ in Whitworth; $\frac{1}{2}$ in BSF
0.866	22 mm
0.875	$\frac{7}{8}$ in AF
0.920	$\frac{1}{2}$ in Whitworth; $\frac{9}{16}$ in BSF
0.938	$\frac{15}{16}$ in AF
0.945	24 mm
1.000	1 in AF
1.010	$\frac{9}{16}$ in Whitworth; $\frac{5}{8}$ in BSF
1.024	26 mm
1.063	$1\frac{1}{16}$ in AF; 27 mm
1.100	$\frac{5}{8}$ in Whitworth; $\frac{11}{16}$ in BSF
1.125	$1\frac{1}{8}$ in AF
1.181	30 mm
1.200	$\frac{11}{16}$ in Whitworth; $\frac{3}{4}$ in BSF
1.250	$1\frac{1}{4}$ in AF
1.260	32 mm
1.300	$\frac{3}{4}$ in Whitworth; $\frac{7}{8}$ in BSF
1.313	$1\frac{5}{16}$ in AF
1.390	$\frac{13}{16}$ in Whitworth; $\frac{15}{16}$ in BSF
1.417	36 mm
1.438	$1\frac{7}{16}$ in AF
1.480	$\frac{7}{8}$ in Whitworth; 1 in BSF
1.500	$1\frac{1}{2}$ in AF
1.575	40 mm; $\frac{15}{16}$ in Whitworth
1.614	41 mm
1.625	$1\frac{5}{8}$ in AF
1.670	1 in Whitworth; $1\frac{1}{8}$ in BSF
1.688	$1\frac{11}{16}$ in AF
1.811	46 mm
1.813	$1\frac{13}{16}$ in AF
1.860	$1\frac{1}{8}$ in Whitworth; $1\frac{1}{4}$ in BSF
1.875	$1\frac{7}{8}$ in AF
1.969	50 mm
2.000	2 in AF
2.050	$1\frac{1}{4}$ in Whitworth; $1\frac{3}{8}$ in BSF
2.165	55 mm
2.362	60 mm

Jacking, towing and roadwheel removal

Jacking

In order to avoid repetition, the procedure for raising the car to be able to carry out work under it is not included before each relevant operation described in this Manual.

It is to be preferred, and is certainly recommended, that the vehicle is positioned over an inspection pit or raised on a lift. Where such equipment is not available, use ramps or jack up the car strictly in accordance with the following guide, and observe the requirement for axle safety stands at all times.

The jack supplied with the car should be used only for emergency roadside wheel changing. Never work under the car with this type of jack, and even when lifting the car on a workshop jack, always supplement it with axle stands.

To repair the car always use (preferably) a trolley jack or a heavy duty bottle or screw jack.

Roadwheel removal and refitting

To remove a roadwheel, unbolt and take off the trim plate from the centre of the wheel. Unscrew each roadwheel nut or bolt (Gordini and Gordlni Turbo) through one half of a turn and then place the car jack (photo) in one of the oval slots at the base of the sills. Use the slot nearest the wheel that is to be removed.

Raise the car until the roadwheel clears the floor and then remove the nuts and take the wheel from the hub.

Refit and tighten the nuts so that they just secure the wheel to the hub. Lower the jack and tighten the wheel nuts or bolts fully. Refit the trimplate.

Spare wheel

On most models, the spare wheel is located wthin the engine compartment (photo). Many operations will require the removal of the spare wheel to give access to the engine or other component which is to receive attention. This requirement is not repeated throughout the Manual as it should be obvious prior to commencing the operations described.

On models equipped with air conditioning, the spare wheel is located on the floor of the luggage compartment. This arrangement is also used on Gordini versions.

Towing

In an emergency, the car may be towed using the front or rear tie-down eyes (photos). When being towed, make sure that the handbrake is fully released and the gearchange lever is in neutral. Make sure that the steering column is unlocked by turning the ignition key.

Cars equipped with automatic transmission may be towed provided an extra 2.0 litres (4.0 Imp pts, 2.1 US qts) of transmission fluid is added, the road speed is restricted to 30 kph (18 mph) and the distance is less than 50 km (30 miles). As this is not really practical, towing with the front wheels off the ground is recommended. This method is preferable even with manual transmission versions.

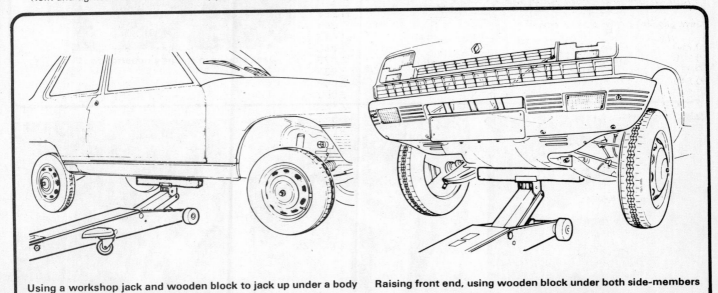

Using a workshop jack and wooden block to jack up under a body sill

Raising front end, using wooden block under both side-members

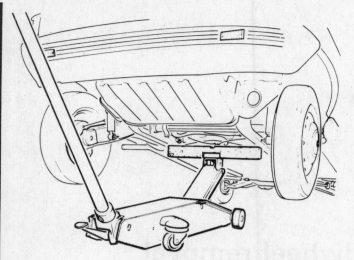

Raising the rear end using a wooden block under both side members

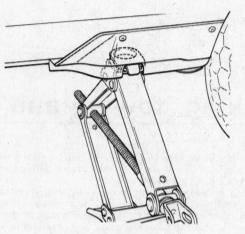

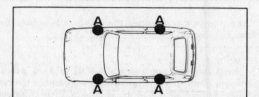

Car tool kit sill jacking points (A)

Car tool kit jack in use

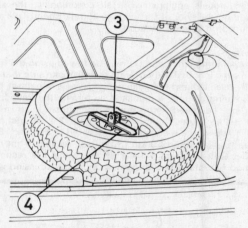

Spare wheel stowed in luggage compartment

3 Bolt   4 Clamp

Jack stowed in engine compartment

Spare wheel stowed in engine compartment

Rear tie-down eye

Front tie-down eye

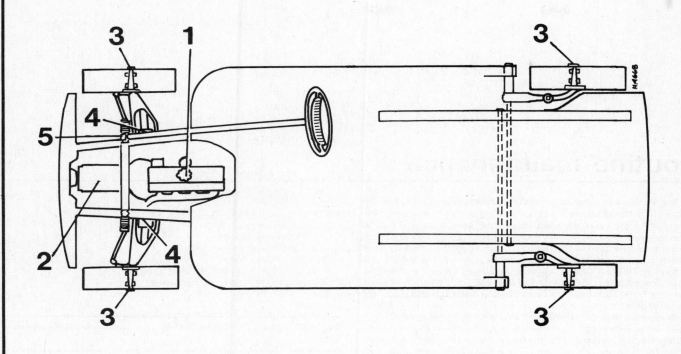

Recommended lubricants and fluids

Component or system	Lubricant type/specification	Duckhams recommendation
1 Engine	Multigrade engine oil, viscosity SAE 15W/50	Duckhams Hypergrade
2 Manual transmission	Gear oil, viscosity SAE 75 or 80	Duckhams Hypoid 80S
2 Automatic transmission	Dexron type ATF	Duckhams Uni-Matic or D-Matic
3 Wheel bearings	Multi-purpose lithium based grease	Duckhams LB 10
4 Driveshaft coupling Spider type Four-ball type	 Elf S747 SJW oil	Duckhams LBM 10
5 Steering gear	Molykote BR2	
5 Power steering	Dexron type ATF	Duckhams Uni-Matic or D-Matic

Routine maintenance

Maintenance is essential for ensuring safety, and desirable for the purpose of getting the best in terms of performance and economy from the car. Over the years the need for periodic lubrication – oiling and greasing – has been drastically reduced, if not totally eliminated. This has unfortunately tended to lead some owners to think that because no such action is required the components either no longer exist or will last forever. This is a serious delusion. If anything, there are now more places, particularly in the steering and suspension, where joints and pivots are fitted. Although you do not grease them any more you still have to look at them – and look at them just as often as you may previously have had to, to grease them. It follows therefore that the largest initial element of maintenance is visual examination.

Commencing January 1985, the makers have extended the service interval for changing the engine oil and filter from every 7500 km (5000 miles) to every 10 000 km (6000 miles).

Major overhaul and servicing has also been extended to every 50 000 km (30 000 miles).

Unless economy is absolutely paramount, it is recommended that the shorter service intervals specified here are adhered to in the interest of maximum component life and safety.

Every 375 km (250 miles) or weekly – whichever comes first

Check coolant level in the expansion tank (photo)
Check tyre pressures, including the spare
Check the windscreen washer fluid level, and top up if necessary (photo), adding a screen wash additive such as Turtle Wax High Tech Screen Wash
Check engine oil level, and top up if necessary (photo)
Check the operation of all lamps, direction indicators, horn and wipers
Check brake hydraulic fluid level, and top up if necessary
Check battery electrolyte level, and top up, if necessary
Check tyres for wear and damage

After the first 1500 km (1000 miles) for new vehicles or those fitted with a reconditioned engine or transmission

Renew the engine oil (photo)
Renew the transmission fluid (photo)
Check torque of the cylinder head bolts
Check valve clearances
Adjust carburettor
Check ignition settings (dwell and timing)

Every 7500 km (5000 miles) or 6 months – whichever comes first

Renew engine oil and filter
Check dwell angle and condition of contact breaker points
Check brake pads for wear
Adjust drum brakes
Check steering and suspension for wear

Check driveshaft joints for wear and condition of bellows
Check condition and tension of drivebelts
Check transmission oil level
Oil all hinges and controls
Check condition of exhaust system
Check clutch adjustment
Check air conditioning hoses for security
Check air conditioning refrigerant level

Every 15 000 km (10 000 miles) or 12 months – whichever comes first

Check drum brake shoes for wear
Check valve clearances
Renew spark plugs
Renew contact breaker (if applicable)
Renew air cleaner element
Renew air pump filter element (emission control AIS)
Clean PCV system hoses and flame trap
Check for hydraulic fluid leaks from brake circuits
Adjust handbrake linkage, if necessary
Check steering angles
Check front wheel alignment
Clean fuel pump
Renew oil in manual transmission
Check headlamp alignment
Check condition of seat belts
Check wheel bearings for play and wear
Check fluid level in the power-assisted steering pump (if applicable) and top up, if necessary

Every 30 000 km (20 000 miles) or 2 years – whichever comes first

Clean EGR system pipes and valve (emission control)
Renew charcoal canister (emission control fuel recovery system)
Renew idle delay valve (emission control accelerated idle system)

Every 2 years

Renew brake hydraulic fluid by bleeding
Renew coolant, and inspect hoses
Clean underbody and make good undersealing where necessary

Every 45 000 km (30 000 miles) or 3 years – whichever comes first

Renew oxygen sensor (emission control, closed loop feedback system)
Renew automatic transmission fluid
Test shock absorbers

View from underneath the front end

1 Suspension lower arm
2 Torsion bar
3 Anti-roll bar

4 Transmission
5 Exhaust pipe
6 Resonance eliminator

7 Undershield
8 Transmission drain plug
9 Gear selector rod

View from underneath the rear end

1 Handbrake equaliser
2 Suspension trailing arm
3 Shock absorber lower
   mounting

4 Silencer
5 Fuel tank
6 Rear foglamp

7 Fuel tank filler pipe
8 Torsion bars
9 Brake pressure regulator

View of engine compartment (R1229) – air cleaner and spare wheel removed

1	Bonnet lock	6	Heater	11	Battery
2	Brake servo	7	Jack – stowed	12	Radiator
3	Brake master cylinder	8	Washer reservoir and pump	13	Coolant expansion bottle
4	Alternator	9	Oil filler cap	14	Radiator sealing cap
5	Carburettor	10	Brake fluid reservoir	15	Vehicle identification oval plate
				16	Vehicle production detail plate

Topping-up the coolant

Filling washer reservoir

Topping-up the engine oil

Topping-up the brake hydraulic fluid

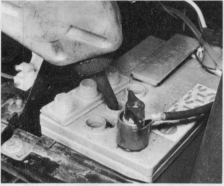

Topping-up the battery

Engine sump drain plug

Transmission drain plug

Chapter 1 Engine

For modifications, and information applicable to later models, see Supplement at end of manual

Contents

Specifications

Part 1 Type 800 (845 cc) engine
General

Application .... R1221 (three-door L) and R1391 (five-door L)
Engine type .... Four-cylinder, in-line pushrod operated overhead valves (ohv)
                           Wet cylinder liners
Displacement .... 845 cc (51.56 cu in)

Bore .... 58.0 mm (2.284 in)
Stroke .... 80.0 mm (3.150 in)
Compression ratio .... 8.0 : 1
Firing order .... 1-3-4-2 (No 1 cylinder at flywheel end)
Power (SAE) .... 38 bhp (27.9 kW) at 5000 rpm
Torque (SAE) .... 40.5 lbf/ft (54 Nm) at 3000 rpm

Crankshaft
Number of main bearings 3
Journal:
    Diameter .... 40.0 mm (1.5760 in)
    Regrind undersize .... 0.25 mm (0.0099 in)
Crankpin:
    Diameter .... 38.0 mm (1.4972 in)
    Regrind undersize .... 0.25 mm (0.0099 in)
Crankshaft endfloat .... 0.05 to 0.23 mm (0.0020 to 0.0091 in)
Thrust washer thickness .... 2.0 mm (0.0788 in)
2.05 mm (0.0808 in)
2.10 mm (0.0827 in)
2.15 mm (0.0847 in)

Camshaft
Number of bearings .... 3 (direct in block)
Maximum endfloat .... 0.06 to 0.14 mm (0.0024 to 0.0055 in)

Pistons and cylinder liners
Liner type and material .... Detachable (wet) cast iron with base seals
Liner protrusion above block .... 0.04 to 0.12 mm (0.0016 to 0.0047 in)
Liner base seal thickness:
    Paper:
        Blue .... 0.07 mm (0.0028 in)
        Red .... 0.10 mm (0.0039 in)
        Green .... 0.14 mm (0.0055 in)
    Excelnyl:
        Blue .... 0.08 mm (0.0032 in)
        Red .... 0.10 mm (0.0039 in)
        Green .... 0.12 mm (0.0047 in)
Piston type .... Light alloy, three ring
Oversizes .... Not available. Standard piston/liner assemblies only from Renault
Gudgeon pin fitting .... Interference fit in connecting rod, free turning in piston
Gudgeon pin length .... 49.0 mm (1.931 in)
Gudgeon pin diameter .... 16.0 mm (0.630 in)
Piston rings .... Two compression, one oil control
Top compression ring .... 1.75 mm (0.069 in) thick
Second compression ring .... 2.0 mm (0.079 in) thick
Oil control ring .... 3.5 mm (0.138 in) thick
   Ring gaps and groove clearances are preset

Crankcase and cylinder block
Material .... Cast iron

Cylinder head
Material .... Light alloy
Height (nominal) .... 94.7 mm (3.728 in)
Minimum height after refacing .... 94.2 mm (3.709 in)
Maximum distortion of mating face .... 0.05 mm (0.002 in)

Valves
Clearance (cold):
    Inlet .... 0.15 mm (0.006 in)
    Exhaust .... 0.20 mm (0.008 in)
Clearance (hot):
    Inlet .... 0.18 mm (0.007 in)
    Exhaust .... 0.25 mm (0.010 in)
Stem diameter .... 7.0 mm (0.276 in)
Head diameter:
    Inlet .... 28.2 mm (1.110 in)
    Exhaust .... 25.0 mm (0.984 in)
Contact face angle .... 90° (included)
Contact face width:
    Inlet .... 1.0 to 1.5 mm (0.040 to 0.059 in)
    Exhaust .... 1.5 to 2.0 mm (0.059 to 0.079 in)
Valve guide bore .... 7.0 mm (0.276 in)
Guide outside diameter (nominal) .... 11.0 mm (0.433 in)

Oversize outside diameter:
   Single groove marking .... 11.10 mm (0.437 in)
   Double groove marking .... 11.25 mm (0.443 in)
Valve springs (single):
   Wire diameter .... 2.7 mm (0.106 in)
   Free length .... 40.4 mm (1.59 in)
   Spring coil inside diameter .... 16.8 mm (0.661 in)

Valve timing
Inlet valve opens .... 20° BTDC
Inlet valve closes .... 56° ABDC
Exhaust valve opens .... 53° BBDC
Exhaust valve closes .... 23° ATDC

Pushrods
Length .... 132.0 mm (5.2 in)
Diameter .... 5.0 mm (0.197 in)

Tappets (cam followers)
Outside diameter:
   Nominal .... 19.0 mm (0.748 in)
   Oversizes .... 19.2 mm (0.756 in), 19.5 mm (0.768 in)

Lubrication
Oil pressure at 4000 rpm .... 2.38 kgf/cm² (34.0 lbf/in²)
Oil filter .... Champion C116
Oil type/specification .... Multigrade engine oil, viscosity SAE 15W/50 (Duckhams Hypergrade)
Oil capacity (including filter change) .... 2.75 litres (4.8 Imp pts, 2.9 US qts)

Torque wrench settings

	Nm	lbf ft
Cylinder head bolts (cold)	64	47
Manifold nuts	30	22
Big-end cap bolts	35	26
Main bearing cap bolts	65	48
Flywheel bolts	41	30
Suspension balljoint nuts	34	25
Rack end fitting bolts	35	26
Engine-to-bellhousing bolts	41	30
Clutch cover to flywheel	20	15
Spark plugs	25	18

Part 2 Type 688 (1108 cc), 689 (956 cc) and 810 (1289 cc) engines

General
Application:
   Type 688 ....
R1227 (three-door TL/GTL)
R1247 (three-door TL/GTL)
R1397 (five-door TL/GTL)

   Type 689 ....
R1222 (three-door TL)
R1392 (five-door TL)

   Type 810 ....
R1224 (three-door TS)
R1225 (three-door GTL)
R1226 (three-door GTL)
R1228 (Le Car GTL)
R1395 (five-door GTL)

Engine type .... Four-cylinder, in-line pushrod operated overhead valves (ohv)
Detachable (wet) cylinder liners

	Type 688	Type 689	Type 810
Displacement	1108 cc (67.6 cu in)	956 cc (58.3 cu in)	1289 cc (78.6 cu in)
Bore	70.0 mm (2.758 in)	65.0 mm (2.561 in)	73.0 mm (2.876 in)
Stroke	72.0 mm (2.837 in)	72.0 mm (2.837 in)	77.0 mm (3.034 in)
Compression ratio	9.5 : 1	9.25 : 1	9.5 : 1

Firing order .... 1-3-4-2 (No 1 cylinder at flywheel end)

	Type 688	Type 689	Type 810
Power (SAE)	47 bhp (34.6 kW) at 5500 rpm	47 bhp (34.6 kW) at 6000 rpm	64 bhp (47.1 kW) at 6000 rpm
Torque (SAE)	57 lbf ft (78 Nm) at 3500 rpm	47 lbf ft (64 Nm) at 3500 rpm	67 lbf ft (91 Nm) at 3500 rpm

Crankshaft
Number of main bearings 5
Journal:
   Diameter:
      Early models .... 46.0 mm (1.811 in)
      Later models .... 54.795 mm (2.157 in)
   Regrind undersize .... 0.25 mm (0.010 in)
Crankpin:
   Diameter .... 43.98 mm (1.731 in)
   Regrind undersize .... 0.25 mm (0.010 in)

Crankshaft endfloat .... 0.05 to 0.23 mm (0.002 to 0.009 in)
Thrust washer thickness .... 2.78 mm (0.109 in)
                                                                                    2.80 mm (0.110 in)
                                                                                    2.85 mm (0.112 in)
                                                                                    2.88 mm (0.113 in)
                                                                                    2.90 mm (0.114 in)
                                                                                    2.93 mm (0.115 in)
                                                                                    2.95 mm (0.116 in)

Camshaft
Number of bearings 4
Maximum endfloat .... 0.06 to 0.12 mm (0.0024 to 0.0047 in)

Pistons and cylinder liners
Liner type and material .... Detachable (wet) cast iron with base seals
Liner protrusion above block .... 0.04 to 0.12 mm (0.0016 to 0.0047 in)
Liner base seal thickness:
    Excelnyl:
        Blue .... 0.08 mm (0.0032 in)
        Red .... 0.12 mm (0.0047 in)
        Green .... 0.10 mm (0.0039 in)
Piston type .... Light alloy, three ring
Oversizes .... Not available. Standard piston/liner assemblies only from Renault
Gudgeon pin fitting .... Interference fit in connecting rod, free turning in piston
Gudgeon pin length:
    Type 688, 689 engines .... 57.0 mm (2.244 in)
    Type 810 engine:
        Early models .... 62.0 mm (2.441 in)
        Later models .... 64.0 mm (2.519 in)
Gudgeon pin outside diameter:
    Type 688, 689 engines .... 18.0 mm (0.709 in)
    Type 810 engine .... 20.0 mm (0.787 in)
Piston rings .... Two compression, one oil control
Top compression ring .... 1.75 mm (0.069 in) thick
Second compression ring .... 2.0 mm (0.079 in) thick
Oil control ring:
    Type 688 and 689 .... 3.5 mm (0.138 in) thick
    Type 810 .... 4.0 mm (0.157 in) thick
    Ring gaps and groove clearances are preset

Crankcase and cylinder block
Material .... Cast iron

Cylinder head
Material .... Light alloy
Height (nominal):
    Type 688 engine .... 70.15 mm (2.761 in)
    Type 689 engine .... 71.55 mm (2.817 in)
    Type 810 engine .... 72.00 mm (2.835 in)
Minimum height after refacing:
    Type 688 engine .... 69.65 mm (2.741 in)
    Type 689 engine .... 71.25 mm (2.805 in)
    Type 810 engine .... 71.50 mm (2.815 in)
Maximum distortion of mating face .... 0.05 mm (0.002 in)

Valves
Clearance (cold):
    Inlet .... 0.15 mm (0.006 in)
    Exhaust .... 0.20 mm (0.008 in)
Clearance (hot):
    Inlet .... 0.18 mm (0.007 in)
    Exhaust .... 0.25 mm (0.010 in)
Valve stem diameter .... 7.0 mm (0.275 in)
Valve head diameter:
    Type 688 engine:
        Inlet .... 33.5 mm (1.319 in)
        Exhaust .... 29.0 mm (1.142 in)
    Type 689 and 810 engines
        Inlet .... 33.5 mm (1.319 in)
        Exhaust .... 30.3 mm (1.193 in)
Contact face angle .... 90° (included)
Contact face width:
    Inlet .... 1.1 to 1.4 mm (0.043 to 0.055 in)
    Exhaust .... 1.4 to 1.7 mm (0.055 to 0.067 in)
Valve guide bore .... 7.0 mm (0.276 in)
Guide outside diameter (nominal) .... 11.0 mm (0.433 in)

Oversize outside diameter:
    Single groove marking .... 11.10 mm (0.437 in)
    Double groove marking .... 11.25 mm (0.443 in)
Valve springs (single):
    Wire diameter .... 3.4 mm (0.13 in)
    Free length .... 42.0 mm (1.7 in)
    Spring coil inside diameter .... 21.6 mm (0.85 in)

Valve timing
Type 689 engine:
    Inlet valve opens .... 18° BTDC
    Inlet valve closes .... 54° ABDC
    Exhaust valve opens .... 53° BBDC
    Exhaust valve closes .... 23° ATDC
Type 688 engine:
    Inlet valve opens .... 12° BTDC
    Inlet valve closes .... 48° ABDC
    Exhaust valve opens .... 52° BBDC
    Exhaust valve closes .... 8° ATDC
Type 810 engine:
    Inlet valve opens .... 22° BTDC
    Inlet valve closes .... 62° ABDC
    Exhaust valve opens .... 65° BBDC
    Exhaust valve closes .... 25° ATDC

Pushrods
Length:
    Early models .... 172.3 mm (6.783 in)
    Later models .... 176.3 mm (6.931 in)
Diameter .... 5.0 mm (0.197 in))

Tappets (cam followers)
Outside diameter .... 19.0 mm (0.748 in)
Oversize diameter .... 19.2 mm (0.756 in)

Lubrication
Oil pressure at 4000 rpm .... 3.57 kgf/cm² (51 lbf/in²)
Oil filter .... Champion C108
Oil type/specification .... Multigrade engine oil, viscosity SAE 15W/50 (Duckhams Hypergrade)
Oil capacity (including filter change) .... 3.25 litres (5.72 Imp pts, 3.44 US qts)

Torque wrench settings

	Nm	lbf ft
Cylinder head bolts (cold)	60	44
Manifold nuts	30	22
Big-end cap bolts:		
688 and 689 engines	35	26
810 engine	45	33
Main bearing cap bolts	64	47
Flywheel bolts	50	37
Suspension balljoint nuts	34	25
Rack end fitting bolts	35	26
Engine-to-bellhousing bolts	41	30
Clutch cover-to-flywheel bolts	20	15
Spark plugs	25	18
Camshaft sprocket bolt	30	22
Camshaft pulley bolt	34	25
Torque converter/driveplate bolts (810 engine)	70	51

Part 3 Type 840 (1397 cc) engines
General
Application .... R1223 (three-door Gordini)
Engine type .... Four-cylinder, pushrod operated overhead valves (ohv). Crossflow head, detachable (wet) cylinder liners
Displacement .... 1397 cc (85.2 cu in)
Bore .... 76.0 mm (2.99 in)
Stroke .... 77.0 mm (3.03 in)
Compression ratio .... 10.0 : 1
Firing order .... 1-3-4-2 (No 1 cylinder at flywheel end)
Power (DIN) .... 93 bhp (69.35 kW) at 6400 rpm
Torque (DIN) .... 85 lbf ft (115 Nm) at 4000 rpm

All other specifications are as for the type 810 engine given in Part 2, with the exception of the following:

Crankshaft
Thrust washer thickness .... 2.80 mm (0.110 in)
    2.85 mm (0.112 in)
    2.90 mm (0.114 in)
    2.95 mm (0.116 in)

Gudgeon pins
Gudgeon pin length .... 64.0 mm (2.519 in)
Gudgeon pin bore .... 12.0 mm (0.472 in)

Cylinder head
Height (nominal) .... 79.3 mm (3.122 in)
    Refacing not permitted

Valves
Clearance (cold or hot):
    Inlet .... 0.20 mm (0.008 in)
    Exhaust .... 0.25 mm (0.010 in)
Valve stem diameter .... 8.0 mm (0.315 in)
Valve head diameter:
    Inlet .... 38.7 mm (1.319 in)
    Exhaust .... 30.3 mm (1.193 in)
Contact face width:
    Inlet .... 1.5 to 1.8 mm (0.059 to 0.070 in)
    Exhaust .... 1.7 to 2.0 mm (0.067 to 0.079 in)
Valve guide bore .... 8.0 mm (0.315 in)
Guide outside diameter (nominal) .... 13.0 mm (0.512 in)
Oversize outside diameter:
    Single groove marking .... 13.10 mm (0.515 in)
    Double groove marking .... 13.25 mm (0.521 in)
Valve springs (dual):
    Wire diameter:
        Outer .... 4.2 mm (0.165 in)
        Inner .... 2.4 mm (0.095 in)
    Free length:
        Outer .... 44.1 mm (1.74 in)
        Inner .... 38.9 mm (1.53 in)
    Spring coil inside diameter:
        Outer .... 25.0 mm (0.99 in)
        Inner .... 18.6 mm (0.73 in)

Valve timing
Inlet valve opens .... 30° BTDC
Inlet valve closes .... 72° ABDC
Exhaust valve opens .... 72° BBDC
Exhaust valve closes .... 30° ATDC

Pushrods
Length:
    Inlet .... 176.0 mm (6.929 in)
    Exhaust .... 203.5 mm (8.012 in)
Diameter .... 6.0 mm (0.236 in)

Torque wrench settings

	Nm	lbf ft
Cylinder head bolts (hot or cold)	68	50
Camshaft sprocket bolt	20	15

Part 4 Type 847 (1397 cc) engine
General
Application .... R1229 (three-door TX)
                                R1399 (Le Car de luxe)
Engine type .... Four-cylinder, in-line pushrod operation overhead valves (ohv). Detachable (wet) cylinder liners
Displacement .... 1397 cc (85.2 cu in)
Bore .... 76.0 mm (2.99 in)
Stroke .... 77.0 mm (3.03 in)
Compression ratio .... 9.25 : 1
Firing order .... 1-3-4-2 (No 1 cylinder at flywheel end)
Power (SAE) .... 51 bhp (37.5 kW) at 5000 rpm
Torque (SAE) .... 55 lbf ft (75 Nm) at 3000 rpm

All other specifications are as for the type 810 engine given in Part 2, with the exception of the following:

Crankshaft
Thrust washer thickness .... 2.80 mm (0.110 in)
                                2.85 mm (0.112 in)
                                2.90 mm (0.114 in)
                                2.95 mm (0.116 in)

Pistons and cylinder liners
Liner protrusion above block (O-ring removed) .... 0.02 to 0.09 mm (0.0008 to 0.0035 in)
Gudgeon pin length .... 64.0 mm (2.52 in)

Gudgeon pin outside diameter .... 20.0 mm (0.79 in)

Cylinder head
Height (nominal) .... 72.2 mm (2.84 in)
Minimum height after refacing .... 71.7 mm (2.82 in)

Valves
Valve head diameter:
    Inlet .... 34.2 mm (1.35 in)
    Exhaust .... 29.0 mm (1.14 in)
Head contact face angle:
    Inlet .... 120°
    Exhaust .... 90°

Valve timing
Inlet valve opens .... 12° BTDC
Inlet valve closes .... 48° ABDC
Exhaust valve opens .... 52° BBDC
Exhaust valve closes .... 8° ATDC

Pushrods
Overall length .... 169.0 mm (6.7 in)
Diameter .... 5.0 mm (0.20 in)

Part 5 Type C6J-7-26 engine
General
Application .... 122B (Gordini Turbo)
Engine type .... Four-cylinder, pushrod operated overhead valves (ohv). Detachable (wet) cylinder liners
Displacement .... 1397 cc (85.2 cu in)
Bore .... 76.0 mm (2.99 in)
Stroke .... 77.0 mm (3.03 in)
Compression ratio .... 8.6 : 1
Firing order .... 1-3-4-2 (No 1 cylinder at flywheel end)
Power (DIN) .... 110 bhp (82.03 kW) at 6000 rpm
Torque .... 108.5 lbf ft (147.1 Nm) at 4000 rpm

All other specifications are as for the type 840 engine with the exception of the following:

Valve timing
Inlet valve opens .... 10° BTDC
Inlet valve closes .... 54° ABDC
Exhaust valve opens .... 54° BBDC
Exhaust valve closes .... 10° ATDC

PART 1 Type 800 (845 cc) engine

1 General description

This engine has a three bearing crankshaft, a light alloy cylinder head and a cast iron block.

The camshaft is driven by a single timing chain to operate the overhead valves through tappets (cam followers) and pushrods.

The timing chain is provided with a tensioner.

The engine has 'wet' cylinder liners which are a push fit in the cylinder block and sealed at the base with special gaskets.

The gearbox is located ahead of the engine. This layout is the converse of that found in conventional vehicle power trains.

The lubrication system consists of an oil sump from which oil is drawn by a pump driven by a gear on the camshaft. The oil is pressurised before being passed through a disposable type cartridge filter to all engine bearings and friction surfaces by means of galleries and passages.

The cylinder walls are splash lubricated.

On engines which incorporate a hydraulic chain tensioner, the engine oil pressure is used to feed this device. Gauze mesh strainers are fitted at the chain tensioner oil feed hole and at the oil pump pick-up.

The engine is equipped with a crankcase ventilation system. For full information, refer to Chapter 3 which also covers the emission control systems fitted to North American and certain other models.

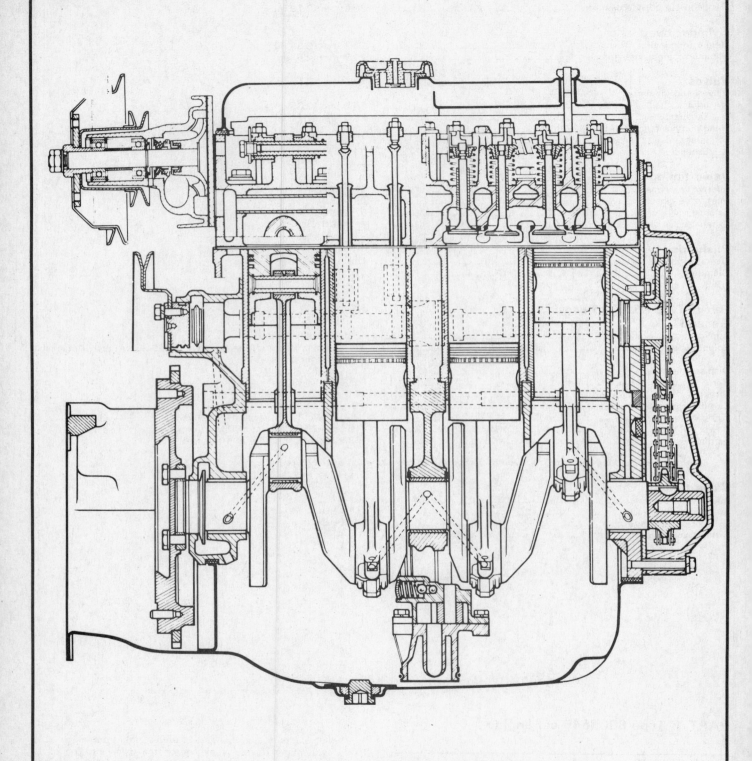

Fig. 1.1 Longitudinal sectional view of the type 800 engine (Sec 1)

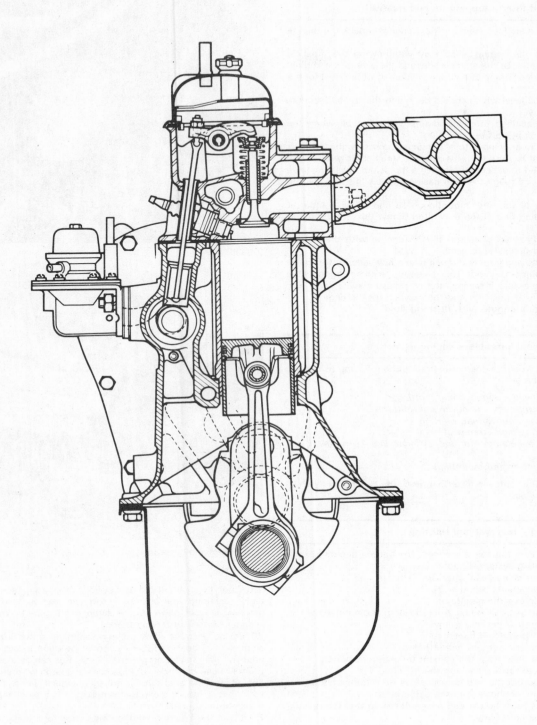

Fig. 1.2 Cross-sectional view of the type 800 engine (Sec 1)

2   Engine oil and filter – topping-up and renewal

1   At regular intervals (see Routine Maintenance) check the engine oil level.

2   Do this when the engine is cold by withdrawing the dipstick, which is located between the spare wheel and the side of the engine. Wipe the dipstick clean, reinsert it into its guide and withdraw it for the second time.

3   Read off the oil level which should be within the cut-out section. Add oil if necessary.

4   Also, at the specified intervals, drain the engine oil when the engine is hot by removing the drain plug.

5   While the oil is draining into a container, unscrew the oil filter (photo) and discard it. An oil filter wrench or small chain wrench will probably be required to unscrew it. If such a tool is not available, drive a heavy screwdriver through the filter casing and use this as a lever to unscrew it.

6   Clean the face of the filter mounting base and smear a little oil on the rubber sealing ring of the new filter. Screw the filter on hand-tight only.

7   Refit the sump drain plug and fill the engine with the correct quantity of a good quality engine oil.

8   Start the engine and note that it will take a few seconds for the oil pressure warning lamp to go out. This is due to the oil having to fill the empty filter casing before it reaches the oil pressure switch.

9   Check for leaks at the filter and then switch off the engine.

10 **Never flush this engine with flushing fluid.**

3   Major operations possible – engine in car

1   The following work may be carried out without having to remove the engine from the car:

  (a) *Cylinder head – removal and refitting*
  (b) *Engine sump pan – removal and refitting*
  (c) *Oil pump – removal and refitting*
  (d) *Big-end bearings – renewal*
  (e) *Piston, connecting rod and cylinder liner – removal and refitting*
  (f) *Renewal of engine mountings*

If the gearbox is first removed (see Chapter 6) the clutch and flywheel will also be accessible.

4   Cylinder head – removal and refitting

1   If the engine is in the car, disconnect the battery negative lead.

2   Drain the cooling system (Chapter 2).

3   Remove the air cleaner (Chapter 3).

4   Remove the drivebelts (Chapter 2).

5   Unbolt and remove the generator.

6   Disconnect the gearchange control rod clamp and remove the rod.

7   Unbolt and remove the rocker cover.

8   Remove the distributor (Chapter 4).

9   Disconnect the coolant and heater hoses.

10 Disconnect the lead from the coolant temperature switch.

11 Uncouple the exhaust pipe from the manifold.

12 Disconnect the throttle and choke cables from the carburettor.

13 Disconnect the fuel hose from the carburettor.

14 Release the radiator tie-bar and gearshift rod so that the radiator can be tilted forwards slightly.

15 Slacken the rocker arm adjuster screw locknuts and back the screws right off so that the pushrods can be withdrawn (photo). Keep the rods in their originally installed order.

16 Release each cylinder head bolt half a turn at a time commencing with the centre ones and working towards each end. Do not unscrew bolt (A) more than one turn (see Fig. 1.4), but all the other bolts should be removed.

17 In order not to break the liner base seals as the cylinder head is removed, swivel the cylinder head around the dowel bolt (A) by tapping the head carefully in a sideways direction using a plastic-faced mallet.

18 Once the head is free, remove the bolt (A) and lift the head from the block.

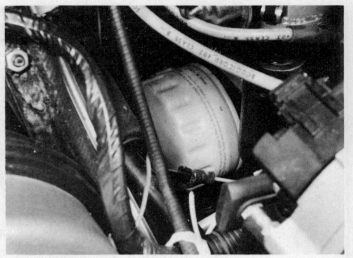

2.5 Oil filter

4.15 Removing pushrods

19 Carefully clean off old gasket from the mating face of the cylinder block, ensuring that the alloy surfaces are not scored during the process. Do not allow dirt or scraped off material to drop into the cylinder bores and remain there.

20 On no account allow the crankshaft to rotate until cylinder liner clamps have been fitted. This should be done in order to retain the liners on their base clamps. Suitable clamps can be made up using the cylinder head bolts, socket wrenches and large washers, or a length of angled steel material suitably drilled. A special clamp is available (MOT 521), but unless this can be borrowed, it will be cheaper to make up a substitute yourself.

21 Clean the cylinder head mating face in preparation for refitting. If full decarbonising and valve grinding is to be carried out, remove the carburettor and manifolds from the cylinder head and refer to Section 8.

22 If there is any evidence of gasket leakage, check the cylinder liner protrusion, as described in Section 27.

23 Remove the cylinder liner clamp.

24 Locate a new cylinder head gasket (without jointing compound) on the cylinder block so that the 'HAUT TOP' mark can be read from above. Make sure that the gasket is of the correct type for the engine.

25 It is recommended that two long studs are used as positioning guides for the cylinder head. These can be made up by cutting the heads from two old cylinder head bolts and screwing them in by two or three turns into each end of the cylinder head.

Are your plugs trying to tell you something?

Normal.
Grey-brown deposits, lightly coated core nose. Plugs ideally suited to engine, and engine in good condition.

Heavy Deposits.
A build up of crusty deposits, light-grey sandy colour in appearance.
Fault: Often caused by worn valve guides, excessive use of upper cylinder lubricant, or idling for long periods.

Lead Glazing.
Plug insulator firing tip appears yellow or green/yellow and shiny in appearance.
Fault: Often caused by incorrect carburation, excessive idling followed by sharp acceleration. Also check ignition timing.

Carbon fouling.
Dry, black, sooty deposits. Fault: over-rich fuel mixture. Check: carburettor mixture settings, float level, choke operation, air filter.

Oil fouling.
Wet, oily deposits. Fault: worn bores/piston rings or valve guides; sometimes occurs (temporarily) during running-in period.

Overheating.
Electrodes have glazed appearance, core nose very white – few deposits. Fault: plug overheating. Check: plug value, ignition timing, fuel octane rating (too low) and fuel mixture (too weak).

Electrode damage.
Electrodes burned away; core nose has burned, glazed appearance. Fault: pre-ignition. Check: for correct heat range and as for 'overheating'.

Split core nose.
(May appear initially as a crack). Fault: detonation or wrong gap-setting technique. Check: ignition timing, cooling system, fuel mixture (too weak).

WHY DOUBLE COPPER IS BETTER FOR YOUR ENGINE.

Unique Trapezoidal Copper Cored Earth Electrode — 50% Larger Spark Area — Copper Cored Centre Electrode

Champion Double Copper plugs are the first in the world to have copper core in both centre <u>and</u> earth electrode. This innovative design means that they run cooler by up to 100°C – giving greater efficiency and longer life. These double copper cores transfer heat away from the tip of the plug faster and more efficiently. Therefore, Double Copper runs at cooler temperatures than conventional plugs giving improved acceleration response and high speed performance with no fear of pre-ignition.

Champion Double Copper plugs also feature a unique trapezoidal earth electrode giving a 50% increase in spark area. This, together with the double copper cores, offers greatly reduced electrode wear, so the spark stays stronger for longer.

 FASTER COLD STARTING

 FOR UNLEADED OR LEADED FUEL

 ELECTRODES UP TO 100°C COOLER

 BETTER ACCELERATION RESPONSE

 LOWER EMISSIONS

 50% BIGGER SPARK AREA

THE LONGER LIFE PLUG

Plug Tips/Hot and Cold.
Spark plugs must operate within well-defined temperature limits to avoid cold fouling at one extreme and overheating at the other.
Champion and the car manufacturers work out the best plugs for an engine to give optimum performance under all conditions, from freezing cold starts to sustained high speed motorway cruising.
Plugs are often referred to as hot or cold. With Champion, the higher the number on its body, the hotter the plug, and the lower the number the cooler the plug.

Plug Cleaning
Modern plug design and materials mean that Champion no longer recommends periodic plug cleaning. Certainly don't clean your plugs with a wire brush as this can cause metal conductive paths across the nose of the insulator so impairing its performance and resulting in loss of acceleration and reduced m.p.g.
However, if plugs are removed, always carefully clean the area where the plug seats in the cylinder head as grit and dirt can sometimes cause gas leakage.
Also wipe any traces of oil or grease from plug leads as this may lead to arcing.

CHAMPION

DOUBLE COPPER

1 This photographic sequence shows the steps taken to repair the dent and paintwork damage shown above. In general, the procedure for repairing a hole will be similar; where there are substantial differences, the procedure is clearly described and shown in a separate photograph.

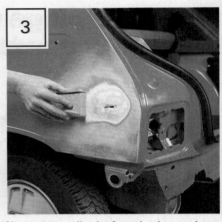

2 First remove any trim around the dent, then hammer out the dent where access is possible. This will minimise filling. Here, after the large dent has been hammered out, the damaged area is being made slightly concave.

3 Next, remove all paint from the damaged area by rubbing with coarse abrasive paper or using a power drill fitted with a wire brush or abrasive pad. 'Feather' the edge of the boundary with good paintwork using a finer grade of abrasive paper.

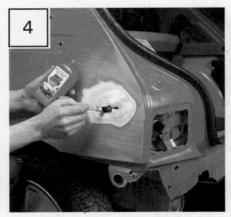

4 Where there are holes or other damage, the sheet metal should be cut away before proceeding further. The damaged area and any signs of rust should be treated with Turtle Wax Hi-Tech Rust Eater, which will also inhibit further rust formation.

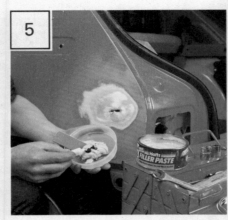

5 *For a large dent or hole* mix Holts Body Plus Resin and Hardener according to the manufacturer's instructions and apply around the edge of the repair. Press Glass Fibre Matting over the repair area and leave for 20-30 minutes to harden. Then ...

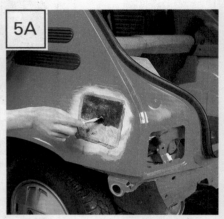

5A ... brush more Holts Body Plus Resin and Hardener onto the matting and leave to harden. Repeat the sequence with two or three layers of matting, checking that the final layer is lower than the surrounding area. Apply Holts Body Plus Filler Paste as shown in Step 5B.

5B *For a medium dent*, mix Holts Body Plus Filler Paste and Hardener according to the manufacturer's instructions and apply it with a flexible applicator. Apply thin layers of filler at 20-minute intervals, until the filler surface is slightly proud of the surrounding bodywork.

5C *For small dents and scratches* use Holts No Mix Filler Paste straight from the tube. Apply it according to the instructions in thin layers, using the spatula provided. It will harden in minutes if applied outdoors and may then be used as its own knifing putty.

6 Use a plane or file for initial shaping. Then, using progressively finer grades of wet-and-dry paper, wrapped round a sanding block, and copious amounts of clean water, rub down the filler until glass smooth. 'Feather' the edges of adjoining paintwork.

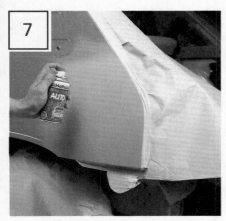

7

Protect adjoining areas before spraying the whole repair area and at least one inch of the surrounding sound paintwork with Holts Dupli-Color primer.

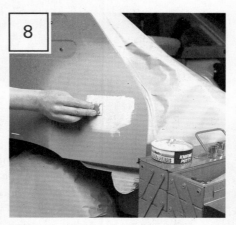

8

Fill any imperfections in the filler surface with a small amount of Holts Body Plus Knifing Putty. Using plenty of clean water, rub down the surface with a fine grade wet-and-dry paper – 400 grade is recommended – until it is really smooth.

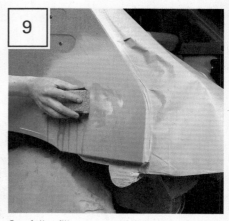

9

Carefully fill any remaining imperfections with knifing putty before applying the last coat of primer. Then rub down the surface with Holts Body Plus Rubbing Compound to ensure a really smooth surface.

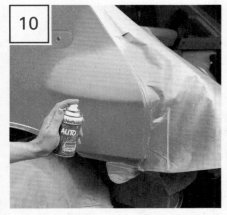

10

Protect surrounding areas from overspray before applying the topcoat in several thin layers. Agitate Holts Dupli-Color aerosol thoroughly. Start at the repair centre, spraying outwards with a side-to-side motion.

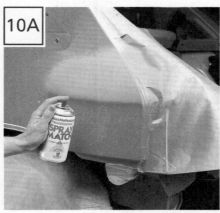

10A

If the exact colour is not available off the shelf, local Holts Professional Spraymatch Centres will custom fill an aerosol to match perfectly.

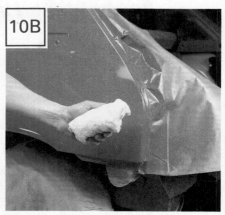

10B

To identify whether a lacquer finish is required, rub a painted unrepaired part of the body with wax and a clean cloth.

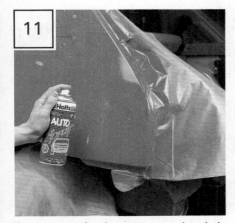

11

If *no* traces of paint appear on the cloth, spray Holts Dupli-Color clear lacquer over the repaired area to achieve the correct gloss level.

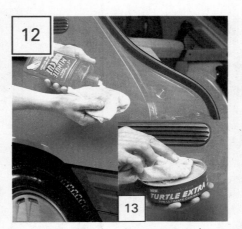

12

13

The paint will take about two weeks to harden fully. After this time it can be 'cut' with a mild cutting compound such as Turtle Wax Minute Cut prior to polishing with a final coating of Turtle Wax Extra.

14

When carrying out bodywork repairs, remember that the quality of the finished job is proportional to the time and effort expended.

HAYNES No1 for DIY

Haynes publish a wide variety of books besides the world famous range of *Haynes Owners Workshop Manuals*. They cover all sorts of DIY jobs. Specialist books such as the *Improve and Modify* series and the *Purchase and DIY Restoration Guides* give you all the information you require to carry out everything from minor modifications to complete restoration on a number of popular cars. In addition there are the publications dealing with specific tasks, such as the *Car Bodywork Repair Manual* and the *In-Car Entertainment Manual*. The *Household DIY* series gives clear step-by-step instructions on how to repair everyday household objects ranging from toasters to washing machines.

Whether it is under the bonnet or around the home there is a Haynes Manual that can help you save money. Available from motor accessory stores and bookshops or direct from the publisher.

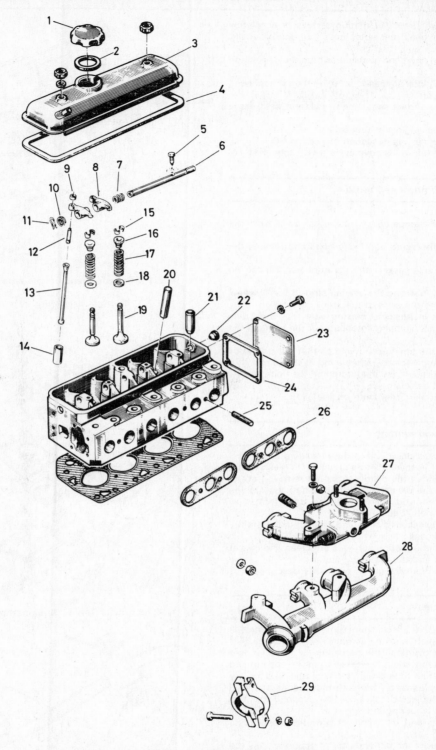

Fig. 1.3 Cylinder head components – type 800 engine (Sec 4)

1	Oil filler cap	11	Spring clip	21	Valve guide
2	Oil seal	12	Adjuster screw	22	Rocker shaft hole plug
3	Rocker cover	13	Pushrod	23	Endplate
4	Rocker cover gasket	14	Tappet (cam follower)	24	Gasket
5	Rocker shaft locating bolt	15	Split collets	25	Stud
6	Rocker shaft	16	Valve spring cap	26	Manifold gasket
7	Coil spring	17	Valve spring	27	Inlet manifold
8	Rocker arm	18	Valve spring seat	28	Exhaust manifold
9	Locknut	19	Valve	29	Exhaust pipe clamp
10	Coil spring	20	Sleeve		

26 Make sure that the cylinder head mating surface is absolutely clean and that the cylinder head bolt holes have had any oil or dirt cleared from them.

27 Lower the cylinder head down the guide studs onto the gasket and block.

28 Remove the temporary guide studs and screw in the cylinder head bolts (threads oiled) finger tight.

29 Tighten the bolts in the correct sequence to the specified torque (see Fig. 1.34).

30 Fit the pushrods in their original sequence.

31 Adjust the valve clearances, as described in Section 30.

32 Refit and reconnect all the items covered in paragraphs 1 to 14.

5 Engine sump pan – removal and refitting

1   Drain the engine oil.

2   Unbolt the anti-roll bar clamps and prise the bar away from the sump pan.

3   Unscrew and remove the sump pan fixing bolts and remove the pan.

4   Remove the sump pan side gaskets and the front and rear sealing strips.

5   Commence refitting by inserting the sealing strip at the flywheel end. Apply gasket cement to the ends of the strip.

6   Stick the side gaskets in position, making sure that their tabs overlap the sealing strip. Apply jointing compound at the joints of the gasket and seal.

7   Fit the sealing strip at the timing chain end so that the strip ends overlap the side gaskets. Apply jointing compound at the joints.

8   Offer up the sump pan and screw in and tighten the bolts evenly.

9   Reconnect the anti-roll bar clamps.

10 Tighten the sump drain plug, refill with engine oil.

6 Oil pump – removal and refitting

1   Remove the sump pan, as described in the preceding Section.

2   The oil pump driveshaft is splined into a drivegear in mesh with a gear on the camshaft. Provided the distributor is not removed at the same time, withdrawal of the oil pump will not disturb the ignition timing. If the drivegear is removed, then it will have to be refitted as described in engine reassembly, Section 29.

3   Unscrew the three pump securing bolts and lift the pump from the machined face of the crankcase.

4   Refit, making sure that the mating surfaces are clean. No gasket is used between the pump and the mounting surface.

5   Refit the sump pan and fill with oil, as previously described.

7 Big-end bearings – renewal

1   Although it is unlikely that these bearings will require renewal, other than at times of complete engine overhaul when the crankshaft main bearings also require overhaul, the procedure is given for two reasons. Firstly, the opportunity should be taken to renew the big-end bearing shells if the connecting rods and pistons are removed for any reason. Secondly, it is possible that the big-ends may require attention if the engine has been subjected to abuse by overloading, over advance ignition or regular labouring in high gear.

2   Remove the sump pan and oil pump as previously described. Disconnect the battery.

3   Rotate the crankshaft until the big-ends are at approximately the same level, which will indicate that the pistons are at roughly the same height in the cylinder bores.

4   Mark the adjacent surfaces of the big-ends caps and rods by centre punching (1 to 4 numbering from the flywheel end) on the side furthest from the camshaft.

5   Remove the big-end cap bolts and tap off the caps with their lower half shells.

6   A worn shell will be obvious by the fact that the lead coloured surface metal will have worn away to expose the copper coloured underlay. The bearing shells are stamped on their backs with standard or undersize details and a replacement set should be purchased to match the original markings. If the crankpin surfaces show signs of scoring then new bearing shells will be a waste of time as the

Fig. 1.4 Cylinder head bolts – type 800 engine (Sec 4)

A   Bolt for pivoting cylinder head

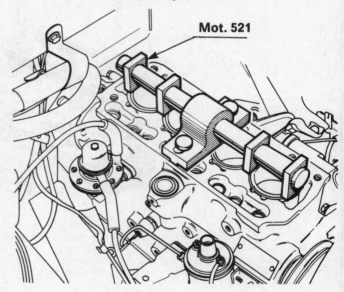

Fig. 1.5 The official Renault liner clamp tool – MOT 521 (Sec 4)

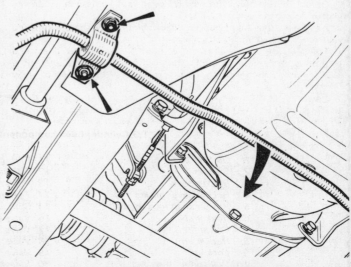

Fig. 1.6 Front anti-roll bar removal (Sec 5)

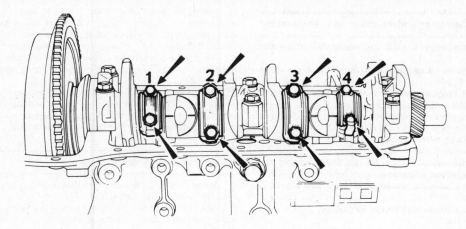

Fig. 1.7 Big-end cap bolts (Sec 7)

crankshaft will be in need of grinding – refer to Section 18.
7   Fit the new shells into perfectly clean recesses in their caps.
8   Apply engine oil to the crankpins and then offer up the caps so that their positioning mark is adjacent to the one on the connecting rod. Pull the rod down tightly onto the crankpin.
9   Fit the big-end cap bolts and tighten to the specified torque.
10 Refit the oil pump, sump pan and refill the engine with oil.

8   Cylinder liner, piston and rod assembly – removal and refitting

1   If the engine is in the car, disconnect the battery and drain the cooling system.
2   Remove the cylinder head, oil pump and the sump, all as previously described.
3   Mark the connecting rod big-end caps and rods at adjacent points by centre punching (1 to 4) numbering from the flywheel end and making sure that the marks are furthest from the camshaft.
4   Unbolt and remove the big-end caps with their shells. If the shells are to be used again, keep them carefully with their respective caps.
5   Using quick drying paint, mark the upper rim of each cylinder liner in respect of position and alignment in the block.
6   Remove the complete liner, piston and rod assembly. This will probably require tapping the bottom edge of each liner with a wooden block or plastic-faced mallet.
7   To dismantle and reassemble the liner, piston and rod refer to the next Section.
8   Before reassembly, thoroughly clean out the remains of the cylinder liner base seals.
9   New seals may be of paper or Excelnyl material and are supplied in colour coded sets (see Specifications).
10 Place a blue seal on the end of each of the cylinder liners and insert them (without piston and rod) into their original positions in the block. If new liners are being fitted then it does not matter how they are installed.
11 Press the liners down by hand and check their protrusion above the block face. Do this either with a dial gauge or a straight edge and feeler blades. The correct protrusion should be as specified.
12 To adjust the protrusion, change the base seals for ones of other thicknesses. With new liners, it is permissible to interchange their positions in the block to ensure that the difference in protrusion between two adjacent liners does not exceed 0.04 mm (0.0016 in).
13 Once the protrusion is correctly established keep the seals with their respective liners and then fit the pistons and rods into the liners. To do this, oil the liner bore and pistons rings liberally and fit a piston ring compressor.
14 With the liner standing upside down on the bench, insert the piston into the bottom end of the liner until the piston ring compressor is resting on the base rim of the liner.
15 Place the assembly in the liner so that the following three conditions are met.

(i)   The machined sides of the connecting rod big-end must be parallel with the flats on top of the liner
(ii)   The number (punch marks) made on the connecting rod at dismantling must be furthest from the camshaft
(iii) The arrow on the piston crown must be towards the flywheel

16 Press the piston further until the ring compressor is released. Fit the bearing shells to the rods.
17 Insert the liner, piston and rod assemblies into the cylinder block, with each liner carrying the selected base seal.
18 Fit a liner clamp.
19 Oil the crankpins and then draw each connecting rod down onto its crankpin.
20 Fit the bearing shells into the big-end caps. The bearing recesses in the cap must be perfectly clean. Fit the caps matching the location numbers made at dismantling. Screw in and tighten the cap bolts to the specified torque.
21 Check that the crankshaft rotates freely.
22 Fit the cylinder head, oil pump and sump pan, as previously described.
23 Fill the engine with oil. Fill and bleed the cooling system (if applicable).

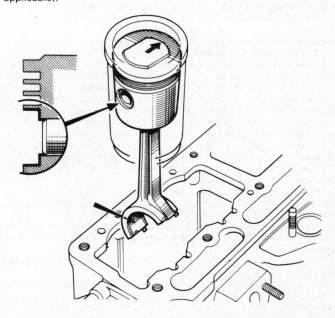

Fig. 1.8 Liner, piston and rod alignment (Secs 8 and 9)

9 Cylinder liner, piston and rod – dismantling and reassembly

1   The piston and rod assembly should be withdrawn from the bottom of the liner.

2   Remove the piston rings upwards off the piston. If they are to be used again, take great care not to expand them too much as they snap very easily. To be safe it is recommended that two or three feeler blades are slid behind the ring and spaced at equidistant points around the piston. The blades will guide the ring over the lands and empty grooves.

3   Gudgeon pin removal is best left to your dealer as the pin is an interference fit in the connecting rod small-end and the rod must be heated before it can be pressed out. However, for those having the necessary equipment, the method of removal and refitting is given.

4   To remove a gudgeon pin, set the piston on a vee block. Heat the small-end of the rod with a fine flame from a gas blowlamp or torch until a stick of solder melts when touched on the rod.

5   Press out the gudgeon pin.

6   Check that the new gudgeon pin turns freely in the piston.

7   When the new gudgeon pin is pressed into position it is important that it is centred in the small-end of the rod and for this reason accurate fitting is best carried out using the special fitting kit MOT 574, but it is possible to make up suitable thrust pads and mandrels to achieve comparable results.

8   Have the piston ready for fitting to the connecting rod with the alignment as shown in Fig. 1.8. Heat the small-end, as previously described, and connect the piston to the rod by pressing in and centring the pin, which was previously smeared with oil.

9   Move the connecting rod in both directions to the limit of its side clearance and check that the gudgeon pin is below the surface of the piston skirt.

10 Fit the oil control ring and two compression rings to the piston and rotate them around the piston to stagger their gaps at 120° to each other. The ring end gaps and groove clearances are preset, and will be within specified limits (Renault manufacture).

10 Engine mountings – renewal

1   Either the engine side mountings or the gearbox front mounting may be removed by unbolting.

2   Support the engine or gearbox securely before removing a mounting, and never release more than one at a time.

11 Engine removal – method

The engine is removed by lifting it out of the engine compartment complete with transmission for later separation.

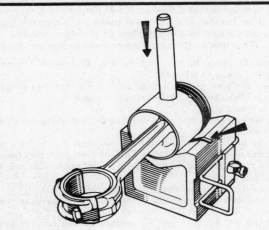

Fig. 1.9 Pressing out a gudgeon pin (Sec 9)

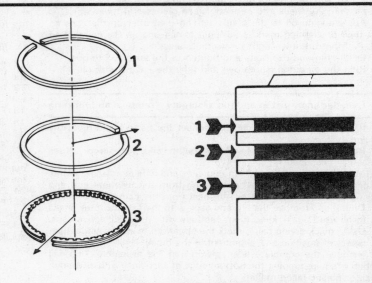

Fig. 1.10 Piston ring location (Sec 9)

1   *Top compression (plain)*   3   *Oil control (slotted)*
2   *Second compression (tapered)*

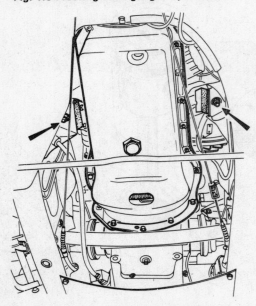

Fig. 1.11 Engine side mountings (Sec 10)

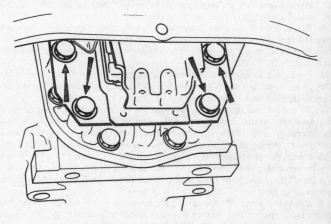

Fig. 1.12 Transmission front mounting (Sec 10)

12 Engine/manual transmission – removal

1   Disconnect the battery. Disconnect the earth lead first.
2   Drain the cooling system (Chapter 2) and the engine oil.
3   Remove the bonnet (photos) – see Chapter 12.
4   Remove the air cleaner. Disconnect the hoses from the fuel pump (photo) and plug them.
5   Disconnect the coolant and heater hoses (photo) and the starter motor leads (photo).
6   Disconnect the HT lead and the LT negative lead from the ignition coil.
7   Disconnect the electrical leads from the coolant temperature and oil pressure switches.
8   Disconnect the throttle and choke control cables (photos), the clutch cable and the speedometer drive cable at the transmission (photos). The latter is retained by a screw and locknut which must be released.
9   Remove the gearchange control rod. On facia mounted types, remove the bolt from the joint of the two sections of the tubular rod and unbolt the cross-brace and the stay from the radiator (photos). On floor-mounted gearchange models, unbolt the control rod bracket bolts on the gearbox and then release the rod from the base of the control lever by extracting the circlip from the end of the cross pivot. Refer to Chapter 6 for full details of gearchange mechanisms.
10   Remove the radiator and the expansion bottle.
11   Remove the downpipe fixing clips from the exhaust manifold (photos).
12   Set the roadwheels in the straight-ahead position and then remove two bolts from the steering shaft flexible coupling to disconnect it (photo).
13   Raise the front of the car and support it securely on axle stands placed under the side-members. Remove the front roadwheels.
14   Unbolt and remove the gearbox shield (photo).

15   Drain the transmission oil.
16   Using a balljoint extractor, disconnect the suspension upper arm balljoints.
17   Disconnect the steering rack end fittings from the tie-rods by removing the pivot bolts (photo).
18   Tilt the tops of the brake drums outwards and withdraw the driveshafts from the sunwheels in the transmission. Take care during this operation not to damage the lips of the oil seals in the transmission as the splined ends of the shaft are withdrawn.
19   Record the location of the height setting shims at the steering rack mountings and unbolt and remove the steering rack assembly (photos).
20   Remove the fan blades and the generator drivebelt.
21   Fit lifting tackle to the engine and transmission. It is recommended that a lifting eye is bolted to the front end of the engine by taking off the two topmost flywheel housing nuts. When a hoist is attached in this position the engine will be well balanced for removal.
22   Use the hoist to just take the weight of the engine/transmission and then unbolt the flexible mountings from the side-members (photo). Remove the transmission flexible mounting.
23   Hoist the engine/transmission out of the engine compartment.

13 Engine/transmission – separation

1   With the engine/transmission out of the car, clean away external dirt using paraffin or a water soluble solvent and a stiff brush.
2   Remove the starter motor.
3   Support the engine in a vertical position and then unscrew and remove the nuts and bolts which hold the engine and flywheel housing together.
4   Take the weight of the transmission and pull it from the engine in a straight line.

12.3a Unscrewing a bonnet hinge nut

12.3b Lifting the bonnet away

12.4 Disconnecting a fuel pump hose

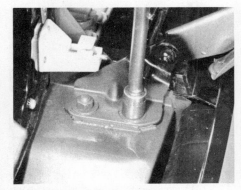
12.5a Radiator top hose disconnected

12.5b Disconnecting starter motor leads

12.8a Throttle operating rod connection

38

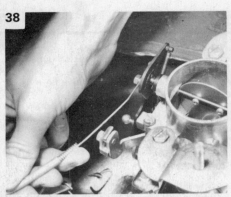

12.8b Choke cable connection

12.8c Clutch cable connection

12.8d Speedometer drive cable at transmission

12.9a Disconnecting gearchange control rod

12.9b Gearchange rod separated

12.9c Removing gearchange rod cross-brace

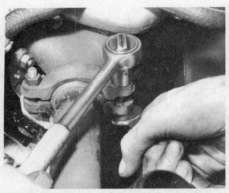

12.11a Releasing exhaust downpipe clamp

12.11b Removing exhaust downpipe clamp

12.12 Disconnecting steering flexible coupling

12.14 Removing gearbox undershield

12.17 Disconnecting steering rack end fittings

12.19a Steering rack mountings

12.19b Removing steering rack shims

12.19c Removing steering rack

12.22 Releasing transmission mounting bolts

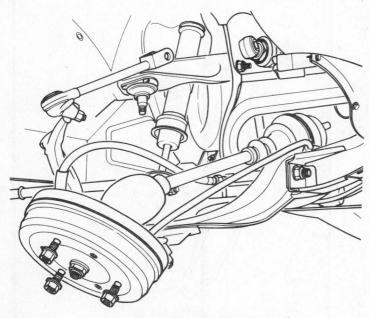
Fig. 1.13 Releasing driveshafts (Sec 12)

3   Although complete overhaul and renovation details are given here the amount of work actually carried out may be limited to the renewal of the worn components, provided the rest of the engine is in good condition. However, the opportunity should be taken to examine every item, with reference to Sections 16 to 27 inclusive.
4   Before commencing work, collect an adequate selection of tools, including spanners, socket wrenches and a torque wrench, rags, brushes, containers and masking tape. Paraffin and lubricating oil will also be required.
5   Don't be afraid of sketching parts and recording details of sequence of assembly rather than trusting to memory.
6   Obtain essential spares beforehand, including a full gasket set, valve springs, hoses, drivebelts and a timing chain.

15   Engine – complete dismantling

1   Unbolt and remove the major external components. These include the following:

   (1)   Generator (Chapter 10)
   (2)   Clutch (Chapter 5)
   (3)   Distributor (Chapter 4)
   (4)   Fuel pump (Chapter 3)
   (5)   Oil filter and dipstick
   (6)   Coolant pump (Chapter 2)
   (7)   Right-hand engine mounting

2   Drain the engine oil, if not done previously.
3   Remove the rocker cover.
4   Remove the camshaft pulley (photo).
5   Remove the cylinder head, as described in Section 4. Fit clamps only if the liners are not to be disturbed.
6   Remove the tappets (photo) and retain them in their originally fitted sequence.
7   Withdraw the oil pump/distributor drivegear from the distributor mounting hole.
8   Remove the sump pan and oil pump, as previously described.
9   Unbolt and remove the timing chain cover (photo).

14   Engine overhaul – general

1   The need for complete dismantling will depend upon any obvious signs of wear or excessive noise.
2   If an engine has covered a very high mileage and the cylinder bores and pistons are worn, with bearing rumble and low oil pressure, it may be more economical to obtain a reconditioned or good secondhand unit rather than carry out a complete overhaul on the old unit.

15.4 Removing camshaft pulley

15.6 Removing tappets (cam followers)

15.9 Removing timing chain cover

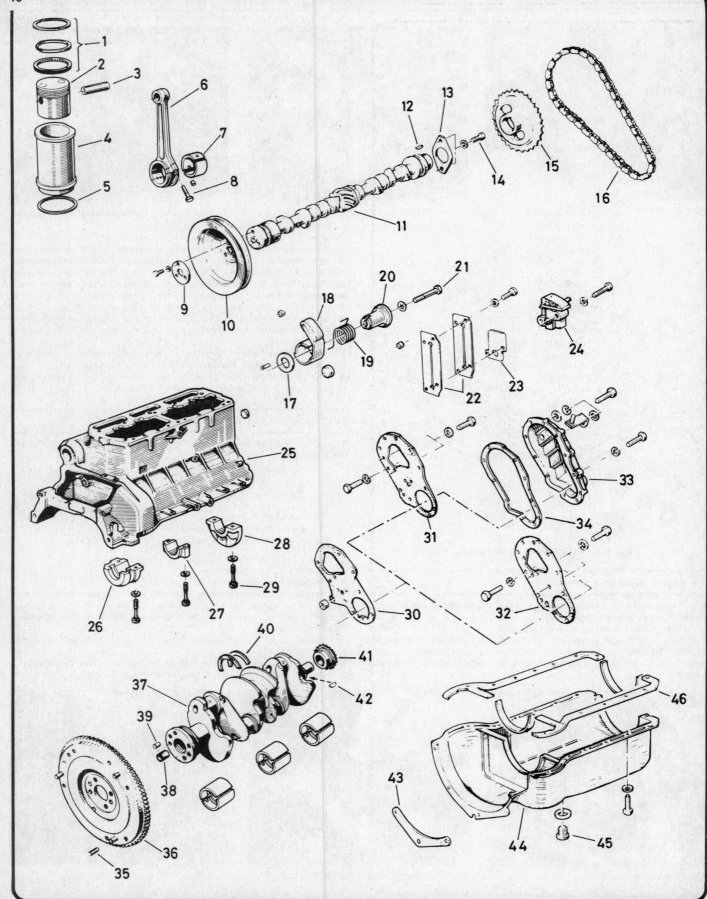

Fig. 1.14 Cylinder block and crankcase components (Sec 15)

1   Piston rings
2   Piston
3   Gudgeon pin
4   Cylinder liner
5   Liner base seal
6   Connecting rod
7   Big-end bearing shells
8   Big-end cap bolt
9   Spacer plate
10   Camshaft pulley
11   Camshaft
12   Woodruff key
13   Camshaft retainer plate
14   Retainer plate bolt
15   Camshaft sprocket
16   Timing chain
17   Washer (mechanical chain tensioner)
18   Slipper (mechanical chain tensioner)
19   Spring (mechanical chain tensioner)
20   Pivot (mechanical chain tensioner)
21   Bolt (mechanical chain tensioner)
22   Oil input plates
23   Tensioner backplate (hydraulic chain tensioner)
24   Hydraulic chain tensioner (alternative)
25   Crankcase
26   Rear main bearing cap
27   Centre main bearing cap
28   Front main bearing cap
29   Cap bolt
30   Endplate (alternative)
31   Endplate alternative)
32   Endplate (alternative)
33   Timing chain cover
34   Gasket
35   Dowel pin
36   Flywheel
37   Crankshaft
38   Pilot bush
39   Dowel pin
40   Thrust washers
41   Chain sprocket
42   Woodruff key
43   Plate
44   Sump pan
45   Oil drain plug
46   Sump gasket

10   Jam the starter ring gear on the flywheel with a large blade such as a cold chisel. Mark the relative position of the flywheel to its mounting hub, bend up the tabs of the lockplates and unscrew the securing bolts.
11   Remove the flywheel (photo).
12   Remove the timing chain tensioner. This may be one of three types, refer to Section 25.
13   Unscrew and remove the camshaft sprocket bolt. Using a suitable extractor pull off the camshaft sprocket and lift it away, complete with timing chain.
14   Unbolt the camshaft retaining plate and withdraw the camshaft from the timing chain end of the crankcase.
15   Unbolt and remove the endplate from the timing chain end of the crankcase. Note the oil filter gauze used when a hydraulic chain tensioner is fitted.
16   Using a two-legged extractor, draw off the crankshaft sprocket.
17   Mark the adjacent surfaces of the connecting rods and their caps on the sides furthest from the camshaft. Number them 1 to 4 with a centre punch, No 1 being at the flywheel end.
18   Unbolt and remove the bearing caps, keeping the shells with their respective caps if the shells are to be used again.
19   Mark the main bearing caps 1 to 3, again No 1 being at the flywheel end.
20   Unbolt and remove the main bearing caps (photo), keeping the bearing shells with their respective caps if they are to be used again.

15.11 Removing the flywheel

15.20 Removing No 3 main bearing cap

21 Push the connecting rod big-ends away from the crankpins and then lift the crankshaft from the crankcase (photo). Retain the bearing shells in their original sequence if they are required for further service. Note the semi-circular thrust washers used either side of the centre main bearing.

22 Mark the position and order in which the cylinder liners are fitted, using quick drying paint, and then remove the liner, piston and rod assemblies from the block.

15.21 Removing crankshaft

16 Examination and renovation – general

1 With the engine dismantled, all components must be thoroughly cleaned and examined for wear as described in the following Sections.

2 If a high mileage has been covered since new or the last engine rebuild, and general wear is evident, consideration should be given to renewing the engine assembly.

3 If a single component has malfunctioned and the rest of the engine is in good condition endeavour to find out the cause of its failure if not readily apparent. For example, if a bearing has failed, check that the adjoining oilways are clear; the new bearing will not last long if it is not being lubricated.

4 If uncertain about the condition of any components, seek a second opinion, preferably from a Renault dealer/mechanic who will obviously have an expert knowledge of your model and be able to advise on the best course of action.

5 Check on the availability of replacement parts before discarding the old ones. Check the new part against the old to ensure that you have the correct replacement.

6 Some of the measurements required will need the use of feeler blades or a micrometer, but in many instances wear will be visually evident or the old component can be compared with a new one.

17 Crankcase, cylinder block and mountings – examination and renovation

1 Examine the casting for cracks, especially at the bolt holes.

2 Check that the threads in the tapped holes are not stripped.

3 Clean out all oil galleries and passages by probing with a length of wire.

4 If the engine flexible mountings show signs of deterioration or deformation, renew them.

18 Crankshaft and main bearings – examination and renovation

1 Carefully examine the surfaces of the main bearing journals and the crankpins for scoring. Using a micrometer check that the journal and crankpin diameters are of the specified dimensions and then, by measuring them at several different positions, establish whether they have worn oval in shape.

2 If any indications of wear are evident, the crankshaft will have to be reground by your Renault dealer or motor engineering works. A set of undersize shell bearings will be supplied with the reground crankshaft and they will allow for the correct running clearance.

3 Clean out the crankshaft oilways using wire or a pressure cleaner, making sure that all dirt and swarf is removed.

4 Examine the pilot bearing in the centre of the crankshaft flange which supports the end of the transmission input shaft. If it is worn or damaged, it must be renewed. To extract the pilot bearing, either tap a thread into it and use a suitable extracting tool or fill it full of grease and drive in a close fitting rod. This will create sufficient hydraulic pressure to push out the bearing.

5 Drive in the new bearing, taking care not to burr its rim.

19 Main and big-end bearings – examination and renovation

1 The main bearing shells themselves are normally a matt grey in colour all over and should have no signs of pitting or ridging or discoloration as this usually indicates that the surface bearing metal has worn away and the backing material is showing through. It is worthwhile renewing the main bearing shells anyway if you have gone to the trouble of removing the crankshaft, but they must, of course, be renewed if there is any sign of damage to them or if the crankshaft has been reground.

2 If the crankshaft is not being reground, yet the bearing shells are being renewed, make sure that you check whether or not the crankshaft has been reground before. This can be determined by looking at the back of the bearing shell which will indicate whether it is undersize or not. The same size shell bearings must be used when they are renewed.

3 The big-end bearings are subject to wear at a greater rate than the crankshaft journals. A sign that one or more big-end bearings are getting badly worn is a pronounced knocking noise from the engine, accompanied by a significant drop in oil pressure due to the increased clearance between the bearing and the journal permitting oil to flow more freely through the resultantly larger space. If this should happen quite suddenly and action is taken immediately (within a few miles), it is possible that the bearing shell may be renewed without any further work needing to be done.

4 If this happens in an engine which has been neglected, and oil changes and oil filter changes have not been carried out as they should have been, it is most likely that the rest of the engine is in a pretty terrible state anyway. If it occurs in an engine which has been recently overhauled, then it is almost certainly due to a piece of grit or swarf which has got into the oil circulation system and finally come to rest in the bearing shell and scored it. In the latter instance, renewal of the shell alone accompanied by a thorough flush through of the lubrication system may be all that is required.

20 Cylinder liner bores – examination and renovation

1 Wear in the cylinder bores will usually become obvious by the amount of smoke being emitted from the exhaust and the poor performance of the engine due to lost compression.

2 The cylinder liners can be renewed complete with matching pistons, rings and gudgeon pins. These are supplied by Renault in kit form.

3 An alternative method of overcoming worn cylinder bores is to fit proprietary piston rings. These are available in sets and include new compression rings and a special type of oil control ring.

4 If this type of ring set is fitted to worn bores, the engine can be expected to resume nearly new performance for several thousand miles.

5 Before fitting these, or any other new piston rings, the cylinder bore must be de-glazed using either a 'glaze-buster' tool or fine glasspaper to give a cross-hatched surface to the bore. This is required to assist the rapid bedding-in of the new rings.

6 If a wear ridge can be detected at the upper end of the cylinder liner then this must either be removed using a ridge reamer or the new top compression ring must be stepped so that it does not strike the ridge when the piston is at TDC.

7 Apart from compression blow-by due to worn piston rings or cylinder bores, badly seating valves will contribute to low compression.

8 To check the compression of each individual cylinder, a

compression gauge may be obtained from most motor accessory stores. This is screwed into the cylinder head in place of the spark plug. If the engine is then 'spun' on the starter motor with the throttle held wide open, the compression reading can be taken for each cylinder.
9   Compare the results with the gauge manufacturer's acceptable pressure range limits and compare one cylinder reading with another. Any large difference between cylinders will indicate the need for attention to the valves (see Section 27).

21 Connecting rods, pistons and rings – examination and renovation

1   If the original pistons are to be used again fitted with new rings, it is essential to clean the ring grooves completely free from carbon and to clear the groove oil return holes. The best tool for clearing the grooves is a piece of broken piston ring.
2   If the pistons are to be changed refer to Section 9.
3   It is rare for the connecting rods to require renewal unless the gudgeon pin is no longer an interference fit in the small end.
4   A bent or distorted connecting rod will only occur if water has entered the carburettor when the engine is running. In this event, apart from new connecting rods, all the engine internal components should be subjected to the closest scrutiny.

22 Camshaft – examination and renovation

1   Check the lobes for wear, pitting or scoring.
2   Check the skew gear teeth for wear or chipping.
3   If the camshaft is worn, it is possible to have it re-profiled by specialist companies at a much lower cost than would be charged for a new camshaft.
4   The camshaft runs directly in the cylinder block without the use of separate bearings. It is rare for the camshaft journals or bearings to wear, but the fit of the camshaft should be checked in the block at time of overhaul.
5   Finally, inspect the condition of the tappets (cam followers). Although they are unlikely to be worn in their bores, the lobe contact face may show signs of dishing. It is possible for the tappets to be resurfaced, but they must be ground absolutely square and the work is best left to your dealer or engine reconditioners.

23 Flywheel – examination and renovation

1   Inspect the clutch friction lining contact area of the flywheel. If this is scored or grooved by failure to renew the driven plate when worn down to its rivets, it may be possible to have it surface ground by your dealer or engine reconditioner. Otherwise a new flywheel will be required.
2   If the contact area on the flywheel is covered in small cracks, these will be due to overheating and will have to be dealt with as for scoring or grooving.
3   It is unlikely that the flywheel starter ring gear will be worn or damaged as a pre-engaged type starter motor does not damage the teeth as an inertia type starter motor does.
4   However, should any teeth be chipped, (which can occur if the starter motor is operated by turning the ignition key while the engine is running) the ring gear should be renewed. This will mean splitting off the old ring gear with a cold chisel and heating the new one before fitting it squarely down onto the shoulder of the flywheel.
5   As the ring gear must be heated to about 350°C (662°F) evenly, so as not to spoil its temper, this is really a job for your dealer or engine reconditioner.

24 Oil pump – examination and renovation

1   The oil pump incorporates a ball type pressure release valve.
2   To remove the valve components, relieve the staking on the sealing plug and then unscrew the plug using an Allen key.
3   Extract the spring and ball.
4   Unscrew the pump cover bolts, remove the cover and withdraw the idler gear and drivegear/shaft assembly.
5   Clean all components and check the gear teeth for wear or

chipping. Make sure, also, that the oil pump shaft bearings in the body are not worn.
6   Reassemble the gears and, using feeler blades, measure the clearance between the tips of the teeth and the pump body. If the clearance is more than 0.20 mm (0.008 in) renew the gears. If the gears are worn, the pressure relief valve ball is scored or pitted, or the pump cover gear endfloat pads are scored, consideration should be given to the purchase of a new pump rather than renew individual components.

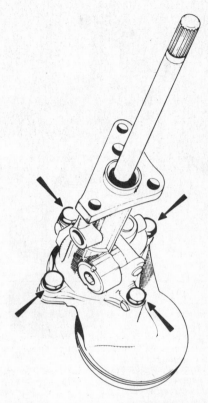

Fig. 1.15 Oil pump cover bolts (Sec 24)

25 Timing chain, sprockets and tensioner – examination and renovation

1   Examine the teeth of the sprockets. If there is any sign of damage or 'hooking' then the sprockets must be renewed.
2   The timing chain should be renewed at overhaul if it has been in service for 50 000 miles (80 000 km) or more. A rough check for chain wear is to support both ends of the chain (link pins vertical) and observe whether the chain takes on a deeply bowed appearance. If it does then the chain is badly worn.
3   Examine the slipper of the chain tensioner. If it is deeply grooved, renew the slipper.
4   One of three types of timing chain tensioner may be fitted and details of their construction are given here in case any individual component requires renewal.

Hydraulic tensioner with manual initial take-up
5   With this type of tensioner, the slipper is retracted and extended by removing the plug (b) and inserting a 3.0 mm Allen key – see Fig. 1.17.

Hydraulic tensioner with automatic initial take-up
6   The slipper on this shoe is held retracted by means of a peg (e) engaging in a notch (c) of the piston (3) – see Figs. 1.18 and 1.19.
7   The piston is locked in the slipper by inserting an Allen key and turning it until the peg engages in the piston notch. The slipper/piston assembly is then inserted into the tensioner body, but do this very gently as too much pressure on the slipper will release it. Heavy

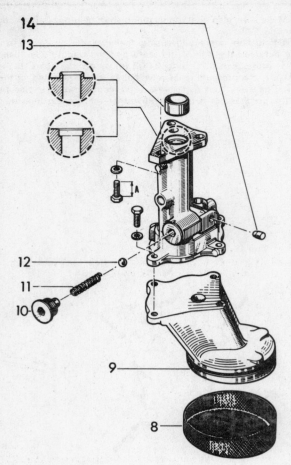

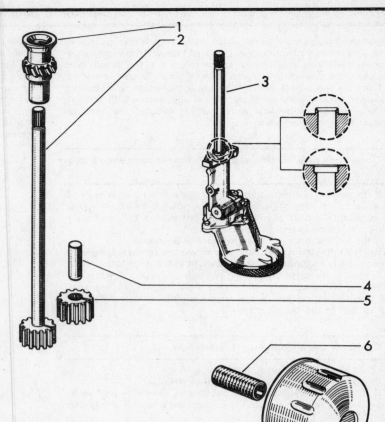

Fig. 1.16 Oil pump components (Sec 24)

1	Distributor/oil pump drivegear	5	Gear	9	Pump body	12 Ball
2	Oil pump driveshaft	6	Hollow stud	10	Plug	13 Sleeve
3	Oil pump assembled	7	Oil filter	11	Spring	14 Plug
4	Idler shaft	8	Filter screen			

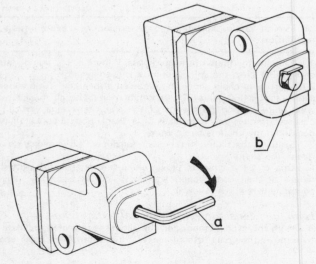

Fig. 1.17 Chain tensioner with manual initial take-up (Sec 25)

a *Allen key*   b *Plug*

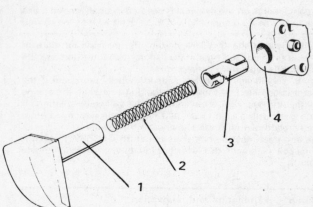

Fig. 1.18 Chain tensioner with automatic initial take-up (Sec 25)

1	Slipper	3	Piston
2	Spring	4	Body

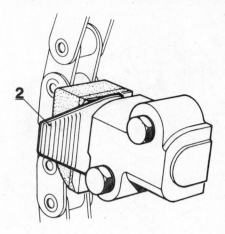

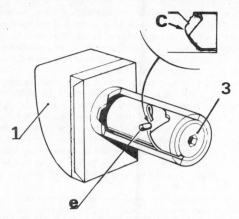

Fig. 1.19 Piston locking arrangement on chain tensioner with automatic initial take-up (Sec 25)

1   *Slipper*   c   *Notch*
3   *Piston*   e   *Peg*

Fig. 1.20 Keeper plate (2) in position on chain tensioner with automatic initial take-up (Sec 25)

pressure will be required to set the tension of the chain during engine rebuilding.

8   New chain tensioner assemblies are supplied with a keeper plate (2.0 mm - 0.079 in thick) inserted between the slipper and the tensioner body to prevent it being released until required. The plate is withdrawn and the slipper depressed and released to press against the timing chain.

Mechanical tensioner

9   This consists of a slipper pivoted on a bolt and tensioned by means of a spring. Releasing the tension of the spring is difficult without the special tool (MOT 761), but prising the tensioner away from the chain using a cranked lever will make it possible to unhook the spring from its hole in the crankcase.

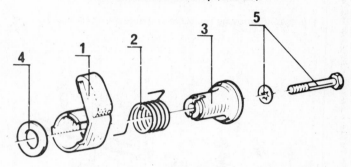

Fig. 1.21 Mechanical type chain tensioner components (Sec 25)

1   *Slipper*   4   *Washer*
2   *Spring*   5   *Star washer and bolt*
3   *Pivot*

26 Rocker gear – examination and renovation

1   Check the shafts for wear at the bearing housing areas.
2   Inspect the rocker arm pressure pads for grooves or circular indentations. Any minor wear of this kind can be removed by the careful use of an oilstone or abrasive cloth, but maintain the contour of the pressure pad.
3   Check that the adjuster screw threads and their heads are in good condition, otherwise renew them.

27 Cylinder head and valves – dismantling, decarbonising and reassembly

1   With the cylinder head removed from the engine, unscrew the spark plugs and unbolt the manifolds, coolant pump and endplate.
2   Prise out the rubber plug from the rocker shaft removal hole in the cylinder head.
3   Unscrew the rocker shaft end plugs, if fitted.
4   Remove the spring clip and coil spring from each end of the rocker shaft.
5   Unscrew and remove the two rocker shaft locating bolts.
6   The rocker shaft can now be removed either by tapping it out of the head, using a rod, or by screwing a bolt into the rocker shaft tapped hole.
7   As the rocker shaft is withdrawn, keep the rocker arms and springs in their originally fitted sequence.
8   Using a suitable valve spring compressor, compress each spring in turn until the split cotters can be removed. Place a small packing block under the valve head to support the valve when using the compressor. It is sometimes found that the valve spring will not compress, due to the fact that the collets are 'stuck' in the spring cap. Do not continue to screw down the compressor in an attempt to free the components, but remove the compressor and place a box spanner or a piece of tubing on the spring cap and give it a tap with a hammer.
9   Once the split collets have been removed, slowly release the

compressor, take off the spring cap, the spring, the spring seat and withdraw the valve. Keep the components in their originally installed order using either a box with divisions or a card with holes punched in it and numbered to take the valves.
10   The cylinder head should now be cleaned of all carbon and combustion deposits. Remember that it is made of light alloy so do not dig or score it with a sharp instrument. The use of a piece of copper tubing which has its end flattened as a scraper is a suitable tool. Finish off with a rotary wire brush in an electric drill, paying particular attention to the inlet and exhaust ports.
11   The carbon must now be removed from the piston crowns. Again remember that the pistons are of light alloy construction and must not be scored. To remove the carbon, turn the crankshaft to bring two pistons to the top of their stroke. Stuff rag into the other two cylinders and tape over the coolant passages and oilways on top of the cylinder block to prevent the entry of dirt.
12   Remove the carbon from the two pistons which are at the top of their stroke. Depending upon the type of cylinder liner clamp used, it may have to be temporarily removed in order to be able to completely remove all the carbon. If you do this, on no account turn the crankshaft while the clamp is off.
13   Remove the carbon from the remaining two pistons once they have been brought to TDC.
14   To complete the cylinder head reconditioning operation, the valves should be ground in. Unless the cylinder head has been removed for renewal of the gasket only, grinding in the valves and renewing the valve springs should be regarded as essential, especially if the car has covered 30 000 miles (48 000 km) or more since the engine was last overhauled.
15   Examination of the valve heads and seats should reveal only light discolouration with black spots which can be removed by grinding in with paste. If the valve head is burned away at the edge or the valve

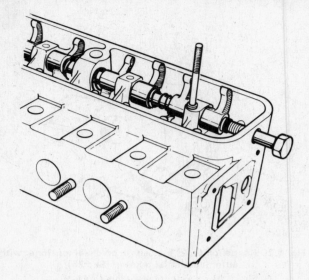

Fig. 1.22 Removing rocker shaft using a bolt (Sec 27)

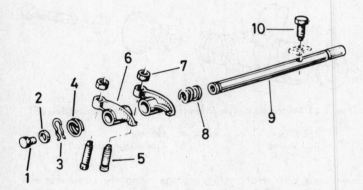

Fig. 1.23 Rocker gear components (Sec 27)

1	Shaft end plug (where fitted)	6	Rocker arm
2	Washer	7	Locknut
3	Clip	8	Spring
4	Spring	9	Rocker shaft
5	Adjuster screw	10	Shaft locating bolt

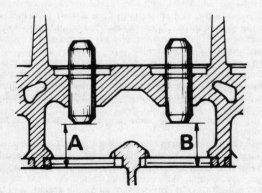

Fig. 1.24 Valve guide installation diagram (Sec 27)

A   Inlet = 14.0 mm (0.551 in)
B   Exhaust = 14.0 mm (0.551 in)

seat is similarly affected, renew the valves and have the seats re-cut. If the mating faces of valve head or seat have a rounded appearance then it is best to have the valves and seats refinished by your dealer or engine reconditioner before grinding in, as this condition is caused by 'hammering' of the valve into its seat over high mileages and makes the metal very hard and difficult to grind in.

16 If the valve has a distinct side-to-side rocking motion when pushed into its guide then new guides must be fitted. These are available with external diameters in oversizes to ensure that an interference fit is maintained in the cylinder head. It is recommended tht the fitting of new valve guides or valve seats is left to your Renault dealer or engine reconditioner.

17 Assuming the valves and seats are in reasonable condition they should be reseated by grinding them using valve grinding carborundum paste. The grinding process must also be carried out when new valves are fitted.

18 The carborundum paste used for this job is normally supplied in a double-ended tin with coarse paste at one end and fine at the other. In addition, a suction tool for holding the valve head so that it may be rotated is also required. To grind in a valve, first smear a trace of coarse paste onto the seat face and fit the suction grinder to the valve head. Then with a semi-rotary motion grind the valve head into its seat, lifting the valve occasionally to redistribute the grinding paste. When a dull matt continuous line is produced on both the valve seat and the valve then the paste can be wiped off. Apply a little fine paste and finish off the grinding process, then remove all traces of the paste. If a light spring is placed over the valve stem behind the head this can often be of assistance in raising the valve from time to time against the pressure of the grinding tool so as to redistribute the paste evenly round the job. The width of the line which is produced after grinding indicates the contact face width, and this width should not exceed the specified maximum. If, after a moderate amount of grinding, it is apparent that the seating line is too wide, it probably means that the seat has already been cut back one or more times previously, or else the valve has been ground several times. Here again, specialist advice is best sought.

19 Double check that all grinding paste has been cleaned from the valves and the seats.

20 At the end of the cylinder head is a cover plate. The cover plate hides the end of the coolant distribution tube in the cylinder head. Although the cover plate and a possible leaking gasket can be renewed with the engine and cylinder head in the car, the distribution tube cannot, nor even be inspected.

21 To replace a leaking cover plate gasket drain the coolant from the system and undo the four securing screws. Clean the mating surfaces and, using gasket cement, replace with the proper gasket and tighten sufficiently.

22 To inspect the coolant distribution tube, a task only worth doing when the cylinder head or engine are being overhauled, requires the cylinder head to be removed from the block. Remove the cover plate, as described, and check to see if the cylindrical steel tube, its end visible through the cover plate end in the circular hole is corroded badly, disintegrated, or otherwise damaged. If it is damaged it will have to be drifted very delicately from the cover plate end through to the coolant pump end. This means removing the coolant pump.

23 The holes drilled in the tube should face towards the exhaust valve seats at an angle of 30° to the vertical, and the end which has the two holes close together should be positioned at the cover plate end. Peen the ends after insertion to prevent any twisting movement. Replace the coolant pump and cover plate.

24 Commence reassembly by oiling the stem of No 1 valve and inserting it into its guide. Over the stem fit the spring seat, spring (closer coils to head) and the spring cap.

25 Using the compressor tool, compress the valve spring and locate the split collets in the cut-out in the valve stem. Retain the collets if necessary with a dab of grease while the compressor is being released. Note the different shapes of the split collets used for inlet and exhaust valves on early models. Fit the remaining valves in a similar way.

26 Push the rocker shaft into the cylinder head and, as this is done, fit the rocker arms and coil springs in their original sequence. Align the rocker shaft so that the two fixing bolts will enter the holes in the shaft when they are screwed in.

27 Fit the end springs and clips to the shaft and screw in the end plugs (if fitted).

28 Fit the rocker shaft removal hole rubber plug.

29 Using new gaskets on clean mating surfaces, fit the manifolds,

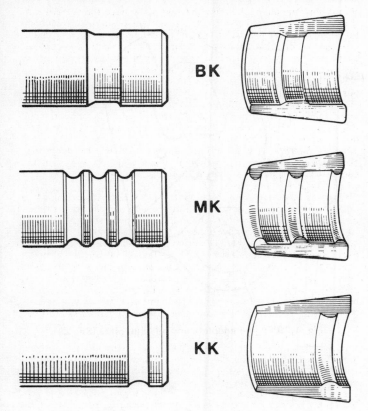

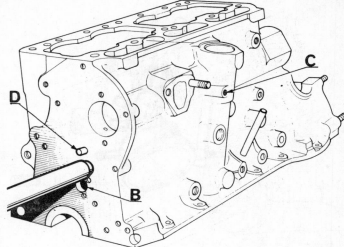

Fig. 1.26 Cylinder block plugs (Sec 29)

B   Hydraulic tensioner oil channel
C   Camshaft centre bearing oil channel
D   Timing chain lubrication jet

Fig. 1.25 Different types of valve collets and valve stem grooves
(Sec 27)

BK Inlet   KK Inlet and exhaust (later models)
MK Exhaust

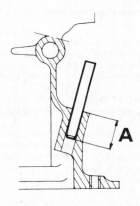

Fig. 1.27 Engine oil dipstick guide tube fitting diagram (Sec 29)

A = 20.5 mm (0.807 in)

coolant pump and end cover plate. Tighten the manifold bolts to the specified torque.
30 Release the rocker arm adjuster screw locknuts and unscrew the screws fully, pending refitting the cylinder head (Section 4) and adjustment of the valve clearances (Section 30).

28 Engine reassembly – general

1   Observe absolute cleanliness during reassembly. Renew all gaskets, oil seals and locking plates as a matter of routine.
2   As reassembly progresses, lubricate each component and its friction surface with engine oil before fitting.
3   Double check that each component has been fitted the correct way with any positioning marks correctly aligned and nuts and bolts tightened to torque where specified.

29 Engine – reassembly

1   With the cylinder block standing on the bench drive in and stake any new aluminium oil gallery plugs which were removed during examination and renovation.
2   On engines having a mechanical chain tensioner, fit the lubrication jet.
3   Drive in the dipstick guide tube in accordance with the fitting diagram (Fig. 1.27).
4   Temporarily fit the cylinder liners and check liner protrusion, as described in Section 8.
5   Fit the main bearing shells into their crankcase seats. These shells have oil holes in them. Make sure that the seats are absolutely clean, otherwise the shells will bind on the crankshaft journals.
6   Oil the shells liberally.
7   Lower the crankshaft into position.

8   Fit the crankshaft semi-circular thrust washers so that the oil grooves are towards the ends of the crankshaft.
9   Fit the plain main bearing shells into their caps and oil them liberally.
10 Fit the caps so that the marks made at dismantling are adjacent. When fitting No 1 bearing cap, apply jointing compound to the block mating face.
11 Tighten the bolts to the specified torque and check that the crankshaft rotates freely.
12 Check the crankshaft endfloat with a dial gauge. Do this by pushing the shaft fully in one direction and then push the shaft fully in the opposite direction and measure the total movement. An alternative method of checking is to use feeler blocks inserted at the centre bearing between the face of the thrust washer and the journal shoulder.
13 If the endfloat is not within the specified tolerances, the thrust washers will have to be changed for ones of alternative thickness.
14 Locate the flywheel on the end of the crankshaft so that the marks made at removal are in alignment.
15 Fit new lockplates and then, having applied a thread-locking compound to clean bolt threads, screw in the bolts evenly and tighten to the specified torque.
16 Fit the bearing shells to their connecting rod big-end recesses which must be absolutely clean.

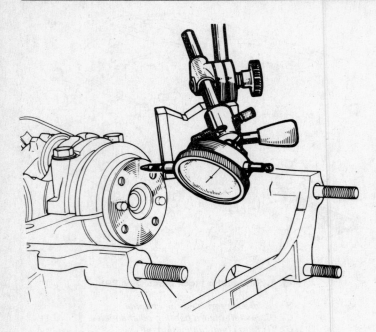

Fig. 1.28 Checking crankshaft endfloat with a dial gauge (Sec 29)

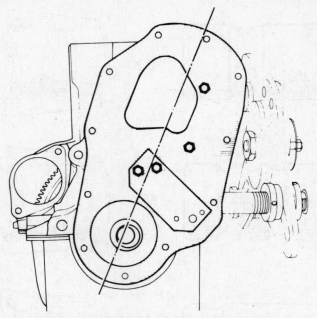

Fig. 1.29 Engine endplate and oil input plate (Sec 29)

17 Install the liner, piston and rod assemblies with selected base seals, as described in Section 8. Make sure that No 1 cylinder is at the flywheel end, the connecting rod big-end numbers are furthest from the camshaft and also the arrow on the piston crown is pointing towards the flywheel.
18 Clamp the cylinder liners in the block.
19 Oil the crankpins and then draw the connecting rods down to connect them to the crankshaft.
20 Fit the bearing shells into their caps, oil them and locate them on the crankpins so that the matching numbers are adjacent.
21 Screw in the big-end cap bolts and tighten to the specified torque. Check that the crankshaft rotates freely.
22 Invert the cylinder block or place it on its side and bolt the oil pump into place.
23 Using a smear of jointing compound, stick the sump gasket strip to the rear main bearing cap.
24 Stick the sump side gasket strips in position so that their rear ends overlap the ends of the rear bearing strip. Apply a bead of jointing compound to the joint of the gaskets.
25 Now fit the gasket strip to the front main bearing gasket. Where its ends overlap the side gaskets, apply a bead of jointing compound.
26 Place the sump pan in position and screw in the fixing bolts evenly. The bolts with the slotted heads are located nearest the flywheel so that a screwdriver can be used on them due to the limited access for inserting a socket or box spanner.
27 The timing chain tensioner preliminary components should now be fitted, the method depending upon the type of tensioner.

Hydraulic chain tensioner
28 Fit the small gauze filter.
29 Fit the engine endplate with the paper gasket smeared with gasket cement, but tighten the bolts only finger tight.
30 Fit the oil input plate with the paper gasket smeared with gasket cement, but tighten the bolts only finger tight.

Mechanical chain tensioner
31 Check that the following components are in position (refer to Fig. 1.30):

  Plug (A)
  Oil jet (B)
  Tensioner positioning dowel (C)

32 Fit the engine endplate with the paper gasket smeared with gasket cement.

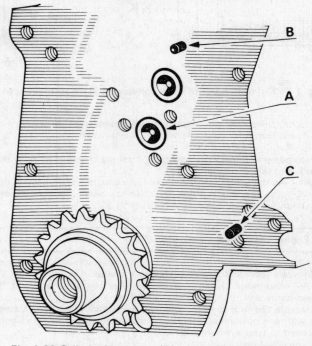

Fig. 1.30 Cylinder block plug (A), oil jet (B) and tensioner positioning dowel (C) on engine with mechanical chain tensioner (Sec 29)

All engines
33 The camshaft sprocket, having been drawn off at dismantling, should now be reinstalled. A press will be required.
34 Locate the retainer plate on the camshaft so that the chamfer on the plate is towards the camshaft.
35 Press the Woodruff key into its groove.
36 Locate the sprocket so that its timing mark is facing outwards and then press the sprocket onto the camshaft so that surfaces (A) and (B) are flush, as shown in Fig. 1.31.
37 Oil the camshaft bearings and push it partially into position.
38 The timing chain should now be fitted. Genuine Renault timing chains are marked with a yellow link (a) and a scribed line (b) to assist setting the timing (Fig. 1.32).

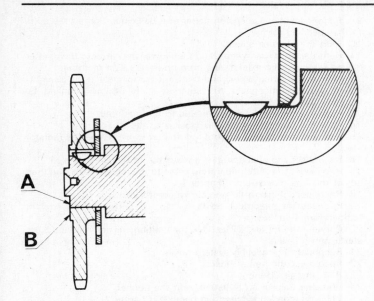

Fig. 1.31 Camshaft sprocket fitting diagram (Sec 29)

A and B flush faces

39 Slip the chain over the camshaft sprocket so that the scribed line is opposite the timing mark on the sprocket.
40 Now turn the camshaft sprocket until a line drawn from the scribed mark on the chain will pass through the centres of the camshaft and crankshaft.
41 Make sure that the Woodruff key is in position in the crankshaft.
42 Engage the crankshaft sprocket within the loop of the timing chain so that the yellow link of the chain is opposite the timing mark on the sprocket.
43 Turn the crankshaft as necessary to align the Woodruff key with the keyway in the sprocket. Push the sprocket onto the crankshaft. Use a bolt, nut and distance piece to draw the crankshaft sprocket fully into position and at the same time push the camshaft home.
44 Where a timing chain is being fitted which does not have link marks, fit it in any position provided a line drawn between the sprocket marks passes through the centres of the camshaft and crankshaft.
45 Working through the holes in the camshaft sprocket, screw in and tighten the camshaft retainer plate bolts.
46 Fit the timing chain tensioner according to type (see Section 25) and set it.
47 Where a hydraulic type tensioner is used, now is the time to fully tighten the engine plate and oil inlet plate bolts (see paragraphs 29 and 30).
48 Bolt on the timing cover with a new gasket.
49 Bolt the camshaft pulley with spacer plate onto the end of the camshaft.
50 Apply oil to the tappets (cam followers) and return them to their original positions in the crankcase.
51 Remove the cylinder liner clamps and fit the cylinder head, as described in Section 4.
52 Adjust the valve clearances, as described in Section 30.
53 Insert the distributor drivegear. Do this by first turning the crankshaft until No 1 piston is at TDC on its firing stroke. This can be verified if the rocker arms for No 4 cylinder are rocking (in balance). The skew gear must now be dropped into its recess in the cylinder block so that when it is fully engaged with the camshaft gear, the distributor drive slot is at 60° to the engine centre line with the larger drive dog segment nearer the flywheel. The gear engages on splines at the end of the oil pump driveshaft, the setting of this shaft is not critical. A certain amount of trial and error will be necessary to achieve the correct setting as the slot will turn as the drivegear is pushed fully home and the gears mesh. Anticipate this by turning the slot a few degrees back from its finally desired setting before pushing it into position. A bolt may be screwed into the end of the distributor drivegear as a means of withdrawing and inserting it.
54 Fit the distributor and turn it until the contact breaker points are just about to open. Tighten the distributor clamp bolt.

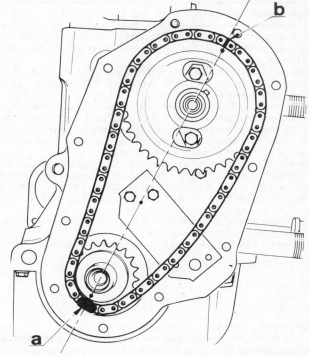

Fig. 1.32 Correctly aligned chain and sprockets (type 800 engine) – No 1 piston at TDC (Sec 29)

a Yellow link   b Scribed line

55 Fit the rocker cover with a new gasket.
56 Centre and fit the clutch assembly.
57 Refit the oil pressure switch and coolant temperature switch.
58 Refit all the ancillaries removed at dismantling (generator, fuel pump, engine mountings etc).
59 Fit a new oil filter (see Section 2).
60 Insert the dipstick into its guide tube.

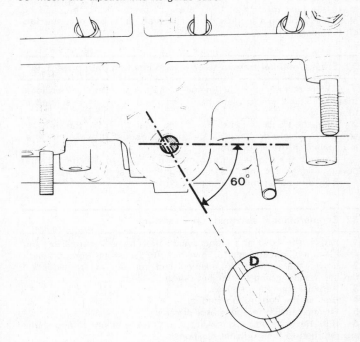

Fig. 1.33 Distributor drive slot (type 800 engine) – No 1 piston at TDC (Sec 29)

D Larger segment towards flywheel

30 Valve clearance – adjustment

1   This operation is necessary after engine overhaul, cylinder head removal and refitting and at the intervals specified in Routine Maintenance.

2   The valve rocker clearances are important as they control the amount a valve opens and when it opens and thus can affect the efficiency of the engine.

3   The clearances should be measured and set by using a feeler blade between the rocker arm and the end of each valve stem. This is done when the valve is closed and the tappet is resting on the lowest point of the cam. The clearances may be adjusted with the engine hot or cold, but note the different clearance values.

4   To enable each valve to be in the correct position for checking with the minimum amount of engine turning the procedure and order of checking should follow the sequence given in the following tables. In the table the valves are numbered 1 to 8, number 1 being nearest the flywheel.

5   A valve is fully open when the rocker arm has depressed the end of the valve stem to its fullest extent.

6   Use the following table, using the sequence indicated.

Valve fully open	Valves to adjust
1 Exhaust	6 Inlet and 8 exhaust
5 Exhaust	7 Inlet and 4 exhaust
8 Exhaust	3 Inlet and 1 exhaust
4 Exhaust	2 Inlet and 5 exhaust

7   Using feeler blades check the gap between the end of the valve stem and the rocker arm. If adjustment is required to give the feeler blade a stiff sliding fit, release the rocker arm adjuster screw locknut and turn the adjuster screw in or out as necessary. When adjustment is complete, tighten the locknut without disturbing the position of the adjuster screw.

8   Repeat the operations on the remaining valves.

9   If the valve clearances are being adjusted at a Routine Maintenance interval, the easiest way to turn the crankshaft is to jack up a front roadwheel, engage top gear and turn the roadwheel in the forward direction of rotation.

10 On cars with automatic transmission use the starter motor to turn the crankshaft to somewhere near its final position having first disconnected the HT lead from the coil to prevent the engine firing. Make the final rotation of the crankshaft by removing the sparking plugs and applying a spanner to the camshaft pulley bolt or to the flats on the camshaft.

31 Engine/manual transmission – reconnection before refitting

1   Before reconnecting the engine to the transmission it is essential that the clutch driven plate has been centralised, as described in Chapter 5.

2   Offer the transmission to the engine, supporting the transmission so that its weight does not hang upon the input shaft while the latter is engaged in the driven plate.

3   Connect the engine and transmission flanges so that the locating dowels engage and then insert and tighten the securing bolts.

4   Bolt the starter motor into position.

32 Engine/manual transmission – refitting

1   Attach the hoist and lifting eye to the engine/transmission and raise it to a height suitable for lowering into the engine compartment.

2   Lower the engine into position and connect the transmission flexible mounting and the engine side mountings.

3   Remove the lifting tackle.

4   Bolt on the cooling fan blades.

5   Fit and tension the generator drivebelt.

6   Refit the steering rack, making sure that the height setting shims are returned to their original positions.

7   Engage the inboard ends of the driveshafts in the transmission sunwheel splines by tilting the tops of the brake drums inwards. Take care not to damage the differential oil seals during this operation.

8   Reconnect the steering rack end fittings to the tie-rods. Tighten the bolts to the specified torque.

9   Reconnect the suspension upper arm balljoints, tighten the bolts to the specified torque.

10 Refit the gearbox shield.

11 Refit the front roadwheels and then lower the car onto them, after having removed the axle stands from under the side members.

12 With the steering wheel and the front roadwheels in the straight-ahead position, reconnect the steering shaft flexible coupling by inserting the two connecting bolts.

13 Reconnect the exhaust downpipe to the manifold.

14 Refit the radiator and the expansion bottle.

15 Refit the gearchange control rod, the cross-brace and the radiator stay.

16 Reconnect the speedometer drive cable to the transmission.

17 Reconnect the clutch operating cable to the release lever and then adjust the free movement (Chapter 5).

18 Reconnect the throttle and choke control cables.

19 Connect the electrical leads to the oil pressure and coolant temperature switches.

20 Connect the HT and LT leads to the ignition coil and reconnect the starter motor leads.

21 Reconnect the cooling system hoses.

22 Reconnect the heater hoses.

23 Refit the air cleaner.

24 With the help of an assistant, refit the bonnet.

25 Refill the cooling system and bleed it (Chapter 2).

26 Refill the engine and transmission with the correct quantity and grade of oil.

27 Reconnect the battery.

33 Engine – starting up after major overhaul

1   Pull the choke fully out and operate the starter. The engine will take longer to fire than usual as the fuel pump and carburettor will have to fill with fuel.

2   Once the engine starts, ease the choke in until the engine is running smoothly at a fast idle. Avoid revving the engine.

3   Check that the oil pressure and ignition warning lamps have gone out.

4   Dispense with the choke as soon as the engine will run without it. You will find that the idle speed screw will have to be turned to increase the idle speed. This will offset the stiffness of the engine which is the result of having fitted new internal components.

5   Once the engine has reached normal working temperature, check and adjust the idle speed and mixture settings (Chapter 3) and the ignition timing (Chapter 4).

6   Restrict the engine and roadspeeds during the first 1000 miles (1600 km) if major internal components have been renewed.

7   At the end of this period, change the engine oil and filter, check the cylinder head bolts and valve clearances.

8   When checking the cylinder head bolts, carry out the following procedure. Have the engine cold with the rocker cover removed. Unscrew the bolt (1) – see Fig. 1.34 – through one quarter of a turn and then retighten to the specified torque. Repeat the procedure one by one on the remaining bolts in the sequence indicated.

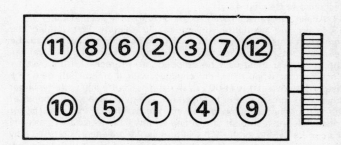

Fig. 1.34 Cylinder head bolt tightening sequence diagram – type 800 engine (Secs 4 and 33)

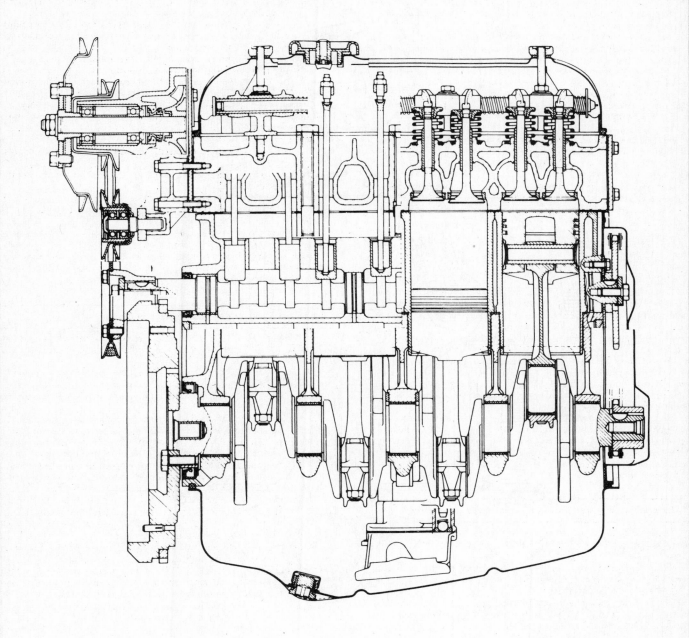

Fig. 1.35 Longitudinal sectional view of type 689 engine (Sec 34)

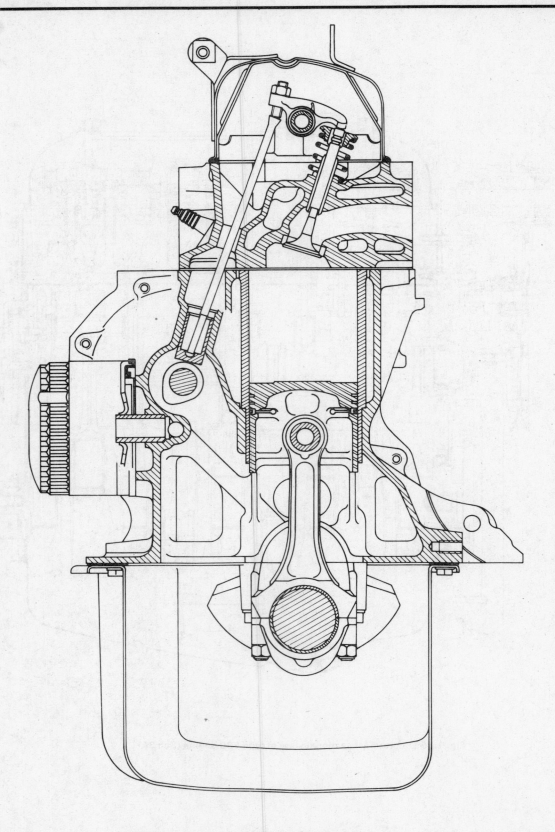

Fig. 1.36 Cross-sectional view of type 689 engine (Sec 34)

PART 2 Type 688 (1108 cc), 689 (956 cc) and 810 (1289 cc) engines

34 General description

This engine is similar to the type 800 described in Part 1, except that it has a five bearing crankshaft.

The crankcase on later models incorporates an oil bath for camshaft lubrication and an inverted type fuel pump operated by a pushrod.

The end of the camshaft is fitted with a pulley and is supported in the flywheel housing.

35 Engine oil – topping-up and renewal

Refer to Section 2. On later models the oil filler cap incorporates breather hose connections (photo).

36 Major operations possible – engine in car

Refer to Section 3.

37 Cylinder head – removal and refitting

Refer to Section 4. Note the sequence for loosening and tightening the cylinder head bolts – Fig. 1.37.

38 Engine sump pan – removal and refitting

1   Although the operations are essentially as described in Section 5, note that the clutch shield must be unbolted and tilted to the right-hand side.

2   When refitting the sump pan, note also that the side gaskets are located on dowel pins and the ends of the gaskets should overlap the front and rear main bearing cap rubber sealing strips. Apply a bead of jointing compound at the joint of gasket and strip.

39 Oil pump – removal and refitting

Refer to Section 6.

40 Big-end bearings – renewal

Refer to Section 7.

41 Cylinder liner, piston and rod assembly – removal and refitting

1   Refer to Section 8 (photos), but note that only Excelnyl liner base seals are used on this engine.

2   These seals are available in the specified thicknesses.

42 Cylinder liner, piston and rod – dismantling and reassembly

Refer to Section 9.

43 Engine mountings – renewal

Refer to Section 10.

44 Engine removal – method

Refer to Section 11.

35.1 Oil filler/breather cap

41.1a Oiling the piston rings

41.1b Piston ring clamp fitted

41.1c Pushing piston into liner

41.1d Liner base seal in position

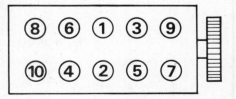
Fig. 1.37 Cylinder head bolt loosening and tightening sequence – type 688, 689 and 810 engines (Secs 37 and 52)

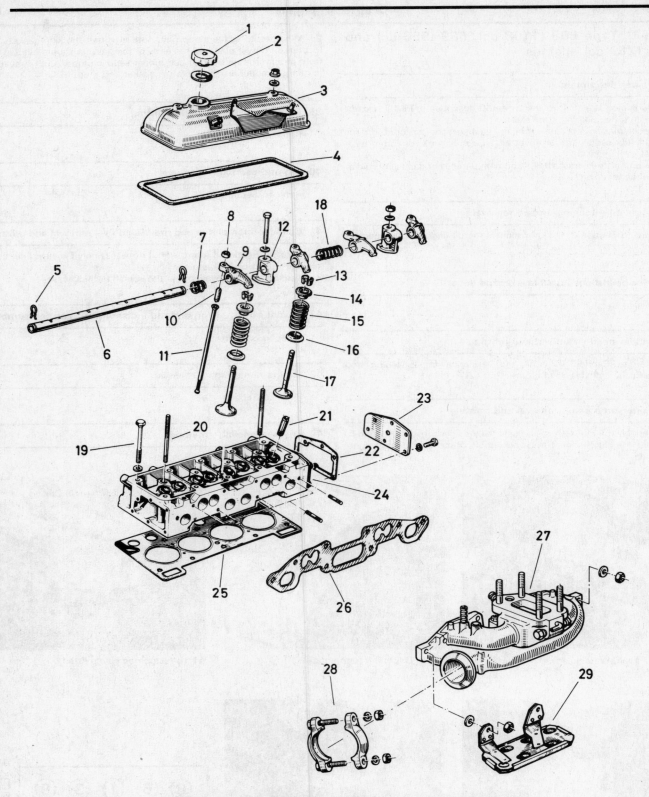

Fig. 1.38 Cylinder head components type 688, 689 and 810 engines (Sec 37)

1	Oil filler cap	9	Rocker arm
2	Seal	10	Adjuster screw
3	Rocker cover	11	Pushrod
4	Gasket	12	Rocker shaft pedestal
5	Clip	13	Split collets
6	Rocket shaft	14	Spring cap
7	Spring	15	Valve spring
8	Locknut		

16	Spring seat
17	Valve
18	Spring
19	Cylinder head bolts
20	Pedestal stud
21	Valve guide
22	Gasket

23	Endplate
24	Cylinder head
25	Gasket
26	Gasket
27	Manifold
28	Exhaust downpipe clamp
29	Shield

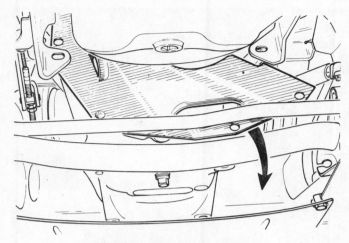

Fig. 1.39 Clutch shield plate (Sec 38)

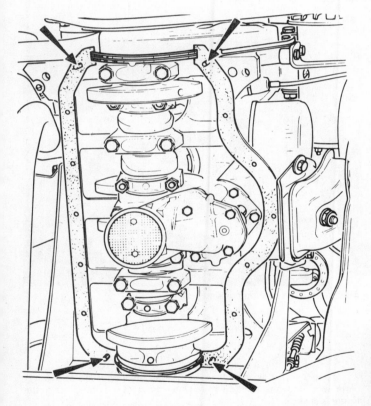

Fig. 1.40 Sump pan gaskets and locating dowels (Sec 38)

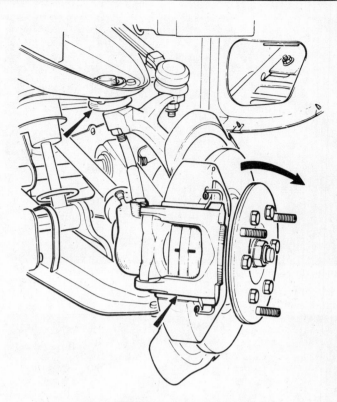

Fig. 1.41 Disconnection points pending removal of
engine/transmission (Sec 45)

Separation

6   Before unbolting the transmission (flywheel housing) bolts,
remove the pulley and its mounting flange from the flywheel end of the
camshaft (photos). The nuts at each side of the camshaft aperture
have lockplates and their tabs must be flattened before the nuts can be
unscrewed.
7   On later models the steering rack end fittings are not of pivot bolt
type but are of more conventional tie-rod and locknut type (refer to
Chapter 11).

45.2a Suspension and tie-rod balljoints

45 Engine/manual transmission – removal and separation

1   The operations are essentially as described in Sections 12 and 13,
but observe the following differences and ignore any reference to fan
blades.
2   Unbolt the front disc calipers (Chapter 9) and tie them up to avoid
straining the flexible hydraulic hose before disconnecting the
suspension upper balljoint (photos).
3   Disconnect the brake servo vacuum hose from the intake
manifold.
4   On North American models, disconnect the hoses and leads from
the emission control systems.
5   Disconnect the radiator fan leads before removing the radiator
(photo).

45.2b Suspension upper balljoint disconnected

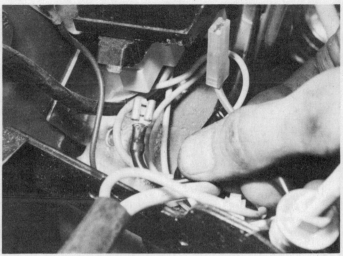

45.5 Electric fan relay leads

45.6a Camshaft pulley mounting flange

45.6b Camshaft bearing housing

46 Engine/automatic transmission – removal

1   The operations are similar to those described for vehicles with manual transmission, but ignore all reference to the clutch cable and fan blades and observe the following additional requirements.
2   Drain the transmission fluid.
3   Disconnect the electrical leads from the transmission governor and the computer.
4   Disconnect the pipe from the vacuum capsule.
5   Disconnect the electrical leads from the reverse lamp switch.
6   Disconnect the speedometer drive cable from the transmission.
7   Extract the circlip at the computer end of the selector rod. Disconnect the rod.
8   Remove the pulley and mounting flange from the torque converter end of the camshaft.

47 Engine/automatic transmission – separation

1   Unbolt and remove the starter motor and the torque converter cover plate.

2   Using a socket wrench inserted through the starter motor or cover plate apertures, unscrew the bolts which connect the driveplate to the torque converter.
3   Access to the three bolts can only be obtained if the driveplate is rotated to bring each bolt into view within the starter motor cover plate apertures. Do this by levering against the teeth of the starter ring gear.
4   Once the bolts are removed, support the weight of the transmission and withdraw it from the engine. The help of an assistant should be obtained to hold the converter in full engagement with the transmission as the transmission is withdrawn. Bolt a keeper plate to one of the converter housing flange bolt holes to retain the torque converter while the transmission is out of the car.

48 Engine overhaul – general

Refer to Section 14.

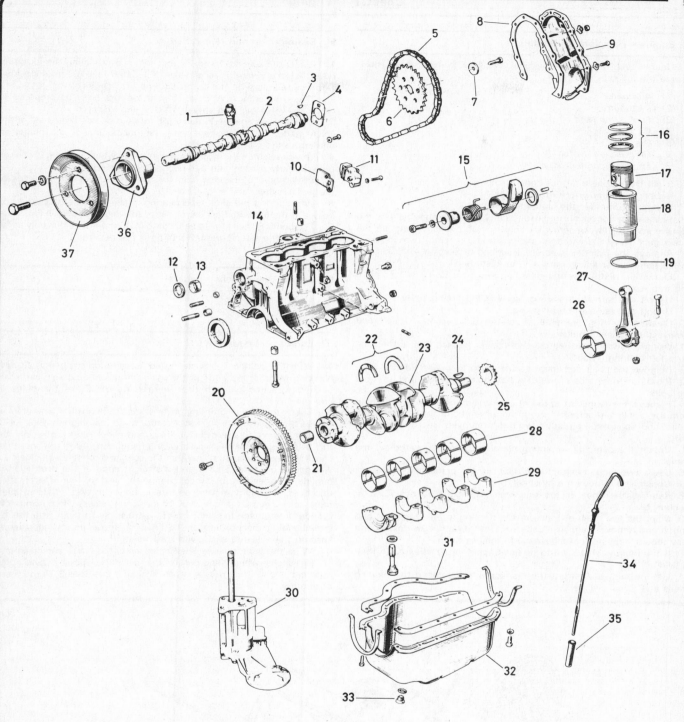

Fig. 1.42 Cylinder block/crankcase components – type 688, 689 and 810 engines (Sec 49)

1	Distributor/oil pump drivegear	11	Hydraulic chain tensioner (alternative)
2	Camshaft	12	Oil seal
3	Woodruff key	13	Camshaft extension housing bearing
4	Camshaft retaining plate	14	Cylinder block/crankcase
5	Timing chain	15	Mechanical chain tensioner (alternative)
6	Camshaft sprocket	16	Piston rings
7	Spacer	17	Piston
8	Gasket	18	Cylinder liner
9	Timing chain cover	19	Liner base seal
10	Tensioner backplate		

20	Flywheel	29	Main bearing caps
21	Pilot bearing	30	Oil pump
22	Crankshaft thrust washers	31	Sump pan gasket
23	Crankshaft	32	Sump pan
24	Woodruff key	33	Oil drain plug
25	Chain sprocket	34	Dipstick
26	Big-end bearing shells	35	Dipstick guide tube
27	Connecting rod	36	Bushed flange
28	Main bearing shells	37	Pulley

49 Engine – complete dismantling

1   Unbolt and remove the engine ancillary components. These include the following:

    (1) Alternator
    (2) Distributor
    (3) Fuel pump (and air pump – N. America)
    (4) Oil filter
    (5) Dipstick
    (6) Oil pressure switch
    (7) Engine mounting brackets

2   Drain the engine oil if not done previously.
3   Unbolt and remove the rocker cover.
4   Unbolt and remove the clutch assembly.
5   Release the rocker arm adjuster screw locknuts and unscrew the adjuster screws fully. Unscrew the rocker shaft pedestal bolts, lift the rocker gear away and withdraw the pushrods, keeping them in order.
6   Remove the cylinder head, as described in Section 4. Fit clamps only if the cylinder liners are not to be disturbed.
7   Extract the distributor drivegear by screwing a 12 mm x 1.75 pitch bolt into it.
8   Unbolt and remove the sump pan and the timing cover.
9   Unbolt and remove the oil pump.
10 Clean away the remnants of all the old gaskets. Unbolt and remove the camshaft pulley.
11 Using a suitable two-legged extractor or hooked tool, extract the camshaft bearing oil seals.
12 Remove the chain tensioner according to type (see Section 25).
13 Bend down the tabs of the camshaft bolt lockplates and unscrew the bolts.
14 Remove the camshaft sprocket and chain and release the chain from the crankshaft sprocket. From the other end of the camshaft the pulley and flange will already have been removed (see Sections 45, 46).
15 Unbolt the camshaft retaining plate and carefully withdraw the camshaft.
16 Use a two-legged extractor to draw off the crankshaft sprocket.
17 Unbolt and remove the flywheel.
18 Remove the liner, piston and rod assemblies as described in Section 8.
19 Mark the five main bearing caps in relation to the crankcase and unbolt and remove them. The caps are located on hollow dowels and may require tapping (not sideways) to release them.
20 If the bearing shells are to be used again, retain them with their individual caps.
21 Lift the crankshaft from the crankcase and remove the bearing shells and thrust washers.

50 Examination and renovation

1   Refer to Sections 16 to 27, but when overhauling the oil pump note that the pressure relief valve is located in a different position when compared with the pump on type 800 engines.
2   When unbolting the cover from the pump body be prepared to catch the valve ball and spring which will be ejected.
3   Although recommended as a job for your dealer, if renewal of the valve guides is undertaken note the positioning of the guides in relation to the valve seats.
4   The camshaft extension bearing in the flywheel housing is of shell type on early models and ball-bearing type on later ones.
5   Both types of bearing can be removed using an extractor or spacers, washers and a long bolt.
6   When fitting the shell type bearing, make sure that the larger oil hole is at the top with the bearing slit positioned as shown in Fig. 1.44.
7   The bearing shell should be located in the cylinder block only as far as indicated in the diagram. Reaming is not required.

51 Engine reassembly – general

    Refer to Section 28.

52 Engine – reassembly

1   With the cylinder block clean and standing on the bench, fit new blanking plugs at the ends of the main oil gallery, and also camshaft bearing threaded plugs if they were removed. Stake the plugs in position.
2   Check that the two timing cover studs are in position and drive in the dipstick guide tube so that it conforms to the diagram (Fig. 1.47).
3   Temporarily fit the cylinder liners and check liner protrusion. Do this by fitting a blue seal and applying hand pressure to the liner then check the liner protrusion is within the specified tolerances by using a dial gauge or feeler blades and a straight-edge. If the protrusion is outside the specified tolerance, change the seal for one of alternative thickness. The difference in protrusion between two adjacent liners must not exceed 0.04 mm (0.0016 in). If this occurs when using new cylinder liner/piston assemblies it is permissible to overcome this by interchanging the position of the liners. Remove the cylinder liners, keeping the selected seals with their liners.
4   Wipe the main bearing shell recesses in the crankcase clean and fit the shells which incorporate the oil holes (photo). Shells for positions 1 and 3 are of one width, shells for positions 2, 4 and 5 are of another.

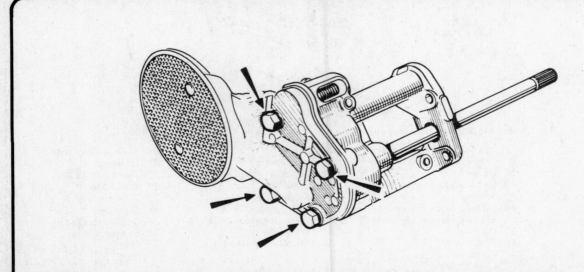

Fig. 1.43 Oil pump cover bolts – type 688, 689 and 810 engines (Sec 50)

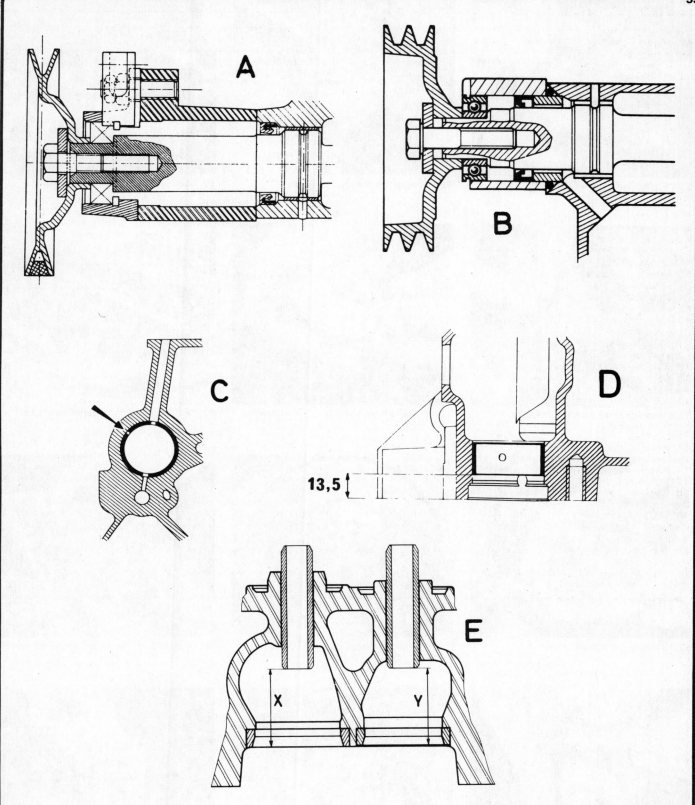

Fig. 1.44 Camshaft extension bearing and valve guide renewal diagrams – type 688, 689 and 810 engines (Sec 50)

A	Early type camshaft extension bearing	C	Camshaft shell bearing oil hole alignment
B	Later type camshaft extension bearing	D	Camshaft shell bearing setting in block
		E	Valve guide fitting

X = 26.6 mm (1.043 in)
Y = 26.2 mm (1.031 in)

60

52.4 Fitting bearing shells to crankcase

52.5 Lubricating the shell bearings

52.6 Lowering crankshaft into position

52.7 Locating crankshaft thrust washers

52.8 Fitting a main bearing cap shell bearing

52.10 Tightening main bearing cap bolts

52.13 Fitting crankshaft oil seal

52.14 Fitting flywheel

52.16 Installing liner, piston and rod assembly

52.19 Fitting a big-end cap shell bearing

52.20 Tightening big-end cap bolts

52.22 Locating oil pump

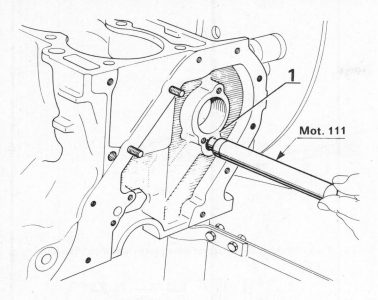

Fig. 1.45 Staking oil gallery plugs (1) (Sec 52)

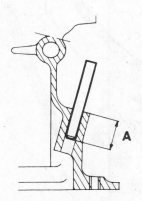

Fig. 1.47 Dipstick guide tube fitting diagram (Sec 52)

A = 10.0 mm (0.39 in)

5 Oil the shell bearings (photo).
6 Oil the crankshaft journals and lower the crankshaft into position (photo).
7 Locate the semi-circular thrust washers so that the oil grooves are facing towards the ends of the crankshaft (photo).
8 Wipe out the main bearing cap recesses and fit the plain shells into them (photo).
9 Fit the caps so that the marks made at dismantling are adjacent.
10 Tighten the cap bolts to the specified torque (photo).
11 Now check the crankshaft endfloat. Do this by using a dial gauge. Push the shaft fully in one direction and then push the shaft fully in the opposite direction and measure the total movement. An alternative method of checking is to use feeler blades inserted at the centre bearing between the face of the thrust washer and the journal shoulder.
12 If the endfloat is not within the specified tolerance, the thrust washers will have to be changed for ones of alternative thickness (see Specifications).
13 Fit the oil seal at the flywheel end of the crankshaft (photo). Smear it with oil before fitting and take great care when fitting not to damage its lips and also to drive it in squarely. Use a tubular item or the old seal and a block of wood to tap it home. If it is noticed that the lips of the old oil seal have worn a groove in the crankshaft flange, don't drive the new seal in so far as the old one so that the lips will bear upon an unmarked surface.

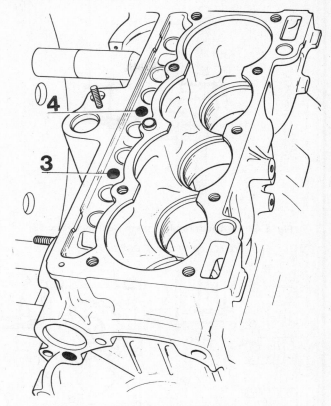

Fig. 1.46 Camshaft bearing threaded plugs (3 and 4) (Sec 52)

14 Fit the flywheel (photo) using new bolts which have had thread locking compound applied to them. Tighten to the specified torque wrench setting.
15 Wipe out the bearing recesses in the connecting rod big-ends and fit the shells.
16 Install the liner, piston and rod assemblies with the selected base seals (photo). Make sure that No 1 cylinder is at the flywheel end, the connecting rod big-end numbers are furthest from the camshaft, and also that the arrow on the piston crown is pointing towards the flywheel.
17 Clamp the cylinder liners to the block.
18 Oil the crankpins and then draw the connecting rods down to connect them to the crankshaft.
19 Fit the bearing shells into their caps (photo), oil them and locate them on the crankpins so that the matching numbers made at dismantling are adjacent to each other.
20 Screw in the big-end cap bolts and tighten to the specified torque (photo).
21 Check that the crankshaft rotates freely.
22 Bolt the oil pump into position (photo). No gasket is used at its mounting flange.
23 Fit the Woodruff key and fit the crankshaft sprocket so that the timing mark faces outwards. Use a bolt, washers and distance piece to draw the sprocket into position.
24 The camshaft sprocket, having been drawn off at dismantling, must now be reassembled.
25 Locate the retainer plate and drive it onto the camshaft shoulder using a piece of tubing.
26 Draw on the sprocket (timing mark outwards) using the fixing bolt and tighten it to the specified torque.
27 Using a feeler blade, check that a clearance (J) exists between the camshaft and the retainer plate – Fig. 1.48.
28 Oil the camshaft bearings and insert the camshaft into position (photo). Do not allow the camshaft lobes to damage the bearings. Screw in and tighten the camshaft retainer plate bolts (photo).
29 Turn the camshaft and the crankshaft until the sprocket timing marks are closest together and in line with the shaft centres (Fig. 1.50).
30 Hold the camshaft sprocket from turning by passing a bar through

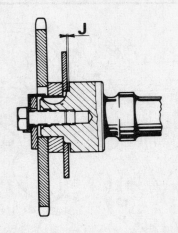

Fig. 1.48 Camshaft retainer plate clearance (Sec 52)

J = 0.06 to 0.11 mm (0.002 to 0.005 in)

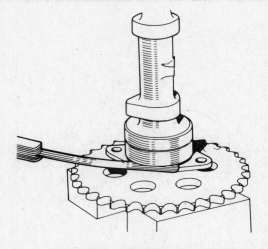

Fig. 1.49 Checking camshaft retainer plate clearance (Sec 52)

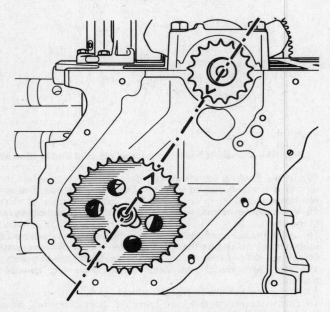

Fig. 1.50 Timing sprockets aligned – type 688, 689, 810 and 840 engines (Secs 52 and 73)

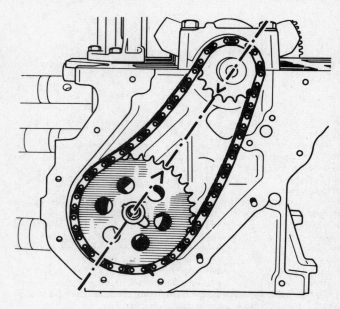

Fig. 1.51 Timing chain fitted (Secs 52 and 73)

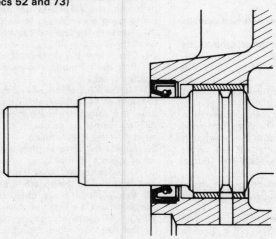

Fig. 1.52 Camshaft oil seal (Sec 52)

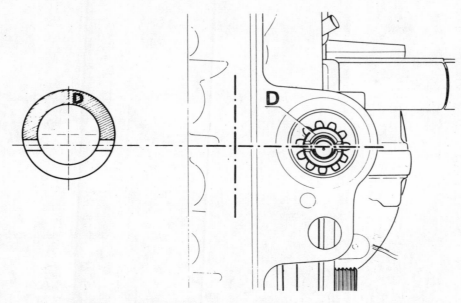

Fig. 1.53 Distributor/oil pump drivegear setting (Sec 52)

D   Larger segment

one of its holes and unscrew the bolt. Remove the sprocket without disturbing the previously set position of the camshaft.

31 Engage the timing chain with the crankshaft sprocket and then locate the camshaft sprocket within the loop of the chain so that it can be pushed into position on the camshaft without having to turn either the crankshaft or camshaft to obtain exact alignment of the timing marks (photo).

32 Fit a lockplate and tighten the camshaft sprocket bolt to the specified torque. Bend up the tab of the lockplate.

33 If a hydraulic type chain tensioner is fitted, locate the oil filter gauge in position.

34 Fit the timing chain tensioner according to type by reference to Section 25.

35 Bolt on the timing cover using a new gasket.

36 Grease the lips of a new camshaft oil seal and drive it fully home.

37 With the engine resting on its side, fit the rubber sealing strips to the front and rear main bearing caps (photos).

38 Fit the side gaskets so that their ends overlap the cap seals (photo).

39 Fit the sump (photo).

40 Oil the tappets (cam followers) and insert them in their originally fitted order.

41 Remove the cylinder liner clamp and fit the cylinder head, as

described in Section 4 (photos). Tighten to the specified torque in the sequence shown in Fig. 1.37.

42 Adjust the valve clearances as described in Section 30 (photos).

43 Turn the crankshaft until No 1 cylinder is at TDC on its firing stroke. This can be verified by observing that the rocker arms for No 4 cylinder are 'rocking' (in balance).

44 Using a 12 mm diameter x 1.75 pitch bolt to hold it, drop the distributor drivegear into its hole (photo). A certain amount of trial and error repositioning will be required to achieve the correct setting of the distributor drive slot as the drivegear will turn as it meshes with the gear on the camshaft. Anticipate this by turning the slot back a few degrees from its desired final setting before pushing it into position. The drivegear is correctly set when the slot is at 90° to the engine centre line with the larger segment of the drive dog towards the flywheel.

45 Fit the distributor and turn it until the contact breaker points are just about to open (No 1 piston still at TDC). Tighten the distributor clamp bolt.

46 Fit the rocker cover using a new gasket (photo).

47 Fit the clutch mechanism to the flywheel, making sure that the driven plate is centralized, as described in Chapter 5.

48 Fit all the engine ancillaries (photos).

49 Fit the engine mounting brackets.

52.28a Inserting camshaft

52.28b Bolting camshaft retaining plate into position

52.31 Fitting camshaft sprocket with chain

64

52.37a Main bearing cap sealing strip

52.37b Main bearing cap seal in position

52.38 Fitting sump side gaskets

52.39 Fitting the sump

52.41a Cylinder head gasket

52.41b Locating cylinder head

52.41c Fitting pushrods

52.41d Fitting rocker gear

52.42a Adjusting a valve clearance

52.42b Checking a valve clearance

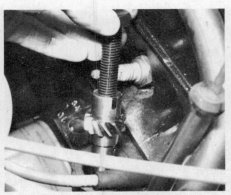

52.44 Using a bolt to install distributor/oil pump drivegear

52.46 Fitting the rocker cover

52.48a Fitting the fuel pump

52.48b Fitting the coolant pump

52.48c Fitting the alternator

53 Valve clearances – adjustment

Refer to Section 30.

54 Engine/manual transmission – reconnection before refitting

Refer to Section 31. Fit new lockplates to the nuts at the sides of the camshaft pulley mounting flange hole. Tighten the nuts and bend up the lockplate tabs.

55 Engine/automatic transmission – reconnection before refitting

1   The operations are a reversal of those described in Section 47, but the driveplate and torque converter must be aligned, as described fully in Chapter 7.
2   Fit new lockplates under the nuts either side of the camshaft pulley mounting flange hole.
3   Tighten the nuts and bend up the tabs of the lockplates.

56 Engine/manual transmission – refitting

1   Reverse the removal operations described in Sections 12 and 45.
2   Apply the footbrake two or three times to position the disc pads against the discs.
3   Reconnect the emission control system.
4   Fit the camshaft extension bearing mounting flange and pulley.

57 Engine/automatic transmission – refitting

1   Reverse the removal operations described in Section 46.
2   Refill the transmission with the correct grade and quantity of oil.
3   Check the adjustment of the kickdown switch, the governor and the selector control, as described in Chapter 7.
4   Apply the footbrake two or three times to position the brake pads against the discs.
5   Reconnect the emission control system.
6   Fit the camshaft extension bearing flange and pulley.

58 Engine – starting up after major overhaul

Refer to Section 33.

PART 3 Type 840 (1397 cc) engine

59 General description

This engine differs from the other power units by having a crossflow cylinder head in which the inlet and exhaust manifolds are on opposite sides of the head.
The timing chain is of duplex type.

60 Engine oil and filter – topping up and renewal

Refer to Section 2.

61 Major operations possible – engine in car

Refer to Section 3.

62 Cylinder head – removal and refitting

1   Disconnect the battery earth lead.
2   Remove the warm air intake and unbolt the exhaust manifold.
3   Drain the cooling system by removing the cylinder block drain plug

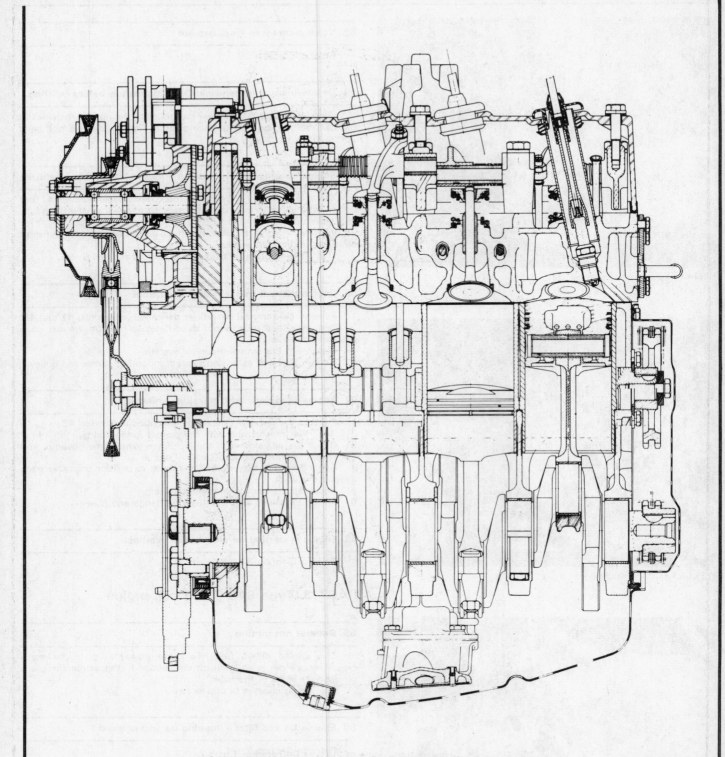

Fig. 1.54 Longitudinal sectional view of the type 840 engine (Sec 59)

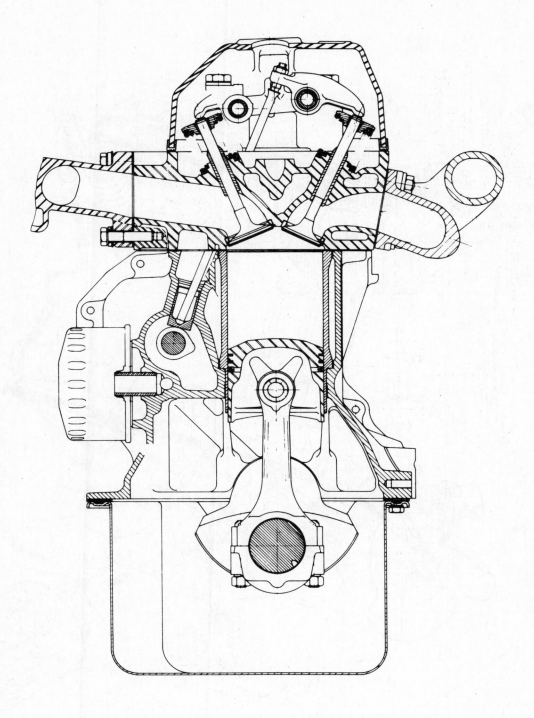

Fig. 1.55 Cross-sectional view of the type 840 engine (Sec 59)

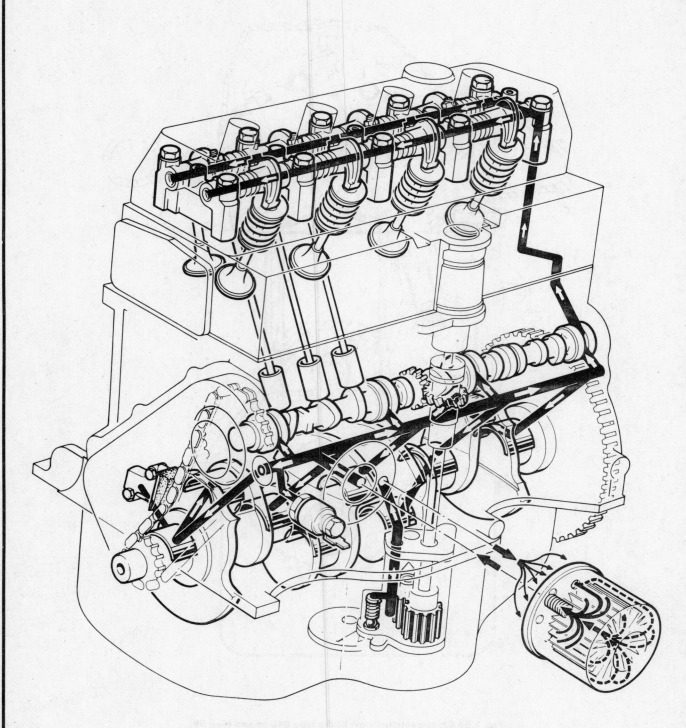

Fig. 1.56 Lubrication system on type 840 engine (Sec 60)

and disconnecting the radiator lower hose. If the coolant is not due for renewal, try and retain it for further use.

4   Remove the air filter elbow.

5   Disconnect electrical connections, hoses and carburettor controls as necessary to clear the cylinder head.

6   Remove the drivebelt and the alternator.

7   Remove the distributor.

8   Unbolt and remove the camshaft pulley and release the drivebelt.

9   Remove the rocker cover.

10   Unscrew the cylinder head bolts, half a turn at a time working from the centre ones towards each end. Do not undo bolt (A) – Fig. 1.58 more than one turn. The four rear cylinder head bolts should be unscrewed and retained in their raised position using a rubber band as a means of securing the rocker gear.

11   Release the cylinder head from the block by levering it sideways using the alternator mounting bracket as a lever until the head pivots on bolt (A). On no account attempt to lever the cylinder head upwards or the cylinder liners will be disturbed and the liner base seals broken. Remove the bolt (A) and remove the cylinder head complete with rocker gear.

12   Fit liner retaining clamps as described in Section 4.

13   Decarbonising and valve grinding may be carried out, as described in Section 27.

14   To ensure a leak-free refitting operation it is important that the installation work is followed precisely.

15   Make sure that all carbon and old gasket material is removed and that the surfaces of the block and head are absolutely clean.

16   Use a locating tool as a positioning dowel. In the absence of the special tool a piece of suitable tubing can be made up and tapped gently into place.

17   Position the cylinder head gasket with the words HAUT/TOP uppermost. Make sure that the gasket is dropped into its correct position first time. *Do not attempt to reposition it or the adhesive with which it is coated will be destroyed.* Should this happen, renew the gasket.

18   Install the cylinder head complete with the four rear bolts in the raised position.

19   Remove the temporary positioning tool.

20   Screw in the bolts in the sequence shown (Fig. 1.57) to the specified torque wrench setting.

21   Fit and tighten the cylinder block drain plug.

22   Fit the drivebelt and camshaft pulley, tighten the fixing bolt to the specified torque.

23   Adjust the valve clearances, as described in Section 30.

24   Fit the distributor, after reference to Chapter 4.

25   Fit the rocker cover with a new gasket, if required

26   Reconnect all leads, hoses and controls.

27   Fit the exhaust manifold with a new gasket and then install the warm air intake.

28   Fill and bleed the cooling system.

63   Engine sump pan – removal and refitting

1   Drain the engine oil.

2   Unbolt the anti-roll bar insulators and tilt the bar downwards.

3   Unbolt the clutch cover plate and swivel it towards the right-hand side.

4   Unscrew the sump fixing screws and then bend the engine rear plate just enough to be able to withdraw the sump pan.

5   Refit by reversing the removal operations.

6   Use new side gaskets, and front and rear sealing strips. Apply silicone sealant to the corner overlaps and refit the sump. Bend the engine rear plate straight.

7   Refill with engine oil.

64   Oil pump – removal and refitting

1   Remove the sump pan as just described.

2   Unbolt the oil pump and remove it from the machined face of the crankcase.

3   Refit by reversing the removal operations, but remember that a gasket is not fitted between the oil pump mounting flange and the crankcase.

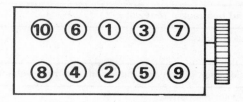

Fig. 1.57 Cylinder head bolt loosening and tightening sequence – type 840 engine (Sec 62)

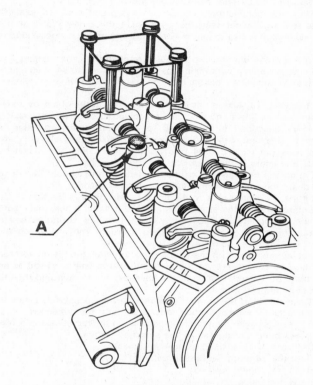

Fig. 1.58 Cylinder head dowel pivot bolt (A) (Sec 62)

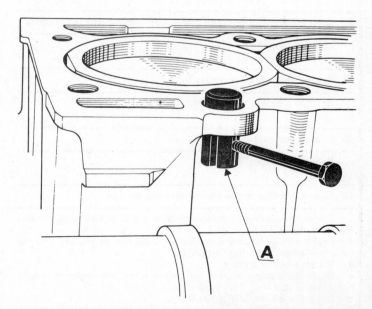

Fig. 1.59 Cylinder head locating tool (A) (Sec 62)

65 Big-end bearings – renewal

Refer to Section 7.

66 Cylinder liner, piston and rod assembly – removal and refitting

1   Disconnect the battery.
2   Drain the cooling system.
3   Remove the sump pan, as described in Section 63.
4   Remove the oil pump, as described in Section 64.
5   Remove the cylinder head, as described in Section 62.
6   Mark the connecting rods and their big-end caps at adjacent points to indicate not only the position in the block (No 1 at the flywheel end), but also to which side of the engine the connecting rods face.
7   Unscrew the big-end cap nuts and remove the caps, keeping the bearing shells paired with their caps if the shells are to be used again.
8   Remove the liner, piston and rod assemblies from the cylinder block.
9   The cylinder liners on this engine are sealed at their base by an O-ring and, as the liners and block are machined to close tolerances, the procedure described in Section 8 for adjusting liner projection is limited to checking that the difference in protrusion between adjacent liners does not exceed 0.04 mm (0.0016 in). Check protrusion by placing the liners in the block without their O-rings.
10 Fitting the new pistons to the connecting rods should be left to your dealer or engine reconditioning company (Section 9).
11 Fitting the piston rods to the liners is described in Section 8.
12 Before refitting the assemblies into the cylinder block, make sure that the components are absolutely clean. Use new O-ring seals and fit them onto the cylinder liners **before** fitting. The arrows on the piston crowns must point towards the flywheel.
13 Use a compressor on the piston rings to install the piston and rod into the liner and always fit the complete piston liner, and rod as an assembly. Do not attempt to fit the liner first on its own and then fit the piston and rod into it.
14 Make sure that the big-end shell recesses are absolutely clean, fit the shells, draw the connecting rods down onto the crankpins.
15 Fit the caps with the matching number on the rod adjacent, screw in the cap bolts and tighten to the specified torque.
16 Refit the cylinder head using a new gasket.
17 Refit the oil pump and sump pan.
18 Refill the engine with oil.
19 Refill and bleed the cooling system.
20 Reconnect the battery.

67 Cylinder liner, piston and rod – dismantling and reassembly

Refer to Section 9.

68 Engine mountings – renewal

Refer to Section 10.

69 Engine removal – method

Refer to Section 11.

70 Engine/manual transmission – removal

1   Remove the bonnet, the radiator grille, the grille crossmember and the front shield.
2   Remove the windscreen washer reservoir and its bracket, and the air intake elbow from the carburettor.
3   Disconnect the battery.
4   Drain the cooling system by disconnecting the radiator bottom hose and unscrewing the cylinder block drain plug.
5   Drain the engine and gearbox oils.
6   Remove the warm air manifold and pipe, then unbolt the exhaust manifold.

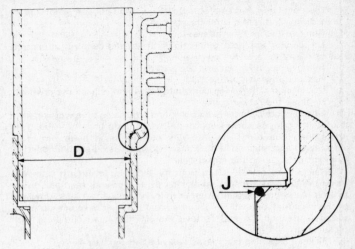

Fig. 1.60 Cylinder liner O-ring base seals (Sec 66)

D = Cylinder outside diameter   J   O-ring

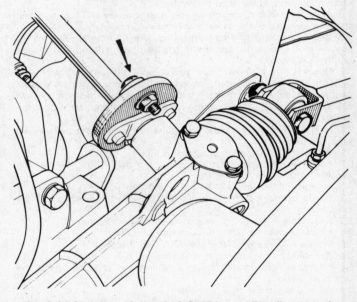

Fig. 1.61 Steering column shaft flexible coupling disconnection point (Sec 70)

7   Disconnect all electrical leads, hoses and controls from the engine and its ancillaries.
8   Mark the leads and hoses to eliminate any doubt later on about reconnection.
9   Unbolt and remove the radiator, complete with electric cooling fan.
10 Remove the expansion bottle.
11 Disconnect the steering column shaft at the flexible coupling. Retain the rubber ring which will be ejected.
12 Raise the front of the car and support it securely with axle stands under the body side-members.
13 Remove the front roadwheels.
14 Unbolt the front brake calipers and tie them up out of the way. There is no need to disconnect the hydraulic pipelines.
15 Disconnect the steering tie-rods from the rack ends. On later models, disconnect the tie-rod end balljoints from the steering arms.
16 Unbolt the steering rack housing taking care to retain the rack height setting shims and record from which side they are removed.
17 Using a thin drift, drive out the roll pins from the inboard ends of the driveshafts.
18 Unscrew the nuts from the suspension upper arm balljoints and then, using a suitable extractor, separate the balljoints from the stub axle carriers.

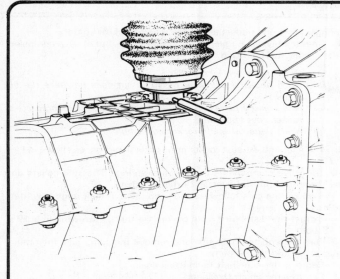

Fig. 1.62 Driving out driveshaft roll pins (Sec 70)

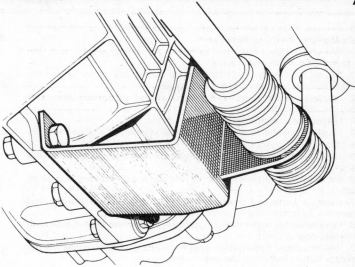

Fig. 1.63 Gearchange control rod bracket (Sec 70)

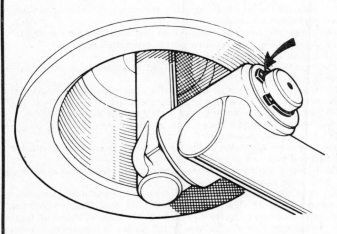

Fig. 1.64 Gearlever/rod joint circlip (Sec 70)

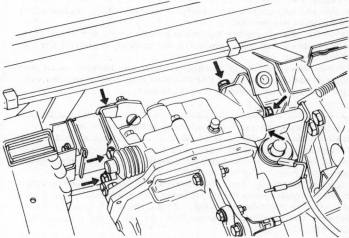

Fig. 1.65 Front crossmember/flexible mounting-to-transmission bolts (Sec 70)

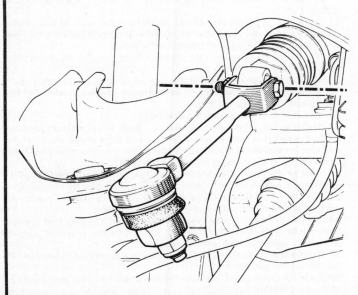

Fig. 1.66 Steering rack end fitting coupling pin (Sec 70)

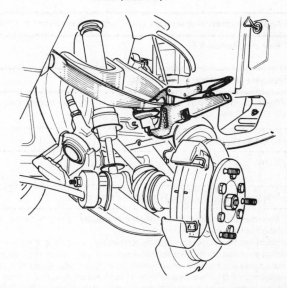

Fig. 1.67 Self-locking grips holding suspension upper arm balljoint (Sec 70)

19 Pull the tops of the stub axle carriers outwards to release the driveshafts from the differential.
20 Working under the car, remove the bolts which hold the gearchange control rod bracket.
21 Extract the circlip which secures the control rod to the base of the gear lever. Remove the control rod.
22 Slacken off the clutch cable adjuster and disconnect the cable from the release fork.
23 Disconnect the speedometer drive cable.
24 Fit lifting chains or slings to the engine/gearbox and just take its weight.
25 Unscrew the nuts from the underside of the engine mounting pads.
26 Remove the front crossmember complete with gearbox mounting pads.
27 Using a suitable hoist, carefully raise the engine/gearbox and remove it from the engine compartment.
28 Installation is a reversal of removal, but observe the following essential points.
29 Bolt the front crossmember and mounting pad assembly to the gearbox before installing the engine/gearbox.
30 Use new roll pins to secure the driveshafts.
31 Remember to refit the steering box shims, also the rubber ring at the flexible coupling.
32 Adjust the clutch.
33 The steering rack end coupling pins must be horizontal after connecting to the tie-rods.
34 Fill the engine, gearbox and cooling system.
35 Apply the brake pedal several times to bring the disc pads up against the disc.
36 When screwing on the suspension upper arm balljoint nut, if the ball-pin tends to rotate, use a pair of self-locking grips to seat the eye of the stub axle carrier tightly on the pin taper.

71 Engine/manual transmission – separation

1 With the engine/gearbox removed from the car, clean away all external dirt using a water-soluble solvent, or paraffin, and a stiff brush.
2 Before unbolting the transmission (flywheel housing) bolts, remove the pulley and its mounting flange from the flywheel end of the camshaft. The nuts at each side of the camshaft aperture have lockplates and their tabs must be flattened before the nuts can be unscrewed.
3 Unbolt the clutch bellhousing from the engine, support the weight of the gearbox and withdraw it from the engine.

72 Engine overhaul – general

Refer to Section 14.

73 Engine – complete dismantling

1 Unbolt and remove the engine ancillary components. These include the following:

    1   Alternator
    2   Distributor
    3   Fuel pump
    4   Oil filter
    5   Dipstick
    6   Oil pressure switch
    7   Engine mounting brackets

2 Drain the engine oil, if not done previously.
3 Unbolt and remove the rocker cover.
4 Unbolt and remove the clutch assembly.
5 Unscrew the rocker arm adjuster screws fully, push the arms aside against spring pressure and withdraw the pushrods. Keep the rods in their originally fitted sequence.
6 Remove the cylinder head, as described in Section 62. With the cylinder head removed, the rocker gear may be lifted from it.
7 The rocker gear can be dismantled by tapping out the shaft locating roll pins. Withdraw the shafts from the pedestals. Keep the

springs, arms and pedestals in their originally fitted order.
8 Reassembly is a reversal of dismantling, but if any confusion arises, note the following.

    (a)   Both shafts are identical
    (b)   No 5 pedestal is similar to No 1, but does not have the oil channel
    (c)   Nos 2 and 4 pedestals are identical, and do not incorporate a rocker cover bolt hole
    (d)   No 3 pedestal has a rocker cover bolt hole

9 The inlet and exhaust rocker arms differ in design, as shown in Fig. 1.71.
10 The valve components include dual springs. The split collets are the same for both the inlet and exhaust valves.
11 Remove the cam followers and keep them in their originally fitted order.
12 Extract the distributor drive pinion. Do this by screwing in a 12 x 1.75 bolt.
13 Turn the engine on its side and remove the sump pan, the timing gear cover and the oil pump.
14 Remove the camshaft bearing oil seals.
15 Remove the chain tensioner.
16 Bend back the lockplate tab and unscrew the camshaft sprocket bolt.
17 Take off the camshaft sprocket and chain. A three-legged puller will probably be needed.
18 Unbolt the camshaft flange plate and withdraw the camshaft.
19 Again using a puller, draw off the crankshaft sprocket.
20 Unbolt and remove the flywheel.
21 Remove the liner, piston and rod assemblies, as described in Section 66.
22 Mark the positons of the main bearing caps (No 1 nearest the flywheel) and which way round they are fitted.
23 Unbolt and remove the caps with their shells. Tape the shells to their respective caps if they are to be used again.
24 Lift out the crankshaft.
25 Remove the bearing shells from the crankcase and identify their location if they are to be used again.
26 Remove the thrust washers which are located either side of the centre main bearing.
27 With the engine dismantled, clean and examine all components and renovate as described in Part 1 of this Chapter. Although recommended as a job for your dealer, if renewal of the valve guides is undertaken note the position of the guides in relation to the valve seats.
28 Commence reassembly by fitting the main bearing shells to their seats in the crankcase. All shells have oil holes, numbers 1 and 3 are of similar type, whilst those for numbers 2, 4 and 5 are of slightly different pattern.
29 Stick the semi-circular thrust washers either side of the centre main bearing in the crankcase using thick grease. Make sure that the white metal side is against the crankshaft web.
30 Fit the bearing shells to the main bearing caps. These shells have no oil holes.
31 Oil the crankshaft shells and lower the crankshaft into position.
32 Fit the main bearing caps in their originally marked order. Tighten the bolts to the specified torque.
33 Check that the crankshaft turns freely.
34 Using a dial gauge or feeler blades, check the crankshaft endfloat by first pushing it fully in one direction and then in the other. If the endfloat is outside the specified tolerance, the thrust washers will have to be changed for ones of different thickness.
35 Grease the lips of a new crankshaft rear oil seal and install it using a suitable piece of tubing. Should the crankshaft seal bearing surface be slightly worn, do not drive the new seal fully home in order to present the seal lips with a new rubbing surface.
36 Fit the flywheel, screw in new retaining bolts having first applied thread locking fluid to the threads. Tighten to the specified torque. Always fit new flywheel bolts at reassembly.
37 Fit the liner, piston and rod assemblies, as described in Section 66.
38 Fit the oil pump.
39 Using a piece of tubing tap the crankshaft sprocket into position. Make sure that the Woodruff key is in position and the sprocket timing mark is facing outwards. If the sprocket is difficult to drive fully home, screw a length of threaded rod into the end of the crankshaft and, using a nut and washer, draw the sprocket onto the shaft.

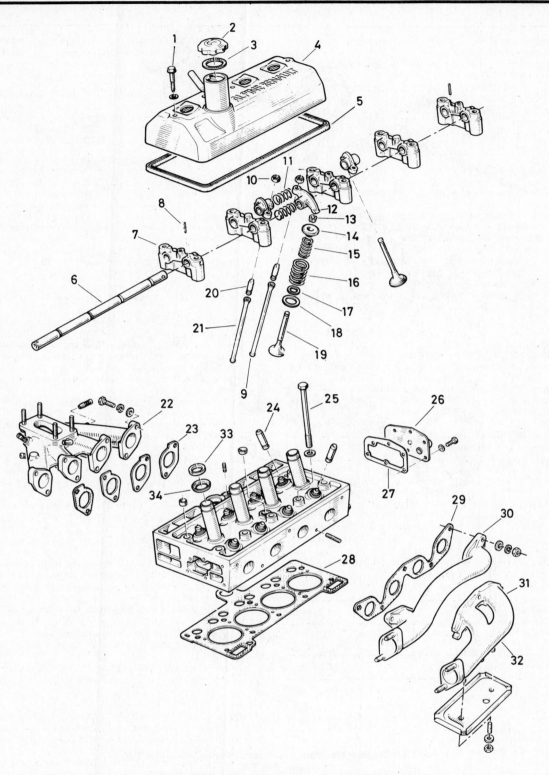

Fig. 1.68 Cylinder head components – type 840 engine (Sec 73)

1	Rocker cover bolt	10	Locknut
2	Oil filler cap	11	Spring
3	Oil seal	12	Rocker arm
4	Rocker cover	13	Split collets
5	Gasket	14	Spring cap
6	Rocker shaft (one of two)	15	Inner valve spring
7	Pedestal	16	Outer valve spring
8	Roll pin	17	Spring seat (inner)
9	Exhaust pushrod (longer)	18	Spring seat (outer)

19	Valve
20	Rocker arm adjuster screw
21	Inlet pushrod (shorter)
22	Inlet manifold
23	Gasket
24	Valve guide
25	Cylinder head bolt
26	Endplate

27	Gasket
28	Gasket
29	Gasket
30	Exhaust manifold
31	Exhaust manifold
32	Heat shield
33	Seal
34	Seal cup

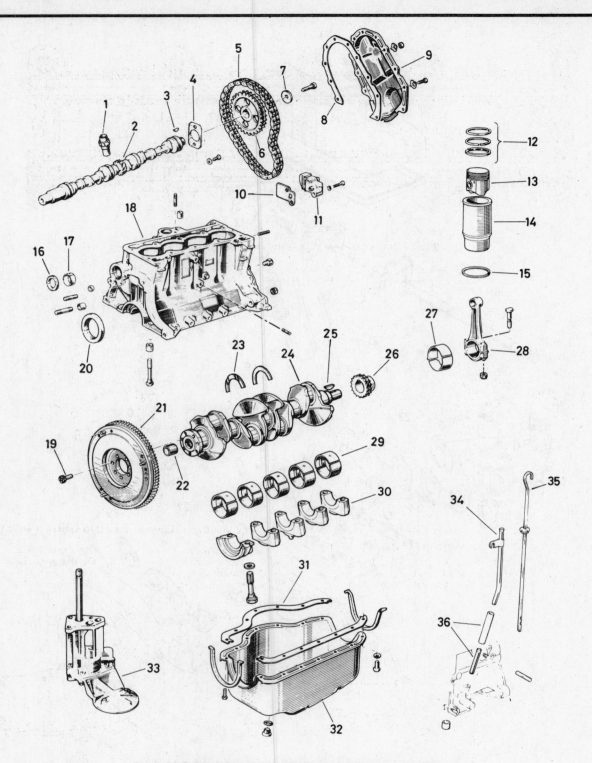

Fig. 1.69 Cylinder block and crankcase components – type 840
engine (Sec 73)

1	Distributor drivegear	10	Tensioner backing plate	19	Flywheel bolt	28	Connecting rod
2	Camshaft	11	Chain tensioner	20	Crankshaft oil seal	29	Main bearing shells
3	Woodruff key	12	Piston rings	21	Flywheel	30	Main bearing caps
4	Camshaft retaining plate	13	Piston	22	Pilot bearing	31	Sump pan gaskets
5	Timing chain	14	Cylinder liner	23	Thrust washers	32	Sump pan
6	Sprocket	15	Liner base seal	24	Crankshaft	33	Oil pump
7	Spacer	16	Oil seal	25	Woodruff key	34	Dipstick guide tube
8	Gasket	17	Camshaft bearing	26	Sprocket		extension
9	Timing chain cover	18	Cylinder block/crankcase	27	Big-end bearing shells	35	Dipstick
						36	Guide tube

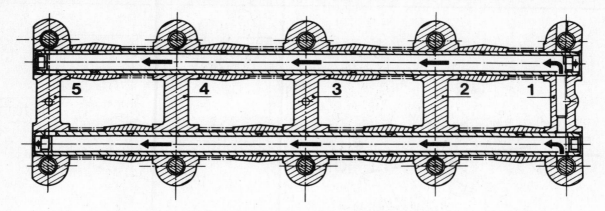

Fig. 1.70 Rocker shaft and pedestal arrangement (Sec 73)

1 Pedestal   3 Pedestal   5 Pedestal
2 Pedestal   4 Pedestal   Arrows show oil flow

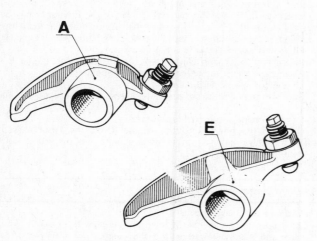

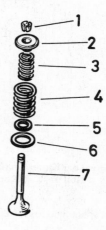

Fig. 1.72 Valve components – type 840 engine (Sec 73)

1 Split collets   5 Inner spring seat
2 Spring cap   6 Outer spring seat
3 Valve spring (inner)   7 Valve
4 Valve spring (outer)

Fig. 1.71 Rocker arm identification (Sec 73)

A Inlet   E Exhaust

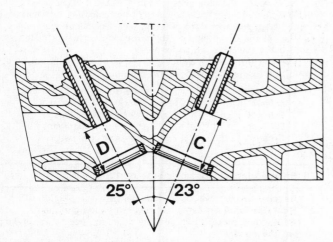

Fig. 1.73 Valve guide fitting diagram – type 840 engine (Sec 73)

C = 37.5 mm (1.476 in)   D = 28.8 mm (1.133 in)

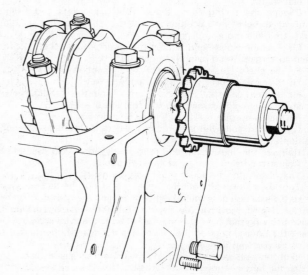

Fig. 1.74 Method of drawing sprocket onto crankshaft (Sec 73)

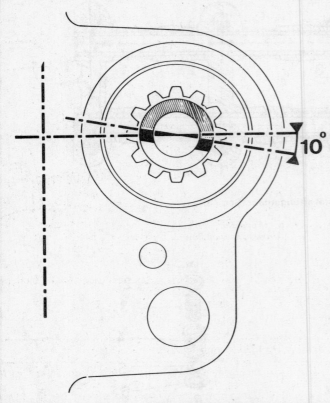

Fig. 1.75 Distributor drivegear fitting diagram (type 840 engine) – No 1 piston at TDC (Sec 73)

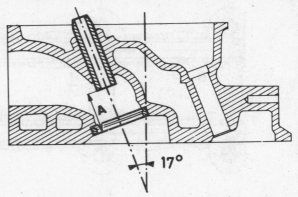

Fig. 1.76 Valve guide fitting diagram – type 847 engine (Sec 78)

A = 25.2 mm (1.0 in) exhaust   A = 30.5 mm (1.2 in) inlet

40 Oil the camshaft bearings and install the camshaft. Bolt on the camshaft flange.
41 Fit the camshaft sprocket so that the timing mark faces outwards, but do not bolt it into position.
42 Turn the crankshaft and the camshaft so that both sprocket timing marks are closest together and a line drawn between the two timing marks would pass through the shaft centres (see Fig. 1.50).
43 Remove the camshaft sprocket without disturbing the setting of the camshaft.
44 Engage the timing chain around both sprockets and push the camshaft sprocket into position on the camshaft so that the timing marks are once more in alignment.
45 Fit a new lockplate and tighten the camshaft sprocket bolt to the specified torque. Bend over the lockplate tab.
46 Fit the chain tensioner as described in Section 25.
47 Fit the timing cover with a new cork gasket.
48 Fit a new camshaft front oil seal. Tape the shoulder on the camshaft to prevent damage to the seal lips..
49 Fit the sump pan, as described in Section 63.
50 Oil the cam followers and return them to their originally recorded positions.
51 Remove the liner clamp and refit the cylinder head (Section 62).
52 Adjust the valve clearances (next Section).
53 The distributor drivegear must now be fitted.
54 Turn the crankshaft until No 1 piston is at TDC on its compression stroke. This can be determined either by feeling the compression being generated in No 1 cylinder by placing a finger over the spark plug hole, or by observing that No 4 cylinder rocker arms are in balance (rocking). Check the timing mark on the flywheel is in line with the mark on the clutch bellhousing flange.
55 With the bolt used for removing the drivegear, insert the drivegear so that the larger segment is towards the flywheel and the driving slot is at an angle of 10° to the centre line of the engine. A certain amount of trial and error repositioning will be required to achieve the correct setting of the drivegear as it will turn as it meshes with the gear on the camshaft. Anticipate this by turning the slot back a few degrees from its desired final setting before pushing it into position.

56 Push the distributor into place so that the offset driving dog engages correctly. Turn the distributor so that the contact points are just about to open, tighten the clamp bolt. If the drivegear has been correctly installed, the contact end of the rotor will be aligned with No 1 contact in the distributor cap. Fit the spark plugs and HT leads.
57 Fit the rocker cover with a new gasket.
58 Install the clutch and centralize it, as described in Chapter 5.
59 Fit the alternator, adjuster link and drivebelt.
60 Fit the fuel pump and dipstick.
61 Screw in the oil pressure switch and screw on a new oil filter, hand tight.
62 Fit the engine mounting brackets.
63 Offer up the gearbox to the engine. Once the input shaft has passed through the clutch driven plate splined hub, insert and tighten the bellhousing-to-engine bolts.

74 Valve clearances – adjustment

1   Remove the rocker cover.
2   Jack-up one of the front wheels and engage top gear.
3   Turn the roadwheel to rotate the crankshaft until No 1 valve (nearest the flywheel) is fully open, being depressed by the rocker arm.
4   Insert a feeler blade of equivalent thickness to the specified valve clearance between the end of the No 3 inlet valve stem and the rocker arm. The feeler blade should be a stiff sliding fit. If it is not, release the adjuster screw locknut and turn the adjuster screw. When the correct clearance is achieved, tighten the locknut without disturbing the setting of the screw.
5   Now adjust the clearance on No 4 exhaust valve.
6   The clearances may be adjusted hot or cold, but note that the inlet and exhaust clearances are different (see Specifications).
7   Repeat the operations on the remaining valves for cylinders 3, 4 and 2 using the table which follows.
8   Viewing from the flywheel end of the engine, inlet valves are on the left and exhaust valves are on the right.

Valves fully open	Valves to adjust
1 Exhaust	*3 Inlet and 4 Exhaust*
3 Exhaust	*4 Inlet and 2 Exhaust*
4 Exhaust	*2 Inlet and 1 Exhaust*
2 Exhaust	*1 Inlet and 3 Exhaust*

75 Engine/manual transmission – refitting

1   Reverse the removal operations described in Section 70.
2   Refit the camshaft extension bearing flange and pulley.
3   Apply the footbrake two or three times to position the brake pads against the discs.

76 Engine – starting up after major overhaul

Refer to Section 33.

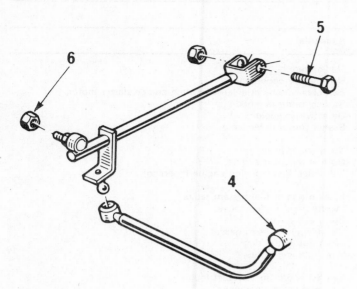

Fig. 1.77 Gearchange disconnection points – type C6J-7-26
engine (Sec 80)

4   *Gearlever linkage point*   6   *Gearlever linkage point*
5   *Gearlever linkage point*

PART 4   Type 847 (1397 cc) engine

77 General description

This engine is used on certain North American Le Car models and
other TX versions.
Servicing and overhaul operations are as for the type 810 engine
described in Part 2, but refer to the Specifications which are applicable
to the type 847 engine for dimensions and tolerances.

78 Examination and renovation

The operations are as described in Part 2, but if new valve guides
are being fitted to the cylinder head, note the guide insertion depth by
reference to Fig. 1.76.

PART 5   Type C6J-7-26 (1397 cc) engine

79 General description

This engine is used in the Gordini Turbo and is very similar to the
type 840 engine previously described, apart from the addition of the
turbocharger.
Refer to the Specifications, however, for the differences between
the two power units.

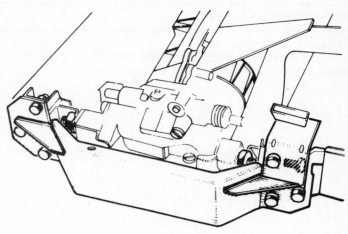

Fig. 1.78 Transmission front crossmember – type C6J-7-26 engine
(Sec 80)

80 Engine/transmission – removal and refitting

1   Although the operations are basically as described in Sections 70
and 75, the following additional work must be carried out.
2   Disconnect the oil cooler pipes and plug them and then unbolt and
remove the radiator and oil cooler as an assembly.
3   Remove the turbocharger/carburettor assembly, as described in
Chapter 3.
4   Disconnect the TDC sensor plug from the socket on the electronic
module.
5   Disconnect the gearchange linkage at the points numbered 4, 5
and 6 (Fig. 1.77). This will eliminate the need for adjustment at
reassembly.
6   Remove the transmission front crossmember.
7   Refitting is a reversal of removal, but note that the steering rack
must be installed before the turbocharger/carburettor.

81 Engine sump pan – removal and refitting

1   Disconnect the battery, drain the engine oil.
2   Remove the engine undershield and the TDC sensor.
3   Remove the fuel pump.
4   Disconnect the gearchange remote control rod.
5   Disconnect the anti-roll bar clamps and prise the bar away from the
sump pan.
6   Remove the sump pan bolts, lower the pan at the flywheel end then
manoeuvre it over the oil pump.
7   Clean the mating faces on the crankcase and sump pan, stick new
gaskets and strips in position and apply jointing compound at their
points of overlap.
8   Refit the sump pan, reconnect the anti-roll bar and gearchange rod.
Check the setting of the latter by reference to Chapter 6, Section 20.
9   Fill the engine with oil, and reconnect the battery.

See overleaf for Fault Diagnosis

Part 6

82 Fault diagnosis – engine

Symptom	Reason(s)
Engine will not turn when starter switch is operated	Flat battery Bad battery conditions Bad connections at solenoid switch and/or starter motor Starter motor jammed Defective solenoid Starter motor defective
Engine turns normally but fails to fire and run	No spark at plugs No fuel reaching engine Too much fuel reaching engine (flooding)
Engine starts but runs unevenly and misfires	Ignition and/or fuel system faults Incorrect valve clearances Burnt out valves Blown cylinder head gasket Worn out piston rings Worn cylinder bores
Lack of power	Ignition and/or fuel system faults Incorrect valve clearances Burnt out valves Blown cylinder head gasket Worn out piston rings Worn cylinder bores
Excessive oil consumption	Oil leaks from crankshaft oil seal, timing cover gasket and oil seal, rocker cover gasket, crankcase or gearbox joint (as applicable) Worn piston rings or cylinder bores resulting in oil being burnt by engine (smoky exhaust is an indication) Worn valve guides
Excessive mechanical noise from engine	Wrong valve to rocker clearance Worn crankshaft bearings Worn cylinders (piston slap) Slack or worn timing chain and sprockets

Chapter 2 Cooling, heating and air conditioning systems

For modifications, and information applicable to later models, see Supplement at end of manual

Contents

Specifications

System type ....

Thermo-syphon, pressurised with belt-driven coolant pump. Belt-driven or electric cooling fan, depending upon model

Thermostat
Opening temperature ....

75° to 86° C (167° to 186° F) depending upon model and operating territory

Thermostat fully open ....

85° to 95° C (185° to 203°F) depending upon opening temperature of thermostat

Coolant capacity
All models except type 800 engines ....

6.3 litres, 11.1 Imp pts, 6.7 US qts

Type 800 engines ....

5.8 litres, 10.2 Imp pts, 6.13 US qts

1 General description

The cooling system is of a thermo-syphon type, assisted by a belt driven coolant pump.

The system is pressurised and incorporates an expansion bottle to accept coolant which is displaced as the engine warms up. When the engine cools, the coolant flows back into the system from the expansion bottle. This system eliminates the need for topping-up as coolant is never lost by expansion.

A thermostat is incorporated in the system to restrict coolant flow during the warm-up period.

Cars having a type 800 engine use a belt-driven radiator cooling fan. Other engine types have a thermostatically controlled electric cooling fan.

Heating and ventilating are standard equipment on all models. Air conditioning is a factory-fitted option on certain models.

2 Maintenance, draining and refilling

1   Regularly check the coolant level in the expansion bottle. When the engine is cold, the level should be at the 'MAX' mark on the bottle. If the level falls, this can only be due to a leak in the system.
2   Periodically check the security of the system hose clips and renew any hoses which have hardened or are starting to crack. When renewing a hose, replace the production clips with ones of worm drive type.

3   If the system is to be drained, have the engine cold to prevent distortion of the cylinder head.
4   Depending upon the type of radiator fitted, a drain plug may or may not be incorporated. Where a drain plug is not fitted the lower hose on the radiator must be disconnected.
5   Before draining the system, unscrew the cap from the expansion bottle and place the heater control to the 'HOT' position.
6   If the coolant is to be retained for further use, place a container of adequate capacity on the floor to receive it during draining.
7   The cylinder block has a drain plug which should also be removed to empty the system completely. The drain plug is located at the crankshaft pulley end of the engine, below the water pump.
8   Provided the coolant has been renewed at the specified intervals (see Routine Maintenance), and is made up with an adequate concentration of anti-freeze, or corrosion inhibitor, flushing should not be required.
9   If the system has been neglected, however, and contains scale, sediment and rust, it should be flushed through by placing a cold water hose in the radiator neck and keeping it there until the water flows clear from the drain holes or radiator bottom hose.
10 If, after a reasonable period, the water still does not run clear, remove the radiator (see Section 7 or 8) and reverse-flush it. In severe cases of neglect, the radiator may be flushed with a good proprietary cleaning agent, such as Holts Radflush or Holts Speedflush. It is important that the manufacturer's instructions are followed carefully.
11 To refill the system, screw in the drain plugs or reconnect the radiator bottom hose and prepare the specified quantity of coolant containing antifreeze or corrosion inhibitor (see Section 4).
12 Pour coolant into the expansion bottle until the level is 32.0 mm (1.25 in) above the 'MAX' mark.

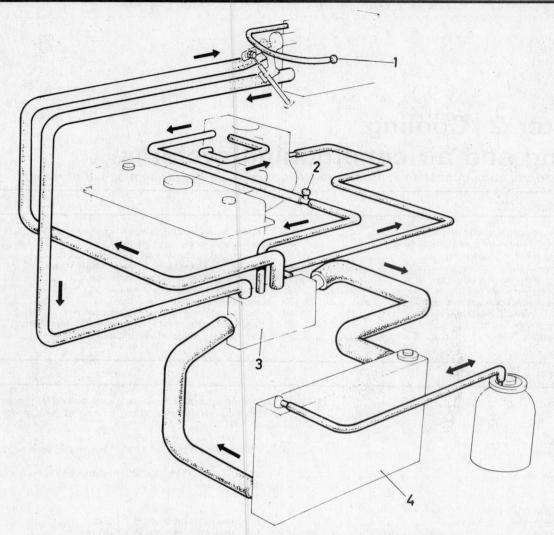

Fig. 2.1 Typical cooling system layout. Note flow to intake manifold below carburettor (Sec 1)

1   Heater matrix bleed screw   2   Centre bleed screw   3   Coolant pump   4   Radiator

Fig. 2.2 Different types of expansion bottle (Sec 2)

Fig. 2.3 Typical drivebelt arrangement (Sec 3)

F   Point to test belt deflection

2.14 Filling the radiator

2.16a Bleed screw

2.16b Heater matrix bleed screw

3.3a Drivebelt idler pulley adjuster

3.3b Alternator drivebelt adjuster link (arrowed)

3.6 Removing a drivebelt

13 Screw on the expansion bottle cap and then open the cooling system bleed screws.

14 Using the same coolant mixture, pour it slowly into the radiator until it is full to the brim (photo).

15 Start the engine and run it at about 1500 rpm. Top up the radiator as the level drops.

16 As soon as coolant is seen to be ejected from the bleed screws, close the screws (photos).

17 Top up the radiator, if necessary, and then fit the radiator cap.

18 Run the engine to the normal operating temperature, switch off and allow it to cool, preferably overnight. Top up the expansion bottle, if necessary, to the 'MAX' level.

3 Drivebelts — tensioning, removal and refitting

1 Two or more drivebelts are used, one to drive the coolant pump from the camshaft pulley and the other to drive the generator from the second groove on the coolant pump pulley.

2 On type 800 engines a cooling fan is fitted to the coolant pump pulley.

3 Belt adjustment is controlled by an idler pulley and adjustment link on one drivebelt and by pivoting the generator for the other belt. Typical examples are shown in the photos.

4 On N. American Le Car models a twin drivebelt is used, adjustment being carried out by pivoting the emission control air pump after releasing its mounting bolts. On cars equipped with power-assisted steering, the pump drivebelt is tensioned by releasing the pump tensioner and mounting bolts (refer to Chapter 11).

5 Correct tensioning of the drivebelts is important. Special tensioning tools are used by Renault dealers, but an acceptable alternative method is explained in the following paragraphs.

6 To remove a belt, slacken the idler pulley adjuster completely or release the generator mounting bolts. The belt may now be prised over the rim of the pulley with the fingers (photo).

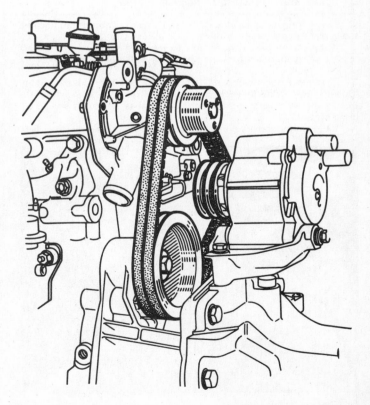

Fig. 2.4 Twin drivebelt arrangement on models with an emission control air pump (Sec 3)

7   Fit the new belt and tension until using moderate finger pressure at the centre of the longest run of the belt it deflects as follows:

Coolant pump belt (type 800 engine)	5.0 to 6.0 mm (0.21 to 0.24 in)
Coolant pump belt (other engines)	4.5 to 5.5 mm (0.17 to 0.23 in)
Dynamo belt	10.0 to 12.0 mm (0.39 to 0.47 in)
Alternator belt	5.0 to 6.0 mm (0.21 to 0.24 in)
Air pump belt	3.5 to 4.5 mm (0.14 to 0.17 in)
Power assisted steering belt	2.0 to 3.0 mm (0.08 to 0.12 in)
Air conditioner compressor belt	2.0 to 3.0 mm (0.08 to 0.12 in)

8   After running the engine for ten minutes a new drivebelt should be re-tensioned to accommodate the initial stretch.

4   Coolant mixtures

1   The cooling system must never be filled with just plain water. Apart from the danger of frost damage, corrosion and rust will occur. A glycol type anti-freeze mixture should be used, as this contains corrosion inhibitors, essential to the protection of the alloy content of the engine.
2   Follow the antifreeze manufacturer's recommendations as to concentration, but generally a 50% solution of antifreeze will give protection down to -20°C (-4°F). Where severe winter conditions are not anticipated a 25% solution will be adequate.
3   If the expansion bottle should ever require topping up, use an antifreeze mixture made up in similar proportions to the original coolant.
4   In climates where antifreeze mixture is not necessary, use a corrosion inhibitor in the cooling system.

5   Thermostat – removal, testing and refitting

1   The thermostat is located in the end of the radiator outlet hose at the coolant pump, and is retained by the hose clip (photo).
2   If the engine overheats, is slow to warm up or the heater fails to reach a satisfactory temperature, the thermostat may be faulty or of an incorrect type.
3   To remove the thermostat for testing, drain the cooling system (Section 2) and disconnect the top hose from the coolant pump. Extract the thermostat from the end of the hose (photo). It should be closed (cold).
4   Various thermostats are used, according to engine type, and they have different opening and fully open temperature ratings. The temperature rating is stamped on the thermostat.
5   Suspend the thermostat in a pan of water and heat the water. As the water approaches the specified temperature, the thermostat valve plate should open. If it does not, renew it.
6   It is important that you ask your dealer for the correct one for your particular car by quoting the vehicle identification number.
7   Refitting is a reversal of removal, fill and bleed the cooling system as described in Section 2.

6   Radiator electric cooling fan and switch

1   On all models with an electric cooling fan for the radiator, the thermostatically controlled switch is located in the right-hand tank of the radiator, except for R1228 models (1977 and later) where both the fan switch and the coolant temperature switch are screwed into the core plate of the cylinder head.
2   The radiator fan is usually withdrawn with the radiator and separated later, refer to the next Section.

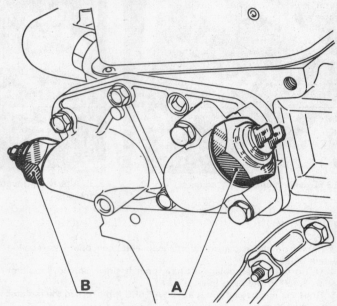

Fig. 2.5 Core plate on R1228 models (Sec 6)
  A   Radiator fan switch
  B   Coolant temperature warning lamp switch

5.1 Thermostat location

5.3 Removing the thermostat from the top hose

7 Radiator (belt-driven fan) – removal, repair and refitting

Note: *If the reason for removing the radiator is concern over coolant loss, note that minor leaks may be repaired by using a radiator sealant, such as Holts Radweld, with the radiator in situ.*

1 Drain the cooling system, as described in Section 2.
2 Disconnect the upper and lower hoses from the the radiator.
3 Mark the setting of the gearchange rod and clamp, and remove the forward section of the rod with the bracket from the top of the radiator.
4 Unbolt and remove the stay.
5 Unscrew the nut from the right-hand bracket at the base of the radiator. The bracket is held by one steering rack mounting stud.
6 Disconnect the radiator side mounting.
7 Lift the radiator from the engine compartment.
8 A leaking radiator may be temporarily repaired with one of the products available for the purpose, but leave permanent repairs to a radiator repair specialist. The material used in the construction of the radiator varies according to date of production and may be of non-ferrous metal, aluminium or plastic and can therefore present a problem to the unskilled.
9 Refitting is a reversal of removal, fill and bleed the cooling system as described in Section 2.
10 Check the front wheel alignment (Chapter 11) in case loosening the steering rack mounting has altered the setting.

8 Radiator (electric fan) – removal, repair and refitting

Note: *If the reason for removing the radiator is concern over coolant loss, note that minor leaks may be repaired by using a radiator sealant, such as Holts Radweld, with the radiator in situ.*

1 Drain the cooling system, as described in Section 2.
2 Disconnect the battery.
3 Disconnect the radiator top and bottom hoses and the hose which runs to the expansion bottle.
4 Disconnect the leads from the cooling fan and the thermostatic fan switch (photo).

5 Unscrew the nuts from the radiator fixing studs. These are located one at the top left-hand side and the other at the base right-hand side. Note the sequence of washers, flexible cushion and spacer tube.

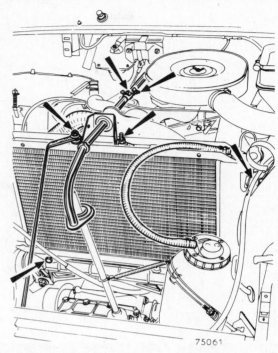

Fig. 2.6 Radiator disconnection points – engines with belt-driven fan (Sec 7)

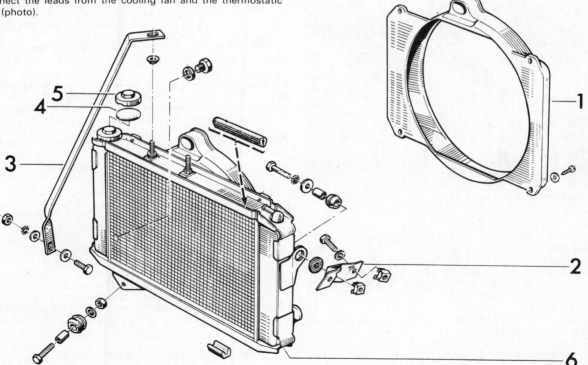

Fig. 2.7 Radiator components – engines with belt-driven fan (Sec 7)

1 Cowl	*3 Stay*	*5 Radiator cap*
2 Side mounting	*4 Radiator cap seal*	*6 Radiator*

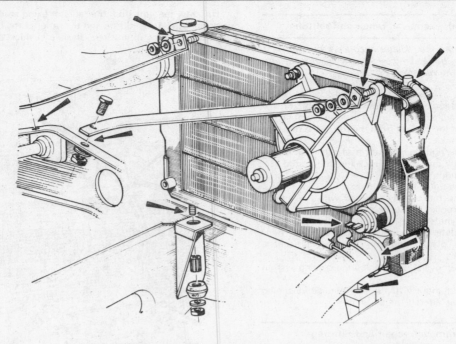

Fig 2.8 Radiator disconnection points – engines with electric fan (Sec 8)

8.4 Bottom hose and radiator thermal switch

6   Lift the radiator complete with fan from the engine compartment.
7   Where necessary, the fan can be unbolted from the radiator and the thermostatic switch unscrewed from the radiator right-hand tank (except R1228 models – see Section 6).
8   Refitting is a reversal of removal. Fill and bleed the cooling system, as described earlier in this Chapter.

9 Coolant temperature switch

1   One of three positions may be used for the coolant temperature sender unit; in the thermostat housing, at the rear of the cylinder head or in the cylinder head core plate, according to engine type.
2   The sender unit (switch) actuates a warning lamp on the instrument panel in the event of the engine overheating. Should the lamp come on and stay on, but further investigation proves the engine temperature to be normal, the switch should be renewed by unscrewing it after the cooling system has been drained (Section 2).

10 Coolant expansion bottle – servicing

1   The interior of the expansion bottle should be cleaned each time the coolant is drained.
2   Check the cap rubber seal and renew if it is deformed or damaged.
3   Should the expansion bottle valve ever be saturated with coolant due to overfilling or by failure to bleed air from the system during filling, it must be renewed.
4   Oily deposits observed within the expansion bottle may be due to a gasket leak in the engine.

11 Coolant pump – removal and refitting

1   Removal of the coolant pump will normally be required because of a leaking shaft gland seal or general wear.
2   Drain the cooling system, as described in Section 2 and disconnect the battery.
3   Disconnect the coolant hoses from the pump.
4   Refer to Section 3 and slacken and remove the drivebelt(s) from the pump pulley.

Type 800 engines without an electric radiator fan

5   Remove the gearchange rod and stay from the radiator.
6   Disconnect the lead from the coolant temperature switch.
7   Release the radiator side and bottom fixing bolts.
8   Unbolt and remove the fan blades and take off the coolant pump pulley (photo).
9   Unbolt and remove the drivebelt tensioner.
10   Unscrew and remove the coolant pump fixing bolts (photo). Release the pump from the block by striking the pump with a plastic-faced hammer. Clean the pump and block mating faces, removing all old gasket

All engine types with an electric cooling fan

11   Disconnect the battery and drain the cooling system.
12   Disconnect the hoses from the coolant pump.
13   Slacken and remove the drivebelt idler/tensioner pulley and the coolant pump pulley.
14   Unscrew and remove the pump fixing bolts and strike the pump with a plastic-faced hammer to release it from the cylinder block.
15   Clean the pump and block mating faces free from old gasket.

11.8 Removing coolant pump pulley

11.10 Coolant pump fixing bolts

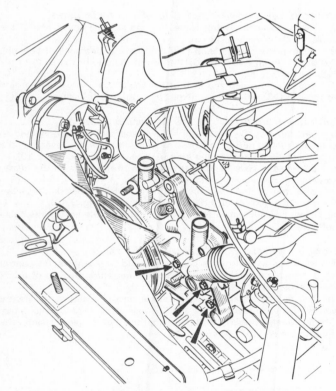

Fig. 2.9 Coolant pump bolts – type 800 engines (Sec 11)

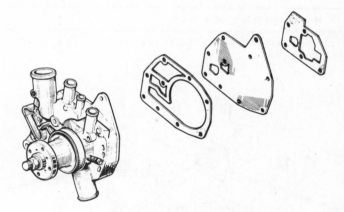

Fig. 2.10 Coolant pump – type 800 engines (Sec 11)

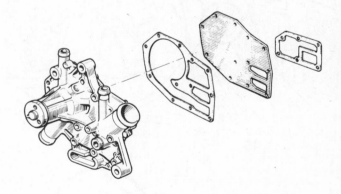

Fig. 2.11 Coolant pump – type 689, 810 and 840 engines (Sec 11)

All types

16 A worn pump will have to be renewed. Overhaul is not possible and spare parts are not available.

17 Refitting is a reversal of removal, but observe the following points:

(a) Use new gaskets without jointing compound
(b) Tension the drivebelts
(c) Fill and bleed the cooling system

12 Heating and ventilator system – description

1 The heater utilises heat from the engine cooling system. Coolant flows from the cylinder head, passes through the heater matrix and returns to the coolant pump.

2 The air which passes over the matrix enters the heater via a grille in the bonnet.

3 Provision is made for demisting the windscreen and side windscreen.

4 Fresh air outlets are provided on the facia panel, the air being drawn from a grille below the windscreen (photo).

5 Stale air is exhausted through outlets at both sides of the tailgate (photo).

12.4 Fresh air intake grille

12.5 Stale air outlet

13 Heater controls – adjustment

1   The facia coolant valve and the air control flap valve are adjusted in a similar way.

Controls on the left-hand side of the facia panel

2   Disconnect the control cable clip and slip the coiled end of the cable from the valve lever pin.
3   Push in the control knob (18), but leave a clearance of between 2.0 and 3.0 mm (0.079 to 0.12 in) from the end of the knob to the facia panel (see Fig. 2.12).
4   Engage the coiled end (12) of the cable with the valve lever and fit the clip (15) without disturbing the setting of the cable.

Slide controls at the centre of the facia panel

5   The cable at the hand control lever end should be connected so that the cranked part of the inner cable is located in the lever, and the outer cable is up against the stop (A) and clipped (see Fig. 2.13).
6   Engage the coiled end of the cable with the lever on the heater valve or air flap valve, as appropriate.
7   Slide the control knob towards the 'CLOSED' position, but leave the specified gap (X) at the end of the slot (see Fig. 2.14).
8   Now close the valve lever with the fingers and secure the cable with clip (4).

Rotary controls at the centre of the facia panel

9   With this type of heater control fitted to later models, the control knob actuates a cranked valve spindle through the medium of a fork and a short cable.
10 The control assembly is accessible once the top of the centre console is pulled towards you and the base of the control panel freed.
11 When reassembling, make sure that the flap spindles (1) enter the operating forks (2) – see Fig. 2.15.

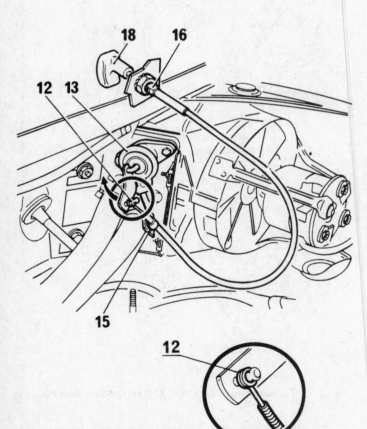

Fig. 2.12 Heater controls – left-hand side of facia (Sec 13)

12 Cable coiled end   16 Back nut
13 Water valve   18 Control knob
15 Cable clip

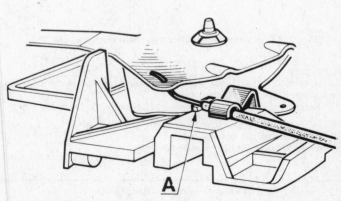

Fig. 2.13 Heater controls – slide type, centre of facia (Sec 13)

A   Outer cable stop

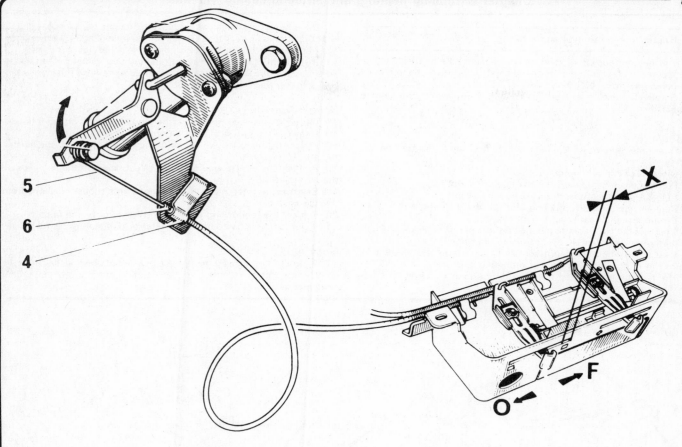

Fig. 2.14 Setting heater control cable – slide type, centre of facia (Sec 13)

4	Cable clip	6	Outer cable	F	Full on
5	Cable coiled end	O	Off	X	5.0 to 6.0 mm (0.2 to 0.24 in)

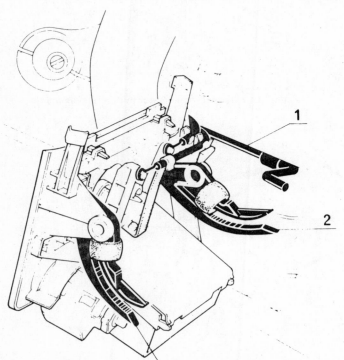

Fig. 2.15 Rotary type heater control (Sec 13)

1   Valve flap spindle
2   Operating fork

14 Heater unit – removal and refitting

1   The heater consists of three major sections, the heater housing, the blower motor and the matrix. Each section may be removed independently from the other.

2   Removal operations are carried out from within the engine compartment.

Renault type

3   Open the bonnet, disconnect the battery and remove the air cleaner.

4   Disconnect the air flap control cable.

5   Pull the electrical leads from the heater blower motor.

6   Release the bleed hose from its retaining clip.

7   Remove the air intake ducting after releasing the hose clip.

8   Disconnect the heater valve control cable.

9   Unscrew the two mounting bolts from the matrix and carefully pull the motor/matrix assembly away from the bulkhead.

10   Four screws hold the fan assembly to the matrix and three nuts secure the motor. Note the rubber mounting cushions.

11   The fan can be released from the motor shaft by using an Allen key.

12   If the heater matrix is to be removed, then the heater hoses should either be clamped near to it or the complete cooling system drained.

13   Remove the heater valve and disconnect the heater hoses.

14   If the matrix is leaking have it repaired by a radiator specialist or obtain a new one. Clogging may be cleared by reverse flushing with a cold water hose.

Sofica type

15   Carry out the operations described in paragraphs 3 to 6 (photos).

16   Unscrew the two fixing bolts from the air intake duct.

17   Prise off the clips which hold the two halves of the casing together.

18   Remove the air flap support panel after prising off the two clips on the air intake side.

19   Remove the three motor fixing screws with rubber cushions from the top casing.

20   Pull off the fan locking sleeve and then remove the fan.

21   If the matrix is to be removed, refer to paragraphs 12 to 14.

Both types

22   Refitting both types of heater is a reversal of removal, but note the correct sequence of fitting of the Sofica type motor mounting components (Fig. 2.24).

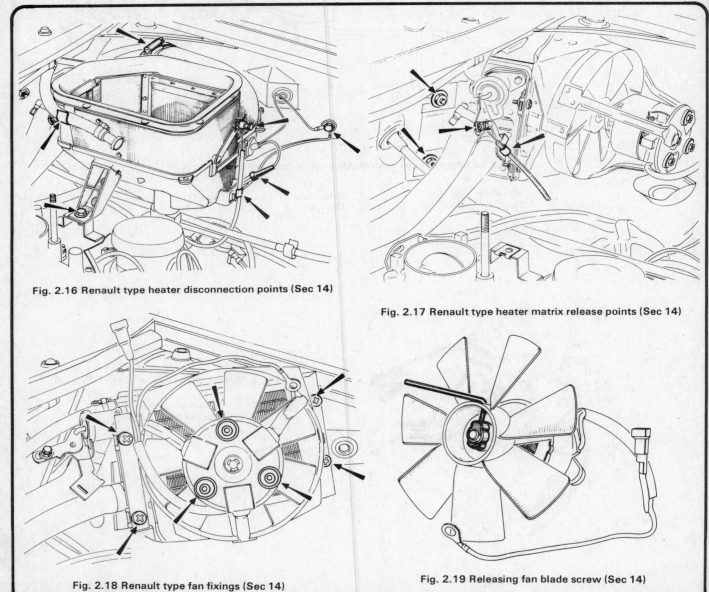

Fig. 2.16 Renault type heater disconnection points (Sec 14)

Fig. 2.17 Renault type heater matrix release points (Sec 14)

Fig. 2.18 Renault type fan fixings (Sec 14)

Fig. 2.19 Releasing fan blade screw (Sec 14)

14.15a Heater control linkage

14.15b Heater air flap control linkage (arrowed)

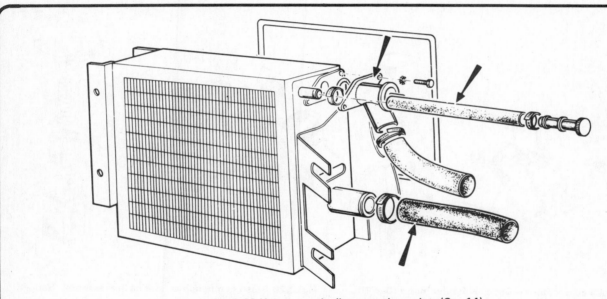

Fig. 2.20 Heater matrix disconnection points (Sec 14)

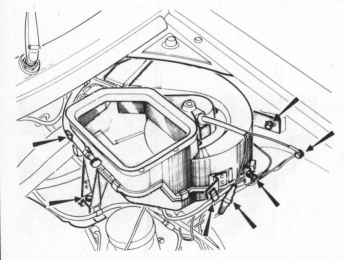

Fig. 2.21 Sofica type heater disconnection points (Sec 14)

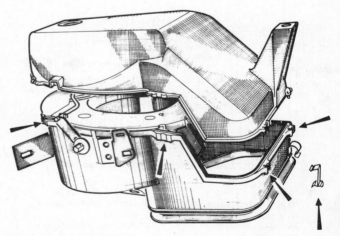

Fig. 2.22 Sofica type heater casing (Sec 14)

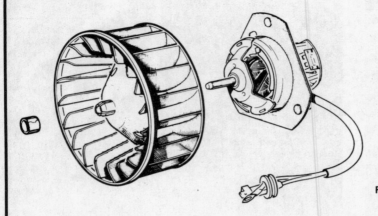

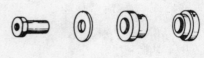

Fig. 2.24 Sofica type fan motor mounting components (Sec 14)

Fig. 2.23 Sofica type heater fan and locking sleeve (Sec 14)

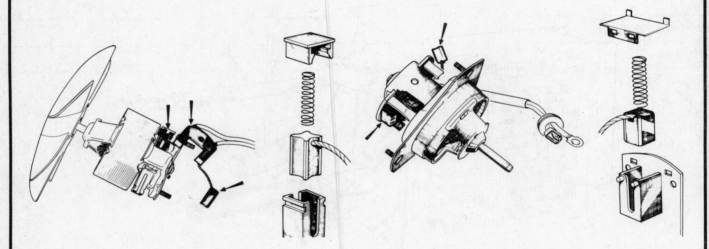

Fig. 2.25 Brush components – Ducellier heater motor (Sec 15)

Fig. 2.26 Brush components – Sofica heater motor (Sec 15)

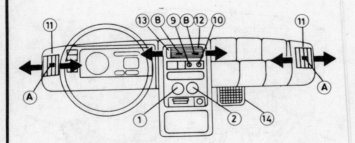

Fig. 2.27 Air conditioner controls (Sec 16)

1   Heated air control
2   Heater temperature control
9   Air conditioner on/off and airflow control
10 Air conditioner temperature control
11 Side cold air grille
12 Centre cold air grille
13 Centre cold air outlet control
14 Air conditioner intake (**Never obstruct this grille**)
A   Up/down grille control
B   Left/right grille control

Fig. 2.28 Air conditioner receiver dryer (Sec 17)

15 Sight glass

15 Heater blower motor brushes – renewal

1   After removal of the heater blower motor, the brushes may be renewed if they are found to be worn.
2   Remove the cap, spring and brush with its lead. With Ducellier motors, the brush leads are secured by crimping. On Sofica motors, the leads are soldered in position. With the latter type of brush, grip the lead with a pair of pliers to act as a heat sink when soldering, and do not allow the solder to flow down the strands of the brush lead or its flexibility will be impaired.

16 Air conditioner – description and operation

1   An air conditioner is available as a factory option on certain North American models.
2   To switch on the air conditioner, turn the control knob (9) clockwise (Fig. 2.27). The further it is turned, the greater the airflow.
3   The temperature control knob (10) should be turned clockwise to reduce the temperature of the airflow.
4   When operating the air conditioner, keep all windows closed, the heater off and the fresh air intake flaps closed.

17 Air conditioner – maintenance and precautions

1   During winter when the air conditioner is not in use, operate it for a few minutes each week to keep it lubricated and in good order.
2   At regular intervals (see Routine Maintenance) inspect the refrigerant through the sight glass of the receiver dryer. The appearance of bubbles in the glass for the first few minutes of operation is normal, but if they continue to be visible the refrigerant level is low and should be topped up by your dealer. Keep the compressor belt tensioned (see Section 3).
3   The refrigerant used is usually Freon 12 which is odourless, non-poisonous, non-inflammable and non-corrosive, except when it comes into contact with a naked flame when a poison gas is created. Avoid contacting the refrigerant with the skin or eyes.
4   On cars equipped with an air conditioner, components of the system (compressor, condensor etc) may be unbolted and moved within the limits of travel of their flexible connecting hoses in order to facilitate engine overhaul.
5   Never disconnect any part of the system yourself, but if this is essential for access to parts being worked on, have the system discharged by your dealer or refrigeration engineer and recharged again on completion of the work.
6   It is important that all disconnected components of the system are sealed pending reconnection to prevent the entry of moisture.
7   Occasionally clean the fins of the condenser free of dirt and flies.

18 Fault diagnosis – cooling, heating and air conditioning systems

Symptom	Reason(s)
Loss of coolant	Leaks in system Blown cylinder head gasket Faulty expansion bottle valve
Oil in coolant	Blown gasket Cracked cylinder Leaking cylinder liner base seals
Engine runs cool	Thermostat missing or stuck open
Engine overheats	Faulty thermostat or one of incorrect rating for car Slipping fanbelt (type 800 engines) Blown cylinder head gasket Faulty electric fan or thermo-switch (except 800 engines) Clogged coolant passages Coolant hose collapsed or kinked Clogged radiator fins Binding brakes Ignition and fuel system settings grossly out of tune Exhaust system partially blocked Low engine oil level
Heater lacks warmth	Clogged heater matrix Control cables incorrectly set Faulty or missing thermostat

Chapter 3 Fuel and emission control systems

For modifications, and information applicable to later models, see Supplement at end of manual

Contents

Specifications

System type .... Rear mounted fuel tank, mechanically or electrically operated fuel pump, single or dual barrel carburettor. Full emission control on N. American models

Fuel capacity
Without overspill device .... 38 litres, 8.36 Imp gal, 10.0 US gal
With overspill device .... 34 litres, 7.48 Imp gal, 8.98 US gal

Octane rating (RON)
High compression (9.5:1 to 10.0:1) .... 97 to 99
Low compression (8.5:1 to 8.8:1) .... 87 to 90
Unleaded fuel must be used on cars equipped with an emission control system

Carburettor settings
Owing to the variety of carburettors used on the Renault 5 we only list basic settings – for further information approach your dealer. The carburettor type and mark should be recorded somewhere on the carburettor.

Solex 32 SE1A and 32 DIS
Intermediate choke position: | **Throttle opening**
Marks 507, 508, 543, 555, 585, 591, 602 and 603 .... 0.65 mm (0.026 in)
Marks 561, 561-3, 586 and 639 .... 0.70 mm (0.028 in)
Full choke position:
Mark 727 .... 0.65 mm (0.026 in)
Mark 798 .... 0.70 mm (0.028 in)
Marks 602, 603, and 687 .... 0.75 mm (0.030 in)
Marks 561-3 and 675 .... 0.80 mm (0.032 in)
Marks 677, 682, 682-1, 702, 741 and 761 .... 0.90 mm (0.035 in)
Marks 678, 678-1, 765 and 781 .... 0.95 mm (0.037 in)
Marks 707 and 707-1 .... 1.10 mm (0.043 in)
Float level:
Marks 677, 678, 678-1, 741 and 798 .... 36.50 mm (1.44 in)
Marks 687, 702, 765 and 781 .... 12.40 mm (0.49 in)
Accelerator pump setting:

Throttle opening at end of pump stroke
Marks 677, 678, 678-1 and 798 .... 7.00 mm (0.28 in)

Zenith 32 1F7
Throttle opening in full choke position .... 0.90 mm (0.035 in)
Accelerator pump stroke .... 22.90 mm (0.90 in)

Weber 32 DIR

Initial throttle opening:
Mark 100	0.85 mm (0.033 in)
Marks II, IIT, 47, 54, 58, 58T, 62 and 75	1.00 mm (0.039 in)
Marks 82 and 87	1.05 mm (0.041 in)
Marks 80 and 90	1.10 mm (0.043 in)
Marks 46 and 56	1.20 mm (0.047 in)
Marks 53 and 55	1.25 mm (0.049 in)
Mark 89	1.35 mm (0.053 in)

Float level:
All marks except 80	7.0 mm (0.28 in)
Mark 80	38.00 mm (1.50 in)

Float travel:
All marks	8.00 mm (0.32 in)

Mechanical choke flap setting:
	Throttle opening
Mark 56	4.0 mm (0.16 in)
Mark 100	4.50 mm (0.18 in)
Marks II, IIT, 46, 47, 53, 55, 58, 58T, 62 and 75	5.0 mm (0.20 in)
Mark 90	5.50 mm (0.22 in)
Marks 82 and 87	6.00 mm (0.24 in)
Marks 54 and 80	6.50 mm (0.26 in)
Mark 89	8.00 mm (0.32 in)

Vacuum choke flap setting:
	Throttle opening
Marks 46, 47, 53 and 62	6.00 mm (0.24 in)
Mark 54	6.50 mm (0.26 in)
Marks 55, 56 and 75	7.00 mm (0.28 in)
Marks II, IIT, 58, 58T, 89, 90 and 100	8.00 mm (0.32 in)
Marks 82 and 87	9.00 mm (0.35 in)
Mark 80	10.0 mm (0.39 in)

Idle speeds

Owing to variations in the technical information available the idle speeds given in this Specification Section should be regarded as a guide.

Solex 32 SEIA	625 to 675 rpm (automatic in 'D')
Solex 32 DIS	675 to 725 rpm
Zenith 32 IF7	625 to 675 rpm
Weber 32 DIR:	
Except N. America	750 to 800 rpm
N. America, except Canada	700 to 800 rpm
Canada	825 to 875 rpm
R1228	800 to 900 rpm
122B	1025 to 1075 rpm

CO percentage in exhaust gas
0.5 to 3.0%

This figure may vary according to model, year of manufacture and territory. It is advisable to consult your dealer.

Air cleaner element
845 cc, 956 cc and 1108 cc engine models:
Round type, 57 mm (2.25 in) high (Tecalamit air cleaner)	Champion W123
Round type, 46.5 mm (1.83 in) high (Lautrette air cleaner)	Champion W164
1289 cc engine models:	
Round type	Champion W123
Cylindrical type	Champion W109
1397 cc engine models	Champion W109

Fuel filter
Champion L101

Torque wrench settings

	Nm	lbf ft
Manifold nuts	30	22

---

1 General description

The fuel system consists of a rear mounted fuel tank, a fuel pump which is mechanically operated from the camshaft on most models, and a carburettor.

The type of carburettor depends upon the particular model and date of production. It may be either single or dual barrel.

On 1981 R1229 RHD models, an electric fuel pump is used.

---

2 Air cleaner – description and element renewal

1 On early models a round air cleaner is fitted with Summer and Winter positions for the air intake nozzle so that cool or warm air (from around the exhaust manifold) may be selected to suit the prevailing ambient temperature.

2 On later models, a cylindrical type of air cleaner is fitted which incorporates a thermostatically controlled flap valve to mix cold and warm air (from around the exhaust downpipe) to maintain the optimum temperature level for the carburettor intake air. The air is ducted to the carburettor (photos).

3 The filter element should be renewed at the intervals specified in Routine Maintenance.

4 On round type air cleaners, unscrew the wing nut, lift off the lid and extract and discard the element.

5 On cylindrical type air cleaners, release the casing securing strap (photos) and hold the casing vertically. Unscrew the wing nut, remove the lid, extract the filter element and discard it (photo).

6 With both types of cleaner, wipe out the casing and insert a new element. Check the lid gasket, refit the lid and screw on the wing nut.

7 The round type of air cleaner casing can be removed after removal of the mounting nuts and cushions. The cylindrical type of air cleaner can be removed once the securing strap and ducts have been released.

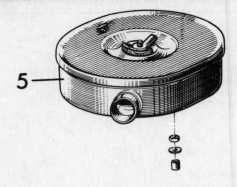

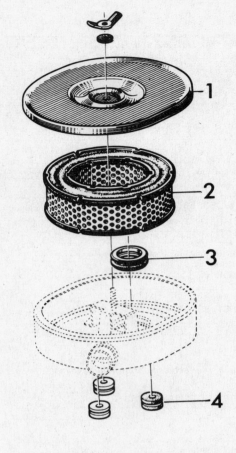

Fig. 3.1 Round type air cleaner (Sec 2)

1 Cover
2 Element
3 Rubber collar
4 Mounting cushions
5 Casing

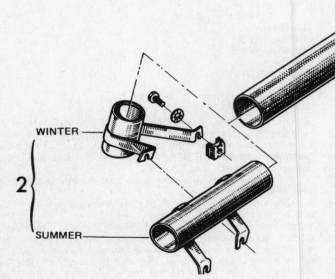

WINTER

SUMMER

2

Fig. 3.2 Air cleaner intake ducts (Sec 2)

1 Intake pipe
2 Winter and summer alternatives

Fig. 3.3 Cylindrical type air cleaner (Sec 2)

A   Retaining strap   D   Lid retaining wing nut

2.2a Hot air collector

2.2b Removing the carburettor intake duct

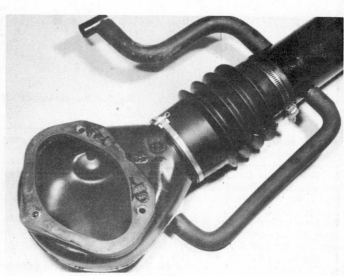

2.2c Carburettor intake duct inverted

2.5a Air cleaner retaining strap anchor clip

2.5b Air cleaner element

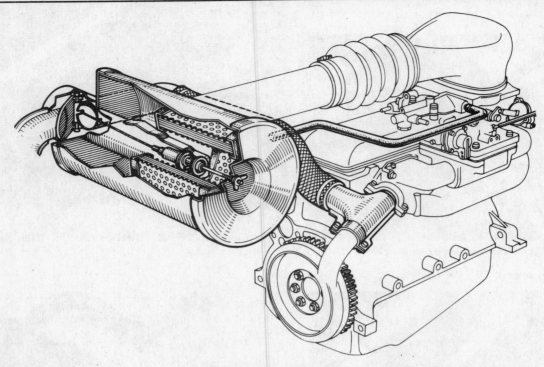

Fig. 3.4 Thermostatically controlled valve in air cleaner (Sec 3)

3 Air cleaner (temperature controlled type) – testing the thermostatically-controlled valve

1 With the air cleaner removed and the filter element extracted, immerse the air cleaner casing in water so that the thermostat (photo) is covered. If the water is cold, the air intake flap should be closed against entry of cold air.

2 Now place the casing in hot water (36°C – 97°F) when the flap should be closed against entry of warm air. If it does not operate in this way, the thermostat must be renewed.

3 Dry the casing and refit it with the filter element.

4 On Gordini Turbo models the thermostatically controlled valve in the air cleaner is adjustable, see Section 19.

4 Fuel pump – servicing and testing

Mechanical type – except on 689 and 810 engines

1 The fuel pump is bolted to the engine crankcase and operated by means of an arm pressed against a cam on the camshaft.

2 The type of pump fitted may vary slightly in design detail according to the manufacturer and date of production.

3 Routine servicing consists of cleaning sediment from the pump interior and filter.

4 Remove the screws which hold the pump cover in position. One or two screws may be used and on certain engines, the pump is mounted in an inverted position which makes the operation more difficult.

5 Take out the filter and mop out the fuel and sediment from the pump interior.

6 Check the cover gasket, renewing it if necessary, and then refit the filter, cover and screws. Do not overtighten the screws.

7 If fuel pump failure is suspected after symptoms of fuel starvation at the carburettor, carry out the following test. Disconnect the fuel supply hose at the carburettor and place its open end in a container. Disconnect the high tension (HT) lead at the coil to prevent the engine from firing and then turn the ignition key to 'START'. As the crankshaft is rotated, regular well defined spurts of fuel should be seen to be ejected from the end of the hose. If not, and it is known that there is fuel in the tank, the pump will have to be removed for overhaul or renewal.

8 If the pump operates correctly, reconnect the fuel hose.

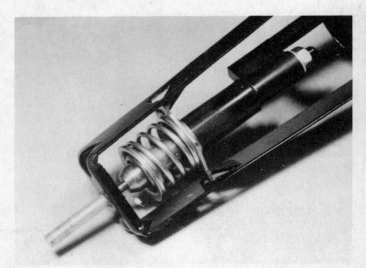

3.1 Air cleaner thermostat

Mechanical type – on 689 and 810 engines

9 The fuel pump on the 689 engine is of an inverted mounted type. On later models the pump is operated by a pushrod instead of a lever, the crankcase having been modified to incorporate a camshaft oil bath.

10 Apart from the pushrod, servicing and testing is as previously described.

11 If an oil bath type crankcase is fitted to a type 810 engine the lever type pump can be used, but a new insulator (three hole fitting) and gaskets will be required.

Electrically operated pump on RHD R1229 models

12 No servicing is possible, but occasionally check the security of electrical connections and fuel hoses.

13 The pump may be tested as described for the mechanical pump, but actuate it by turning the ignition key to position '3' not 'START'.

5 Fuel pump – removal, overhaul and refitting

Lever type mechanical pump

1 Disconnect the fuel hoses from the pump. Plug the end of the hose from the tank to prevent loss of fuel.
2 Unscrew the pump flange fixing nut and setscrew and pull the pump from the crankcase. Discard the gaskets, but retain the insulating spacer.
3 Clean away all external dirt and obtain a repair kit for your particular pump.
4 Remove the pump cover and extract the filter. Mark the alignment of the upper and lower body sections and extract the flange screws.
5 Drive out the operating lever pivot pin. This may be secured by staking or circlips, according to type. Remove the lever and spring.
6 Lift out the diaphragm and rod.
7 If the valves appear damaged the complete pump should be renewed.
8 The repair kit will only contain a new diaphragm, arm, spring and gaskets so more extensive repairs requiring other items cannot be undertaken.
9 Commence reassembly by fitting the diaphragm and operating arm. To do this insert the spring into the pump body followed by the diaphragm and its rod. Compress the diaphragm spring and then locate the operating arm spring. Push the operating arm into position so that it engages over the machined stop on the rod. Insert the pivot pin and secure with circlips or by careful staking.
10 Fit the two sections of the pump body together so that the marks made before dismantling are in alignment. Move the rocker arm until the diaphragm is flush with the joint and then fit the flange screws finger tight. Move the rocker arm further to bring the diaphragm to the bottom of its stroke and then tighten the flange screws evenly in diametrically opposite sequence.
11 Fit the filter and the cover using a new gasket.
12 Operate the rocker arm and feel for suction and delivery pressure at the inlet and outlet ports of the pump.
13 Use new flange gaskets either side of the insulating spacer and make sure that the operating arm locates correctly on the cam.
14 Reconnect the fuel hoses.

Pushrod type mechanical pump

15 The operations are similar to those just described, except that the pump is held by two setscrews.
16 The operating pushrod is loosely located between the cam and the pump.

Electrically operated pump

17 This type of pump is located in front of the fuel tank on the right-hand crossmember.
18 A feed and earth lead are connected to the switch with flexible fuel feed inlet and outlet hoses.
19 To remove the pump, disconnect the leads, disconnect the hoses and plug the one from the tank. Remove the two mounting nuts.
20 If the pump is faulty, renew it as an assembly.
21 Refitting the pump is a reversal of removal.

Fig. 3.5 Exploded view of inverted type fuel pump (Sec 5)

1 Mounting base
2 Spring
3 Body
4 Filter
5 Gasket
6 Cover
7 Repair kit

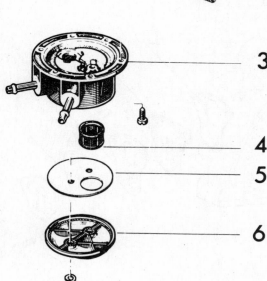
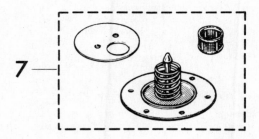

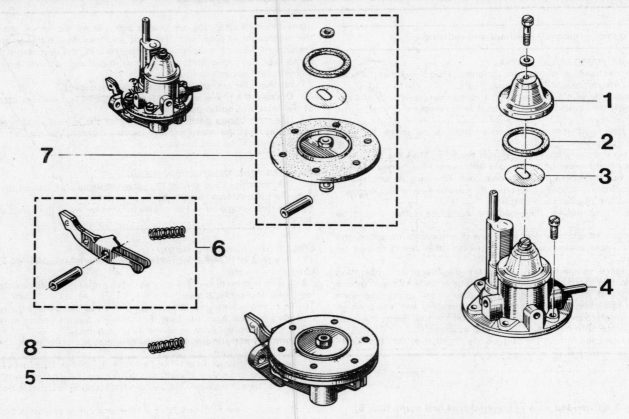

Fig. 3.6 Exploded view of typical fuel pump (Sec 5)

1	Cover	3	Filter	5	Lower body	7	Diaphragm (repair kit)
2	Seal	4	Upper body	6	Operating lever (repair kit)	8	Spring (operating lever)

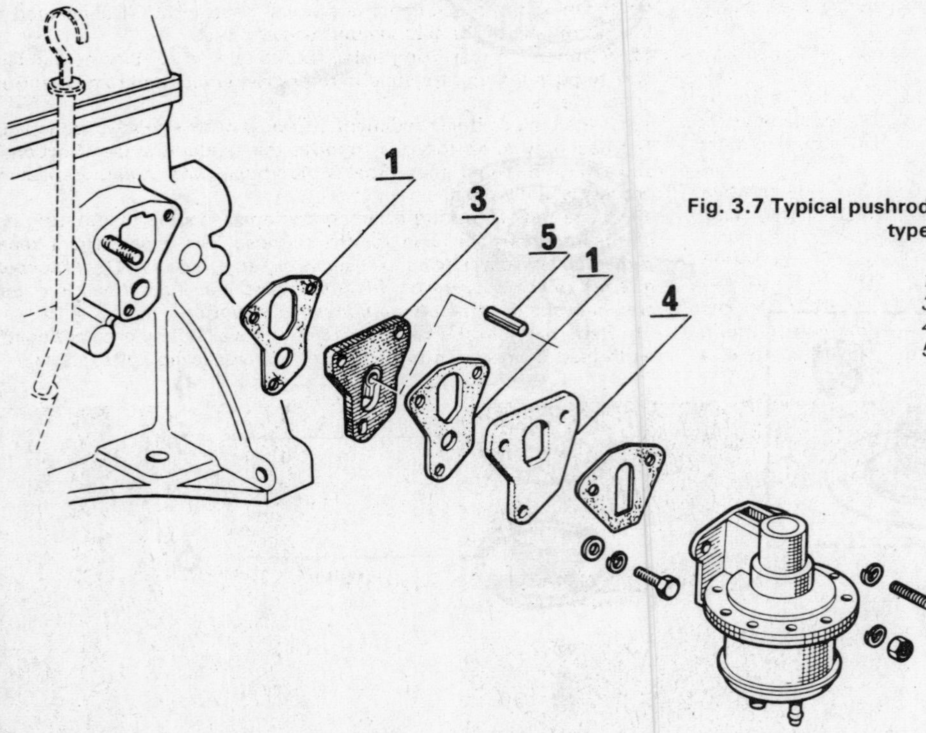

Fig. 3.7 Typical pushrod operated fuel pump as fitted to oil bath type crankcases (Sec 5)

1 Gasket
3 Insulator
4 Plate
5 Operating rod

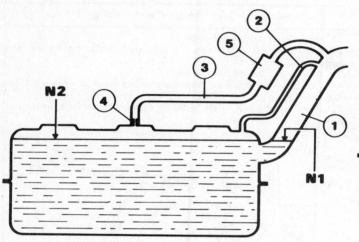

Fig. 3.8 Fuel tank anti-overspill system – early type (Sec 6)

1   Filler pipe   4   Jet
2   Breather pipe   5   Chamber
3   Anti-overspill pipe   N1,N2 Fuel levels stabilised

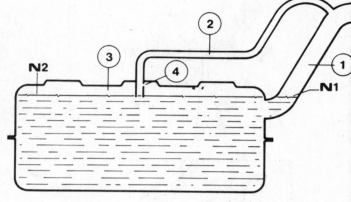

Fig. 3.9 Fuel tank anti-overspill system – later type (Sec 6)

1   Filler pipe   4   Jet
2   Breather pipe   N1,N2 Fuel levels stabilised
3   Air

6   Fuel tank – removal and refitting

1   Four different types of fuel tank have been fitted:

(a)   Fuel tank without an overspill device
(b)   Fuel tank with an anti-overspill device – October 1975 on
(c)   Fuel tank with an anti-overspill device – January 1976 on
(d)   Tank with a fuel vapour recovery system – North American vehicles

2   With the first type of anti-overspill system (Fig 3.8), the breather pipe (2) restricts the volume of fuel entering the tank during refilling. The filler pipe (1) will contain a quantity of fuel during the refilling process.
3   Fuel vapour is extracted through the calibrated jet (4) so allowing the fuel levels N1 and N2 to stabilize.
4   During an increase in ambient temperature, or if the vehicle is parked on a slope, the jet (4), anti-overspill pipe (3) and chamber (5) permit vapour to escape and the rise in fuel level (due to heat expansion) to stabilize.
5   With the second type of overspill system (Fig. 3.9), the breather pipe (2) restricts the volume of fuel entering the tank during refilling. The filler pipe (1) remains full of fuel during the operation.
6   The calibrated jet (4) enables the fuel levels N1 and N2 to stabilize.
7   The jet (4), anti-overspill pipe (2), filler pipe (1) and the filler cap vent hole allow fuel vapour to escape, so preventing any increase in the air pressure (3) which would occur as the fuel expanded – due to

a rise in ambient temperature. Similar conditions occur when the car is parked on a slope.
8   In North American cars, the fuel tank is fitted with a fuel vapour recovery system which is designed to prevent any emission of fuel vapour to the atmosphere. The system is described in detail in Section 14.
9   To remove the fuel tank, take off the tank shield and drain the fuel. Early models are fitted with a drain plug (photo) and a tank shield, later models are not and fuel will have to be syphoned out.
10   Release the filler pipe clip.
11   Take out the front fixing bolt (photo) and then tilt the tank forward so that access can be obtained to the fuel supply hose, the vent hose and the tank sender unit leads. Disconnect all these items. On North American vehicles additional hoses will have to be disconnected as they form part of the fuel vapour recovery system.
12   Remove the rear fixing bolts, tilt the tank to enable the fuel filler pipe to pass through the hole in the side-member and remove it from under the car.
13   If the tank contains sediment, it should be thoroughly cleaned out. The best way to do this is to remove the sender unit (see Section 7) and pour in some fuel. Shake vigorously and drain. Repeat as necessary until clean.
14   If the tank is leaking a temporary repair may be made using one of the products available for the purpose, but a permanent repair should be left to a specialist – usually radiator repairers. *On no account attempt to solder or weld a fuel tank yourself as it must be thoroughly steamed out to eliminate all danger of explosion.*
15   Refit the tank by reversing the removal operations, noting the earth lead connections under one of the rear fixing bolts (photo).

6.9 Fuel tank drain plug

6.11 Fuel tank front fixing bolts

6.15 Earth lead under a fuel tank rear fixing bolt

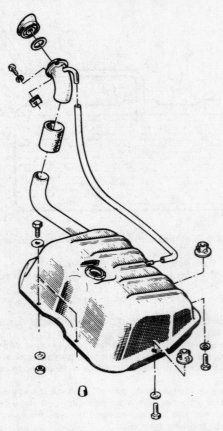

Fig. 3.10 Fuel tank components without anti-overspill or evaporative control system (Sec 6)

7 Fuel tank sender unit – removal and refitting

1   Disconnect the battery earth lead.
2   Peel back the mat from the luggage compartment floor and remove the circular plate.
3   Disconnect the electrical lead.
4   Turn the unit with a screwdriver or a flat blade to release it from the securing tangs.
5   Withdraw the unit carefully, taking care not to damage the float or arm.

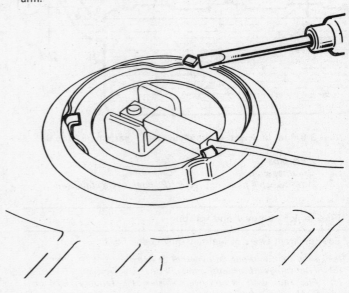

Fig. 3.11 Removing fuel tank sender unit (Sec 7)

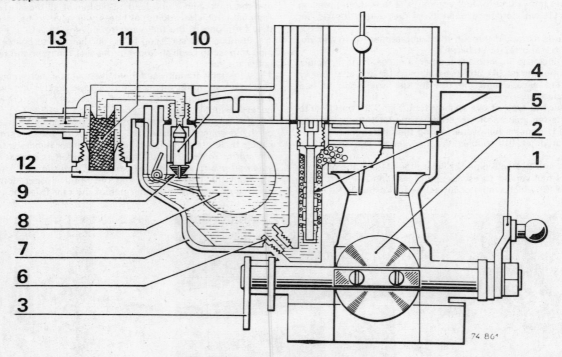

74 861

Fig. 3.12 Sectional view of Weber carburettor (Sec 8)

1 Throttle lever	4 Choke valve plate	8 Float	11 Filter gauze
2 Throttle butterfly valve plate	5 Emulsion tube	9 Tongue	12 Filter plug
3 Accelerator pump cam	6 Main jet	10 Fuel inlet needle valve	13 Fuel inlet
	7 Float chamber		

6   The unit can be checked if an ohmmeter is connected between the terminal and the sender unit body.

7   Move the float arm through a quarter of its stroke at a time and check the resistance reading against the figures given.

Float arm position	Resistance
Full stroke	*0 to 14 ohms*
Three-quarter stroke	*50 ohms*
Half stroke	*82 to 112 ohms*
Quarter stroke	*162 ohms*
Closed	*260 to 300 ohms*

8   Refitting is a reversal of removal, but check that the rubber sealing ring is in good order, otherwise renew it.

8 Carburettors – general

1   One of several different carburettors may be fitted depending upon engine capacity and date of production.

2   The Solex or Zenith units are of single barrel downdraught type, while the Weber is of dual barrel design.

3   All the carburettors have the throttle valve spacer block heated by engine coolant.

4   All carburettors have a manually operated choke with the exception of the Weber unit fitted to the Gordini Turbo which has a coolant heated automatic choke.

5   When exchanging a carburettor, renewing components or even obtaining a repair kit at time of overhaul, make sure that you quote the exact details of your vehicle including the identification number and the original carburettor type and reference numbers, as it is very important that the type of carburettor originally specified for your car with its individual calibration is retained.

6   Some Weber carburettors are fitted with a solenoid operated fuel cut-off valve (anti run-on valve).

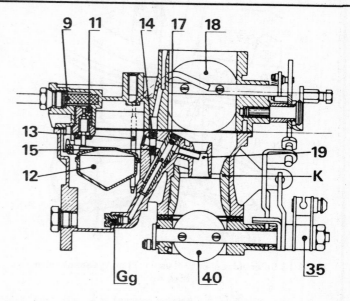

Fig. 3.14 Sectional view of Zenith 32 IF7 carburettor (Sec 8)

9 Filter	*18 Choke valve plate*
11 Needle valve	*19 Secondary choke tube*
12 Float	* venturi*
13 Auxiliary jet	*35 Throttle lever*
14 Degassing jet	*40 Throttle butterfly valve plate*
15 Air compensator jet	*Gg Main jet*
17 Atomiser	*K Choke tube*

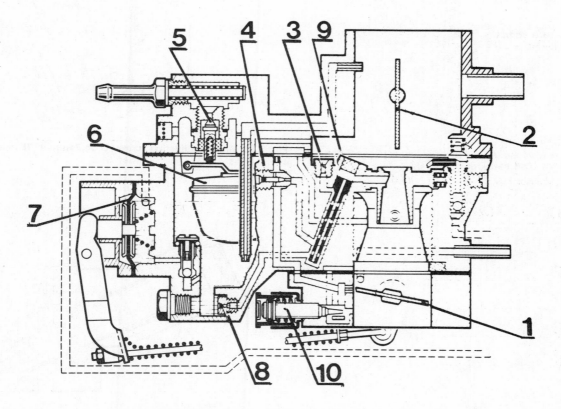

Fig. 3.13 Sectional view of Solex 32 DIS carburettor (Sec 8)

1 Throttle butterfly	*4 Idle jet*	*7 Accelerator pump*	*9 Emulsion tube*
2 Choke valve plate	*5 Fuel inlet needle valve*	*8 Main jet*	*10 Fuel mixture screw*
3 Air compensating jet	*6 Float*		

Fig. 3.15 Solenoid fuel cut-off valve (Z) on Weber carburettor (Sec 8)

P   Retaining screws

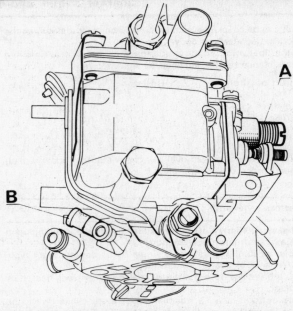

Fig. 3.16 Idle speed screw (A) and mixture screw (B) on Solex 32 SEIA (Sec 9)

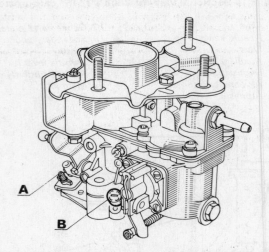

Fig. 3.17 Idle speed screw (A) and mixture screw (B) on Solex 32 DIS carburettor (Sec 9)

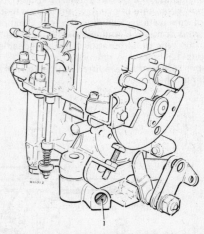

Fig. 3.18 Mixture adjusting screw (1) on Zenith 32 IF7 carburettor (Sec 9)

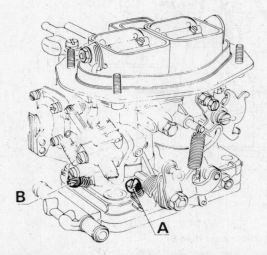

Fig. 3.19 Idle speed screw (A) and mixture screw (B) on Weber 32 DIR carburettor (Sec 9)

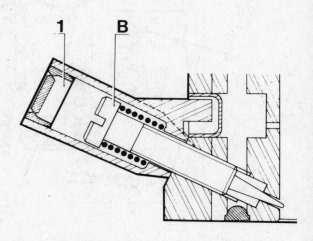

Fig. 3.20 Sectional view of typical carburettor adjuster screw fitted with tamperproof cap (Sec 9)

1   Tamperproof cap end plug   B   Screw

9 Idle speed and mixture – adjustment

1   Have the engine at normal operating temperature with the choke and all electrical accessories off. On N. American cars with an air injection system, clamp off the air injection hose (see Section 14) before starting up.
2   On later models, a plastic tamperproof cap is fitted to the adjustment screws. Prise out the cap plugs with a scriber. This plug should not be removed in countries with strict emission regulations.
3   Refer to Figs. 3.16 to 3.19 for the locations of the carburettor adjustment screws.

Adjustment with an exhaust gas analyser

4   Turn the speed screw (A) to obtain the specified idle speed.
5   Connect the exhaust gas analyser in accordance with the manufacturer's instructions.
6   Turn the mixture screw (B) to obtain a CO level of 2%
7   Re-adjust the throttle speed screw, if necessary, to set the specified idle speed.

Adjustment without an exhaust gas analyser

This method of adjustment is not accurate enough for use in countries having strict emission control regulations.
8   Turn the throttle speed screw (A) until the engine is running at the specified idle speed.
9   Turn the mixture screw (B) until the idle speed is at its highest. Repeat the two adjustments until the engine is running at the specified idle speed.

10   Turn the screw (B) in to weaken the mixture until the engine speed drops by about 30 rpm. Do not turn the screw in too far to cause the engine to idle roughly.

General

11   On completion of adjustment a new tamperproof cap should be fitted.

10 Carburettor (Solex 32 SEIA) – in car adjustments

Accelerator pump stroke

1   Remove the air cleaner and then, with the throttle in the idle position, bring the roller (6) into contact with cam (7) – Fig. 3.21.
2   Tighten the screw (8) so that it just touches the plunger (9). Give the screw a further $\frac{1}{2}$ to 1 complete turn.
3   Check that dimension (A) between the valve and the top of the float chamber (when the throttle lever is at idle) is as specified (see Fig. 3.22). If it is not, the stem of the valve should be bent slightly.

Choke cold start setting (carburettor mark 707 only)

4   With the choke set in the cold start position, there should be the specified clearance (J) – Fig. 3.23. If the clearance is incorrect, release the screw (L) and move the dashpot bracket. Retighten the screw.
5   As soon as the engine starts on the full choke setting, the choke valve plate should open so that a twist drill of the specified diameter will pass between the edge of the plate and the venturi wall. If necessary, loosen the locknut and turn the screw (K) to adjust, Fig. 3.24.

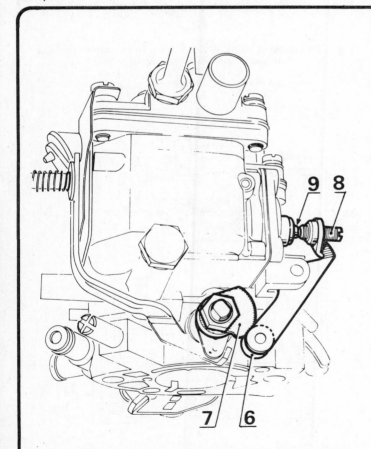

Fig. 3.21 Accelerator pump stroke adjustment – Solex 32 SE!A (Sec 10)

6	Roller	8	Screw
7	Cam	9	Plunger

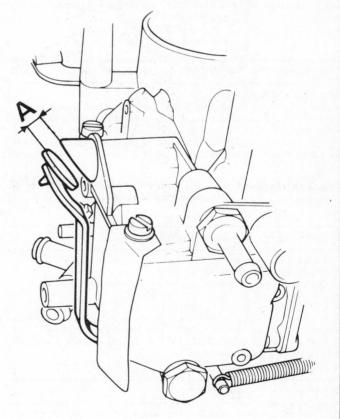

Fig. 3.22 Float chamber vent valve (Sec 10)

A = 3.0 mm (0.12 in)

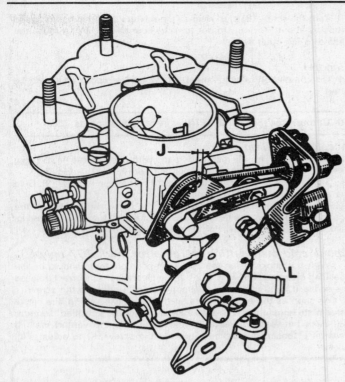

Fig. 3.23 Solex 32 SEIA mark 707 carburettor choke cold start setting (Sec 10)

J = 1.0 mm (0.04 in)
L = Dashpot bracket screw

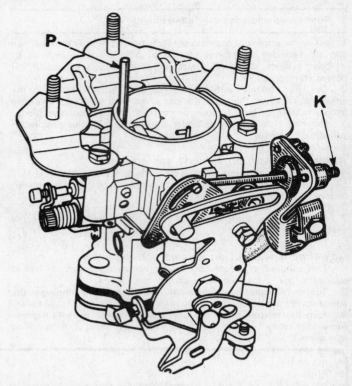

Fig. 3.24 Checking Solex 32 SEIA mark 707 carburettor choke cold start valve plate opening (Sec 10)

K   Adjuster screw
P   3.5 mm (0.137 in) twist drill as gauge rod

11 Carburettor (Weber 32 DIR) – in car adjustments

Fast idle adjustment

1   Make sure that the specified idle speed has been correctly set.
2   With the ignition switched off disconnect the negative lead from the solenoid flap valve (17) (Fig. 3.25).
3   Now actuate the solenoid flap valve by running a jump lead from the battery negative terminal to the previously disconnected solenoid terminal.
4   Start the engine and turn the screw (V) to obtain an engine speed of between 1450 and 1550 rpm.
5   Switch off the engine and re-make the original connections.

12 Carburettor – removal and refitting

1   Remove the air cleaner.
2   Disconnect the choke control cable.
3   Disconnect the accelerator control cable from the carburettor.
4   Disconnect the distributor vacuum pipe.
5   Disconnect the fuel hoses (photo).
6   Unscrew the two mounting nuts (Solex and Zenith) or four nuts (Weber) and remove the carburettor from the manifold (photo).
7   Refit by reversing the removal operations, but always use a new gasket on clean mating surfaces.

13 Carburettor – overhaul

1   Under normal circumstances, overhaul means removing the fixing screws and separating the top cover and throttle block from the main body of the carburettor so that the float chamber can be cleaned out and the jets and other passages cleaned with compressed air.
2   If the carburettor has been in service for a high mileage or the throttle spindles and their bushes have become worn, it is recommended that a new carburettor is obtained. It is unlikely that the individual parts will be available to recondition the carburettor yourself and the money saved in using less fuel will soon pay for the new unit.

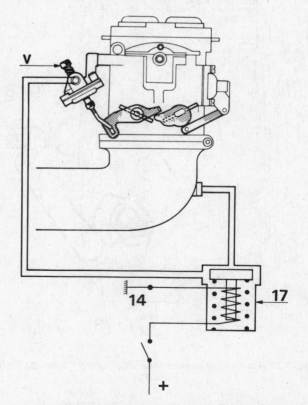

Fig. 3.25 Weber carburettor fast idle adjustment (Sec 11)

14 Negative lead   *17 Solenoid flap valve*
V   Fast idle adjuster screw

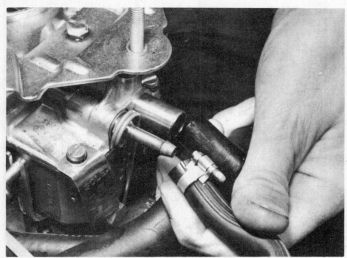

12.5 Typical fuel hose attachment to carburettor

12.6 Unscrewing typical carburettor fixing nuts

3   When reassembling the carburettor, carry out the following adjustments as work proceeds and use all the new gaskets, seals and other items supplied in the special repair kit for each carburettor.

Solex 32 SEIA carburettor
Initial throttle opening (fast idle) adjustment
4   Invert the carburettor.
5   Close the choke to the full or intermediate position as indicated in the table in the Specifications according to carburettor model. The choke position will be determined when the detent ball is felt to engage in the hole in the cam lever as the lever is swivelled.
6   Using a twist drill or gauge rod, measure the gap between the edge of the throttle valve plate and the venturi wall.
7   Adjust if necessary to specification by turning the screw (2) – Fig. 3.28.

Solex 32 DIS carburettor
Intake throttle opening (fast idle) adjustment
8   Hold the choke valve plate fully closed and then invert the carburettor.
9   Using a twist drill or gauge rod, measure the gap between the edge of the throttle valve plate and the venturi wall.
10 Adjust to the specification by breaking off the tamperproof cap (7) and turning the screw (Fig. 3.29). Fit a new white tamperproof cap in place of the original black one fitted in production.

Accelerator pump stroke adjustment
11 When the accelerator pump rod is at the end of its stroke, the throttle valve plate should be open the specified amount. Measure this gap between the edge of the throttle valve plate and the venturi wall with a twist drill or gauge rod. Where adjustment is required, release

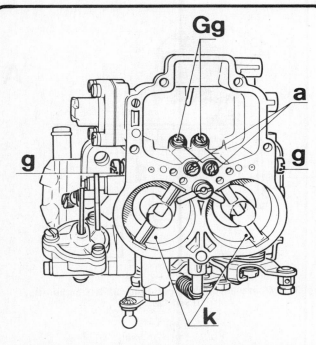

Fig. 3.26 Jet locations in Weber carburettor (Sec 13)

  a   Air compensator jets   Gg Main jets
  g   Idling jets   K   Choke tubes

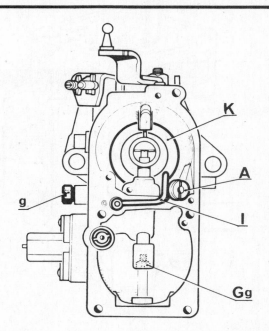

Fig. 3.27 Jet location in Solex 32 DIS carburettor (Sec 13)

  A   Air compensating jet   Gg Main jet
  K   Venturi (choke tube)   g   Idle jet
  I   Accelerator pump ejector
      nozzle

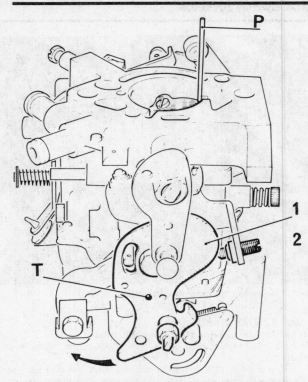

Fig. 3.28 Checking initial throttle opening on Solex 32 SEIA (Sec 13)

P   Twist drill as gauge rod
T   Intermediate choke position detent
1   Cam
2   Adjuster screw

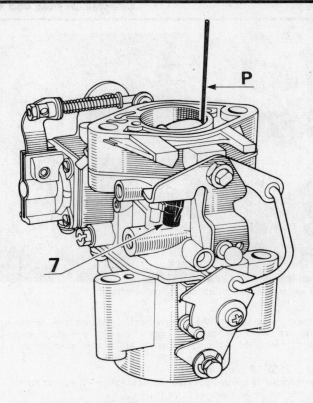

Fig. 3.29 Checking initial throttle opening on Solex 32 DIS carburettor (Sec 13)

P   Twist drill as gauge rod
7   Tamperproof cap on adjuster screw

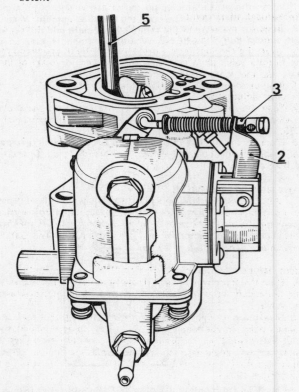

Fig. 3.30 Accelerator pump rod stroke adjustment on Solex 32 DIS carburettor (Sec 13)

2   Diaphragm lever
3   Locknut
5   Twist drill as gauge rod

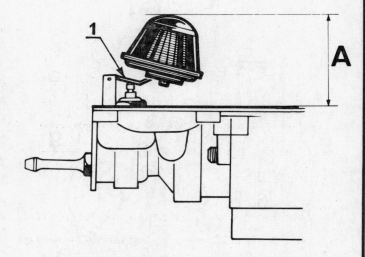

Fig. 3.31 Float adjusting diagram Solex 32 DIS carburettor (Sec 13)

1   Float arm
A = 35.5 to 37.5 mm
(1.4 to 1.5 in)

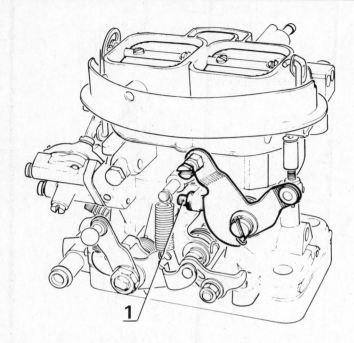

Fig. 3.32 Initial opening adjuster screw (1) on Weber 32 DIR carburettor (Sec 13)

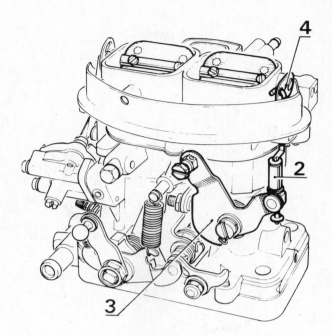

Fig. 3.33 Choke flap part open setting (mechanical) on Weber 32 DIR carburettor (Sec 13)

2   Sleeve/spring   3   Cam
          4   Link rod

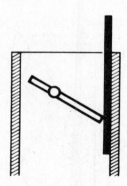

Fig. 3.34 Position of twist drill for checking throttle valve plate opening (Sec 13)

the locknut on the pump rod and turn the adjuster nut. Lock the nut on completion.

Float height adjustment
12 Hold the carburettor cover upside down so that the float arm depresses the fuel inlet needle valve.
13 Measure the dimension (A) between the float base and the surface of the cover gasket — see Fig. 3.31.
14 If dimension (A) is not as specified, bend the float arm gently.

Weber 32 DIR carburettor
Initial throttle opening adjustment
15 Close both choke valve plates completely.
16 Using a twist drill or gauge rod, measure the throttle valve plate gap between the edge of the valve plate and the venturi wall.
17 If adjustment is required, release the locknut and turn the screw (1) — Fig. 3.32.

Choke flap part open setting
18 This setting consists of two parts — mechanical and vacuum.

Mechanical adjustment
19 Close the choke valve plates completely. Check that the sleeve (2) is in contact with the cam (3) — Fig. 3.33.
20 Invert the carburettor and using a twist drill or gauge rod measure the throttle valve plate port opening between the edge of the valve plate and the venturi wall.
21 If adjustment is needed, bend the link rod (4).
Vacuum adjustment
22 Push the rod (5) to its stop then close the choke valve plates by moving the cam (3) until the spring (8) is slightly compressed — Fig. 3.35.
23 Measure the throttle valve plate gap as described in paragraph 20.
24 If adjustment is needed, extract the threaded plug (6) and turn the grub screw (7).

Float chamber vent valve
25 Check that the choke valve plate is fully open and then depress the float chamber vent valve stem (1) and measure the throttle valve plate opening between the edge of the plate and the venturi wall — Fig. 3.36. This should be between 0.35 and 0.65 mm (0.014 and 0.025 in). If adjustment is needed, turn the nut (E).

Float height adjustment
26 Hold the top cover vertical so that the float hangs down with its arm tab in contact with the needle valve ball, but not depressing it into the valve.
27 Measure the dimension (A) from the cover gasket surface to the nearest point on the float (Fig. 3.37). If it is not as specified, bend the float arm gently, but make sure that the tongue (4) is kept at right angles to the needle valve centre line. When the float is correctly set, check the float stroke (dimension B). If this is not as specified, bend the tongue (5).

Zenith 32 IF7 carburettor
Initial throttle opening
28 Close the choke valve plate until the hole (T) snaps over the detent ball. Now measure the choke valve plate opening using a twist drill or gauge rod. If the gap is not as specified, release the locknut (2) and turn the screw (1) — Fig. 3.38.

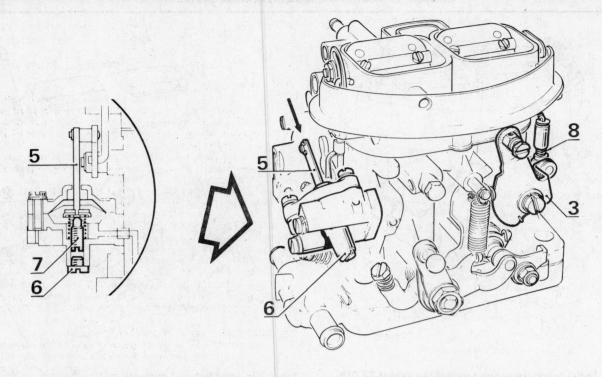

Fig. 3.35 Choke flap part open setting (vacuum) on Weber 32 DIR carburettor (Sec 13)

| 3 Cam | 5 Link rod | 6 Blanking screw | 7 Adjuster screw |

8 Sleeve/spring

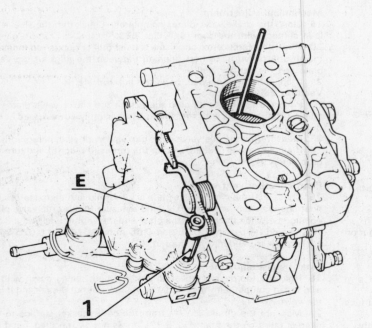

Fig. 3.36 Checking float chamber vent valve on Weber carburettor (Sec 13)

1 Valve stem *E Adjuster nut*

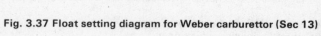

Fig. 3.37 Float setting diagram for Weber carburettor (Sec 13)

1 Fuel inlet valve
2 Valve ball
3 Float arm
4 Tongue
5 Tongue
A = 7.0 mm (0.28 in)
B = 8.0 mm (0.32 in)

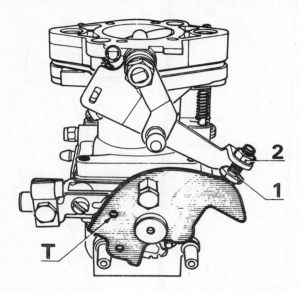

Fig. 3.38 Initial opening Zenith 32 IF7 carburettor (Sec 13)

1 *Fast idle screw*	2 *Locknut*

T   *Choke full open detent*

14 Emission control systems – description

1   The purpose of any emission control system is to reduce the level of noxious gases and fuel vapour being vented into the atmosphere.
2   All models have a positive crankcase ventilation system (PCV) which permits crankcase breathing and eliminates blow-by gases which pass the piston rings, by drawing them into the intake manifold and then burning them during the normal engine combustion process.
3   Later models have a temperature controlled air cleaner to keep intake air at the optimum temperature to ensure clean burning and to prevent icing of the carburettor.

4   The more sophisticated systems are only fitted to models destined for operation in North America and a few other territories which have stringent anti-pollution regulations.
5   These systems include the following:

Air injection system
6   This system is used to reduce the emission of hydrocarbons, carbon monoxide and nitric oxide in the exhaust gases and consists of an air pump, diverter/relief valve, air shut-off/check valve and air injection manifold. Air is introduced into the cylinder head around the exhaust ports.
7   The rotary vane type pump is belt driven from the engine and delivers compressed air at a maximum pressure of 4.3 psi to each of the four exhaust ports.
8   The diverter/relief valve controls the air pressure delivered to the injection manifold and releases excessive pressure to the atmosphere. During deceleration the diverter/relief valve shuts off the compressed air supply to the injection manifold and the compressed air is released to the atmosphere.
9   The air shut-off valve is controlled by the choke cable and forms an integral part with the check valve. When the choke is operated the valve shuts off the air flow from the air pump to the injection manifold.
10   The check valve is a diaphragm-spring operated non-return valve. Its purpose is to protect the air pump from the exhaust gas pressures both under normal operation and in the event of the drivebelt failing.

Exhaust gas recirculation (EGR) system
11   This system reduces the emission of nitric oxide contained in the exhaust gas by lowering the peak combustion temperatures inside the engine. This is achieved by recirculating a metered quantity of exhaust gas through the intake manifold.
12   A control signal is taken from a tapping in the carburettor body. Various valves in the system circuit prevent operation of the EGR valve if the coolant temperature is below 45°C (113°F) during warm-up, at idle or under full load conditions.

Fuel evaporative control system (fuel vapour recovery system)
13   This system employs an activated charcoal absorption canister through which the fuel tank and the carburettor float chamber are vented.

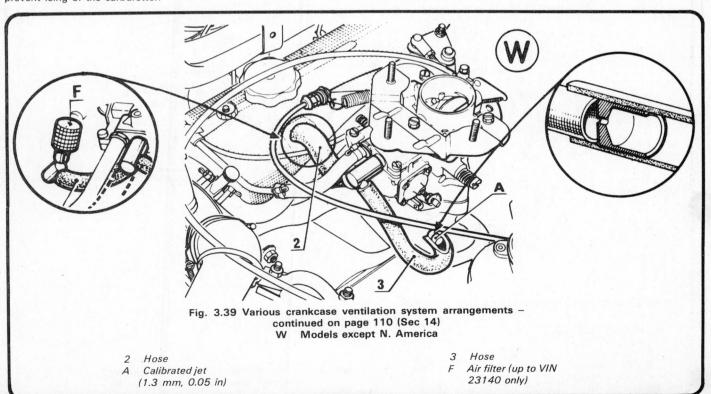

**Fig. 3.39 Various crankcase ventilation system arrangements –
continued on page 110 (Sec 14)
W   Models except N. America**

2 *Hose*	3 *Hose*
A *Calibrated jet*	F *Air filter (up to VIN*
(1.3 mm, 0.05 in)	*23140 only)*

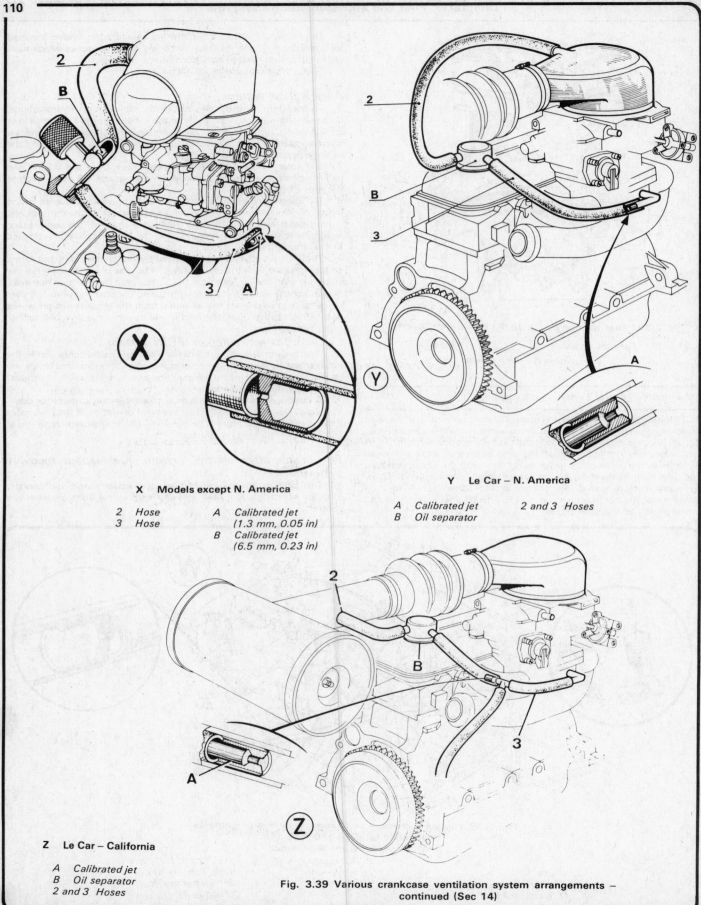

X Models except N. America

2 Hose
3 Hose

A Calibrated jet
(1.3 mm, 0.05 in)
B Calibrated jet
(6.5 mm, 0.23 in)

Y Le Car – N. America

A Calibrated jet
B Oil separator

2 and 3 Hoses

Z Le Car – California

A Calibrated jet
B Oil separator
2 and 3 Hoses

Fig. 3.39 Various crankcase ventilation system arrangements –
continued (Sec 14)

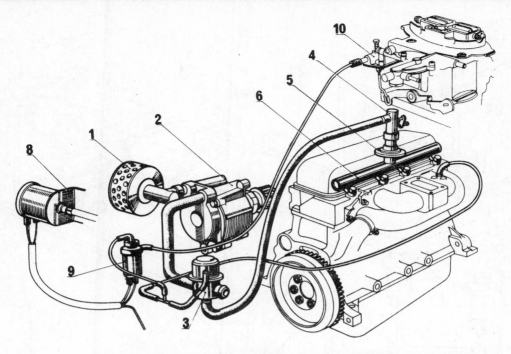

Fig. 3.40 Air injection system – early models (Sec 14)

1	Air pump filter	4	Air shut-off valve
2	Air pump	5	Check valve
3	Relief/diverter valve	6	Air injection manifold

8	Centrifugal governor	
9	Throttle valve positioner solenoid	
10	Throttle valve positioner diaphragm unit	

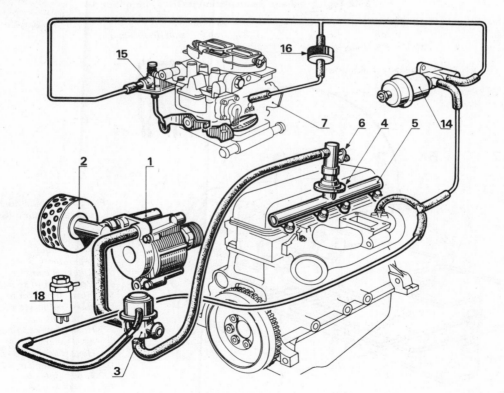

Fig. 3.41 Typical later model air injection system (Sec 14)

1	Air pump	5	Air injection manifold
2	Air filter	6	Air shut-off valve
3	Relief/diverter valve	7	Carburettor
4	Check valve	14	Vacuum valve

15	Throttle plate opener
16	Idle delay valve
18	Throttle valve positioner solenoid

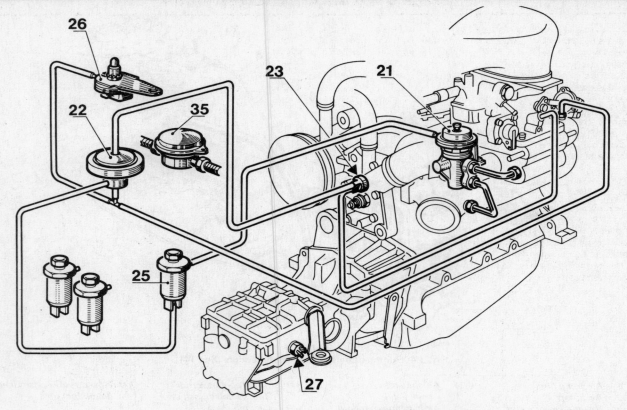

Fig. 3.42 Typical exhaust recirculation (EGR) system (Sec 14)

21 EGR valve
22 Amplifier

23 Coolant temperature
   switch
25 Solenoid flap valve

26 Vacuum switch
27 Transmission (fourth-speed)
   switch

35 Service indicator

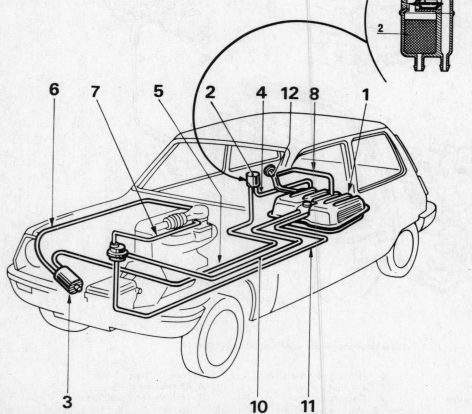

Fig. 3.43 Typical fuel vapour recovery system (Sec 14)

1 Fuel tank
2 Vapour/liquid
  separator
3 Charcoal canister
4 Hose (tank to separator)
5 Hose (separator to canister)
6 Hose (carburettor to
  air intake)
7 Hose (float chamber to
  air cleaner)
8 Hose (filler pipe to tank)
10 Fuel return pipe
11 Fuel supply pipe
12 Fuel filler pipe

14 Fuel vapour passes through a separator to the charcoal canister where it is stored until the engine is started and the canister is purged, the vapour being drawn into the carburettor intake and burned during the normal combustion cycle.

15 With this system, a non-vented fuel filler cap is fitted. There is also a valve to equalise tank internal pressure as the fuel level falls.

16 A one-way valve is incorporated in the tank to pump return pipeline and this prevents fuel circulation when the engine is not running and also has a fuel cut-off facility should the car roll over.

17 On some carburettors the method of venting the float chamber to the charcoal canister is by means of a solenoid operated valve. The valve is operated by a switch, mounted on the idle stop, and a relay.

Ignition advance control system (mechanical contact breaker)

18 A switch linked to the choke cable closes when the choke is operated. When closed the switch supplies current to the vacuum solenoid valve which then opens and allows the carburettor vacuum to act upon the distributor vacuum advance unit. This arrangement allows the ignition timing to be advanced during cold engine operation. When the choke is released the switch contacts open and the system is de-energised.

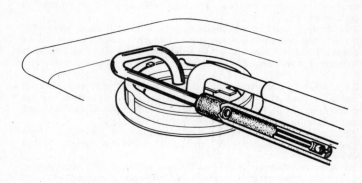

Fig. 3.44 Fuel return pipe one-way valve (Sec 14)

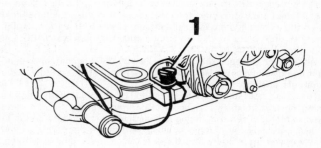

Fig. 3.46 Carburettor vent valve switch (1) mounted on idle stop (Sec 14)

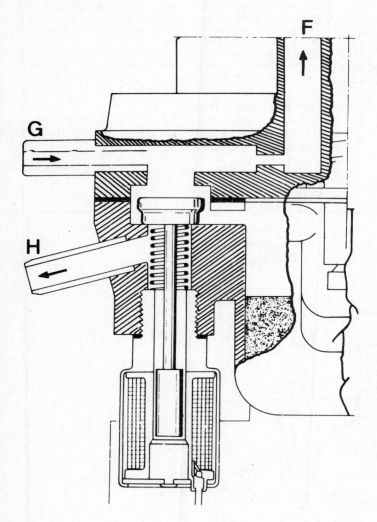

Fig. 3.45 Solenoid operated carburettor vent valve (Sec 14)

F and G Vents to atmosphere
H   Vent to charcoal canister

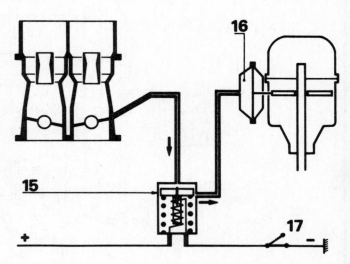

Fig. 3.47 Ignition advance control system (Sec 14)

15 Solenoid valve for
    vacuum control
16 Distributor vacuum unit
17 Solenoid control switch

Accelerated idle system

19 The purpose of this system is to hold the primary throttle plate open slightly for a few seconds after removing the foot from the accelerator pedal.

20 On early models the circuit incorporates a vacuum valve (14) housing two pressure capsules – one of which is subject to barometric pressure and the other to intake vacuum (Fig. 3.49). The difference between the two capsules controls the projection of the operating rod (T).

21 On later models the circuit is of simplified design and does not include a vacuum valve, only a delay valve (19) and a throttle plate opener (Fig. 3.50). The system prevents accumulation of unburned fuel vapour during deceleration on the overrun.

22 Vacuum in the intake manifold acts upon the diaphragm of the throttle plate opener, this in turn slightly opens the primary throttle valve plate.

23 A modified system is used on Californian models, incorporating an electronic governor (14) located inside the car under the left-hand parcel shelf, a solenoid valve (17) and a throttle plate opener (15) on the carburettor (Fig. 3.51).

24 The system operates when a magnetic pick-up in the speedometer transmits impulses to the electronic governor which actuates the solenoid valve at roadspeeds between 26 and 30 kph (16.2 and 18.6 mph).

25 Once the throttle is released during deceleration, the throttle valve plates in the carburettor start to close, vacuum in the intake manifold acts on the throttle plate opener diaphragm (15) which holds open the primary throttle plate to give an engine speed of between 1400 and 1600 rpm.

26 When the roadspeed drops below 26 kph the solenoid valve is no longer energised, vacuum is cut off and the throttle plate returns to the normal idle position.

27 To assist hot starting which can be a problem with engines running on lean mixtures, a vacuum operated primary throttle plate opener is fitted. When the engine is switched off, the return spring in the device pushes the plunger against the throttle plate linkage and partially opens the primary throttle plate. Once the engine is running, vacuum from the intake manifold actuates the diaphragm unit which withdraws the plunger and releases the throttle linkage so that the valve plate can resume the idle position.

Vacuum advance system (breakerless ignition system)

28 The system is designed to advance the ignition timing when the engine oil temperature is below 15°C (59°F). Under these conditions, the thermoswitch (18) is closed and the solenoid valve (26) is energised to close the vacuum circuit from the carburettor (Fig. 3.52). The relay (33) is energised and the secondary impulse sender (B1) operates – resulting in advanced ignition timing, but without actuation of the distributor vacuum unit.

29 When the engine oil temperature rises above 15°C (59°F) the thermoswitch (18) is open and the solenoid valve (26) is not energised so that the vacuum from the carburettor primary venturi acts normally on the distributor vacuum unit. The relay (33) is not energised and the main impulse sender (B) operates to give the normal ignition advance.

Catalytic converter

30 To further reduce the emission of carbon monoxide and hydrocarbons, a catalytic converter is incorporated in the exhaust system of Californian models.

31 The converter is basically a honeycomb-like core housed within a stainless steel casing. The core is coated with a catalyst which converts unburnt carbon monoxide and hydrocarbons into carbon dioxide and water by a chemical reaction.

32 Certain precautions are necessry on cars equipped with one of these devices. Only unleaded fuel should be used, the carburettor should never be run on an over-rich setting. Never allow misfiring to occur when the fuel tank is nearly empty.

33 The catalytic converter can get very hot after descending long gradients with the throttle pedal released. Never park over long dry grass or other combustible material.

Closed loop feedback system

34 This system is fitted to late (1980) Californian models and incorporates the following components:

(a) Modified Weber carburettor
(b) Oxygen sensor located in the exhaust downpipe
(c) Electronic control unit located on the floor behind the driver's seat
(d) Vacuum solenoid regulator

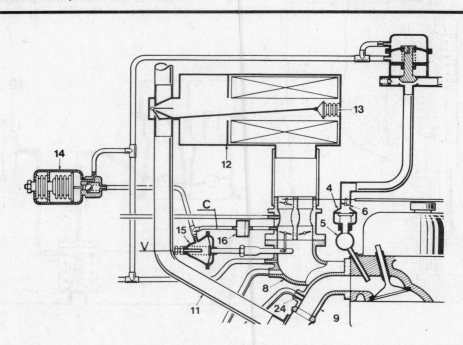

Fig. 3.48 Earlier type accelerated idle system (Secs 14 and 16)

4 Check valve	9 Exhaust manifold	14 Vacuum valve	24 Calibrated orifice
5 Air mixture manifold	11 Warm air intake duct	15 Throttle opener	C Bleed channel
6 Air shut-off valve	12 Air cleaner	16 Idle delay valve	V Adjuster screw
8 Intake manifold	13 Air cleaner thermostat		

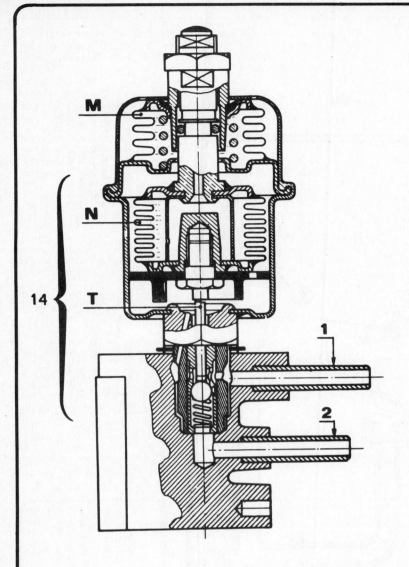

Fig. 3.49 Sectional view of vacuum valve (14) in early accelerated idle system (Sec 14)

M Capsule (atmospheric pressure)
N Capsule (intake manifold vacuum)
T Operating rod
1 Vacuum connection
2 Throttle opener connection

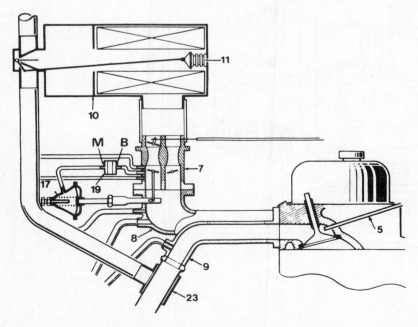

Fig. 3.50 Later type accelerated idle system (Sec 14)

5   Air injection manifold
7   Venturi wall
8   Intake manifold
9   Exhaust manifold
10 Air cleaner
11 Thermostatic valve
17 Throttle plate opener
19 Delay valve
23 Warm air collection point
M   Black side of valve
B   White side of valve

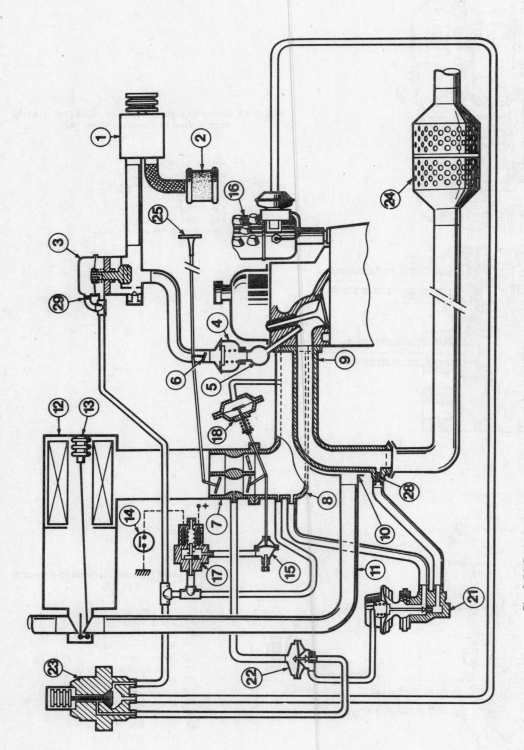

Fig. 3.51 Emission control system incorporating accelerated idle system with electronic governor (Sec 14)

1 Air pump	9 Exhaust manifold	16 Distributor
2 Air pump filter	10 Warm air collector point	17 Fast idle solenoid
3 Diverter/relief valve	11 Warm air intake duct	valve
4 Check valve	12 Air cleaner	18 Primary throttle plate
5 Air injection manifold	13 Air cleaner thermostat	opener
6 Air shut-off valve	14 Electronic governor	21 EGR valve
7 Carburettor	15 Throttle plate opener	22 Vacuum switch
8 Intake manifold		

23 Thermovalve	
24 Catalytic converter	
25 Choke operating knob	
28 Calibrated orifice	
(3.5 mm, 0.14 in)	
29 Calibrated orifice	
(0.4 mm, 0.016 in)	

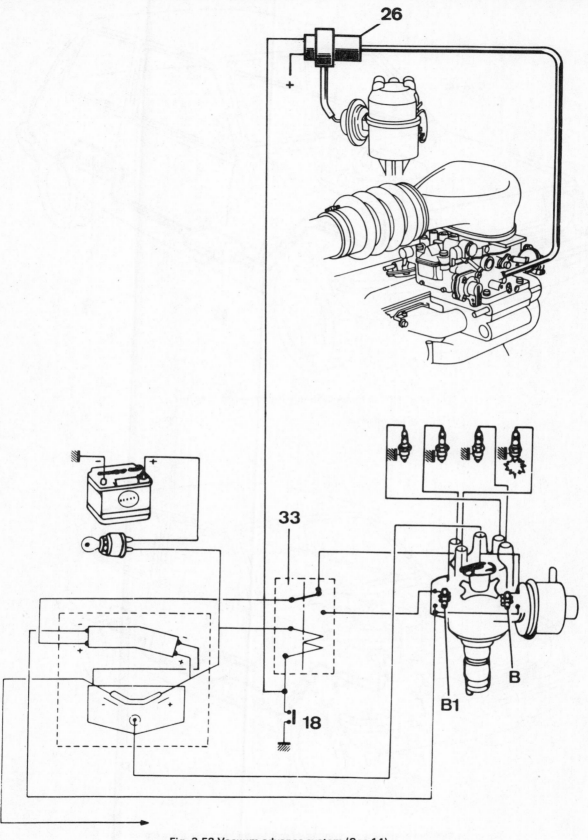

26

33

18

B1

B

Fig. 3.52 Vacuum advance system (Sec 14)

B	Main impulse sender	18	Thermo switch	33	Relay
B1	Secondary impulse sender	26	Solenoid valve		

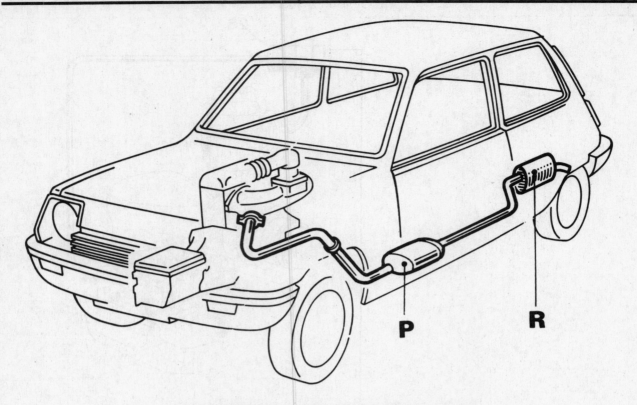

Fig. 3.53 Exhaust system with converter (Sec 14)

P   *Catalytic converter*   R   *Silencer*

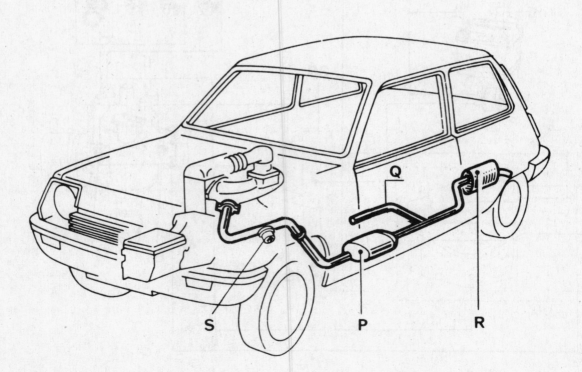

Fig. 3.54 Exhaust system with catalytic converter and anti-resonance pipe (Sec 14)

P   *Catalytic converter*   Q   *Anti-resonance pipe*   R   *Silencer*   S   *Sensor plug socket*

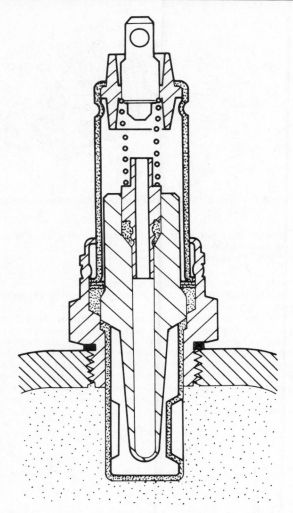

Fig. 3.55 Oxygen sensor – closed loop feedback carburettor (Sec 14)

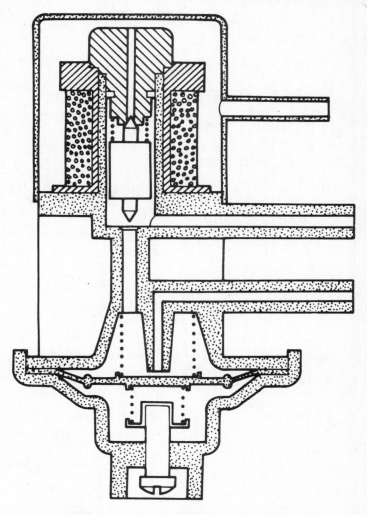

Fig. 3.56 Vacuum solenoid regulator – closed loop feedback carburettor (Sec 14)

35 The oxygen sensor monitors the fuel/air mixture in the exhaust and sends a signal to the electronic control unit.

36 The electronic control unit receives signals not only from the oxygen sensor, but also the position of the choke (cold start) control and the ignition coil LT circuit (engine speed).

37 The vacuum solenoid regulator is energised by signals from the control unit. By altering the vacuum conditions in the intake manifold the mixture is either weakened or enriched to ensure the most suitable fuel/air ratio is maintained to keep the exhaust-emission CO levels at permissible levels under all operating conditions.

15 Emission control system (Canadian specification) – description

1 On models with a type 810 engine destined for operation in Canada, the emission control system is simplified and includes the following device.

Throttle opener

2 The vacuum capsule (6) in the system opens the circuit to the diaphragm (5) during deceleration at a pre-determined intake manifold vacuum (Fig. 3.57) The diaphragm holds the throttle open at an engine speed of 1500 rpm.

3 A calibrated jet controls the bleed for the return to normal idling speed.

4 On later models the throttle opener circuit incorporates a delay valve instead of a bleed channel. This lengthens the time taken for

engine speed to return to idle in the interest of reduced exhaust emission.

5 A dashpot is fitted to the carburettor to slow the return of the throttle to idle during deceleration.

16 Emission control system – maintenance

General

1 At regular intervals (see Routine Maintenance), check the security and condition of the system hoses and electrical connections.

2 An essential factor for efficient operation of the emission control system is to ensure that the ignition and fuel systems are correctly adjusted. The air cleaner element should also be renewed at the specified intervals.

3 Carry out the following work at the intervals specified in Routine Maintenance.

Positive crankcase ventilation (PCV) system

4 Disconnect the hoses and clean them out. Make sure that the calibrated restricting jet is not clogged and refit it correctly in its pipeline leading to the intake manifold.

5 Wash out the oil separator on the rocker cover with paraffin and blow dry.

Air injection system (AIS)

6 Check the drivebelt and adjust or renew it, as described in Chapter 2, Section 3.

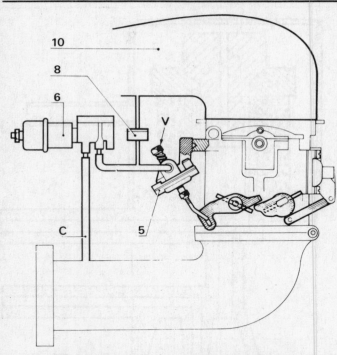

**Fig. 3.57 Throttle opening system – Canadian specification
(Sec 15)**

5	Throttle valve plate opener	10	Air intake duct
6	Vacuum capsule	C	Original bleed channel (blocked)
8	Delay valve	V	Fast idle screw

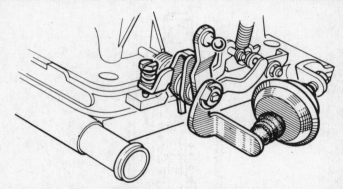

**Fig. 3.58 Dashpot on Weber carburettor – Canadian specification
(Sec 15)**

7 Remove the cover from the air pump air cleaner, take out the
element and discard it.
8 Fit a new element and refit the cover.

Exhaust gas recirculation (EGR) system

9 Remove the EGR valve, dismantle and clean away all combustion
deposits with a wire brush.
10 Dismantle the connecting pipes and thoroughly clean them out,
paying particular attention to the intake manifold passage.
11 The EGR system has a sealed maintenance indicator fitted into the
speedometer cable and located in the engine compartment.
12 It is recommended that the system is serviced by your dealer,
when he will cut the seal, unclip the cover and turn the knob (B)
through a $\frac{1}{4}$ turn towards the 'O' mark to reset the mileage indicator
and turn off the warning lamp which comes on at the end of a
maintenance cycle (Fig. 3.61).

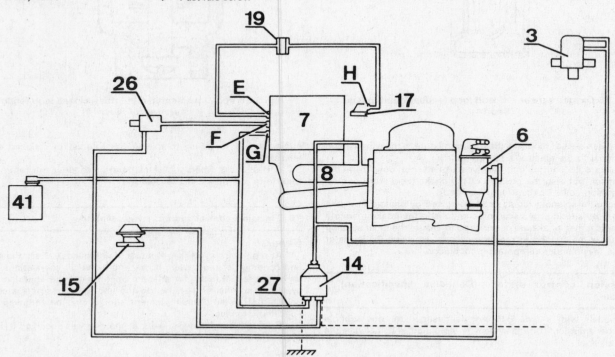

Fig. 3.59 Typical emission control system hose arrangement – without air conditioning (Sec 16)

3	Diverter/relief valve	14	EGR solenoid valve	26	Vacuum advance solenoid valve	E	Red cable
6	Distributor	15	EGR valve	27	Calibrated orifice (5.5 mm, 0.22 in)	F	Black cable
7	Carburettor	17	Throttle valve plate opener	40	Air conditioning solenoid valve	G	Brown cable
8	Intake manifold	19	Delay valve	41	Charcoal canister	H	Blue cable

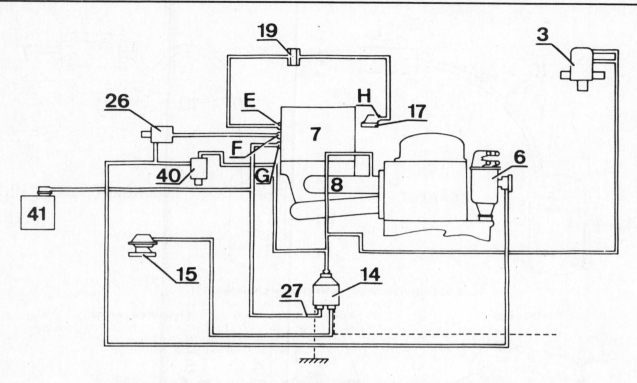

Fig. 3.60 Typical emission control system hose arrangement with air conditioning (Sec 16)

Key as Fig. 3.59

Fuel evaporative control system

13 Identify the hose connections on the charcoal canister within the engine compartment and then disconnect them.

14 Renew the canister and reconnect the hoses. Do not allow the carburettor vent hose to have a low point, but support it in a continuous sweep.

15 Check the condition of the rubber seal in the fuel tank filler cap and renew it if there is any doubt as to its condition.

Accelerated idle system

16 Although no maintenance is normally required to this system, any doubt as to its correct operation should be checked out in the following way.

17 Have the engine at normal operating temperature with the radiator fan running.

18 Disconnect the vacuum pipe from the vacuum valve (Fig. 3.48). Connect a pipe directly to the throttle plate opener from the intake manifold.

19 Increase the engine speed to 2500 rpm and then release the throttle. Check that the accelerated idle speed is between 1800 and 2000 rpm before dropping to idle. If this is not so, adjust the screw (V) on the throttle opener.

20 The idle delay valve (16) must be renewed at the specified mileage intervals.

Throttle opener (Canadian models)

21 If the delay valve (8) – Fig. 3.57 is renewed, make sure that the end coloured brown is towards the intake manifold.

Closed loop feedback system

22 A maintenance indicator is located on the speedometer cable and mounted on the air cleaner bracket.

23 Its function is similar to that used to indicate maintenance intervals for the EGR system, but its purpose is to act as a reminder to renew the oxygen sensor.

24 When renewing the sensor, use sealant on the threads and check that there are no leaks in the exhaust system as they would affect the operation of the sensor.

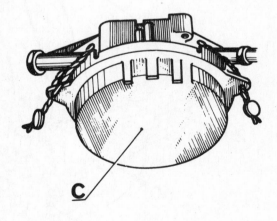

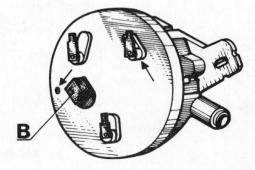

Fig. 3.61 EGR maintenance indicator (Sec 16)

C   *Indicator cover*
B   *Reset knob*

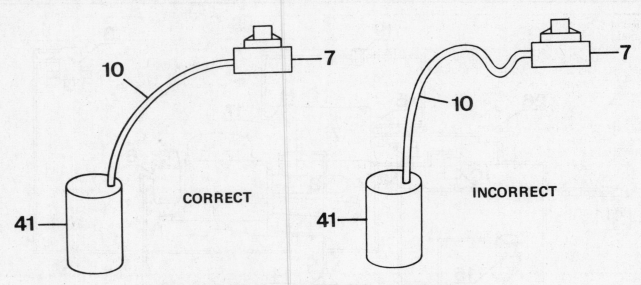

CORRECT

INCORRECT

Fig. 3.62 Correct routing of carburettor vent hose (Sec 16)

7 Carburettor   10 Vent hose   41 Charcoal canister

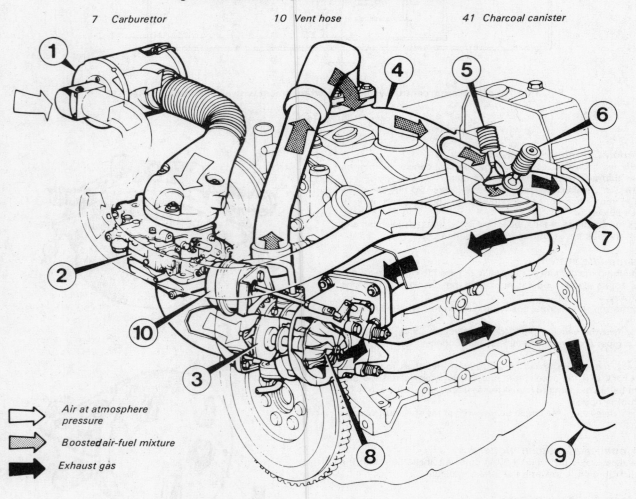

Air at atmosphere pressure

Boosted air-fuel mixture

Exhaust gas

Fig. 3.63 Gordini turbocharger (Sec 17)

1 Air cleaner   5 Inlet valve   8 Exhaust driven turbine
2 Carburettor   6 Exhaust valve   9 Exhaust downpipe
3 Inlet air compressor   7 Exhaust manifold   10 Wastegate control capsule
4 Inlet manifold

17 Gordini Turbo carburettor and turbocharger – description and precautions

1   On these 1397 cc models, a Garrett type T3 turbocharger is fitted in conjunction with a Weber 32 DIR 75 carburettor.

2   This arrangement gives greater power and acceleration with outstanding flexibility due to increased torque, but without any great increase in fuel consumption.

3   The layout of the components of the turbocharged engine is shown in Fig. 3.64. The main circuits are intake, crankcase ventilation, fuel and vacuum/pneumatic.

4   After any repair or overhaul which has required disconnection of the oil feed circuit, the turbocharger lubrication circuit must be primed in the following way.

5   Disconnect the TDC sensor plug from the socket (B) on the electronic module (Fig. 3.65).

6   Disconnect the oil feed pipe at the turbocharger end and fill the pipe with the specified oil.

7   Reconnect the oil pipe and reconnect the plug (B)

8   Spin the engine on the starter motor until the oil warning lamp goes out.

18 Turbocharger – removal and refitting

1   Remove the warm air intake duct.

2   Remove the strut (1) – Fig. 3.67.

3   Remove the channel (11) – Fig. 3.68.

4   Disconnect the downpipe clamp.

5   Unscrew and remove the nuts (2).

6   Take off the clips (3) and the hose (15).

7   Disconnect the oil feed pipe (4) at the flange, also the oil return pipe.

8   Remove the socket-headed screws (6).

9   Never attempt to support the turbocharger by holding the control rod (T), or the diaphragm inside the capsule may be damaged.

10 Lift the turbocharger carefully from the engine compartment.

11 To refit the turbocharger, lower it into position and engage it in its flexible trunking.

12 Refit and tighten the clips (3).

13 Screw in the socket-headed screws (6), using new sealing gaskets.

14 Fit the nuts (2).

15 When tightening the downpipe flange nuts, it is important not to

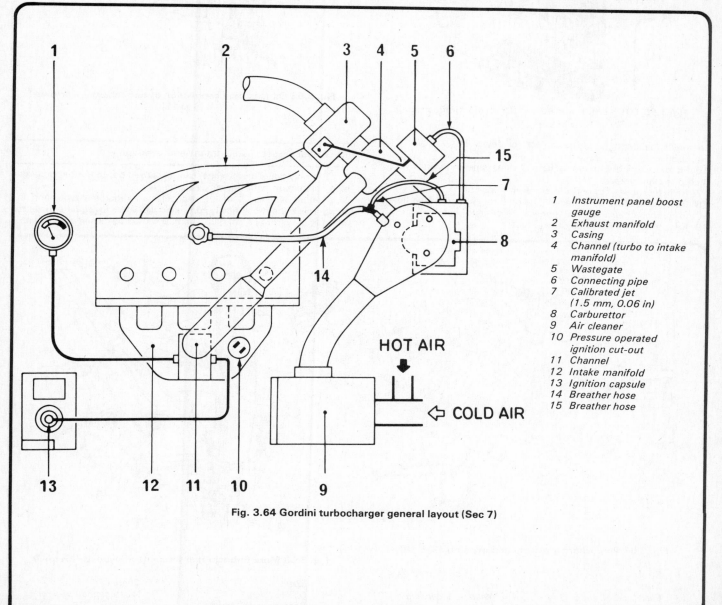

1   Instrument panel boost gauge
2   Exhaust manifold
3   Casing
4   Channel (turbo to intake manifold)
5   Wastegate
6   Connecting pipe
7   Calibrated jet (1.5 mm, 0.06 in)
8   Carburettor
9   Air cleaner
10 Pressure operated ignition cut-out
11 Channel
12 Intake manifold
13 Ignition capsule
14 Breather hose
15 Breather hose

HOT AIR

COLD AIR

Fig. 3.64 Gordini turbocharger general layout (Sec 7)

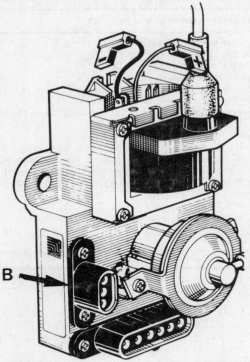

Fig. 3.65 TDC sensor plug socket (B) on electronic module (Sec 17)

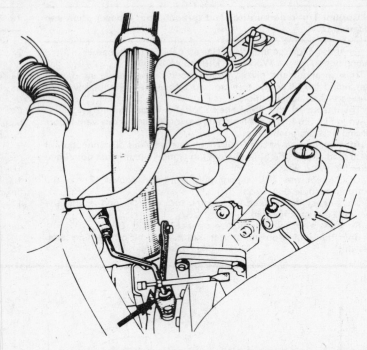

Fig. 3.66 Oil feed pipe connection at turbocharger – arrowed (Sec 17)

compress the length (L) of the coil springs below 24.0 mm (0.94 in) – Fig. 3.69.

16 Fit the channel (11) using new O-rings smeared with hydraulic fluid or rubber grease.

17 Refit the hose (15) and the oil return pipe (5).

18 Pour some of the specified engine oil through the oil feed hole (4) of the turbocharger and then connect the oil feed pipe.

19 Reconnect the warm air intake duct.

19 Turbocharger – adjustment and overhaul

1 The only adjustment which can be carried out to the turbocharger is in connection with the air cleaner.

2 The air cleaner is of the temperature regulated type, and incorporates a thermostatically controlled flap valve to regulate the entry and mix of warm and cold air. The flap should be closed against entry

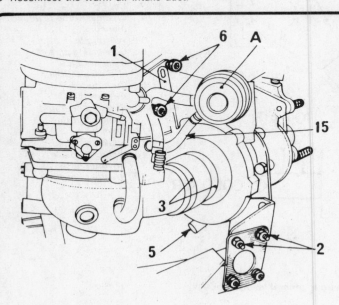

Fig. 3.67 Turbocharger disconnection points (Sec 18)

1	Strut	6	Socket-headed screws
2	Nuts	15	Hose
3	Clips	A	Wastegate capsule
5	Oil return pipe		

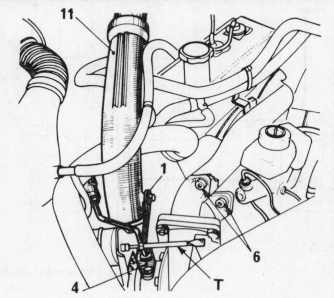

Fig. 3.68 More turbocharger disconnection points (Sec 18)

1	Strut	11	Channel
4	Oil feed pipe	T	Wastegate control rod
6	Socketheaded screws		

of cold air at temperatures below 26°C (79°F) and against entry of warm air at temperatures above 32°C (89.6°F).

3   The thermostat in the air cleaner may be tested by immersing it in water and heating to observe the correct opening temperatures. If necessary, turn the adjuster screw (R) to alter the calibration – Fig. 3.70.

4   The turbocharger itself should be treated as a sealed unit and any fault left to your dealer for rectification.

20   Throttle cable – removal and refitting

Type 840 engine

1   Disconnect the cable from the throttle lever at the carburettor.
2   Unscrew the nuts on the end fitting and slip the cable out of the support bracket.
3   Take off the tension spring.
4   Working inside the car at the accelerator pedal, remove the clevis pin from the clevis fork.
5   Extract the C-clip and withdraw the cable through the bulkhead grommet into the car.
6   Refit by reversing the removal operations, and lubricate pivots and swivels.
7   Adjust the nuts at the end fitting so that, with the accelerator pedal fully depressed, the throttle is fully open (lever against stop on carburettor) and yet, when the pedal is released, the lever can return to idle with just the minimum of slackness in the cable to allow for engine movement on its flexible mountings.
8   When correctly adjusted, the compensator coil spring should be compressed as shown in Fig. 3.72.

All other engine types

9   The removal and refitting operations are similar to those described earlier in this Section, but note that the cable is clamped at the carburettor swivel and a tension spring is used.
10   Always hold the swivel with a spanner while tightening the clamp nut to prevent the cable distorting.

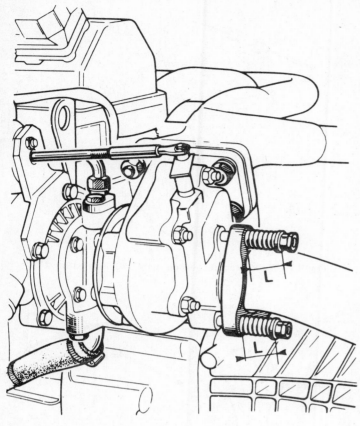

Fig. 3.69 Turbocharger downpipe flange nut tightening (Sec 18)

L = 24.0 mm (0.94 in)

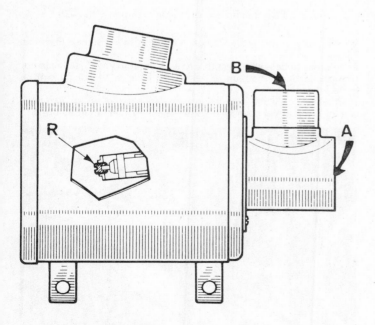

Fig. 3.70 Air cleaner thermostat (Sec 19)

R   *Adjuster screw*
A   *Cold air intake*
B   *Warm air intake*

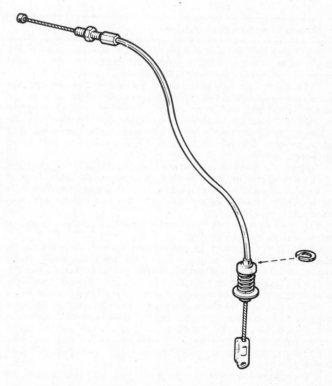

Fig. 3.71 Throttle cable – type 840 engine (Sec 20)

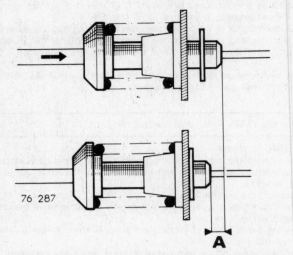

Fig. 3.72 Throttle cable compensator spring compressed (Sec 20)

A = 2.0 mm (0.079 in)

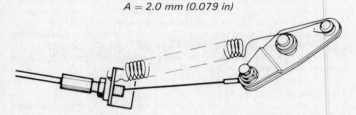

Fig. 3.74 Throttle cable clamp at carburettor (Sec 20)

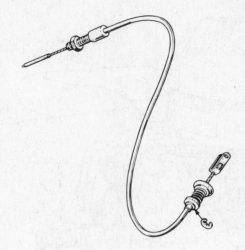

Fig. 3.73 Throttle cable – except type 840 engine (Sec 20)

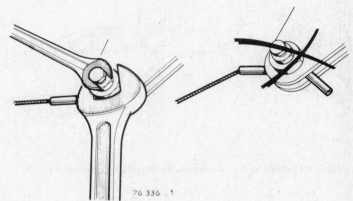

Fig. 3.75 Tightening throttle cable clamp nut (Sec 20)

21 Manifolds and exhaust system

1   The intake and exhaust manifolds are on opposite sides of the cylinder head on the type 840 engine (crossflow design). On all other engines the manifolds are mounted on the same side.
2   The majority of engines have the intake manifold heated from the engine cooling system so that before the manifold can be removed, the cooling system will have to be drained. Provided the system is cold and depressurised by removing the expansion chamber cap, the coolant hoses can be disconnected from the manifold and tied up as high as possible. This will reduce coolant loss, but after refitting bleed the cooling system.
3   Whenever a manifold is removed (photos), discard the gasket and before refitting ensure that the mating flanges are perfectly clean.
4   Various types of exhaust systems are fitted, according to vehicle model, but all cars for use outside North America include a silencer and an expansion box.
5   Some North American versions incorporate a catalytic converter and an anti-resonance pipe.
6   To check the condition of the exhaust system, raise the car as necessary, then start the engine and examine the entire length of the exhaust, while an assistant temporarily places a wad of cloth over the tailpipe. If a leak is evident, stop the engine, and use a good proprietary repair kit to seal it. Holts Flexiwrap and Holts Gun Gum exhaust repair systems can be used for effective repairs to exhaust pipes and silencer boxes, including ends and bends. Holts Flexiwrap is an MOT-approved permanent exhaust repair. If the leak is large, or if serious damage is evident, it may be better to renew the relevant exhaust section. Smear an exhaust sealant such as Holts Firegum on all exhaust joints before assembly.
7   It is recommended that even to renew one section of an exhaust system, the complete system is removed. This facilitates cutting away the necessary pipes and refitting the new sections under comfortable working conditions.
8   New exhaust pipe/front expansion boxes are supplied complete

with a captive connecting flange for fitting to stud type manifold flanges.
9   In order to be able to use this type of assembly with early clamp type connections, the captive flange will have to be cut off with a hacksaw or torch.
10 Always keep the exhaust system flexible mountings in good condition (photo), renewing any that have perished or are deformed.

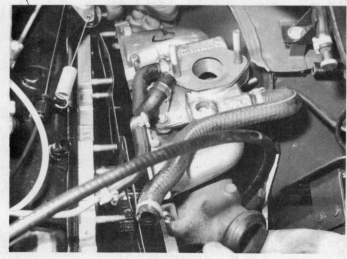

21.3a Removing intake manifold

21.3b Unscrewing exhaust manifold bolts

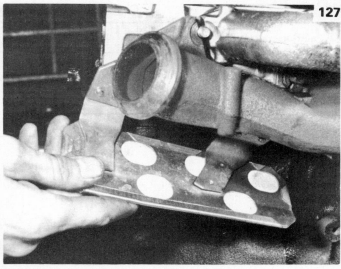

21.3c Heat shield clipped to exhaust manifold

21.3d Releasing exhaust downpipe clamp

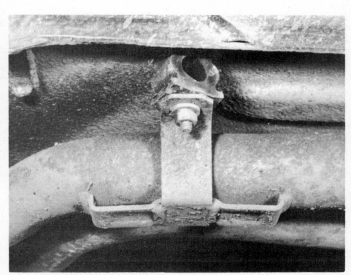

21.10 Exhaust pipe flexible mounting (typical)

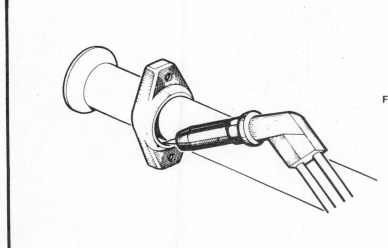

Fig. 3.76 Cutting off exhaust pipe captive flange (Sec 21)

22 Fault diagnosis – fuel system

Unsatisfactory engine performance and excessive fuel consumption are not necessarily the fault of the fuel system or carburettor. In fact they more commonly occur as a result of ignition and timing faults. Before acting on the following it is necessary to check the ignition system first. Even though a fault may lie in the fuel system it will be difficult to trace unless the ignition is correct. The faults below, therefore, assume that this has been attended to first (where appropriate).

Symptom	Reason(s)
Smell of petrol when engine is stopped	Leaking fuel lines or unions Leaking fuel tank
Smell of petrol when engine is idling	Leaking fuel line unions between pump and carburettor Overflow of fuel from float chamber due to wrong level setting, ineffective needle valve or punctured float
Excessive fuel consumption for reasons not covered by leaks or float chamber faults	Worn jets Over-rich jet setting Sticking mechanism
Difficult starting, uneven running, lack of power, cutting out	One or more jets blocked or restricted Float chamber fuel level too low or needle valve sticking Fuel pump not delivering sufficient fuel

23 Fault diagnosis – emission control system

Symptom	Reason(s)
PCV system Fumes escaping from engine	Clogged calibrated jet split or collapsed hoses Split or collapsed hoses
Fuel evaporative control system Fuel odour or rough running	Choked carbon canister Split or collapsed hoses Poor filler cap seal
Air injection system Fume emission from exhaust	Air pump drivebelt incorrectly tensioned Damaged air supply pipes Defective air pump Faulty valves Clogged pump air filter
EGR system Rough idling	Dirty or faulty EGR valve Split or collapsed hoses Leaking valve gasket
Catalytic converter Fume emission from exhaust	Impact damage to casing Clogged catalyst
Closed loop feedback system Erratic risk or weak mixture	Leaks in exhaust system Poor sensor seal Loose system wiring Faulty control unit

Chapter 4 Ignition system

For modifications, and information applicable to later models, see Supplement at end of manual

Contents

Specifications

Part 1 – Mechanical breaker system
System type .... Battery, coil, mechanical breaker distributor

Distributor
Type .... Ducellier or SEV Marchal
Rotor rotation .... Clockwise
Firing order .... 1–3–4–2 (No 1 cylinder nearest radiator)
Contact points gap .... 0.4 mm (0.016 in)
Dwell angle .... 54 to 60°
Dwell percentage .... 60 to 66%

Ignition timing
Vacuum pipe disconnected from distributor and plugged – engine at idle unless otherwise stated. Refer also to the tag on the distributor HT lead

European models	Engine	Initial setting
R1221:		
Up to 1982	800	5° to 7° BTDC
1982 and later	800	3° to 5° BTDC
R1222	689	4° to 6° BTDC
R1223:		
Static	840	1° BTDC to 1° ATDC
At 1050 rpm	840	5° to 7° BTDC
122B	C6J-7-26 (840)	13° to 15° BTDC
R1224	810	1° BTDC to 1° ATDC
R1225:		
Manual	810	5° to 7° BTDC
Automatic	810	9° to 11° BTDC
R1226	810	5° to 7° BTDC
R1227	688	4° to 6° BTDC
R1229:		
Manual:		
Up to 1982	C2J-P-7-13 (847)	9° to 11° BTDC
1982 and later	847	1° BTDC to 1° ATDC
Automatic	847	9° to 11° BTDC
R1247:		
GTL	688	4° to 6° BTDC
TL	688	3° to 5° BTDC
R1391:		
Up to 1982	800	5° to 7° BTDC
1982 and later	800	3° to 5° BTDC

R1392	689	4° to 6° BTDC
R1395:		
Manual	810	5° to 7° BTDC
Automatic	810	9° to 11° BTDC
R1397	688	4° to 6° BTDC
North American models		
R1226	810	5° to 7° BTDC
R1228	810	1° BTDC to 1° ATDC
R1229	847	1° to 5° BTDC
R1399	847	1° to 5° BTDC

Spark plugs
Type – European models
845 cc and 956 cc engine models	Champion L87YCC or RL87YC
1108 cc engine models	Champion L86CC or RL86C
1289 cc engine models:	
Engine code 810-19	Champion RN9YCC or RN9YC
Engine code 810-26	Champion L87YCC or RL87YC
1397 cc engine models (except Turbo):	
Engine code 840	Champion RS9YCC or RS9YC
Engine code 847	Champion RN9YCC or RN9YC
1397 cc engine models (Turbo)	Champion BN2

Type – North American models
1289 cc engine models (except California):	
1976 to 1977	Champion L92YC
1977 to 1978	Champion L87YC
1979	Champion L92YC
1289 cc engine models (California):	
1977 to 1979	Champion L92YC
1397 cc engine models:	
1980 to 1982	Champion N12YC
1983	Champion RN12YC

Electrode gap – all models
Champion Double Copper plugs (CC suffix)	0.8 mm (0.032 in)
All other Champion plugs	0.6 mm (0.024 in)

Part 2 – Electronic ignition
System type	Battery, coil, electronic control unit, impulse generator and distributor

Distributor
Trigger plate rotation	Clockwise
Firing order	1–3–4–2 (No 1 cylinder nearest radiator)
Trigger plate gap	0.3 to 0.6 mm (0.012 to 0.024 in)

Ignition timing
At engine speed at 750 rpm with the vacuum pipe disconnected from the distributor and plugged.
US	2° to 4° BTDC
Canada	1° BTDC to 1° ATDC
Other territories	9° to 11° BTDC

Spark plugs – see above

All models
Torque wrench settings
	Nm	lbf ft
Spark plugs	25	18

PART 1 – MECHANICAL BREAKER SYSTEM

1   General description

In order that the engine may run correctly it is necessary for an electrical spark to ignite the fuel/air mixture in the combustion chamber at exactly the right moment in relation to engine speed and load.

Basically the ignition system functions as follows. Low tension voltage from the battery is fed to the ignition coil, where it is converted into high tension voltage. The high tension voltage is powerful enough to jump the spark plug gap in the cylinder many times a second under high compression pressure, providing that the ignition system is in good working order and that all adjustments are correct.

The ignition system consists of two individual circuits known as the low tension (LT) circuit and high tension (HT) circuit.

The low tension circuit (sometimes known as the primary circuit) consists of the battery, lead to ignition switch, lead to the low tension or primary coil windings and the lead from the low tension coil windings to the contact breaker points and condenser in the distributor.

The high tension circuit (sometimes known as the secondary circuit) consists of the high tension or secondary coil winding, the heavily insulated ignition lead from the centre of the coil to the centre of the distributor cap, the rotor arm, the spark plug leads and the spark plugs.

The complete ignition system operation is as follows. Low tension voltage from the battery is changed within the ignition coil to high tension voltage by the opening and closing of the contact breaker points in the low tension circuit. High tension voltage is then fed, via a contact in the centre of the distributor cap, to the rotor arm of the distributor. The rotor arm revolves inside the distributor cap, and each time it comes in line with one of the four metal segments in the cap, the opening and closing of the contact breaker points causes the high tension voltage to build up, jump the gap from the rotor arm to the appropriate metal segment and so via the spark plug lead, to the spark plug where it finally jumps the gap between the two spark plug electrodes, one being earthed.

The ignition timing is advanced and retarded automatically to ensure the spark occurs at just the right instant for the particular load at the prevailing engine speed.

The ignition advance is controlled both mechanically and by a vacuum operated system. The mechanical governor mechanism consists of two weights which move out under centrifugal force from the central distributor shaft as the engine speed rises. As they move outwards they rotate the cam relative to the distributor shaft, and so advance the spark. The weights are held in position by two light springs, and it is the tension of these springs which is largely responsible for correct spark advancement.

The vacuum control comprises a diaphragm, one side of which is connected, via a small bore tube, to the carburettor, and the other side to the contact breaker plate. Depression in the induction manifold and carburettor, which varies with engine speed and throttle opening, causes the diaphragm to move so rotating the contact breaker plate and advancing or retarding the spark.

2   Contact breaker points (non-cassette type without external gap adjuster) – renewal and adjustment

1   To renew the contact points, prise down the spring clips and move the distributor cap to one side.
2   Pull the rotor from the distributor shaft (photo) and take off the plastic shield (if applicable).
3   If the contact points are being examined at the specified interval (see Routine Maintenance) pitting and metallic build-up will have taken place on the points faces. This is a normal condition. Do not attempt to dress the points on an oilstone or with abrasive material as even if the faces appear to be smooth and flat you will have upset their critical contours which will spoil an otherwise correct ignition setting.
4   Should examination of the points reveal excessive erosion, suspect a faulty condenser or poor earth connection somewhere in the ignition circuit.
5   Remove the spring clip from the contact breaker pivot post (photo) and take off the insulating washer.

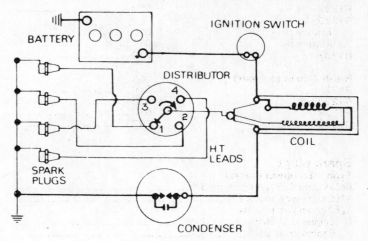

Fig. 4.1 Diagrammatic view of the ignition circuit (Sec 1)

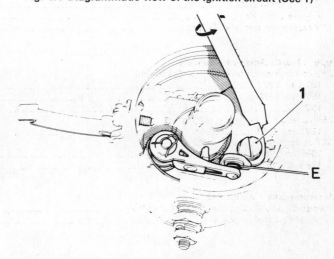

Fig. 4.2 Adjusting contact breaker points – SEV (Sec 2)

1   Anchor screw   E   Gap

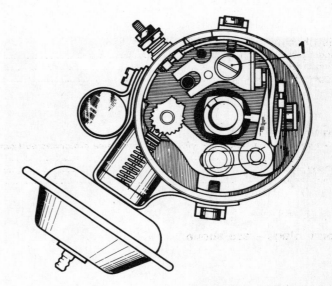

Fig. 4.3 Contact breaker – Ducellier (Sec 2)

1   Anchor screw

2.2 Removing rotor

2.5 Removing spring from pivot post

2.6 Disconnecting LT lead

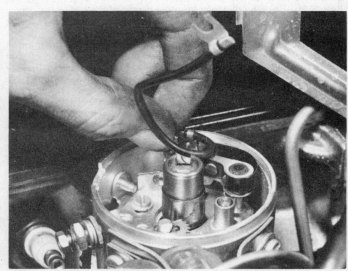

2.7 Removing contact breaker spring arm

2.11 Checking contact points gap

2.12 Tightening fixed contact securing screw

6   On some distributors, the contact breaker spring arm is retained by a nut on a terminal post to which the condenser lead is also anchored (photo). On other distributors, the end of the spring arm is held by its own tension against the condenser terminal tag in a plastic terminal block. To release the contact breaker spring arm, prise it forwards and upwards out of the terminal block.

7   Once released, slide the contact breaker up off its pivot post (photo).

8   Remove the fixed contact fixing screw and take out the contact.

9   Refit the new fixed contact, but leave the securing screw loose.

10 Fit the new spring arm contact, making sure that the insulating washer and spring clip are refitted.

11 The crankshaft must now be turned to bring one of the distributor shaft cam peaks squarely on the plastic cam follower of the spring contact arm. Now move the fixed contact until a feeler gauge of the specified size will provide a sliding fit between the faces of the contacts (photo). A cut-out is provided in the fixed arm for leverage purposes enabling the use of a small screwdriver. If the contact fixing screw is kept just nipped up, precise adjustment of the gap will be made that much easier.

12 Fully tighten the fixed contact securing screw on completion (photo).

13 Apply a smear (no more) of petroleum jelly to the shaft cam peaks and apply one drop of oil to the breaker arm pivot and two drops to the felt pad on top of the distributor shaft.

14 Fit the rotor, shield and cap.

15 Check the dwell angle and timing, as described in Sections 5 and 6.

3   Contact breaker points (non-cassette type with external gap adjuster) — renewal and adjustment

1   Later models are equipped with a distributor which has an externally accessible points gap adjuster.

2   To remove the contact breaker, first take off the distributor cap and the rotor. Remove the plastic shield (photo).

3   Unscrew the adjuster nut (A) and the two baseplate screws (B) — Fig. 4.4.

4   Take out the cover (photo) and prise out the retaining clip (C), noting that the hole is uppermost (Fig. 4.5 and photo).

5   Remove the adjuster rod and spring (photo).

6   Remove the securing screw (photo) and take out the fixed contact.

7   Remove the spring retaining clip from the top of the pivot post (photo), disconnect the LT wire (photo) and remove the spring contact arm.

8   Fit the new contact breaker points by reversing the removal operations. Lubricate and adjust the gap as described in paragraphs 11 to 15 of Section 2, noting that the fixed contact is moved to adjust the gap by turning the nut on the external adjuster (photo).

9   Note also that the setting of the serrated segment must not be altered, otherwise the advance characteristics will be upset.

3.2a Removing the distributor cap

3.2b Rotor

3.2c Plastic shield

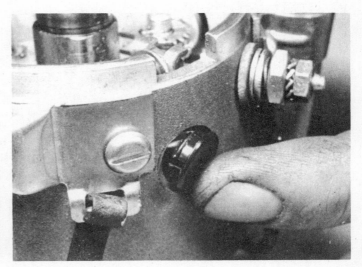

3.4a Plug over spring clip

3.4b Spring clip

3.5 Adjuster rod spring (arrowed)

3.6 Fixed contact screw

3.7a Pivot post retaining clip and insulating washer (arrowed)

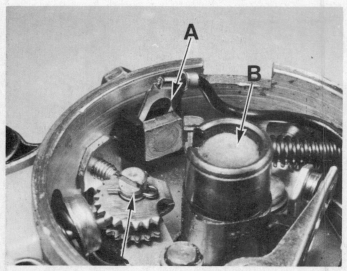

3.7b LT connecting wire (A), felt lubrication pad (B), advance curve toothed segment (C)

3.8 Adjusting contact breaker gap

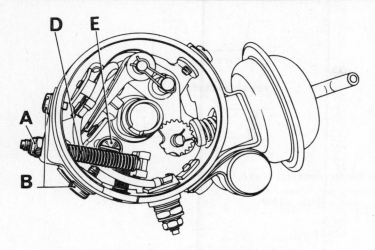

Fig. 4.4 Distributor with external gap adjuster (Sec 3)

A   Adjuster nut   D   Adjuster rod and springs
B   Baseplate screws   E   Fixed contact retaining screw

Fig. 4.5 Adjuster rod retaining clip (C) (Sec 3)

4   Contact breaker points (cassette type) – renewal and adjustment

1   On models equipped with a distributor having cassette type points, the gap (dwell angle) is preset during production and it should be only a matter of changing the cassette to provide the optimum ignition setting. In practice, it is recommended that after the cassette has been renewed, the dwell angle (Section 5) is checked. Any adjustment required can be carried out by inserting a 3.0 mm Allen key through the hole provided in the distributor body.
2   Although a cassette is expensive, when compared with a conventional contact breaker set, it does have the advantage that the spark jumps vertically within the distributor cap. This eliminates any possibility of voltage reduction at the spark plug as happens with a conventional distributor if worn bushes allow any play in the distributor shaft.
3   To renew the cassette, release the distributor cap and move it to one side.
4   Take off the rotor arm.

5   Pull the lead from the spade terminal at the base of the condenser.
6   Pull the cassette upwards, complete with condenser and plastic mounting block, and remove it from the distributor.
7   Pull the plug connector from the spade terminals located on top of the condenser.
8   Remove and discard the old cassette and engage the new one in the advance lugs of the condenser plastic mounting block.
9   Make sure that the cassette is the correct way up with its socket-headed adjuster screw opposite to the Allen key hole in the distributor body. The cassette is reversible to suit distributors which rotate either clockwise or anti-clockwise.
10   Hold the cassette/mounting block assembly over the distributor ready to fit, but if the rotor cut-out in the top of the distributor shaft is in alignment with the heel (follower) of the contact breaker, rotate the crankshaft slightly to alter the position of the cut-out, otherwise one of the cam peaks may damage the cassette contact heel as the assembly is fitted. Fit the connector plug.
11   Push the cassette/mounting block assembly fully down into the distributor recess. Make sure that the sides of the assembly engage in their grooves and check that the plastic connecting plug is fully seated with the condenser in a downward direction.
12   Fit the rotor and distributor cap.
13   Check the dwell angle and timing, as described in Sections 5 and 6.

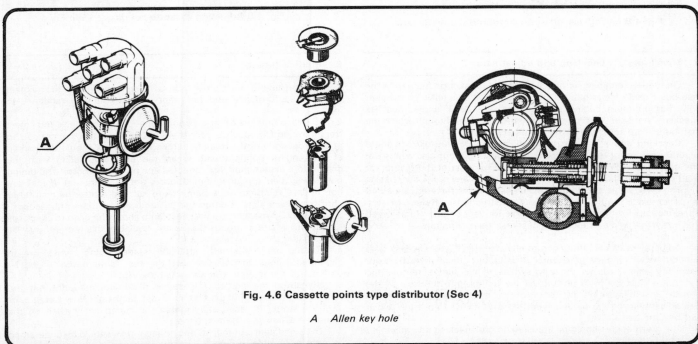

Fig. 4.6 Cassette points type distributor (Sec 4)

A   Allen key hole

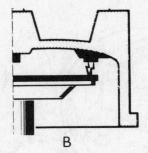
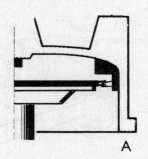

Fig. 4.7 Spark path within distributor (Sec 4)

　　A　*Conventional points distributor*
　　B　*Cassette points type distributor*

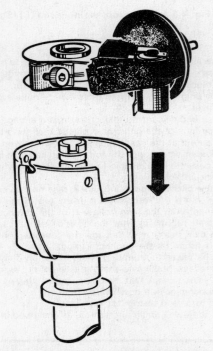

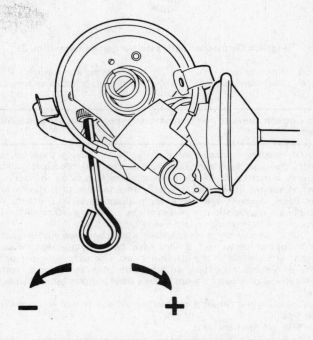

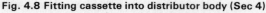

Fig. 4.8 Fitting cassette into distributor body (Sec 4)

Fig. 4.9 Adjusting cassette points gap (Sec 4)

5　Dwell angle – checking and adjustment

1　On modern engines, setting the contact breaker points gap in the distributor using feeler gauges can be regarded as a basic adjustment only. For optimum engine performance, the dwell angle must be checked. The dwell angle is the number of degrees through which the distributor cam turns while the points are closed.

2　Checking and adjusting the dwell angle not only gives a more accurate setting of the contact breaker points gap but also evens out any gap variations which could be caused by wear of the distributor shaft or its bushes or by a difference in height of any of the cam peaks.

3　The dwell angle should be checked using a dwell meter connected in accordance with the maker's instructions. Refer to the Specifications for the correct dwell angle for your engine. If it is found that the dwell angle is too large, increase the points gap, if it is too small, reduce the gap.

4　Adjustment of the points gap to alter the dwell angle is easy with distributors which have an external adjuster, but on units which do not have this facility, you will have to switch off the engine, remove the distributor cap and rotor and adjust the points with the heel of the breaker arm follower on the centre of one of the cam peaks. Where fine adjustment has to be achieved this is a trial and error job which can be time consuming.

5　The dwell angle should be adjusted before checking and adjusting the ignition timing.

6　Ignition timing

1　Ignition timing must always be as specified in order to maintain optimum performance and fuel economy without any tendency to 'pink'.

2　It is recommended that a stroboscope is used to check and adjust the timing on all models except the R1223. A stroboscope connected in accordance with the manufacturer's instructions should be pointed at the engine timing marks when the engine is idling with the distributor vacuum pipe disconnected and plugged (photo). The timing marks will then appear to be stationary and in alignment. If they are not, release the distributor clamp plate nut and rotate the distributor until the marks align. Tighten the nut and remove the stroboscope.

3　On R1223 models, a simple test lamp should be used to check the timing and where a stroboscope is not available, this method may be used for the other models as well.

4　Rotate the crankshaft until the static timing marks are in alignment (firing stroke). Connect the test lamp between the (-) terminal of the ignition coil and a good earth.

5　Switch on the ignition, release the distributor mounting nut and turn the distributor until the test lamp just comes on. Now turn it back until the lamp just goes out. Tighten the clamp nut, switch off the ignition and remove the test lamp.

6　The significance of the various timing marks should be understood in order to be able to time the ignition successfully.

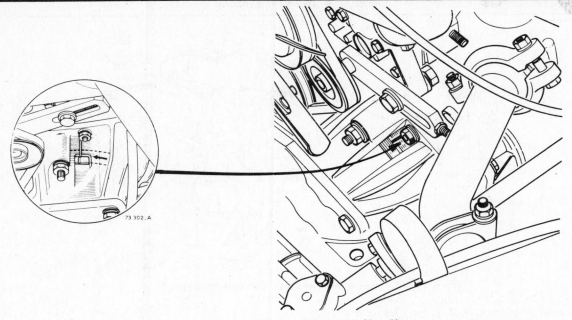

Fig. 4.10 Single timing mark (Sec 6)

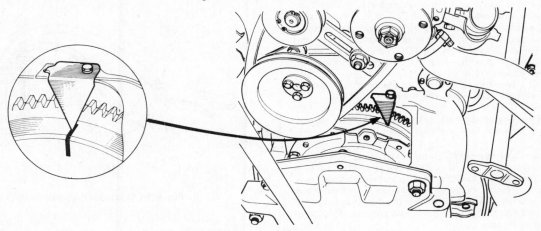

Fig. 4.11 Alternative type of single timing mark (Sec 6)

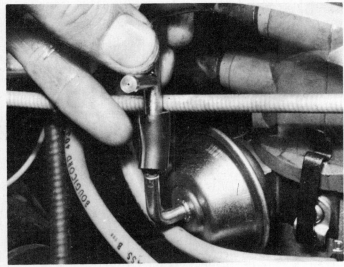

6.2 Disconnecting distributor vacuum pipe

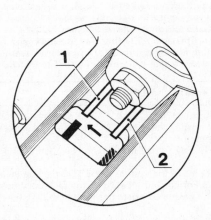

Fig. 4.12 Dual timing marks (Sec 6)

1   TDC   2   4° BTDC

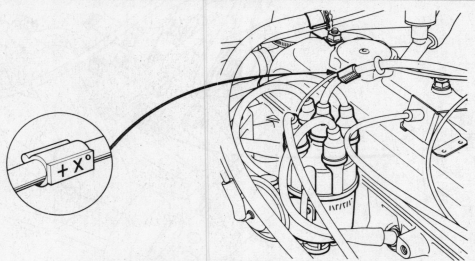

Fig. 4.13 Clip showing required static ignition timing (Sec 6)

7   Observe the cut-out in the flywheel housing. If only one pointer is evident with one mark on the flywheel then No 1 piston is at TDC when the marks are in alignment. If a strobe dephaser is not available, it is recommended that a static advance timing mark is made on the periphery of the flywheel **in advance** of the TDC mark. Do this after reference to the Specifications, noting the particular advance setting, in degrees, for your car. Consider 2.0 mm is equivalent to 1° and measure the flywheel in advance from the TDC mark. Make a punch mark in the flywheel and fill it with a drop of quick drying white paint. This will be your permanent static advance mark.
8   On models having two timing pointers on the flywheel housing, then pointer (1), indicates TDC while (2) indicates 4° BTDC – Fig. 4.12.
9   On the flywheel housing of some models a bold TDC mark may be found, along with a series of less prominent marks, each of which corresponds to 1°.
10 It must be emphasised that when using a test lamp to time the ignition then No 1 piston must be in its firing position. Check this in one of two ways, either remove No 1 spark plug and with a finger over the hole feel the compression being generated as the crankshaft is rotated (by hand or with the starter), or remove the distributor cap and check that the contact end of the rotor is aligned with the position of No 1 contact in the distributor cap.
11 On later models, the ignition timing (static advance) is marked on a clip attached to the centre HT lead of the distributor cap for each particular engine.
12 On 122B Gordini Turbo models, an anti-pinking device is fitted. The throttle butterfly limit switch activates a timer relay to give 4° ignition advance for approximately one second. A vacuum sensitive switch cuts off the advance where vacuum below the air cleaner reaches between 650 and 750 mbar. The positive feed to the timer relay in the system is routed through the 'choke on' warning lamp so that the anti-pinking device will only operate if the choke is fully off.

7   Diagnostic socket and TDC pick-up

1   Commencing in 1978, R1222, R1223 and R1225 models were fitted with a diagnostic socket and TDC pick-up. The socket is located on the coolant pump.
2   This device is only of use to garages equipped with a diagnostic bay.
3   An essential part of the system is the TDC pick-up located on the flywheel housing. For efficient operation, the pick-up should be set in its clamp so that a clearance exists between it and the flywheel of 1.0 mm (0.04 in).
4   With the right test equipment connected to the socket, the following checks can be made:
  Condition of contact breaker points
  Dwell angle
  Ignition timing
  Engine speed
  Centrifugal and vacuum advance curves

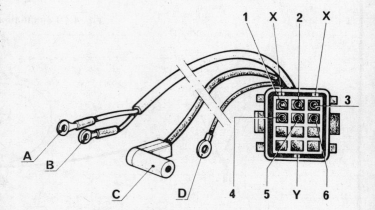

Fig. 4.14 Diagnostic socket (Sec 7)

A   To ignition coil (–) terminal (black/red)
B   To ignition coil (+) terminal (grey/blue)
C   To TDC pick-up
D   Earth (yellow)
X   One-way locator
Y   One-way locator

1   TDC pick-up (red)
2   Distributor earth (yellow)
3   Contact breaker (black)
4   TDC pick-up (white)
5   TDC pick-up screening
6   Ignition coil (+) (grey)

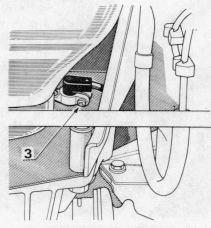

Fig. 4.15 TDC pick-up (Sec 7)

3   Clamp screw

9.5 Removing distributor

11.1 Ignition coil. Note cooling system bleed screw (arrowed)

8 Condenser – testing

1   A faulty condenser can cause difficult starting, severely pitted contact breaker points and misfiring.
2   The simplest test for a condenser is to substitute a new one, however some indication that the original component is faulty may be obtained if the ignition is switched on and the points separated with an insulated tool.
3   If the result is a vivid blue flash instead of the normal small spark, then the condenser must be renewed.

9 Distributor – removal and refitting

1   In order to make refitting the distributor easier, it is recommended that the engine is set so that No 1 piston is at TDC (refer to Section 6, paragraph 9). Mark the relative position of the contact end of the rotor to the rim of the distributor body and the distributor mounting flange to the cylinder block.
2   Disconnect the leads from the spark plugs and coil.
3   Disconnect the LT lead from the terminal on the side of the distributor body (non-cassette type) or from the spade terminal (cassette type).
4   Disconnect the vacuum pipe from the distributor.
5   Remove the distributor clamp plate nut and withdraw the distributor straight out of the cylinder block (photo), retain the rubber sealing ring.
6   Refitting is a reversal of removal. Note that the distributor driveshaft dog is offset so provided this is aligned to mesh with the slot in the end of the oil pump driveshaft the distributor can be pushed directly into the cylinder block.
7   Align the rotor and mounting flange marks made before removal and tighten the clamp plate nut.
8   Reconnect the HT and LT leads and the vacuum pipe.
9   Check the ignition timing (refer to Section 6).

10 Distributor – overhaul

1   Renewal of the contact breaker assembly, condenser, rotor and distributor cap should be regarded as the limit of overhaul. Few other spares are available except the vacuum unit and fitting a new one of these will not serve much purpose unless it is adjusted to operate on the specified advance curve. This is a job for your dealer or automotive electrician.
2   When the distributor has seen extended service and the shaft bushes and centrifugal advance mechanism become worn, obtain a new unit.

11 Ignition coil

1   The maintenance of the coil is minimal, and is limited to periodically wiping its surface clean and dry and checking that the leads are secure (photo). The high voltages generated by the coil can easily leak to earth over its surface and prevent the spark plugs from receiving electrical pulses.
2   Keep the coil mounting bracket tightly fixed.

12 Spark plugs and HT leads

1   The correct functioning of the spark plugs is vital for the correct running and efficiency of the engine. It is essential that the plugs fitted are appropriate for the engine (the correct type is specified at the beginning of this Chapter). If this type is used, and the engine is in good condition, the spark plugs should not need attention between scheduled service renewal intervals. Spark plug cleaning is rarely necessary, and should not be attempted unless specialised equipment is available, as damage can easily be caused to the firing ends.
2   At the intervals specified in 'Routine maintenance' at the beginning of this manual, the plugs should be removed and renewed.
3   To remove the plugs, first open the bonnet and pull the HT leads from them. Grip the rubber end fitting, not the lead, otherwise the lead connection may be fractured.
4   Brush out any accumulated dirt or grit from the spark plug recess in the cylinder head as it may drop into the combustion chamber when the plug is removed.
5   Unscrew the spark plugs with a deep socket or a box spanner. Do not allow the tool to tilt, otherwise the ceramic insulator may be cracked or broken.
6   Examination of the spark plugs will give a good indication of the condition of the engine.
7   If the insulator nose of the spark plug is clean and white, with no deposits, this is indicative of a weak mixture or too hot a plug (a hot plug transfers heat away from the electrode slowly, a cold plug transfers heat away quickly).
8   The plugs fitted as standard are specified at the beginning of this Chapter. If the top and insulator nose are covered with hard black-looking deposits, then this is indicative that the mixture is too rich. Should the plug be black and oily, then it is likely that the engine is fairly worn, as well as the mixture being too rich.
9   If the insulator nose is covered with light tan to greyish brown deposits, then the mixture is correct and it is likely that the engine is in good condition.
10 The spark plug gap is of considerable importance, as, if it is too large or too small, the size of the spark and its efficiency will be seriously impaired. For the best results the spark plug gap should be

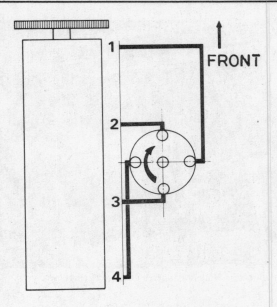

Fig. 4.16 HT lead connections (Sec 12)

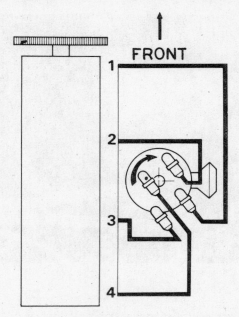

Fig. 4.17 Alternative connections (Sec 12)

8   Extract the two fixing screws from the rear face of the assembly and pull the switch from the lock.
9   Reassembly and refitting are reversals of removal and dismantling.

set in accordance with the Specifications at the beginning of this Chapter.
11 To set it, measure the gap with a feeler gauge, and then bend open, or close, the outer plug electrode until the correct gap is achieved. The centre electrode should never be bent as this may crack the insulation and cause plug failure if nothing worse.
12 Special spark plug electrode gap adjusting tools are available from most motor accessory stores.
13 Note that, as the cylinder head is of aluminium alloy, it is recommended that a little anti-seize compound (such as Copaslip) is applied to the plug threads before they are fitted.
14 Screw each plug in by hand. This will make sure that there is no chance of cross threading. On R1223 and 122B engines the spark plugs are of taper seat design and have no sealing washers. It is important that all plugs are tightened into clean, grit-free seats to the specified torque. If a torque wrench is not available, just nip up each plug. It is better to undertighten than over do it and strip the threads from the light alloy cylinder head.
15 When reconnecting the spark plug leads, make sure that they are refitted in their correct order. No 1 cylinder being nearest the radiator (see Figs. 4.16 and 4.17).
16 The plug leads require no routine attention other than being kept clean and wiped over regularly. At intervals, however, pull each lead off the plug in turn and remove it from the distributor. Water can seep down into the joints giving rise to a white corrosive deposit which must be carefully removed from the end of each cable.

13 Ignition/steering lock switch – removal and refitting

1   Disconnect the battery earth lead.
2   Take off the cover panel from under the switch.
3   Disconnect the wiring harness plug.
4   Turn the key to the 'garage' (G) position and then withdrawn the key (photo).
5   Remove the securing screw (1) from the top surface of the lock – Fig. 4.18.
6   Using a thin rod, depress the plunger (2) and push the lock assembly from behind to remove it.
7   To separate the lock from the ignition switch insert the key and turn it to the S or ST position. Remove the key.

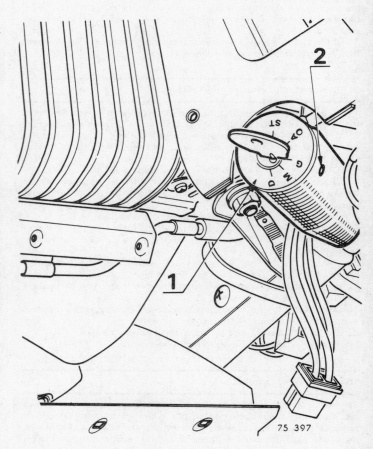

Fig. 4.18 Ignition switch/steering lock (Sec 13)

1   Fixing screw
2   Locking plunger

13.4 Ignition key positions (typical)

14 Fault diagnosis – mechanical breaker system

Symptom	Reason(s)
Engine fails to start	Loose battery connections Discharged battery Oil on contact breaker points Disconnected ignition leads Faulty condenser Damp HT leads or distributor cap
Engine starts and runs but misfires	Faulty spark plug Cracked distributor cap Cracked rotor arm Worn advance mechanism Incorrect spark plug gap Incorrect points gap Faulty condenser Faulty coil Incorrect timing Poor earth connections
Engine overheats, lacks power	Seized centrifugal weights Perforated or loose distributor vacuum pipe Incorrect ignition timing
Engine 'pinks'	Timing too advanced Advance mechanism stuck in advance position Broken counterweight spring Too low fuel octane rating

PART 2 – ELECTRONIC IGNITION SYSTEM

15 Description and precautions

1 This type of ignition system is fitted to certain later models (122B and R1229 – 1982 and later).

2 The contact breaker in the conventional distributor is replaced by an impulse generator.

3 The trigger plate in the distributor rotates and as one arm of the plate approaches the impulse sender coil the control voltage increases.

4 When the arm of the trigger plate reaches the point where it is directly aligned with the impulse sender coil the control voltage, having reached maximum positive charge, then changes to negative charge.

5 As the arm of the trigger plate moves away from the impulse sender coil, the voltage drops to zero.

6 The control voltage generated in this manner is relayed to the control unit which reacts by regulating the form of current received and initiating a control current. The control unit then creates a break in this current which results in a high voltage at the ignition coil.

7 The high voltage is distributed to the spark plugs by the rotor, as in mechanical breaker systems.

8 A relay controlled by an oil temperature switch activates a secondary impulse sender if the engine oil temperature is below 15°C (59°F). The secondary impulse sender advances the ignition by 3° (6° at the flywheel).

9 Components of the electronic ignition system include a compact control unit and coil assembly, and an inductive type distributor. The components cannot be repaired, and if diagnosed as faulty they must be renewed as units.

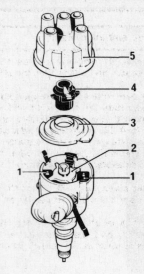

Fig. 4.19 Main components of the breakerless type distributor
(Sec 15)

1   Impulse senders
2   Trigger plate
3   Seal
4   Rotor
5   Distributor cap

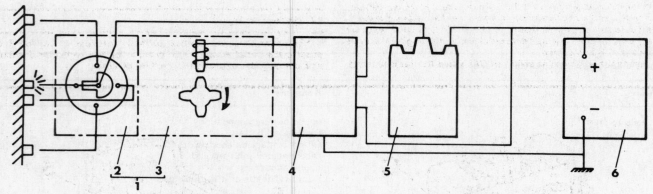

Fig. 4.20 Diagrammatic layout of breakerless ignition system (Sec 15)

1   Distributor   3   Impulse sender   5   Coil
2   Distributor cap   4   Control unit   6   Battery

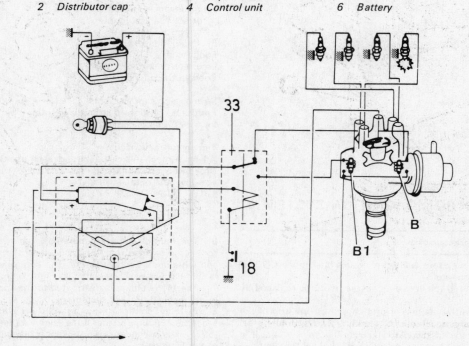

Fig. 4.21 Breakerless ignition circuit (Sec 15)

B   Main impulse sender   B1 Secondary impulse sender   18 Oil temperature switch   33 Relay

10 Do not pull a lead from a spark plug as a means of stopping the engine as the distributor trigger plate may be damaged.

11 To prevent personal injury and damage to the ignition system, the following precautions must be observed when working on the ignition system.

12 Do not attempt to disconnect any plug lead or touch any of the high tension cables when the engine is running, or being turned by the starter motor.

13 Ensure that the ignition is turned *OFF* before disconnecting any of the ignition wiring.

14 Ensure that the ignition is switched *OFF* before connecting or disconnecting any ignition testing equipment such as a timing light.

15 Do not connect a suppression condenser or test lamp to the coil negative terminal.

16 Do not connect any test appliance or stroboscopic lamp requiring a 12 volt supply to the coil positive terminal.

17 If the HT cable is disconnected from the distributor, the cable must immediately be connected to earth and remain earthed if the engine is to be rotated by the starter motor, for example if a compression test is to be done.

18 The ignition coil of an electronic system must never be replaced by the ignition coil from a contact breaker type ignition system.

19 If an electric arc welder is to be used on any part of the vehicle, the car battery must be disconnected while welding is being done.

20 If a stationary engine is heated to above 80°C (176°F) such as may happen after paint drying, or steam cleaning, the engine must not be started until it has cooled.

21 Ensure that the ignition is switched *OFF* when the car is washed.

16 Distributor – maintenance and adjustment

1 This type of distributor is virtually maintenance-free. Occasionally wipe the cap free of oil and grease, and check that the HT leads are secure in their sockets.

2 If the impulse senders are ever renewed the trigger plate gap will have to be adjusted. To do this, rotate the crankshaft until one arm of the trigger plate is in alignment with one of the impulse sender studs.

3 Release screws 5 and 6 (Fig. 4.23) and using a feeler gauge of the specified size adjust the trigger plate gap so that the gauge is a sliding fit. Retighten the screws and check the gap at the other trigger arm positions. If the gaps are not consistent the distributor is worn and must be renewed.

4 Having adjusted the trigger plate gap, now adjust the secondary impulse sender timing offset from the main sender by an angle of 3 degrees (Fig. 4.25).

5 Do this by aligning one arm of the trigger plate with a stud, releasing the screws (6) and (7) and then moving the secondary impulse sender so that the centre point of the stud (9) is offset by 3°. Tighten the screws.

17 Ignition timing

The operations are identical to those described in Section 6, but observe the initial advance specification for this particular distributor and use only the stroboscopic method of timing.

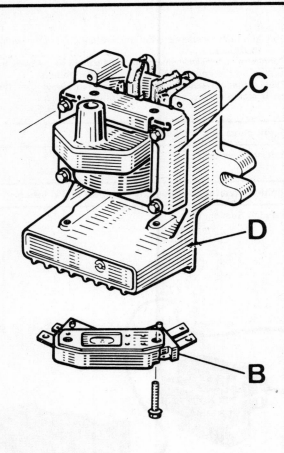

Fig. 4.22 Electronic control unit (B), support (D) and coil (C) (Sec 15)

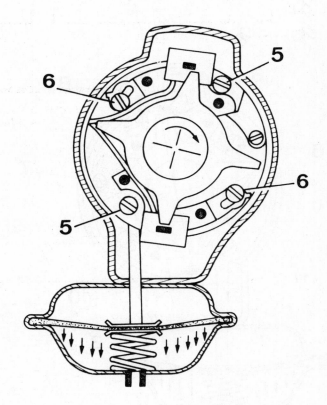

Fig. 4.23 Trigger plate arm in alignment with impulse sender coil stud (Sec 16)

5 *Securing screw*   6 *Securing screw*

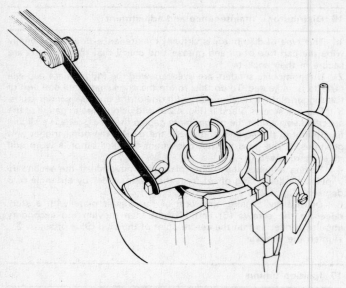

Fig. 4.24 Checking trigger plate gap (Sec 16)

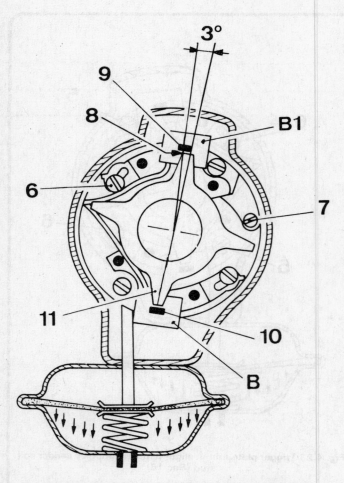

Fig. 4.25 Secondary impulse sender offset diagram (Sec 16)

B	Main impulse sender	8	Corner of trigger plate arm
B1	Secondary impulse sender	9	Coil stud
6	Screw	10	Coil stud
7	Screw	11	Trigger plate arm

18 Distributor – removal and refitting

Refer to Section 9.

19 Diagnostic socket

Refer to Section 7.

20 System components – testing

1   The individual components of the transistorized ignition system may be checked if, by reference to the Fault Diagnosis Section, a component is suspected of being faulty.

Impulse sender
2   Connect an ohmmeter between one of the terminals of the impulse sender and earth. If the needle moves, the coil is faulty and must be renewed.

Ignition coil and control unit
3   Turn the ignition key to ON.
4   Connect a voltmeter between the two terminals of the ignition coil.
5   Pass a magnet quickly to and fro by the ignition coil. If the needle moves, renew the coil. If the needle does not move the electric control unit must be at fault.

Distributor
6   Should a fault be suspected in the distributor, pull the wiring plug from the distributor.
7   Connect a spare TDC sensor (diagnostic plug) to the two terminals of the plug on the control unit. Switch on the ignition.
8   Pass a magnet quickly towards and then away from the TDC sensor. If arcing occurs, renew the distributor.

21 Spark plugs and HT leads

Refer to Section 12.

22 Ignition/steering lock switch – removal and refitting

Refer to Section 13.

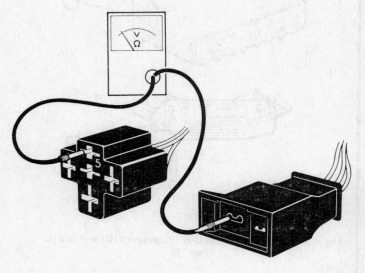

Fig. 4.26 Impulse sender test circuit (Sec 20)

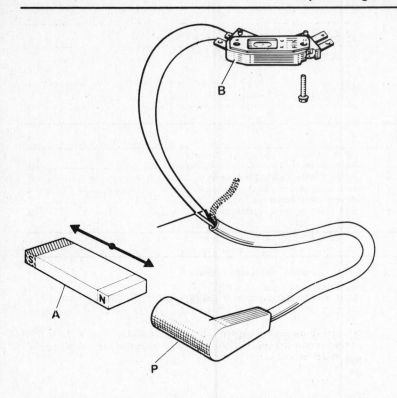

Fig. 4.27 Distributor test circuit (Sec 20)

A *Magnet*
B *Electronic control unit*
P *TDC sensor*

23 Fault diagnosis – electronic ignition system

Symptom	Reason(s)
Engine will not start from cold	Loose wire or connection Faulty impulse sender Faulty coil Faulty electric control unit
Engine starts when cold but stalls after engine oil reaches 15°C (59°F)	Faulty impulse sender

Chapter 5 Clutch

Contents

Specifications

Type .... Single dry plate with cable operation

Driven plate diameter .... 160.0, 170.0, 180.0 or 190.0 mm (6.3, 6.7, 7.1 or 7.5 in)

Pedal free movement
Measured at release lever .... 3.0 to 4.0 mm (0.12 to 0.16 in)

Torque wrench settings	Nm	lbf ft
Flywheel housing to engine	41	30
Flywheel housing to gearbox:		
8.0 mm bolts	25	18
10.0 mm bolts	35	26
Clutch cover to flywheel	20	15

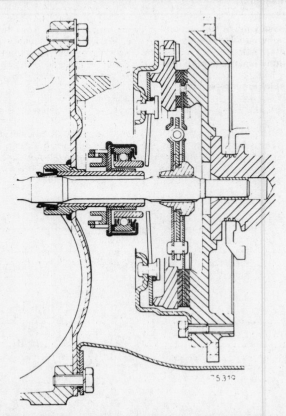

Fig. 5.1 Sectional view of clutch with ball pivot type release arm
(Sec 1)

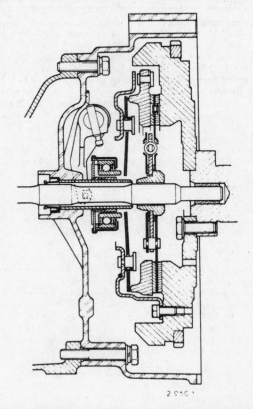

Fig. 5.2 Sectional view of clutch with cross-shaft type release arm
(Sec 1)

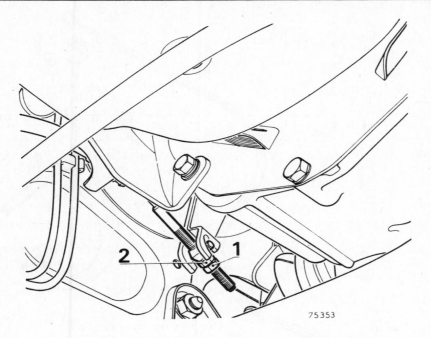

75353

Fig. 5.3 Clutch cable adjuster at release arm (Sec 2)

1   Locknut   2   Adjuster nut

1   General description

A single dry plate clutch is used on all models with manual transmission. The clutch components may differ slightly between models and it is important that when ordering spares the exact vehicle identification details are given.

Clutch operation is by means of a foot pedal and cable. The cable arrangement differs according to the method of operation of the gearchange lever – floor or facia mounting.

Depressing the clutch pedal causes the cable to move the release arm which in turn actuates the release bearing. The release bearing bears upon the fingers of the diaphragm type spring of the clutch pressure plate.

The diaphragm spring then releases or engages the driven plate (friction disc) which slides on the splines of the gearbox primary shaft.

The clutch driven plate is free to spin between the pressure plate and the flywheel when released and is held tightly between these components when engaged so connecting the drive from the engine to the transmission.

As the friction material on the driven plate wears, the clearance between the release bearing and the diaphragm spring decreases. This clearance must be maintained at the specified dimension by regular adjustment (see Section 2).

2   Clutch – adjustment

1   At the specified intervals (see Routine Maintenance) check the free movement at the end of the release lever. Do this by pressing the release arm from the fully released position to the point where it is just making the release bearing contact the diaphragm spring fingers.
2   If the free movement is not within the specified limits release the locknut on the threaded rod at the end of the clutch cable at the release lever and turn the adjuster nut. Retighten the locknut.
3   On early LHD models with a facia mounted gearchange lever, adjustment is carried out by turning the nuts on the short rod attached to the top of the swivel arm at the transmission.
4   When the nuts are at the end of the rod and no further adjustment is possible, the clutch driven plate will have to be renewed (see Section 5).

3   Clutch cable – renewal

1   Working at the clutch release lever, unscrew the nuts from the threaded end of the cable and disconnect the cable from the lever.
2   On early LHD vehicles with a facia mounted gearchange lever, the end of the cable is detached by disconnecting the clevis fork.
3   Free the cable grommet at the engine compartment rear bulkhead.
4   Working inside the car, remove the parcel shelf from above the pedals (see Chapter 12).
5   Disconnect the clutch pedal return spring.
6   Prise off the clip from the end of the pedal cross-shaft and slide the pedal from the shaft.
7   Extract the clevis pin from the pedal arm and disconnect the cable.
8   Ease the outer cable out of the pedal support bracket.
9   Refit the new cable by reversing the removal operations. Apply grease to the pedal bushes and cross-shaft, and adjust the clearance on completion as described in the preceding Section.

4   Clutch pedal – removal and refitting

This is described in the preceding Section during renewal of the clutch cable.

5   Clutch – removal

1   Access to the clutch is obtained by removing the gearbox, as described in Chapter 6.
2   Mark the relationship of the cover to the flywheel.
3   Unscrew the cover bolts half a turn at a time in diagonally opposite sequence until the pressure of the diaphragm spring is released. Withdraw all the bolts and lift the clutch mechanism from the flywheel.
4   Take care that the driven plate does not drop to the floor during removal.

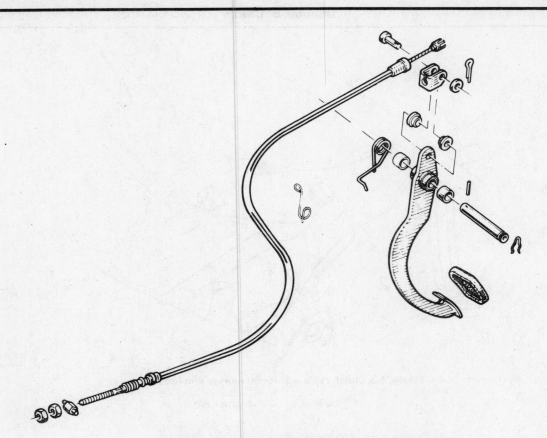

Fig. 5.4 Typical RHD clutch pedal and cable (Sec 3)

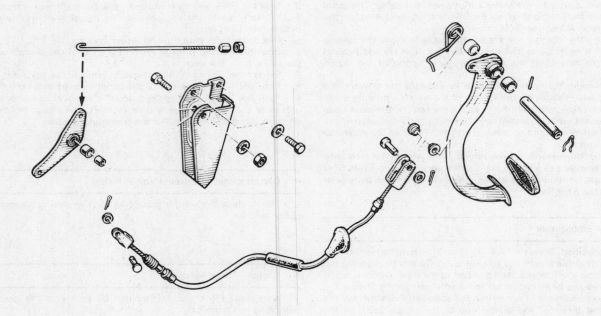

Fig. 5.5 Early LHD clutch pedal and cable (Sec 3)

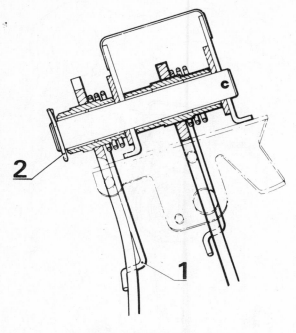

Fig. 5.6 Pedal cross-shaft (Sec 3)

1   Pedal return spring   2   Clip

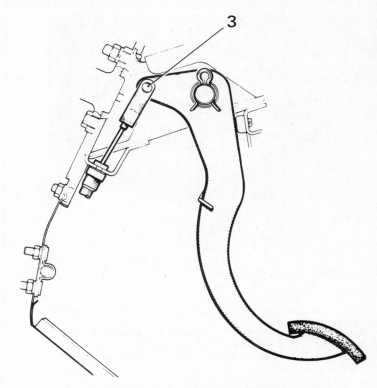

Fig. 5.7 Clutch cable attachment to pedal arm (Sec 3)

3   Clevis pin

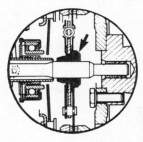

Fig. 5.8 Driven plate has larger diameter boss (arrowed) towards flywheel (Sec 7)

7.2 Assembling the clutch

6   Clutch – inspection and renovation

1   With the clutch removed, examine the faces of the driven plate. A well worn clutch will have the rivet heads which hold the friction material flush with the linings. If the plate is in this condition a new driven plate will be required. Do not attempt to re-line the plate yourself, it seldom proves satisfactory.

2   Examine the ends of the diaphragm spring fingers. If a step has been worn in them by the release bearing then the complete pressure plate cover must be renewed.

3   Inspect the surfaces of the flywheel and pressure plate machined faces. If they are scored or show evidence of tiny cracks, renew the pressure plate cover. The flywheel may be renovated subject to certain precautions, refer to Chapter 1.

4   The release bearing should be renewed automatically at the time of clutch overhaul (see Section 8).

5   If oil staining was evident when the clutch components were removed then this is probably due to failure of the input shaft oil seal. This must be renewed before refitting the clutch, refer to Section 9.

7   Clutch – refitting

1   Thoroughly clean the machined faces of the flywheel and pressure plate, freeing them from any protective coating.

2   Offer the driven plate to the flywheel so that the larger diameter of the driven plate boss is towards the flywheel (photo).

3   Locate the pressure plate cover. If the original cover is being refitted, align the marks made at dismantling. Screw in the bolts evenly, but only finger tight, so that the driven plate is just held against the flywheel.

4   The driven plate must now be centralised. To do this use one of the clutch alignment tools available from most motor accessory stores or an old input shaft if one is available. Alternatively, a round bar may be used having steps on it so that its end will engage in the flywheel pilot bush and also provide a sliding fit in the splined centre hole in the driven plate hub. An ordinary round bar may be formed to suit the purpose by winding adhesive tape around it.

5   Insert the tool through the clutch cover and driven plate hub engaging the end of the tool in the pilot bush. This action will force the driven plate to move on the flywheel face and centralise it (photo).

7.5 Centralising the clutch driven plate

6   Tighten the cover bolts to the specified torque and withdraw the centralising tool.
7   Before refitting the gearbox, apply a smear of molybdenum disulphide grease to the splines of the input shaft.
8   On completion, adjust the clutch free movement as previously described in this Chapter.

8   Clutch release bearing – renewal

1   Renewal of the release bearing is normally carried out at the time of clutch renewal. If the bearing becomes noisy when the clutch pedal is depressed, this may be the result of 'riding' the pedal with the foot when driving along.

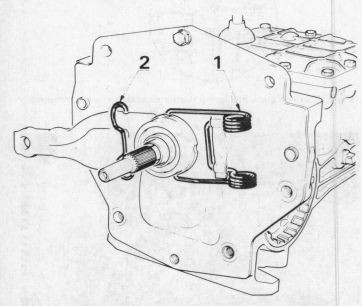

Fig. 5.9 Release bearing with ball pivot type release lever (Sec 8)

1 and 2 Springs

Release bearing with ball pivot release lever

2   Remove the gearbox as described in Chapter 6.
3   Disengage the ends of the spring (1) from the bearing holder and release arm (Fig. 5.9).
4   Withdraw the release bearing assembly.

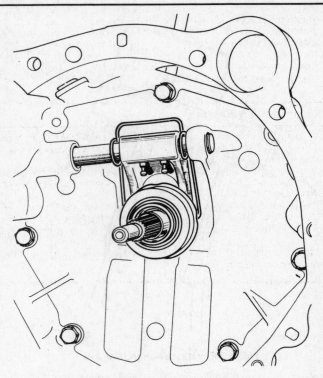

Fig. 5.10 Release bearing with cross-shaft pivot release lever (Sec 8)

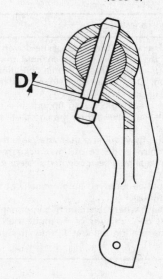

Fig. 5.11 Release fork pin projection on cross-shaft (Sec 8)

D = 1.0 mm (0.039 in)

5   Unhook the spring (2) and remove the release fork from the ball stud pivot.
6   Refitting is a reversal of removal, but apply a little molybdenum disulphide grease to the ball of the pivot stud before fitting the release lever.

Release bearing with cross-shaft pivot release lever

7   Remove the gearbox, as described in Chapter 6.
8   Unhook the ends of the springs from the release bearing holder and withdraw the bearing assembly.
9   If the release lever and cross-shaft must be removed the fork pins will have to be extracted. A special tool (EMB 384) is available for this purpose, although it is possible to remove them by using a lever which has a fork formed at one end.

10 Withdraw the fork/lever assembly with the spring.

11 Refitting is a reversal of removal, but when fitting the pins the shoulder of the pin should remain proud by the specified amount (Fig. 5.11).

12 The cross-shaft bushes should be smeared with molybdenum disulphide grease before entering the cross-shaft.

9 Input shaft oil seal – renewal

1 If, at the time of clutch overhaul, there is evidence of oil leakage from the input shaft oil seal, then the oil seal must be renewed. Unbolt the flywheel housing.

2 The oil seal should be driven out by partially removing the guide tube. If the guide tube is renewed, make sure that the hole in the tube is in line with the web (4) – Fig. 5.12.

3 Drive in the guide tube until it contacts the housing flange.

4 Drive in the new oil seal and spread the seal lips inside the release bearing guide by using a suitable piece of tubing with a well chamfered end.

5 Before bolting the flywheel housing to the gearbox, fit a new paper gasket smeared with gasket compound.

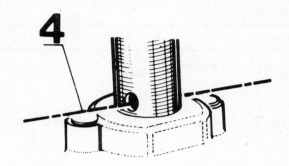

Fig. 5.12 Alignment of hole in clutch release bearing guide tube (Sec 9)

4 Housing web

6 On cars with a type 689 engine, note the location of the shorter bolt when fitting the flywheel housing to the gearbox – see Fig. 5.15.

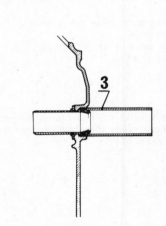

Fig. 5.13 Installing input shaft oil seal (Sec 9)

3 Tubular drift

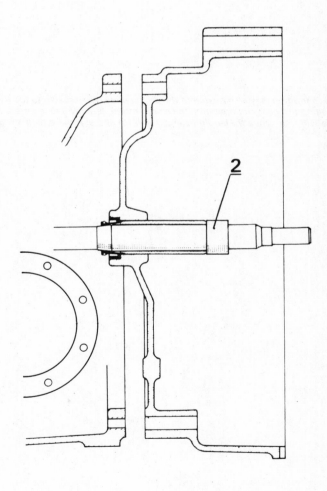

Fig. 5.14 Spreading oil seal lips (Sec 9)

2 Chamfered tubular drift

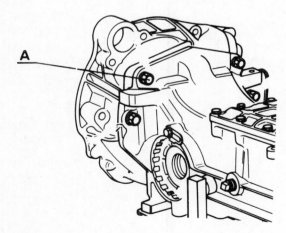

Fig. 5.15 Shorter flywheel housing bolt (A) (Sec 9)

10 Fault diagnosis – clutch

Symptom	Reason(s)
Judder when taking up drive	Loose engine or gearbox mountings Badly worn friction linings or contaminated with oil Worn splines on gearbox input shaft or driven plate hub Worn input shaft
Clutch spin (failure to disengage) so that gears cannot be meshed	Incorrect release bearing to pressure plate clearance Rust on splines (may occur after vehicle standing idle for long periods)* Damaged or misaligned pressure plate assembly Cable stretched or broken
Clutch slip (increase in engine speed does not result in increase in vehicle road speed – particularly on gradients)	Incorrect release bearing to pressure plate finger clearance Friction linings worn out or oil contaminated
Noise evident on depressing clutch pedal	Dry, worn or damaged release bearing Incorrect pedal adjustment Weak or broken pedal return spring Excessive play between driven plate hub splines and input shaft splines
Noise evident as clutch pedal released	Distorted driven plate Broken or weak driven plate cushion coil springs Incorrect pedal adjustment Weak or broken clutch pedal return spring Distorted or worn input shaft Release bearing worn

*This condition may also be due to the driven plate being rusted to the flywheel or pressure plate. It is possible to free it by applying the handbrake, engaging top gear and operating the starter motor. If really badly corroded, then the engine will not turn over, but in the majority of cases the driven plate will free. Once the engine starts, rev it up and slip the clutch several times to clear the rust deposits.

Chapter 6 Manual transmission

For modifications, and information applicable to later models, see Supplement at end of manual

Contents

Specifications

General

Type .... Mounted ahead of engine, four or five forward speeds and reverse. Synchromesh on all forward gears.

Application: **Gearbox type**
R1222 .... 354 or HA1
R1223 .... 385 or NG5
122B NG5
R1227 .... 354 or HA1
R1229 .... 354 or HA1
R1392 .... 354 or HA1
R1397 .... 354 or HA1
All other models 354

Gearbox ratios (typical)
The ratios vary slightly according to model. Quote the transmission suffix number when ordering spare parts – the number may be found on the identification plate on the gearbox housing.

Type 354:
    R1221 and R1222 models:
        1st .... 3.67 : 1
        2nd .... 2.24 : 1
        3rd .... 1.46 : 1
        4th .... 1.03 : 1
        Reverse .... 3.23 : 1
    R1224 models:
        1st .... 3.67 : 1
        2nd .... 2.37 : 1
        3rd .... 1.52 : 1
        4th .... 1.03 : 1
        Reverse .... 3.23 : 1
    R1225 models:
        1st .... 3.83 : 1
        2nd .... 2.23 : 1
        3rd .... 1.45 : 1
        4th .... 1.02 : 1
        Reverse .... 3.54 : 1
Type 385:
    R1223 models:
        1st .... 3.82 : 1
        2nd .... 2.24 : 1
        3rd .... 1.48 : 1
        4th .... 1.04 : 1
        5th .... 0.86 : 1
        Reverse .... 3.08 : 1
Type HA1:
    R1222, R1227, R1229, R1397 models:
        1st .... 3.83 : 1
        2nd .... 2.23 : 1
        3rd .... 1.46 : 1
        4th .... 1.17 : 1
        5th .... 0.95 : 1
        Reverse .... 3.54 : 1

Type NG5:

R1223 and 122B models:	
1st	3.82 : 1
2nd	2.18 : 1
3rd	1.41 : 1
4th	1.03 : 1
5th	0.86 : 1
Reverse	3.08 : 1

Final Drive Ratios

Type 354	3.62 : 1 or 4.13 : 1
Type 385	3.87 : 1
Type HA1	3.44 : 1 or 4.13 : 1
Type NG5	3.78 : 1

Oil type/specification

Gear oil, viscosity SAE 75 or 80 (Duckhams Hypoid 80S)

Oil capacity

Type 354	1.8 litres, 3.06 Imp pts 1.9 US qts
Type 385	1.7 litres, 2.99 Imp pts 1.8 US qts
Type HA1	2.0 litres, 3.52 Imp pts 2.1 US qts
Type NG5	2.0 litres, 3.52 Imp pts 2.1 US qts

Torque wrench settings

	Nm	lbf ft
Type 354:		
Top cover bolts	12	9
Front cover bolts	25	18
Primary shaft bearing thrust plate	25	18
Reverse gear lever bolt	29	21
Speedometer drive worm nut	115	85
Secondary shaft bearing	25	18
Reverse lamp switch	30	22
Rear cover bolts	25	18
Bellhousing-to-gearbox bolts:		
8.0 mm	25	18
10.0 mm	35	26
Bellhousing-to-engine bolts	41	30
Types 385 and HA1:		
Half casing connecting bolts:		
7.0 mm	25	18
8.0 mm	30	22
Bellhousing to gearbox:		
8.0 mm	25	18
10.0 mm	35	26
Reverse gear lever bolt	25	18
Crownwheel bolts	109	80
Speedometer drive worm nut	122	90
Primary shaft bolt	122	90
Reverse lamp switch	26	19
Cover bolts	12	9
Bellhousing-to-engine bolts	41	30

1 General description

One of four types of manual transmission may be fitted, depending upon model and date of production (see Specifications).

The transmission is of four- or five-speed type with synchromesh on all forward gears.

Owing to the fact that the type 800 (845 cc) engine revolves in the opposite direction when compared with the other engine types, the crownwheel and pinion must be located on the opposite side within the transmission casing.

The primary shaft transmits motion via four forward gears to the secondary or pinion shaft on which is the main gear cluster and synchromesh. The reverse gear is on a third shaft fixed to the gear casing. Motion is then transmitted when a gear is engaged, by the pinion gear on the end of the pinion shaft to the crownwheel and then to the driveshafts. Gear selector forks are mounted in the casing and are operated by a gearchange lever which is mounted at the side or on the top of the casing.

These forks select gears on the primary shaft which then mesh with the appropriate gear on the pinion shaft.

Various gear ratios have been used. The speedometer is gearbox driven. Although relatively simple transmission units there are nevertheless a few words of warning which must be stated before any potential dismantlers start work, to let them know what they are letting themselves in for.

First of all decide whether the fault you wish to repair is worth all the time and effort involved. Second, if the transmission unit is in a very bad state then the cost of the necessary components parts may well exceed the cost of an exchange factory unit. Third, be absolutely sure that you understand how the transmission unit works.

Returning to the second point just mentioned, it is possible to dismantle the unit with tools from a normal tool kit but only so far. Fortunately this is the point, if further dismantling is decided to be necessary, to check whether an exchange unit would be a cheaper method of repair. Renault cannot supply individual component parts, rather parts assembled into units, past this point.

Check very carefully the availability and cost of transmission unit parts before dismantling.

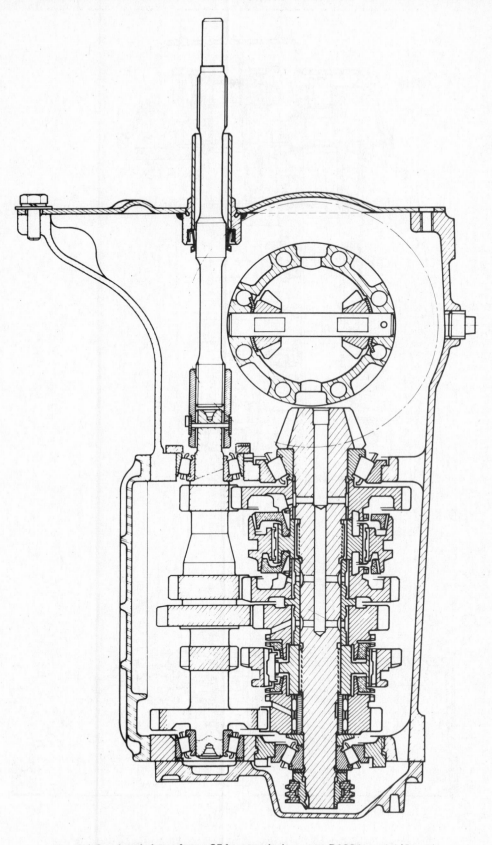

Fig. 6.1 Sectional view of type 354 transmission – not R1221 model (Sec 1)

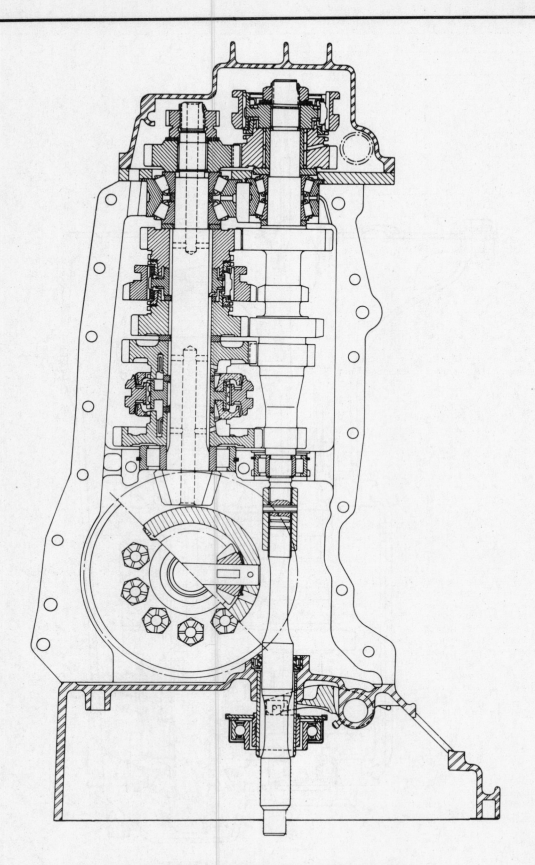

Fig. 6.2 Sectional view of type 385 transmission (Sec 1)

2 Maintenance

1 The oil level in the transmission should be checked at the intervals specified in Routine Maintenance.
2 Remove the combined oil level/filler plug from the side of the transmission.
3 The oil should just be level with the bottom of the plug hole, if it is not, top it up with the specified oil.
4 Also, at the specified intervals, drain the transmission oil while it is hot and refill it with fresh lubricant.

3 Transmission – method of removal

1 The transmission (gearbox/final drive) may be removed complete with the engine from above or, on its own, from below the car.
2 To remove the transmission complete with the engine, refer to Chapter 1.

4 Transmission (Type 354) – removal and refitting

All models

1 Apply the handbrake, jack up the front of the car and support on firmly based axle stands.
2 Unbolt and remove the transmission undershield.
3 On R1225 models, remove the engine undershield.
4 Drain the transmission oil.
5 Disconnect the battery.
6 Disconnect the earth strap from the transmission.
7 Disconnect the speedometer cable from the transmission.
8 On models with a facia-mounted gear lever, disconnect the return spring, drive out the roll pin (1), unscrew the two bolts (2) and pull out the front section of the rod (Fig. 6.4). On R1221 models, remove the radiator tie-rod. Unclip the starter cable.
9 On models with a floor-mounted gear lever unbolt the two bracket fixing bolts on the transmission.

R1221 models

10 On R1221 models, disconnect the plastic brake cable guides from the side-members. Tap out the cable end fittings from the tubular crossmember.
11 It is possible that, if the steering rack housing has been set high (shims – see Chapter 11), the transmission cannot be removed unless the tubular crossmember is first removed. Careful measuring will determine this. To remove the tubular crossmember, unscrew the top bolts (1) Fig. 6.6 and tilt the crossmember in the direction of the arrow. Refit the top bolts and then remove the bottom bolts. Tap the crossmember out towards the rear of the car. Refit the bottom bolts.
12 Release the brake hydraulic hoses from their clips.
13 Using a balljoint extractor, disconnect the suspension arm upper balljoints.
14 Disconnect the tie-rod ends.
15 Pull the stub axle carriers outwards and downwards and release the inboard ends of the driveshafts from the final drive.
16 Take care not to damage the differential oil seal lips during this operation.
17 Disconnect the clutch operating cable from its clevis fork.
18 Unbolt the exhaust pipe support bracket.
19 Support the front of the transmission on a jack and remove the front mounting.
20 If the inboard ends of the driveshafts have not freed from the final drive, lever the transmission first to the left and then to the right and pull the driveshafts towards the front of the car.
21 Unscrew the nuts which secure the transmission flange to the engine.
22 Withdraw the transmission, supporting its weight to prevent strain on the primary shaft while it is still engaged in the clutch mechanism.

All other models

23 Remove the top two starter motor fixing bolts.
24 Unbolt the brake caliper and tie it up out of the way. There is no need to disconnect the hydraulic hose.
25 Disconnect the tie-rod ends.

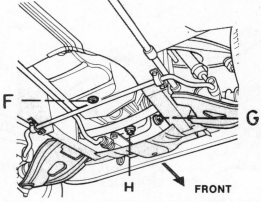

Fig. 6.3 Oil drain plugs (Sec 2)

F   Engine sump drain plug
G   Transmission oil level/filler plug
H   Transmission drain plug

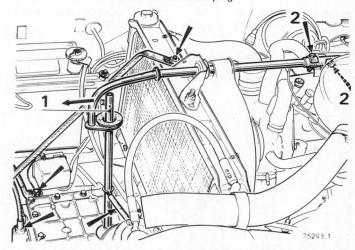

Fig. 6.4 Facia gearchange lever disconnection points (Sec 4)

1   Roll pin   2   Pinch bolts

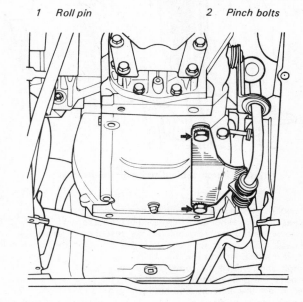

Fig. 6.5 Floor-mounted gearchange lever bracket (Sec 4)

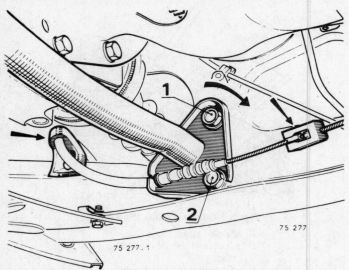

Fig. 6.6 Handbrake cable guides and tubular crossmember bolts (1 and 2) on R1221 models (Sec 4)

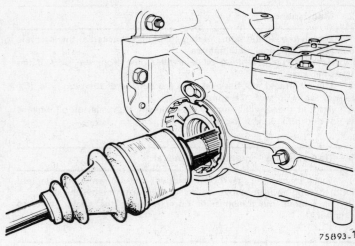

Fig. 6.7 Disconnecting driveshaft at inboard end (Sec 4)

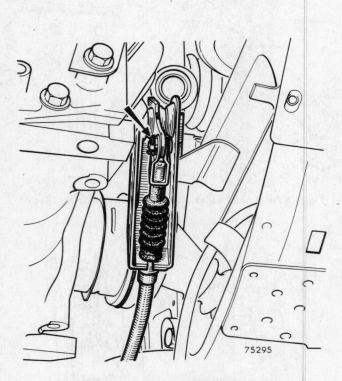

Fig. 6.8 Clutch cable disconnection (Sec 4)

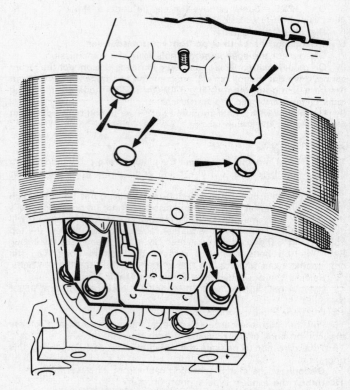

Fig. 6.9 Transmission front mounting (Sec 4)

26 Disconnect the suspension upper arm balljoints.
27 Release the driveshafts, as described in paragraphs 15, 16 and 20.
28 Remove the tubular crossmember, as described in paragraph 11.
29 Release the locknut and unscrew the drivebelt tensioner bolt. Remove the tensioner and the drivebelt.
30 Unbolt and remove the camshaft pulley.
31 Remove the pulley driveplate.
32 Disconnect the exhaust pipe bracket.
33 Remove the remaining accessible starter fixing bolts and withdraw the starter motor as far as possible.
34 Take the weight of the front of the transmission and unbolt the front mounting bracket.

35 Remove the transmission-to-engine flange bolts.
36 Remove the starter after unscrewing the bottom bolt using a socket extension with a universal joint or a cranked ring spanner.
37 Unscrew the side reinforcement fixing bolts. Remove the clutch cover plate.
38 Lower the engine/transmission and withdraw the transmission from the car.

Refitting

39 Refitting is a reversal of removal, lightly grease the primary shaft splines and refill the transmission with oil. Adjust the clutch (Chapter 5).

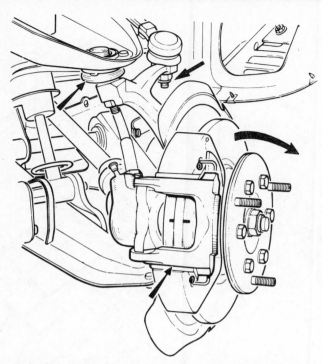

Fig. 6.10 Stub axle carrier disconnection points for withdrawal of driveshaft (Sec 4)

5 Transmission (type 385) – removal and refitting

1 The operations are very similar to those described in the preceding Section, but observe the following differences and additional work required.
2 Remove the radiator grille.
3 Remove the windscreen washer reservoir mounting plate.
4 Release the radiator mountings then lift and tilt it over the engine.
5 Drive out the roll pins from the inboard ends of the driveshafts. It may be necessary to depress the clutch pedal in order to reach one of the bellhousing bolts.
6 Refitting is a reversal of removal, make sure that the driveshaft roll pin holes are aligned and when the roll pins are installed, seal their ends with RTV or similar sealant.

6 Transmission (type HA1) – removal and refitting

1 The operations are generally similar to the type 354 transmission, but observe that the following additional work is required.
2 Remove the air cleaner and its bracket.
3 Unbolt the power-assisted steering pump and move it to one side without disconnecting the hydraulic hoses.
4 Remove the camshaft bearing from the flywheel housing.
5 Release the radiator and move it aside without disconnecting the coolant hoses, to give access to the transmission flexible mounting.
6 Support the engine/transmission and remove the mounting bolts, including the one marked (V) – Fig. 6.15.
7 Unscrew the transmission-to-engine flange bolts, tilt the transmission downward by lowering the jack and withdraw it from the car.
8 Refitting is a reversal of removal.

7 Transmission (type NG5) – removal and refitting

1 Removal of this type of transmission is carried out in a similar manner to that described for type 385. The turbocharger need not be removed.
2 Unbolt and remove the stay (A) – Fig. 6.16.
3 Tilt the engine/transmission downward to permit the clutch control to pass beneath the steering gusset.

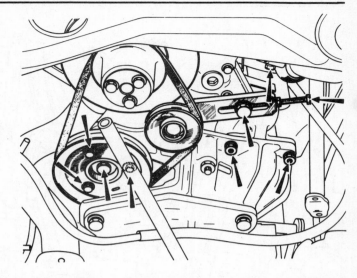

Fig. 6.11 Belt tensioner, camshaft pulley and starter bolt removal (Sec 4)

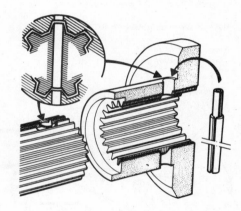

Fig. 6.12 Driveshaft double roll pins (Sec 5)

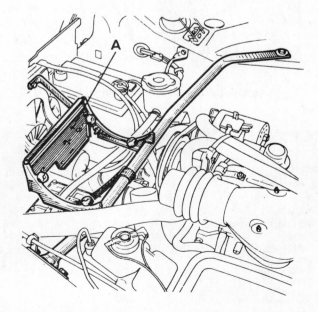

Fig. 6.13 Air cleaner bracket (A) (Sec 6)

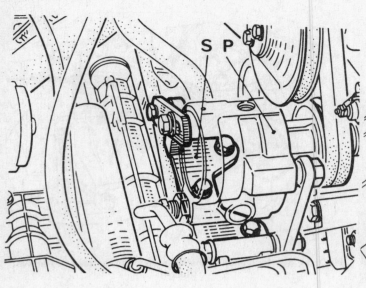

Fig. 6.14 Power-assisted steering pump (Sec 6)

P   Pump
S   Mounting bracket

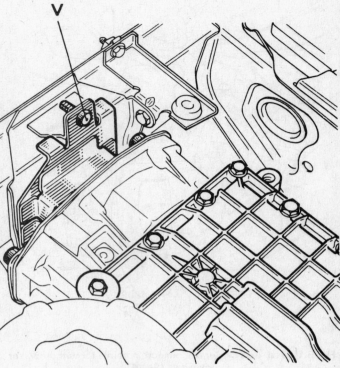

Fig. 6.15 Transmission (type HA1) front mounting (Sec 6)

V   Special bolt

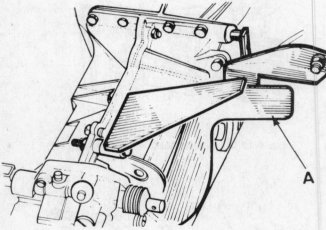

Fig. 6.16 Stay (A) on type NG5 transmission (Sec 7)

8   Transmission (type 354) – overhaul

1   With the transmission removed from the car, clean away external dirt and grease using paraffin, or a water-soluble solvent, and a stiff brush.

2   On all models except the R1221, unbolt and remove the clutch bellhousing (photos). If the clutch release mechanism is to be dismantled, refer to Chapter 5.

3   Mark the position of the differential adjusting ring nuts relative to the casing. Use a pin punch to dot mark them. Undo the locking tab nut and remove (photo). Now gently tap each ring nut round using a hammer and screwdriver or pinch wrench if one is available (photo). Count the number of turns the ring nut has to go through to remove. This will enable exact repositioning upon reassembly.

4   To free the primary or clutch shaft, and thereby the differential, pull out the roll pin which locks the two halves of the primary shaft together (photo). Withdraw the shaft (photo). This will now allow the differential to come out of the end of the casing (clutch end) (photo).

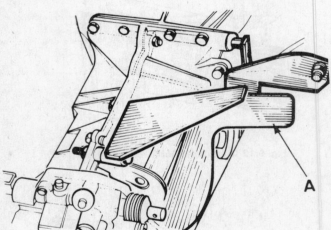

8.2a Removing a bellhousing bolt

8.2b Separating the bellhousing from transmission casing

8.3a Releasing differential adjusting ring nut lockbolt

8.3b An alternative method of unscrewing a differential adjusting ring nut

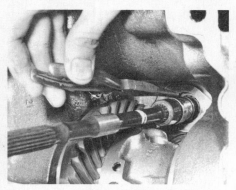

8.4a Removing primary/clutch shaft roll pin

8.4b Withdrawing clutch shaft

8.4c Removing differential

8.5 Removing top cover

8.6 Detent springs

8.7a Removing end cover

8.7b Primary shaft setting shims

8.8 Primary shaft bearing retaining plate

5 Now remove the top cover (photo). Retain the washers and setscrews. Undo all screws progressively.

6 When the cover is removed three springs will appear on the casing edge. Remove these (photo). A small plunger (1st/2nd gear) will be on top of one of these. A small selector shaft locking ball will be below all of these. Turn the casing upside down allowing these to drop out. Retain them.

7 Remove the end cover, its setscrews and washers (photo). Pick out the primary shaft setting shims (photo).

8 Unlock and remove the primary shaft rear bearing retaining plate (bellhousing end). It is held by two setscrews (photo). On some later models a lockplate is not used, instead the bolt threads are held with thread locking fluid.

9 Punch out (parallel pin punch) the two roll pins holding the reverse gear idler shaft. Then remove the reverse gear selector shaft (photo).

10 Punch out the roll pins holding the two other gear selector shafts. Remove the 3rd/4th selector shaft and retain the locking disc which appears between the 3rd/4th and reverse gear selector shafts (photos).

Remove the 1st/2nd selector shafts (photo). All shafts pull out through the primary end of the gear casing.

11 Select two speeds by sliding the two synchro sleeves along so that neither shaft will turn.

12 Using a very wide but thin spanner, unlock and unscrew the speedometer drive nut from the secondary shaft (photo). Then release the two gears selected.

13 Tap gently with a hide-headed hammer the end of the final drive pinion towards the differential end. Remove the taper-roller bearing shims with the final drive pinion (photo).

14 Push the primary shaft towards the differential end so to free its rear bearing cage. Pull out its front bearing plus shims for it is a free fit (photo).

15 Pull out of the top of the casing the primary shaft. This will enable the reverse gear shaft to be pulled out of the casing, then the gear itself (photos).

16 Now lift out the 3rd/4th and 1st/2nd selector forks (photo).

17 Mark with punched dot marks the secondary shaft adjusting nut

8.9 Removing reverse selector shaft

8.10a Removing 3rd/4th selector shaft

8.10b Removing selector shaft locking disc

8.10c Removing 1st/2nd selector shaft

8.12 Unscrewing speedometer drive worm nut

8.13 Removing final drive pinion

8.14 Removing primary shaft rear bearing outer track and shims

8.15a Removing primary shaft

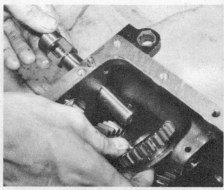

8.15b Removing reverse idler shaft and gear

8.16 Removing selector forks

8.17 Removing secondary shaft adjusting ring followed by 4th gear and its thrust washer

8.18a Removing gear cluster (2nd, 3rd and reverse)

8.18b Removing gear cluster (1st gear)

lockplate as you have the differential housing. Remove the locktab and nut and then unscrew the adjusting nut counting the number of turns. Remove the 4th speed gear thrust washer, and the 4th gear from the end of the casing (photo).

18 Remove the rest of the gear cluster from the top of the casing (photos).

19 Further dismantling is possible of the gear clusters and the final drive as well as the gear selectors. However, it is not recommended to undertake any further dismantling to the bearings and to the final drive because of the necessity of presses to undertake the work properly. If at this stage it is found necessary to replace any bearings or the final drive you must seek the services of a Renault agent with suitable equipment. Take him the parts needing work.

20 To refit the synchro units correctly, mark the two parts of the synchronising 1st/2nd and 3rd/4th, then separate them. This will obviously not apply when renewing individual gears. Reassembly is covered in Section 10.

21 The top cover is easily dismantled, if necessary.

9 Inspection of transmission components

Once decided that the transmission unit will have to be stripped down because of some minor irritant or major fault it is still not

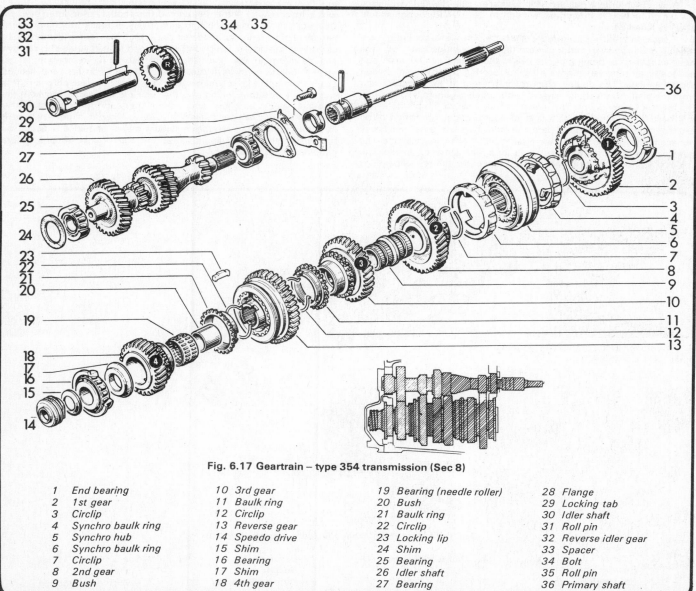

Fig. 6.17 Geartrain – type 354 transmission (Sec 8)

1 End bearing	10 3rd gear	19 Bearing (needle roller)	28 Flange
2 1st gear	11 Baulk ring	20 Bush	29 Locking tab
3 Circlip	12 Circlip	21 Baulk ring	30 Idler shaft
4 Synchro baulk ring	13 Reverse gear	22 Circlip	31 Roll pin
5 Synchro hub	14 Speedo drive	23 Locking lip	32 Reverse idler gear
6 Synchro baulk ring	15 Shim	24 Shim	33 Spacer
7 Circlip	16 Bearing	25 Bearing	34 Bolt
8 2nd gear	17 Shim	26 Idler shaft	35 Roll pin
9 Bush	18 4th gear	27 Bearing	36 Primary shaft

necessary to strip the unit completely. For example there is no need to remove the reverse gear cluster shaft if the synchromesh is being renewed on an otherwise properly functioning gearbox. Consequently you should go slowly once the three major components are removed from the unit because you may be doing unnecessary work. You may also have to face the fact that even when dismantled you will do better to reassemble the box there and then (do it properly though) and exchange it for a replacement unit from Renault. The economics of renewing large components is not always on when compared to a complete exchange unit. Remember also that exchange units are likely to be more readily available than individual component parts and that they will carry a guarantee.

Once dismantled into its three major components, the primary shaft and final drive, inspection should be detailed. Clean the inside of the unit thoroughly first with a suitable solvent and wipe dry.

1   Check the casting for cracks or damage, particularly near the bearing housings and on the mating surfaces.

2   Check all the gears for chips and possible cracks and renew where necessary. You should be able to tell whether this could be so from the diagnosis before dismantling.

3   Check all the shafts and splines for wear and flat spots and renew if necessary. The gears through which the shafts pass should be a good slide fit and not rock about.

4   Check the synchromesh rings and assembly. All models are prone to early synchromesh failure which should really be renewed as a matter of course, as it is cheap enough to do so. The springs should also be renewed.

5   Check the bearings: Primary shaft bearings are generally very reliable and long-lived and these are the only bearings apart from the double taper-roller bearing on the pinion shaft which can be easily and economically renewed. Check them for scoring and 'wobble'. Pinion shaft bearings: The double taper-roller bearing at the opposite end from the final drive is easily renewed although it is generally long-lived. Renew it if in any doubt. The pinion bearing next to the pinion wheel will have to be renewed at a cost of approximately one third of an exchange unit. If this unit is defective and there are other necessary replacements within the transmission unit, then reassemble the gearbox and exchange the whole unit for a replacement transmission. It is not economic to do otherwise. The two outer differential bearings

should be inspected in the same way. These may be renewed by the home mechanic but he may have difficulty in setting up the final drive in the casing afterwards. Again these bearings are usually reliable.

6   Any failure within the final drive unit will mean renewal of the whole unit, crownwheel assembly included. Under certain circumstances it will mean changing the bearing and speedo drive gear. See the Specifications at the start of the Chapter. We did not dismantle the crownwheel and pinion because it is not a task which can be undertaken, at least at the reassembly stage, by the home mechanic. The cost of purchasing a new crownwheel without a new pinion is approximately half that of a new exchange transmission unit. Purchasing the two together, crownwheel assembly and pinion assembly, to enable them to mesh and set-up correctly is approximately the cost of the exchange transmission and you will not get the guarantee.

7   Check that the nylon speedometer drive gearwheel is in good condition and running easily in its bush.

8   Check the selector forks for wear. Measure them with a pair of calipers and compare their ends with the thickest point; if in doubt renew. They should be only fractionally worn.

9   Check the gear shift mechanism. The tongue which also slots into the top of the selectors wears quite rapidly often resulting in non-selected gears and sloppy action.

Special Note: Such is the construction of these transmission units that they are, generally speaking, very reliable, but often noisy. They all whine from new to some degree and this should not frighten owners. Obviously, it is not possible to detect any increase in whine over a period of time only to suddenly think that it is doing it more than perhaps it should. However, this is no good reason in itself to remove and disassemble the unit. The usual reason for discontent is the gradual failure of the synchromesh, particularly on first and second gears. This again is not really good reason for disassembly until it is completely non-functioning and the whine is excessive. Provided the unit still selects its gears, keeps them there and functions smoothly there is no mechanical reason for worry. Only at a point where it becomes unbearable for the individual owner should this action be taken. See the 'Fault diagnosis' at the end of this Chapter before jumping to conclusions.

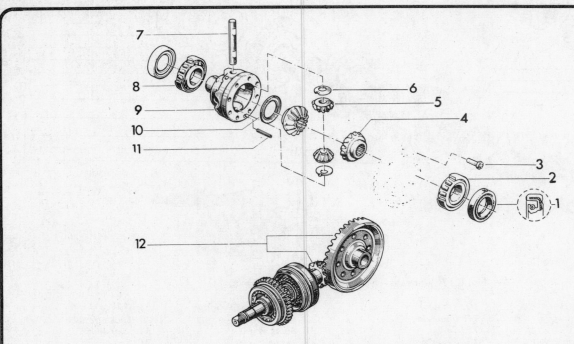

Fig. 6.18 Differential/final drive components (Sec 10)

1 Oil seal	4 Differential gear	7 Pinion shaft	10 Spacer
2 Bearing	5 Pinion gear	8 Bearing	11 Roll pin
3 Crownwheel bolt	6 Spacer	9 Differential carrier	12 Differential, complete

10 Transmission (type 354) – reassembly

1   Make sure all the components are spotlessly clean.Then look at the component drawings relevant to this gearbox. Picture the assemblies in your mind.

2   Make sure the top cover is assembled, complete. Reassemble it in a reverse sequence to its disassembly.

3   Reassemble the two synchro-hubs. For the 1st/2nd unit fit the recessed inner of the hub facing towards the 2nd speed sliding gear. Fit the two springs correctly. If original parts are fitted match up the two marks. For the 3rd/4th fit the two springs, positioning each one correctly with the three keys in their recesses. Fit the sliding gear with the groove facing the inner part of the hub with the biggest offset.

4   Put the gear casing on its end; bellhousing end down.

5   Fit the secondary/pinion shaft gear cluster into the casing (photos).

6   Now fit to 4th gear and ring its split needle roller cage. Hold the cage halves in light grease. Fit the gear sleeve thrust washer and 4th speed gear (photos).

7   Screw in the bearing adjusting ring nut. Tighten and lock it using the same number of turns counted on removal and having the dot marks aligned (photos).

8   Turn the gearbox onto its lower side.

9   Insert the 1st/2nd and 3rd/4th selector forks (photo).

10   Insert the reverse gear and its shaft. Punch its roll pins but not too far (photos).

11   Put in the primary shaft, pushing the reverse gear up and down its shaft to allow it to fit. Punch the reverse gear shaft roll pins home (photos).

12   Refit the rear endplate of the primary shaft and lock it (photo).

13   Insert the pinion shaft gently through the gear cluster. Once inserted tap the taper-roller bearing onto the shaft at the other end (photos).

14   Select two speeds and lock the gearbox. Refit the speedometer skew gear (photo). Tighten fully. Select neutral. The secondary shaft must now revolve easily and without play. If not something has gone wrong. To rectify, unlock the secondary shaft adjusting ring nut and loosen or tighten appropriately. Then relock. If new bearings have been fitted a preload on the secondary shaft of 1 to $3\frac{1}{2}$ lbs will indicate correct fitment. Use a spring balance round the 3rd/4th groove.

15   Now refit the selector shafts in the exact reverse order. 1) 1st/2nd selector shaft and roll pin. 2) 3rd/4th selector shaft and roll pin. 3) Locking disc between the selector shafts (photos).

16   Drop the three locking balls above the selector shafts through the edge of the casing. Follow here with the springs and the 1st/2nd spring plunger (photos).

17   Use a new gasket and refit the top cover (photo). Move the end of the selector lever (longest finger) in the top cover towards its nearest

10.5A Locating secondary shaft gear cluster (1st gear)

10.5b Locating secondary shaft gear cluster (2nd, 3rd and reverse)

10.6a Fitting needle roller bearing to 4th gear

10.6b Locating 4th gear

10.7a Screwing in bearing adjusting ring nut

10.7b Fitting bearing ring nut lockplate and bolt

10.9 Locating 1st and 2nd selector forks

10.10a Fitting reverse idler gear

10.10b Installing reverse idler shaft and roll pins

10.11a Installing primary shaft assembly

10.11b Primary shaft correctly fitted

10.11c Reverse idler shaft roll pins ready for driving home

10.12 Primary shaft endplate

10.13a Installing final drive pinion

10.13b Fitting pinion shaft bearing and shim

10.13c Tapping taper-roller bearing home on pinion shaft

10.14 Tightening speedometer drivegear worm nut

10.15a Fitting selector shafts

10.15b Fitting selector fork roll pin

10.15c Fitting selector shaft locking disc

10.15d Check that all gears mesh and the roll pins are home

10.16a Detent balls

10.16b Detent springs

10.17 Refitting top cover and gasket

10.18 Primary shaft bearing shims

10.19 Refitting end cover and gasket

10.20 Fitting differential

10.21a Screwing in remaining differential bearing ring nut

10.21b Differential bearing ring nut locked

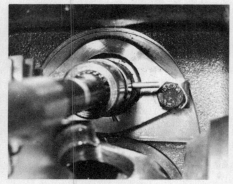

10.22 Clutch/primary shaft connecting roll pin

10.23 Connecting bellhousing using a new gasket

corner and, having used some gasket cement on both the casing and the cover, place the gasket on the casing and tighten the top cover. If it does not go on easily take it off and slide the reverse gear along so that it rests on the 4th gear on the primary shafts. Make sure the gearbox is neutral. Try again; the selector lever should slide into its correct notch.

18 Now refit the primary shaft front bearing. Tap the outer track ring flush with the casing. Refit the same number of shims which were removed (photo).

19 Refit the end cover. Use a new gasket and gasket cement (photo).

20 Refit the differential inside the housing (photo). Make sure the crownwheel is on the correct side. See the appropriate diagram – Fig. 6.19.

21 Screw in the differential adjusting ring nuts the same number of

turns that were used in its removal (photo). Make sure the dot punch marks align. If new bearings have been used your number of turns and dot alignment marks are not valid. Screw in the ring marks until the differential becomes 'slightly hard' to turn. Then check the preload. Revolve the differential to settle the bearings and then use a spring balance to test. It needs 2 to 7 lb to turn the differential easily. Adjust the ring nut until all is well. Refit the lock tab and set screw (photo).

22 Refit the clutch shaft to the primary shaft using a new roll pin (photo).

23 Now assemble the bellhousing and bolt it to the gearbox (photo) or fit the cover plate of the R1221. Bolt the relevant part to the gearbox casing in the reverse sequence of its removal.

24 Check that the gears can be selected easily.

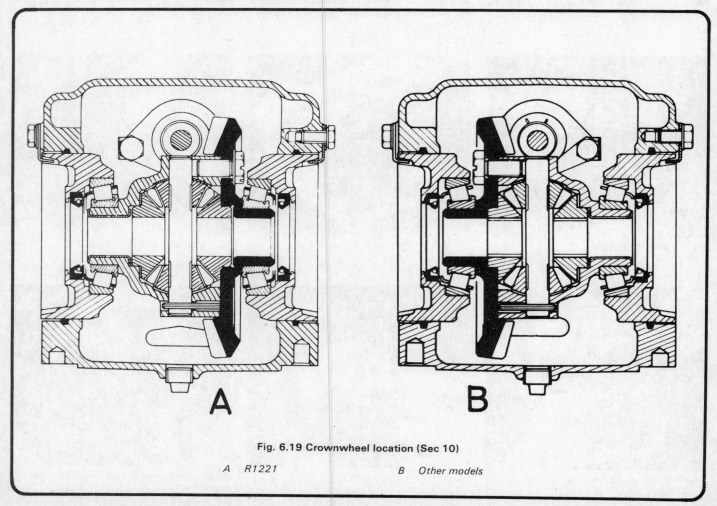

Fig. 6.19 Crownwheel location (Sec 10)

A R1221   *B Other models*

11 Reverse stop plate modification (type 354 transmission)

1 Models built up to and including 1976 have a reverse stop plate fixed under the floor panel beneath the gearchange control lever.
2 Later models have a spring located inside the gearcase cover on the selector shaft.
3 If a new type transmission is being fitted, make sure that the reverse stop plate is removed from the car.

12 Transmission (type 385) – dismantling

1 With the transmission removed from the car clean away all external dirt using a water soluble solvent, or paraffin, and a stiff brush.
2 Unscrew and remove the reversing lamp switch.
3 Unbolt the clutch bellhousing from the main transmission case.

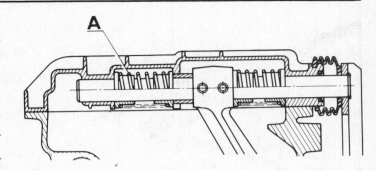

Fig. 6.20 Selector shaft reverse stop spring (A) (Sec 11)

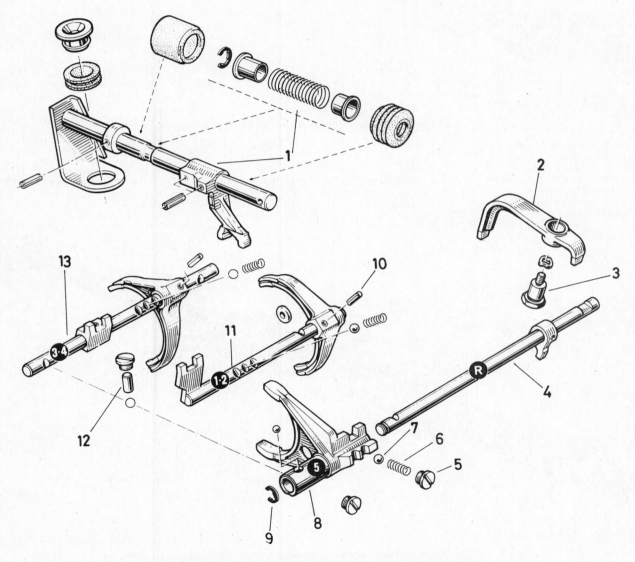

Fig. 6.21 Selector components – type 385 transmission (Sec 12)

1 Gearchange control rod	5 Detent plug	8 5th speed selector fork	11 1st/2nd selector fork
2 Reverse selector swing lever	6 Detent spring	9 Circlip	12 Interlock plunger, ball and plug
3 Pivot bolt	7 Detent ball	10 Roll pin	13 3rd/4th selector shaft and fork
4 5th/reverse selector shaft			

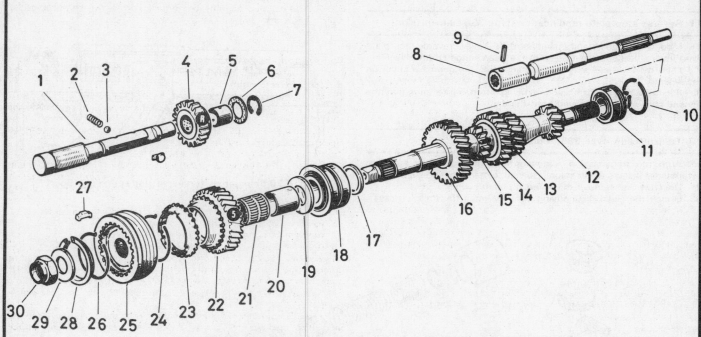

Fig. 6.22 Primary geartrain components – type 385 transmission (Sec 12)

1	Reverse idler shaft	9	Roll pin	17	Adjuster washer	24 Synchro spring
2	Spring	10	Circlip	18	Bearing	25 5th speed synchro
3	Locking ball	11	Bearing	19	Shim	26 Synchro spring
4	Reverse idler gear	12	1st speed gear	20	Spacer/sleeve	27 Synchro sliding key
5	Spacer/sleeve	13	2nd speed gear	21	Needle bearing	28 Circlip
6	Friction washer	14	3rd speed gear	22	5th speed gear	29 Washer
7	Circlip	15	Reverse gear	23	Baulk ring	30 Nut
8	Input (clutch) shaft	16	4th speed gear			

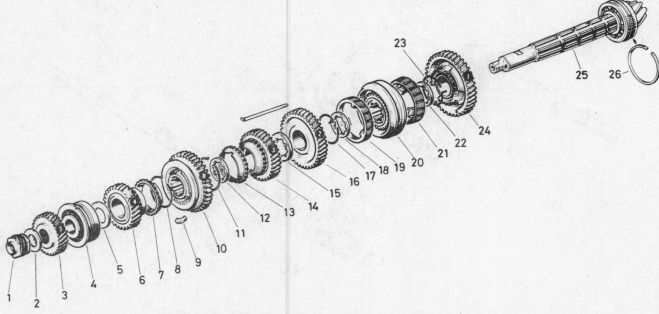

Fig. 6.23 Secondary geartrain components – type 385 transmission (Sec 12)

1	Speedo drive worm gear/nut	8	Synchro spring	15	Stop washer	21 Baulk ring
2	Washer	9	Sliding key	16	2nd speed gear	22 Stop washer
3	5th speed gear	10	3rd/4th synchro, with reverse	17	Synchro spring	23 Synchro spring
4	Bearing	11	Synchro spring	18	Stop washer	24 1st speed gear
5	Washer	12	Stop washer	19	Baulk ring	25 Secondary (pinion shaft)
6	4th speed gear	13	Baulk ring	20	1st/2nd synchro	26 Circlip
7	Baulk ring	14	3rd speed gear			

4 Select neutral and then unscrew 5th speed detent plug and extract the spring and ball.
5 Remove the detent plug, plunger and ball from 3/4th selector shaft and from the 5th/reverse selector shaft.
6 Unbolt and remove the end cover from the transmission case. Retain 5th speed selector fork ball.
7 Engage 5th and 3rd or 4th gears simultaneously by moving two selector shafts at once. This will lock up the geartrains.
8 Unscrew the nut at the 5th speed synchro hub on the end of the primary shaft.

Primary shaft – dismantling
9 Mark the relationship of 5th speed synchro sliding sleeve to its hub, using a dab of quick drying paint.
10 Remove the circlip from the reverse shaft.
11 Withdraw 5th speed synchro with sleeve, hub and selector fork.
12 Remove the baulk ring.
13 Remove 5th gear and spacer. The primary shaft cannot be dismantled further, with the exception of renewing the bearings. These can be removed using a suitable puller, once the primary shaft has been removed and the clutch shaft has been separated from the primary shaft by driving out its connecting roll pin.

Casing – dismantling
14 Mark the setting of the differential ring nuts, remove the locking plates and unscrew the ring nuts, noting the number of turns required.
15 Unscrew the half-casing connecting bolts and separate the two sections.
16 Lift out the secondary geartrain with stop peg for the outer track of the double taper-roller bearing.
17 Lift out the primary shaft and the final drive assembly.
18 Drive out the roll pin from the 3rd/4th selector fork. Remove shaft, fork, ball and spring. Take out the locking disc from between the shafts.
19 Withdraw reverse selector shaft back as far as possible and drive out the roll pin from the 1st/2nd selector fork. Remove the shaft, fork, ball and spring.
20 Remove the reverse selector swing lever.
21 Drive out the roll pins from the dog on the reverse selector shaft. Remove the shaft and the dog.

Reverse idler shaft – dismantling
22 To remove the reverse idler gear, extract the shaft circlip, pull out the shaft and take off the reverse idler gear, the friction washer and sleeve. Make sure that you catch the ball and locking spring.

23 The bearing tracks may be removed from the half-casings by driving them out with a piece of tubing.

Secondary shaft – dismantling
24 Grip the shaft vertically by the 1st speed gear in the jaws of a vice protected by soft metal covers.
25 Move the synchro sleeve to 1st gear position.
26 Unlock the speedo drive worm and remove it. Remove the washer and 5th gear.
27 Remove the double taper-roller bearing, and the washer used for pinion protrusion adjustment.
28 Remove 4th gear and baulk ring.
29 Remove 3rd/4th synchro unit (with reverse). A press or puller will be needed to draw off the synchro hub. If the synchro is to be taken apart, mark the relationship of hub to sleeve with a dab of quick drying paint.
30 Remove the retaining key for the gearwheel stop washers.
31 Remove the stop washer.
32 Remove 3rd gear and baulk ring.
33 Remove 2nd gear stop washer, 2nd gear and baulk ring.
34 Remove 1st/2nd synchro unit. A press or puller will be needed to draw off the synchro hub. If the synchro is to be taken apart, mark the relationship of hub to sleeve with a dab of quick drying paint.
35 Remove 1st speed baulk ring, stop washer and 1st speed gear itself.
36 There is not much point in dismantling the roller bearing, although the rollers and outer track will slip out easily enough. The inner track is bonded to the pinion. The bearing and shaft are renewed as an assembly.

Primary shaft bearing – removal
37 Remove the circlips from the primary shaft and also the bearing adjusting shims before drawing off the bearings. Retain the primary shaft setting washer once the front bearing has been removed.

Differential/final drive – dismantling
38 Using a suitable puller, extract the taper-roller bearings.
39 Unscrew and remove the crownwheel securing bolts, discard them and purchase new ones for use at reassembly.
40 Drive out the roll pin which retains the planet wheel shaft. Separate the differential components.

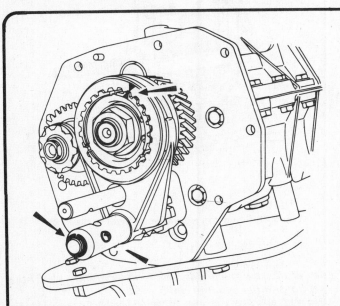

Fig. 6.24 5th speed synchro alignment marks and reverse shaft circlip (Sec 12)

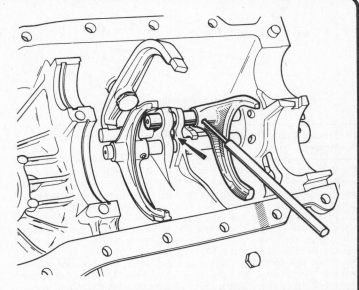

Fig. 6.25 Removing 3rd/4th selector fork roll pin (Sec 12)

Locking disc arrowed

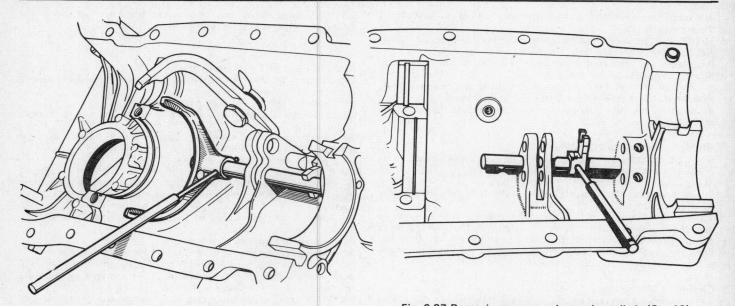

Fig. 6.26 Removing 1st/2nd selector fork roll pin (Sec 12)

Fig. 6.27 Removing reverse selector dog roll pin (Sec 12)

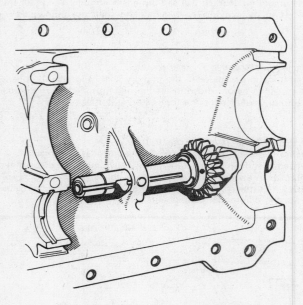

Fig. 6.28 Removing reverse idler shaft (Sec 12)

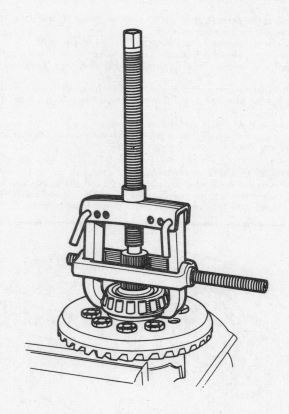

Fig. 6.29 Removing a differential bearing (Sec 12)

13 Transmission (type 385) – examination and renovation of components

1   With the transmission completely stripped examine all components for wear and damage. The need for renewal of synchro units will usually be evident from the history of noisy gearchanging or to the fact that the synchromesh was easily 'beaten' during changes.

2   Wear in the 3rd or 4th speed synchro can be checked by measuring the clearance between the baulk ring and the hub face with the ring pressed hard on to its cone. Refer to figures for specified clearances (Figs. 6.30 and 6.31).

3   When reassembling a synchro align the hub and sleeve marks made at dismantling. With the ends of both springs engaged in the same key, make sure that they run in opposite directions in relation to each other.

4   Renewal of a synchro unit or the secondary shaft/crownwheel is a rather complicated procedure if some original components are to be used again.

Renewal of crownwheel and pinion (secondary shaft) but retaining original synchro units

5   Measure across two splines on the original shaft as shown (Fig. 6.35) at a point 60.0 mm (2.36 in) from the rear face of the pinion gear. Take measurements at several different pairs of splines and then record the largest dimension. Compare with the following table and purchase the specified colour-coded shaft.

Spline measurement
Less than 16.63 mm (0.655 in)
16.63 mm (0.655 in) or greater

Secondary (pinion) shaft required
Red/blue

Yellow

Renewal of synchro units but retaining original secondary (pinion) shaft

6   Carry out the spline measuring procedure previously described and compare the dimensions with the following table. Purchase the specified colour-coded synchro unit.

Spline measurement
Less than 16.63 mm (0.655 in)
16.63 mm (0.655 in)

1st/2nd hub
Red/Yellow

White

3rd/4th hub
Blue/White

Red

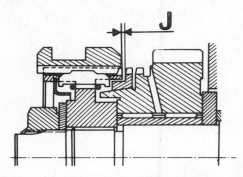

Fig. 6.31 5th speed synchro wear checking diagram (Sec 13)

J = 0.20 mm (0.008 in) maximum

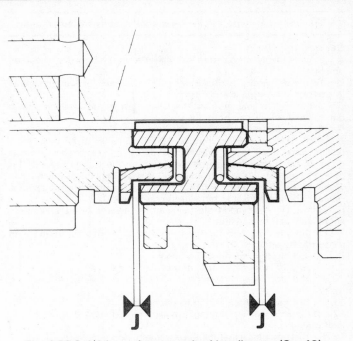

Fig. 6.30 3rd/4th synchro wear checking diagram (Sec 13)

J = 0.20 mm (0.008 in) maximum

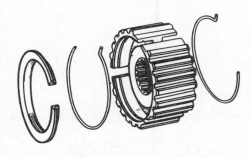

Fig. 6.33 5th speed synchro components (Sec 13)

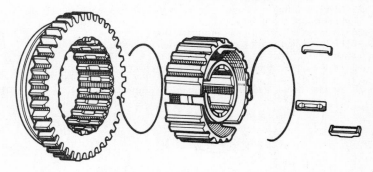

Fig. 6.32 3rd/4th synchro components (Sec 13)

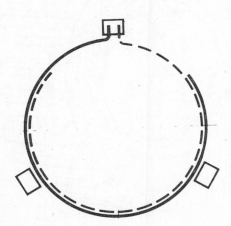

Fig. 6.34 Synchro spring installation diagram (Sec 13)

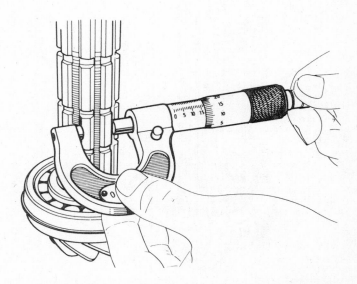

Fig. 6.35 Measuring two splines on secondary (pinion) shaft (Sec 13)

14 Transmission (type 385) — reassembly ready for adjustment

Secondary shaft

1   Engage the synchro spring in 1st gear so that it runs over the three notches.

2   To the secondary (pinion) shaft which will have its bearing clipped in position, fit 1st gear and its baulk ring.

3   Slide on 1st gear stop washer then turn it and retain it with a dummy key which can be made up.

4   Remove the pinion bearing outer track retaining clip.

5   Heat 1st/2nd synchro hub to 100°C (212°F) in an oven or in boiling water. Fit it to the shaft so that one of its unsplined sections is opposite the dummy key and the chamfer on the splines towards 1st gear. The hub should be pressed on to the shaft until it just touches the stop washer. Then allow the hub to cool with the pressure still applied. Release the pressure and remove the dummy key.

6   Fit the 1st/2nd synchro sleeve (chamfer towards 2nd gear) and the alignment marks opposite).

7   Fit the stop washer, turning it so that its splines are in line with those on the shaft.

8   Fit the synchro spring to 2nd gear.

9   Fit 2nd gear and its baulk ring to the shaft.

10   Fit the stop washer, turning it so that its splines are in line with those on the shaft.

11   Fit 3rd gear and baulk ring to the shaft.

12   Fit the stop washer, turning it to align its splines with those on the final drive pinion.

13   Fit the retaining key for the gearwheel stop washers.

14   Press 3rd/4th synchro onto the shaft until it just contacts the 3rd gear stop washer. The notch on the hub must face towards 3rd gear and be in alignment with the stop key.

15   Make sure that the three notches on the synchro baulk ring are in alignment with the three keys.

16   To the shaft fit 4th gear and baulk ring.

17   Fit the pinion protrusion adjusting washer which was removed at dismantling.

18   Fit the double taper roller bearing.

19   Fit 5th gear.

20   Fit the washer and the speedometer worm drive gear.

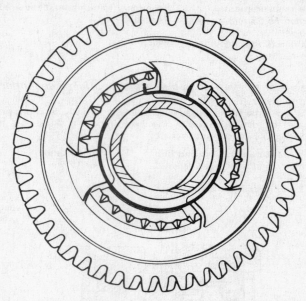

Fig. 6.36 1st speed gear spring correctly engaged (Sec 14)

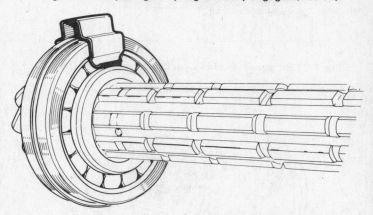

Fig. 6.37 Secondary shaft bearing clipped in position (Sec 14)

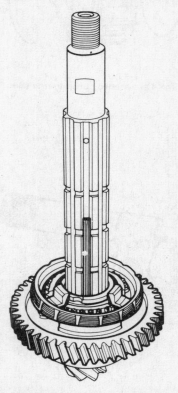

Fig. 6.38 1st speed gear stop washer retained by dummy key (Sec 14)

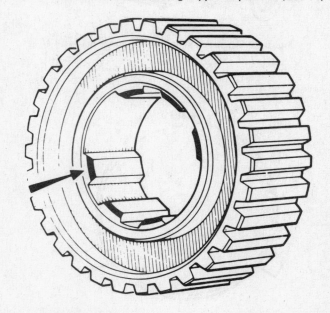

Fig. 6.39 1st/2nd synchro hub chamfer (Sec 14)

21 Grip the secondary gear train/shaft by 1st gear in the jaws of a vice fitted with jaw protectors.

22 Move the synchro sleeve to engage 1st gear and, with the geartrain locked, tighten the speedometer worm nut to the specified torque, but do not stake it in position at this stage.

Differential – reassembly

23 Into the differential case fit the impregnated washer so that the oil groove is on the sunwheel side. A spacer washer is sometimes used if there is excessive play between the sunwheel and planet gear teeth.

24 Apply oil to one sun wheel and install it.

25 Bolt the crownwheel to the differential case, using new self-locking bolts, tighten to the specified torque.

26 Fit the sun wheel O-rings.

27 Fit the planet gears and their friction washers so that the locking pegs engage in the holes in the case.

28 Insert the planet wheel shaft.

29 Fit the shaft roll pin so that its end is about 5.0 mm (0.2 in) below the surface of the case.

30 Apply oil to the second sun wheel and insert it inside the crownwheel.

31 Fit the taper-roller bearings to each side of the differential.

32 If the primary shaft bearings were removed press on the new ones now.

33 Check the differential bearing adjuster nuts and renew their oil seals and felt washers where necessary.

34 Before any further reassembly can be carried out, the adjustments described in the following Section must be completed. This is vital if any new components have been installed in the transmission.

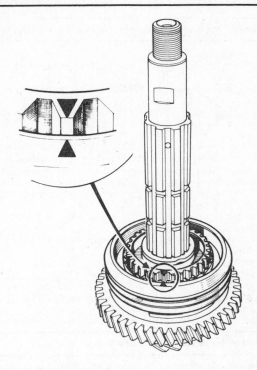

Fig. 6.40 1st/2nd synchro sleeve chamfer (Sec 14)

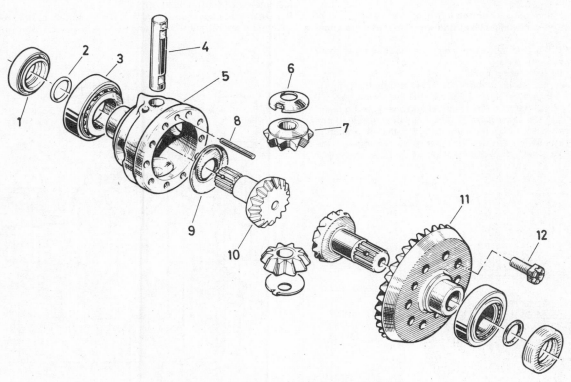

Fig. 6.41 Differential components (Sec 14)

1 Bearing ring nut	4 Planet wheel shaft	7 Planet gear	10 Sun wheel
2 Seal	5 Differential case	8 Roll pin	11 Crownwheel
3 Bearing	6 Friction washer	9 Special (impregnated) washer	12 Crownwheel bolt

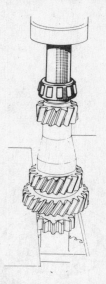

Fig. 6.42 Pressing on primary shaft bearing (Sec 14)

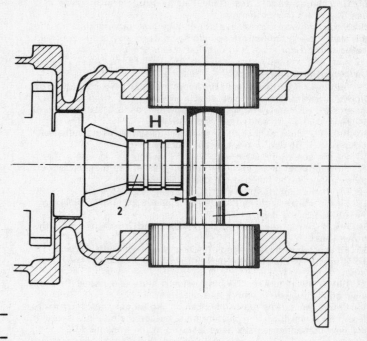

Fig. 6.44 Special tools for checking pinion projection (Sec 15)

1	B. Vi 239-01	C	0.50 mm (0.020 in)
2	B Vi 419	H	42.5 mm (1.673 in)

15 Transmission (type 385) – adjustments

1   The following adjustments will require the use of special tools. Where these cannot be borrowed the work will have to be entrusted to your Renault dealer.

Pinion protrusion adjustment

2   The position of the pinion face must be at a specified distance (A) from the centre of the crownwheel. This is set by the thickness of the washer (arrowed) – Fig. 6.43.

3   Locate the secondary shaft into the left-hand half-casing.

4   Connect the right-hand half-casing and insert a few bolts finger tight.

5   Temporarily fit the end cover to hold the double taper-roller bearing in position.

6   Now tighten the half-casing bolts.

7   Install the mandrel (special tool B.Vi 239-01) and then locate the spacer (special tool B.Vi 419) against the face of the pinion gear.

8   Measure the gap (C) between the mandrel and spacer using feeler blades (Fig. 6.44). If the dimension is less than that specified the secondary shaft will have to be dismantled and a thinner adjusting washer substituted between the double taper-roller bearing and the secondary shaft shoulder. If the dimension is greater than that

specified, change the washer to a thicker one. Washers are available in thicknesses of between 3.50 and 4.10 mm (0.138 and 0.162 in) in increments of 0.05 mm (0.002 in).

9   Once the adjustment is correct, dismantle the casing, remove the secondary shaft then tighten and stake the speedo worm nut.

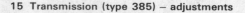

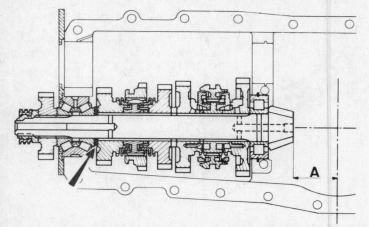

Fig. 6.43 Setting diagram – pinion end face to crownwheel centre (Sec 15)

A = 53.0 mm (2.086 in)
Adjuster washer arrowed

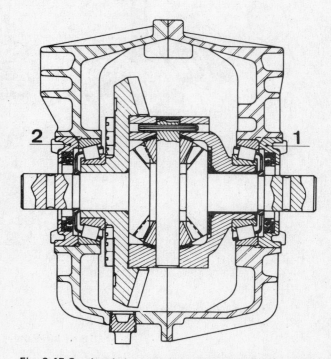

Fig. 6.45 Sectional view of differential/final drive (Sec 15)

1   Differential case side
2   Crownwheel side

Differential bearing adjustment

10 Check that the bearing outer tracks have been fully installed into their casing seats and are just below the casing surface.

11 Install the final drive/differential with bearings into the left-hand half-casing.

12 Connect the right-hand half-casing and insert and tighten all the connecting bolts to the specified torque.

13 Carefully screw in each bearing ring nut until they just contact the bearing tracks.

14 If the original bearings are being used the differential bearing adjuster ring nuts should be further screwed in until all play is eliminated when the differential is turned. When turning the ring nuts, turn the nut on the differential case side (1) more than the other one (2) on the crownwheel side to create backlash (Fig. 6.45).

15 Mark the position of the ring nuts in relation to the casing.

16 Dismantle the casing and remove the differential.

17 If new bearings are being used, they must be installed with a preload. Proceed exactly as described for adjustment of used bearings, but continue to screw in the ring nuts until the differential becomes stiff to turn.

18 Using a cord wrapped round the differential case and a spring balance, check the pull required to keep the differential rotating. The pull recorded on the spring balance should be 0.9 kg (2.0 lb). Adjust the ring nuts as necessary to achieve this figure, using the nut on the differential case side to increase the preload.

19 Mark the position of the ring nuts in relation to the casing, then dismantle the casing.

Primary shaft bearing adjustment

20 Place the bearing tracks and the original adjusting washer on to the shaft.

21 Locate the primary shaft meshed with the secondary shaft in the left-hand half-casing.

22 The alignment of the 3rd and 4th gearwheels on both shafts must show a similar recess dimension as shown in the diagram (Fig. 6.47). Where necessary, change the thickness of the adjusting washer (1) which is located between 4th gear and the bearing on the primary shaft.

23 Now remove the secondary shaft leaving the primary shaft in position.

24 Fit the right-hand half-casing, but without bolts.

25 Fit the original spacer and shims. The primary shaft should turn freely and the spacer should stand proud of the casing by the thickness of the end cover gasket which is 0.20 mm (0.008 in). Adjust the spacer projection if necessary by adding or removing shims.

26 On completion of adjustment, remove the right-hand half-casing, lift out the primary shaft from the left-hand half-casing.

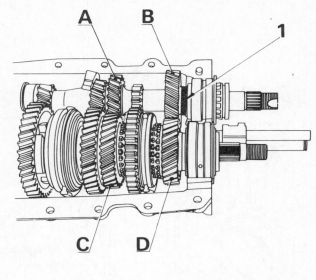

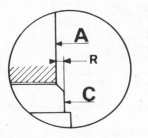 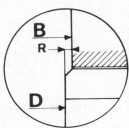

Fig. 6.47 Primary/secondary shaft alignment (Sec 15)

A   Primary shaft 3rd gear   D   Secondary shaft 4th gear
B   Primary shaft 4th gear   R   Recess dimension
C   Secondary shaft 3rd gear   1   Adjusting washer

16 Transmission (type 385) – final reassembly

1 Connect the input (clutch) shaft to the primary shaft by tapping in the roll pin.

2 Into the casing, insert the reverse selector shaft, passing it through the fork which must have its boss towards the final drive end of the transmission.

3 Fix the fork to the shaft with the roll pin and make sure that the slot in the roll pin is towards the transmission end (front) cover.

4 Fit the reverse swivel lever, engaging it with the notch in the reverse selector shaft. Tighten the bolt to the specified torque.

5 Insert 1st/2nd selector shaft locking ball and spring.

6 Push 1st/2nd selector shaft into position.

7 Fit the 1st/2nd fork to its shaft so that its longer boss is towards the clutch housing end. Fix the fork to the shaft with the roll pin, making sure that the slot in the roll pin is towards the transmission end (front) cover.

8 Fit the locking disc between the shafts.

9 Fit 3rd/4th selector shaft locking ball and spring.

10 Insert 3rd/4th selector shaft and fork (projecting hub towards final drive) and fix it with a roll pin. Make sure that the slot in the roll pin is towards the transmission end cover.

11 Into the casing install the primary shaft and differential/final drive.

12 Install the secondary shaft and geartrain with the stop peg for the double taper-roller bearing outer track.

13 Bolt on the remaining half-casing.

14 Screw in the differential ring nuts to their previously marked positions. Now feel the crownwheel to pinion backlash by turning the input shaft back and forth by hand. If it is obviously excessive, unscrew the ring nut on the differential case side and screw in the nut on the opposite side. Final adjustment should be made using a dial gauge until the backlash is between 0.12 and 0.25 mm (0.005 and 0.010 in).

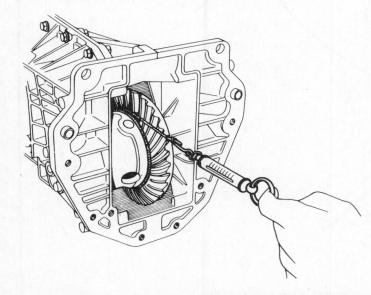

Fig. 6.46 Checking differential bearing preload (Sec 15)

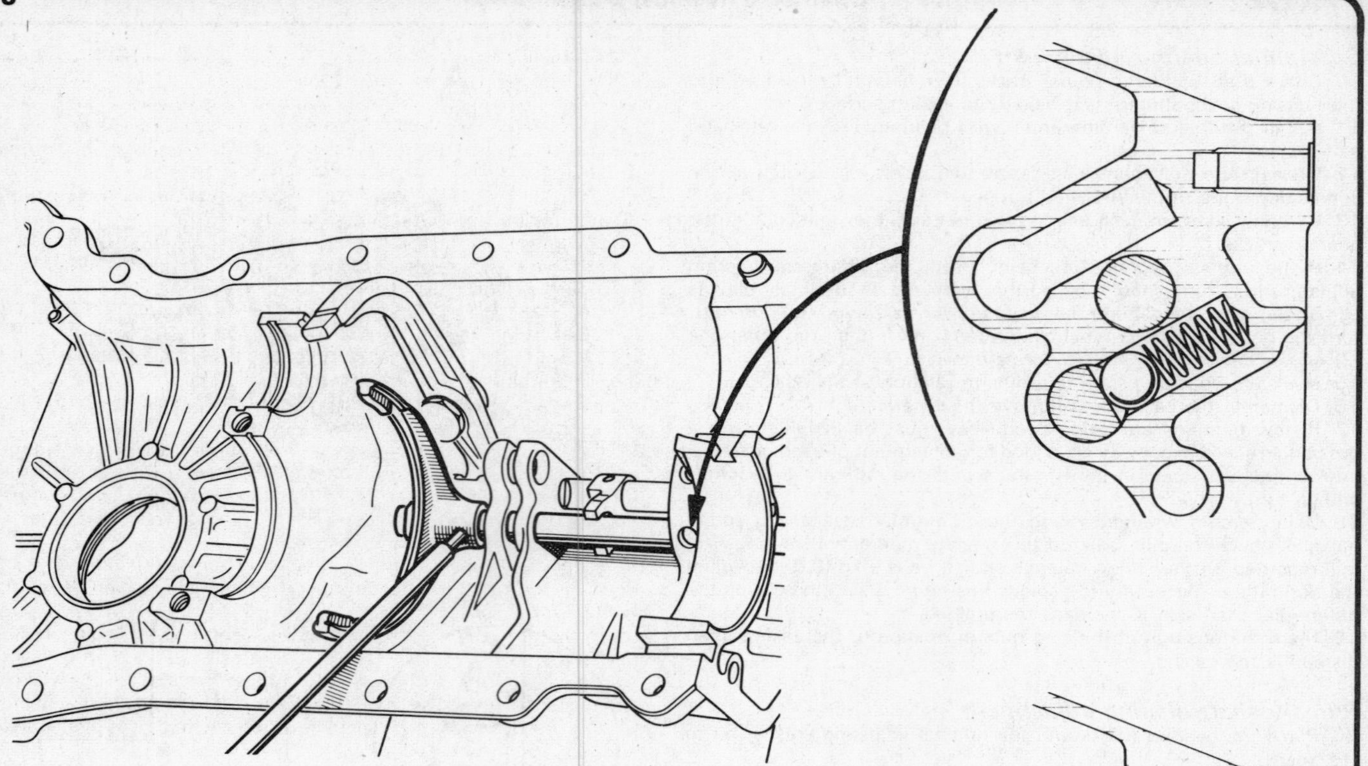

Fig. 6.48 1st/2nd selector shaft locking ball location (Sec 16)

Roll pin being driven out

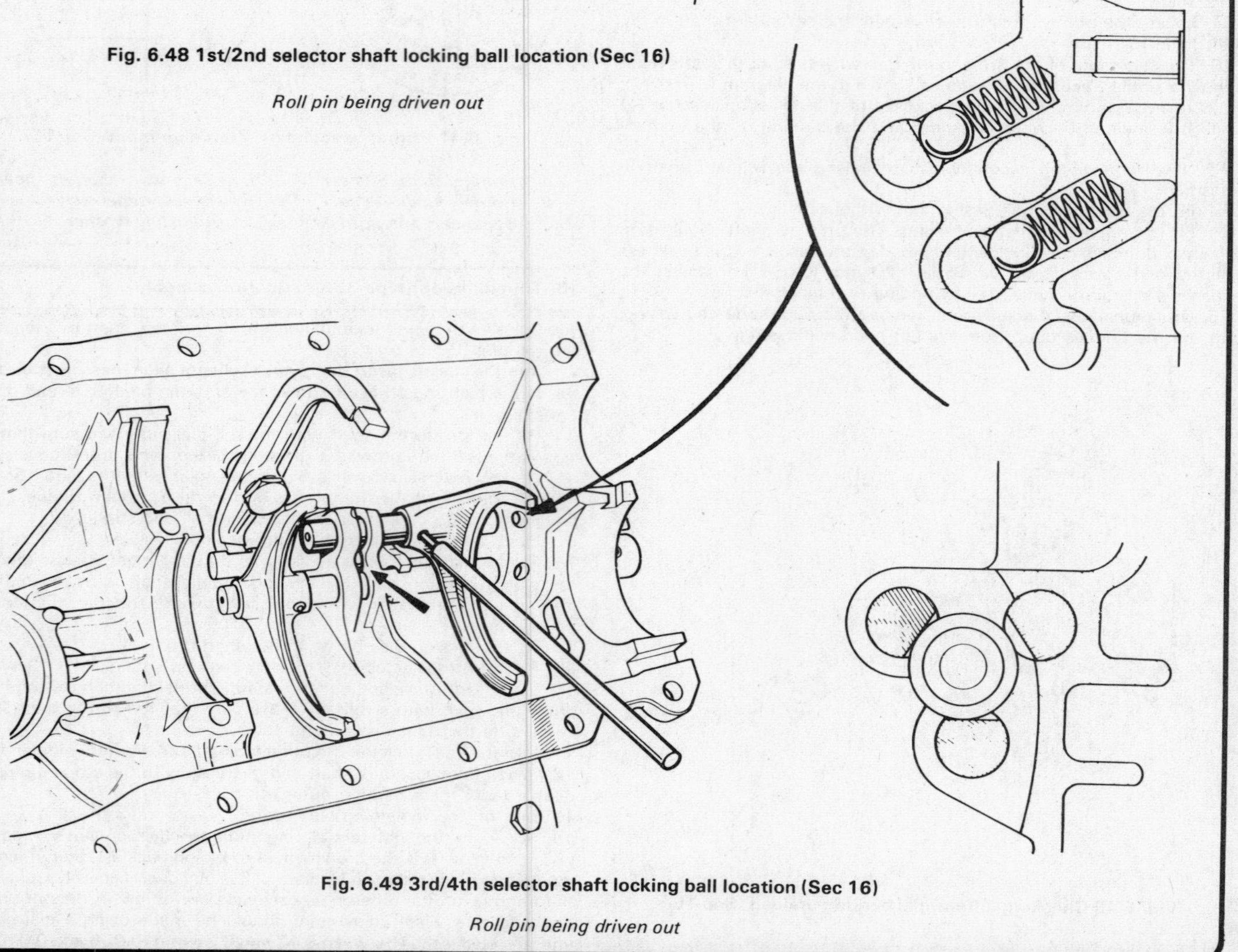

Fig. 6.49 3rd/4th selector shaft locking ball location (Sec 16)

Roll pin being driven out

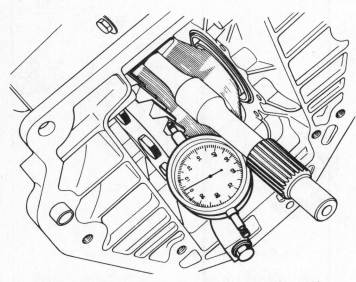

Fig. 6.50 Checking pinion/crownwheel backlash (Sec 16)

15 Lock the ring nuts with their locking plates.
16 Fit 5th speed gearwheel and spacer to the primary shaft.
17 Fit the baulk ring followed by 5th speed synchro and selector fork.
18 Fit the circlip to the end of the reverse shaft.
19 Select 5th speed and 3rd or 4th speed simultaneously to lock the transmission, and then tighten the nut on the end of the primary shaft. Return the gears to neutral.
20 Locate a new gasket and bolt on the end cover.
21 Refit the detent ball, plunger and plug to 3rd/4th and 5th selector shafts.
22 Locate a new gasket and bolt on the clutch bellhousing. Tape the shaft splines to prevent damage to the oil seal lips as the bellhousing is installed.
23 Screw in the reversing lamp switch.
24 Check that all bolts have been tightened to the specified torque.
25 Fit the clutch release lever and bearing.
26 Fill the transmission with the specified oil after it has been refitted to the car.

17 Transmission (type HA1) – overhaul

1 Overhaul is essentially the same as that described earlier in this Chapter for the type 354 transmission, with the exception of 5th speed gear which is described in this Section.
2 With the cover removed from the transmission, extract the detent ball and spring from 5th speed selector shaft.
3 Unbolt and remove the front cover and its gasket.
4 Move the synchro sleeves on two gears (1st and reverse) to lock them both and so prevent the gearshafts from turning.
5 Unscrew the bolt (1) from the end of the primary shaft (Fig. 6.51).
6 Unscrew and remove the reverse lamp switch.
7 Extract the circlip (2) from the reverse dog (3) and then push the dog slightly towards the differential (Fig. 6.52).
8 Withdraw the 5th speed selector fork (4) and shaft, but only move them a short distance.
9 Remove the 5th speed synchro from the secondary shaft and then turn the selector shaft and fork through 90° towards the bottom of the transmission, so that the interlock ball for reverse dog can be removed.
10 Remove the 5th speed selector shaft and fork from the transmission, retain the interlock ball.
11 Remove 5th speed synchro, the spring and baulk ring then the 5th speed sliding gear, the needle roller bearing, spacer and flange from the primary shaft.
12 Unbolt and detach the 5th gear housing and tilt it upwards and forwards to remove.
13 Unlock and remove the speedo drive worm nut and then take the spring washer and 5th speed fixed gear from the secondary shaft.
14 The gear cluster can now be removed from the transmission casing.
15 If the speedometer drive gear must be removed, the only way to do it is to break it up.
16 When fitting the new speedometer drive gear, make sure that the lugs have fully entered their location.
17 Reassembly is a reversal of dismantling, smear the shaft nut and bolt threads with thread locking fluid and tighten to the specified torque.

18 Transmission (type NG5) – overhaul

1 This later type of transmission used on Gordini models is covered in Chapter 13, Supplement.

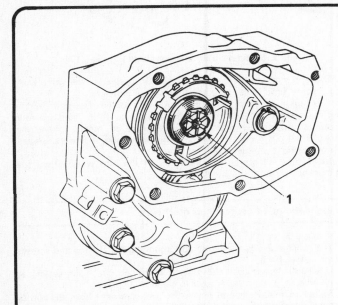

Fig. 6.51 Unscrewing primary shaft bolt type HA1 transmission (Sec 17)

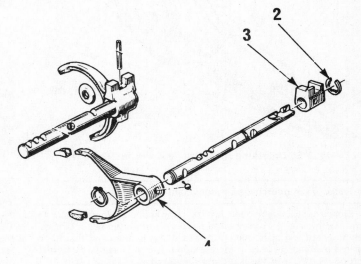

Fig. 6.52 Selector components (Sec 17)

2 Circlip   3 Reverse dog
4 5th speed selector fork

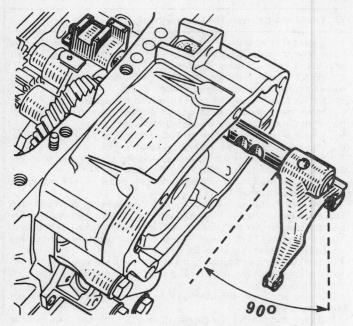

Fig. 6.53 5th speed selector shaft and fork (Sec 17)

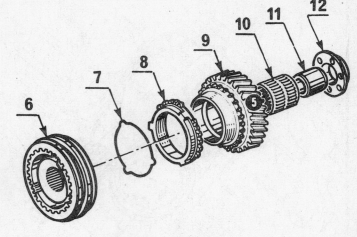

Fig. 6.54 5th speed gear components (Sec 17)

6	Synchro unit	10	Needle roller bearing
7	Spring	11	Spacer
8	Baulk ring	12	Flange
9	5th speed sliding gear		

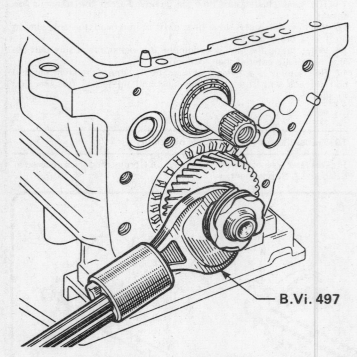

Fig. 6.55 Unlocking speedo drive worm nut (Sec 17)

Fig. 6.56 Speedo driven gear lugs (D) (Sec 17)

3   The end bush on the gearchange rod is changed in the same way. At the same time make sure the bias spring is fitted.

4   The bulkhead bush is more difficult to replace. The gearchange tube must be removed from under the facia. It is fixed by four setscrews. Again the gearchange rod must be halved under the bonnet. Poke out the bush and push in a new one, inside its keeper. Reassembly is a simple reverse process.

5   Make sure all grommets are fitted to the bodywork where the shaft passes through the bulkhead.

19 Facia panel gearchange mechanism

1   Sloppy gear changes and rattling gear knobs are usually due to worn bushes. The gearchange rod passes through two nylon bushes, both mounted in rubber, one on the radiator or centre cross brace and one in a gearchange tube in the bulkhead. The rod itself has a further bush on its end, over the lever into the gearbox.

2   To replace the cross brace bushes on the radiator, disconnect the gearchange rod in its middle and push out the rod. Lever out the nylon bush through the rubber one and discard both. Lubricate the new nylon and rubber bush as a pair with washing up liquid. Insert one into the other and then push them into the bracket. Reassemble the gearchange rod.

20 Floor-mounted gearchange mechanism

Four-speed type

1   The mechanism is dismantled by removing the circlips and screws shown in Fig. 6.58.

2   Occasionally lubricate the moving parts and check the setting of the reverse stop plate (refer also to Section 11).

3   Select reverse gear and check the measurement from the top of the stop button on the end of the gearshift lever to the bottom of the stop plate (see Fig. 6.59 – dimension A).

4   If the measurement is not within the specified range adjust the stop plate height using washers placed between the stop plate and the body (dimension R).

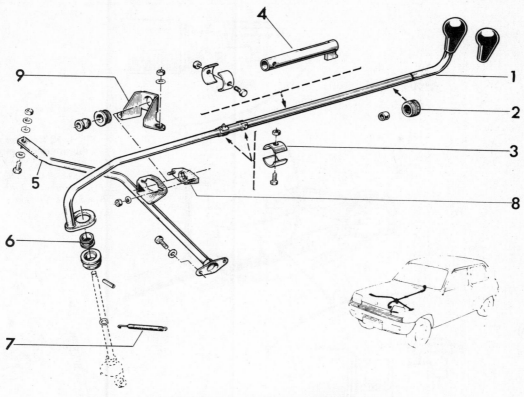

Fig. 6.57 Fascia panel gearchange lever (Sec 19)

1	Gearchange control	4	Tube	7	Anti-rattle spring	9	Top bush bracket
2	Bulkhead bush	5	Crossmember (except	8	Top bush bracket		(R1221)
3	Clamp		R1221)		(except R1221)		
		6	Bush				

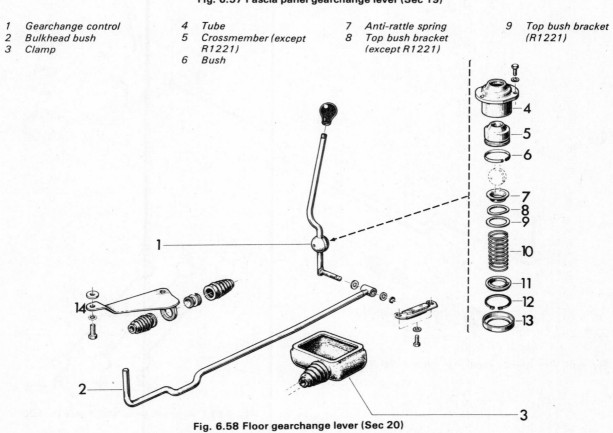

Fig. 6.58 Floor gearchange lever (Sec 20)

1	Control lever	5	Dust cover	9	Spacer	12	Circlip
2	Secondary rod	6	Clip	10	Spring	13	Base cup
3	Boot	7	Cup	11	Seal	14	Bracket
4	Balljoint cap	8	Wave washer				

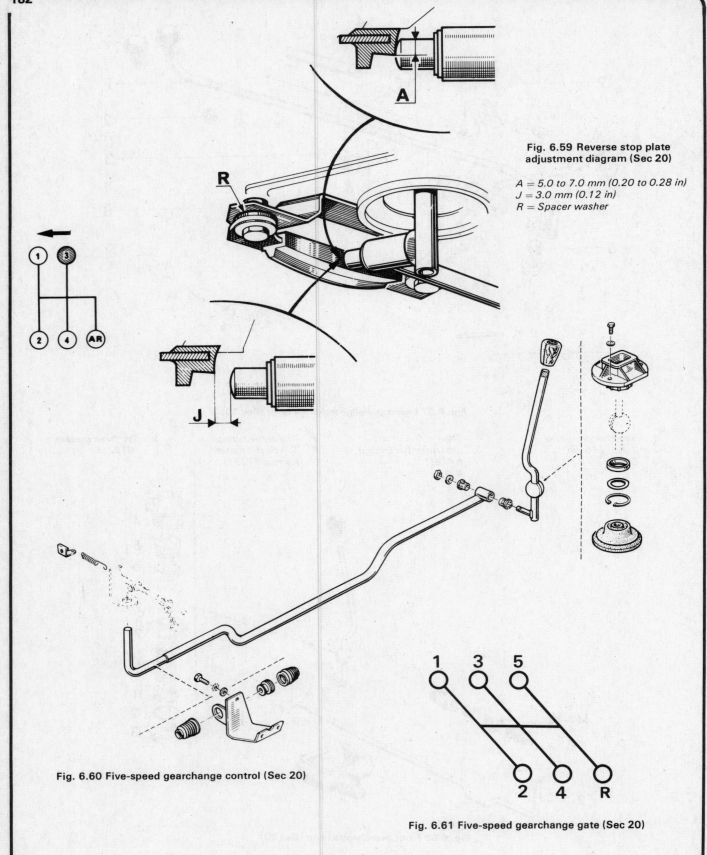

Fig. 6.59 Reverse stop plate adjustment diagram (Sec 20)

$A = 5.0$ to 7.0 mm (0.20 to 0.28 in)
$J = 3.0$ mm (0.12 in)
$R = $ Spacer washer

Fig. 6.60 Five-speed gearchange control (Sec 20)

Fig. 6.61 Five-speed gearchange gate (Sec 20)

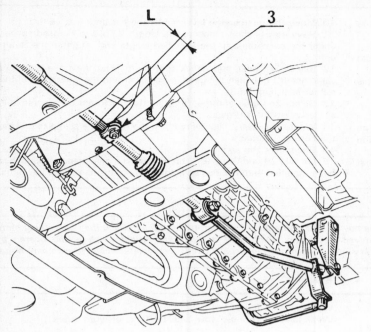

Fig. 6.62 Five-speed gearchange control (Sec 20)

3   Clamp bolt
L   Length of exposed splines – 12.0 mm (0.47 in)

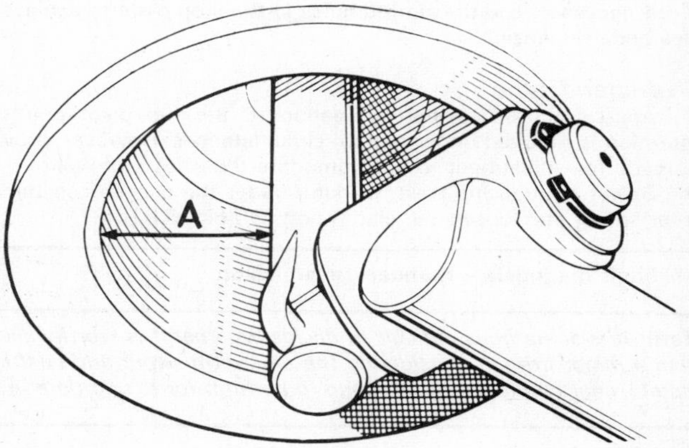

Fig. 6.63 Gearchange lever setting diagram (Sec 20)

A = 7.0 mm (0.28 in)

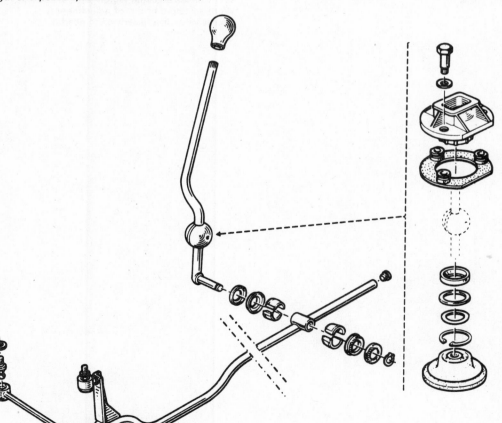

Fig. 6.64 Gearchange linkage – R1229 and Gordini (Sec 20)

5   Now select 3rd gear position and press the lever over toward the 1st-2nd gear position.

6   With the gear lever in this position measure the distance (J) between the stop plate and the end of the stop button which should be as specified.

7   If necessary use the slotted holes in the stop plate to achieve this clearance dimension.

Five-speed type

8   Apart from occasional lubrication of the rod pivot points, no attention is required under normal circumstances. However, provision is made for adjustment to accommodate the effects of wear.

9   Select neutral and then, working under the car, detach the gear lever spring and loosen the clamp bolt (3) (Fig. 6.62).

10   Move the gearchange lever inside the car until it is vertical.

11   Have an assistant measure the length (L) of the exposed splines under the car. Adjust to the specified length and retighten the clamp bolt.

12   Select 3rd gear and check that there is at least the specified clearance (A) between the gearchange lever and the inner edge of the rubber seal (Fig. 6.63).

13   Select 2nd gear and then 5th gear to check that the clearance is as described for 3rd gear.

14   Where necessary, slightly readjust the rod at the clamp to provide the correct clearance.

15   Reconnect the spring.

16   On R1229 and Gordini Turbo models, the gearchange linkage has been modified and includes balljoints. Do not dismantle the balljoints.

21 Fault diagnosis – manual transmission

Note: *It is sometimes difficult to decide whether it is worthwhile removing and dismantling the gearbox for a fault which may be nothing more than a minor irritant, considering the amount of work and cost involved. Gearboxes which howl, or where the synchromesh can be 'beaten' by a quick gear change, may continue to perform for a long time in this state. A worn gearbox usually needs a complete rebuild to eliminate noise.*

Symptom	Reason(s)
Ineffective synchromesh. Jumps out of one or more gears (on drive or overrun)	Worn synchro units Weak lockball springs, worn selector forks or worn gears
Noisy, rough, whining and vibration	Oil level low or incorrect grade Worn bearings and gears Crownwheel and bevel pinion out of adjustment
Difficulty in engaging gears	Worn or maladjusted clutch Worn selectors or out of adjustment Excessive or insufficient oil in gearbox

Chapter 7 Automatic transmission

Contents

Specifications

General
Automatic models	R1225, R1229, R1395 and R1399
Transmission type identification numbers	4139-40 and 4139-43

Speed change points (typical)
First and second:
Light throttle (1st to 2nd)	20 kph (12 mph)
Full throttle (1st to 2nd)	55 kph (34 mph)
Kickdown (2nd to 1st)	50 kph (31 mph)

Second and third:
Light throttle (2nd to 3rd)	35 kph (22 mph)
Full throttle (2nd to 3rd)	100 kph (62 mph)
Kickdown (3rd to 2nd)	85 kph (53 mph)

Gear ratios
1st	2.26:1
2nd	1.40:1
3rd	0.97:1
Reverse	1.94:1
Final drive	3.56:1

Fluid type/specification
Dexron type ATF (Duckhams Uni-Matic or D-Matic)

Fluid capacity
From dry	5 litres (8.75 Imp pts, 5.28 US qts)
At routine fluid change	2.5 litres (4.4 Imp pts, 2.64 US qts)

Torque wrench settings
	Nm	lbf ft
Selector rod clamp nut	37	27
Fluid sump pan bolts	8	6
Hydraulic distributor bolts	7	5
Converter-to-driveplate bolts	34	25
Driveplate-to-crankshaft flange bolts	68	50

1 General description

The type 4139 automatic transmission incorporates a three-speed epicyclic geartrain and a hydraulic torque converter.

The gear selector lever is floor-mounted with a safety catch to prevent unintentional selection of first gear hold or reverse. Gear selection is electronically controlled.

The main components of the automatic transmission and their function are as follows.

Torque converter
Provides a smooth fluid drive connection between the engine and the geartrain.

Final drive
Hypoid bevel crownwheel and pinion, and differential gear for transmitting the drive from the gear output shaft to the roadwheels.

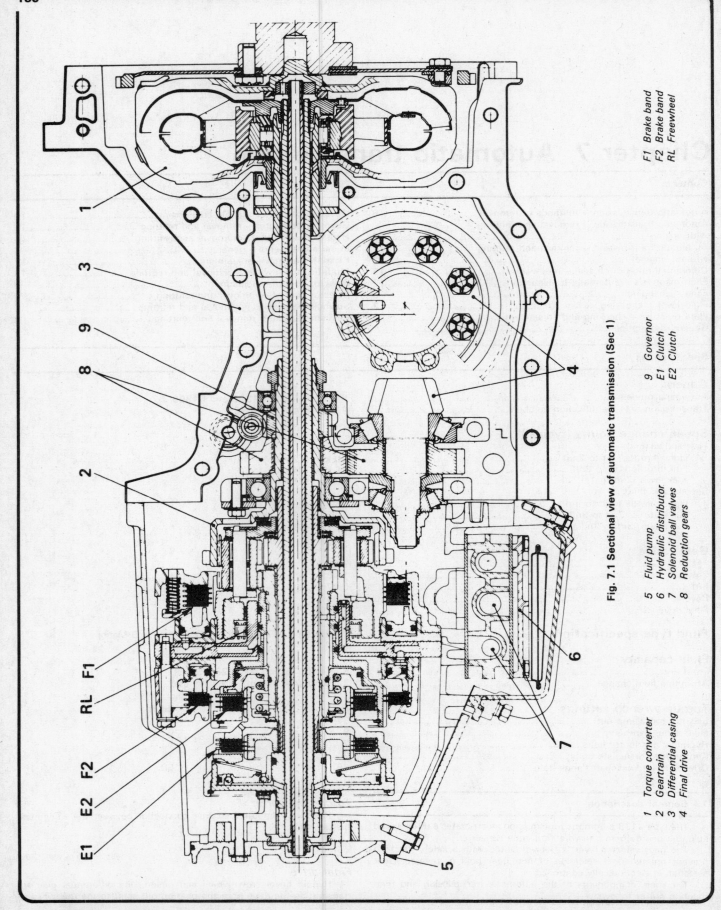

Fig. 7.1 Sectional view of automatic transmission (Sec 1)

1 Torque converter
2 Geartrain
3 Differential casing
4 Final drive
5 Fluid pump
6 Hydraulic distributor
7 Solenoid ball valves
8 Reduction gears
9 Governor
E1 Clutch
E2 Clutch
F1 Brake band
F2 Brake band
RL Freewheel

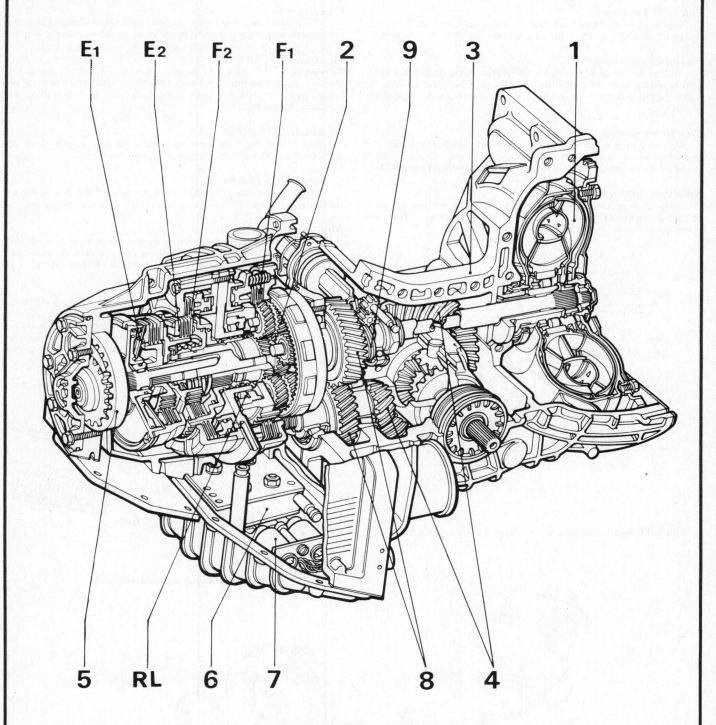

Fig. 7.2 Cut-away view of automatic transmission (Sec 1)

1	Torque converter	5	Fluid pump	9	Governor	F1	Brake
2	Geartrain	6	Hydraulic distributor	E1	Clutch	F2	Brake
3	Differential housing	7	Solenoid ball valves	E2	Clutch	RL	Geartrain freewheel
4	Crownwheel and pinion	8	Reduction gear cluster				

Epicyclic geartrain

Operated by mechanical, hydraulic and electric control elements, the geartrain provides three forward speed ratios and one reverse.

Governor/computer

This assembly gives the signal for gearchanging depending upon vehicle road speed and engine torque loadings. The governor is really a low output alternator driven by a worm gear from the final drive pinion.

Kickdown switch

This switch is operated by the accelerator pedal at the extreme end of its travel. The switch earths a circuit in the computer which causes a lower gear to be selected immediately for rapid acceleration.

Solenoid-operated ball valves

These valves open or close the hydraulic passages for gear changing purposes. The valves receive instruction from the governor/computer in the form of electrical impulses.

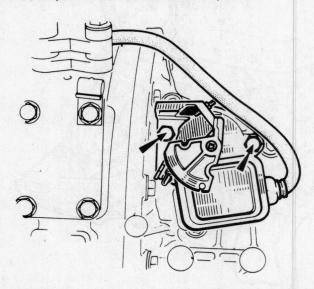

Fig. 7.3 Governor/computer – mounting bolts arrowed (Sec 1)

Freewheel

This allows torque to be transmitted between the engine and the roadwheels without any braking effect being available from the engine.

Fluid pump

Engine driven, the pump supplies pressurised fluid to supply the torque converter, to lubricate the gears and for use in the transmission brakes and clutches. The fluid pump is located at the rear of the transmission casing.

Hydraulic distributor

This varies the fluid pressure to suit varying engine loads as monitored by the vacuum capsule and pilot valve.

Clutches and brakes

These are of the multi-disc oil bath type. They are hydraulic receivers which lock or release certain units in the epicyclic geartrain.

Multi-function switch

The cam in this switch is moved by the speed selector lever and opens or closes various electrical circuits which switch those for the starter circuit, reverse lamp circuit and the solenoid ball valves.

Maintenance

The maintenance and adjustment operations described here should be all that is necessary to keep the transmission in perfect working order, but dismantling and repair when necessary should be left to your dealer who will have the necessary special tools and equipment. Removal and installation of the transmission is well within the capabilities of the home mechanic.

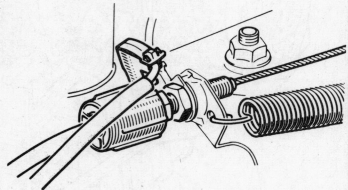

Fig. 7.4 Kickdown switch (Sec 1)

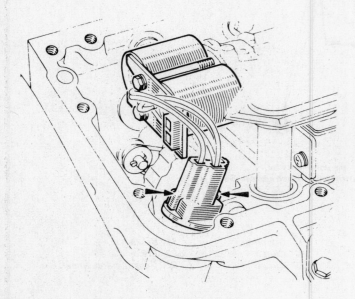

Fig. 7.5 Solenoid-operated ball valves (Sec 1)
Wiring plug retaining clips arrowed

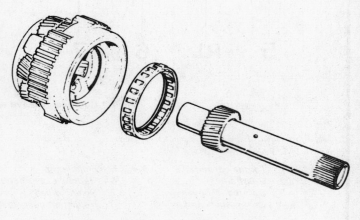

Fig. 7.6 Freewheel (Sec 1)

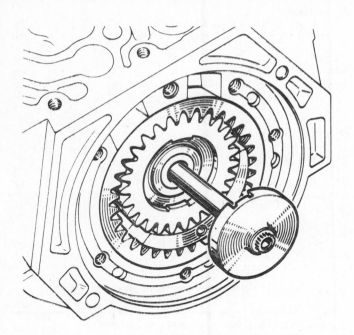

Fig. 7.7 Fluid pump (Sec 1)

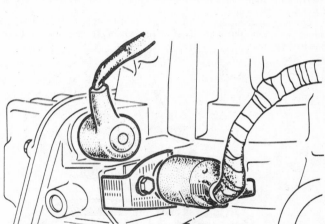

Fig. 7.8 Hydraulic distributor (Sec 1)

2 Fluid level – checking

Cold

1 If the transmission is cold, start the engine with the selector lever in P (park) and let it run for two or three minutes to allow the torque converter to fill.

2 Withdraw the dipstick, wipe it clean, re-insert it and withdraw it for the second time (photo). Check that the fluid level is within the cut-out on the edge of the dipstick at the COLD mark (photo). Top-up as necessary, but do not overfill.

Hot

3 Checking the fluid hot means after the car has been operating for at least half an hour on the road. With the engine idling, withdraw the dipstick, wipe it, re-insert it and withdraw it for the second time. The fluid level should be within the cut-out at the HOT mark on the dipstick. Top-up as necessary, but do not overfill.

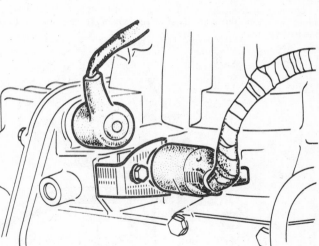

Fig. 7.9 Multi-function switch (Sec 1)

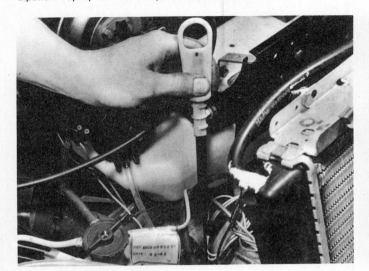

2.2a Withdrawing the dipstick

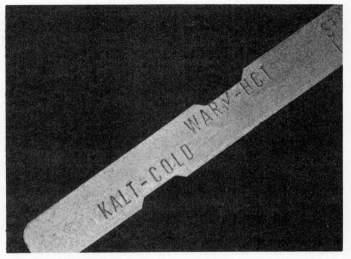

2.2b Dipstick markings

3   Fluid – changing

1   The automatic transmission fluid should be changed at the intervals recommended in Routine Maintenance. On a new vehicle the fluid will be changed under the terms of the first service schedule at between 500 and 1000 miles (800 and 1600 km).
2   Have the transmission fluid at normal operating temperature.
3   Remove the dipstick, unscrew the drain plug and allow the fluid to drain completely.
4   Refit the drain plug and refill with fresh fluid through the dipstick guide tube. When filling, use a funnel with an integral filter as it is very important not to allow any grit to enter the system.
5   Once the specified quantity of fluid has been poured into the transmission, check the level as previously described.

4   Selector control – adjustment

1   With the selector lever in P (Park) it should be tilting forward through 10°. If necessary move the bearing brackets within the limits of their elongated bolt holes to achieve this setting.
2   Now set the selector lever in neutral.
3   Working under the car, withdraw the shield and seal from the base of the selector lever.
4   Check that the gap (A) is as specified in Fig. 7.10. If it is not, release the clamp nut and adjust as necessary. Tighten the nut to the specified torque.

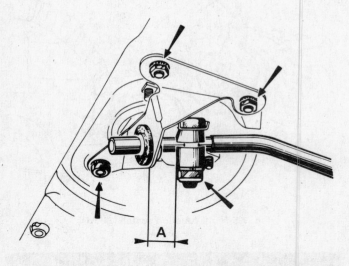

Fig. 7.10 Selector control rod clamp (Sec 4)

A = 16.0 to 18.0 mm (0.63 to 0.71 in)

5   Selector control – removal and refitting

1   Set the control lever in neutral.
2   Working under the car, extract the circlip from the end of the control finger.
3   Release the control rod clamp nut and the bracket nuts.
4   Working inside the car, remove the selector gate, the selector lever housing and the selector lever support assembly.
5   Refitting is a reversal of removal, adjust as described in the preceding Section.

6   In-car adjustments – general

The following adjustments and other operations will only require carrying out if the symptoms suggested in Fault Diagnosis indicate the need.

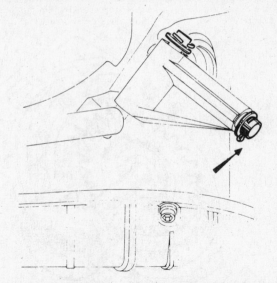

Fig. 7.11 Selector rod control finger circlip (Sec 5)

7   Solenoid ball valves – removal and refitting

1   Drain the transmission fluid.
2   Remove the automatic transmission undershield.
3   Unscrew the fixing bolts and remove the sump pan.
4   Unclip the wiring plug.
5   Unbolt the valve retaining plate and withdraw the ball valves. Do not mix them up and record their original locations.
6   Refitting is a reversal of removal.

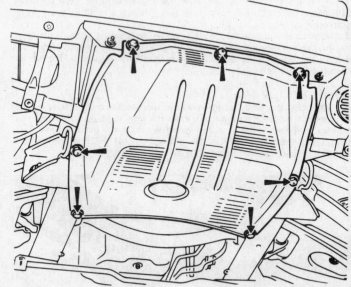

Fig. 7.12 Undershield retaining bolts (Sec 7)

8   Fluid pressure – checking and adjustment

1   Before carrying out this test, have the transmission fluid hot after a mimimum of half an hour's operation on the road.
2   A suitable pressure gauge and union must be available for screwing into the tapped hole after removal of the fluid pan plug (1) Fig. 7.13.
3   Raise the front of the car so that the roadwheels are clear of the ground. Start the engine and run at 2500 rpm in 'Drive'. The fluid pressure indicated on the gauge should be between 52 and 55 lbf/in² (3.6 and 3.8 bars).

4   Adjustment should be made where necessary by turning the screw on the vacuum capsule. One complete turn of the screw increases the pressure by 0.1 bar (1.5 lbf/in²).

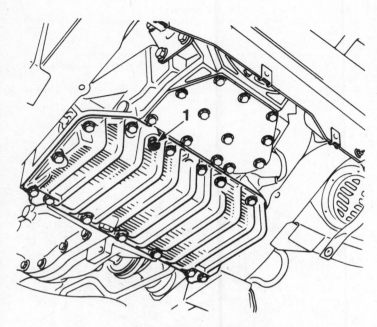

Fig. 7.13 Fluid pressure take-off plug (1) (Sec 8)

9   Vacuum capsule – removal and refitting

1   Drain the transmission fluid.
2   Unscrew the capsule clamp bolt and remove the capsule.
3   Refitting is a reversal of removal, but use a new seal.
4   Refill the transmission with fluid and then carry out the pressure test previously described, adjusting the capsule screw if necessary.
5   It should be noted that on R1225 models the vacuum capsule has no connection with the inlet manifold.

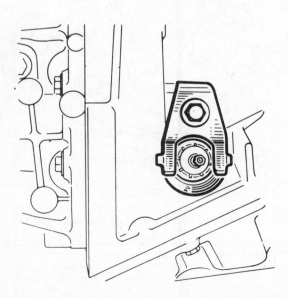

Fig. 7.14 Vacuum capsule and retaining clamp (Sec 9)

10   Governor/computer – cable adjustment

1   Check that the cable release nut (G) is screwed fully in at the governor end (Fig. 7.15).
2   Depress the accelerator pedal fully and then, working at the carburettor, tension the cable by turning the sleeve stop nut until the quadrant (S) at the governor is against its stop (Fig. 7.16).
3   Tighten the carburettor cable adjuster locknut.
4   Working at the governor/computer, slacken the cable sleeve nut (G) until a clearance (J) is obtained between the quadrant (S) and the stop peg (E) when the accelerator pedal is fully depressed with the throttle butterfly valve wide open (Figs 7.15 and 7.16). Tighten the cable sleeve locknut.

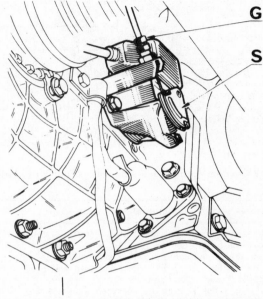

Fig. 7.15 Governor/computer cable adjuster sleeve (G) and quadrant (S) (Sec 10)

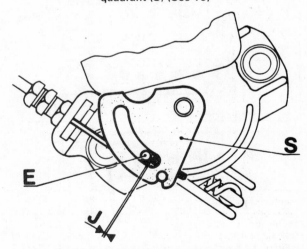

Fig. 7.16 Governor/computer setting diagram (Secs 10 and 11)

E   Stop peg   *S   Quadrant*
J = 0.4 mm (0.016 in)

11   Governor/computer – removal and refitting

1   Release the expansion bottle and move it to one side to provide better access to the governor/computer.
2   Disconnect the cable from the quadrant (S) (Fig. 7.16).
3   Remove the two governor mounting bolts.

4   Disconnect the bridge and junction box.
5   Extract the two harness fixing screws.
6   Remove the governor/computer complete with wiring harness.
7   Refitting is a reversal of removal, adjust the cable as described in the preceding Section.

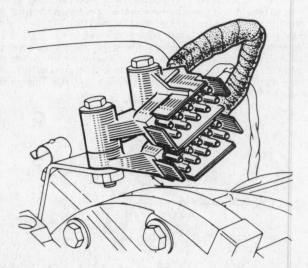

Fig. 7.17 Governor/computer wiring harness and plugs (Sec 11)

12 Kickdown switch – adjustment

1   The kickdown switch is located on the rocker cover.
2   Remove the switch cover.
3   Release the locknut on the cable sleeve adjuster.
4   Turn the switch nut so that the accelerator cable will move the stop collar (B) through distance (A) when the accelerator pedal is fully depressed (Fig. 7.18). Tighten the sleeve adjuster and also the locknut and refit the switch cover.

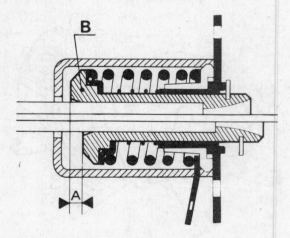

Fig. 7.18 Kickdown switch setting diagram (Sec 12)

A = 3.0 to 4.0 mm (0.12 to 0.16 in)
B   Stop collar

13 Multi-function switch – removal and refitting

1   The multi-function switch is located on the transmission.
2   Pull the connector from the switch.
3   Unscrew the switch clamp bolt and withdraw the switch.
4   Refitting is a reversal of removal.

14 Hydraulic distributor – removal and refitting

1   Drain the transmission fluid.
2   Remove the shield from under the transmission.
3   Remove the sump pan and gasket.
4   Unbolt and remove the filter gauze/seal assembly. Retain the fluid suction pipe seal.
5   Pull the wiring socket from the switch.
6   Remove the solenoid ball valves, as described earlier.
7   Unscrew only those bolts arrowed in Fig. 7.20 and withdraw the hydraulic distributor.
8   Refitting is a reversal of removal, but use a new sump gasket and tighten all bolts to the specified torque.

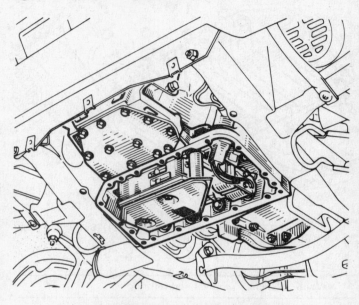

Fig. 7.19 Fluid sump pan removed (Sec 14)

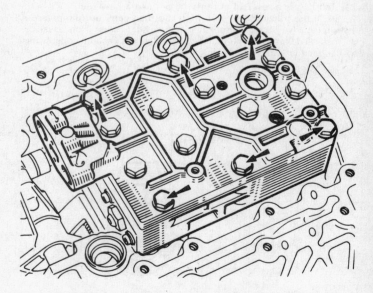

Fig. 7.20 Hydraulic distributor securing bolts (Sec 14)

15 Differential ring nut oil seal – renewal

1   Drain the transmission fluid and remove the driveshaft, as described in Chapter 8.
2   Mark the setting of the ring nut in relation to the transmission casing.

3   Remove the ring nut lockplate.
4   Using a suitable pin wrench, unscrew and remove the ring nut and oil seal.
5   Renew the oil seal and refit the ring nut to its orginal position. Fit the lockplate.
6   Install the driveshaft and refill the transmission with fluid.

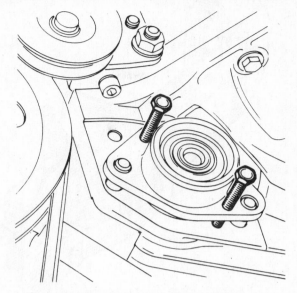

Fig. 7.22 Removing camshaft bearing (Sec 17)

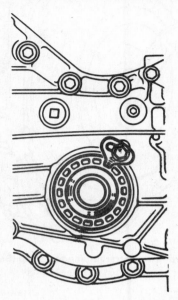

Fig. 7.21 Differential ring nut lockplate (Sec 15)

16 Automatic transmission – methods of removal

The automatic transmission may be removed on its own, leaving the engine in the car, or lifted out complete with engine. Both methods are described in the following Sections.

17 Automatic transmission – removal and refitting without engine

1   Release the cooling system expansion bottle from its mounting and move it to rest on the engine. Remove the camshaft pulley drivebelt. Disconnect the battery, remove the air cleaner and the starter motor.
2   An extended camshaft is fitted to the Type 810 engine used in conjunction with automatic transmission and, in consequence, the camshaft pulley and bearing must be removed before further work is carried out.
3   The camshaft bearing can be drawn off using two suitable bolts (M6 x 50 with 35.0 mm thread length).
4   Disconnect all the wiring harness from the transmission. Drain the transmission fluid.
5   Disconnect the lead from the governor/computer.
6   Disconnect the speedometer cable from the transmission.
7   Raise the front end of the car and remove the roadwheels.
8   Remove the brake calipers and pads and tie them up out of the way without disconnecting the hydraulic hoses.
9   Using a balljoint splitter, disconnect the tie-rod ends from the steering arms.
10   Remove the steering rack housing, taking great care to mark the location of the height setting shims.
11   Again using the balljoint splitter, separate the upper suspension arm balljoints from the stub axle carriers.
12   Pull the tops of the stub axle carriers outwards to free the driveshafts from the transmission.
13   Disconnect the gear selector control rod.
14   Remove the shield plate from the lower face of the torque converter bellhousing.
15   Unscrew and remove the three bolts that connect the driveplate on the crankshaft to the torque converter (photo). It will be necessary

17.15 Unscrewing torque converter/driveplate bolts

to turn the crankshaft to bring the bolts into view in the aperture left by removal of the bellhousing shield plate.
16   Note the torque converter/driveplate alignment marks (Fig. 7.25). Failure to align them correctly will result in the engine timing being 120° out.
17   Place a trolley jack under the transmission.
18   Unbolt and remove the front crossmember.
19   Disconnect the transmission mountings.
20   Using a hacksaw, cut off the web (A) Fig. 7.27 to ease removal of the unit.
21   Unscrew and remove the torque converter-to-engine connecting bolts.
22   Support the engine on a second jack or use a hoist.
23   Withdraw the transmission from the engine, keeping the torque converter fully engaged within the converter housing.
24   Lower the transmission and remove it from under the car. The car will require raising under its jacking points to be able to do this.
25   Refitting is a reversal of removal, but use a new O-ring (B) – Fig. 7.28 – and make sure that the two positioning dowels are in position.
26   When offering the transmission to the engine, raise the engine slightly to facilitate connection. Smear the centre boss on the torque converter with molybdenum disulphide grease.
27   Reconnect the stub axles to the suspension arm balljoints and as they are pushed into position, engage the driveshafts with the transmission.

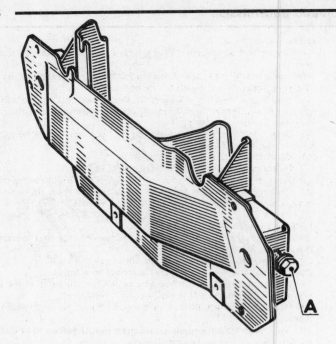

Fig. 7.23 Front crossmember (Sec 17)

A   Side-member bolt

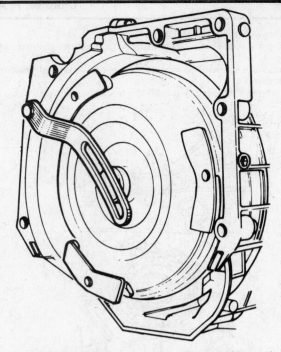

Fig. 7.24 Torque converter retained by strap (Sec 17)

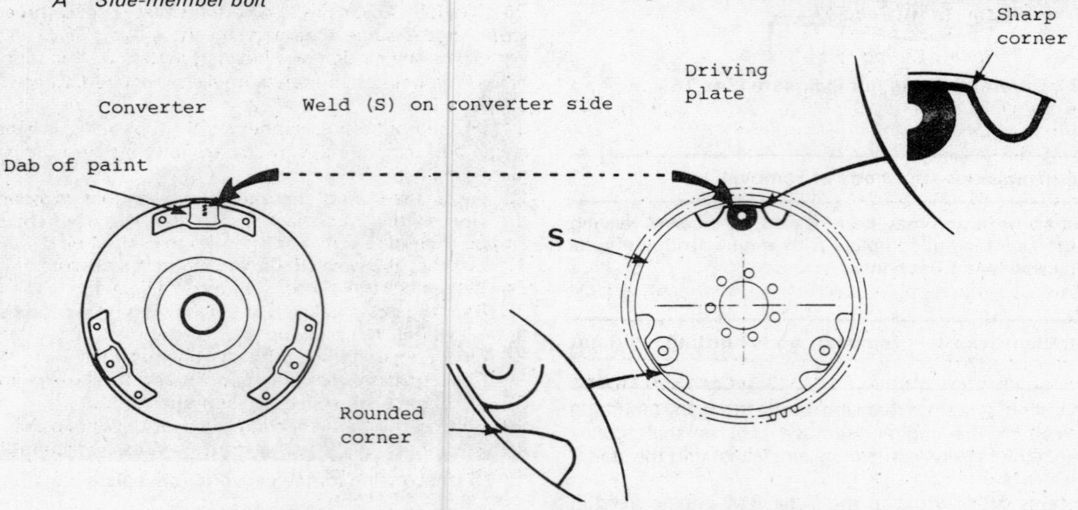

Converter   Weld (S) on converter side

Dab of paint

Driving plate

Sharp corner

S

Rounded corner

Fig. 7.25 Driveplate/torque converter alignment marks (Sec 17)

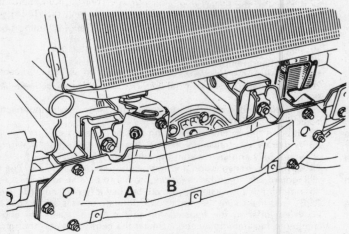

Fig. 7.26 Front crossmember retaining bolts (Sec 17)

A   Bolt to remove   B   Bolt to slacken only

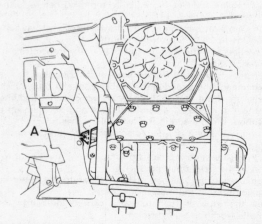

Fig. 7.27 Cut web (A) flush to ease transmission removal (Sec 17)

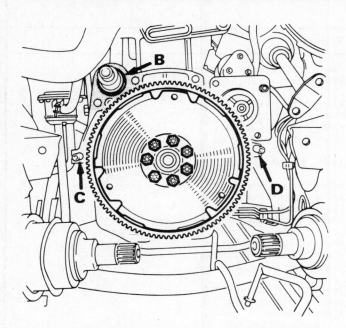

Fig. 7.28 Check that the locating dowels (C and D) are in position (Sec 17)

Renew O-ring (B)

28 Refit the brake calipers and the disc pads. Apply the brake pedal hard several times to position the pads against the discs.
29 Refit the steering rack housing with the original shims.
30 Reconnect the tie-rod ends to the steering arms.
31 Reconnect the speedometer cable and all electrical leads.
32 Refit the camshaft bearing and pulley. Then fit the drivebelt and tension it correctly.
33 Move the expansion bottle back to its original position.
34 Refill the transmission with fluid. Reconnect the battery and refit all other components.

18 Automatic transmission – removal and installation with engine

1   Disconnect the battery.
2   Disconnect the lamp leads and remove the front shield.
3   Remove the radiator grille.
4   Remove the headlamps.
5   Remove the bonnet and the bonnet lock.
6   Remove the radiator grille cross support.
7   Unbolt and remove the shield from under the automatic transmission.
8   Remove the battery cover and the battery.
9   Drain the cooling system.
10 Disconnect the electrical leads from the electric radiator fan and from the fan thermostatic switch.
11 Remove one mounting bolt from each bracket at the base of the radiator. The other mounting bolts need only be released, as they engage in slots.
12 Remove the radiator and the expansion bottle together.
13 Remove the air filter.
14 Disconnect all electrical leads, hoses and control wires from the engine.
15 Using a balljoint splitter, disconnect the tie-rod end balljoints from the steering arms on the stub axle carriers.
16 Unbolt the flexible coupling at the lower end of the steering column shaft. Retain the rubber cushion from the centre of the pinion coupling flange.
17 Unbolt and remove the steering rack housing, noting the location of the mounting shims.
18 Drain the automatic transmission fluid.
19 Disconnect the speed selector control rod.
20 Raise the front end of the vehicle and remove the roadwheels.
21 Remove the calipers from the discs and tie them up out of the way. There is no need to disconnect the hydraulic hoses.
22 Using a balljoint splitter, disconnect the suspension upper arm balljoint from the stub axle carrier.
23 Pull the tops of the stub axle carriers outwards and release the driveshafts from the transmission.
24 Unscrew the engine mounting nuts from the body.
25 Fit a suitable lifting sling and attach it to a hoist.
26 Unbolt and remove the front crossmember (six bolts at the front, one entered from the left-hand side-member).
27 Hoist the engine/transmission carefully out of the engine compartment.
28 The transmission is removed from, and reconnected to, the engine as described in the preceding Section.
29 To install the combined assembly, first tie the speed selector control rod to the left-hand side of the engine compartment.
30 Carefully lower the engine/transmission into the engine compartment, at the same time aligning the inboard ends of the driveshafts with the transmission and locating the engine mounting studs in their holes. The help of an assistant will be required. Keep the transmission supported.
31 Fit the front crossmember, bolting up the right-hand side, then the single bolt from the side-member, finishing with the bolts on the left-hand side.
32 Lower the front of the transmission so that its mountings slide into the slots in the crossmember. Tighten the front mountings and the engine mounting nuts and then remove the hoist.
33 Connect the driveshafts with the transmission.
34 Reconnect the suspension arm balljoints.
35 Refit the brake calipers and pads. Apply the footbrake hard several times to bring the pads up against the discs.
36 Refit the steering box with the original shims.
37 Reconnect the flexible coupling and the tie-rod end balljoints.
38 Reconnect the speed selector control rod.
39 Bolt on the roadwheels and lower the car to the ground.
40 Reconnect all hoses, electrical wires and control cables to the engine and transmission.
41 Fit the air cleaner.
42 Install the radiator with its expansion bottle.
43 Fit the windscreen washer reservoir and connect the radiator tie-rod with the washer reservoir bracket to the steering rack housing.
44 Connect the hoses and electrical leads to the radiator.
45 Install the battery.
46 Fit the front shield and radiator grille cross support.
47 Connect the lamp wires.
48 Install the radiator grille, the bonnet, the bonnet lock and cable.
49 Fill the engine and transmission with the correct grade and quantity of oil.
50 Fill the cooling system.
51 Adjust the speed selector control if necessary.

19 Fault diagnosis – automatic transmission

Symptom	Reason(s)
Creep in N	Selector linkage requires adjustment Internal clutch fault
Slip when moving off in forward or reverse gears	Incorrect fluid level Incorrect fluid pressure Faulty pressure regulator Faulty torque converter
Slip when moving off in forward gear	Faulty freewheel
Slip when changing gear	Incorrect fluid pressure Faulty hydraulic distributor Faulty pressure regulator Internal clutch or brake fault
Snatch when changing gear	Governor cable adjustment Faulty hydraulic distributor Faulty pressure regulator
Incorrect speed change points	Incorrectly adjusted governor cable or kickdown switch Faulty computer Faulty solenoid ball valve Faulty kickdown switch Faulty multi-function switch
No forward or reverse drive	Incorrectly adjusted selector linkage Faulty pressure regulator Faulty fluid pump Faulty torque converter
No drive in third or reverse gears	Faulty hydraulic distributor
No drive in A or first gear hold	Internal clutch fault
No reverse or engine braking in first gear hold	Faulty hydraulic distributor Internal brake fault
No first speed drive	Faulty solenoid ball valve Faulty hydraulic distributor Faulty freewheel Faulty multi-function switch
No second speed drive	Faulty solenoid ball valve Faulty hydraulic distributor Internal brake fault
No third speed drive	Faulty governor/computer Faulty solenoid ball valve Faulty hydraulic distributor
Will not change out of first speed	Faulty governor/computer Faulty hydraulic distributor
Will not change out of third speed	Blown system fuse Faulty governor/computer Faulty solenoid ball valve Faulty hydraulic distributor
'Park' cannot be engaged	Selector linkage requires adjustment Faulty manual valve mechanical control
Smoky exhaust	Split vacuum hose or faulty vacuum capsule
Starter inoperative	Selector linkage requires adjustment Faulty multi-function switch
Reverse lamps inoperative	Faulty multi-function switch

Chapter 8 Driveshafts, hubs, wheels and tyres

For modifications, and information applicable to later models, see Supplement at end of manual

Contents

Specifications

Driveshafts

Type .... Open, tubular with spider coupling or four balljoint at the ends, according to model

Coupling lubricant type:
- Spider type .... Elf S747 (Duckhams LBM 10)
- Four-ball type .... SJW oil

Front hub bearings

Type .... Inner and outer ball with single lip or double seal on inner bearing
Lubricant type .... Multi-purpose lithium based grease (Duckhams LB 10)

Rear hub bearings

Type .... Inner and outer tapered roller bearings with single lip or double seal on inner bearing
Lubricant type .... Multi-purpose lithium based grease (Duckhams LB 10)
Bearing endfloat .... 0.01 and 0.05 mm (0.0004 and 0.002 in)

Roadwheels

Type .... Pressed steel or light alloy, according to model
Size:
- Pressed steel .... 4, 4½ or 5½, according to model
- Alloy 5¼

Tyres

Type .... Radial ply

Pressures (cold)

	Front	Rear
Normal use:		
135 SR 13	1.6 bar (24 lbf/in^2)	2.0 bar (29 lbf/in^2)
135 HR 13	1.7 bar (25 lbf/in^2)	1.9 bar (28 lbf/in^2)
145 SR 13	1.6 bar (24 lbf/in^2)	2.0 bar (29 lbf/in^2)
145 HR 13	1.7 bar (25 lbf/in^2)	1.9 bar (28 lbf/in^2)
155/70 SR 13	1.7 bar (25 lbf/in^2)	1.9 bar (28 lbf/in^2)
155/70 HR 13	1.7 bar (25 lbf/in^2)	1.8 bar (26 lbf/in^2)
175/60 HR 13	1.7 bar (25 lbf/in^2)	1.8 bar (26 lbf/in^2)
High speeds or heavy loads	Increase rear tyre pressures by 0.3 bar (4lbf/in^2)	

Torque wrench settings

	Nm	lbf ft
Driveshaft nut (except R1223 and 122B)	117	86
R1223 and 122B	156	115
Roadwheel nuts or bolts	58	43
Suspension upper balljoint nut	34	25
Suspension lower balljoint nut	49	36
Steering tie-rod end balljoint nut	33	24
Caliper mounting bolts	64	47

1 General description

The driveshafts which transmit the power from the transmission to the front roadwheels are of tubular, open type with a 'spider' type coupling at the roadwheel end.

On all models except the R1223 (Gordini) and 122B (Gordini Turbo) the driveshaft joint at the inner end is also of Spider type. On the two models mentioned the inboard joint is of four ball type. Refer also to Section 3, paragraph 60.

The front hubs run on an inner and outer ball-race.

The rear hubs run on inner and outer tapered roller bearings.

The roadwheels are generally of pressed-steel type with the exception of certain special models which have wheels of light alloy construction.

Tyres of radial ply construction are fitted, the section depending upon the model and date of production.

2   Driveshaft – removal and refitting

1   Remove the trim plate from the roadwheel.
2   Raise the side of the car being worked on and support it securely.
3   Remove the roadwheel.
4   Have an assistant apply the footbrake hard and unscrew the driveshaft nut (photo). This is very tight and will require the use of a long knuckle bar. Remove the washer (photo).
5   On cars having drum front brakes, disconnect the hydraulic hose clip (1) – see Fig. 8.1.
6   On cars with disc front brakes, unbolt the caliper and tie it up out of the way.
7   On R1223 and 122B models, drive out the roll pins from the inboard driveshaft joint. The roll pins are of double type (inner and outer).
8   Using a balljoint separating tool, disconnect the suspension upper arm balljoint and the tie-rod end balljoint.
9   Tilt the upper end of the stub axle carrier outwards and press the stub axle from it. If it is tight, use a suitable three-legged extractor to do the job. To remove the driveshaft, grip the inboard joint and pull it from the transmission (photo). Do not grip its tubular section and pull, as this could cause the couplings to come apart. Should this happen the couplings would have to be reassembled, as described in Section 3.

2.4a Driveshaft nut

2.4b Driveshaft washer

2.9 Driveshaft inboard end being removed from the transmission

2.11 Connecting driveshaft to stub axle carrier

2.14 Tightening driveshaft nut to the specified torque

10 Before refitting a new driveshaft, a check must be made to establish the type of oil seal which is fitted to the old bearing. If a lip type double seal is used then grease the seal lips and fit the driveshaft by reversing the removal operations. If the old bearing does not have a lip type oil seal remove the deflector already fitted to the new driveshaft and substitute the spare one supplied.

11 Apply molybdenum disulphide grease to the driveshaft splines before connecting to the stub axle carrier (photo). It is recommended that the hub is drawn onto the shaft splines as the pressure must be sufficient to force the outer bearing into the stub axle carrier as well. In the absence of the special tool (T.AV 409-01) it should be possible to make up an internally threaded sleeve to serve the same purpose.

12 Engage the inboard end of the driveshaft in the transmission sunwheel. On R1223 and 122B models, make sure that the roll pin holes are in alignment. Drive in new roll pins and seal the ends with a blob of RTV (room temperature vulcanising) sealant.

13 Reconnect the balljoint nuts.

14 Fit the washer and driveshaft nut to the stub axle. Tighten the nut to the specified torque (photo).

15 On drum brake models fit the hydraulic hose clip.

16 On disc brake models fit the caliper.

17 Top up the transmission oil.

18 Refit the roadwheel and lower the car to the floor.

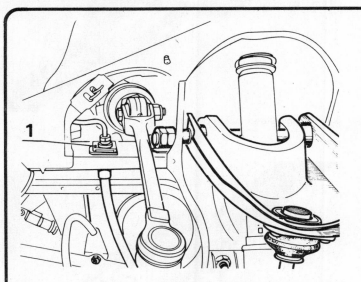

Fig 8.1 Front drum brake hydraulic hose clip (1) (Sec 2)

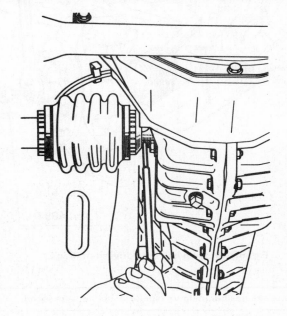

Fig. 8.2 Driving out a driveshaft roll pin (Sec 2)

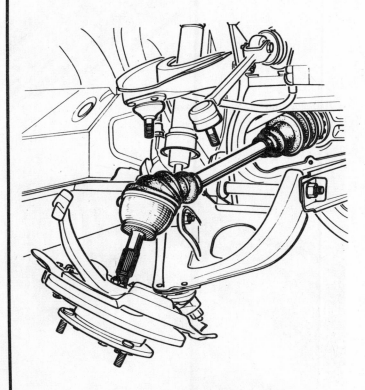

Fig. 8.3 Removing a driveshaft (Sec 2)

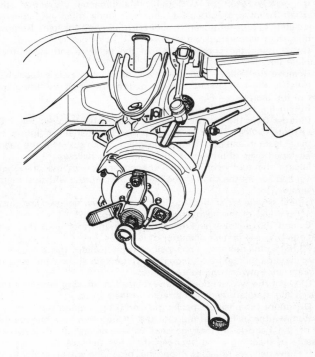

Fig. 8.4 Forcing driveshaft from hub (Sec 2)

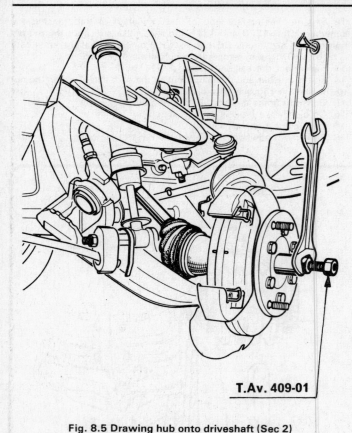

T.Av. 409-01

Fig. 8.5 Drawing hub onto driveshaft (Sec 2)

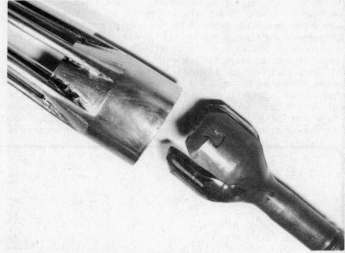

3.7a Fitting bellows tool to driveshaft

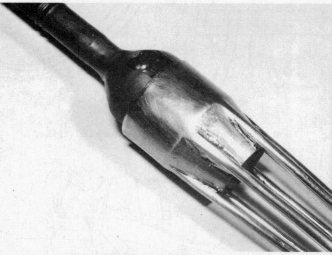

3.7b Bellows fitting tool located on driveshaft

3   Driveshaft flexible bellows (spider coupling) – renewal

Outboard joint (type GE 76 and GE 86)

1   If, as the result of a Routine Maintenance inspection, the driveshaft bellows are found to be split, they must be renewed immediately to prevent the entry of dirt or water into the joint. Remove the driveshaft as previously described.

2   Cut through the crimped band of the bellows and along their complete length.

3   Remove the bellows and wipe away as much grease as possible.

4   Release the bell-shaped section of the driveshaft by lifting the ends of the starplate – Fig. 8.7.

5   Retain the thrust ball and spring.

6   In order to fit the new bellows, a special tool is required, Fig. 8.8. A substitute device can be made up by bending a sheet of light alloy in conical fashion and pop riveting the seam. Make sure that the seam is well taped over to prevent it cutting the new bellows.

7   Locate the tool over the bell-shaped section of the driveshaft (photo) and secure the shaft in the jaws of a vice fitted with soft metal protectors.

8   Smear engine oil around the inside of the new bellows and push the narrow end of the bellows onto the tool (photo).

9   Extend the bellows and ease them up the tool until they are positioned on the largest diameter of it.

10   Fit the spring and thrust ball inside the joint spider, move the roller cages towards the centre and locate the starplate so that the ends of the plate are between the roller cages.

11   Connect the two sections of the driveshaft, making sure that the ends of the starplate engage correctly in their slots.

12   Distribute the pack of special grease (180g) around the joint.

13   Remove the bellows fitting tool and at the same time engage the lips of the bellows in their grooves in the driveshaft. Release air pressure by inserting a rod between shaft and bellows lip.

14   Fit new bellows retaining clips. The metal one will be easier to fit without damaging the bellows if two pieces of rod are drilled and the rods slipped onto the ends of the clip and used as prising tools (Fig. 8.14).

3.8 Fitting new bellows

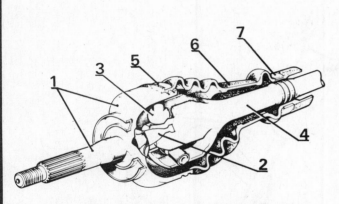

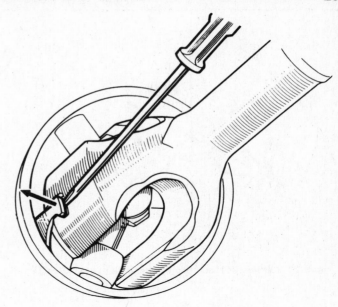

Fig. 8.6 Cutaway view of outboard coupling (Sec 3)

1	Bell-shaped section	5	Crimped tool
2	Starplate	6	Flexible bellows
3	Spider	7	Retaining band
4	Yoke		

Fig. 8.7 Raising an end of the starplate (Sec 3)

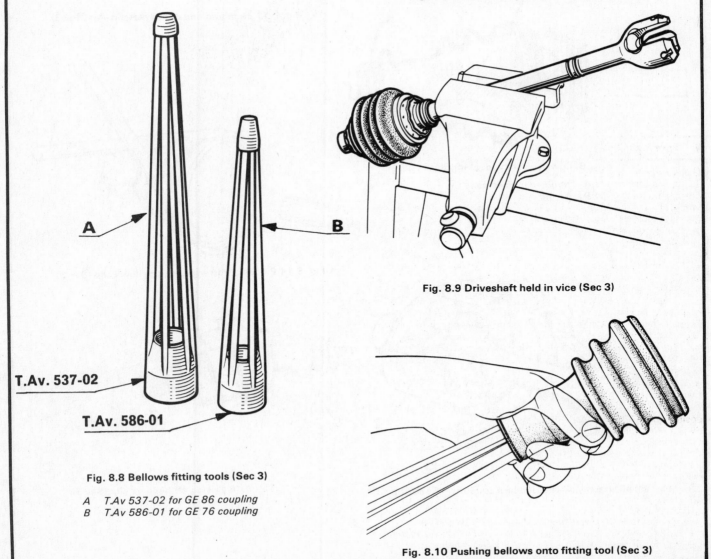

Fig. 8.9 Driveshaft held in vice (Sec 3)

T.Av. 537-02

T.Av. 586-01

Fig. 8.8 Bellows fitting tools (Sec 3)

A   T.Av 537-02 for GE 86 coupling
B   T.Av 586-01 for GE 76 coupling

Fig. 8.10 Pushing bellows onto fitting tool (Sec 3)

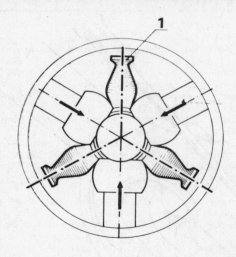

Fig. 8.11 Starplate (1) located between roller cages (Sec 3)

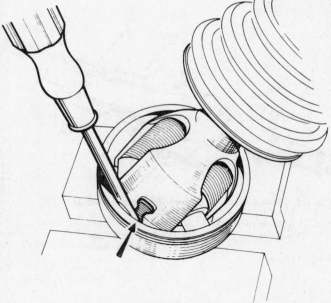

Fig. 8.12 Engaging end of starplate in slot (Sec 3)

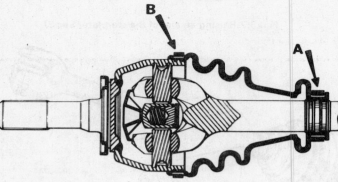

Fig. 8.13 Bellows correctly located (Sec 3)

A   Rubber retaining band
B   Spring clip

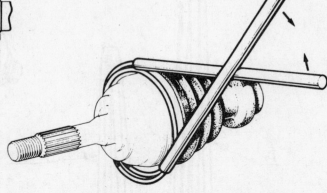

Fig. 8.14 Pieces of rod used to fit bellows clip (Sec 3)

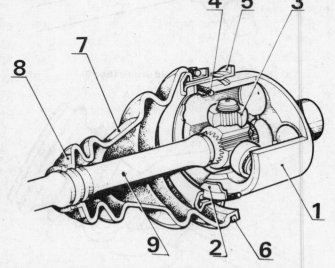

Fig. 8.15 Cutaway view of inboard coupling – GI 62 (Sec 3)

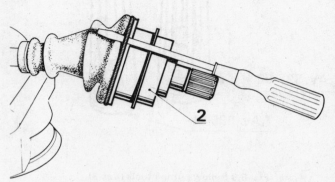

Fig. 8.16 Prising off bellows clip (Sec 3)

1	Yoke	6 Retaining clip
2	Anti-separation plate	7 Flexible bellows
3	Spider	8 Rubber retaining band
4	O-ring seal	9 Driveshaft
5	Cover	

2   Yoke

Inboard joint (type GI 62)

15 Remove the driveshaft as previously described.
16 Prise off the bellows retaining spring.
17 Cut the bellows over their entire length.
18 Wipe away as much grease as possible.
19 Using a pair of pliers, lift up each end of the anti-separation plate and then remove the yoke. Tape around the spider to prevent the rollers being displaced, as they and their needle bearings are matched in production.
20 Extract the retaining circlip and then press the shaft from the spider. Provided the spider is well supported, it should be possible to drive it out using a hammer and brass or copper rod.
21 Lubricate the driveshaft and slide on the new bellows with retaining collar.
22 Drive the spider onto the shaft and fit the circlip.
23 Centralise the spring (2) and the cup (1) on the spider and fit the yoke (Fig. 8.19).
24 Make up a wedge in accordance with the diagram (Fig. 8.20) and fit it between the anti-separation plate and the yoke.
25 Tap the anti-separation plate carefully into its original position using the wedge and then remove the wedge.
26 Distribute 140g of the special grease evenly between the bellows and the yoke.
27 Locate the lips of the bellows in their grooves and then release some of the air from the bellows by inserting a rod under the bellows lip.
28 Adjust the length of the bellows to conform with Fig. 8.22 and fit the bellows clips.

Inboard joint (type GI 69)

29 Remove the driveshaft as previously described.
30 Tape over the oil seal rubbing surface at the inboard end of the shaft to prevent it being scratched or damaged.
31 Cut the retaining band and the bellows along their entire length.
32 Wipe away as much grease as possible.
33 Prise up the three cover lugs (1) and then remove the yoke (Fig. 8.24).
34 Do not displace the rollers, as they are matched in production, but tape them to secure them.
35 Extract the circlip and press or drive the shaft from the spider.
36 Before fitting the new bellows, lubricate the driveshaft. Slide on the new bellows and retaining band.
37 Drive the spider onto the shaft and fit the circlip. Remove the temporary tape.
38 Fit the yoke and secure the ends of the three lugs by bending them over with a brass drift.
39 Spread the special grease (130g) on the yoke and inside the bellows.
40 Locate the lips of the bellows in their grooves and release any excessive air pressure by inserting a rod under the bellows lip.
41 Adjust the length of the bellows to conform with Fig. 8.26.
42 Fit the bellows metal clip as described in paragraph 14 of this Section.

Four-ball type

43 Remove the driveshaft as previously described.
44 Cut off the two bellows securing bands.

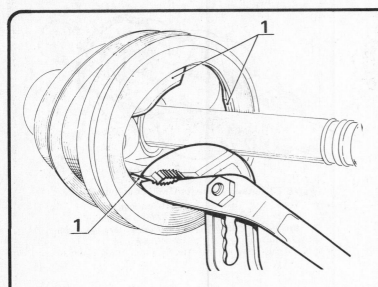

Fig. 8.17 Raising ends of anti-separation plate (1) (Sec 3)

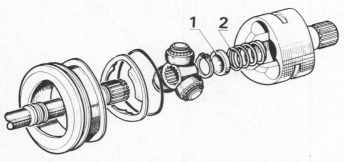

Fig. 8.19 Thrust cup (1) and spring (2) on type GI 62 coupling (Sec 3)

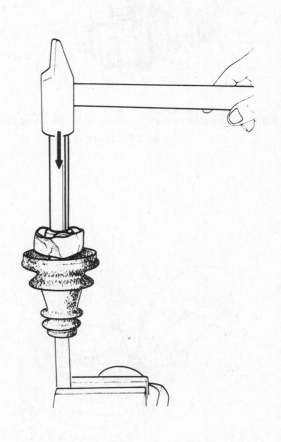

Fig. 8.18 Fitting spider to splined shaft (Sec 3)

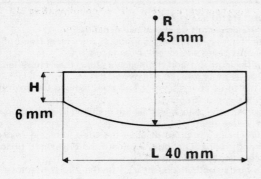

Fig. 8.20 Wedge fabrication diagram (Sec 3)
Material 2.5 mm thick

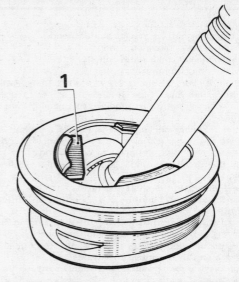

Fig. 8.21 Using wedge (1) to fit anti-separation plate (Sec 3)

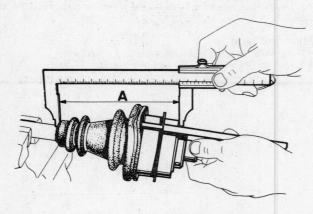

Fig. 8.22 Bellows setting diagram – GI 62 coupling (Sec 3)
A = 153.5 mm (6.04 in)

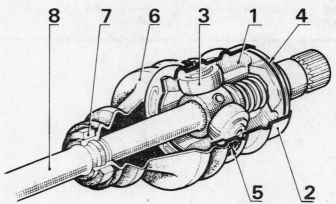

Fig. 8.23 Cutaway view of GI 69 coupling (Sec 3)

1 Yoke
2 Cover
3 Spider roller cages
4 O-ring seal
5 Retaining clip
6 Flexible bellows
7 Rubber retaining band
8 Driveshaft

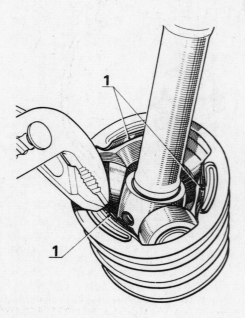

Fig. 8.24 Prising up coupling cover lugs (1) (Sec 3)

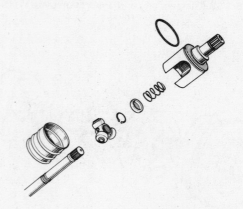

Fig. 8.25 GI 69 Coupling components (Sec 3)

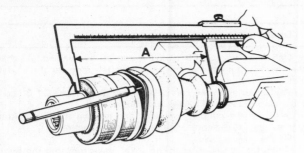

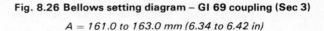

Fig. 8.26 Bellows setting diagram – GI 69 coupling (Sec 3)

A = 161.0 to 163.0 mm (6.34 to 6.42 in)

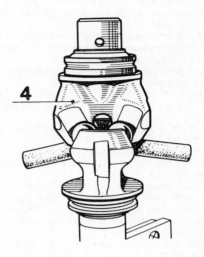

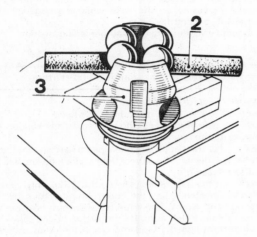

Fig. 8.28 Coupling upper jaw (4) in position (Sec 3)

Fig. 8.27 Fitting coupling balls (Sec 3)

2   Rubber hose   3   Jaws

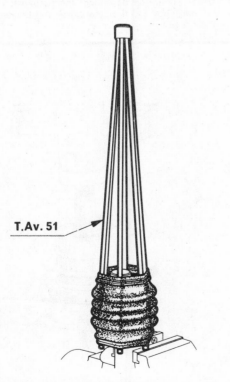

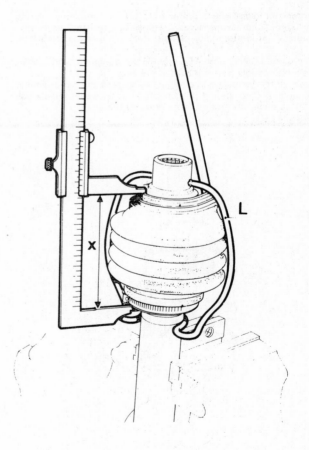

Fig. 8.29 Bellows fitting tool (Sec 3)

T.AV 51 four ball coupling

Fig. 8.30 Bellows on four ball coupling clamped and correctly set (Sec 3)

L   Clamp   X = 113.0 mm (4.5 in)

45 Using a centre punch, mark the position of the jaws in relation to each other.

46 Using tape, mark each ball in relation to its jaw, as each ball is individually ground into its ramp diameter during manufacture.

47 Cut off the faulty bellows.

48 Separate the coupling, clean the jaws and the balls.

49 To fit the new bellows, grip the driveshaft in the jaws of a vice as close as possible to the coupling jaw.

50 Obtain a piece of rubber tubing about 14.0 mm (0.55 in) in length and 12.5 mm (0.5 in) diameter and place it across the shaft jaws.

51 Arrange the four balls opposite to their tracks.

52 Offer up the upper jaw, withdraw the tubing as the jaw is pushed downward to engage the balls.

53 Fit either the special tool (T.Av. 51) or a satisfactory substitute (see paragraph 6) so that it fully covers the coupling and rests on the vice.

54 Lubricate the inside of the bellows and slide them fully onto the coupling. Withdraw the tool.

55 Engage the bellows in their grooves, fit the bellows lower clip.

56 Insert a piece of rod between the upper bellows lip and pour in 210g of the specified SJW oil.

57 Squeeze the bellows to expel some of the trapped air and then fit the clamp supplied with new driveshafts or make up a suitable substitute using a cranked rod and two hose clips. This device is to prevent the coupling sections separating. Keep the clamp in position until the driveshaft is back in the car.

58 Position the jaws so that the distance between their machined faces is 113.0 mm (4.45 in).

59 Remove the temporary air release rod and fit the second bellows clip.

Special nut

60 In order to overcome component supply problems during production some manual transmission versions are fitted with driveshafts which incorporate a Lobro type ball coupling at the roadwheel end.

61 For the same reason, some TX models are equipped with a shaft having a six-ball coupling at the roadwheel end.

62 Renewal of the bellows and overhaul operations are as for similar types of couplings described in this Chapter, but note that the six-ball coupling has a circlip to retain the ball hub to the shaft.

4   Driveshaft coupling – overhaul

1 Only the Type GI 69 coupling can be overhauled. Wear in the other driveshaft joints can only be rectified by renewal of the complete shaft.

2 The spider and yoke can be renewed on the type G1 69 coupling by carrying out the following operations.

3 Separate the coupling sections and remove the spider from the shaft splines, as described in the preceding Section.

4 Fit the new spider.

5 When fitting the cover to the yoke, make sure that the two 'pips' on the cover are opposite a cut-out in the yoke. Check that the O-ring is in position on the yoke, and then fit the yoke into the cover.

6 Maintain pressure on the yoke while the edge of the cover is crimped evenly around the yoke.

7 Reassemble as described in the preceding Section.

5   Front stub axle carrier – removal and refitting

Cars with front drum brakes

1 Remove the trim plate from the roadwheel.

2 Raise the side of the car being worked on and support it securely.

3 Remove the roadwheel.

4 Have an assistant apply the brake pedal hard so that the driveshaft nut can be unscrewed. This is very tight and a long knuckle bar will be required to release it.

5 Check that the handbrake is fully off (R1221 only) and then back off the shoe adjusters. Mark the hub to drum relationship.

6 Unscrew and remove the three screws which hold the brakedrum to the hub. Remove the drum. If it refuses to budge screw two 6 mm x 100 pitch bolts into the tapped holes in the drum to force it off.

7 Unscrew and remove the driveshaft nut.

8 Withdraw the hub assembly using either a slide hammer or a three-legged puller.

9 Unscrew and remove the backplate bolts.

10 Using a balljoint separator disconnect the suspension upper and lower suspension balljoints and the steering tie-rod balljoint. Support the suspension lower arm.

Fig. 8.31 Coupling cover in alignment with yoke cut-out (Sec 4)

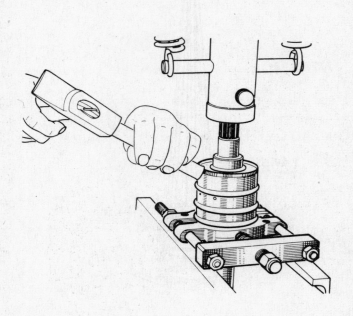

Fig. 8.32 Crimping cover to yoke (Sec 4)

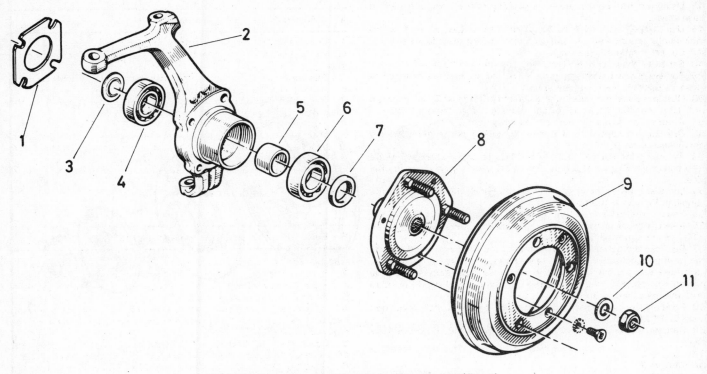

Fig. 8.33 Components of front hub – drum brakes (Sec 5)

1	Bearing closure plate	4	Inner bearing	7	Seal	10	Thrust washer
2	Stub axle carrier	5	Spacer	8	Hub	11	Driveshaft nut
3	Seal	6	Outer bearing	9	Brake drum		

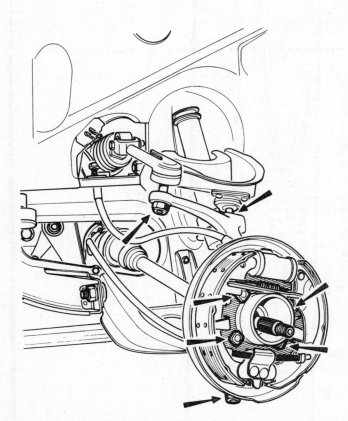

Fig. 8.34 Disconnection points for removal of stub axle carrier (Sec 5)

11 Lift the brake assembly over the end of the driveshaft and then remove the stub axle carrier.

12 Refitting is a reversal of removal, tighten nuts and bolts to the specified torques. Adjust the front brakes (Chapter 9).

Cars with front disc brakes

13 Remove the trim plate from the roadwheel.

14 Raise the side of the car being worked on and support it securely.

15 Remove the roadwheel.

16 Have an assistant apply the footbrake hard and unscrew the driveshaft nut. This is very tight and will require the use of a long knuckle bar.

17 Unbolt the brake caliper and tie it up out of the way without disconnecting the hydraulic flexible hose.

18 Using a slide hammer or a three-legged puller draw off the hub/disc assembly.

19 Using a balljoint separator, disconnect the suspension upper and lower suspension balljoints and the steering tie-rod balljoint. Support the suspension lower arm.

20 Withdraw the stub axle carrier.

21 Refitting is a reversal of removal, tighten the nuts and bolts to the specified torque. Depress the brake pedal two or three times to position the disc pads against the disc.

6 Front hub bearings – removal and refitting

If either bearing is worn, renew both bearings at the same time.

Outer bearing

1 With the hub or hub/disc withdrawn, as described in the preceding Section, the outer bearing will be found attached to the shoulder of the hub. Use a two-legged extractor to withdraw it.

2 Fit the new bearing (sealed face towards the roadwheel) and apply a piece of tubing to the bearing inner track to drive it home. Refit the hub or hub/disc, as described in the preceding Section, making sure that the bearing spacer is in position.

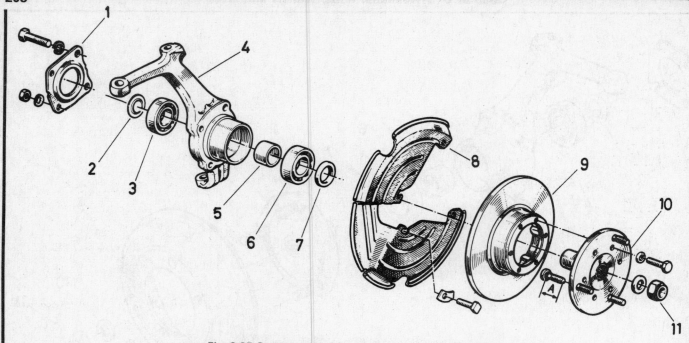

Fig. 8.35 Components of front hub – disc brakes (Sec 5)

1 Bearing closure plate
2 Seal
3 Inner bearing

4 Stub axle carrier
5 Spacer
6 Outer bearing

7 Seal
8 Shield
9 Disc

10 Hub
11 Driveshaft nut

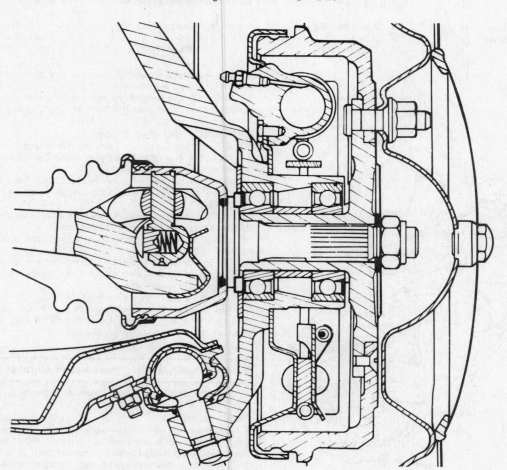

Fig. 8.36 Sectional view of front hub – drum brakes (Sec 6)

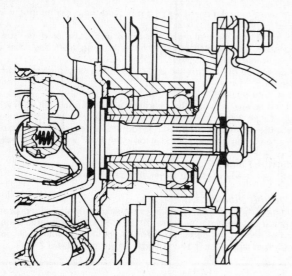

Fig. 8.37 Sectional view of front hub (disc brakes) except R1223 and 122B models (Sec 6)

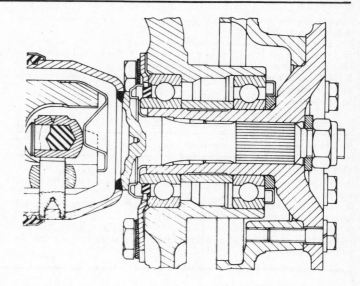

Fig. 8.38 Sectional view of front hub on R1223 and 122B models (Sec 6)

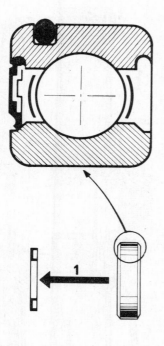

Fig. 8.39 Types of front hub inner bearings with driveshaft deflector (Sec 6)

1   Single lip sealing   2   Dual lip sealing

Inner bearing

3   Remove the stub axle carrier, as described in the preceding Section. Take off the bearing closure plate on cars with front drum brakes.
4   Press or drive the bearing from the stub axle carrier.
5   Check that the new bearing is compatible with the type of driveshaft deflector fitted, otherwise the deflector will have to be changed.
6   Press in the new bearing by applying a tubular sleeve to the bearing outer track.
7   Apply some multi-purpose grease to the space between the inner and outer bearings.
8   Locate the closure plate, having first coated its mating flange with sealant.
9   Refit the stub axle carrier, as described in the preceding Section, making sure that the bearing spacer is in position.

7   Rear hub bearings – adjustment

1   Raise the side of the car concerned and remove the roadwheel.
2   Tap off the grease cap. This can be very difficult to remove but can usually be achieved using a tool with a sharp blade which will dig into the surface of the cap. An alternative way is to tighten a worm-drive clip around the cap and to use this as an impact point for the removal tool.
3   Extract the split pin.
4   Take off the nut retainer.
5   Using a torque wrench, tighten the stub axle nut, while rotating the brake drum, to a torque of 30 Nm (22 lbf ft).
6   Unscrew the nut through one eighth of a turn. This should give an endfloat of between 0.01 and 0.05 mm (0.0004 and 0.002 in). Check this with a dial gauge or feeler blades placed behind the nut. Readjust

the nut slightly if necessary. Failure to achieve the correct endfloat indicates worn bearings.

7   Without disturbing the position of the nut, fit the nut retainer so that two slots are in alignment with the hole in the shaft. Insert a new split pin and bend its ends around the nut, not over it.

8   Fill the grease cap one third full with wheel bearing grease and tap it into position.

9   Refit the roadwheel and lower the car.

8   Rear hub bearings – renewal

With single lip oil seal

1   Raise the side of the car being worked on and secure with safety stands.

2   Back the shoe adjusters right off. The method of doing this varies according to model, refer to Chapter 9.

3   Remove the grease cap, as described in the preceding Section, then extract the split pin and take off the nut retainer, the nut and the thrust washer.

4   Remove the brake drum. As it is removed the outer bearing will be displaced.

5   Prise out the oil seal from the drum and draw or drive out the bearing outer tracks. Remove the inner bearing from the stub axle using a suitable puller.

6   Wipe out all the old grease and drive in the new tracks and fit the inner bearing.

7   Fit a new oil seal.

8   Fill the space between the bearing tracks one third full with wheel bearing grease. Work some grease into the bearing rollers.

9   Refit the drum and outer bearing, adjust as described in Section 7. Fit the grease cap, having filled it one third full with wheel bearing grease.

10   Adjust the brake shoes.

11   Refit the roadwheel and lower the car to the floor.

With double lip oil seal

12   The operations are very similar to those described in the preceding paragraphs, but note the deflector fitted inboard of the inner bearing.

13   Renew this at the same time as the conventional oil seal, noting that its larger diameter is towards the brake backplate.

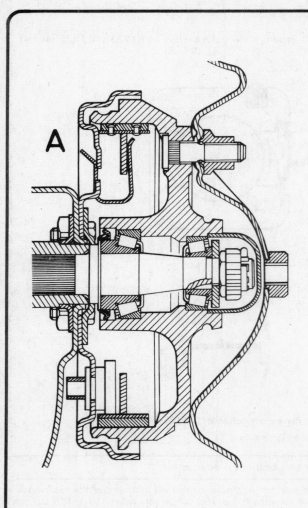
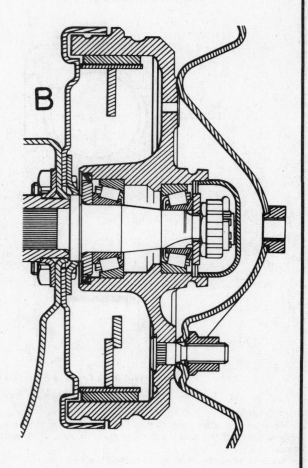

Fig. 8.40 Sectional views of rear hub with single lip sealing (Sec 8)

A   R1221   B   Other models

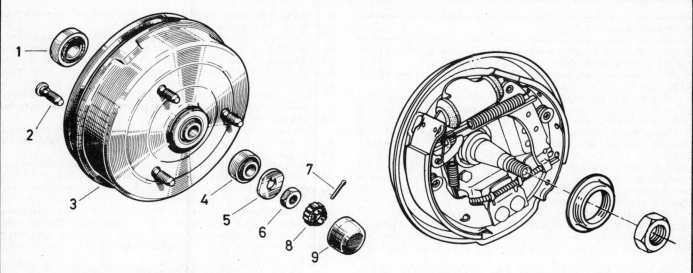

Fig. 8.41 Rear hub components (Sec 8)

1 Inner bearing   6 Nut
2 Wheel stud   7 Split pin
3 Brake drum   8 Nut retainer
4 Outer bearing   9 Grease cap
5 Thrust washer

Fig. 8.43 Deflector fitting direction (double lip sealing) on rear hub
(Sec 8)

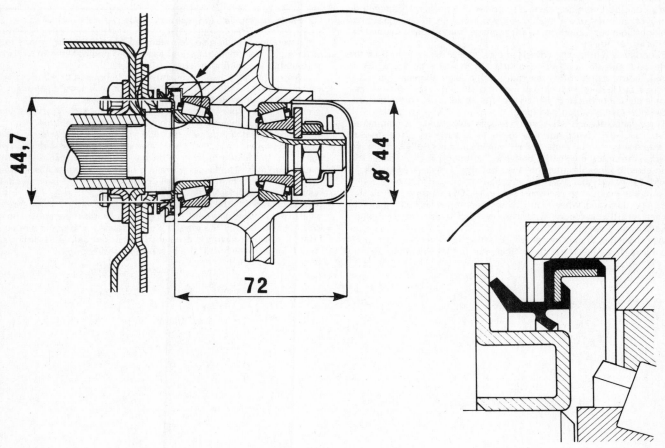

Fig. 8.42 Sectional view of rear hub with double lip sealing (Sec 8)

All measurements are in mm

9 Roadwheels and tyres

The roadwheels are of pressed-steel construction, except for some top of the range models which have light alloy wheels.

The roadwheels are secured by nuts on all models except the R1223 and 122B which have bolts.

Wheels and tyres should give no real problems in use provided that a close eye is kept on them with regard to excessive wear or damage. To this end, the following points should be noted.

Ensure that tyre pressures are checked regularly and maintained correctly. Checking should be carried out with the tyres cold and not immediately after the vehicle has been in use. If the pressures are checked with the tyres hot, an apparently high reading will be obtained owing to heat expansion. Under no circumstances should an attempt be made to reduce the pressures to the quoted cold reading in this instance, or effective underinflation will result.

Underinflation will cause overheating of the tyre owing to excessive flexing of the casing, and the tread will not sit correctly on the road surface. This will cause a consequent loss of adhesion and excessive wear, not to mention the danger of sudden tyre failure due to heat build-up.

Overinflation will cause rapid wear of the centre part of the tyre tread coupled with reduced adhesion, harsher ride, and the danger of shock damage occurring in the tyre casing.

Regularly check the tyres for damage in the form of cuts or bulges, especially in the sidewalls. Remove any nails or stones embedded in the tread before they penetrate the tyre to cause deflation. If removal of a nail *does* reveal that the tyre has been punctured, refit the nail so that its point of penetration is marked. Then immediately change the wheel and have the tyre repaired by a tyre dealer. Do *not* drive on a tyre in such a condition. In many cases a puncture can be simply repaired by the use of an inner tube of the correct size and type. If in any doubt as to the possible consequences of any damage found, consult your local tyre dealer for advice.

Periodically remove the wheels and clean any dirt or mud from the inside and outside surfaces. Examine the wheel rims for signs of rusting, corrosion or other damage. Light alloy wheels are easily damaged by 'kerbing' whilst parking, and similarly steel wheels may become dented or buckled. Renewal of the wheel is very often the only course of remedial action possible.

The balance of each wheel and tyre assembly should be maintained to avoid excessive wear, not only to the tyres but also to the steering and suspension components. Wheel imbalance is normally signified by vibration through the vehicle's bodyshell, although in many cases it is particularly noticeable through the steering wheel. Conversely, it should be noted that wear or damage in suspension or steering components may cause excessive tyre wear. Out-of-round or out-of-true tyres, damaged wheels and wheel bearing wear/maladjustment also fall into this category. Balancing will not usually cure vibration caused by such wear. ·

Wheel balancing may be carried out with the wheel either on or off the vehicle. If balanced on the vehicle, ensure that the wheel-to-hub relationship is marked in some way prior to subsequent wheel removal so that it may be refitted in its original position.

General tyre wear is influenced to a large degree by driving style – harsh braking and acceleration or fast cornering will all produce more rapid tyre wear. Interchanging of tyres may result in more even wear, but this should only be carried out where there is no mix of tyre types on the vehicle. However, it is worth bearing in mind that if this is completely effective, the added expense of replacing a complete set of tyres simultaneously is incurred, which may prove financially restrictive for many owners.

Front tyres may wear unevenly as a result of wheel misalignment. The front wheels should always be correctly aligned according to the settings specified by the vehicle manufacturer.

Legal restrictions apply to the mixing of tyre types on a vehicle. Basically this means that a vehicle must not have tyres of differing construction on the same axle. Although it is not recommended to mix tyre types between front axle and rear axle, the only legally permissible combination is crossply at the front and radial at the rear. When mixing radial ply tyres, textile braced radials must always go on the front axle, with steel braced radials at the rear. An obvious disadvantage of such mixing is the necessity to carry two spare tyres to avoid contravening the law in the event of a puncture.

In the UK, the Motor Vehicles Construction and Use Regulations apply to many aspects of tyre fitting and usage. It is suggested that a copy of these regulations is obtained from your local police if in doubt as to the current legal requirements with regard to tyre condition, minimum tread depth, etc.

10 Fault diagnosis – driveshafts, hubs, wheels and tyres

1   Reference should also be made to Chapter 11 since many faults occurring in the driveshafts and associated components may also be attributable to steering or suspension faults.

2   Worn driveshaft joints will show up initially as a clicking or ticking sound when cornering or manoeuvring on full lock. Eventually the noise will occur even when driving straight ahead.

3   Worn driveshaft splines will produce a clunking noise when moving off from rest, or when going from drive to overrun.

4   Worn hub bearings will produce a moaning or rumbling sound, especially when the bearing concerned is on the outside when cornering. When the bearing is on the inside when cornering, it will become quieter. (Thus a defective hub bearing on the left-hand side of the car will be at its noisiest when negotiating a right-hand bend, but may quieten completely on a left-hand bend).

5   Wheels and tyres that are out of balance or not perfectly true can give rise to quite alarming shaking and vibration, especially on the front wheels. Even if the wheels were balanced when new tyres were fitted, it is worth having the balance rechecked before assuming that something is wrong with the suspension or steering.

Chapter 9 Braking system

For modifications, and information applicable to later models, see Supplement at end of manual

Contents

Specifications

System type

All models except R1221 and 122B	Four wheel hydraulic, with single or dual circuit. Disc front, drum rear, handbrake on rear wheels. Vacuum servo available. Pressure regulating valve on dual circuit systems.
R1221	Four wheel hydraulic single circuit with drums all round. Handbrake on front wheels.
122B	Four wheel hydraulic, dual circuit with discs all round. Vacuum servo unit, pressure regulating valve and pressure drop indicator. Handbrake on rear wheels.

Front drum brakes (R1221)

Wheel cylinder diameter	23.8 mm (0.94 in)
Drum inside diameter	228.5 mm (9.0 in)
Maximum inside diameter after grinding	229.5 mm (9.04 in)

Rear drum brakes

Wheel cylinder diameter:	
R1221	20.6 mm (0.81 in)
Other models	22.0 mm (0.87 in)
Drum inside diameter:	
R1221	160.25 mm (6.31 in)
Maximum inside diameter after grinding	161.25 mm (6.35 in)
Other models	180.25 mm (7.10 in)
Maximum inside diameter after grinding	181.25 mm (7.14 in)

Front disc brakes

Caliper cylinder diameter:	
Except R1223 and 122B	45.0 mm (1.77 in)
R1223	48.0 mm (1.89 in)
122B	36.0 mm (1.42 in)
Disc diameter	228.0 mm (8.98 in)
Disc thickness	10.0 mm (0.39 in)
Minimum thickness after refacing	9.0 mm (0.35 in)
Minimum pad thickness including backing plate	7.0 mm (0.28 in)

Master cylinder

Cylinder diameter:	
Single type	19.0 mm (0.75 in)
Dual type:	
All models except R1223 and 122B	20.6 mm (0.81 in)
R1223 and 122B	19.0 mm (0.75 in)

Vacuum servo diameter

Vacuum servo diameter	152.0 mm (5.99 in)

Brake fluid type/specification

Brake fluid type/specification	Hydraulic fluid to SAE J1703 (Duckhams Universal Brake and Clutch Fluid)

Brake regulating valve cut-off pressures (driver seated, no luggage)

	Full	Fuel tank Half-full	Empty
Models up to 1973:			
R1221	25 to 28 bar (363 to 406 lbf/in²)	24 to 27 bar (348 to 392 lbf/in²)	23 to 26 bar (334 to 377 lbs/in²)
R1222	25 to 28 bar (363 to 406 lbf/in²)	23 to 26 bar (334 to 377 lbf/in²)	22 to 25 bar (319 to 362 lbf/in²)
Models 1974 and later:			
R1221 and R1391	20 to 24 bar (290 to 348 lbf/in²)	18 to 22 bar (261 to 319 lbf/in²)	16 to 20 bar (232 to 290 lbf/in²)
R1223	37 to 43 bar (537 to 624 lbf/in²)	35 to 41 bar (508 to 595 lbf/in²)	33 to 39 bar (479 to 566 lbf/in²)
122B:			
Front	25 bar (363 lbf/in²)	23 bar (334 lbf/in²)	21 bar (305 lbf/in²)
Rear	18 bar (261 lbf/in²)	16 bar (232 lbf/in²)	14 bar (203 lbf/in²)
R1247	21 to 25 bar (305 to 363 lbf/in²)	19 to 23 bar (276 to 334 lbf/in²)	17 to 21 bar (247 to 305 lbf/in²)
R1228 (US) and R1229 (US)	28 to 32 bar (405 to 465 lbf/in²)	26 to 30 bar (376 to 436 lbf/in²)	24 to 28 bar (347 to 407 lbf/in²)
All other models	24 to 28 bar (348 to 406 lbf/in²)	22 to 26 bar (319 to 377 lbf/in²)	20 to 24 bar (290 to 348 lbf/in²)
1983 models:			
R1221 and R1391	24 to 28 bar (348 to 406 lbf/in²)	22 to 26 bar (319 to 377 lbf/in²)	20 to 24 bar (290 to 348 lbf/in²)

Torque wrench settings

	Nm	lbf ft
Bleed screws	8	6
Flexible hose end fitting	20	15
Rigid pipe unions:		
Steel	14	10
Copper	12	9
Caliper bracket bolts	67	49
Disc fixing bolts	26	19
Disc shield screws	18	13
Caliper guide bolts	35	26
Roadwheel nuts or bolts	58	43
Driveshaft nut:		
Except R1223 and 122B	117	86
R1223 and 122B	156	115

1 General description

The braking system is of four wheel hydraulic type. The front brakes on R1221 models are of drum type, while on all other models, disc brakes are used.

The rear brakes on all models except the Gordini Turbo are of drum type with manual or automatic adjustment. Four wheel disc brakes are fitted to the Gordini Turbo.

The handbrake is mechanically operated and activates the front brakes on R1221 models and the rear brakes on all other models.

The hydraulic circuit may be of single or double type, depending upon the model or date of production.

The hydraulic circuit incorporates a pressure regulating valve to prevent rear wheel lock up during heavy braking. Dual circuit models have a pressure drop indicator which monitors any pressure difference between the two circuits which could be caused by a leak.

A vacuum servo unit is standard equipment on some models and optionally available on others.

2 Maintenance and adjustment

1 Inspect the fluid level in the master cylinder reservoir at regular intervals (see Routine Maintenance). Topping-up in order to make up for the small volume of additional fluid needed as the brake friction material wears down should only be required at infrequent intervals. The addition of fluid frequently, or in large quantities, must be due to a leak in the system which should be rectified immediately.
2 Inspect the wear in the brake shoes or disc pads at the intervals specified in Routine Maintenance with reference to Sections 3, 4 and 5.

3 Also at the intervals specified in Routine Maintenance adjust the drum brakes with manual adjusters.

Square-head type manual eccentric adjusters
4 Check that the handbrake is fully off, chock the other roadwheels and raise the one being worked upon.
5 Preferably using the special brake spanner made for the job (obtainable from your Renault dealer), turn one of the two hexagon adjusters on the brake backplate until the wheel locks. It is recommended that the adjuster for the leading shoe is adjusted first, followed by the trailing shoe. The leading shoe is the one nearest the front of the car.
6 Back off the adjuster just enough for the wheel to turn without any tendency to rub or bind. The rear brake adjusters allow very little room for fitting anything but the special spanner. It may be necessary to grind down other types of spanner to make them thin enough to fit.
7 Repeat the procedure on the other adjuster and then on the remaining drum brakes.
8 Apply freeing fluid and a smear of grease regularly to the adjusters on the backplate, as they are particularly prone to rusting and seizure.

Rear brakes with starwheel type adjuster
9 Prise out the plastic plug located on the brake backplate just above the rear suspension arm. Raise the roadwheel off the floor.
10 Insert a screwdriver through the aperture left by removal of the plug and engage it in the teeth of the starwheel adjuster. Prise the starwheel until the shoe linings lock the drum. Now back off the adjuster until the roadwheel rotates freely without binding or rubbing.
11 Repeat the operation on the opposite rear brake.

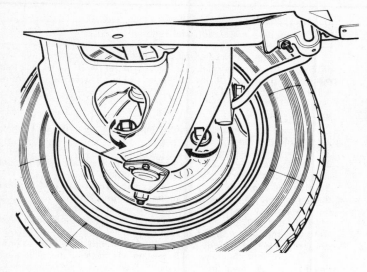

Fig. 9.1 Front drum brake adjusters – arrows indicate shoe expansion (Sec 2)

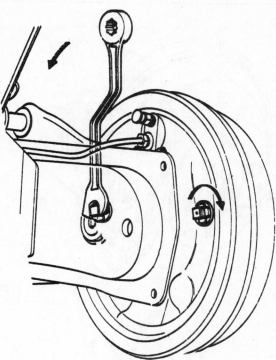

Fig. 9.2 Rear drum brake adjusters – arrows indicate shoe expansion (Sec 2)

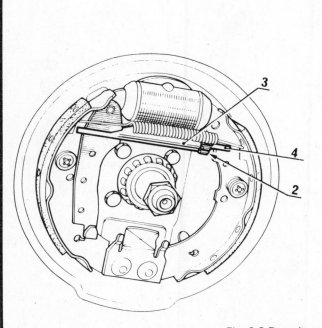

Fig. 9.3 Rear drum brake starwheel adjuster (Sec 2)

1 Aperture in backplate	3 Long strut
2 Starwheel	4 Short strut

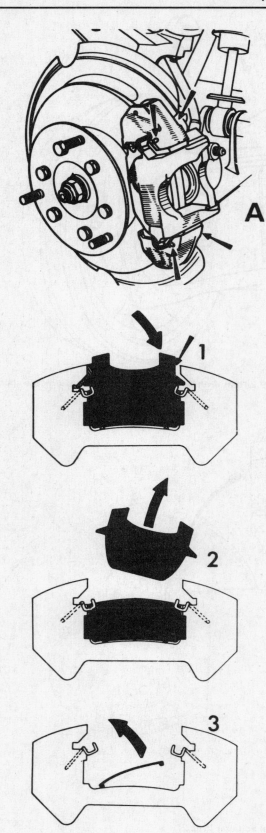

3 Disc pads – inspection and renewal

1   Remove the roadwheel and view the pads end on. The thickness of the pad (friction material plus backing plate) must not be less than the specified amount. If any pad is less than the specified minimum thickness all the pads (axle set) must be renewed.

Bendix type

2   Remove the spring clips (photo) and tap out one of the sliding keys with a thin rod (photo).
3   Remove the second key.
4   The caliper may now be taken from the disc and supported to one side so as not to strain the flexible hose (photo).
5   Remove the pads from the caliper support bracket and take out the springs which are located underneath them (photo).
6   Brush away dust or mud, **taking care not to inhale any.**
7   Refit the pad springs and the new pads, (friction surface to disc). Note that the longer spring is outboard.
8   Using a wide flat blade depress the piston into its cylinder in order to accommodate the new thicker pads. Depressing the piston will cause the fluid level in the master cylinder reservoir to rise, so anticipate this by removing some fluid using a clean battery hydrometer or poultry baster.
9   Engage one side of the caliper between the spring and the keyway on the caliper support bracket and then fit the other side of the caliper by depressing both springs.
10   Tap in the first key and then the second one.
11   Refit the spring clips.
12   Refit the roadwheel and lower the car.
13   Repeat the operations on the opposite wheel.
14   On completion, apply the footbrake two or three times to bring the pads in contact with the discs. Top up the reservoir fluid.

Girling type

15   With the car raised and the roadwheel removed, grip the caliper and move it outwards.

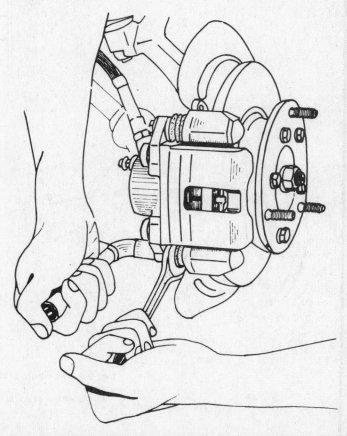

Fig. 9.4 Front disc pad removal sequence (Sec 3)

A	Remove spring clips	2	Pad removed
1	Prising pad out	3	Anti-rattle spring

Fig. 9.5 Removing caliper guide bolts – Girling (Sec 3)

3.2a Sliding key spring clip (Bendix)

3.2b Removing lower sliding key (Bendix)

3.4 Removing caliper from the disc (Bendix)

3.5 Removing disc pads (Bendix)

3.17 Caliper (Girling)

16 Using an Allen key or an open-ended spanner, unscrew and remove the guide bolts.

17 Free the sliding caliper (photo).

18 Extract the pad springs and withdraw the pads.

19 Using a wide flat blade, depress the piston fully into its cylinder. Anticipate a rise in the reservoir fluid level by removing some fluid (see paragraph 8).

20 Fit the new pads and springs making sure that the pad with the black backplate is located on the inboard side, and the springs are located with their offset nearest the disc.

21 Fit the caliper over the pads and fit the lower guide bolt.

22 Apply pressure to the caliper and screw in the upper guide bolt. Tighten the guide bolts (lower one first) to the specified torque.

23 Depress the brake pedal several times to position the pads against the disc.

24 Repeat the operations on the opposite wheel.

25 Top up the master cylinder fluid reservoir.

4 Front shoe linings – inspection and renewal

1 On early models, the brake drum must be removed before the shoe linings can be inspected. On later models, an inspection hole is provided in the brake backplate.

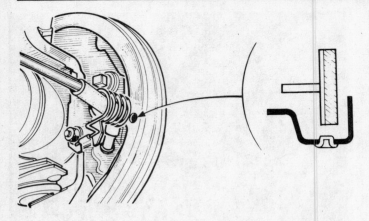

Fig. 9.6 Front shoe lining inspection hole (Sec 4)

2   Check that the handbrake (R1221) is fully released. Raise the car and remove the wheel.
3   Extract the drum retaining screws, back off the shoe adjusters.
4   Mark the relationship of drum to hub and remove the drum. If the drum is stuck, screw in two 6.0 mm x 100 pitch screws into the tapped holes provided to force it off.
5   If the linings are so worn that their rivet heads are flush with the linings, the shoes must be renewed. If the linings are in good condition, brush away the dust from the shoes and drums **taking care not to inhale it.**
6   To remove the shoes, first disconnect the shoe steady springs. These can usually be released if a ½ in square drive extension tool or similar is pushed into the spring and the spring compressed. At the same time rotate the spring to release its hooked end.
7   Note, and sketch if necessary, how the brake shoes are located in respect of leading and trailing shoes and their ends. You will notice how the friction lining covers more of the shoe at one end than the other, the new shoes must be fitted in exactly the same way.
8   Prise the upper ends of the shoes apart, pull the shoes towards you and then allow them to move together in front of the wheel cylinder.
9   Disconnect the shoe upper return spring.
10 Pull the upper ends of the shoes downwards and release the lower ends of the shoes from behind the anchor block. As the shoe is withdrawn, unhook the handbrake cable from the shoe lever.
11 Do not touch the brake pedal while the shoes are removed or the wheel cylinder pistons will be ejected.
12 Purchase a boxed set of shoes, complete with linings. Do not re-line the original shoes yourself as this seldom proves satisfactory.
13 Set the new shoes out on the bench in their correct relative positions, with the handbrake lever fitted to the new shoe.
14 Fit the shoe lower return spring and then offer the shoes to the backplate. Engage the handbrake cable with the lever and then prise the lower ends of the shoes apart so that they can be slipped behind the anchor block.
15 Hold the upper ends as close together as possible and connect the shoe upper return spring.
16 Prise the upper ends of the shoes apart and locate the ends of the shoe webs on the wheel cylinder pistons.
17 Fit the shoe steady springs.
18 Refit the drum, with the marks made at dismantling in alignment.
19 Fit the roadwheel and adjust the brakes as described earlier in this Chapter.
20 Lower the car and then repeat the operations on the opposite brake.

---

5   Rear shoe linings – inspection and renewal

1   On rear drum brakes having starwheel adjusters or self-adjusting brakes, the brake backplate is fitted with an inspection hole. The plug may be removed from the hole and lining wear checked.
2   On models with eccentric cam, square-headed adjusters, the brake drum will have to be removed in order to check lining wear.

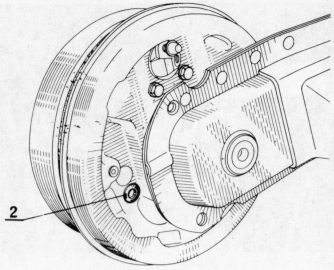

Fig. 9.7 Backplate plug (2) on self-adjusting rear brake (Sec 5)

3   Where the lining has worn down and the rivet heads are flush with the surface of the lining then the shoes must be renewed. If the linings are in good condition, brush away the dust from the shoes and the drum interior, **taking care not to inhale it.**
4   Raise the car and remove the roadwheel.
5   On all models except R1221, slacken the handbrake secondary cable.
6   On models with manually-adjusted brakes, slacken the adjusters right off.
7   On models with self-adjusting brakes, the brake shoe adjustment can be slackened by removing the blanking plug either from the brake drum or the brake backplate. If a screwdriver is inserted through the backplate hole, depress the handbrake lever on the shoe to free its 'pip' from the shoe and then prise the lever towards the drum.
8   If the hole in the brake drum is used, insert a 5.0 mm (0.20 in) rod so that the rod contacts the sector (D). Now rotate the drum in a forward direction which will cause the rod to release the toothed sector (D) from the lever (C) – see Fig. 9.10.
9   Remove the grease cap. This is very tight and, in the absence of the special tool, it can usually be tapped off with a cold chisel with a sharp blade which will 'bite' into the surface of the cap. Alternatively, a worm drive clip can be tightened around the cap and this used as the point of impact for a drift.
10 Extract the split pin.
11 Remove the nut retainer.
12 Unscrew the stub axle nut and take off the thrust washer.
13 Remove the brake drum. As it is withdrawn, catch the outer bearing.
14 Renewal of the brake shoes is very similar to the procedure described in Section 4, but the following differences should be noted.

Brake with eccentric type adjusters or self-adjusting
15 Spring clips are used for shoe steady purposes instead of coil spring type retainers. Remove these by releasing their ends from the small square holes in the backplate and sliding them from the shoe webs.

Brake with starwheel type adjusters
16 Spring and cup type shoe steady devices are used. To remove, grip the edges of the top cup with a pair of pliers, depress it against the pressure of the spring and turn it through 90°. Release the cup gently and remove the coil spring and steady pin.

Refitting
17 With self-adjusting type brakes it is recommended that the toothed sector is moved on the toothed lever until any further movement would prevent the brake drum from sliding over the shoes.
18 Fit the drum, outer bearing, thrust washer and screw on the nut. Tighten the nut to 30 Nm (22 lbf ft) while rotating the drum. Now

219

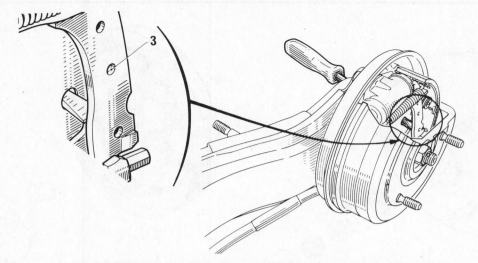

Fig. 9.8 Releasing handbrake lever on self-adjusting rear brakes (Sec 5)

3 Pip

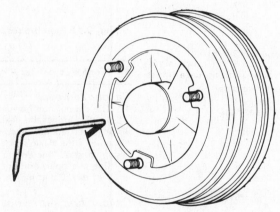

Fig. 9.9 Releasing toothed sector on self-adjusting rear brakes (Sec 5)

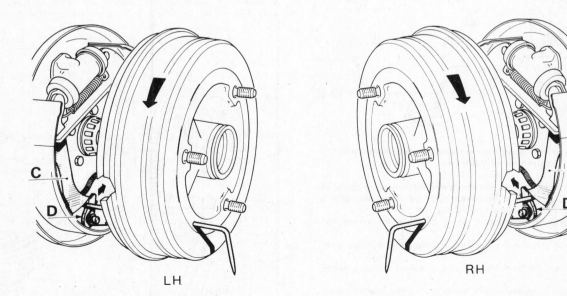

LH   RH

Fig. 9.10 Rotating rear drum to release toothed sector (Sec 5)

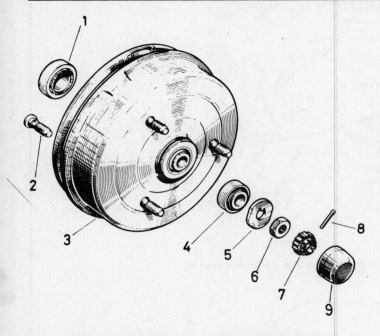

Fig. 9.11 Rear brake drum components (Sec 5)

1 Inboard bearing	6 Nut
2 Wheel stud	7 Nut retainer
3 Brake drum	8 Split pin
4 Outboard bearing	9 Grease cap
5 Thrust washer	

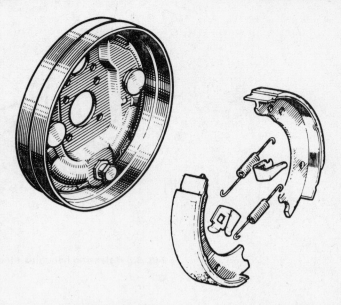

Fig. 9.12 Rear brakes with spring clip type shoe steady (Sec 5)

6   Front disc caliper – removal, overhaul and refitting

Caliper removal

1   The caliper can be removed as described in Section 3.
2   To disconnect the flexible hose, either support the end of the hose in an open-ended spanner and 'unwind' the caliper from it, or disconnect the flexible hose at its junction with the rigid pipe – after first pulling out the spring clip.
3   Cap the open ends of the pipes to prevent loss of fluid and the entry of dirt. Bleed nipple dust caps are useful for this purpose.

Caliper bracket removal

4   With the caliper removed, the caliper bracket can be withdrawn if necessary.
5   On all models except R1223, unscrew the two deflector bolts (A) – see Fig. 9.15.
6   Unscrew the two caliper fixing bolts and remove the bracket from the stub axle carrier. Setting shims are not used under the bracket.

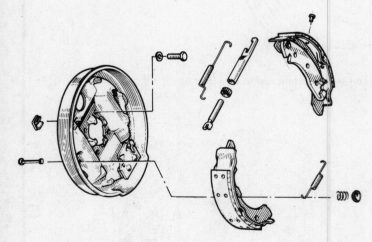

Fig. 9.13 Cup and spring type shoe steady on rear brake with starwheel adjuster (Sec 5)

unscrew the nut through $\frac{1}{8}$ of a turn which should give an endfloat of between 0.01 and 0.05 mm (0.0004 and 0.002 in). Check this with a dial gauge or feeler blades placed behind the nut.
19   Fit the nut retainer so that two of its cut-outs are in line with the split pin hole.
20   Insert a new split pin and bend its ends around the nut, not over the end.
21   Fill the grease cap one third full with the specified grease and tap it into position.
22   Adjust the brakes as described in Section 2. If the brakes are of self-adjusting type, apply the footbrake pedal several times to bring the shoes to their closest possible adjustment clearance to the drum.
23   Adjust the handbrake as described in Section 20.
24   Refit the roadwheel and lower the car.

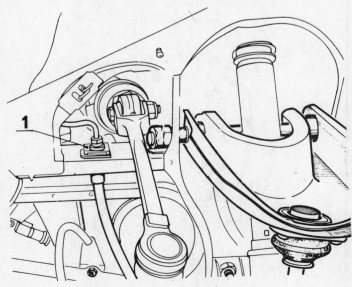

Fig. 9.14 Front disc caliper flexible hose connection (1) (Sec 6)

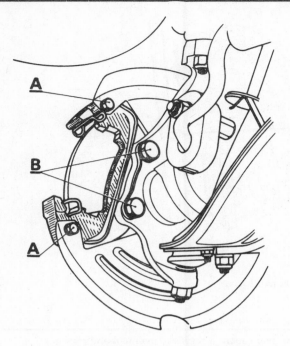

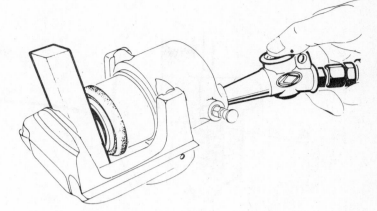

Fig. 9.16 Ejecting caliper piston (Sec 6)

Fig. 9.15 Caliper bracket removal (Sec 6)

A   Deflector bolts   B   Caliper fixing bolts

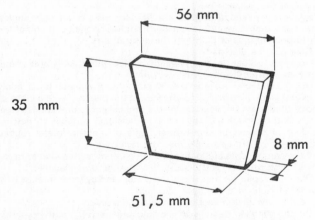

Fig. 9.17 Caliper carrier leg expanding wedge (Sec 6)

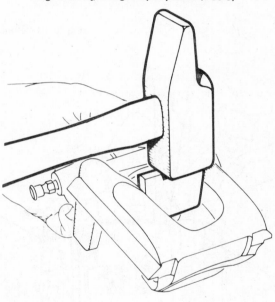

Fig. 9.18 Using wedge to expand caliper carrier legs (Sec 6)

7   Some caliper mounting bolts do not have lockwashers under their heads, but are secured with thread locking compound. The latter type of bolt should be cleaned and its thread smeared with thread locking fluid before refitting and tightening to the specified torque.

Overhaul
Bendix

8   With the caliper removed, take off the rubber dust excluder.

9   Eject the piston by applying air from a tyre pump to the fluid inlet port. Only low air pressure is required for this and take care that the piston is not ejected with so much force that it is damaged against the caliper. Insert a piece of wood or hardboard to protect it.

10 Pick out the seal from its groove in the cylinder using a pointed instrument – but make sure that the cylinder walls are not scratched.

11 Examine the condition of the piston and cylinder surfaces. If they are scored, pitted or show bright metal-to-metal rubbed areas, renew the caliper complete. To do this, the hydraulic cylinder will have to be separated from its carrier. In order to do this, the legs of the carrier will require spreading slightly. Make up a wedge to the dimensions shown in Fig. 9.17 and drive it between the legs. Using a thin rod, depress the spring-loaded plunger and withdraw the cylinder. Refit the new cylinder, making sure that the peg locates in its hole in the carrier.

12 Where the piston and cylinder are found to be in good condition, clean them with methylated spirit or clean hydraulic fluid – nothing else.

13 Obtain a repair kit which will contain all the necessary seals and other items.

14 Manipulate the new seal into its groove using the fingers only.

15 Dip the piston in clean hydraulic fluid and insert it carefully into its cylinder.

16 Fit the new dust excluder.

Girling

17 The operations are very similar to those just described for the Bendix type, except that the cylinder is not detachable from the carrier and is renewable as an assembly.

18 The dust excluder has a spring clip to retain it in position.

Refitting

19 Before refitting the caliper, it is recommended that it is filled with clean hydraulic fluid to facilitate the bleeding operation.

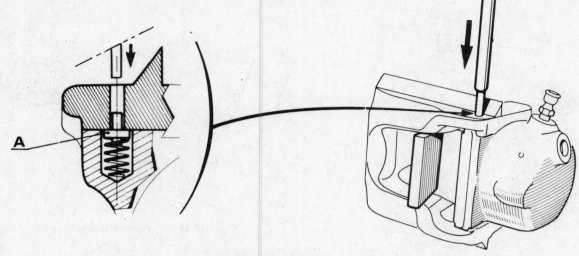

Fig. 9.19 Cylinder retainer plunger (A) (Sec 6)

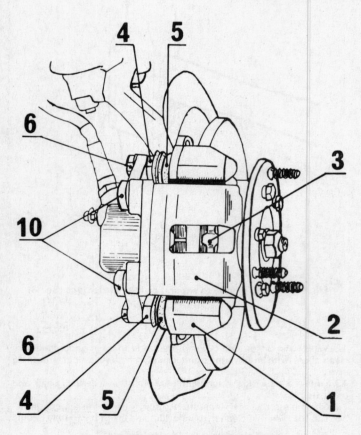

Fig. 9.20 Girling type caliper (Sec 6)

1	Caliper bracket	5	Dust excluders
2	Sliding caliper	6	Guide bolts
3	Pad retaining spring	10	Cylinder assembly bolts
4	Guide		(never remove)

20 Use a new copper sealing washer when connecting the flexible hose to the caliper.
21 Refit the caliper bracket, tightening the bolts to the specified torque.
22 Fit the pads and caliper, as described in Section 3.
23 Bleed the system (refer to Section 17).

7   Rear disc caliper – removal, overhaul and refitting

1   Rear disc brakes are only fitted to the 122B Gordini Turbo.
2   Disconnect the handbrake cable from the operating lever on the caliper.
3   Unbolt the caliper from its bracket.
4   Support the end fitting of the flexible hose in an open-ended spanner and then 'unwind' the caliper from it. Cap the open end of the hose to prevent loss of fluid and the entry of dirt.
5   Take out the disc pads.
6   Grip the caliper in the jaws of a vice fitted with soft metal protectors and remove the dust excluder.
7   Using a suitable tool unscrew the piston. As the piston turns, apply low air pressure from a tyre pump to eject the piston. Place a piece of wood or hardboard between the piston and caliper to prevent damage.
8   Check the condition of the piston and cylinder surfaces. If they are scratched or scored or show other signs of metal-to-metal rubbed areas, the complete assembly must be renewed.
9   If the components are in good condition, remove the seal from the groove in the cylinder, and discard this and the dust excluder.
10 Obtain a repair kit and wash the piston and cylinder interior with methylated spirit or clean hydraulic fluid.
11 Fit the new piston seal using the fingers only.
12 Dip the piston in clean hydraulic fluid and insert it into the cylinder.
13 Press the piston in carefully by hand pressure and then use a screwing action until it will not enter the cylinder any further.
14 Now align the piston so that the line (R) is on the same side as the bleed screw (P) – Fig. 9.26.
15 Smear rubber grease around the end of the piston and fit a new dust excluder.
16 Fit the pads and caliper and bleed the system, as described in Section 17.

8   Front wheel cylinder – removal, overhaul and refitting

1   Raise the car and remove the roadwheel.
2   Remove the brake drum, as described in Section 4.
3   Prise the upper ends of the shoes apart and hold them in that position using a strut.
4   Unscrew the backplate fixing nuts to give access for removal of the wheel cylinder bolts. Remove these.
5   Disconnect the flexible hose at its junction with the rigid pipeline and plug or cap the ends to prevent loss of fluid and the entry of dirt.
6   Remove the wheel cylinder and unscrew the flexible hose from it.
7   Remove the internal components. These can usually be shaken out or, if necessary, use low air pressure from a tyre pump to eject them.
8   Check the piston and cylinder surfaces for scoring or bright metal-

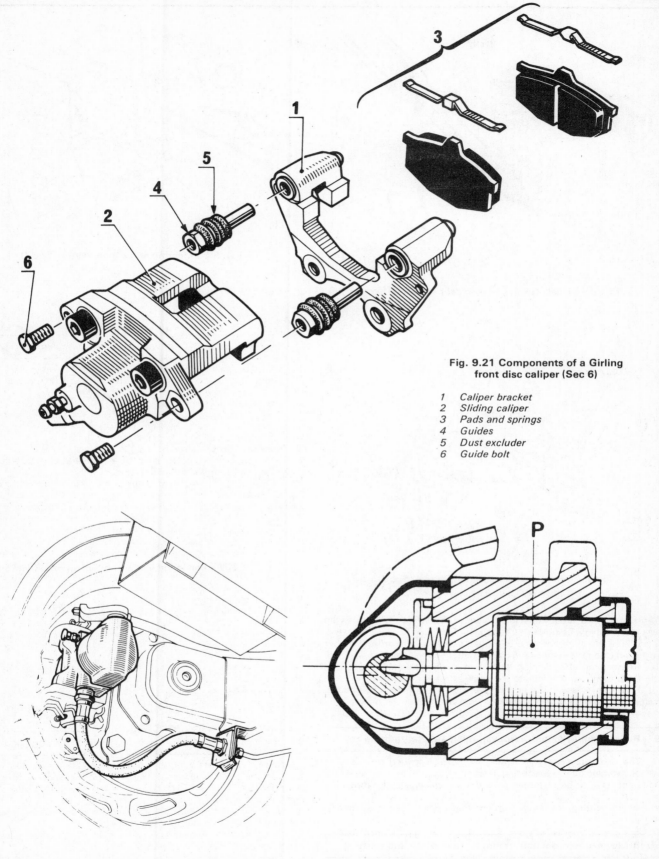

Fig. 9.21 Components of a Girling front disc caliper (Sec 6)

1 Caliper bracket
2 Sliding caliper
3 Pads and springs
4 Guides
5 Dust excluder
6 Guide bolt

Fig. 9.22 Rear disc caliper (Sec 7)

Fig. 9.23 Sectional view of rear disc caliper (Sec 7)
P   Piston

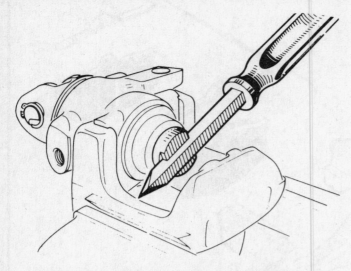

Fig. 9.24 Unscrewing rear disc caliper piston (Sec 7)

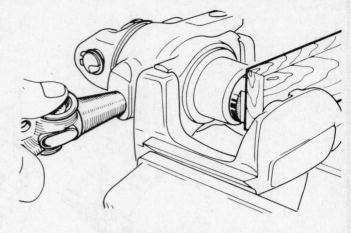

Fig. 9.25 Ejecting rear caliper piston (Sec 7)

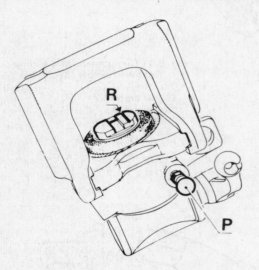

Fig. 9.26 Rear caliper alignment marks (Sec 7)

Align line R with bleed screw P

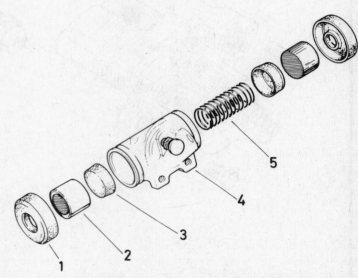

Fig. 9.27 Exploded view of a front wheel cylinder (Sec 8)

1	Dust excluder	4 Cylinder
2	Piston	5 Spring
3	Cup seal	

to-metal rubbed areas. If evident, renew the wheel cylinder as an assembly, otherwise obtain a repair kit.

9   Where the components are in good condition, discard the rubber seals and clean the pistons and cylinder interior in clean hydraulic fluid.

10 Reassemble after dipping each item in clean hydraulic fluid. Use the fingers only to manipulate the seals into the cylinder.

11 Refit the wheel cylinder by reversing the removal operations. Remember to bleed the hydraulic system and adjust the brakes.

9 Rear wheel cylinder – removal, overhaul and refitting

1   The operations are very similar to those described for the front wheel cylinder in the preceding Section, except that the backplate does not have to be disturbed to reach the wheel cylinder mounting bolts.

2   When refitting, adjust the hub endfloat as described in Section 5.

10 Brake disc – inspection, removal, renovation and refitting

Front disc

1   Whenever the brake pads are checked for wear, inspect the condition of the discs. Light scoring or grooving is normal, but deep

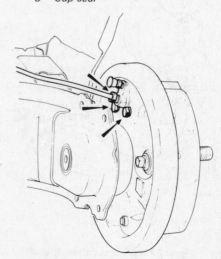

Fig. 9.28 Rear wheel cylinder union and mounting nuts (Sec 9)

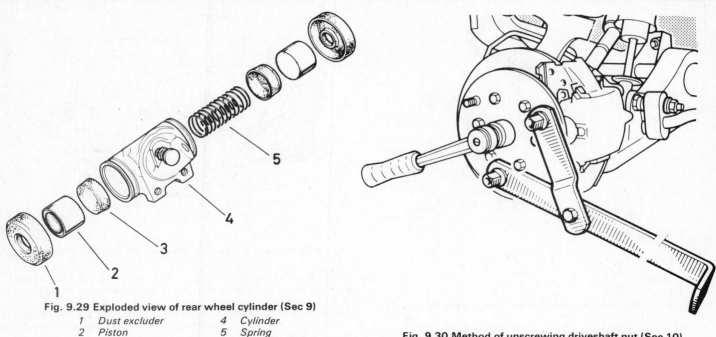

Fig. 9.29 Exploded view of rear wheel cylinder (Sec 9)

    1   Dust excluder   4   Cylinder
    2   Piston   5   Spring
    3   Cup seal

grooving will indicate the need for refacing – provided that the final thickness is not reduced below the specified minimum.
2   To remove a disc, raise the car and remove the roadwheel.
3   With the help of an assistant to apply the brake pedal fully, unscrew the hub nut. Alternatively, make up a lever similar to the one in Fig. 9.30 to prevent the hub rotating. The hub nut is very tight and will require the use of a long knuckle bar to release it.
4   Withdraw the caliper without disconnecting the hydraulic hose and tie it up out of the way.
5   Unbolt and remove the caliper bracket.
6   Using a slide hammer or suitable puller, withdraw the hub/disc.
7   Unscrew the disc fixing bolts and separate the hub from the disc.
8   Refitting is a reversal of removal, tighten the bolts and nuts to the specified torques.
9   If the new disc is coated with anti-corrosion compound, clean this off using a suitable solvent before refitting the caliper.
10 On completion apply the footbrake several times to position the pads against the disc.

Rear disc
11 This type of brake is fitted only to the 122B Gordini Turbo. The operations are similar to those described in earlier paragraphs of this Section except that a grooved disc cannot be reground but must be renewed.
12 Adjust the hub bearing endfloat as described in Section 5.

---

11   Brake drum – inspection and renovation

1   When removing the drum, as described earlier in this Chapter for inspection of the shoe linings for wear, always check the condition of the drum internal friction surface for grooving. This can be caused by the rivet heads scoring the drum if the shoes are not renewed when the linings are worn out. In severe cases of neglect, the drums can become pocketed and make their withdrawal difficult.
2   The drum may be reground internally provided the specified maximum diameter is not exceeded, otherwise a new drum will be required.

---

12   Master cylinder (single type) – removal, overhaul and refitting

1   Drain the hydraulic fluid from the master cylinder reservoir by syphoning or using an old battery hydrometer or poultry baster.
2   Disconnect the pipelines from the master cylinder by unscrewing the union nuts.

Fig. 9.30 Method of unscrewing driveshaft nut (Sec 10)

3   Working inside the car, disconnect the brake pedal pushrod from the pedal arm.
4   Unscrew the master cylinder mounting flange bolts and withdraw the cylinder from the engine compartment.
5   To dismantle the master cylinder, extract the circlip after having depressed the piston slightly to relieve the pressure on the circlip.
6   Remove the stop washer, the complete piston assembly and other internal components shown in Fig. 9.32.
7   Inspect the piston and cylinder bore surfaces for scoring, corrosion or bright metal-to-metal rubbed areas. Where evident a new master cylinder must be fitted.
8   If the components are in good condition, discard the rubber seals and obtain a repair kit. This will contain new seals and other renewable items.
9   Wash the piston and cylinder in methylated spirit or clean hydraulic fluid – nothing else.
10 Fit the new seal or complete piston assembly (depending on how supplied) using the fingers only to manipulate it into position. Dip the components in clean hydraulic fluid as reassembly proceeds.

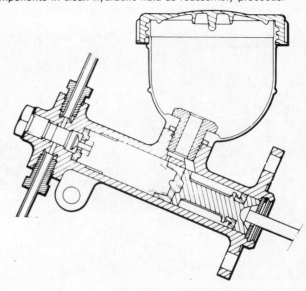

Fig. 9.31 Sectional view of single type master cylinder (Sec 12)

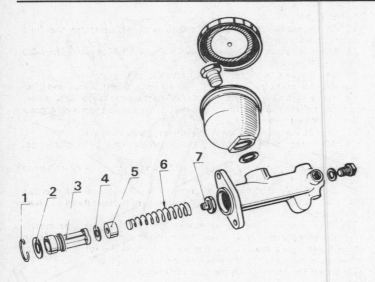

Fig. 9.32 Exploded view of single type master cylinder (Sec 12)

1	Circlip	5	Cup washer
2	Stop washer	6	Spring
3	Piston	7	Valve
4	Washer		

11 Refit the remaining internal components and fit the master cylinder by reversing the removal operations.
12 Bleed the braking system as described in Section 17.

---

13 Master cylinder (tandem type) – removal, overhaul and refitting

1 A master cylinder with an integral pressure drop indicator (see Section 15) cannot be overhauled, but must be renewed complete.
2 Drain the fluid from the master cylinder reservoir by syphoning or by using an old battery hydrometer or poultry baster.
3 Disconnect the pipelines from the master cylinder (photo) by unscrewing the union nuts.
4 If a pressure drop indicator is fitted, unscrew the retaining nuts.
5 If a vacuum servo unit is fitted, unbolt the master cylinder from the servo. On RHD models, the fluid reservoir is remote from the master cylinder (photo) and the feed pipes must be disconnected.

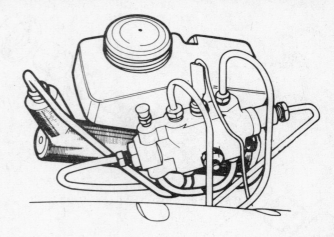

Fig. 9.33 Master cylinder with pressure drop indicator (Sec 13)

6 If a servo unit is not fitted, disconnect the master cylinder pushrod from the brake pedal arm, and unbolt the master cylinder from the pedal bracket.
7 One of two types of master cylinder may be fitted, the two designs differing by the angle of the pipeline union tapped hole at the front end of the master cylinder.

Early type
8 Pull the fluid reservoir from its rubber sealing sleeves by pulling upwards and using a side-to-side rocking motion.
9 Remove the pipeline which connects to the three way union (RHD).
10 Using a thin rod, depress the pistons by about 5.0 mm (0.20 in) and then unscrew the stop bolt (3), Fig. 9.36.
11 Holding the pistons depressed, extract the circlip (4) and the stop washer (5).
12 Release the pressure on the piston assemblies and withdraw the primary piston (6).
13 If the secondary piston will not shake out, eject it by applying air from a tyre pump to the cylinder fluid port.
14 Check the condition of the piston and cylinder surfaces. If they appear to be scored or show signs of bright metal-to-metal rubbing, renew the master cylinder complete.
15 If the components are in good condition, clean them in methylated spirit or clean hydraulic fluid – nothing else.
16 Obtain a repair kit which will contain new piston assemblies complete, separate seals are not supplied.

13.3 Tandem master cylinder and servo (RHD)

13.5 Remotely mounted master cylinder reservoir (RHD)

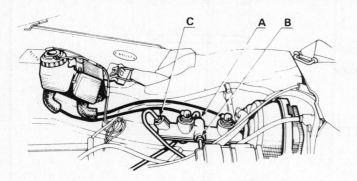

Fig. 9.34 RHD tandem master cylinder (Sec 13)

A   To RH front caliper
B   To LH front caliper
C   To pressure regulating valve

Later type

17 To dismantle this type of master cylinder, remove the fluid reservoir and the rubber sleeves.
18 Make up a tool in accordance with Fig. 9.39 from a length of 6.0 mm (0.24 in) rod.
19 Use the tool to compress the piston/spring assemblies.
20 Grip the end of a 3.5 mm (0.138 in) twist drill in a vice and offer the master cylinder to it so that the drill enters the secondary piston roll pin. Rotate the master cylinder on the drill and then give a good pull to extract the roll pin.
21 Repeat the operations for the primary piston roll pin.
22 Withdraw the compressing tool and withdraw both piston assemblies.
23 Check the condition of piston and cylinder bore as described in paragraphs 14 to 16.
24 Reassembly is a reversal of dismantling. Manipulate the seal lips into the cylinder after having dipped the piston assemblies in clean hydraulic fluid.
25 When inserting the piston assemblies into the later type master cylinder make sure that the roll pin slots in the pistons are aligned with their holes in the master cylinder body. Drive in the roll pins so that their slots are towards the pushrod end of the cylinder.
26 Bleed the hydraulic system on completion.

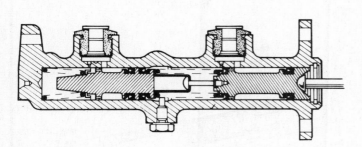

Fig. 9.35 Sectional view of tandem master cylinder – early type (Sec 13)

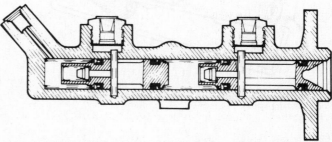

Fig. 9.37 Sectional view of tandem master cylinder – later type (Sec 13)

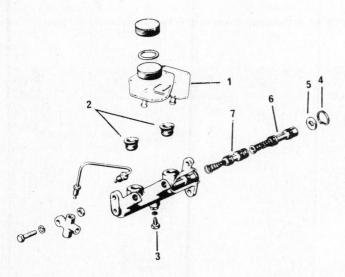

Fig. 9.36 Exploded view of tandem master cylinder (Sec 13)

1   Fluid reservoir
2   Rubber sleeves
3   Stop bolt
4   Circlip
5   Stop washer
6   Primary piston
7   Secondary piston

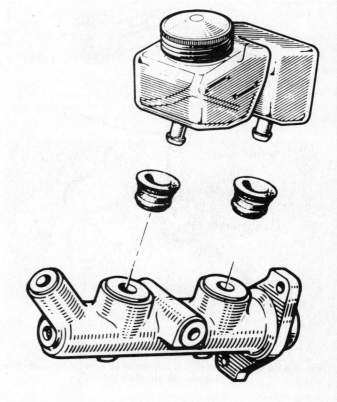

Fig. 9.38 Later type master cylinder (Sec 13)

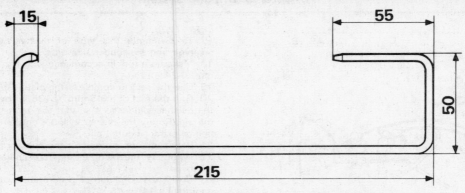

Fig. 9.39 Tool for compressing later type tandem master cylinder pistons (Sec 13)

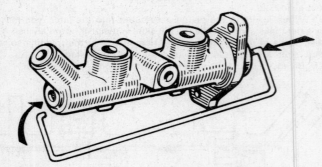

Fig. 9.40 Compressing master cylinder pistons (Sec 13)

Fig. 9.42 Later type master cylinder with piston assemblies (Sec 13)

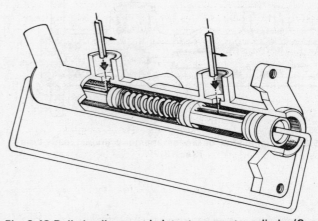

Fig. 9.43 Roll pin alignment in later type master cylinder (Sec 13)

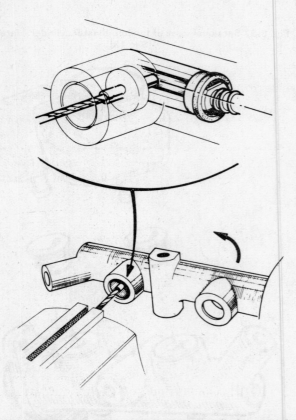

Fig. 9.41 Using a twist drill to extract master cylinder secondary piston roll pin (Sec 13)

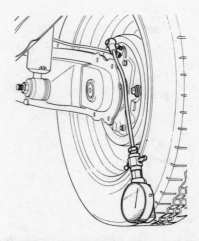

Fig. 9.44 Pressure gauge for checking pressure regulating valve cut-off pressure (Sec 14)

14 Pressure regulating valve – checking, adjusting and renewal

1   This valve (photo) restricts the pressure applied to the rear wheel brakes to prevent rear wheel lock up under heavy applications of the foot pedal.

2   Adjustment can only be carried out satisfactorily if a suitable pressure gauge is screwed into one of the rear wheel cylinders in place of a bleed screw. The gauge must have a bleed screw itself to be able to release   trapped air.

3   Bleed the gauge and system using the gauge bleed screw.

4   Depress the brake pedal several times and with an assistant, record the pressure indicated on the gauge. This should be within the ranges given. The car should be empty apart from the driver and a pre-determined quantity of fuel.

5   When adjustment is required, release the locknut on the threaded rod of the valve and turn the adjuster nut (A) clockwise to increase pressure or anti-clockwise to reduce – see Fig. 9.45.

6   Check the cut-off pressure on the gauge several times and then remove it and bleed the system.

7   A faulty valve cannot be repaired, or even overhauled, but will have to be renewed as an assembly.

8   To remove the valve, disconnect and cap the pipelines, disconnect the control rod and unbolt the valve.

9   Fit the new valve by reversing the removal operations. Bleed the system, check the cut-off pressure and adjust if necessary, remove the gauge and bleed the system again.

14.1 Pressure regulator unit

15 Pressure drop indicator – description, removal and refitting

1   This device is incorporated in the dual circuit type braking system and consists of a piston which is held in balance by the equal hydraulic pressures of the two circuits. In the event of the pressure dropping in one circuit due to a leak, the piston is displaced and completes an electrical circuit which illuminates a warning lamp on the instrument panel.

2   Air in the system or a fault in the master cylinder can also cause the pressure drop indicator to operate.

3   A more sophisticated type of indicator device is fitted to some models. This incorporates a bypass to enable the pressure in the rear circuit to be increased should a leak occur in the front circuit.

4   A faulty pressure drop indicator cannot be overhauled, it must be replaced by a new unit.

5   To remove the indicator, syphon the fluid from the master cylinder reservoir and disconnect the pipelines from it.

6   Disconnect the electrical lead from the terminal on the pressure indicator.

7   Unscrew the mounting nut and remove the device.

8   When refitting, set the pressure drop indicator at an angle of about 30° to the centre line of the master cylinder before tightening its mounting nut.

9   Reconnect the pipelines.

10   Reconnect the switch electrical lead.

11   Bleed the hydraulic system (see Section 17). If a bypass pressure drop indicator is fitted, bleed the device after all the other bleed screws have been bled.

16 Flexible and rigid hydraulic lines – inspection and renewal

1   At regular intervals, examine all components of the brake hydraulic system.

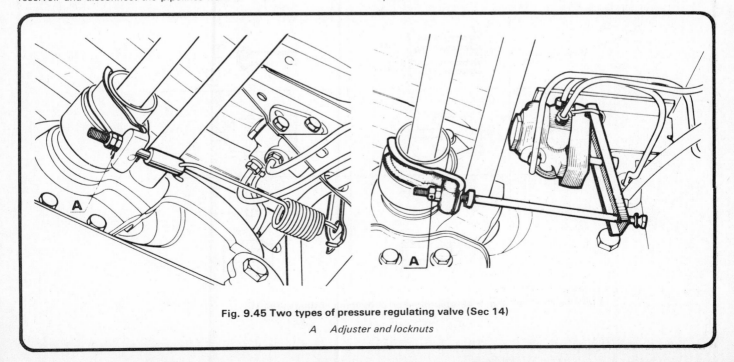

Fig. 9.45 Two types of pressure regulating valve (Sec 14)

A   Adjuster and locknuts

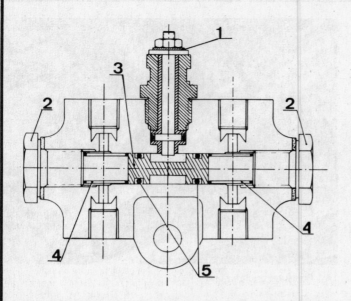

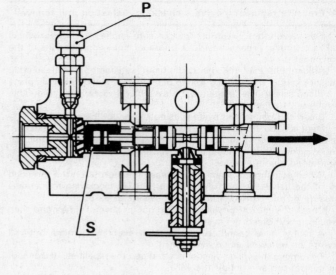

Fig. 9.46 Sectional view of pressure drop indicator (Sec 15)

1 Electrical terminal   4 Springs
2 End plugs   5 Seals
3 Piston

Fig. 9.47 Sectional view of pressure drop indicator with bypass (Sec 15)

P Bleed screw   S Bypass valve

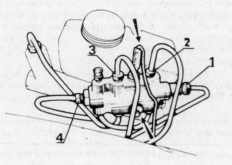

Fig. 9.48 Pressure drop indicator connections (Sec 15)

1 To RH front caliper
2 To LH front caliper
3 To rear brakes
4 Additional circuit outlet (downstream of pressure regulating valve)

	A	B
PIPE ENDS	steel / copper	steel or copper
THREADED BORES		
UNIONS	UNPAINTED 10 mm hex.	GREEN or BLACK 11 or 12 mm hex.

Fig. 9.49 Identification of hydraulic fittings (Sec 16)

A UNF   B Metric

2   First examine all the unions for signs of leaks. Then look at the flexible hoses for signs of fraying and chafing (as well as for leaks). This is only a preliminary inspection of the flexible hoses as exterior condition does not necessarily indicate interior condition which will be considered later.

3   The steel pipes must be examined equally carefully. They must be thoroughly cleaned and examined for signs of dents or other percussive damage, rust and corrosion. Rust and corrosion should be scraped off and, if the depth of pitting in the pipes is significant, they will need renewing. This is most likely in those areas underneath the chassis and along the rear suspension arms where the pipes are exposed to the full force of road and weather conditions.

4   If any section of pipe is to be removed, first of all take off the fluid reservoir cap, place some polythene film over the filler neck aperture and secure with an elastic band. Sealing the system in this manner will minimise the amount of fluid dripping out of the system when the pipes are removed.

5   Rigid pipe removal is usually quite straightforward. The unions at each end are undone and the pipe drawn out of the connection. The clips which may hold it to the car body are bent back and it is then removed. Underneath the car exposed unions can be particularly stubborn, defying the efforts of an open-ended spanner. As few people will have the special split ring spanner required, a self-grip wrench is the only answer. If the pipe is being renewed new unions will be provided. If not, one will have to put up with the possibility of burring over the flats on the union and use a self-grip wrench for refitting also.

6   Flexible hoses are always fitted to a rigid support bracket where they join a rigid pipe, the bracket being fixed to the chassis or rear suspension arm. The rigid pipe unions must first be removed from the flexible union. Then the locknut securing the flexible pipe to the bracket must be unscrewed, releasing the end of the pipe from the bracket. As these connections are usually exposed they are more often than not rusted up and a penetrating fluid is virtually essential to aid removal. When undoing them, both halves must be supported as the bracket is not strong enough to support the torque required to undo the nut and can easily be snapped off.

7   Once the flexible hose is removed, examine the internal bore. If clear of fluid it should be possible to see through it. Any specks of rubber which come out, or signs of restriction in the bore, mean that the inner lining is breaking up and the pipe must be renewed.

8   Rigid pipes can usually be purchased at any local garage where they have the pipe, unions and special tools to make them up. They will need to know the pipe length required and the type of flare used at the ends of the pipe. These may be different at each end of the same pipe.

9   Installation of the pipes is a reversal of the removal procedure. The pipe profile must be preset before fitting. Any acute bends must be put in by the garage on a bending machine, otherwise there is the possibility of kinking them and restricting the fluid flow.

10 With the pipes refitted, remove the polythene from the reservoir, top up and bleed the system as described in Section 17.

11 The threads on hydraulic component connections may be of UNF or metric type depending upon the make of component and date of production. It is important to compare new parts with the original ones to verify compatability. Always screw a threaded component into its tapped hole by hand first, to make sure that the threads are correct.

12 If new brake pipes are being made note the difference in flare contour between metric and other types.

13 A metric union does not seat fully at its shoulder when screwed in as a UNF type would. Do not attempt to force the union right home by applying excessive force.

17 Hydraulic system – bleeding

1   If the entire system is being bled, the sequence of bleeding should be carried out by starting at the bleed screw furthest from the master cylinder and finishing at the one nearest to it. Unless the pressure bleeding method is being used, do not forget to keep the fluid level in the master cylinder reservoir topped up to prevent air from being drawn into the system which would make any work done worthless.

2   Before commencing operations, check that all system hoses and pipes are in good condition with all unions tight and free from leaks.

3   Take great care not to allow hydraulic fluid to come into contact with the vehicle paintwork as it is an effective paint stripper. Wash off any spilled fluid immediately with cold water.

4   If the system incorporates a vacuum servo, destroy the vacuum by giving several applications of the brake pedal in quick succession.

Bleeding – two-man method

5   Gather together a clean jar and a length of rubber or plastic tubing which will be a tight fit on the brake bleed screws.

6   Engage the help of an assistant.

7   Push one end of the bleed tube onto the first bleed screw and immerse the other end in the jar which should contain enough hydraulic fluid to cover the end of the tube.

8   Open the bleed screw one half turn and have your assistant depress the brake pedal fully then slowly release it. Tighten the bleed screw at the end of each pedal downstroke to obviate any chance of air or fluid being drawn back into the system.

9   Repeat this operation until clean hydraulic fluid, free from air bubbles, can be seen coming through into the jar.

10 Tighten the bleed screw at the end of a pedal downstroke and remove the bleed tube. Bleed the remaining screws in a similar way.

Bleeding – using one way valve kit

11 There are a number of one-man, one-way brake bleeding kits available from motor accessory shops. It is recommended that one of these kits is used wherever possible as it will greatly simplify the bleeding operation and also reduce the risk of air or fluid being drawn back into the system, quite apart from being able to do the work without the help of an assistant.

12 To use the kit, connect the tube to the bleed screw and open the screw one half turn.

13 Depress the brake pedal fully and slowly release it. The one-way valve in the kit will prevent expelled air from returning at the end of each pedal downstroke. Repeat this operation several times to be sure of ejecting all air from the system. Some kits include a translucent container which can be positioned so that the air bubbles can be seen being ejected from the system.

14 Tighten the bleed screw, remove the tube and repeat the operations on the remaining brakes.

15 On completion, depress the brake pedal. If it still feels spongy repeat the bleeding operations, as air must still be trapped in the system.

Bleeding – using a pressure bleeding kit

16 These kits are also available from motor accessory shops and are usually operated by air pressure from the spare tyre.

17 By connecting a pressurised container to the master cylinder fluid reservoir, bleeding is then carried out by simply opening each bleed screw in turn and allowing the fluid to run out, rather like turning on a tap, until no air is visible in the expelled fluid.

18 By using this method, the large reserve of hydraulic fluid provides a safeguard against air being drawn into the master cylinder during bleeding which often occurs if the fluid level in the reservoir is not maintained.

19 Pressure bleeding is particularly effective when bleeding 'difficult' systems or when bleeding the complete system at the time of routine fluid renewal.

20 Where a vacuum servo is fitted, it is recommended that the brake pedal is depressed slowly and held down with a wooden strut after opening the first bleed screw.

21 Where a pressure drop indicator is fitted which incorporates a bypass, remember to bleed from the bleed screw on this device.

All methods

22 When bleeding is completed, check and top up the fluid level in the master cylinder reservoir.

23 Check the feel of the brake pedal. If it feels at all spongy, air must still be present in the system and further bleeding is indicated. Failure to bleed satisfactorily after a reasonable repetition of the bleeding operations may be due to worn master cylinder seals.

24 Discard brake fluid which has been expelled. It is almost certain to be contaminated with moisture, air and dirt making it unsuitable for further use. Clean fluid should always be stored in an airtight container as it absorbs moisture readily (hygroscopic) which lowers its boiling point and could affect braking performance under severe conditions.

18 Vacuum servo unit – description and servicing

1   On certain models, braking assistance is provided by a vacuum-operated servo which acts in series with the master cylinder to provide assistance to the driver when the brake pedal is depressed. This reduces the effort required by the driver to operate the brakes under all conditions of braking when the engine is running.

2   The unit operates from the vacuum of the inlet manifold and is essentially a booster diaphragm and a control valve assembly.

3   The servo unit and master cylinder are connected together so that the servo unit piston rod acts as the master cylinder pushrod. The pushrod connected to the brake pedal operates the servo valve.

4   The servo piston is attached to a diaphragm which ensures an airtight seal between the two principal parts of the servo casing. The forward chamber is held under vacuum from the inlet manifold; when the brake pedal is not being depressed, the same vacuum is also applied to the rear chamber.

5   When the brake pedal is depressed, the vacuum port to the rear chamber is closed and the chamber is vented to atmosphere. The resultant pressure difference of atmospheric pressure on the rear of the diaphragm and a vacuum on its front, causes the diaphragm to move forward to operate the master cylinder pushrod.

6   A control system inside the servo provides a reaction force on the brake pedal which is proportional to the pressure being applied to the master cylinder.

7   A vacuum servo is very reliable and does not normally require overhaul except after a very high mileage. Because special tools are required to dismantle it, it is recommended that an exchange unit be obtained when overhaul becomes necessary.

8   Normal servicing includes checking the condition of the vacuum hose and the one-way valve sealing grommet and also renewal of the air cleaner element at the intervals specified in Routine Maintenance.

9   To renew the filter element, disconnect and unscrew the clevis fork from the end of the pedal pushrod.

10   Prise off the dust excluder and using a pointed tool, pick out the old filter. On some models, a retaining spring is fitted to the filter.

11   Fit the new filter element and reconnect the pushrod clevis.

12   Now check dimension (L) as shown in the diagram Fig. 9.51. Adjust as necessary by turning the clevis fork. On completion, tighten the locknut.

13   To renew the one-way valve grommet on the servo, disconnect the vacuum hose from it and then pull and twist the valve from the grommet. Remove the grommet.

14   Fit the new grommet, apply a smear of rubber grease to the one-way valve and push it into the grommet. Use a twisting motion to prevent any possibility of the grommet being pushed into the servo interior.

19 Vacuum servo unit – removal and refitting

1   Disconnect the battery.

2   Disconnect and remove the master cylinder as described in Section 13.

3   Disconnect the vacuum hose from the servo.

4   Disconnect the pushrod from the brake pedal.

5   Unscrew the brake servo mounting nuts and remove the servo.

6   If a new or reconditioned servo is being fitted, check the dimension X Fig. 9.53, which is measured between the end of the servo operating rod and the mounting face for the master cylinder.

7   Where necessary, turn nut P to adjust.

8   Refitting is a reversal of removal.

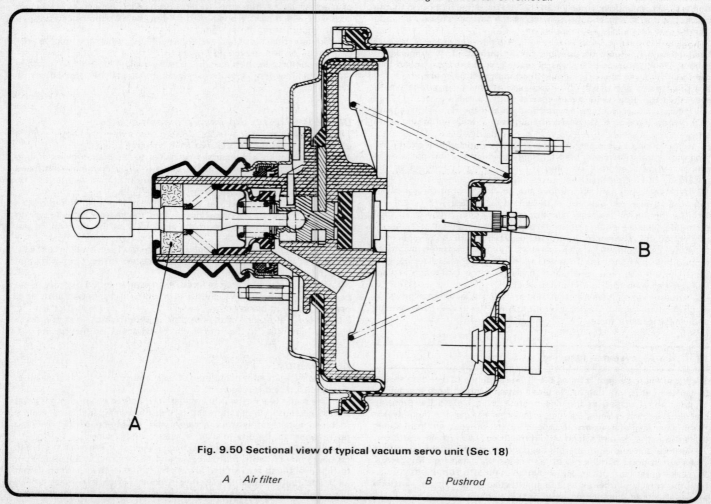

Fig. 9.50 Sectional view of typical vacuum servo unit (Sec 18)

A   Air filter   B   Pushrod

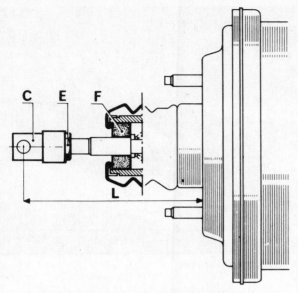

Fig. 9.51 Vacuum servo pushrod setting (Sec 18)

C	Clevis fork	L	RHD – 102.0 mm
E	Locknut		(4.02 in)
F	Air filter	L	LHD – 120.0 mm
			(4.73 in)

Fig. 9.52 Servo one-way valve and grommet (Sec 18)

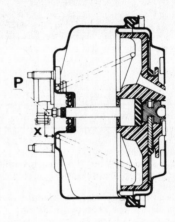

Fig. 9.53 Servo pushrod setting diagram (Sec 18)

P   Pushrod nut   X = 9.0 mm (0.35 in)

20 Handbrake – adjustment

1   Handbrake adjustment is normally automatic whenever the brakes shoes are adjusted. However, over a period of time, due to cable stretch, supplementary adjustment may be required.
2   On R1221 models where the handbrake operates on the front wheels, raise the front of the car. On all other models raise the rear of the car.
3   Release the handbrake fully.
4   Release the locknut on the cable equalizer (photo) and tighten the adjuster nut until the shoes are just heard to scrape against the drum. The handbrake lever should be able to be pulled over six notches of the ratchet to fully apply the brakes. If this is satisfactory, tighten the locknut.

5   Keep the cable groove in the equaliser and the threads of the cable end fitting well smeared with grease at all times to reduce rust and corrosion.
6   On models fitted with a handbrake 'ON' switch (photo), check the function of the switch. Any adjustment may be made by carefully bending the contact strip on the switch.

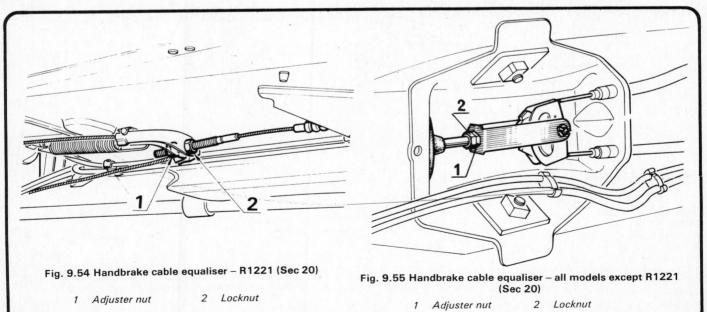

Fig. 9.54 Handbrake cable equaliser – R1221 (Sec 20)

1   Adjuster nut   2   Locknut

Fig. 9.55 Handbrake cable equaliser – all models except R1221 (Sec 20)

1   Adjuster nut   2   Locknut

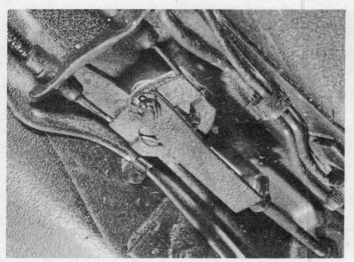

20.4 Handbrake cable equaliser

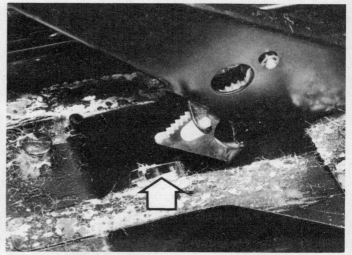

20.6 Handbrake 'ON' switch

21 Handbrake cables – renewal

Primary cable

1   Release the handbrake cable fully.
2   Disconnect the primary cable from the equaliser under the car.
3   Disconnect the cable from the handbrake control lever. Renew the rubber grommet if necessary.
4   Refit the new cable by reversing the removal operations and adjust the handbrake as described in the preceding Section.

Fig. 9.56 Handbrake cable connector – R1221 (Sec 21)

Secondary cable

Model R1221

5   Disconnect the equaliser from the primary cable.
6   Two independent cables are used. Separate the right-hand and left-hand cables at the connector.
7   Remove the guide and the sleeve stop.
8   Remove the brake drum on the side from which the cable is to be removed.
9   Unhook the cable from the lever on the brake shoe.
10 Fit the new cable by reversing the removal operations.
11 Adjust as described in Section 20.

All other models

12 Disconnect the cable equaliser and remove the cable from the equaliser groove.
13 Pull the cable from its sleeve stop.
14 Remove both rear brake drums, unhook the cables from the levers on the brake shoes.
15 Refit by reversing the removal operations, adjust the handbrake and the shoes as described earlier in this Chapter.

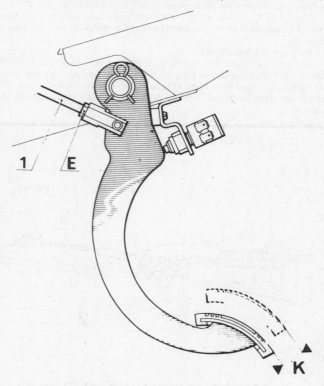

Fig. 9.57 Brake pedal setting diagram (Sec 22)

1   Pushrod   K   Free movement 5.0 mm (0.20 in)
E   Locknut

22 Brake pedal (manual transmission) – removal and refitting

1   Remove the sill embellisher from inside the front door step.
2   Remove the parcel shelf and pillar trim panel.
3   Prise the clip from the end of the pedal cross-shaft.
4   Disconnect the clutch pedal return spring.
5   Disconnect the brake pedal pushrod from the pedal arm.
6   Push the cross-shaft far enough out of its bearings to be able to drop both pedals.
7   Refit by reversing the removal operations, apply grease to the bearings and check the clutch pedal adjustment, as described in Chapter 5.
8   Check the brake pedal free movement (K) and adjust by turning the pushrod as shown in Fig. 9.57.

9   Check the servo pushrod dimension on vehicles so equipped by reference to Section 18.
10 Adjust the brake stop-lamp switch so that the stop lamps come on when the brake pedal has been depressed through 2.0 mm (0.078 in) of its free movement.

23 Brake pedal (automatic transmission) – removal and refitting

1   The operations are similar to those described in the preceding Section, except that the cross-shaft supports only one pedal, a clutch pedal not being fitted.

24 Fault diagnosis – braking system

Before diagnosing faults from the following chart, check that any braking irregularities are not caused by:
(a)   Uneven or incorrect tyre pressures
(b)   Incorrect mix of radial and crossply tyres
(c)   Wear in the steering mechanism
(d)   Misalignment of the chassis geometry

Symptom	Reason(s)
Pedal travels a long way before the brakes operate	Brake shoes set too far from the drums due to faulty adjusting mechanism, or when worn to limit
Stopping ability poor, even though pedal pressure is firm	Linings/pads and/or drums/disc badly worn or scored One or more wheel hydraulic cylinders or caliper pistons seized Brake linings/pads contaminated with oil or hydraulic fluid Wrong type of linings/pads fitted (too hard) Brake shoes/pads wrongly assembled Faulty servo unit (where fitted)
Car veers to one side when the brakes are applied	Brake linings/pads on one side are contaminated Hydraulic wheel cylinder/caliper on one side partially or fully seized A mixture of lining materials fitted between sides Unequal wear between sides caused by partially seized wheel cylinders/pistons
Pedal feels spongy	Air in the hydraulic system
Pedal feels springy when the brakes are applied	Brake linings/pads not bedded into the drums/discs (after fitting new ones) Master cylinder or brake backplate mounting bolts loose Severe wear in brake drums/discs causing distortion when brakes are applied
Pedal travels right down with little or no resistance and brakes are virtually non-operative	Leak in hydraulic system If no signs of leakage are present, the master cylinder internal seals are failing to sustain pressure
Binding, juddering, overheating	One or a combination of causes given in the foregoing sections Handbrake over-adjusted Handbrake cable(s) seized

Chapter 10 Electrical system

For modifications, and information applicable to later models, see Supplement at end of manual

Contents

Specifications

System type	Battery with dynamo or alternator and pre-engaged starter
Battery	36 Ah, 12V negative earth
Alternator Minimum brush length	35A or 50A, according to model 7.0 mm (0.28 in)
Dynamo Minimum brush length	22A 11.0 mm (0.43 in)

Voltage regulator
Type:
    Models up to 1980
    Models after 1980
	
	Sealed, remotely-sited
	Integral with alternator brush holder plate

Starter motor Minimum brush length	Pre-engaged 11.5 mm (0.45 in)

Windscreen wipers
Wiper arms (1977 to 1985)
Wiper blades:
    1972 to 1977
    1977 on
	
	Champion CCA4
	
	Champion X-3303
	Champion X-3603

Fuses (typical) – early models

Number	Circuit protected	Fuse (A)
1	LH front side (parking) and tail lamps, instrument panel	5
2	RH front side (parking) and tail lamps, cigar lighter lamp	5
3	Windscreen wiper/washer	8
4	Cigar lighter, courtesy lamp	5
5	Heater blower motor and radio	5
6	Direction indicator/hazard warning relay	5
7	Spare	
8	Reverse lamps, heated rear window, stop-lamps, tailgate wiper, air conditioner relay	16

Fuses (typical) – later models

Number	Circuit protected	Fuse (A)
1	Reverse lamp switch, heated rear window switch, rear screen wiper 'park' and timer	16
2	Automatic transmission	1.5
3	Windscreen wiper/washer switch	8
4	Car radio, stop-lamp switch, heater booster fan	8
5	Cigar lighter, interior lamp	8
6	Windscreen wiper 'park'	5
7	RH side (parking) and tail lamps, cigar lighter illumination	5
8	LH side (parking) and tail lamps, instrument panel illumination	5
9	Flasher relay	5
10	Rear foglamp switch/Air conditioner	5/16
11	LH electric window	16
12	RH electric window	16

Bulbs (typical)

	Wattage
Headlamp:	
Standard (bulb type)	45/40
Halogen (bulb type)	55
Sealed beam type	unit 6012 or 6052
Front side (parking) lamp	5
Direction indicator lamp	21
Stop/tail lamp	21/5
Reversing lamp	21
Interior lamp	5
Instrument panel and warning lamps	2
Side marker lamp	5

---

1 General description

The electrical system is of 12V negative earth type and consists of a battery, dynamo (early models) or alternator (later models) and a pre-engaged starter motor.

The electrical accessories fitted vary according to model. Generally a more comprehensive range is fitted to later models and include as standard equipment a heated rear window, reversing lamps, rear fog lamps and on certain versions, a radio, electrically-operated front windows and central door lock system.

---

2 Battery – maintenance

1 Although the battery will not normally require topping-up at other than very infrequent intervals, it is worthwhile checking the electrolyte level at the weekly inspection in case the generator (dynamo or alternator) is overcharging. This can be assumed if the battery requires topping-up very frequently and severe gassing is noticed when the cell plugs are removed. The top of the battery casing will also be covered in electrolyte condensate.

2 The cause of such overcharging will be due almost certainly to a faulty voltage regulator.

3 When normal topping-up is required, use only distilled or demineralised water or melted ice condensate from a freezer.

4 Depending upon the type of battery, top up the electrolyte to the indicator or battery case mark. If the level is not marked, top up until the electrolyte level is just above the top of the battery plates.

5 Keep the top of the battery casing dry and the battery terminals free from corrosion by smearing them with petroleum jelly.

6 If the terminals should become corroded through neglect, scrape them clean and neutralise the deposits by applying household ammonia or sodium bicarbonate, leave for a few minutes then wash off.

7 Periodically, remove the battery, inspect the battery tray and if corroded, clean it thoroughly and apply undersealing compound or similar material.

8 Regularly check that the battery lead connections are tight, particularly the earth bonds to engine/transmission and body.

9 The acid used in battery electrolyte should never require replenishment as only the water evaporates. If for any reason, such as spillage, fresh electrolyte is needed **do not attempt to mix the acid and water yourself**, but leave the job to the experts – your Renault dealer or a battery specialist.

10 On cars regularly covering a reasonable mileage, the battery will not require charging from an outside source, but if the starter is used repeatedly for stop/start motoring or only short journeys are made with much use of the electrical equipment, then a mains charger will be required to recharge the battery, preferably overnight.

11 If a battery suddenly exhibits a tendency to lack power for starting purposes if the battery is new, have the charging rate checked. If the battery is old, check the voltage which should be 12.5 V or more.

12 Use a hydrometer to check the specific gravity of the cells. If one or more cells give very different readings from the others then the time has probably come for renewal.

13 When measuring the specific gravity, use the following table as a guide.

State of charge	Specific gravity
Fully charged	*1.28*
Half charged	*1.22*
Discharged	*1.11*

14 If a new battery is to be purchased, make sure that the overall size is the same as the original or that the battery location will accept the new one.

15 Check that the terminal positions are in the same place as the original, otherwise the leads may not be long enough to reach the new terminals.

16 Finally, make sure that the new battery terminal posts are compatible with the original clamps or connectors.

---

3 Battery – removal and refitting

1 The battery is located within the engine compartment.

2 Disconnect the negative lead from the battery followed by the positive one.

3 The battery may be held in position by a frame and tie-bolts or by a base clamp, according to the type of battery fitted.

4 Remove the retainer and lift the battery from the car. Take care not to spill the electrolyte.

5 Refitting is a reversal of removal.

---

4 Dynamo – description, maintenance and testing

1 The dynamo consists of an armature running in bearings. It is surrounded by field coils bolted to the outer casing or yoke. At one end

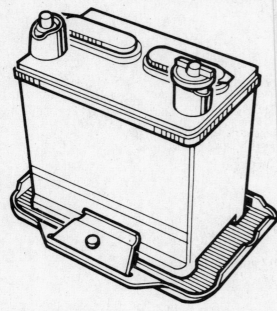

Fig. 10.1 Battery with base clamp (Sec 3)

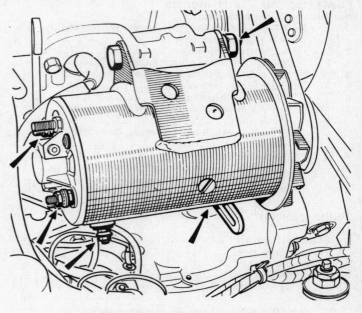

Fig. 10.2 Dynamo disconnection points (Sec 5)

of the armature is the commutator consisting of copper segments. Two carbon brushes, spring loaded and in holders, run on the commutator.

2   The only maintenance required is to check that the drivebelt is correctly tensioned. The armature runs in ball-bearings with sealed in lubrication. Some owners may wish to check the carbon brush length and this can be done by seeing that the ends are not below the ends of the brush holders. If they are, new brushes should be fitted.

3   A dynamo normally works properly, or not at all. There are few instances of poor performance. A quick check can be made if a voltmeter is available. Disconnect both leads from the dynamo and join the two terminals together with a piece of bare wire. From the centre of the wire run a lead via the voltmeter to earth. With the engine running at a fast tickover there should be a reading of about 15 volts. If there is no voltage then suspect the carbon brushes. If the voltage

is low then suspect the field windings or armature. Either of the latter will require overhaul or renewal.

5   Dynamo – removal and refitting

1   Disconnect the battery negative and then positive leads.
2   Disconnect the leads from the dynamo terminals.
3   Release the mounting and belt tensioner bolts, push the dynamo in towards the engine and slip the drivebelt off the pulley.
4   Withdraw the mounting bolt and lift the dynamo from the engine compartment.
5   Refitting is a reversal of removal, tension the drivebelt as described in Chapter 2.

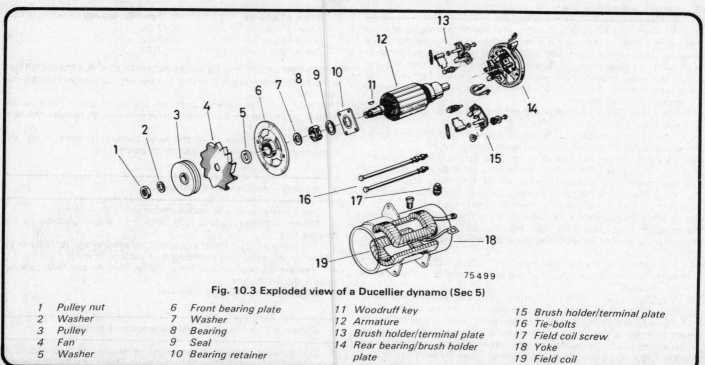

Fig. 10.3 Exploded view of a Ducellier dynamo (Sec 5)

1   Pulley nut
2   Washer
3   Pulley
4   Fan
5   Washer
6   Front bearing plate
7   Washer
8   Bearing
9   Seal
10 Bearing retainer
11 Woodruff key
12 Armature
13 Brush holder/terminal plate
14 Rear bearing/brush holder plate
15 Brush holder/terminal plate
16 Tie-bolts
17 Field coil screw
18 Yoke
19 Field coil

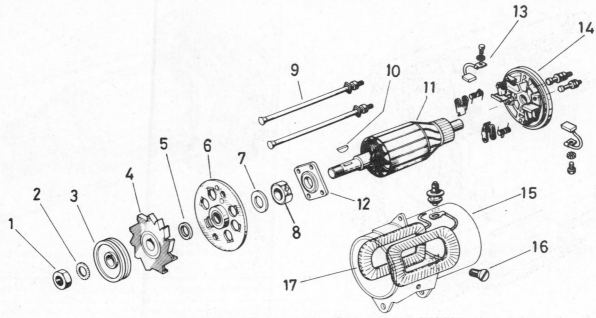

Fig. 10.4 Exploded view of Paris-Rhone dynamo (Sec 6)

1	Pulley nut	6	Front bearing plate
2	Washer	7	Washer
3	Pulley	8	Bearing
4	Fan	9	Tie-bolts
5	Washer	10	Woodruff key

11	Armature	15	Yoke
12	Bearing retainer	16	Field coil screw
13	Brush	17	Field coil
14	Rear bearing/brush holder plate		

6 Dynamo – overhaul

1 With the dynamo removed, clean away external dirt.
2 Unscrew and remove the nuts from the tie-bolts.
3 Pull off the rear cover/bearing assembly.
4 This is far enough to go to be able to check the brushes for wear. If their length is down to 11.0 mm (0.43 in), or less, renew them.
5 The new brushes are supplied complete with leads, renewal is simply a matter of releasing the terminal screws, but note the location of the insulating washers on the output terminal.
6 Remove the yoke complete with field coils. Examine the commutator, if it is black in colour, clean it with a solvent-soaked rag. Any light scoring can be cleaned up with fine glasspaper (not sandpaper). Now check the commutator segment insulators. If they are flush with the surface of the commutator, they should be slightly undercut using a thin hacksaw blade. Make sure that the undercut is square within the groove.
7 If the commutator, armature or bearings show signs of wear or damage, serious consideration should be given to obtaining a new or reconditioned unit, as individual spares are difficult to obtain and not an economical proposition.
8 If further dismantling is needed for any reason, the pulley and front bearing may be removed once the pulley nut is unscrewed. To do this, place an old drivebelt in the pulley groove and grip the belt around the pulley in the jaws of a vice. This method of holding the pulley still while the nut is unscrewed will eliminate the possibility of damage to the pulley rims.
9 Reassembly is a reversal of dismantling. Pack the rear bearing with some high melting point grease.

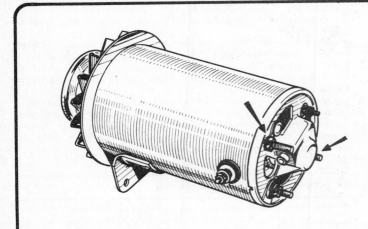

Fig. 10.5 Dynamo tie-bolt nuts (Sec 6)

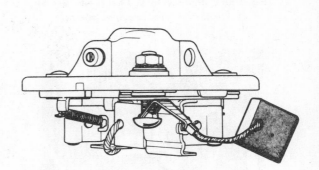

Fig. 10.6 Ducellier dynamo brushes (Sec 6)

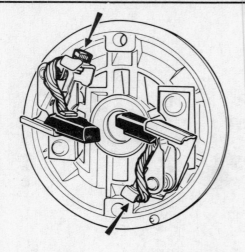

Fig. 10.7 Paris-Rhone dynamo bushes (Sec 6)

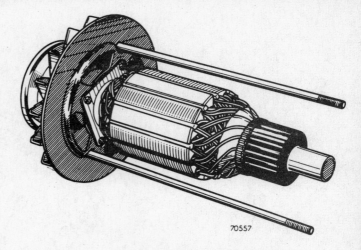

Fig. 10.8 Dynamo with yoke removed (Sec 6)

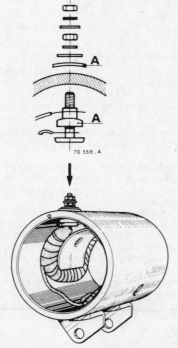

Fig. 10.9 Dynamo yoke and field coils (Sec 6)

A   Insulators fitted to output terminal

9.2 Alternator connections

7   Alternator – description, maintenance and precautions

1   The alternator fitted to all later models has the advantage of generating current at much lower engine speeds than is the case with a dynamo.

2   Maintenance consists of maintaining the correct drivebelt tension (see Chapter 2).

3   The following precautions must be taken to avoid damage to the sensitive diodes within the unit:

(a) *Never earth the 'EXC' terminal or connecting lead from the alternator or voltage regulator*
(b) *Never disconnect a battery or voltage regulator lead while the engine is running*
(c) *Always disconnect the battery before removing the alternator*
(d) *Do not use an electric welder on the car unless the battery is disconnected*
(e) *Disconnect the battery leads before using a mains charger*

8   Alternator – testing

1   The use of a voltmeter and an ammeter will be required for these tests.

2   Connect the voltmeter between the battery terminals. With the engine idling, the reading should be 14V if all electrical accessories are switched off.

3   Increase the engine speed to 2000 rpm and the reading should be 15V.

4   Hold this engine speed and switch on the headlamps, heated rear window, heater blower and wiper/washer, the reading should fall to between 13 and 14V.

5   To check the alternator output, connect an ammeter in series and then start the engine.

6   Increase the engine speed to 2500 rpm, and then switch on as many electrical accessories as possible, one at a time. The alternator output should increase each time an accessory is switched on, but will not exceed the rated output of the particular alternator fitted to your model (see the alternator index plate).

9   Alternator – removal and refitting

1   Disconnect the battery negative and then positive leads.

2   Disconnect the leads from the alternator terminals (photo).

3   Release the alternator mounting and belt adjuster strap bolts and push the unit in towards the engine so that the drivebelt can be slipped off the pulley.

4   Remove the mounting and strap bolts and lift the alternator from the engine.

5   Refitting is a reversal of removal. Tension the drivebelt as described in Chapter 2.

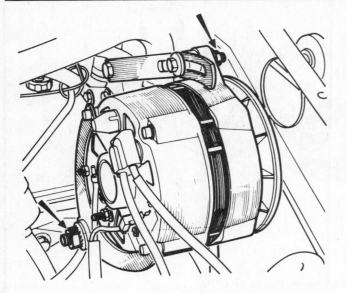

Fig. 10.10 Alternator (R1221) disconnection points (Sec 8)

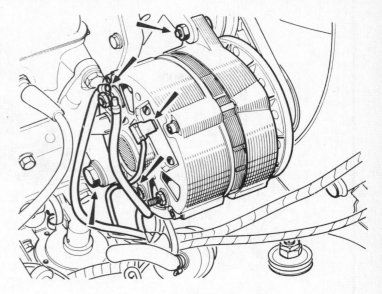

Fig. 10.11 Alternator disconnection points –
all models except R1221 (Sec 8)

10 Alternator – overhaul

1 The operations described are similar for all makes of alternator, but the different designs of components should be noted from the illustrations.
2 With the alternator removed from the car, clean away external dirt.
3 Extract the screws or retaining nuts to obtain access to the brush holder or brushes. These vary according to make of alternator.
4 If the brushes are worn below the specified minimum length then they must be renewed.
5 Place an old drivebelt in the pulley groove and grip the belt around the pulley in the jaws of a vice. This will prevent the pulley turning

while the pulley retaining nut is unscrewed. Remove the pulley.
6 Unscrew and remove the tie-bolts.
7 Insert a screwdriver into the cut-outs between the stator and drive end bracket. Do not insert it to more than a depth of 2.0 mm (0.079 in) otherwise the stator windings may be damaged.
8 Extract the three screws which hold the front bearing retainer, tap the end of the rotor shaft on a block of wood to separate the rotor from the drive end bracket.
9 Examine the slip rings, if they are discoloured, wipe them clean with a solvent-soaked rag.

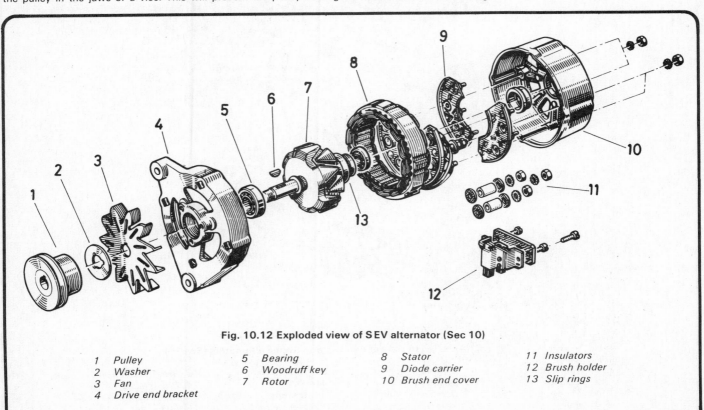

Fig. 10.12 Exploded view of SEV alternator (Sec 10)

1 Pulley	5 Bearing	8 Stator	11 Insulators
2 Washer	6 Woodruff key	9 Diode carrier	12 Brush holder
3 Fan	7 Rotor	10 Brush end cover	13 Slip rings
4 Drive end bracket			

242

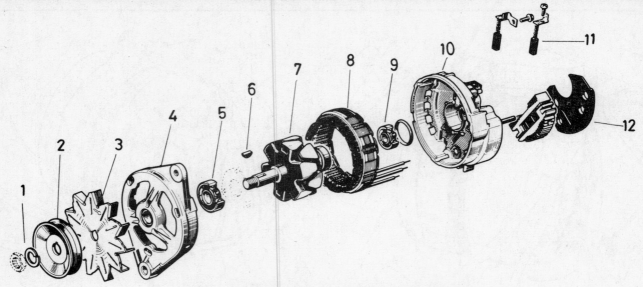

Fig. 10.13 Exploded view of Ducellier alternator (Sec 10)

1	Pulley nut	4	Drive end bracket	7	Rotor	10	Brush end cover
2	Pulley	5	Bearing	8	Stator	11	Brushes
3	Fan	6	Woodruff key	9	Bearing	12	Diode carrier

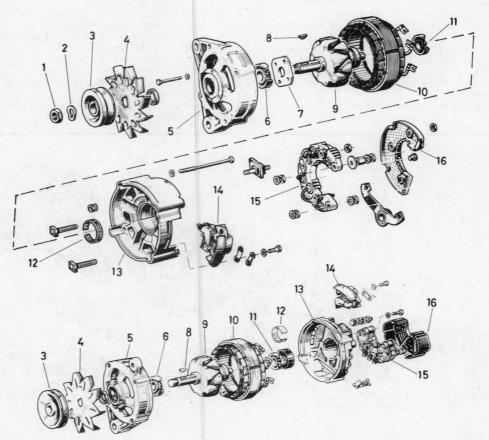

Fig. 10.14 Exploded view of typical Paris-Rhone alternators (Sec 10)

1	Pulley nut	5	Drive end bracket	9	Rotor	13	Brush end bracket
2	Washer	6	Bearing	10	Stator	14	Brush holder
3	Pulley	7	Bearing retainer	11	Bearing	15	Diode carrier
4	Fan	8	Woodruff key	12	Needle race	16	End cover

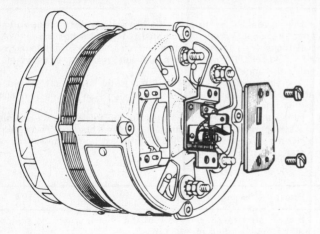

Fig. 10.15 Brush cover plate – SEV alternator (Sec 10)

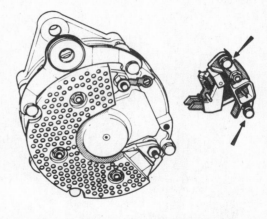

Fig. 10.16 Brush holder – Paris-Rhone alternator (Sec 10)

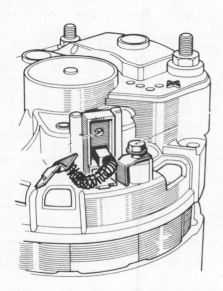

Fig. 10.17 Brush – Ducellier alternator (Sec 10)

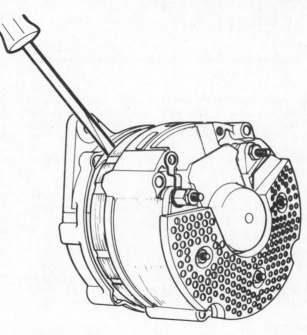

Fig. 10.18 Removing alternator drive end bracket (Sec 10)

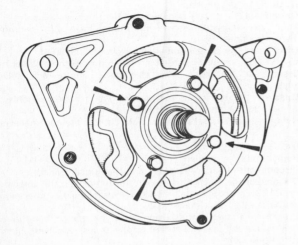

Fig. 10.19 Alternator front bearing retainer screws (Sec 10)

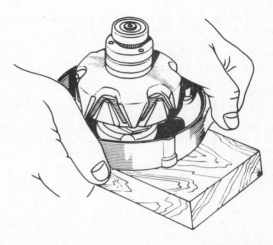

Fig. 10.20 Separating motor from drive end bracket (Sec 10)

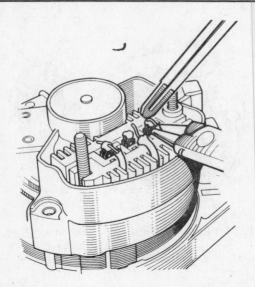

Fig. 10.21 Soldering brush leads – Ducellier alternator (Sec 10)

10 If the slip rings are scored, the bearings worn or dry or the rotor or stator wiring damaged, consideration should be given to the purchase of a new or reconditioned unit. Apart from the fact that small alternator parts are difficult to obtain it will be more economical to do so.

11 Reassembly is a reversal of removal, but note the method of assembling the diode carrier very carefully.

SEV type

12 It is important to position the diode carrier insulating washers and sleeves correctly, and route the diode wires so that they do not touch the rotor.

Ducellier type

13 The diode carrier wires will have to be soldered in position. Grip the wire close to the point of soldering with a pair of pliers as a heat sink and solder as quickly as possible so that excessive heat is not conducted down the wire.

Paris-Rhone type

14 The diode carrier is held by nuts. Remember to fit the link.

11 Voltage regulator

Models up to 1980

1 This is of remotely-sited, sealed type.
2 Never mix up the leads if they are disconnected.
3 No adjustment is possible, and if a fault develops fit a new unit.

Models 1980 and later

4 On SEV and Paris-Rhone type alternators fitted to later models, an integral voltage control unit is used.
5 The regulator is bolted to the brush holder assembly and is renewable as a sealed unit. Do not overtighten the regulator mounting screws because the printed circuit could be damaged and the brush holder soldered connections broken.

12 Starter – description

1 The starter is of the pre-engaged type, ie the drive pinion is brought into mesh with the starter ring gear on the flywheel before the main current is applied.
2 When the starter switch is operated, current flows from the battery to the solenoid, which is mounted on the top of the starter motor body. The plunger in the solenoid moves inwards, so causing a

centrally pivoted lever to push the drive pinion into mesh with the starter ring gear. When the solenoid plunger reaches the end of its travel, it closes an internal contact and full starting current flows to the starter field coils. The armature is then able to rotate the crankshaft, so starting the engine.
3 A special freewheel clutch is fitted to the starter drive pinion so that as soon as the engine fires and starts to operate on its own it does not drive the starter motor.
4 When the starter switch is released, the solenoid is de-energised and a spring moves the plunger back to its rest position. This operates the pivoted lever to withdraw the drive pinion from engagement with the starter ring gear.

13 Starter – testing in car

1 If the starter motor fails to turn the engine when the switch is operated, there are four possible reasons:

   (a) *The battery is discharged or faulty*
   (b) *The electrical connections between switch, solenoid, battery and starter motor are somewhere failing to pass the necessary current from the battery, through the starter to earth*
   (c) *The solenoid has an internal fault*
   (d) *The starter motor is electrically defective*

2 To check the battery, switch on the headlights. If they go dim after a few seconds the battery is discharged. If the lamps glow brightly, operate the ignition/starter switch and see what happens to the lights. If they do dim it is indicative that power is reaching the starter motor but failing to turn it.
3 If when the ignition/starter switch is operated, the lights stay bright, power is not reaching the starter motor. Check all battery and starter motor connections for clean contacts and tightness. Check that the engine and transmission earth bonds are making a good clean contact.
4 It may be that a clicking noise was heard each time the ignition/starter switch was operated. This is the solenoid switch operating, but it does not necessarily follow that the main contact is closing properly. (If no clicking has been heard from the solenoid it is certainly defective). The solenoid contact can be checked by putting a voltmeter or bulb between the main cable connection on the starter side of the solenoid and earth. When the switch is operated there should be a reading or a lighted bulb. If not, the switch has a fault.

14 Starter – removal and refitting

R1221 models

1 Remove the air cleaner.
2 Disconnect the battery negative and then positive leads.
3 Clamp the coolant hoses which run to the base of the carburettor and then disconnect them.
4 Disconnect the exhaust downpipe from the manifold.
5 Unbolt and remove the exhaust manifold from the cylinder head.
6 Disconnect the leads from the starter motor and solenoid terminals.
7 Unscrew the starter motor mounting bolts and withdraw the starter from the engine compartment.
8 Refitting is a reversal of removal, but check the coolant level.

All models except R1221 model

9 Remove the air cleaner.
10 Disconnect the battery negative and then positive leads.
11 Disconnect the leads from the starter motor and the solenoid.
12 On R1223 models, unbolt the exhaust manifold. On other models, unbolt the inlet/exhaust manifold.
13 Unscrew the starter motor fixing bolts. These are difficult to reach and will require the use of a socket extension with a universal joint or a cranked ring spanner.
14 Unbolt and remove the engine mounting stay and then the starter motor rear support bolt.
15 Withdraw the starter from the engine compartment (photo).
16 Refitting is a reversal of removal.

14.15 Removing the starter

15 Starter — overhaul (general)

1   The starter motor is a very reliable component and when it becomes worn or faulty it is usually more economical to exchange it for a new or reconditioned unit rather than overhaul it, even if individual spare parts are available.

2   For those wishing to undertake the work, however, the following Sections cover the operations involved.

16 Starter (Ducellier type) — overhaul

1   With the starter removed from the car, extract the nuts and take off the rear cover. Unscrew the bolt from the end of the armature shaft. Disconnect the lead from the solenoid.

2   Drive out the pivot pin from the pinion fork. Make sure that it is driven out from the side indicated in Fig. 10.23.

3   Withdraw the armature and solenoid.

4   Check the state of the brushes. If they have worn down to the minimum specified length, they must be renewed. Do this by unsoldering the old ones and soldering the new ones. Use a pair of pliers as a heat sink by gripping the brush lead close to the soldering point. Do not allow the solder to run down the lead or it will lose its flexibility.

5   Check the condition of the armature. If it is discoloured, clean it with a solvent-soaked rag or a piece of fine glasspaper. If the insulators between the segments are flush with the surface of the commutator, undercut them squarely to a depth of 1.0 mm (0.039 in) using a thin hacksaw blade or similar.

6   If the solenoid is to be renewed, withdraw it and release the bolt (A) which holds the core (B) — see Fig. 10.25.

7   Fit the fork and spring to the new solenoid and tighten the bolt (A). The solenoid fork travel must be adjusted as described in paragraphs 16 and 17 when reassembly is complete.

8   If the pinion/clutch assembly is to be renewed, drive the stop collar up the armature shaft with a piece of tubing to expose the circlip. Extract the circlip and slide the pinion off the shaft. Fit the new pinion assembly, stop collar and circlip. Draw the stop collar over the circlip.

9   Commence reassembly by applying a little grease to the armature shaft front bush.

10 Fit the armature and solenoid into the front end housing. Tighten the solenoid fixing nuts and drive in the fork pivot pin.

11 Fit the steel washer and then the fibre washer onto the armature shaft.

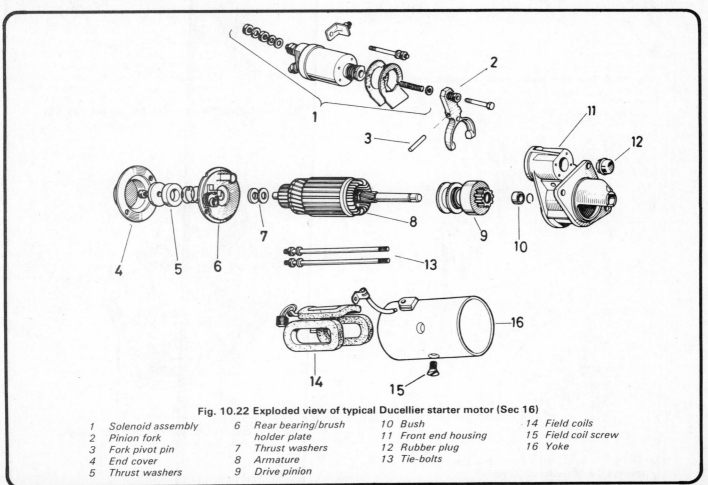

Fig. 10.22 Exploded view of typical Ducellier starter motor (Sec 16)

1 Solenoid assembly	6 Rear bearing/brush	10 Bush	14 Field coils
2 Pinion fork	holder plate	11 Front end housing	15 Field coil screw
3 Fork pivot pin	7 Thrust washers	12 Rubber plug	16 Yoke
4 End cover	8 Armature	13 Tie-bolts	
5 Thrust washers	9 Drive pinion		

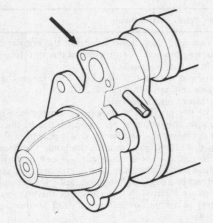

Fig. 10.23 Removing solenoid fork pivot pin (Sec 16)

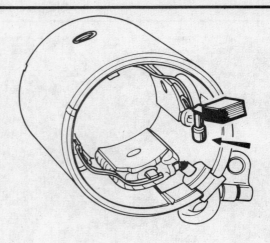

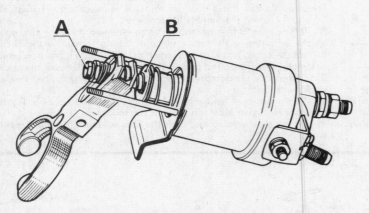

Fig. 10.25 Ducellier starter motor solenoid (Sec 16)
A   Core bolt   B   Core

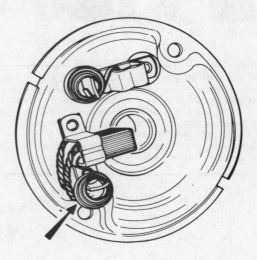

Fig. 10.24 Ducellier starter motor brushes (Sec 16)

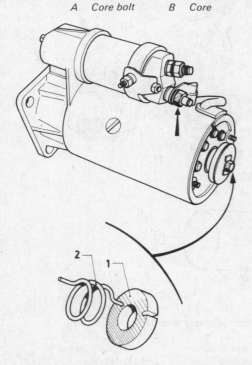

Fig. 10.26 Ducellier starter motor rear plate
spring (2) and washer (1) (Sec 16)

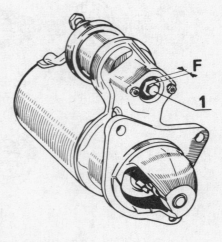

Fig. 10.27 Ducellier solenoid core bolt (1)-to-adjuster
nut clearance (F) (Sec 16)

12 Apply a little grease to the armature shaft rear bush.
13 Slide the yoke into position.
14 Fit the rear plate/brush holder into position. Use two pieces of wire hooked at their ends to hold the brush springs in a retracted position until they are over the commutator. This is a difficult job as the field coil brush must be located in its guide as the rear plate is offered into position.
15 Fit the coil spring and plastic washer, noting the location of the slots. Screw in the shaft end bolt and fit the rear cover.
16 If a new solenoid or associated component was fitted, adjust the travel of the fork. To do this, prise out the rubber plug from the front of the solenoid and then check that there is only a minimal clearance between the bolt head (1) and the adjusting nut (Fig. 10.27), and that the pinion assembly is resting against the armature.
17 Using thumb pressure, push the end of the solenoid bolt as far as it will go and then check that the clearance (G, Fig. 10.28), pinion to stop, is between 0.5 and 1.5 mm (0.020 and 0.060 in). If necessary, turn the adjuster nut to obtain the correct clearance.

17 Starter (Paris-Rhone type) – overhaul

1 With the starter removed from the car, disconnect the lead from the solenoid terminal.
2 Remove the rear cover or cap either by tapping it off (small type) or by removing the two nuts from the ends of the tie-bolts.

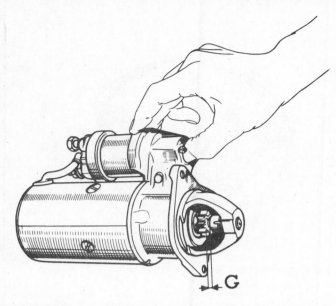

Fig. 10.28 Ducellier starter pinion-to-stop clearance (G) (Sec 16)

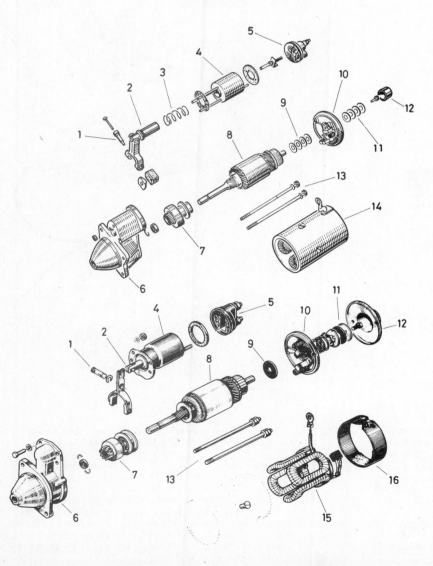

Fig. 10.29 Exploded view of alternative Paris-Rhone starter motors (Sec 17)

1   Solenoid fork pivot pin
2   Pinion fork
3   Spring
4   Solenoid
5   Solenoid end cover
6   Front end housing
7   Drive pinion/clutch
8   Armature
9   Thrust washers
10 Rear bearing plate/brush holder
11 Thrust washers
12 Rear cap
13 Tie-bolts
14 Yoke
15 Field coils
16 Cover band

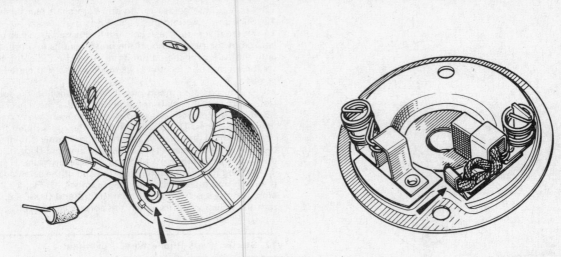

Fig. 10.30 Typical Paris-Rhone starter motor brushes (Sec 17)

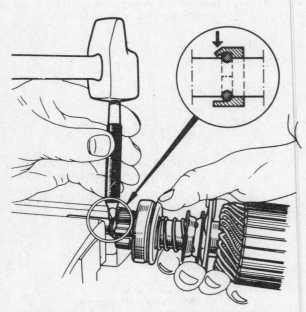

Fig. 10.31 Removing stop collar from Paris-Rhone (type D8E74) starter motor (Sec 17)

3   Remove the tie-bolts or tie-bolt nuts, according to type, and take off the rear plate/brush holder assembly.
4   Withdraw the yoke.
5   Drive out the solenoid fork pivot pin and remove the solenoid fixing nuts.
6   Repeat the operations described in paragraphs 4 and 5 of the preceding Section.
7   If the solenoid is to be renewed, this is simply unbolted and the new one fitted in position.
8   If the pinion/clutch assembly is to be renewed, the operations are as described in paragraph 8 of the preceding Section for all starters except the D8E74 version. On this, the stop collar is held in position on the armature shaft by split collets and the collar can only be removed by cutting it off with a sharp chisel. When refitting this type, use a new stop collar and crimp it in position to trap the split collets.
9   Commence reassembly by applying grease to the front bush then fit the armature and solenoid into the front end housing.
10   Tighten the solenoid mounting nuts and drive in the fork pivot pin.
11   Locate the washers on the rear of the armature shaft. Note the difference in rear bearing components according to starter motor type. Lubricate the rear bush.

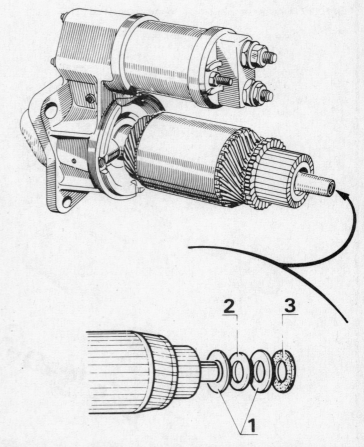

Fig. 10.32 Thrust washer arrangement on Paris-Rhone starter motors – types D8E81 and D8E121 (Sec 17)

1   Steel washer   3   Fibre washer
2   Wave washer

12   Fit the rear plate/brush holder. Use two pieces of wire hooked at their ends to hold the brush springs in a retracted position until they are over the commutator. This is a difficult job as the field coil brush must be located in its guide as the rear plate is offered into position.
13   Fit the washers or washer/spring assembly according to starter motor model, tighten the shaft end bolt.

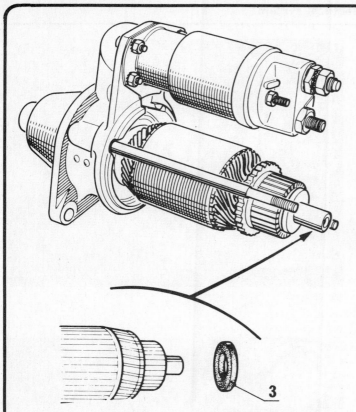

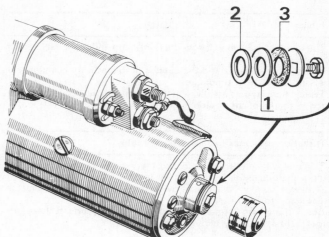

Fig. 10.34 Rear bearing washer arrangement on Paris-Rhone starter motors – types D8E81 and D8E121 (Sec 17)

1   Steel washer   3   Fibre washer
2   Wave washer

Fig. 10.33 Thrust washer arrangement on Paris-Rhone starter motors – types D8E74, D8E130 and D8E131 (Sec 17)

3   Fibre washer

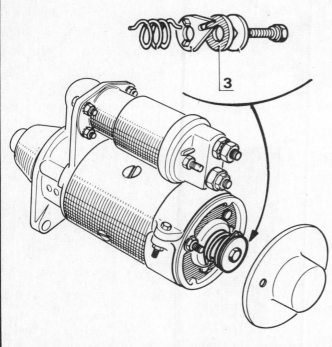

Fig. 10.35 Rear bearing washer arrangement on Paris-Rhone starter motors – types D8E74, D8E130 and D8E131 (Sec 17)

3   Fibre washer

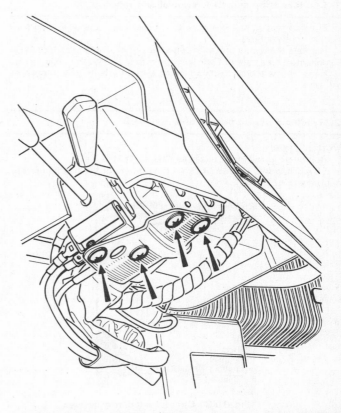

Fig. 10.36 Steering column switch cover plate screws (Sec 20)

14 Screw in the tie-bolts or tighten the tie-bolt nuts and fit the rear cover or cap.
15 Reconnect the solenoid lead.

18 Fuses

1   The fuse box is located below the right-hand end of the facia panel (photo).
2   The number of fuses and the circuits protected vary according to model and the date of production.
3   Typical fuse layouts are given in the Specifications, spare fuses are located in the lid of the fusebox.

19 Direction indicator/hazard warning relay

1   This unit is located in a clip in the steering column shroud (photo). Should a fault develop, first check the fuse.
2   A blown bulb in the circuit will cause the direction indicator warning lamp to flash very rapidly.
3   Check the wiring connections and lamp earth bonds. If these are in order, renew the relay with one of similar type.

20 Steering column switch – removal and refitting

1   Disconnect the battery earth lead.
2   Remove the screws which retain the lower shroud to the steering column upper section.
3   Remove the switch plate securing screws and disconnect the switch wiring plug.
4   Remove the switch.
5   Refitting is a reversal of removal.

21 Courtesy lamp switch – removal and refitting

1   The courtesy lamps switches are secured into the door pillars by a single screw (photo).
2   Remove the screw and withdraw the switch. If the leads are to be disconnected take care not to allow them to slide into the pillar cavity.
3   Keep the switch contacts smeared with petroleum jelly to prevent corrosion.

22 Headlamp sealed beam unit – renewal

Circular type
1   Remove the radiator grille (see Chapter 12).
2   Extract the four screws (A) from the corners of the headlamp trim panel (see Fig. 10.37).

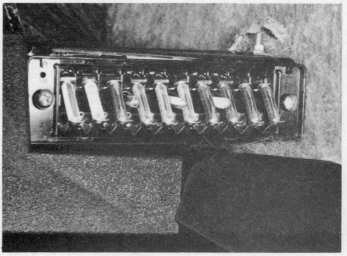

18.1 Fuses

19.1 Steering column lower shroud. Flasher relay arrowed

Fig. 10.37 Circular headlamp screws

A   Headlamp trim panel screw   F   Headlamp horizontal
E   Headlamp vertical   adjustment screw
    adjustment screw

21.1 Courtesy lamp switch

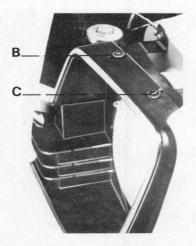

Fig. 10.38 Headlamp trim panel (Sec 22)

B   Retaining screw   C   Retaining screw

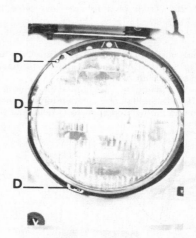

Fig. 10.39 Circular headlamp (Sec 22)

D   Retaining ring screws

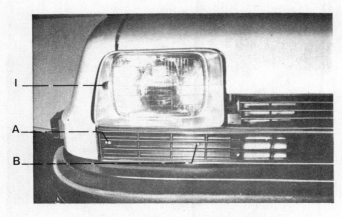

Fig. 10.40 Rectangular headlamp (Sec 22)

A   Grille panel screw   I   Horizontal beam adjustment
B   Grille panel screw   screw

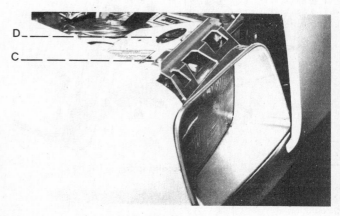

Fig. 10.41 Rectangular headlamp (Sec 22)

C   Trim panel screw   D   Trim panel screw

3   Open the bonnet and loosen, but do not remove the screws B and C from the top of the headlamp trim panel (see Fig. 10.38). Tilt the top of the panel forward and disengage it from the lamp.
4   Loosen, but do not remove, the three screws (D) in the headlamp retaining ring (see Fig. 10.39). Depress the ring and turn it in an anti-clockwise direction. Remove the ring and the headlamp unit after disconnecting the wiring plug at the rear of the lamp.
5   Refit the new unit by reversing the removal operations.
6   The headlamp beam should not have changed from its original setting, but it is worth having the alignment checked by your dealer.

Rectangular type
7   Remove the screws A and B from the grille below the headlamp (see Fig. 10.40).
8   Open the bonnet and extract the screws C and D from the top of the headlamp trim panel (see Fig. 10.41). Remove the trim panel.
9   Remove the headlamp unit retaining screws and withdraw the unit. Disconnect the wiring plug from the rear of the lamp.
10 Refitting is a reversal of removal, but refer to paragraph 6.

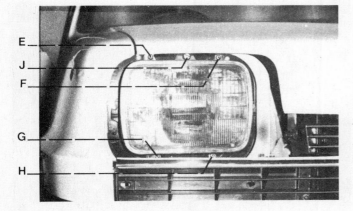

Fig. 10.42 Rectangular headlamp (Sec 22)

E   Rim fixing screw   H   Rim fixing screw
F   Rim fixing screw   J   Vertical beam adjustment
G   Rim fixing screw   screw

23 Headlamp bulb − renewal

1   Remove the radiator grille (see Chapter 12).
2   Open the bonnet.
3   Unhook the spring (B) from its slot (M) − see Fig. 10.43.
4   Pivot the headlamp forwards and move it towards the centre of the car to remove it.

5   Disconnect the wiring plug (photo) and prise back the bulb retaining springs (photo).

6   Renew the bulb (photo) and reassemble by reversing the removal operations.

7   Provided the same type of bulb is being fitted, the headlamp beam should not have altered, although it is worth having the beam alignment checked by your dealer.

8   Do not touch a halogen type bulb with your fingers, this will shorten its life. If this should happen inadvertently, wipe the bulb glass with a rag soaked in methylated spirit to remove any residual grease.

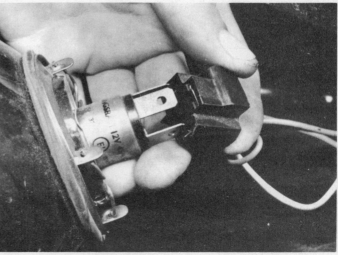

23.5a Headlamp connecting plug

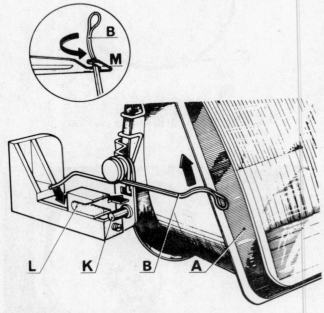

Fig. 10.43 Bulb type headlamp fixing (Sec 23)

A Lamp unit	K Pivot pin
B Spring	L Bearing slot
	M Hook

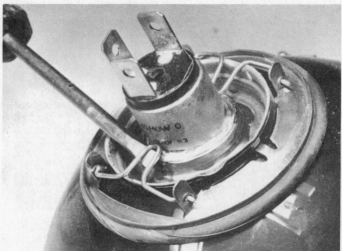

23.5b Prising back headlamp bulb clip

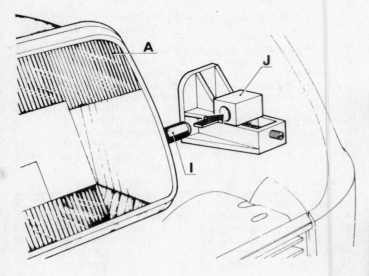

Fig. 10.44 Bulb type headlamp outboard pivot (Sec 23)

A Lamp unit	I Pivot pin
	J Bearing block

23.6 Renewing headlamp bulb

24 Headlamp beams – alignment

Note: *Holts Amber Lamp is useful for temporarily changing the headlight colour to conform with the normal usage on Continental Europe*

1   It is recommended that the headlamp beams are checked for alignment periodically by your dealer or a service station equipped with optical beam setting equipment.

2   In an emergency, the relative positions of the centre points of the headlamps may be measured and the measurements transposed onto a wall. Wait for darkness.

3   With the car standing on level ground perpendicular to the wall and 7.62 m (25 ft) from it, switch the headlamps to main beam. The centers of the beams' brightest spots should be on the marks on the wall. If not, turn the adjuster screws as necessary (photo and Figs. 10.36 and 10.45).

24.3 Headlamp adjuster screw

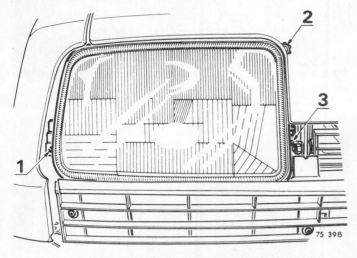

Fig. 10.45 Bulb type rectangular headlamp adjuster screws (Sec 24)

   1   Horizontal adjuster screw   3   Lamp unit height adjusting
   2   Vertical adjuster screw   screw

25 Bulbs (excluding headlamps) – renewal

Exterior

Front side (parking) and direction indicator lamps

1   Extract the lens retaining screws and remove the lens (photo).

2   Depress the bulb and turn it anti-clockwise, then remove it from its holder.

3   Fit a new bulb of similar type to the original.

Side marker lamp

4   Renewal is as for front parking lamp.

Rear lamp cluster

5   Extract the three lens retaining screws and withdraw the lamp lens (photo).

6   Twist the appropriate bulb from its holder and renew it with one of similar type.

Rear fog, reverse and number plate lamps

7   The bulbs are accessible after extracting the lens screws in a similar way to that described for other exterior lamps (photos).

Interior

Courtesy lamp

8   Pull the lens from the lamp base.

9   Pull the bulb from its contacts and renew with one of similar type (photo).

Instrument panel and warning lamps

10   Remove the instrument panel as described in Section 27. Twist the bulbholders from the rear of the panel and take out the wedge type bulbs from the holders (photo).

25.1 Front parking and direction indicator bulbs

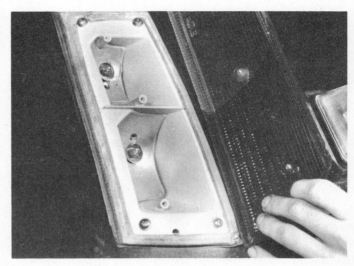

25.5 Rear lamp cluster

25.7a Reversing and rear number plate lamp bulbs

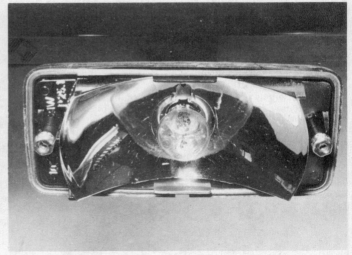

25.7b Rear foglamp bulb

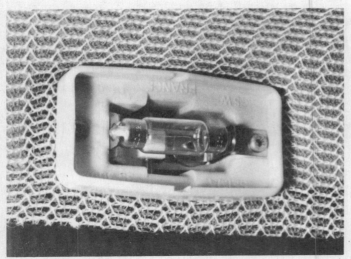

25.8 Interior lamp

25.10 Instrument panel bulb and holder

26 Horn

1   Should the horn fail to work the first thing to do is make sure that current is reaching the horn terminal. This can be done by connecting a 12 volt test lamp to the feed wire and pressing the horn button with the ignition switch on. If the bulb lights then the fault must lie in the horn or the horn mounting. The tightness and cleanliness of the horn mounting is important as the circuit is made to earth through the fixing bolt. The connections should, of course, be a clean, tight fit on the horn terminals.

2   If no current is reaching the horn check wiring connections as indicated in the wiring diagram.

3   If it is found that the fault lies in the horn unit, check whether an adjusting screw is fitted; if there is one, turn the screw until the horn operates correctly. Should there not be an adjusting screw, the horn must be renewed.

4   Removal of all types of horn is simply a matter of unscrewing the retaining nut and disconnecting the electrical wire. The horn is located on the front cross panel adjacent to the gearbox (photo).

5   The horn switch is combined with the lighting switch on the steering column.

26.4 Horn

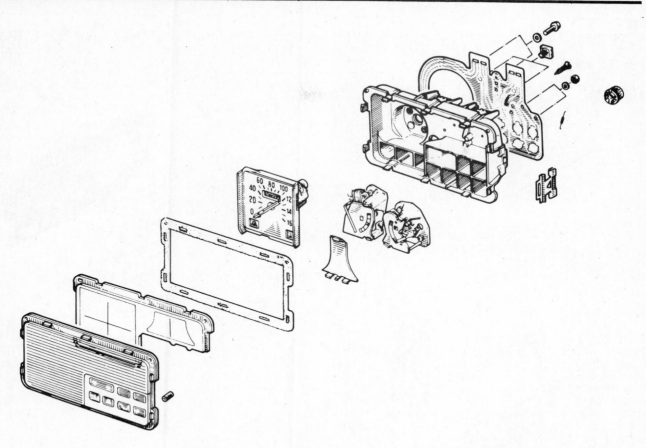

Fig. 10.46 Instrumentation – R1221, R1222 and R1225 models (Sec 27)

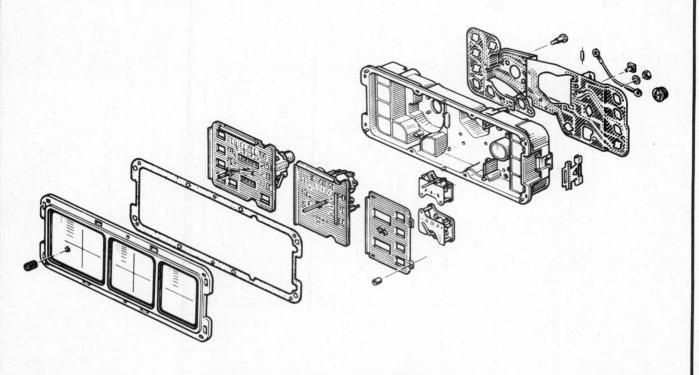

Fig. 10.47 Instrumentation – R1223 and R1224 (Sec 27)

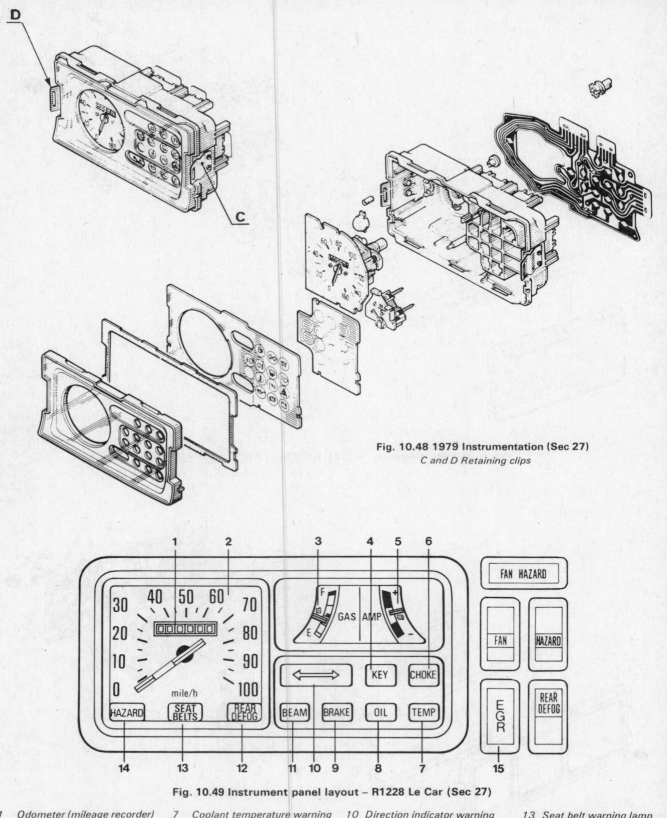

Fig. 10.48 1979 Instrumentation (Sec 27)
C and D Retaining clips

Fig. 10.49 Instrument panel layout – R1228 Le Car (Sec 27)

1   Odometer (mileage recorder)
2   Speedometer
3   Fuel gauge
4   Ignition key (not removed) warning lamp
5   Charge indicator
6   Choke 'ON' lamp
7   Coolant temperature warning lamp
8   Oil pressure warning lamp
9   Handbrake 'ON' and low hydraulic fluid level combined warning lamp
10 Direction indicator warning lamp
11 Headlamp main beam warning lamp
12 Heated rear window indicator lamp
13 Seat belt warning lamp
14 Hazard warning system indicator lamp
15 EGR system maintenance internal reminder lamp

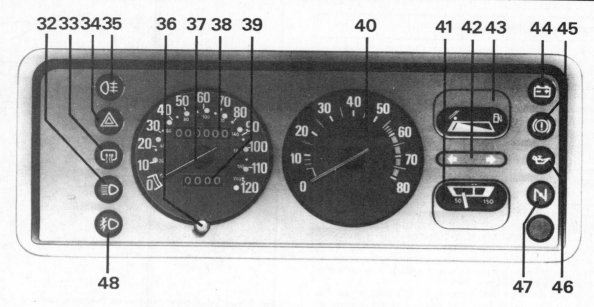

Fig. 10.50 Instrument panel layout – R1223 Gordini (Sec 27)

32 *Headlamp main beam warning lamp*
33 *Heated rear screen warning lamp*
34 *Hazard warning lamp system indicator*
35 *Rear foglamp indicator*
36 *Mileage trip recorder zero knob*
37 *Speedometer*
38 *Odometer (total mileage recorder)*
39 *Trip mileage recorder*
40 *Tachometer (rev counter)*
41 *Coolant temperature gauge*
42 *Direction indicator warning lamp*
43 *Fuel gauge*
44 *Charge warning lamp*
45 *Handbrake 'ON' and low hydraulic fluid lever combined warning lamp*
46 *Oil pressure warning lamp*
47 *Choke*
48 *Front foglamp warning lamp*

27.5 Removing instrument panel

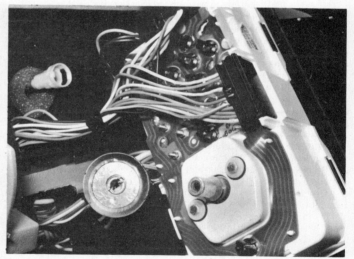

27.6 Rear view of instrument panel

27 Instrument panel – removal and refitting

1   Disconnect the battery earth lead.
2   Disconnect the speedometer cable from the gearbox.
3   The steering wheel need not be removed to remove the instrument panel, but if preferred for better access, refer to Chapter 11.
4   Withdraw the hood from the instrument panel. This is done by prising the upper lip downwards to disengage the retaining lugs.
5   Insert a screwdriver or thin blade carefully at the sides of the instrument panel to release the retaining clips and pull the panel from the facia panel (photo). Have an assistant feed the speedometer cable through the bulkhead grommet until the panel is sufficiently withdrawn to be able to disconnect the drive cable from the speed-

ometer head. Do this by squeezing the retaining collar.
6   Disconnect the panel wiring plugs (photo).
7   Individual instruments may be removed by unscrewing the retaining nuts. The panel glass is retained by clips. Take care not to damage the printed circuit.
8   Reassembly and refitting are reversals of removal and dismantling.

28 Rocker switches – removal and refitting

These are located on the facia panel at the side of the instrument panel. According to model, the switches may be removed individually or the complete switch sub-panel withdrawn. In either case the units are retained by plastic lugs.

29 Speedometer drive cable – renewal

1 Disconnect the cable from the gearbox.
2 Withdraw the instrument panel from the facia panel as described in Section 27 until the speedometer cable can be disconnected from the speedometer head (photo).
3 Withdraw the cable assembly into the engine compartment.
4 The new cable is supplied complete. Refit it by reversing the removal operations, making sure that the squared ends of the inner cable engage positively in the sockets of gearbox and speedometer head.

30 Windscreen and tailgate wiper blades and arms – removal and refitting

1 To remove a blade, pull the arm from the glass until it locks.
2 Swivel the blade and remove it (photo). On some types, a plastic U-clip must first have its ends compressed and be withdrawn before the blade can be removed from the arm.
3 It is recommended that the wiper blades are renewed as soon as they cease to wipe the glass clean. Rubber inserts or the complete blade can be purchased as replacements.
4 Before removing a wiper arm, mark its parked position on the screen with a piece of masking tape. This will facilitate alignment at refitting.
5 To remove an arm, flip up the nut cover and unscrew the nut (photo). Remove the arm from the spindle splines.
6 Refitting the arm and blade is a reversal of removal.

31 Windscreen wiper motor and linkage – removal and refitting

1 Remove the wiper/blade assemblies (Section 30).
2 Unscrew and remove the drive spindle housing retaining nuts. Take off the caps and seals.
3 Working within the engine compartment, disconnect the wiring plug.
4 Unscrew the motor support plate mounting nuts and withdraw the complete assembly in a sideways direction from under the scuttle.
5 Refitting is a reversal of removal.

32 Windscreen wiper assembly – overhaul

1 With the wiper motor and linkage removed from the car, unscrew the nut which holds the crankarm to the motor spindle (photo).
2 Remove the motor mounting screws and detach the motor from the support plate.
3 One of two types of motor may be fitted, either one with direct reduction drive or one with worm reduction gear.

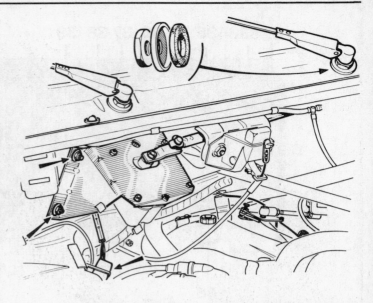

Fig. 10.51 Location of windscreen wiper assembly (Sec 31)
Worm drive reduction gear shown

Motor with direct reduction gear
4 Remove the support plate.
5 Remove the motor cover.
6 Check the condition of the gears. If they are worn or damaged it is doubtful whether replacement is an economical proposition, rather renew the motor complete.
7 If the brushes are well worn, they can be renewed complete with brush carrier by unsoldering the leads and then soldering the new ones in position.
8 Pack the gears with clean multi-purpose grease before reassembly. Align the flat on the shaft with the locating 'pip' to obtain the 'park' position.

Motor with worm reduction gear
9 Remove the cover plate and check the condition of the gears. If worn or damaged, it will probably be more economical to renew the assembly complete.
10 If the brushes are well worn, they can be removed after unsoldering them, but take care not to alter the position of the field coil, otherwise the 'park' position will be lost. If the field coil is changed, feed current to the motor through the 'park' track until the motor stops. Reassemble the remaining components, refitting the gear so that the 'park' brushes line up with the gap in the 'park' track.

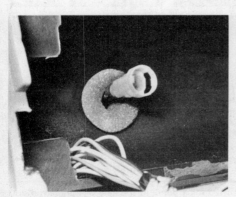

29.2 Speedometer drive cable connector

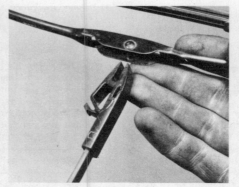

30.2 Typical windscreen wiper blade/arm connection

30.5 Wiper arm retaining nut

Fig. 10.52 Exploded view of direct drive windscreen wiper motor (Sec 32)

32.1 Wiper crankarm and link

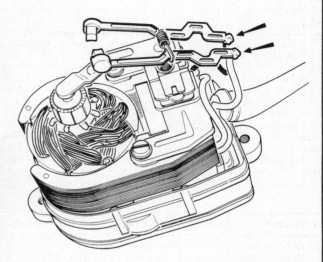

Fig. 10.53 Brush carrier soldered leads onto direct drive
windscreen wiper motor (Sec 32)

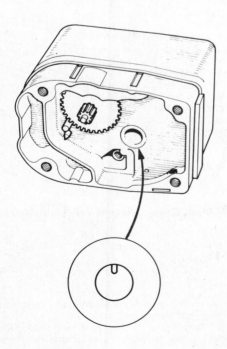

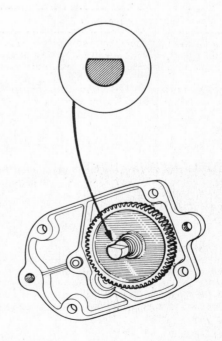

Fig. 10.54 Shaft flat and 'pip' for 'park' alignment on direct drive windscreen wiper motor (Sec 32)

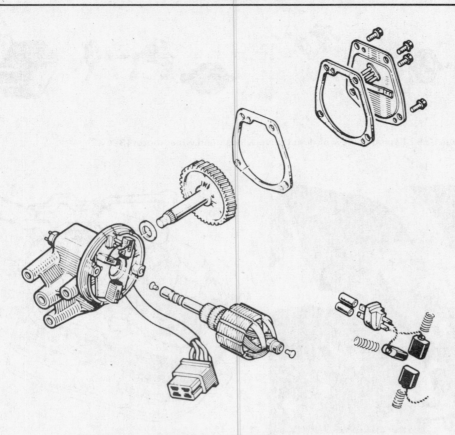

Fig. 10.55 Exploded view of worm drive reduction gear windscreen wiper motor (Sec 32)

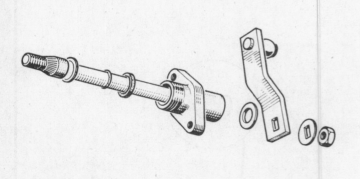

Fig. 10.56 Typical windscreen wiper wheelbox spindles (Sec 32)

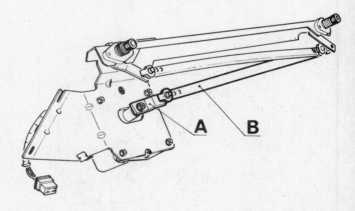

Fig. 10.57 Correct alignment of windscreen wiper assembly
(Sec 32)

A   Crankarm   B   Link

General
11 The wiper arm drive spindles can be taken apart and if unworn, greased and reassembled using a new sealing washer.
12 When connecting the linkage to the motor, make sure that the crankarm (A) and the main link (B) are in exact alignment (see Fig. 10.57). Alter the position of the crankarm on the motor shaft splines if necessary to achieve this setting.

---

33 Tailgate wiper motor – removal and refitting

1   Remove the wiper arm assembly (see Section 30).

2   Unscrew and remove the nut from around the driving spindle, take off the cap and sealing washer.
3   Open the tailgate fully and disconnect the wiper motor leads at the connecting plugs. Remove the cover and disconnect the earth lead (photo).
4   Remove the motor mounting bolts and withdraw the motor.
5   The tailgate motor is a sealed unit and if faulty must be renewed complete.
6   Refitting is a reversal of removal, but make sure that the motor is in the 'parked' position – having been switched off by the wiper switch not the ignition key – before fitting the wiper arm and blade.

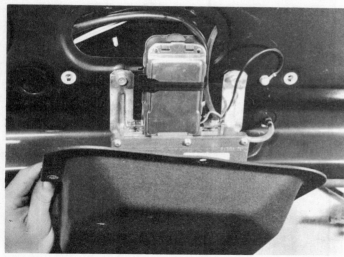

33.3 Tailgate wiper motor and cover

34 Heated rear window

1 The heating elements applied to the glass interior surface should be treated with respect.

2 Clean the glass only with warm water and detergent, and wipe in the direction of the element lines. Take care not to scratch the elements with rings on the fingers or by careless stowage of luggage.

3 Do not stick labels over the elements.

4 To repair a break in the element, use one of the conductive paints which are now readily available from motor accessory stores. Follow the manufacturer's instructions very carefully.

5 Connecting leads are of push-on spade type (photo).

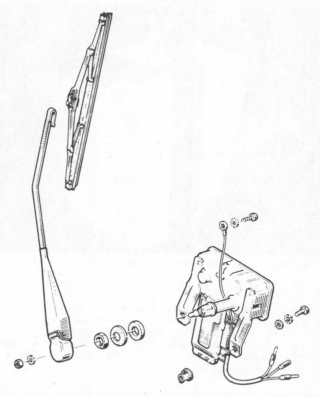

Fig. 10.58 Tailgate wiper motor and arm (Sec 33)

34.5 Heated rear window earth lead

35 Digital clock

1 A digital clock is fitted above the windscreen on Gordini models.

2 The clock body is held in place by two screws.

3 The clock indicates the time when the ignition is switched on. To set the time, rock switch A to the left for rapid figure change and when the time is approaching the correcting setting, rock the switch to the right for fine adjustment (see Fig. 10.59).

Fig. 10.59 Digital clock – Gordini models (Sec 35)

A   Setting switch

36 Electric window winders

1 These are fitted to the front doors of 1983 and Gordini Turbo models (see Chapter 12, Section 15).

2 The winder motors must be renewed as complete assemblies if faulty.

37 Windscreen and tailgate washers

1 Both systems are pressurized by electrically-driven pumps.

2 The windscreen washer fluid reservoir is located within the engine compartment while the one for the tailgate is positioned at the side of the luggage compartment (photos).

3 Keep the reservoirs topped up with water to which a screen cleaning fluid has been added. In severe winter conditions, pour a little

37.2a Windscreen washer fluid reservoir and pump

37.2b Tailgate washer fluid reservoir

methylated spirit, or a proprietary anti-freeze solution into the reservoirs to prevent the water freezing. Never use a coolant anti-freeze mixture or the car paintwork will be damaged.
4   The washer jets may be adjusted to provide an acceptable wash pattern on the glass by inserting a pin into the hole in the jet ball and moving the ball as required.

38 Headlamp washer/wiper system

1   The system is fitted as standard equipment to certain models, and is available as an option on others.
2   The motor and linkage can be removed once the wiper arms have been withdrawn from their spindles.
3   Remove the wiper arms, the front grille and bumper assembly.
4   Disconnect the leads from the wiper motor.
5   Unbolt and remove the linkage, the drive spindles and the motor.
6   When reassembling, set the motor in the 'park' position before fitting the wiper arms to their spindles. The arms should be positioned up against their stops on the headlamps.

39 Radio (models up to 1977) – fitting

1   First check that the operating voltage and polarity of the car are compatible with the radio receiver.
2   Disconnect the battery.

3   Remove the console fixing screws and the blanking plate from the radio aperture.
4   Tilt the console until the radio can be pushed into place with its spacing washers.
5   Fit the embellisher, washers, screw on the fixing nuts and push on the tuning knobs.
6   An angle support bracket is recommended at the base of the receiver.
7   Connect the power feed wire to the grey spare lead located under the right-hand side of the instrument panel. Power to the radio is only available when the ignition key is turned to A or M. Connect the aerial lead.

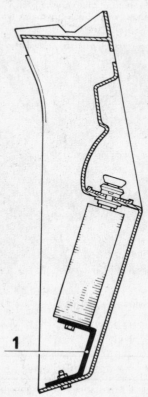

Fig. 10.61 Typical radio location in centre console – early models (Sec 39)

1   Angle bracket

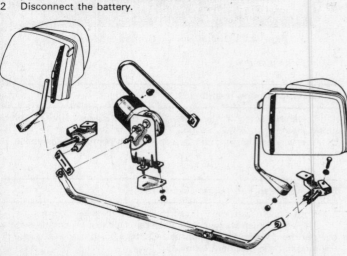

Fig. 10.60 Headlamp wash/wipe system (Sec 38)

8   Connect the earth lead from the radio to an instrument panel screw or to the cigar lighter earth screw.

9   Fit the loudspeaker into the place provided at the base of the console. Connect the loudspeaker wires.

10 Where stereo speakers are required, they should be installed in the rear quarter trim panels above the rear seat with their wires running under the floor covering.

11 To remove the trim panel, the seat and armrest will have to be removed (Chapter 12) and a screwdriver used to unclip the panel.

40 Radio (models 1978 and later) – fitting

Refer also to Chapter 13, Section 9

1   On models built up until 1980, remove the centre console by unscrewing its two mounting nuts or extracting the retaining clip. These fixings are accessible after removal of the loudspeaker grille. Slide the console up and tilt it rearwards.

2   On later models, extract the retaining screw from the centre fresh air grille and remove the grille.

3   Reach in and withdraw the power feed wire with the earth lead attached.

4   The loudspeaker leads are located behind the console and are accessible once the radio blanking plate has been prised out.

5   If an aerial has not yet been fitted, it should be installed, as described in the next Section.

6   Connect the power feed, earth, aerial and speaker leads to the

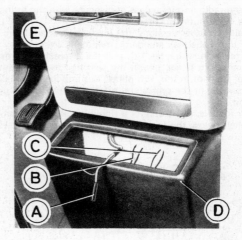

Fig. 10.62 Radio lead location – later models (Sec 40)

A Power feed with earth tag	D Centre console
B Loudspeaker lead	E Facia panel retaining screw
C Loudspeaker lead	

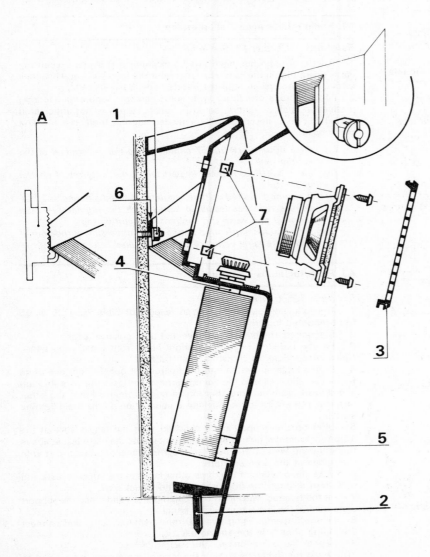

Fig. 10.63 Typical mounting of radio and speaker in centre console – later models (Sec 40)

1   Console fixing nuts
2   Locating peg
3   Grille
4   Spacers
5   Rubber insulator
6   Bracket
7   Plastic clips
A   Console clip

radio, push the radio into its recess and secure with the fitting kit, the control knob bezel nuts and then fit the knobs.

7   On certain two-door versions, the loudspeakers are fitted into the rear quarter trim panels as standard equipment. Where they are not, remove the rear seat (Chapter 12), pull the armrest upwards. Unclip and remove the trim panel, unbolt the seat belt lower mounting and slide it out of the slot in the trim panel. Cut and fit the speakers into the quarter panels, fit the grilles and run the speaker wires under the floor covering.

8   On other models, a location for a single loudspeaker is provided in the parcel shelf below the facia panel or, for stereo speakers, in the front door trim panels.

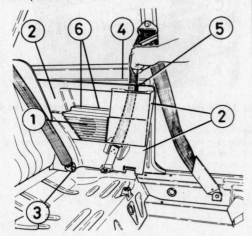

Fig. 10.64 Typical rear speaker arrangement – later models (Sec 40)

1   Armrest/speaker panel   *4   Trim panel channel*
2   Clips   *5   Seat belt slot*
3   Seat belt anchor bolt   *6   Scribed knock-out tabs*

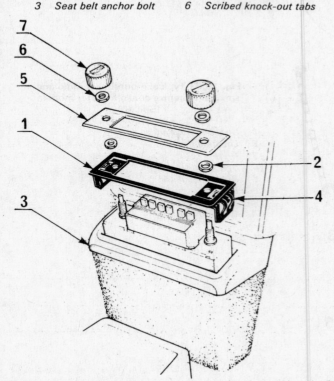

Fig. 10.65 Typical radio control and mounting parts (Sec 40)

1   Bracket   *5   Escutcheon plate*
2   Nut   *6   Nut*
3   Centre console   *7   Control knobs*
4   Spring clips

41 Aerial – installation

Refer also to Chapter 13, Section 9

1   The recommended location for an aerial is on the roof just above the centre of the windscreen.
2   Remove the interior rear view mirror, if fitted to the passenger compartment roof.
3   Carefully drill a hole in the selected position above the centre of the windscreen, of sufficient diameter to suit the aerial base fitting.
4   The hole should be centred in the aperture left by removal of the mirror stem, so it is best to drill a small pilot hole from the inside outwards to start with.
5   Scrape the paint away from the inside around the hole to provide a good earth.
6   Feed the aerial cable through the hole (not forgetting to slide on the aerial base mounting ring). Tape it to some wire or cord so that it can be drawn through the windscreen pillar, behind the glove compartment and connected to the radio.
7   Fit the aerial mounting screw and adjust the aerial to the correct angle.
8   Refit the mirror, if applicable.
9   Whenever a radio or aerial is installed, trim the installation as described in the manufacturer's literature. In the absence of such instructions, tune in to a weak station. Insert a very thin screwdriver and turn the trim screw one way or the other until maximum volume is obtained.

42 Radio interference – suppression

Refer also to Chapter 13, Section 9

1   If, after a radio has been fitted, interference is evident when the car is operating on the road, then carry out the following modifications in the sequence given until the interference is eliminated.
2   Most models are fitted with some ignition suppression during production such as carbon-cored HT leads, and it is not anticipated that all the items described will be needed but only tried on a 'trial and error' basis.

(a) *Fit a 60μF + 10 000pF condenser to the + terminal of the ignition coil*
(b) *Fit a 3.3μF condenser in parallel to the + terminal on the alternator*
(c) *If a remotely-sited voltage regulator is fitted, connect a 3.3μF bypass type condenser in series with the regulator + feed terminal and earth the condenser mounting tag*
(d) *Fit a braided earth strap between the underside of the bonnet and the engine compartment front panel*

43 Front foglamps – fitting

Models 1976 and later

1   The following operations are in respect of Cibie Type 35 or 95 front-mounted foglamps.
2   Disconnect the battery negative and then positive leads.
3   Fix the required relay to the right-hand front inner wing panel. Make connections as shown in Fig. 10.66.
4   Fit the foglamp switch into the instrument panel. From one of its terminals tape a wire to the wiring harness and pass the wire through a bulkhead grommet into the engine compartment. From the other terminal, run a wire to the sidelight E connection on the main lighting switch.
5   Offer up the support plate supplied with the lamps so that the 10.5 mm diameter hole is at the bottom, whilst the plate is just above the stiffening web on the headlamp carrier panel and in contact with the flange of the horn aperture.
6   Mark the position of the three other holes in the support plate and drill them through the front panel of the wheel arch.
7   Fit the tapered washer on the foglamp stem and place the support plate behind the headlamp carrier panel.
8   Fit the foglamp, using two 6.0 mm diameter bolts, and connect the wiring already in the engine bay.
9   Repeat the operations for the second lamp.
10 Adjust the foglamps so that the tops of the beams are parallel to the ground.

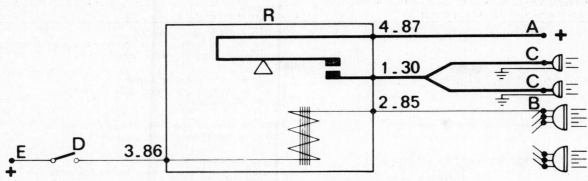

Fig. 10.66 Auxiliary front foglamp wiring circuit (Sec 43)

R Relay
Relay connections:

Terminal 2 (wire 85) to dipped beam headlamp wire at rear of RH headlamp (B)
Terminal 1 (wire 30) to foglamp (C)
Terminal 3 (wire 86) to operating switch (D)
Terminal 4 (wire 87) to positive feed
Remaining terminal on operating switch is connected to sidelamp terminal (E) on main lighting switch of car

Earlier models
11 When fitting foglamps to earlier models, use brackets (Part Nos 7701 400 521) which are connected to the fronts of the horn grilles.

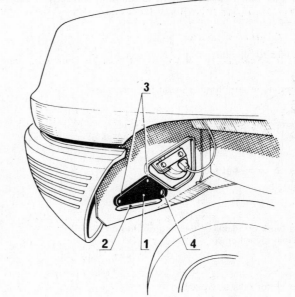

Fig. 10.67 Front foglamp mounting bracket (Sec 43)

1 Reinforcement plate
2 Headlamp carrier panel
3 6.5 mm diameter holes
4 10.5 mm diameter hole

44 Fault diagnosis – electrical system

Symptom	Reason(s)
Starter fails to turn engine	Battery discharged Battery defective internally Battery terminal leads loose or earth lead not securely attached to body Loose or broken connections in starter motor circuit Starter motor switch or solenoid faulty Starter brushes badly worn, sticking, or brush wires loose Commutator dirty, worn or burnt Starter motor armature faulty Field coils earthed

Symptom	Reason(s)
Starter turns engine very slowly	Battery in discharged condition Starter brushes badly worn, sticking or brush wires loose Loose wires in starter motor circuit
Starter spins but does not turn the engine	Starter engagement yoke siezed Pinion or flywheel gear teeth broken or worn Battery discharged
Starter noisy or excessively rough engagement	Pinion or flywheel gear teeth broken or worn Starter motor retaining bolts loose
Battery will not hold charge for more than a few days	Battery defective internally Electrolyte level too low or electrolyte too weak due to leakage Plate separators no longer fully effective Battery plates severely sulphated Drivebelt slipping Battery terminal connections loose or corroded Alternator not charging Short in lighting circuit causing continual battery drain Regulator unit not working correctly
Ignition light fails to go out, battery runs flat in a few days	Drivebelt loose and slipping or broken Generator brushes worn, sticking, broken or dirty Generator brush springs weak or broken Internal fault in generator Regulator incorrectly set Open circuit in wiring of cut-out and regulator unit

Failure of individual equipment to function correctly is dealt with alphabetically, item-by-item, under the headings listed below

Horn

Horn operates all the time	Horn push either earthed or stuck down Horn cable to horn push earthed
Horn fails to operate	Cable or cable connection loose, broken or disconnected Horn has an internal fault
Horn emits intermittent or unsatisfactory noise	Cable connections loose

Lights

Lights do not come on	If engine not running, battery discharged Wire connections loose, disconnected or broken Light switch shorting or otherwise faulty
Lights come on but fade out	If engine not running battery discharged Light bulb filament burnt out or bulbs broken Wire connections loose, disconnected or broken Light switch shorting or otherwise faulty
Lights work erratically – flashing on and off, especially over bumps	Battery terminals or earth connection loose Lights not earthing properly Contacts in light switch faulty

Wipers

Wiper motor fails to work	Blown fuse Wire connections loose, disconnected or broken Brushes badly worn Armature worn or faulty Field coils faulty
Wiper motor works very slowly and takes excessive current	Commutator dirty, greasy or burnt Armature bearings dirty or unaligned Armature badly worn or faulty
Wiper motor works slowly and takes little current	Brushes badly worn Commutator dirty, greasy or burnt Armature badly worn or faulty
Wiper motor works but wiper blades remain static	Wiper motor gearbox parts badly worn

Fig. 10.68 Wire identification

Each wire is identified by a number followed by a letter(s) indicating its colour, a number giving its diameter and finally a number giving the unit destination

Colour code		Wire diameters		Harness identification	
B	Blue	No	mm	A	Front
Bc	White	1	0.7	B	Rear
Be	Beige	2	0.9	C	Lighting switch
C	Clear	3	1.0	D	Indicator switch
G	Grey	4	1.2	E	Generator
J	Yellow	5	1.6	K	Starter
M	Maroon	6	2.1	P	Negative lead
N	Black	7	2.5	Q	Positive lead
Or	Orange	8	3.0	T	Console
R	Red	9	4.5		
S	Pink				
V	Green				
Vi	Violet				

Example :

Or as shown in the diagram on the right:
Unit 40 (L.H.door pillar switch) with wire
133 - N - 2 - 41 connected to Unit 41.

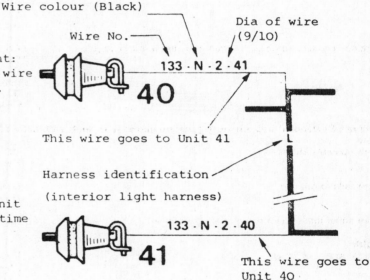

Wire 133 is seen again connected to Unit
41 (R.H.door pillar switch) but this time
it is numbered: 133 - N - 2 - 40

Key to wiring diagram for R1221 L and R1222 TL models

1 LH front sidelight
2 LH front direction indicator
3 LH front headlight
6 RH front headlight
7 RH front direction indicator
8 RH front sidelight
9 Temperature switch (R1221)
10 Cooling fan motor (R1221)
20 Horn
21 Reversing lamps switch (R1221)
22 Dynamo or alternator
23 Battery
24 Dynamo or alternator regulator
25 Cooling fan motor relay (R1222)
26 Coolant temperature switch
27 Starter
28 Distributor
30 Heating-ventilating fan motor
31 Ignition coil
32 Oil pressure sender switch
33 Windscreen wiper motor
40 LH cowl side earth (ground)
41 LH door pillar switch
44 Fusebox
45 Stoplight switch

46 Instrument panel
47 RH door pillar switch
48 Front – rear harness junction
49 Combination lighting switch – front harness junction
50 Direction indicator switch – front harness junction
51 Flasher unit
53 Rear screen switch (R1222)
54 Heating-ventilating fan switch
55 Windscreen wiper switch
60 Interior light
61 Combination lighting switch
62 Direction indicator switch
63 Ignition-starter switch
65 Rear screen (R1222)
66 Fuel tank
67 LH rear direction indicator
68 LH rear and stop-lights
69 LH rear reversing lamp (R1222)
70 Number plate lights
71 RH rear reversing lamp (R1222)
72 RH rear and stop-lights
73 RH rear direction indicator

For wiring harness identification refer to Fig. 10.68

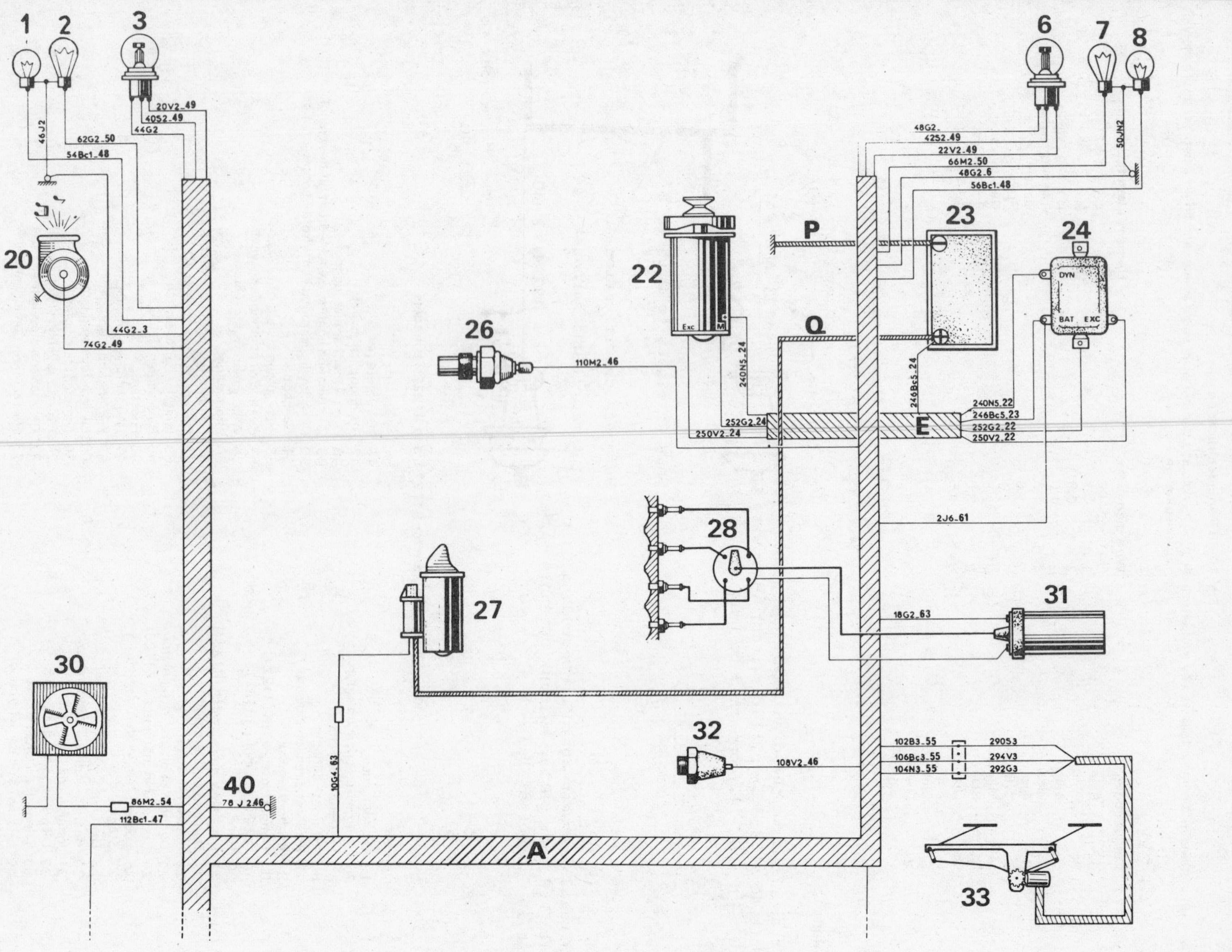

Fig. 10.69 Wiring diagram for R1221 L models

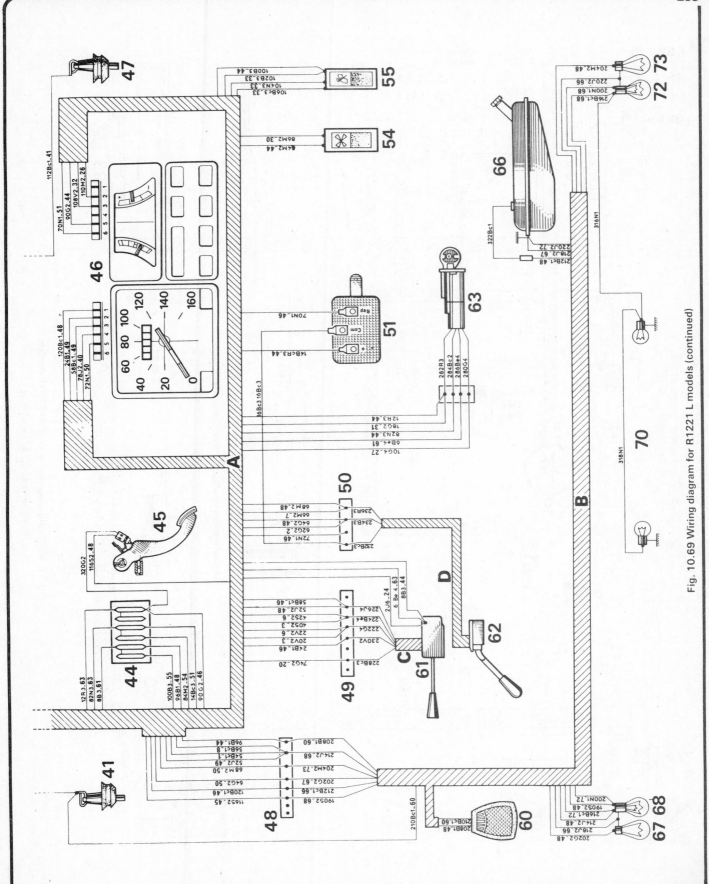

Fig. 10.69 Wiring diagram for R1221 L models (continued)

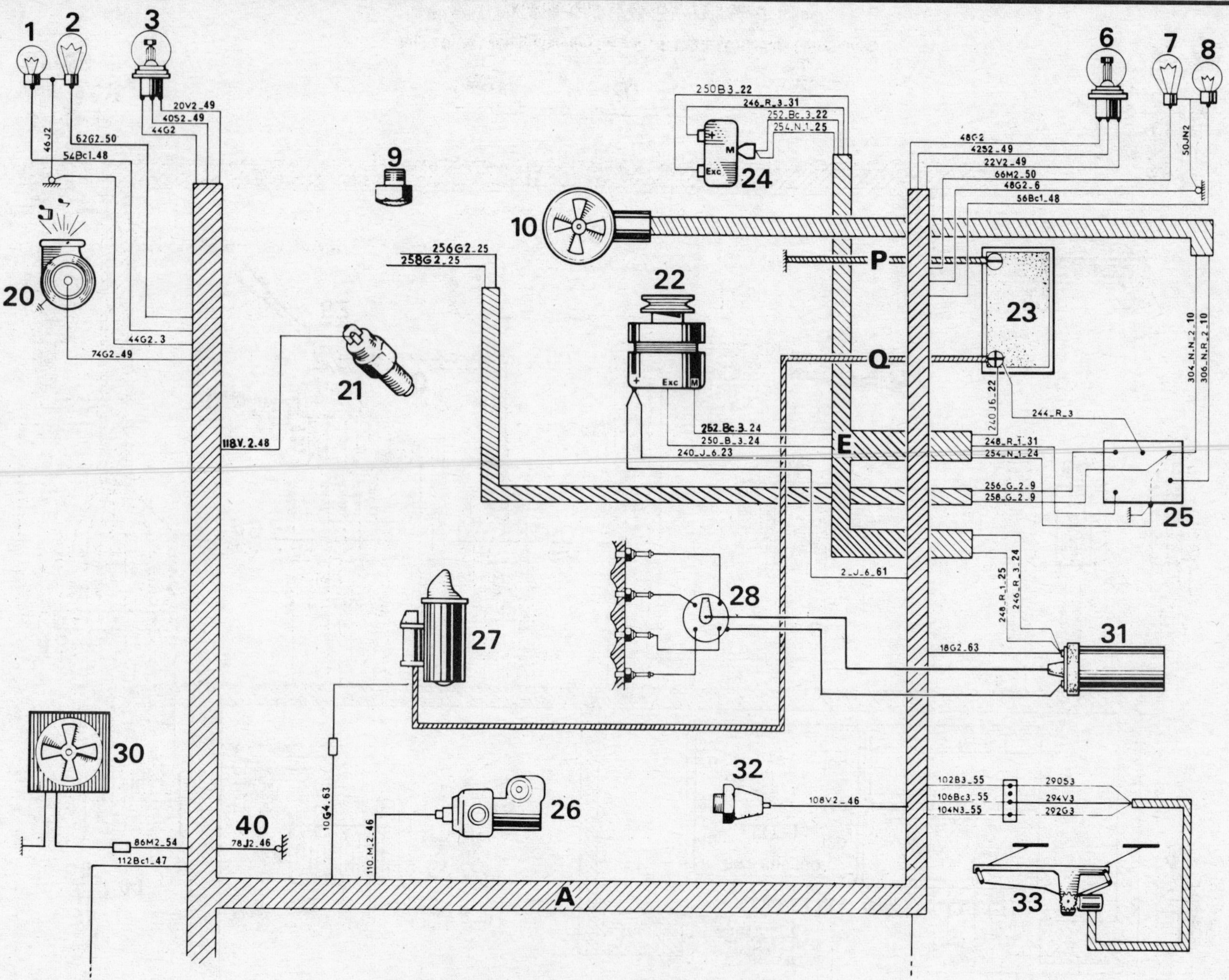

Fig. 10.70 Wiring diagram for early R1222 TL models

Key the same as for R1221 L models

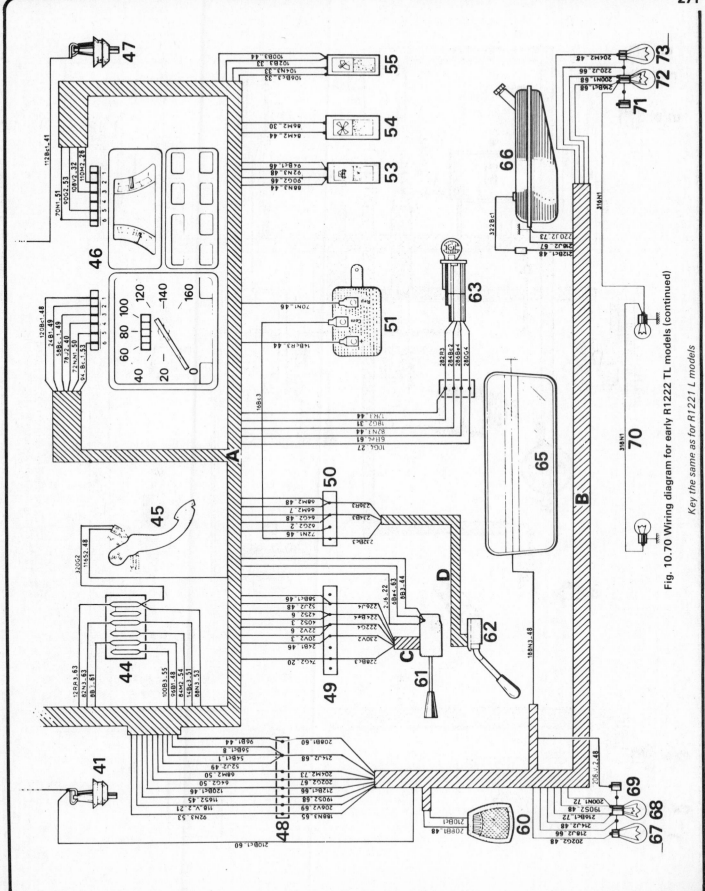

Fig. 10.70 Wiring diagram for early R1222 TL models (continued)

Key the same as for R1221 L models

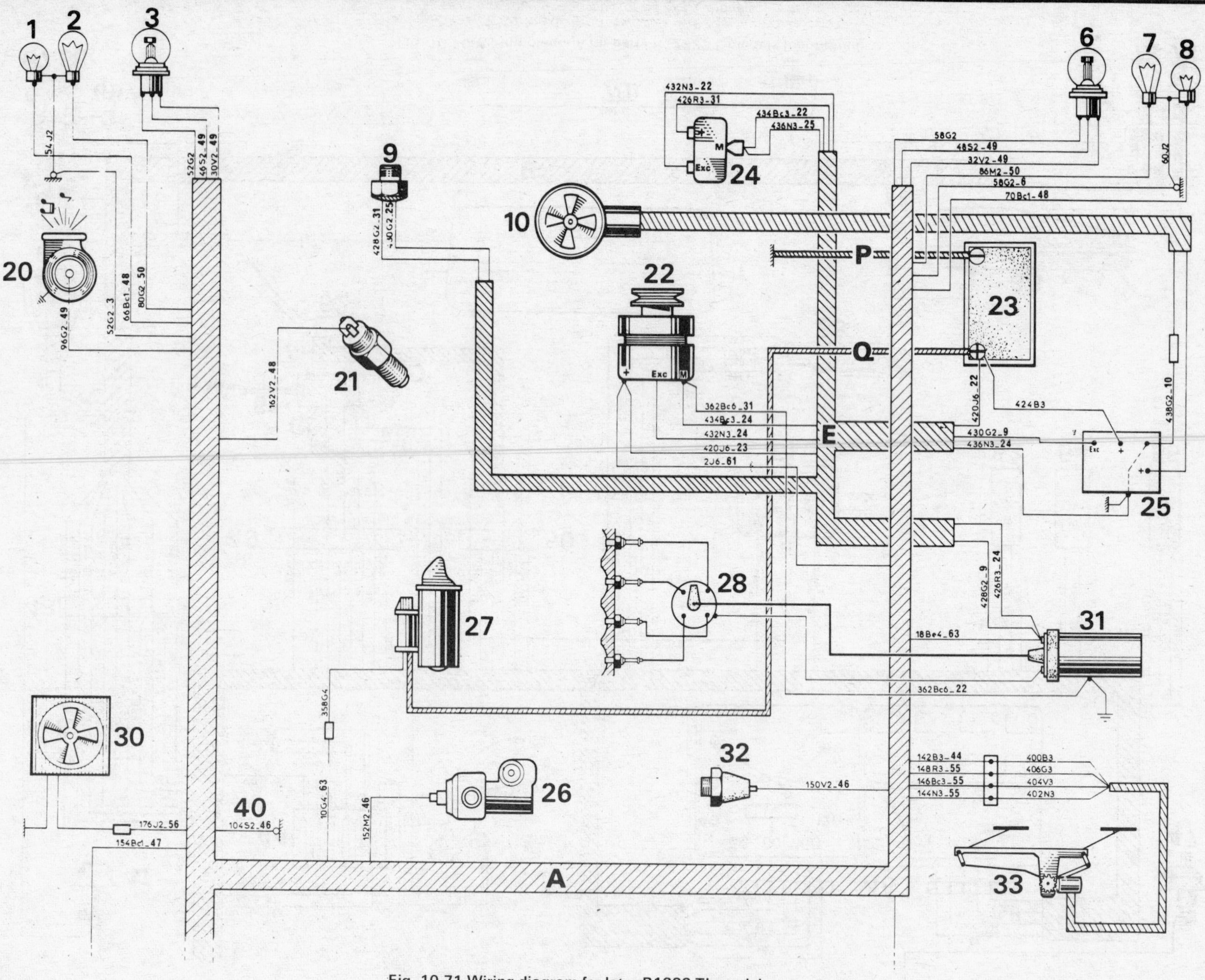

Fig. 10.71 Wiring diagram for later R1222 TL models

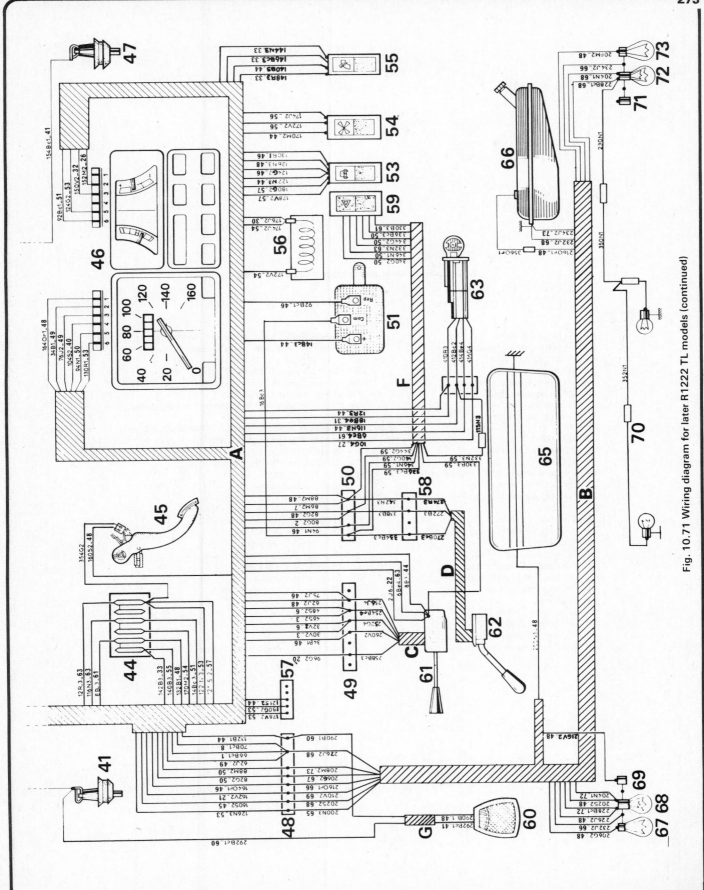

Fig. 10.71 Wiring diagram for later R1222 TL models (continued)

Key to wiring diagram for later R1222 TL models

1	LH front sidelight	49	Combination lighting switch – front harness junction
2	LH front direction indicator	50	Direction indicator switch – front harness junction
3	LH front headlight	51	Flasher unit
6	RH front headlight	53	Rear screen switch (R1222)
7	RH front direction indicator	54	Heating-ventilating fan switch
8	RH front sidelight	55	Windscreen wiper switch
9	Temperature switch	56	Heater blower fan resistance (for two-speed function)
10	Cooling fan motor	57	Connector
20	Horn	58	Direction indicator switch – harness junction
21	Reversing lamp switch	59	Hazard warning lights switch
22	Dynamo or alternator	60	Interior light
23	Battery	61	Combination lighting switch
24	Dynamo or alternator regulator	62	Direction indicator switch
25	Cooling fan motor relay	63	Ignition-starter switch
26	Coolant temperature switch	65	Rear screen
27	Starter	66	Fuel tank
28	Distributor	67	LH rear direction indicator
30	Heating-ventilating fan motor	68	LH rear and stop-lights
31	Ignition coil	69	LH rear reversing lamp
32	Oil pressure sender switch	70	Number plate lights
33	Windscreen wiper motor	71	RH rear reversing lamp
40	LH cowl side earth (ground)	72	RH rear and stop-lights
41	LH door pillar switch	73	RH rear direction indicator
44	Fusebox		
45	Stop-light switch		
46	Instrument panel		
47	RH door pillar switch		
48	Front-rear harness junction		*For wire harness identification refer to Fig. 10.68*

Key to wiring diagram for R1223 Gordini models – 1981 and later

1   LH sidelight and direction indicator lamps
2   RH sidelight and direction indicator lamps
7   LH headlight
8   RH headlight
9   LH horn
10 RH horn
12 Alternator
13 LH side earth (ground)
14 RH side earth (ground)
15 Starter
16 Battery
18 Ignition coil
20 Windscreen washer pump
21 Oil pressure switch
22 Thermal switch on radiator
23 Thermal switch on cylinder head
26 Windscreen wiper plate
27 Master cylinder
28 Heating-ventilating fan motor
29 Instrument panel
30 Connector No 1 – instrument panel
31 Connector No 2 – instrument panel
34 Hazard- warning lights switch
35 Rear screen demister switch
36 Heating-ventilating fan resistance
39 Additional panel instruments
40 LH door pillar switch
41 Fusebox
44 Fusebox
52 Stop-lights switch
53 Ignition – starter – anti-theft switch
54 Heater controls illumination
57 Car radio feed
58 Windscreen wiper-washer switch

59 Lighting switch
60 Direction indicator switch
62 LH interior light
63 RH interior light
64 Handbrake 'On' warning light switch
65 Fuel gauge tank unit
66 Rear screen demister
68 LH rear light assembly
69 RH rear light assembly
70 Number plate light
71 Choke 'On' warning light switch
72 Reversing lights switch
73 Rear light assemblies earth (ground)
74 Flasher unit
75 Heating-ventilating fan switch
76 Instrument lighting rheostat
77 Wire junction – diagnostic socket
78 Rear screen wiper motor
79 Rear screen washer pump
81 Junction block – front and rear harnesses
82 Junction block – front and console harnesses
93 Wire junction – LH front wing marker light
94 Wire junction – RH front wing marker light
100 LH inner wing panel gusset earth
106 Rear foglight switch
123 Clock
129 Front foglights switch
171 Rear screen wiper-washer switch
192 Tailgate earth (ground)
204 Starter relay
214 Front foglights relay
215 RH front foglight
216 LH front foglight

For wire harness identification refer to Fig.10.68

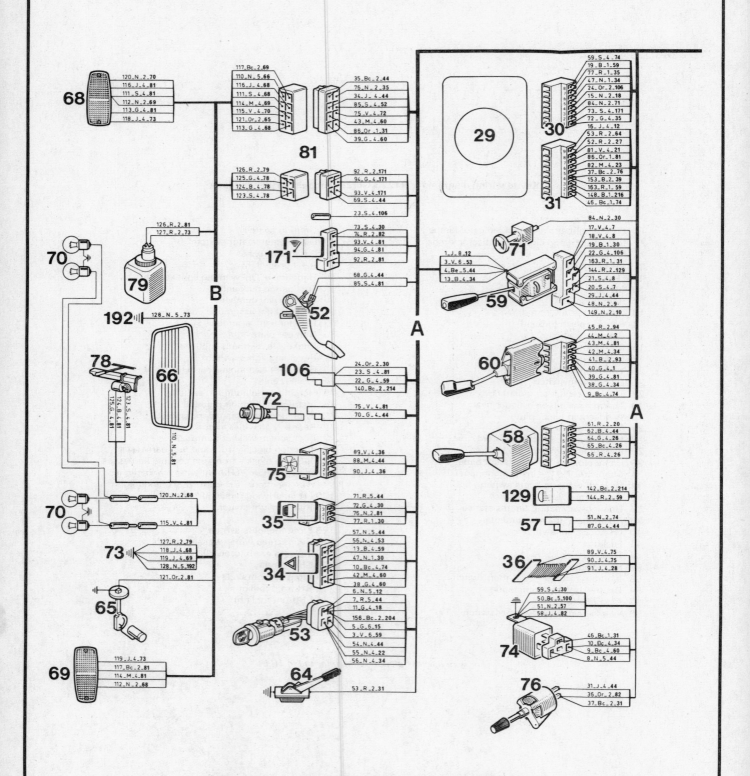

Fig. 10.72 Wiring diagram for R1223 Gordini models – 1981 and later

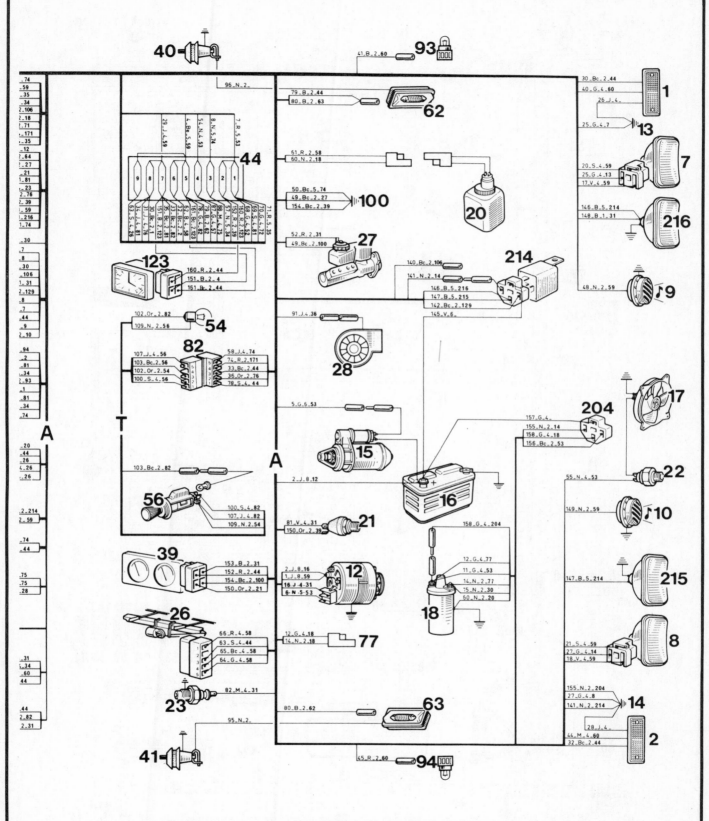

Fig. 10.72 Wiring diagram for R1223 Gordini models – 1981 and later (continued)

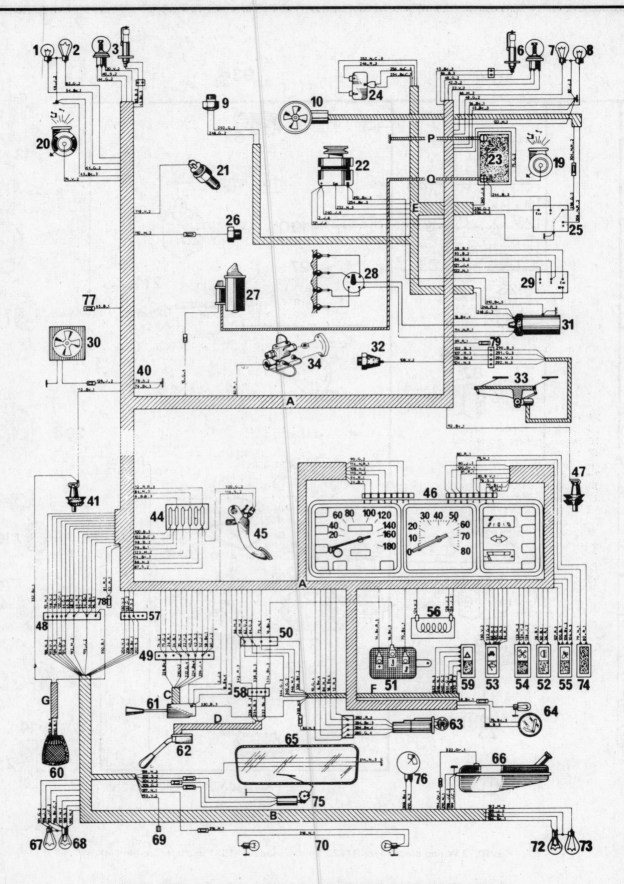

Fig. 10.73 Wiring diagram for early R1224 TS and R1227 TL/GTL models

Key to wiring diagram for early R1224 TS and R1227 TL/GTL models

1 LH front sidelight
2 LH front direction indicator
3 LH front headlight
6 RH front headlight
7 RH front direction indicator
8 RH front sidelight
9 Temperature switch on radiator
10 Cooling fan motor
19 RH horn
20 LH horn
21 Reversing lights switch
22 Alternator
23 Battery
24 Regulator
25 Cooling fan motor relay
26 Water temperature switch
27 Starter
28 Distributor
29 QI driving lights relay
30 Heating-ventilating fan motor
31 Ignition coil
32 Oil pressure switch
33 Windscreen wiper motor
34 Brake pressure drop indicator
40 LH cowl side earth (ground)
41 LH door pillar switch
42 Wire junction
43 Wire junction
44 Fusebox
45 Stop-lights switch
46 Instrument panel
47 RH door pillar switch
48 Junction – front and rear harnesses
49 Junction – front harness and combination lighting switch harness

50 Junction – front harness and hazard-warning lights system warning
51 Flasher unit
52 QI driving lights switch
53 Rear screen demister and rear screen wiper switch
54 Heating-ventilating fan switch
55 Windscreen wiper switch
56 Heating-ventilating fan resistance
57 Junction block – front and rear harnesses
58 Junction block – direction indicator and hazard-warning lights system harnesses
59 Hazard-warning lights system switch
60 Interior light
61 Combination lighting switch
62 Direction indicators switch
63 Ignition-starter switch
64 Cigar lighter
65 Rear screen demister
66 Fuel tank unit
67 LH rear direction indicator
68 LH rear light and stop-light
69 Reversing lights wire
70 Number plate lights
72 RH rear light and stop-light
73 RH rear direction indicator
74 Brake pressure drop indicator warning light switch
75 Rear screen wiper motor
76 Rear screen washer pump
77 Push-in plug and socket for LH side front direction indicator repeater
78 Push-in plug and socket for brake pressure drop warning light
79 Push-in plug and socket for RH side front direction indicator repeater

For wiring harness identification refer to Fig. 10.68

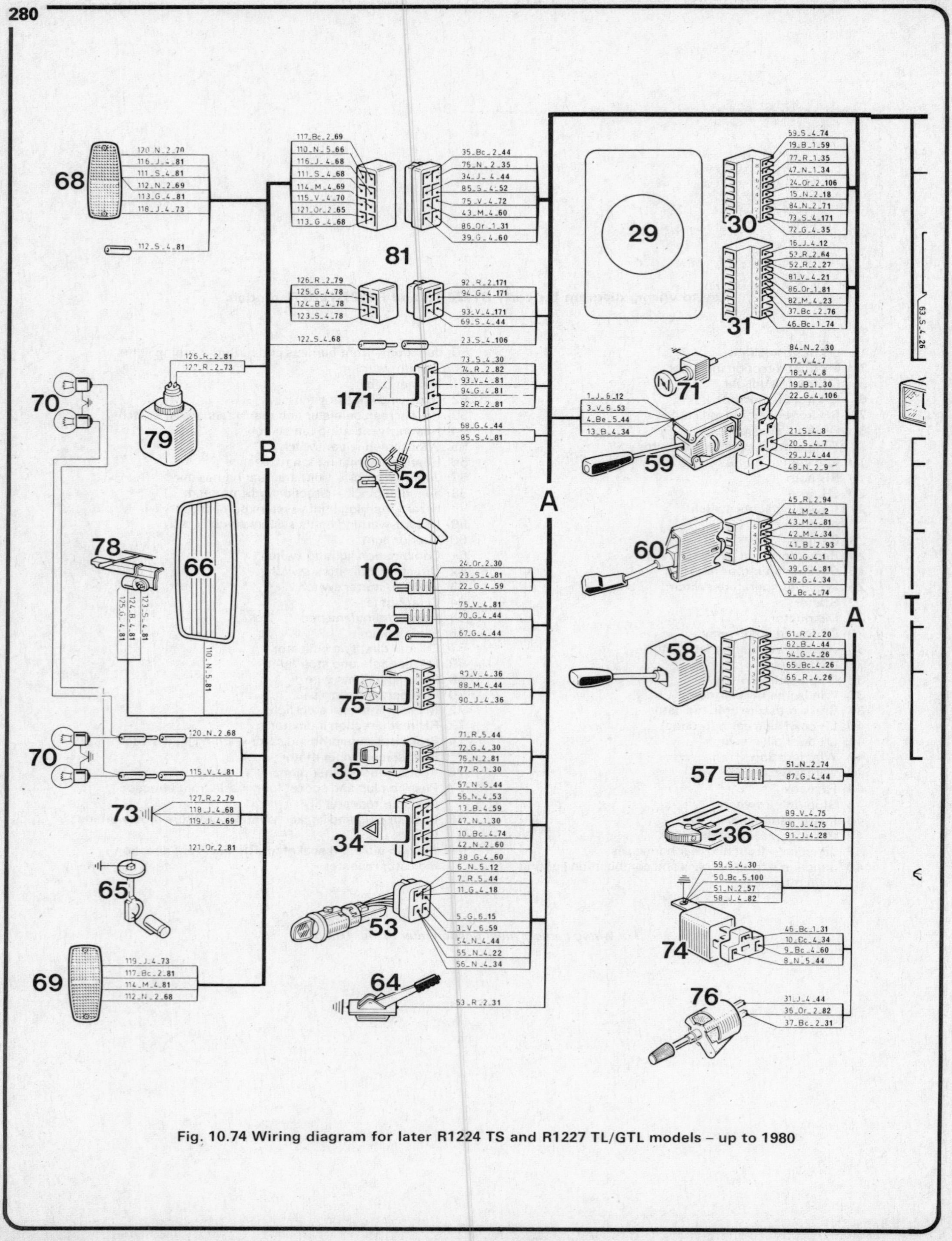

280

68

120.N.2.70
116.J.4.81
111.S.4.81
112.N.2.69
113.G.4.81
118.J.4.73

112.S.4.81

117.Bc.2.69
110.N.5.66
116.J.4.68
111.S.4.68
114.M.4.69
115.V.4.81
121.Or.2.65
113.G.4.68

81

35.Bc.2.44
75.N.2.35
34.J.4.44
85.S.4.52
75.V.4.72
43.M.4.60
86.Or.1.31
39.G.4.60

29

59.S.4.74
19.B.1.59
77.R.1.35
47.N.1.34
24.Or.2.106
15.N.2.18
84.N.2.71
73.S.4.171
72.G.4.35

30

16.J.4.12
53.R.2.64
52.R.2.27
81.V.4.21
86.Or.1.81
82.M.4.23
37.Bc.2.76
46.Bc.1.74

31

63.S.4.26

126.R.2.79
125.G.4.78
124.B.4.78
123.S.4.78

92.R.2.171
94.G.4.171
93.V.4.171
69.S.4.44

122.S.4.68

23.S.4.106

125.R.2.81
127.R.2.73

70

79

73.S.4.30
74.R.2.82
93.V.4.81
94.G.4.81
92.R.2.81

171

68.G.4.44
85.S.4.81

84.N.2.30

71

17.V.4.7
18.V.4.8
19.B.1.30
22.G.4.106

1.J.6.12
3.V.6.53
4.Be.5.44
13.B.4.34

59

21.S.4.8
20.S.4.7
29.J.4.44
48.N.2.9

B

52

A

78

66

123.S.4.81
124.B.4.81
125.G.4.81

110.N.5.81

106

24.Or.2.30
23.S.4.81
22.G.4.59

60

45.R.2.94
44.M.4.2
43.M.4.81
42.M.4.34
41.B.2.93
40.G.4.1
39.G.4.81
38.G.4.34
9.Bc.4.74

A

72

75.V.4.81
70.G.4.44
67.G.4.44

58

61.R.2.20
62.B.4.44
64.G.4.26
65.Bc.4.26
65.R.4.26

75

93.V.4.36
88.M.4.44
90.J.4.36

57

51.N.2.74
87.G.4.44

35

71.R.5.44
72.G.4.30
76.N.2.81
77.R.1.30

36

89.V.4.75
90.J.4.75
91.J.4.28

34

57.N.5.44
56.N.4.53
13.B.4.59
47.N.1.30
10.Bc.4.74
42.N.2.60
38.G.4.60

74

59.S.4.30
50.Bc.5.100
51.N.2.57
58.J.4.82

46.Bc.1.31
10.Bc.4.34
9.Bc.4.60
8.N.5.44

53

6.N.5.12
7.R.5.44
11.G.4.18
5.G.6.15
3.V.6.59
54.N.4.44
55.N.4.22
56.N.4.34

65

121.Or.2.81

69

119.J.4.73
117.Bc.2.81
114.M.4.81
112.N.2.68

73

127.R.2.79
118.J.4.68
119.J.4.69

70

120.N.2.68
115.V.4.81

64

53.R.2.31

76

31.J.4.44
36.Or.2.82
37.Bc.2.31

Fig. 10.74 Wiring diagram for later R1224 TS and R1227 TL/GTL models – up to 1980

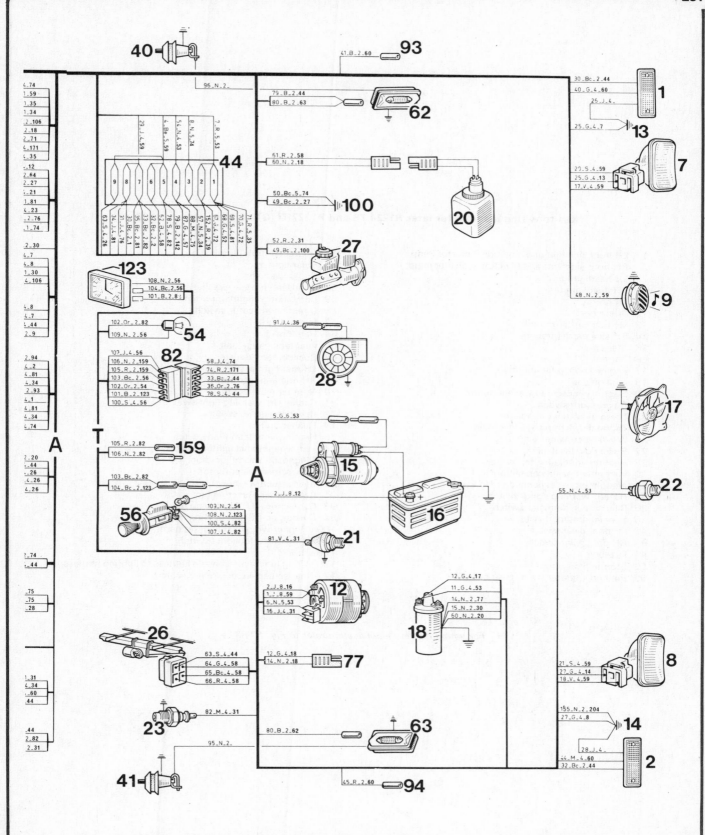

Fig. 10.74 Wiring diagram for later R1224 TS and R1227 TL/GTL models – up to 1980 (continued)

Key to wiring diagram for later R1224 TS and R1227 TL/GTL models – up to 1980

1	LH front sidelight and direction indicator lamp	54	Heater controls illumination
2	RH front sidelight and direction indicator lamp	56	Cigar lighter
7	LH headlight unit	57	Radio feed wire
8	RH headlight unit	58	Windscreen wiper-washer switch
9	LH horn	59	Combination lighting switch
12	Alternator	60	Direction indicator switch
13	LH side earth (ground)	62	Interior light
14	RH side earth (ground)	64	Handbrake
15	Starter	65	Fuel tank gauge unit
16	Battery	66	Rear screen demister
17	Engine cooling fan motor	68	LH rear light assembly
18	Ignition coil	69	RH rear light assembly
20	Electric windscreen washer pump	70	Number plate lights
21	Oil pressure switch	71	Choke 'On' warning light switch
22	Thermal switch on radiator	72	Reversing lights switch
23	Thermal switch on cylinder head	74	Flasher unit
26	Windscreen wiper plate	75	Heating-ventilating fan switch
27	Brake fluid level indicator	76	Instrument panel lighting rheostat
28	Heating-ventilating fan motor	77	Diagnostic socket junction
30	Instrument panel connector No 1	78	Rear screen wiper motor
31	Instrument panel connector No 2	79	Rear screen washer pump
34	Hazard-warning lights switch	81	Rear harness junction block
35	Rear screen demister switch	93	Connector – LH front wing marker
36	Supplementary resistance	94	Connector – RH front wing marker
40	LH door pillar switch	100	LH inner wing panel gusset earth
41	RH door pillar switch	106	Connector – foglights switch
44	Fusebox	123	Clock
52	Stop-lights switch	159	Wiring junction – console harness to lighting harness
53	Ignition – starter – anti-theft switch	171	Rear screen wiper-washer switch

For wiring harness identification refer to Fig. 10.68

Key to wiring diagram for late R1224 TS, R1227 TL/GTL and R1395 GTL/Auto models – 1982 and later

*The wiring diagram has a grid for ease of unit identification. Figures 1 to 9 run horizontally and letters
A to D run vertically*

*Example: Unit No 1 (LH front direction indicator)
This unit will be found in the rectangle bordered by letter A vertically and figure 9 horizontally*

1	LH sidelight and/or direction indicator lamp	A9
2	RH sidelight and/or direction indicator lamp	D9
7	LH headlight	A9
8	RH headlight	D9
9	LH horn	B9
12	Alternator	D8
13	LH front earth (ground)	A9
14	RH front earth (ground)	D8
15	Starter	D8
16	Battery	C8
17	Engine cooling fan motor	B9
18	Ignition coil	C7
20	Windscreen washer pump	D8
21	Oil pressure switch	C7
22	Thermal switch on radiator	C8
26	Windscreen wiper motor	B7
27	ICP (brake fluid pressure drop indicator)	A7
28	Heating-ventilating fan motor	B7
29	Instrument panel	C4
30	Connector No 1 – instrument panel	B4
31	Connector No 2 – instrument panel	C4
34	Hazard- warning lights switch	D5
35	Rear screen demister switch	C5
40	LH front door pillar switch	A5
41	RH front door pillar switch	D5
44	Accessories plate or fusebox	A6
52	Stop-lights switch	A6
53	Ignition – starter – anti-theft switch	A5
54	Heater control panel illumination	D6
56	Cigar lighter	D6
57	Feed to car radio	D6
58	Windscreen wiper-washer switch	B5
59	Lighting and direction indicators switch	A5
60	Direction indicators switch or connector	B5
62	LH side or central interior light	A4
63	RH interior light	D4

64	Handbrake switch	B3
65	Fuel gauge tank unit	B2
66	Rear screen demister	C3
68	LH rear light assembly	A1
69	RH rear light assembly	D1
70	Number plate lights	B1
71	Choke 'On' warning light	A5
72	Reversing lights switch	A8
74	Flasher unit	B5
75	Heating-ventilating fan switch	C6
76	Instrument panel lighting and warning lights rheostat	C5
77	Wire junction – diagnostic socket	C7
78	Rear screen wiper motor	C2
79	Rear screen washer pump	D3
81	Junction block – front and rear harnesses	A3
85	Junction block – window or electro-magnetic lock harness	B5
89	Rear foglight	B1
93	Junction – LH side repeater	A7
94	Junction – RH side repeater	D7
100	Scuttle gusset earth (ground)	B7
101	Fuel tank mounting earth (ground)	C3
106	Rear foglight switch	D5
123	Clock	C6
130	Gearbox earth	A8
144	Junction – interior light wiring	D5 & A5
146	Temperature switch or thermal switch	B8
171	Rear screen wiper-washer switch	C5
174	LH headlight wiper motor	C9
176	Headlight wiper-washers time switch	C9
179	Junction – windscreen washer/headlight washer pump	C8
192	Tailgate earth (ground)	B3
223	Reversing lights	B1 & C1

For wiring harness identification refer to Fig. 10.68

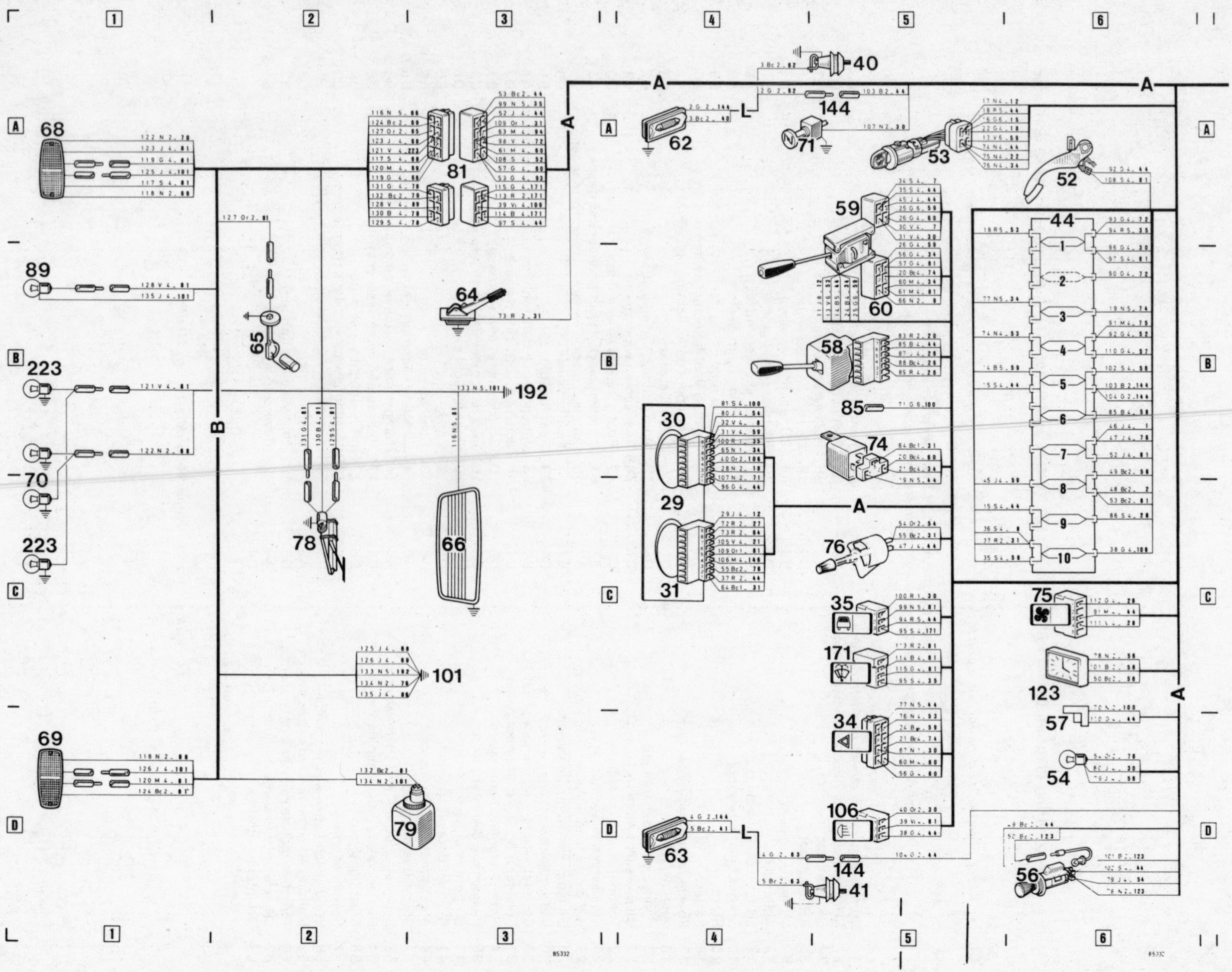

Fig. 10.75 Wiring diagram for late R1224 TS, R1227 TL/GTL and R1395 GTL/Auto models – 1982 and later

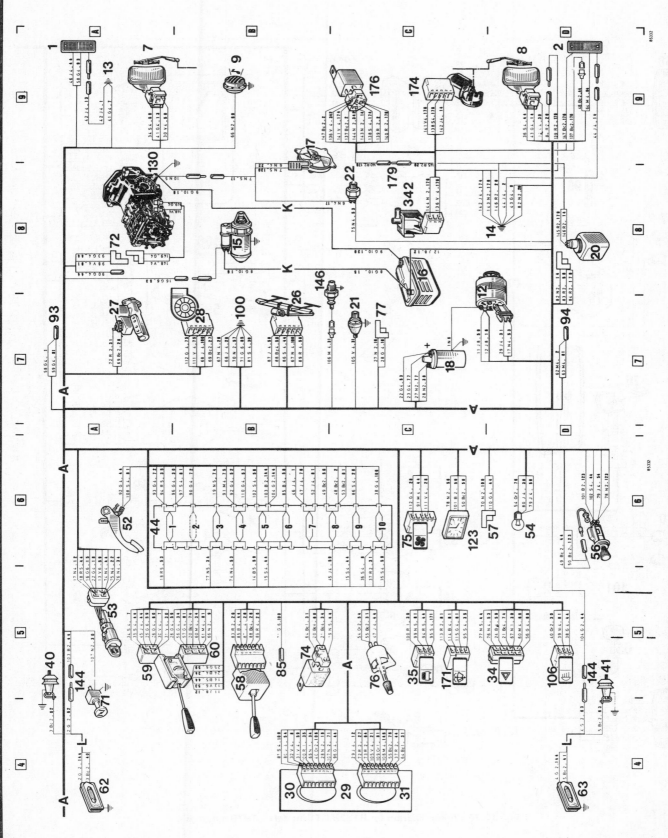

Fig. 10.75 Wiring diagram for late R1224 TS, R1227 TL/GTL and R1395 GTL/Auto models – 1982 and later (continued)

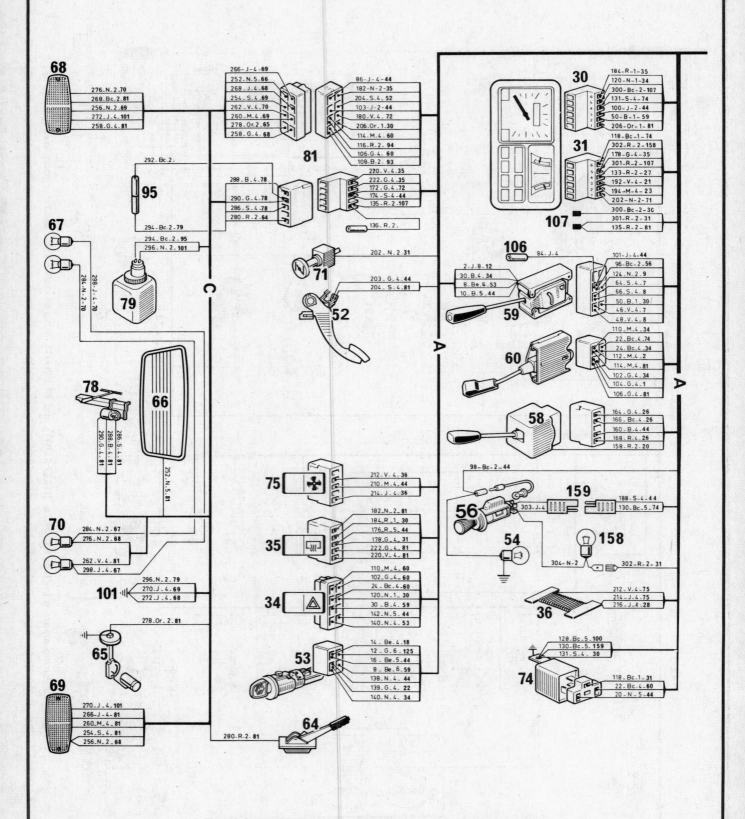

Fig. 10.76 Wiring diagram for R1225 GTL models – 1979 automatic

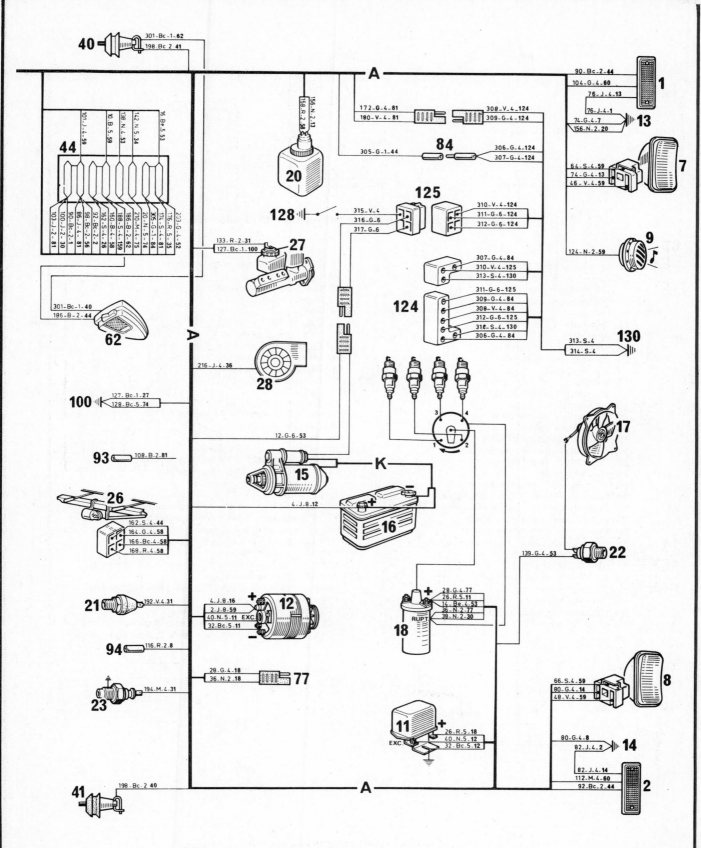

Fig. 10.76 Wiring diagram for R1225 GTL models – 1979 automatic (continued)

Key to wiring diagram for R1225 GTL models – 1979 automatic

1	LH sidelight and direction indicator lamp	58	Windscreen wiper-washer switch
2	RH sidelight and direction indicator lamp	59	Lighting switch
7	LH headlight unit	60	Direction indicators switch
8	RH headlight unit	62	Interior light (LH)
9	LH horn	64	Handbrake
11	Regulator	65	Fuel gauge tank unit
12	Alternator	66	Rear screen demister
13	LH side earth (ground)	67	Luggage compartment illumination
14	RH side earth (ground)	68	LH rear light assembly
15	Starter	69	RH rear light assembly
16	Battery	70	Number plate light
17	Engine cooling fan motor	71	Choke switch
18	Ignition coil	74	Flasher unit
20	Windscreen washer pump	75	Heating-ventilation fan switch
21	Oil pressure switch	77	Diagnostic socket
22	Thermal switch on radiator	78	Rear screen wiper motor
23	Thermal switch on cylinder head	79	Rear screen washer pump
26	Windscreen wiper plate	81	Junction block – front and rear harness
27	Master cylinder	84	Junction block – front harness and
28	Heating-ventilating fan motor		auto-transmission harness
30	Connector No 1 – instrument panel	93	Wire junction – LH front wing marker
31	Connector No 2 – instrument panel	94	Wire junction – RH front wing marker
34	Hazard- warning lights switch	95	Wire junction – rear screen washer pump
35	Rear screen demister switch	100	LH inner wing panel gusset earth (ground)
36	Heating-ventilating fan motor rheostat	101	Fuel tank mounting earth (ground)
40	LH door pillar switch	106	Rear foglights switch
41	RH door pillar switch	107	Brake circuit warning light bulb checking switch
44	Accessories plate (fusebox)	124	Automatic transmission
52	Stop-lights switch	125	Automatic transmission starting inhibitor switch
53	Anti-theft switch	128	Kickdown switch
54	Heater controls illumination	130	Automatic transmission earth
56	Cigar lighter	158	Automatic transmission selector illumination
		159	Wire junction – console harness to lighting harness

For wire harness identification refer to Fig. 10.68

Key to wiring diagram for R1228 Le Car GTL models – except California

1	LH front sidelight	55	Windscreen wiper switch
2	LH front direction indicator	56	Heating-ventilating fan motor resistance
3	LH front reflector/side marker	59	Warning light system switch
4	RH front reflector/side marker	60	Overhead interior light
5	RH front illuminating reflector	61	Combination lighting switch
6	RH front headlight	62	Direction indicator switch
7	RH front direction indicator	63	Ignition-starter switch
8	RH front sidelight	64	Cigarette lighter
9	Temperature switch on radiator	65	Heated rear window
10	Cooling fan motor	66	Fuel tank
11	Solenoid valve	67	LH rear direction indicator
12	Solenoid valve (Ign. dist. vacuum advance)	68	LH rear tail and stop-light
13	Centrifugal switch	69	Reversing light wire
14	Timer relay	70	Number plate light
19	RH horn	72	RH rear tail and stop-light
20	LH horn	73	RH rear direction indicator
21	Reversing light switch	75	Rear window wiper motor
22	Alternator	76	Rear window washer pump
23	Battery	80	LH rear reflector/side marker
24	Regulator	81	RH rear reflector/side marker
25	Cooling fan motor relay	82	Seat belt contact
26	Coolant temperature switch	83	Handbrake 'On' warning switch
27	Starter	84	Heating controls illumination
28	Distributor	85	Front harness – windscreen wiper harness connection
30	Heating-ventilating fan motor	86	Front harness – rear harness connection
31	Ignition coil	87	Front harness – rear harness connection
32	Oil pressure sender switch	88	Front harness – combination lighting switch harness connection
33	Windscreen wiper motor	89	Front harness
34	Brake pressure indicator	90	Front harness
35	Lighting rheostat	91	Key reminder light
36	Buzzer	92	Front harness connection – solenoid valves connection
37	Diodes	93	Switch identification illumination
38	Seat belt light	94	Choke control
40	Instrument panel earth (ground)	95	Harness splice (+)
41	LH door switch	96	Push-in plug socket for seat belt and switch
44	Fusebox	97	Push-in and socket for brake pressure drop indicator
45	Stoplight switch	98	Push-in plug and socket for rear window wiper/pump
46	Instrument panel	99	LH reversing light
47	RH door switch	100	RH reversing light
51	Flasher unit		
53	Rear window demister and wiper switch		
54	Heating-ventilating fan switch		

For wire harness identification refer to Fig. 10.68

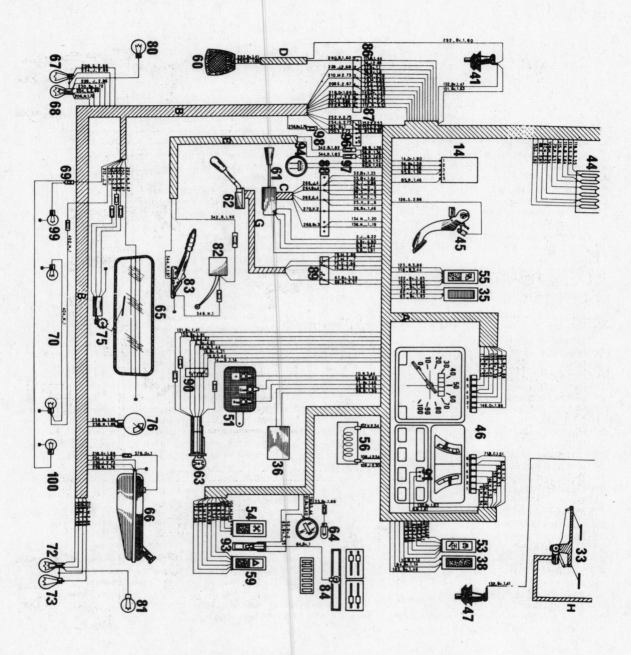

Fig. 10.77 Wiring diagram for R1228 Le Car GTL models – except California

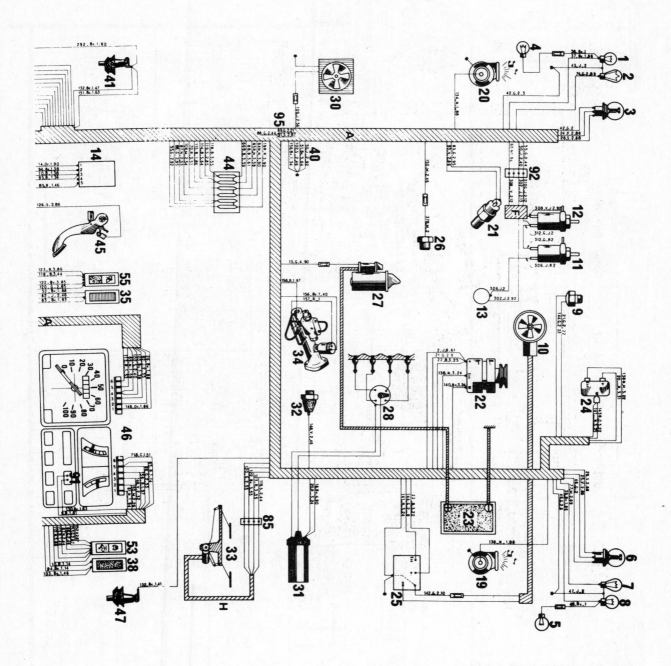

Fig. 10.77 Wiring diagram for R1228 Le Car GTL models – except California (continued)

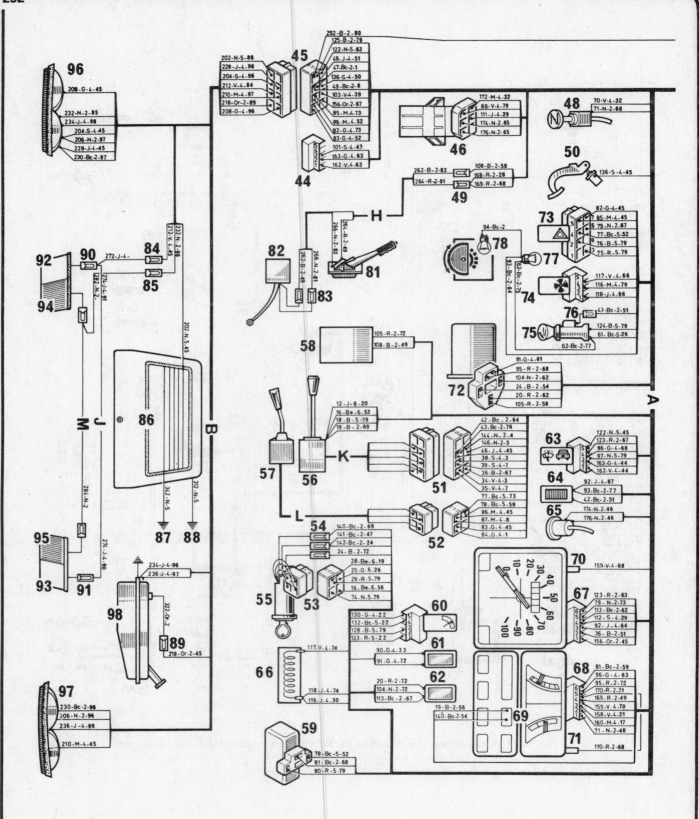

Fig. 10.78 Wiring diagram for R1228 Le Car GTL models – California

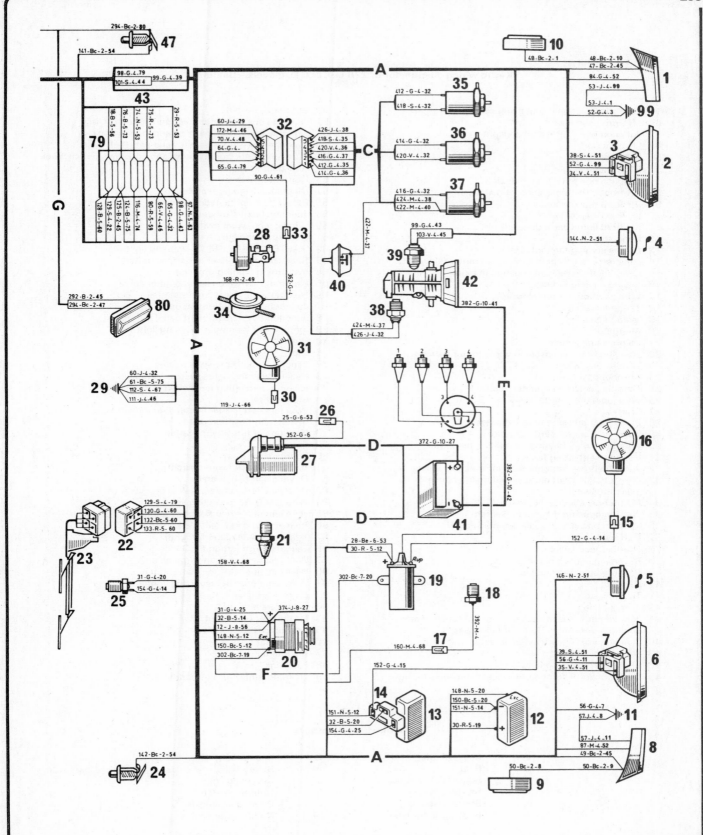

Fig. 10.78 Wiring diagram for R1228 Le Car GTL models – California (continued)

Key to wiring diagram for R1228 Le Car GTL models – California

1 LH front directional signal and sidelight
2 LH front headlight
3 Junction box – LH front headlight
4 LH front horn
5 RH front horn
6 RH front headlight
7 Junction box – RH front headlight
8 RH front directional signal and sidelight
9 RH front marker light
10 LH front marker light
11 RH front lights earth (ground)
12 Regulator
13 Engine cooling fan motor relay
14 Junction box – engine cooling fan motor relay
15 Wire junction – engine cooling fan motor
16 Engine cooling fan motor
17 Wire junction – thermal switch
18 Thermal switch
19 Ignition coil
20 Alternator
21 Oil pressure switch
22 Junction box – windscreen wiper motor harness
23 Windscreen wiper
24 RH door pillar switch
25 Thermal switch on cylinder head
26 Wire junction – starter relay
27 Starter
28 Brake fluid pressure drop indicator
29 LH scuttle gusset earth (ground)
30 Wire junction – heating-ventilating fan motor
31 Heating-ventilating fan motor
32 Junction box – front harness and solenoid valve
33 Wire junction front harness and maintenance indicator switch
34 Maintenance indicator switch
35 Throttle opening diaphragm switch
36 Vacuum advance capsule solenoid valve
37 EGR valve
38 Fourth speed switch
39 Reversing lights switch
40 Vacuum operated switch
41 Battery
42 Transmission
43 Wire junction
44 Junction box – front harness and rear screen wiper
45 Junction box – front and rear harnesses
46 Junction box – gearchange detector
47 LH door pillar switch
48 Choke 'ON' warning light
49 Wire junction – front harness and safety belt wiring

50 Stop-light switch
51 Junction box – front harness and lighting switch
52 Junction box – front harness and steering box
53 Junction box – front harness and anti-theft switch
54 Wire junction – front harness and anti-theft switch wires
55 Anti-theft switch
56 Lighting switch
57 Directional signals switch
58 Safety belt 'not fastened' buzzer
59 Junction box – flasher unit
60 Windscreen wiper switch
61 EGR warning light
62 'FASTEN SEATS BELTS' warning light
63 Rear screen demister and wiper switch
64 Instrument lighting rheostat
65 Electronic switch on speedometer cable
66 Heating-ventilating fan resistance
67 Junction box – instrument panel
68 Junction box – instrument panel
69 Ignition key 'reminder' warning light
70 Diode
71 Diode
72 Junction box – time switch relay
73 Hazard-warning lights system switch
74 Heating-ventilating fan switch
75 Cigar lighter
76 Wire junction – cigar lighter illumination
77 Switch identification plate
78 Heating controls identification
79 Fusebox
80 Interior light
81 Handbrake 'ON' warning light
82 Driver's safety belt stalk
83 Wire junction – driver's safety belt stalk
84 Wire junction – reversing lights
85 Wire junction – number plate lights
86 Rear screen demister
87 Rear screen demister (ground)
88 Tailgate earth (ground)
89 Wire junction – fuel tank gauge unit
90 Wire junction – LH reversing light
91 Wire junction – RH reversing light
92 LH reversing light
93 RH reversing light
94 LH number plate light
95 RH number plate light
96 LH rear light
97 RH rear light
98 Fuel tank
99 LH front lights earth (ground)

List of wiring harnesses

A Engine front
B Rear
C Solenoid flap valves
D Starter positive
E Starter negative
F Body earth (ground)
G Interior light
H Safety belts
J Reversing lights
K Lighting switch
L Directional signals
M Number plate lights

Key to wiring diagram for R1229 Le Car and TX models – 1981 automatic

The wiring diagram has a grid to make it easier to find units. This grid is marked horizontally 1 to 9 and vertically A to D

Example: Unit No 1 (LH front direction indicator)

This unit will be found in the rectangle bounded vertically by letter A and horizontally by number 9

1	LH front sidelight and direction indicator lamp	A9	60	Direction indicator switch	D5
2	RH front sidelight and direction indicator lamp	D9	62	LH interior light	A8
7	LH headlight	A9	63	RH interior light	D8
8	RH headlight	D9	64	Handbrake	A7
9	LH horn	B9	65	Fuel tank gauge unit	D2
12	Alternator	A8	66	Rear screen demister	B2
13	LH side earth (ground)	A9	68	LH rear light assembly	A1
14	RH side earth (ground)	D9	69	RH rear light assembly	D1
15	Starter	C7	70	Number plate lights	B1
16	Battery	B8	71	Choke 'On' warning light switch	A7
17	Engine cooling fan motor	C9	74	Flasher unit	B6
18	Ignition coil	B8	75	Heating-ventilating fan switch	C6
20	Windscreen washer pump	D9	76	Instrument panel lighting rheostat	B6
21	Oil pressure switch	A8	77	Wire junction – diagnostic socket	C9
22	Thermal switch on radiator	C9	78	Rear screen wiper motor	B2
26	Windscreen wiper motor	C7	79	Rear screen washer pump	C2
27	Brake master cylinder	B7	81	Junction block – front and rear harnesses	A2
28	Heating-ventilating fan motor	B7	82	Junction block – front harness to	
29	Instrument panel	A5		console wiring	C5
30	Connector No 1 – instrument panel	A5	85	Junction block – front harness to	
31	Connector No 2 – instrument panel	A5		auto-transmission harness	C8
34	Hazard-warning lights switch	C6	93	Wire junction – LH front wing light	A8
35	Rear screen demister switch	C6	94	Wire junction – RH front wing light	D8
36	Heating-ventilating fan resistance	A7	106	Rear foglight switch	A6
37	LH window switch	B3	112	Window winder relay	C3
38	RH window switch	B3	123	Clock	D5
40	LH door pillar switch	A8	124	Automatic transmission	D7
41	RH door pillar switch	D8	125	Starter safety switch	C8
42	LH window motor	A3	128	Kickdown switch	C8
43	RH window motor	D3	130	Auto-transmission earth (ground)	D7
44	Fusebox	B4	142	Wire junction – window winder harness	C3
52	Stop-lights switch	B7	144	Wire junction – interior light wiring	D8
53	Ignition – starter – anti-theft switch	A6	146	Thermal switch	D8
54	Heater control panel illumination	C5	158	Auto-transmission selector illumination	D4
56	Cigar lighter	D4	171	Rear screen wiper-washer switch	C6
57	Radio feed	D6	192	Tailgate earth (ground)	B2
58	Windscreen wiper-washer switch	B5	204	Starter relay	C7
59	Combination lighting switch	C5	223	Reversing lights	B1 & C1

List of wiring harnesses

A	Front
B	Rear
F	LH window
G	RH window
N	Automatic transmission

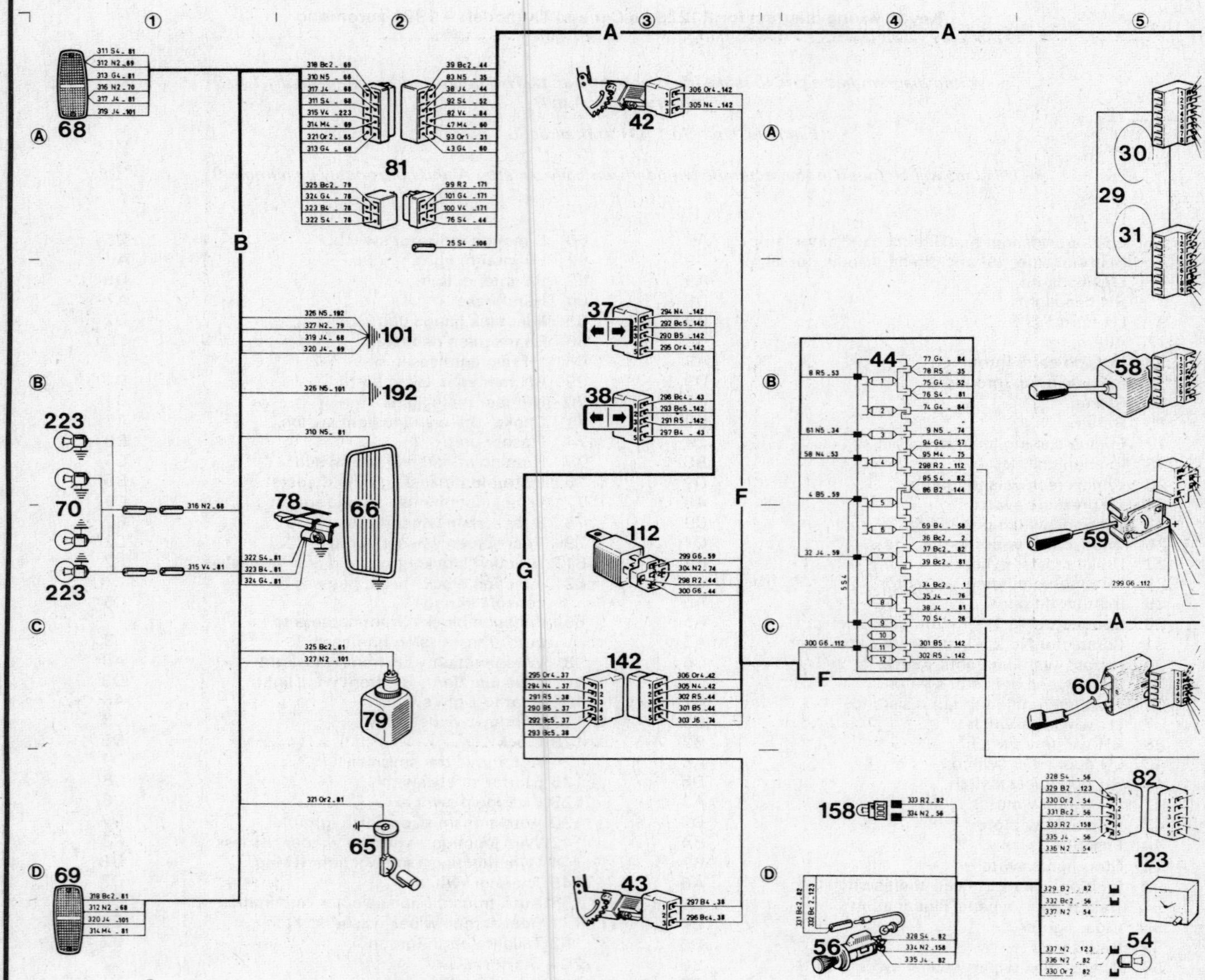

Fig. 10.79 Wiring diagram for R1229 Le Car and TX models – 1981 automatic

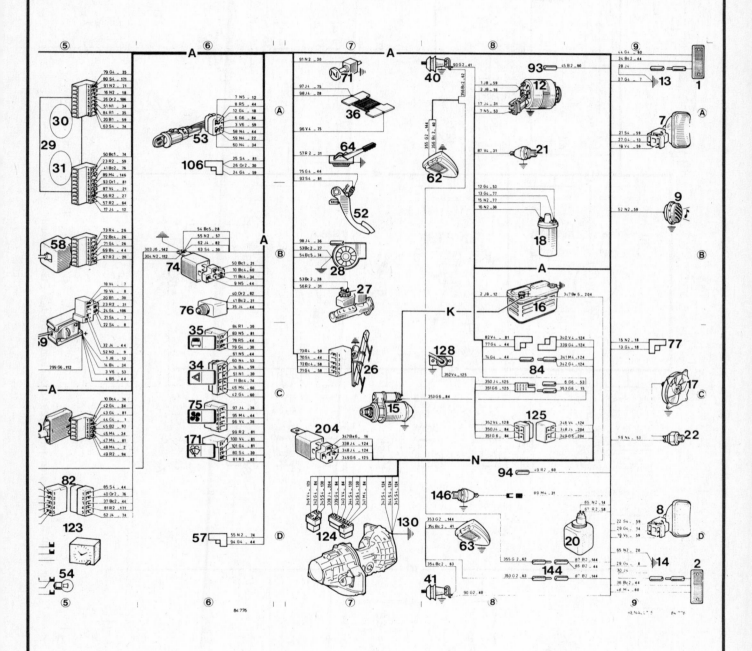

Fig. 10.79 Wiring diagram for R1229 Le Car and TX models – 1981 automatic (continued)

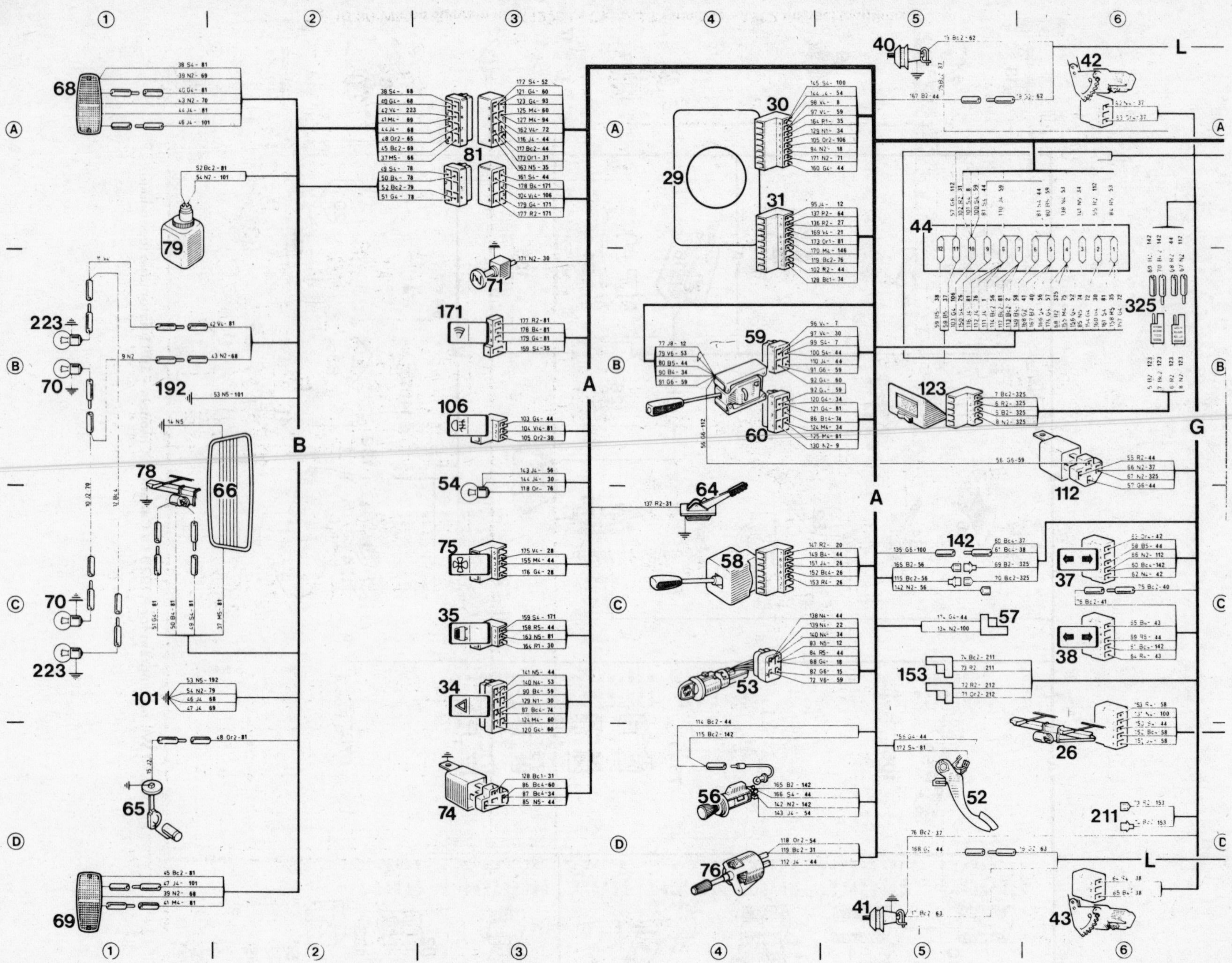

Fig. 10.80 Wiring diagram for R1229 Le Car and TX models – 1982 manual

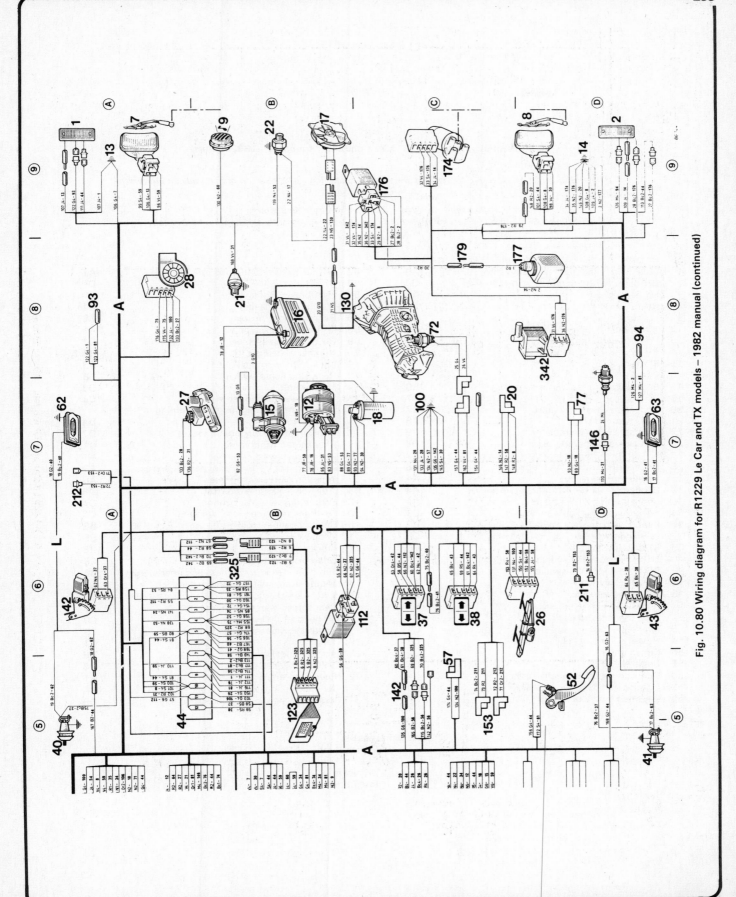

Fig. 10.80 Wiring diagram for R1229 Le Car and TX models – 1982 manual (continued)

Key to wiring diagram for R1229 Le Car and TX models – 1982 manual

The wiring diagram has a grid for ease of unit identification. Figures 1 to 9 run horizontally and letters
A to D run vertically

Example: Unit No 1 (LH front direction indicator)
This unit will be found in the rectangle bordered by letter A vertically and figure 9 horizontally

1	LH sidelight and/or direction indicator lamp	A9	62	LH side or central interior light	A7
2	RH sidelight and/or direction indicator lamp	D9	63	RH interior light	D7
7	LH headlight	A9	64	Handbrake 'ON' switch	C4
8	RH headlight	D9	65	Fuel gauge tank unit	D1
9	LH horn	B9	66	Rear screen demister	C3
12	Alternator	B7	68	LH rear light assembly	A1
13	LH front earth (ground)	A9	69	RH rear light assembly	D1
14	RH front earth (ground)	D9	70	Number plate light	B1 & C1
15	Starter	B7	71	Choke 'On' warning light	B3
16	Battery	B8	72	Reversing lights switch	C8
17	Engine cooling fan motor	B9	74	Flasher unit	D3
18	Ignition coil	C7	75	Heating-ventilating fan switch	C3
20	Windscreen washer pump	C7	76	Instrument panel lighting and warning lights rheostat	D4
21	Oil pressure switch	B8			
22	Thermal switch on radiator	B9	77	Wire junction – diagnostic socket	D7
26	Windscreen wiper motor	D6	78	Rear screen wiper motor	B1
27	ICP (brake fluid pressure drop indicator)	B7	79	Rear screen washer pump	A1
28	Heating-ventilating fan motor	A8	81	Junction block – front and rear harnesses	A3
29	Instrument panel	A4	93	Junction – LH side repeater	A8
30	Connector No 1 – instrument panel	A4	94	Junction – RH side repeater	D8
31	Connector No 2 – instrument panel	A4	100	Scuttle gusset earth (ground)	C7
34	Hazard-warning lights switch	C3	101	Fuel tank mounting earth (ground)	C1
35	Rear screen demister switch	C3	106	Rear foglight switch	B3
37	LH window switch	C6	112	Window relay	C6
38	RH window switch	C6	123	Clock	B5
40	LH front door pillar switch	A5	130	Gearbox earth (ground)	C8
41	RH front door pillar switch	D5	142	Junction – window harness and interior light	C5
42	LH window motor	A6	146	Temperature switch or thermal switch	D7
43	RH window motor	D6	153	Wire – speaker to radio	C5
44	Accessories plate or fusebox	B5	171	Rear screen wiper-washer switch	B3
52	Stop-lights switch	D5	174	LH headlight wiper motor	C9
53	Ignition – starter – anti-theft switch	C4	176	Headlight wiper-washers time switch	C9
54	Heater control panel illumination	C3	192	Tailgate earth	B1
56	Cigar lighter	D4	211	RH rear speaker	D6
57	Radio feed	C5	212	LH rear speaker	D6
58	Windscreen wiper-washer switch	C4	223	Reversing lamps	B1 & C1
59	Lighting and direction indicators switch	B4	325	Junction – clockwise	B6
60	Direction indicator switch	B4	342	Headlamp washer solenoid valve	D8

List of harnesses

A	Engine front
B	Rear
G	Windows
L	Interior light

Key to wiring diagram for 122B Gordini Turbo models – 1982

The wiring diagram has a grid for ease of unit identification. Figures 1 to 9 run horizontally and letters A to D run vertically

Example: Unit No 1 (LH front direction indicator)
This unit will be found in the rectangle bordered by letter A vertically and figure 9 horizontally

1	LH sidelight and/or direction indicator lamp	A9	68	LH rear light assembly	A1
2	RH sidelight and/or direction indicator lamp	D9	69	RH rear light assembly	D1
7	LH headlight	A9	70	Number plate lights	B1 & C1
8	RH headlight	D9	71	Choke 'On' warning light switch	B3
12	Alternator	C7	72	Reversing lights switch	C8
13	LH front earth (ground)	A9	74	Flasher unit	D3
14	RH front earth (ground)	D9	75	Heating-ventilating fan switch	C2
15	Starter	B7	76	Instrument lighting rheostat	D3
16	Battery	B7	78	Rear screen wiper motor	B1
17	Engine cooling fan motor	B9	79	Rear screen washer pump	A1
20	Windscreen washer pump	D8	81	Junction block – front to rear harnes	A2
21	Oil pressure switch	D6	93	Wire junction – LH repeater light	A8
22	Thermal switch on radiator	B9	94	Wire junction – RH repeater light	D8
23	Thermal switch on cylinder head	D6	97	Bodyshell earth (ground)	D7
26	Windscreen wiper motor	D6	100	Inner wing panel scuttle gusset earth (ground)	D5
27	ICP (brake fluid pressure drop indicator)	A7	101	Fuel tank mounting earth (ground)	C1
28	Heating-ventilating fan motor	B7	106	Rear foglight switch	C2
29	Instrument panel	A4	112	Windows relay	C5
30	Connector No 1 – instrument panel	A4	123	Clock	B5
31	Connector No 2 – instrument panel	B4	130	Gearbox earth (ground)	B8
34	Hazard-warning lights switch	C2	142	Junction – window harness and interior light	C6
35	Rear screen demister switch	C2	171	Rear screen wiper-washer switch	B2
37	LH door switch	C6	174	LH headlight wiper motor	C9
38	RH door switch	C6	176	Headlight wiper-washers timer	C9
39	Additional instruments	C4	177	Headlight washers pump	D8
40	LH door pillar switch	A5	179	Junction – windscreen washer/headlight washers pump	C8
41	RH door pillar switch	D5	192	Tailgate earth	B1
42	LH window winder	A6	210	Junction block – AEI harness	C7
43	RH window winder	D6	214	Front foglights relay	A8
44	Accessories plate or fusebox	B6	215	RH front foglight	C9
52	Stop-lights switch	B2	216	LH front foglight	A9
53	Ignition – starter – anti-theft switch	D2	223	Reversing lights	B1 & C1
54	Heater controls illumination	C5	232	Boost pressure gauge	D7
56	Cigar lighter	D4	241	Air horns compressor	B9
57	Radio feed	C5	272	Throttle butterfly switch	C8
58	Windscreen wiper-washer switch	C4	296	Air horns compressor relay	A7
59	Lighting and direction indicators switch	B4	319	Ignition cut-out relay	C8
60	Direction indicator switch or connector	B4	321	AEI module	C7
62	LH side or front centre interior light	A7	325	Wire junction – clock	B6
63	RH interior light	D7	371	AEI timer relay	D8
64	Handbrake 'ON' warning light	D2			
65	Fuel tank sender unit	D1			
66	Rear screen demister	C1			

List of harnesses

A	Front
B	Rear
R	Engine

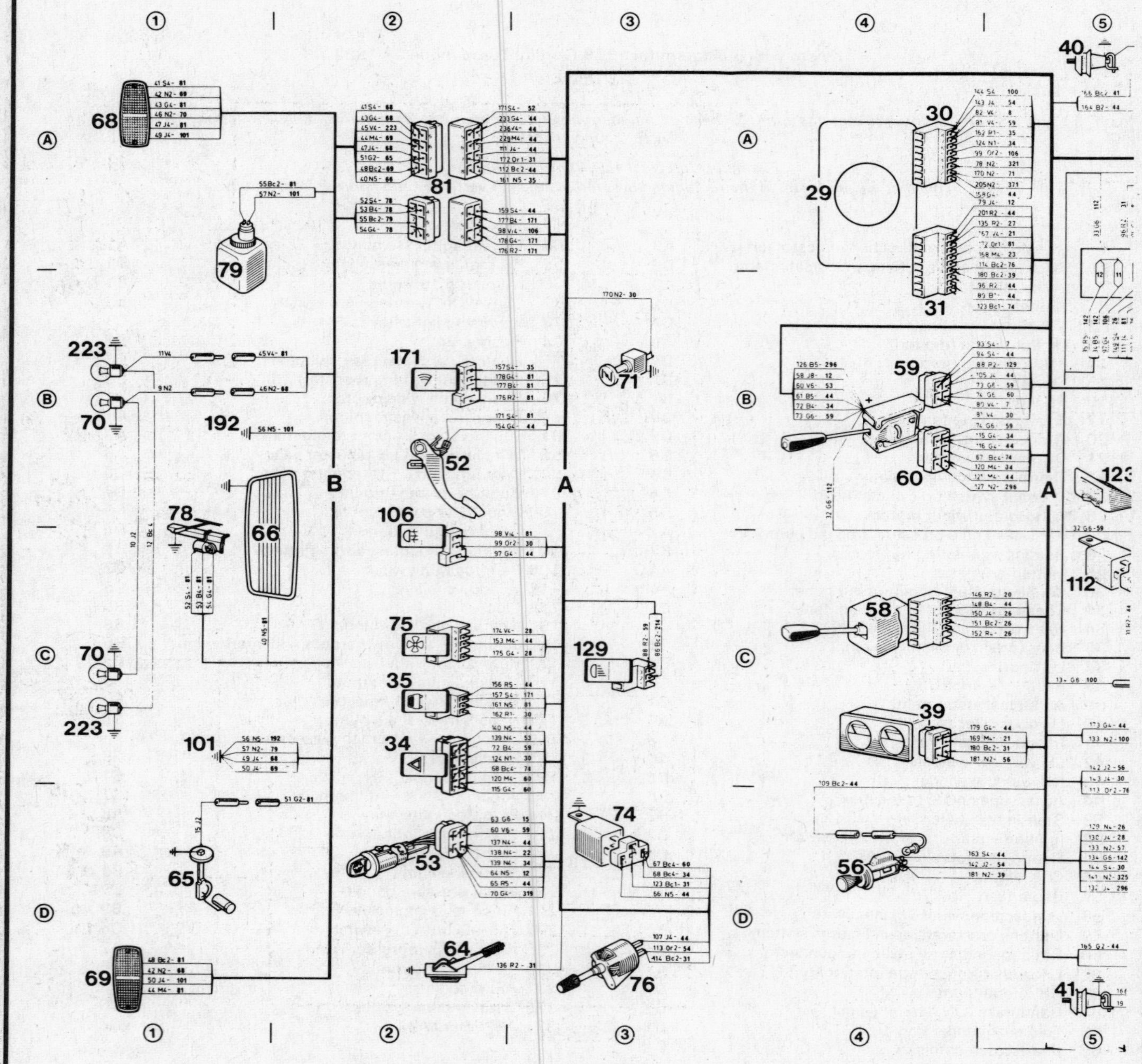

Fig. 10.81 Wiring diagram for 122B Gordini Turbo models – 1982

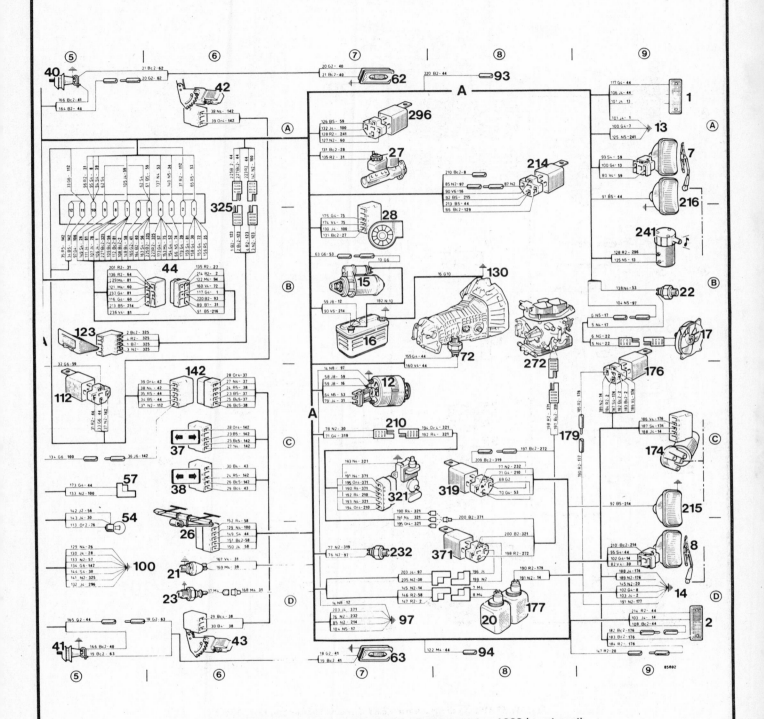

Fig. 10.81 Wiring diagram for 122B Gordini Turbo models – 1982 (continued)

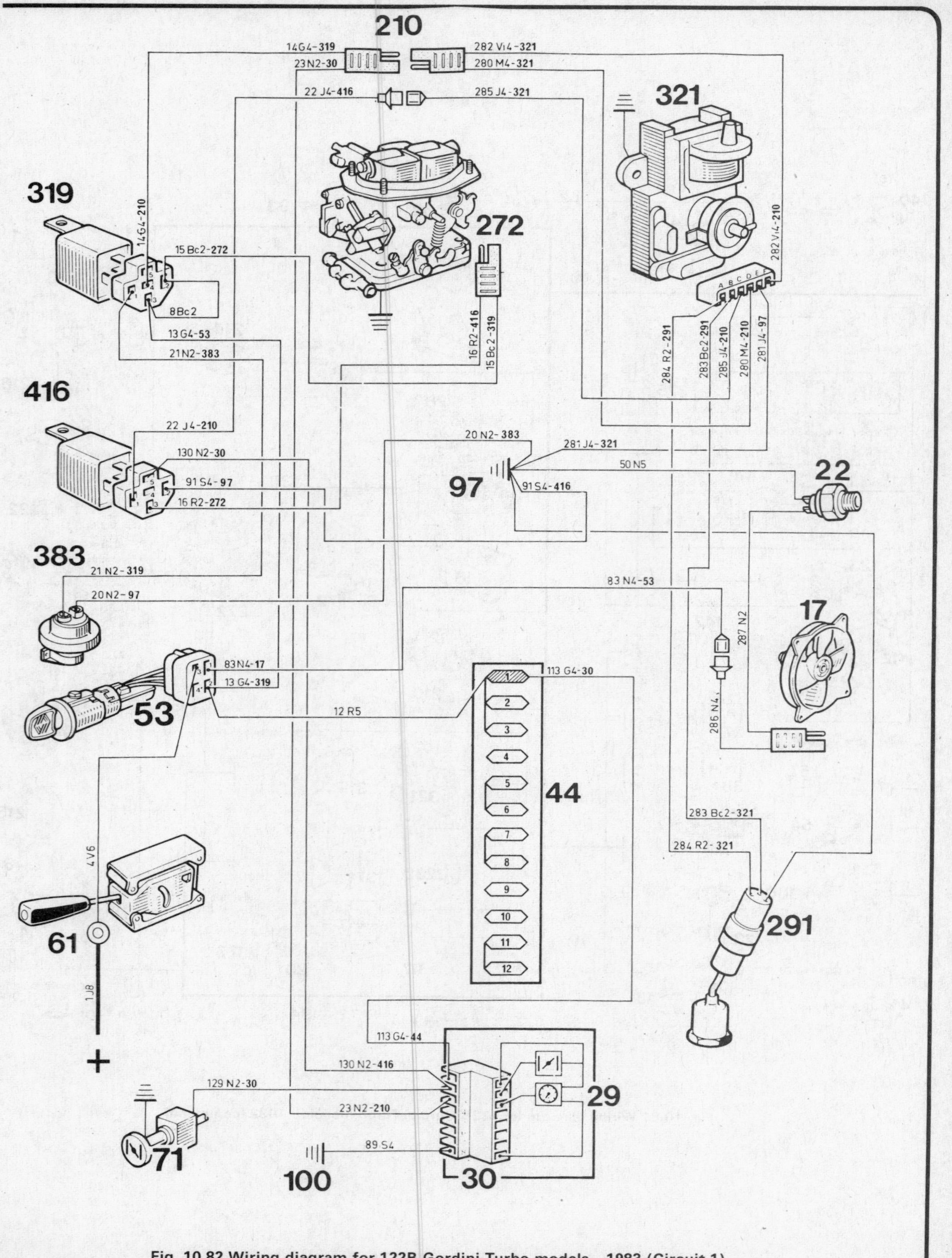

210

14G4-319
23N2-30
282 Vi4-321
280 M4-321
22 J4-416
285 J4-321

321

319

14 G4-210
15 Bc2-272
8Bc2
13 G4-53
21N2-383

272

16 R2-416
15 Bc 2-319

282 Vi4-210

A B C D E F
284 R2-291
283 Bc2-291
285 J4-210
280 M4-210
281 J4-97

416

22 J4-210
130 N2-30
91 S4-97
16 R2-272

20 N2-383
281 J4-321
50 N5
91 S4-416

97

22

383

21 N2-319
20 N2-97

83 N4-53

287 N2
286 N4

17

83N4-17
13 G4-319

53

12 R5

113 G4-30

44
2
3
4
5
6
7
8
9
10
11
12

4 V6

61

1 J8

+

113 G4-44
130 N2-416
129 N2-30
23 N2-210
89 S4

71

100

30

29

283 Bc2-321
284 R2-321

291

Fig. 10.82 Wiring diagram for 122B Gordini Turbo models – 1983 (Circuit 1)

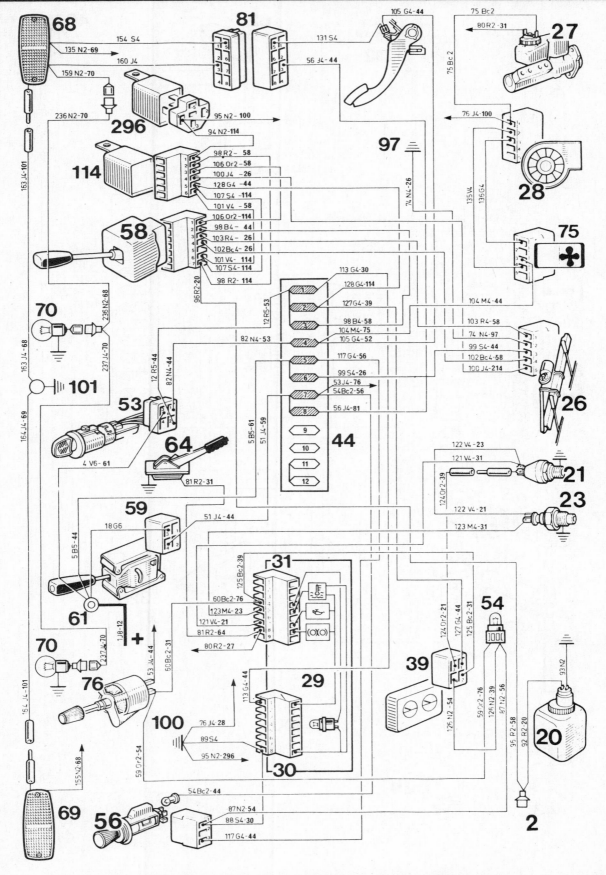

Fig. 10.82 Wiring diagram for 122B Gordini Turbo models – 1983 (Circuit 2)

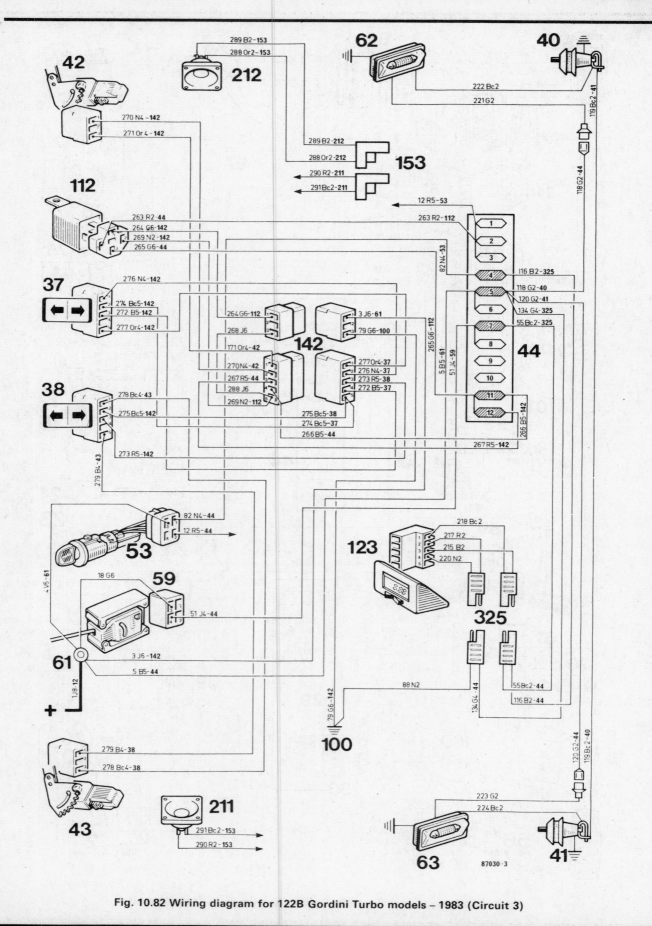

Fig. 10.82 Wiring diagram for 122B Gordini Turbo models – 1983 (Circuit 3)

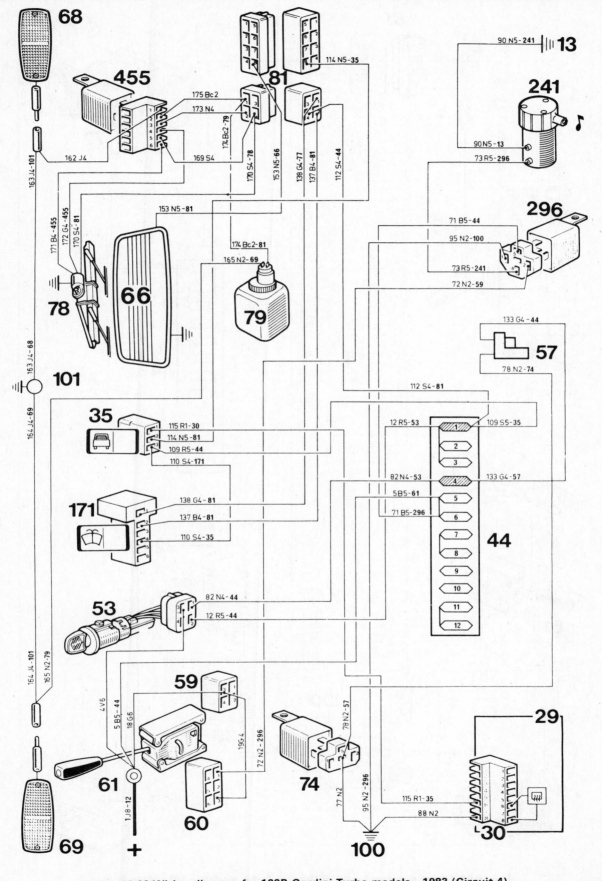

Fig. 10.82 Wiring diagram for 122B Gordini Turbo models – 1983 (Circuit 4)

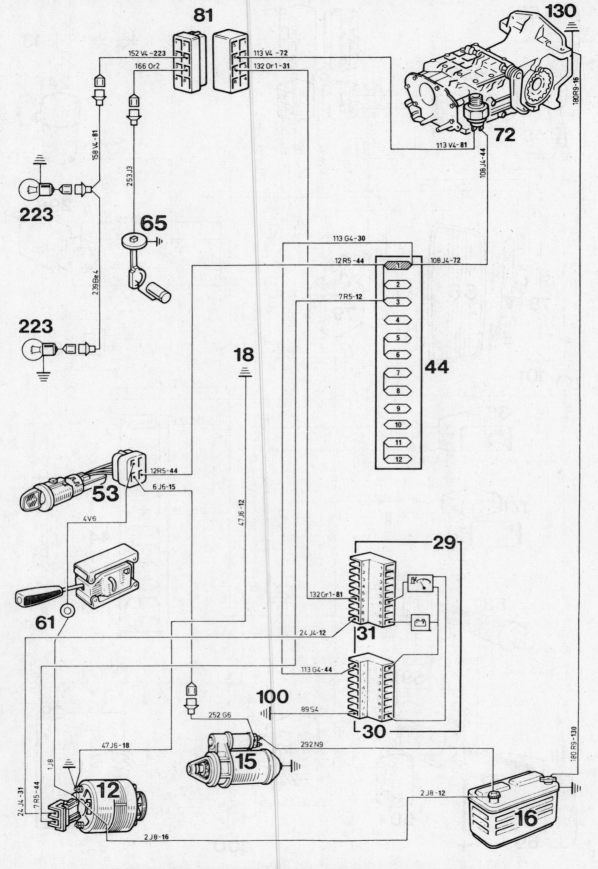

Fig. 10.82 Wiring diagram for 122B Gordini Turbo models – 1983 (Circuit 5)

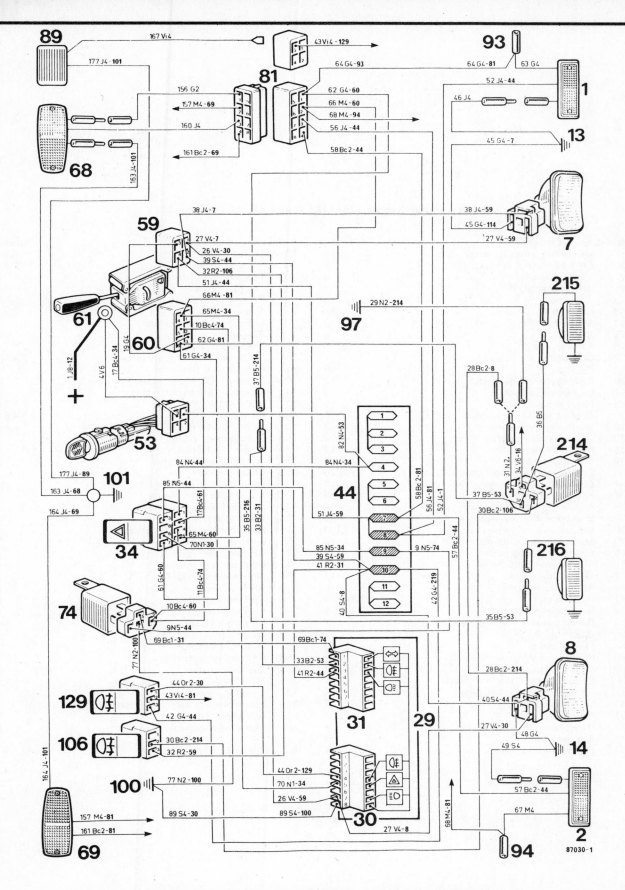

Fig. 10.82 Wiring diagram for 122B Gordini Turbo models – 1983 (Circuit 6)

87030-1

Key to wiring diagrams for 122B Gordini Turbo models – 1983

Number	Component	Circuit	Number	Component	Circuit
1	LH parking/indicator lamp	6	68	LH rear lamps	2,4,6
2	RH parking/indicator lamp	2,6	69	RH rear lamps	2,4,6
7	LH headlamp	6	70	Rear number plate lamp	2
8	RH headlamp	6	71	Choke 'ON' lamp	1
12	Alternator	5	72	Reversing lamp switch	5
13	LH earth	4,6	74	Flasher unit	2,4,6
14	RH earth	6	76	Instrument panel rheostat	2
15	Starter	5	78	Rear screen wiper	4
16	Battery	5	79	Rear screen washer	4
17	Cooling fan	1	81	Junction (front and rear harness)	2,4,5,6
18	Ignition coil	5	89	Rear fog warning lamp	6
20	Windscreen washer pump	2	93	Junction (LH repeater lamp)	6
21	Oil pressure switch	2	94	Junction (RH repeater lamp)	6
22	Fan thermal switch	1	97	Body earth	1,2,6
23	Coolant temperature switch	2	100	Scuttle earth	1,2,3,4,5,6
26	Windscreen wiper motor	2	101	Fuel tank earth	2,4,6
27	Brake pressure drop indicator	2	106	Rear foglamp switch	6
28	Heater blower	2	112	Power window relay	3
29	Instrument panel	1,2,4,5,6	114	Windscreen wiper timer	2
30	Connector (instrument panel)	1,2,4,5,6	123	Cruise control	3
31	Connector (instrument panel)	2,5,6	129	Front foglamp switch	6
34	Hazard warning switch	6	130	Auto transmission earth	5
35	Rear screen demister switch	4	142	Junction (power windows)	3
37	LH power window switch	3	153	Radio speakers	3
38	RH power window switch	3	171	Rear screen wash/wipe switch	4
39	Supplementary instruments	2	210	Junction (AEI)	1
40	LH courtest lamp switch	3	211	RH rear panel speaker	3
41	RH courtesy lamp switch	3	212	LH rear panel speaker	3
42	LH window winder	3	214	Front foglamp relay	6
43	RH window winder	3	215	RH front foglamp	6
44	Fusebox	1,2,3,4,5,6	216	LH front foglamp	6
53	Ignition/starter switch	1,2,3,4,5,6	223	Reversing lamps	5
54	Heater controls illumination	2	241	Horn compressor	4
56	Cigar lighter	2	272	Throttle spindle switch	1
57	Feed to radio	4	291	Pinking detector	1
58	Windscreen wiper/wash switch	2	296	Horn compressor relay	2,4
59	Combination switch	2,3,4,6	319	Ignition cut-out	1
60	Connector (direction indicators)	4,6	321	AEI module	1
61	Ignition switch feed terminal	1,2,3,4,5,6	325	Junction – clock	3
62	LH interior lamp	3	383	Safety pressure switch (turbocharger)	1
63	RH interior lamp	3	416	Anti-knock relay	1
64	Handbrake 'ON' switch	2	455	Rear screen wiper timer relay	4
65	Fuel tank sender	5			
66	Rear screen demister	4		*Not all items fitted to all models*	

Note: *Circuit 6 – wire 31N2 is connected to wire 28 Bc2 or 29N2, depending on the version*

Key to wiring diagram for all 1983 models – except 122B Gordini Turbo

Number	Component	Circuit	Number	Component	Circuit
1	LH parking/indicator lamp	1,8,9,13	81	Junction block (front and rear) harness)	1,2,3,5,7,8,9,13
2	RH parking/indicator lamp	1,6,8,9,13	89	Rear fog warning lamp	1
7	LH headlamp	1,11,12	93	Junction (LH repeater lamp)	1
8	RH headlamp	1,11,12	94	Junction (RH repeater lamp)	1
9	LH horn	1	97	Body earth	9
12	Alternator	3,7,9,11,12,13,14	100	Scuttle earth	1,2,3,4,5,8,9,12,13
13	LH front earth	1,8,9,10,13	101	Fuel tank earth	1,2,5,8,9,13
14	RH front earth	1,2,6,8,9,10,11,12,13	106	Rear foglamp switch	1
15	Starter motor	3,7,13,14	110	Cooling fan relay	11,12
16	Battery	3,7,9,13,14	112	Power window relay	4
17	Cooling fan	6,11,12,13,14	114	Windscreen wiper timer relay	5
18	Ignition coil	3,11,13,14	123	Clock	2
19	Distributor	3,11,14	124	Auto transmission relay	7,14
20	Windscreen washer pump	2,6,10,11	128	Kickdown switch	7,14
21	Oil pressure switch	3,11,12,13,14	130	Transmission earth	3,6,7,13,14
22	Fan thermal switch	6,13	140	Junction box	4,5
23	Coolant temperature switch	3,11,12,14	142	Junction (windows/interior lamps)	4
26	Windscreen wiper motor	2,10	146	Fan thermal switch	1,13
27	Brake pressure drop indicator	2	147	Ignition coil resistor	13
28	Heater blower	2,10	153	Radio speakers	4
29	Instrument panel	2,3,4,5,8,9,11,12,13,14	155	LH rear interior lamp	2
30	Connector (instrument panel)	1,2,3,4,5,8,9,11,12,13,14	158	Selector illumination (auto transmission)	5
31	Connector (instrument panel)	1,2,3,8,11,12,13,14	162	Air condtioner relay	11
34	Hazard warning lamp switch	1,8	164	Fuel pump	9
35	Rear screen demister switch	5	169	Junction (solenoid valve)	13,14
37	LH power window switch	4	171	Rear screen wash/wipe switch	5
38	RH power window switch	4	172	Impulse generator	8
40	LH courtesy lamp switch	4,10	174	RH headlamp wiper	6
41	RH courtesy lamp switch	4,10	176	Headlamp wiper timer relay	6
42	LH window winder motor	4	177	Headlamp washer pump	6
43	RH window winder motor	4	192	Tailgate earth	1
44	Fusebox	1 to 14	195	Idle cut-out	13,14
52	Stop-lamp switch	2,9	204	Starter relay	7,14
53	Ignition/start switch	1 to 14	210	Junction (AEI)	9,13
54	Heater control panel illumination	2,8	212	LH rear panel speaker	4
56	Cigar lighter	2,4	213	RH rear panel speaker	4
57	Feed to radio	5,12	223	Reversing lamps	3,7,9,13
58	Windscreen wash/wipe switch	2,6,10,11	262	Heater control panel	11
59	Combination switch	1,2,4,6,8,9,10,11,12,13	273	Flow meter	8
60	Connector (direction indicator)	1,8,13	278	Carburettor (cold start)	14
61	Ignition switch feed terminal	1 to 14	283	Advance solenoid valve	13,14
62	LH interior lamp	4,10	285	Cold start relay	14
63	RH interior lamp	4,10	319	Ignition cut-out relay	13
64	Handbrake 'ON' switch	2	321	AEI module	9
65	Fuel tank sender unit	3	323	Normalur cruise control	4
66	Rear screen demister	5	325	Junction (clock)	4
68	LH rear lamp	1,2,5,8,9,13	340	Driving aid computer	8
69	RH rear lamp	1,2,5,8,9,13	342	Headlamp washer solenoid valve	6
70	Rear number plate lamp	2	351	Cooling fan thermal switch (pump)	11,12,14
71	Choke 'ON' warning lamp	3,14	353	Thermal switch (15°C)	13,14
72	Reversing lamp switch	3,9,13	355	Defuming valve	13,14
74	Flasher unit	1,5,8,12	358	Defuming valve relay	13,14
75	Heater blower switch	2,10	359	Recycling valve	14
76	Instrument panel rheostat	2	360	Idle switch	13,14
77	Junction – diagnostic socket	3,9,11,13	361	Air conditioner control box	11
78	Rear screen wiper motor	5	362	Junction (air conditioner)	11
79	Rear screen washer pump	5	392	Junction (starter relay)	7,14
80	Junction block (cooling)	11,12,13,14	411	Direction indicator control (dual control)	8

Not all items fitted to all models

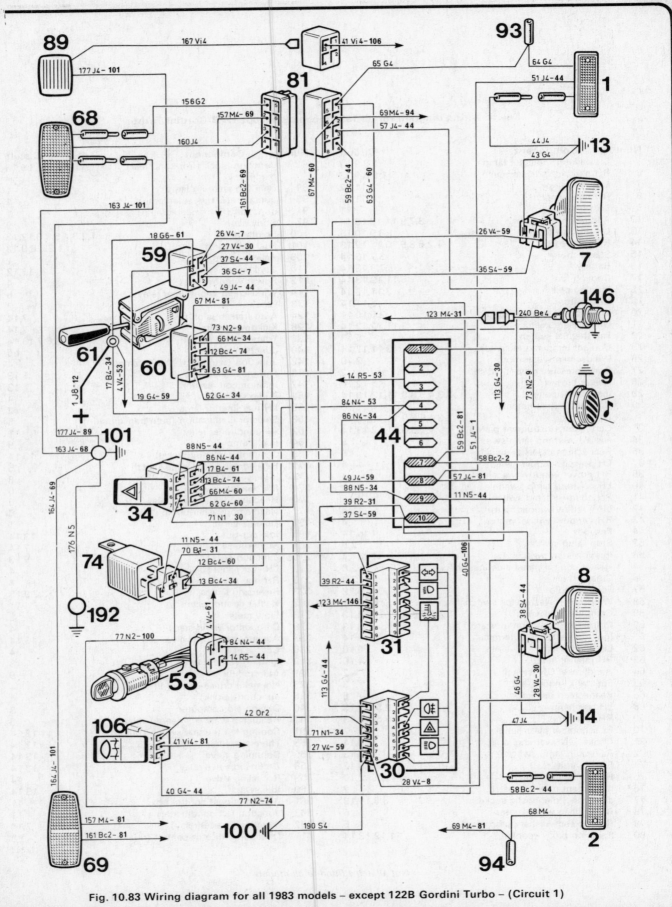

Fig. 10.83 Wiring diagram for all 1983 models – except 122B Gordini Turbo – (Circuit 1)

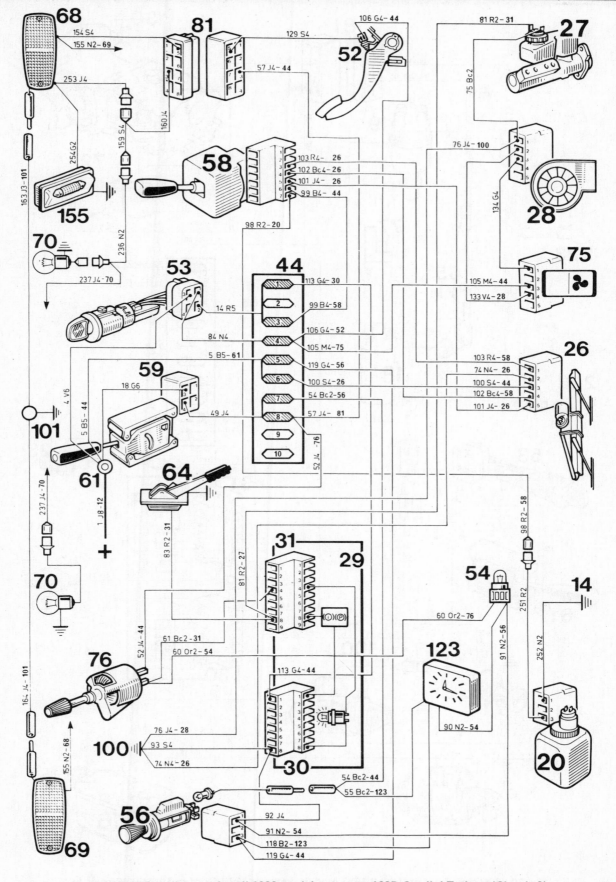

313

Fig. 10.83 Wiring diagram for all 1983 models – except 122B Gordini Turbo – (Circuit 2)

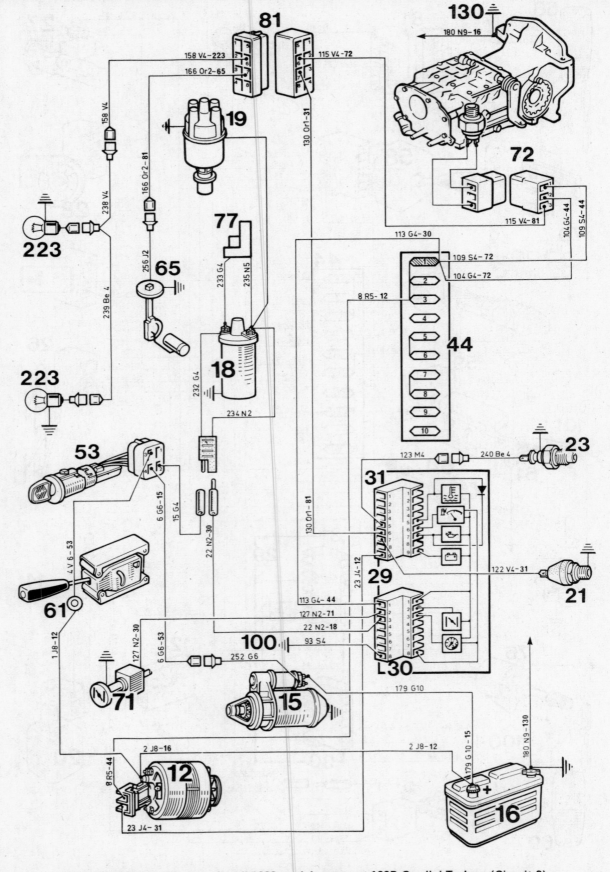

Fig. 10.83 Wiring diagram for all 1983 models – except 122B Gordini Turbo – (Circuit 3)

315

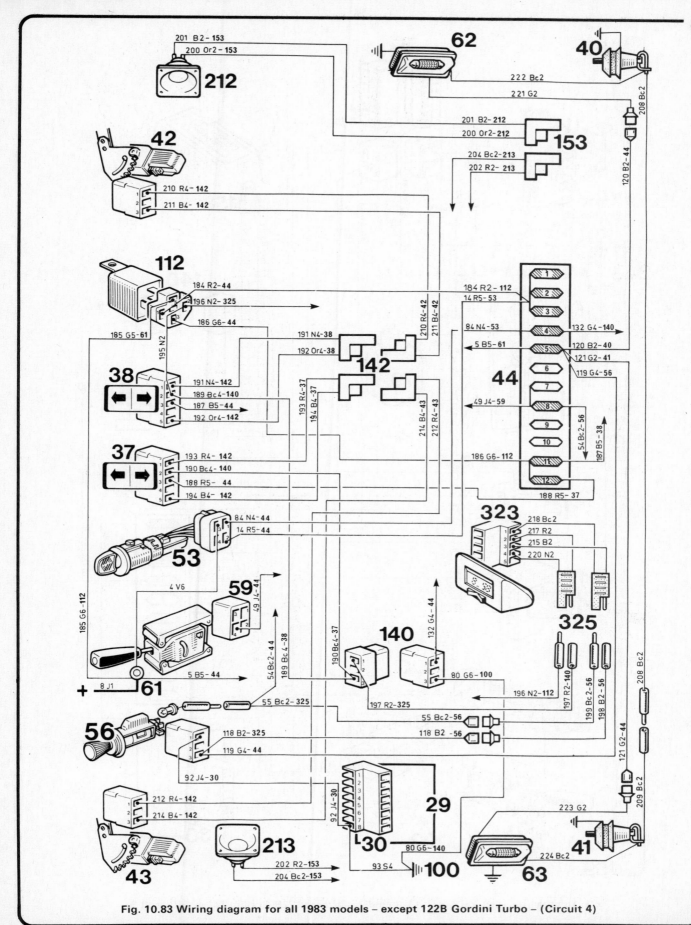

Fig. 10.83 Wiring diagram for all 1983 models – except 122B Gordini Turbo – (Circuit 4)

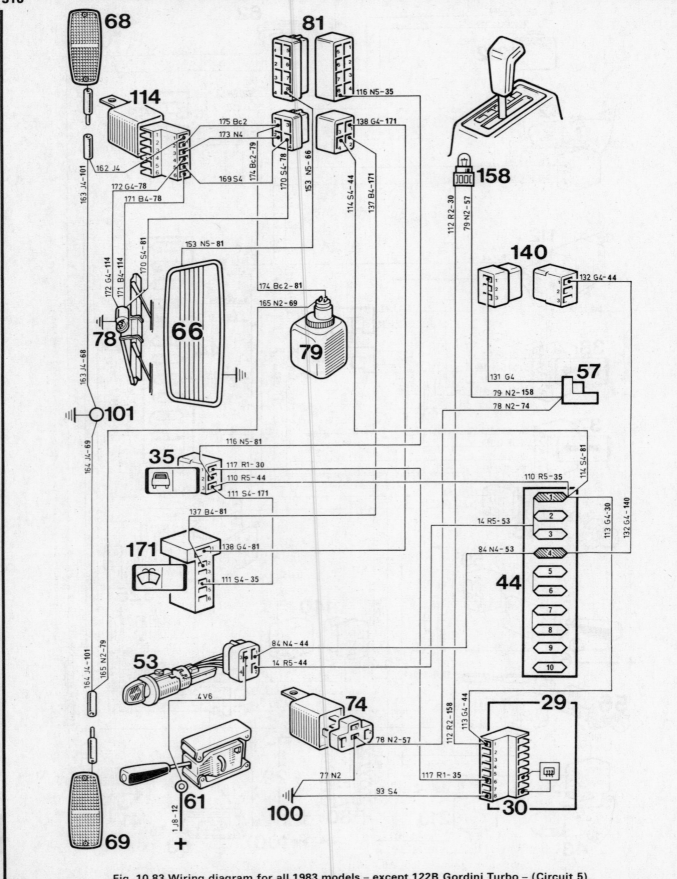

Fig. 10.83 Wiring diagram for all 1983 models – except 122B Gordini Turbo – (Circuit 5)

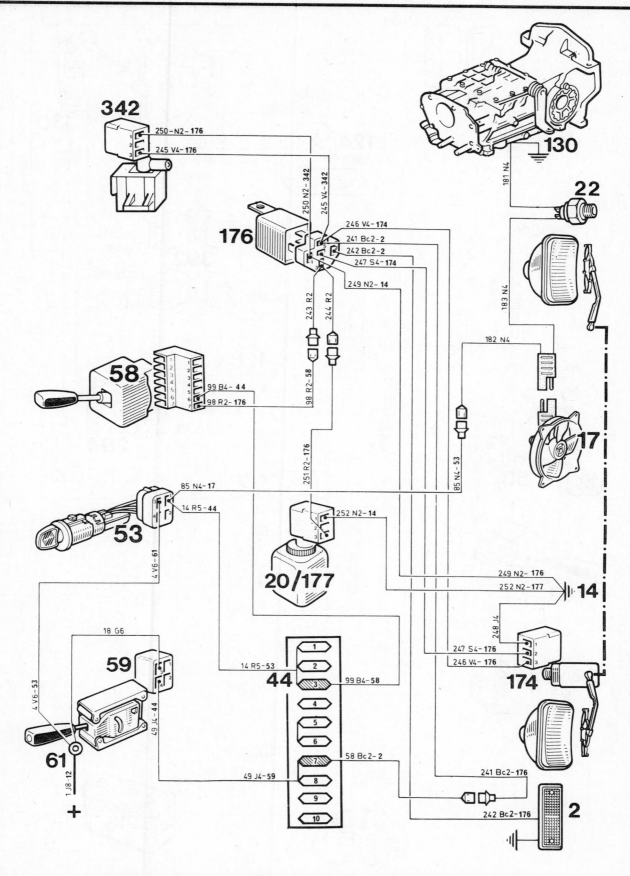

Fig. 10.83 Wiring diagram for all 1983 models – except 122B Gordini Turbo – (Circuit 6)

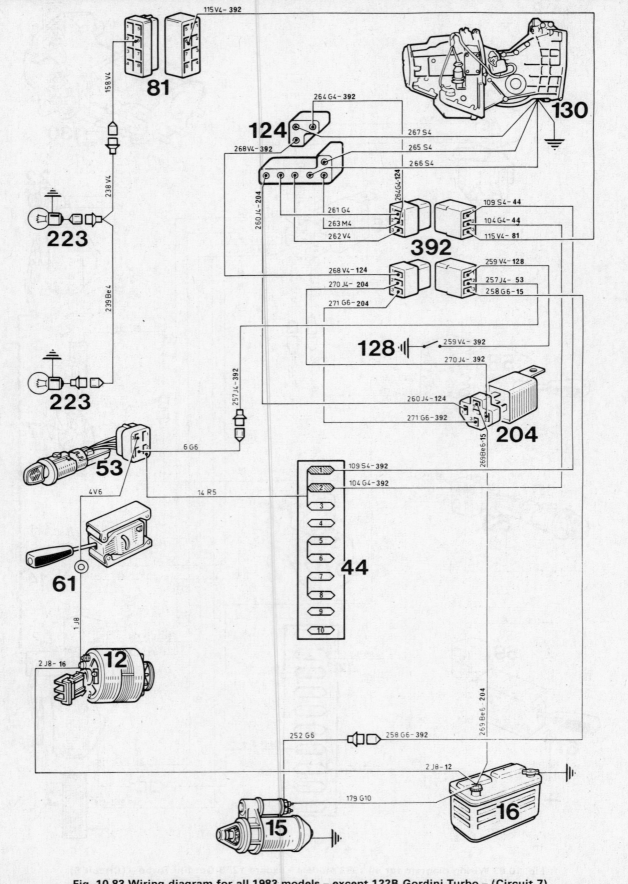

Fig. 10.83 Wiring diagram for all 1983 models – except 122B Gordini Turbo – (Circuit 7)

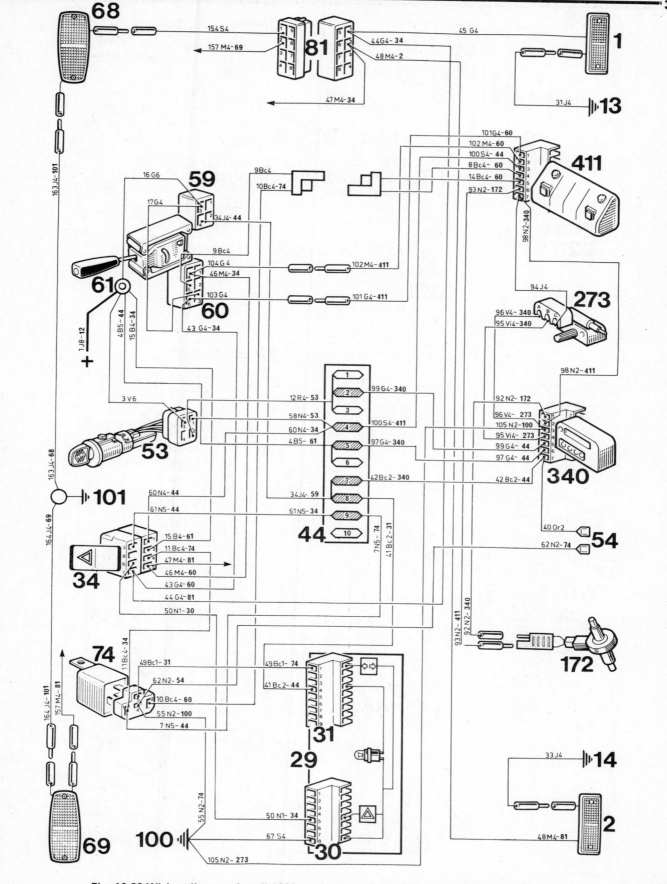

Fig. 10.83 Wiring diagram for all 1983 models – except 122B Gordini Turbo – (Circuit 8)

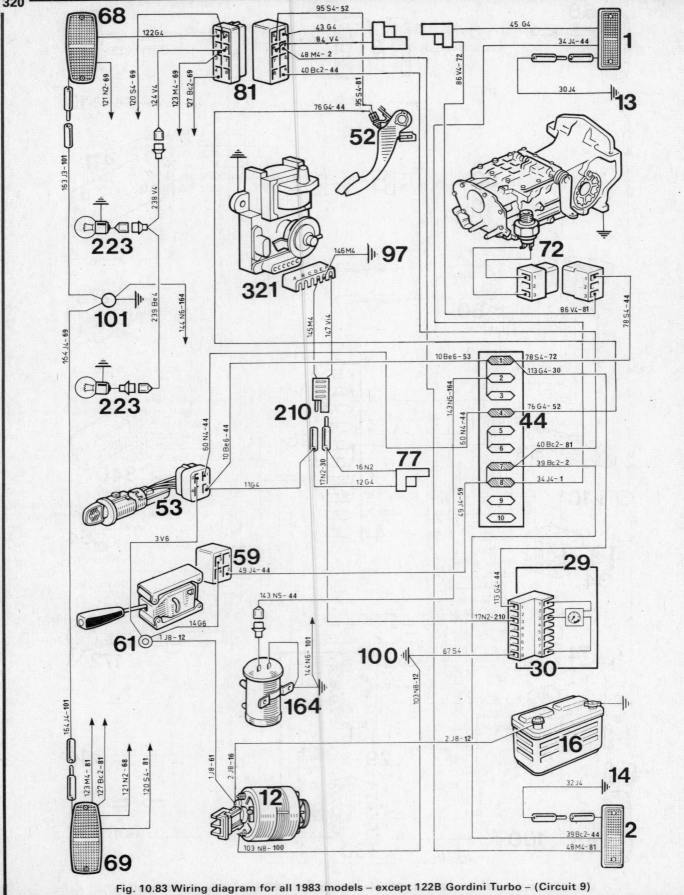

Fig. 10.83 Wiring diagram for all 1983 models – except 122B Gordini Turbo – (Circuit 9)

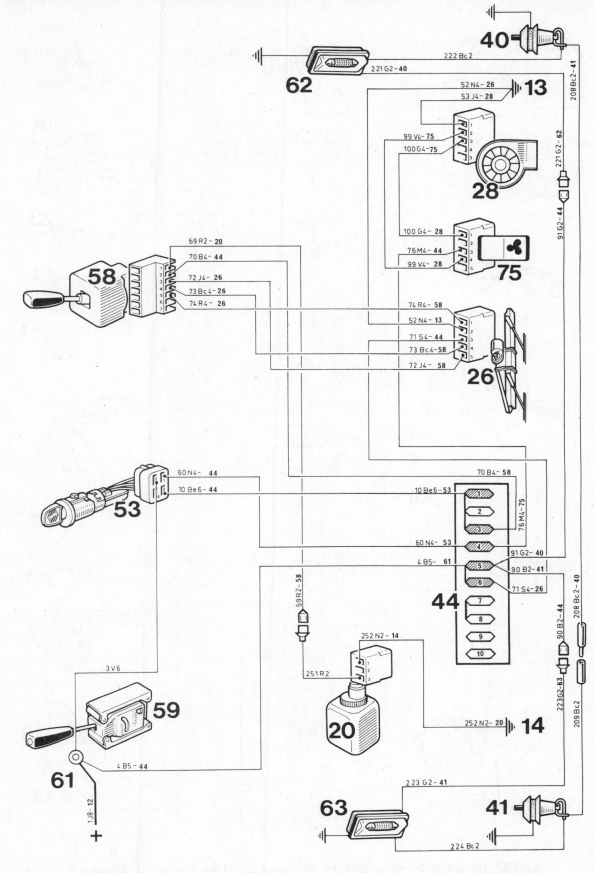

Fig. 10.83 Wiring diagram for all 1983 models – except 122B Gordini Turbo – (Circuit 10)

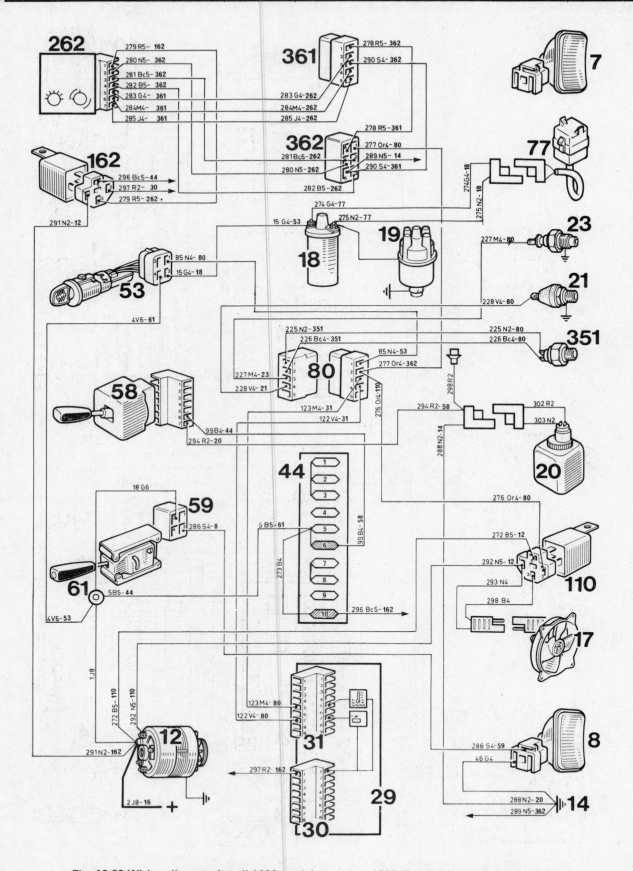

Fig. 10.83 Wiring diagram for all 1983 models – except 122B Gordini Turbo – (Circuit 11)

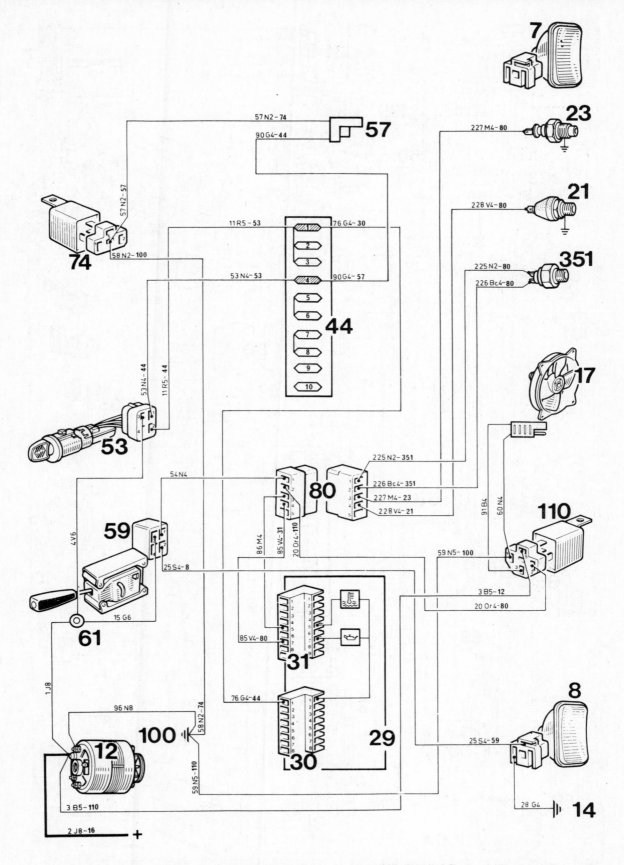

Fig. 10.83 Wiring diagram for all 1983 models – except 122B Gordini Turbo – (Circuit 12)

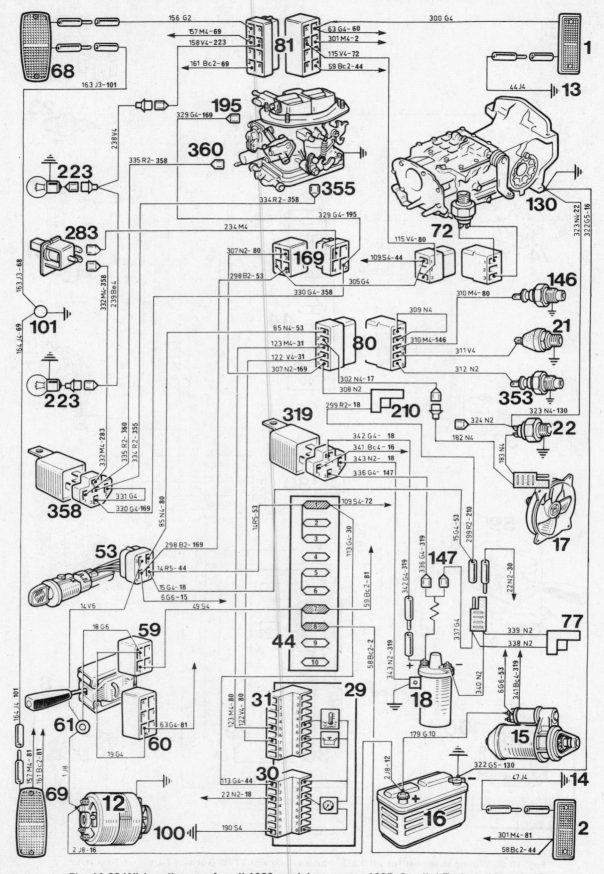

Fig. 10.83 Wiring diagram for all 1983 models – except 122B Gordini Turbo – (Circuit 13)

325

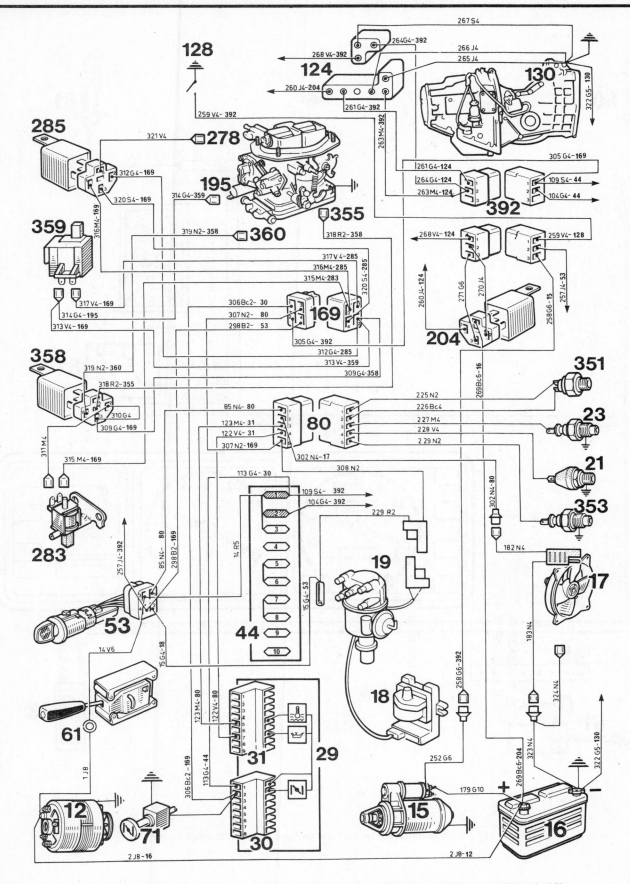

Fig. 10.83 Wiring diagram for all 1983 models – except 122B Gordini Turbo – (Circuit 14)

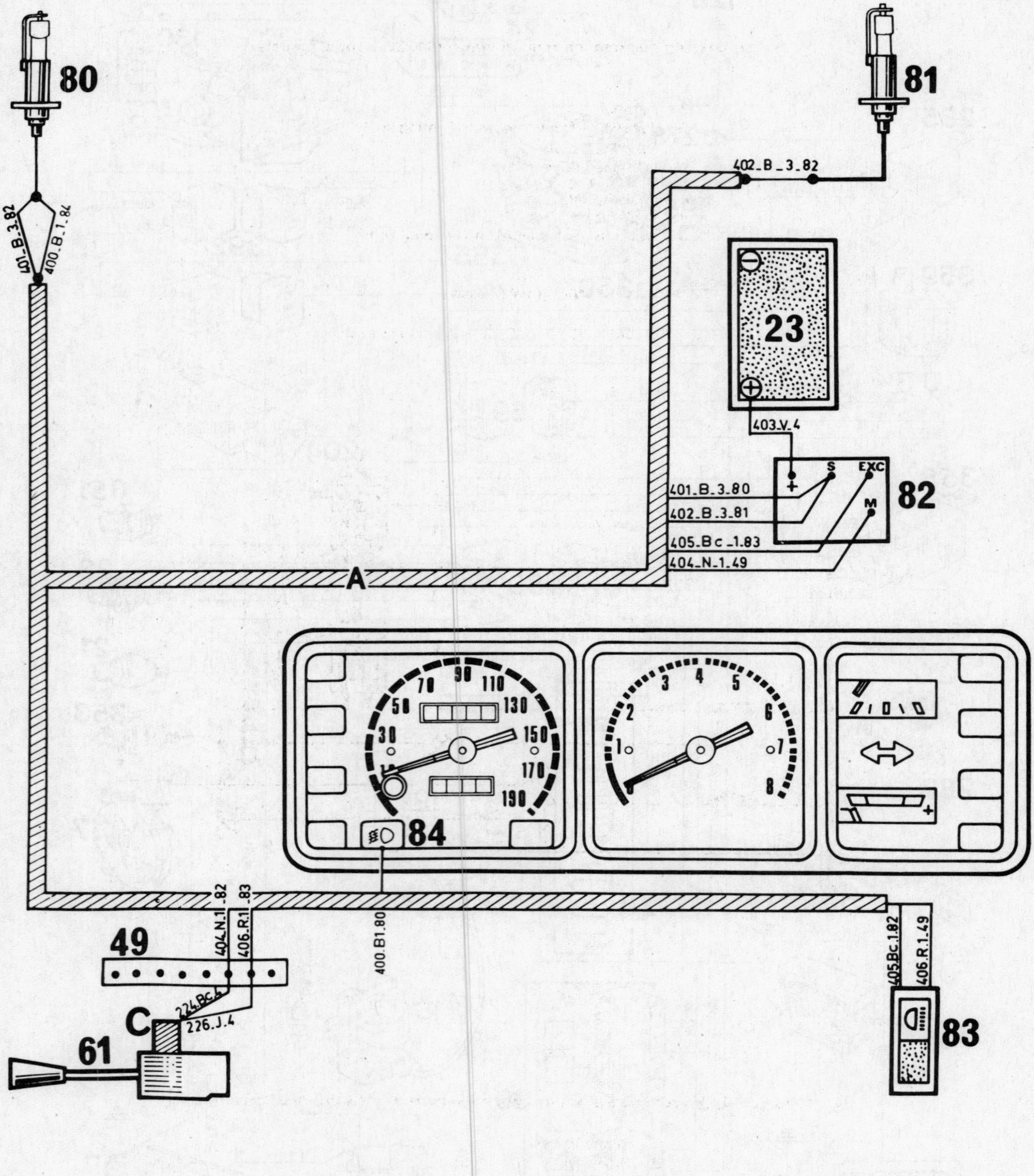

Fig. 10.84 Wiring diagram for front foglamp – R1223 Gordini models

Key to wiring diagram for front foglamp – R1223 Gordini models

23 Battery
49 Junction – front harness to lighting switch
61 Lighting switch
80 LH foglamp
81 RH foglamp
82 Foglamp relay
83 Foglamp switch
84 Instrument panel foglamp warning light

Wiring harnesses

A Front C Lighting switch

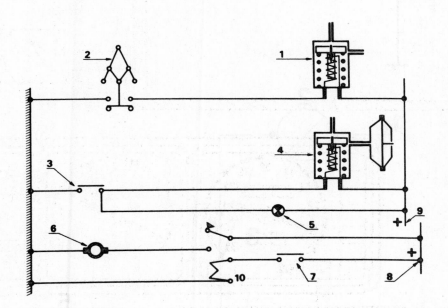

Fig. 10.85 Wiring diagram for the exhaust emission system – North American models

1 Solenoid valve
2 Governor
3 Choke 'ON' switch
4 Solenoid valve (distributor vacuum unit)
5 Choke warning lamp
6 Radiator cooling fan
7 Coolant temperature switch
8 Battery + terminal
9 Ignitional coil + terminal
10 Relay

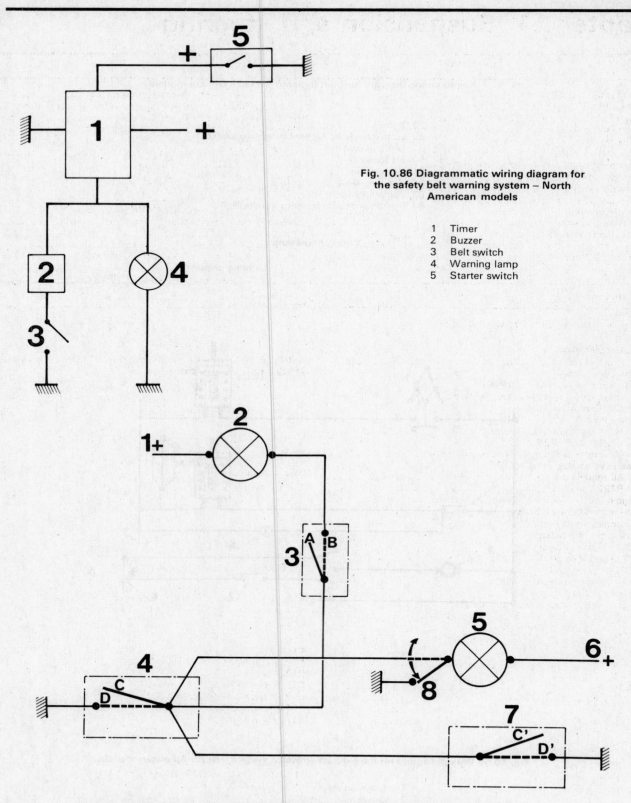

Fig. 10.86 Diagrammatic wiring diagram for the safety belt warning system – North American models

1 Timer
2 Buzzer
3 Belt switch
4 Warning lamp
5 Starter switch

Fig. 10.87 Wiring diagram for the ignition key reminder system – North American models

1	Feed to lamp control	6	Courtesy lamp to fusebox
2	Key reminder lamp	7	RH courtesy lamp switch (pillar)
3	Warning lamp switch to reminder device	8	Courtesy lamp switch (lamp base)
4	LH courtesy lamp switch (pillar)	A	Key removed mode
5	Courtesy lamp	B	Key in lock mode

C LH door closed
C′ RH door closed
D LH door open
D′ RH door open

Chapter 11 Suspension and steering

Contents

Specifications

Refer also to the Specifications in Chapter 8

Front suspension

Type .... Independent, upper and lower wishbone arms, torsion bars, telescopic shock absorbers and anti-roll bar

Steering angles (models up to 1979):
Front suspension compressed (see Section 3)
   Camber (non-adjustable):
      All models except R1223 and 122B .... $0°$ to $1°$ positive
      Maximum difference between sides .... $1°$
      R1223 and 122B .... $2°30'$ negative to $0°30'$ positive
      Maximum difference between sides .... $0°30'$
   Castor (adjustable by shims):
      All models except R1223 and 122B .... $12°$ to $13°$
      R1223 and 122B .... $10°30'$ to $12°30'$
   Kingpin inclination (non-adjustable) .... Equal both sides
   Maximum difference between sides .... $1°$
Steering angles (models 1979 and later):
Suspension not compressed
   Camber (non-adjustable):
      All models except R1223 and 122B .... 0 to $1°$ positive
      R1223 and 122B .... $0°10'$ negative to $0°50'$ positive
   Maximum difference side to side .... $1°$
   Kingpin inclination:
      All models except R1223 and 122B .... $13°14'$
      R1223 and 122B .... $14°20'$
   Maximum difference side to side .... $1°$
   Castor (adjustable by shims) – refer to Fig. 11.51:

H5-H2	**Castor**
20.0 mm	R1223 and 122B $11°30'$, others $6°$
40.0 mm	R1223 and 122B $11°$, others $5°30'$
60.0 mm	R1223 and 122B $10°30'$, others $5°$
80.0 mm	R1223 and 122B $10°$, others $4°30'$
100.0 mm	R1223 and 122B $40°$
120.0 mm	R1223 and 122B $3°30'$

Front wheel alignment:
   Models up to 1979:
      All models except R1223 and 122B .... 1.0 to 5.0 mm (0.039 to 0.20 in) toe-out
      R1223 and 122B .... 0 to 3.0 mm (0 to 0.12 in) toe-out
   Models 1979 and later .... 0 to 2.0 mm (0 to 0.079 in) toe-out

Rear suspension

Type .... Independent, torsion bars, trailing arms, telescopic shock absorbers, anti-roll bar on certain models

Suspension angles (suspension not compressed):
   Models up to 1975:
      Camber (non-adjustable) .... 0 to $1°30'$ positive
      Rear wheel alignment .... 0 to 4.0 mm (0 to 0.16 in) toe-in
   Models 1976 and later:
      Camber (non-adjustable) .... 0 to $1°30'$ negative
      Rear wheel alignment .... 1.0 mm (0.039 in) toe-in to 1.0 mm (0.039 in) toe-out

Steering gear

Type .... Rack-and-pinion with universally-jointed shaft
Ratio:
    Models up to 1979 .... 16.7 : 1
    Models 1979 and later .... 20 : 1
Turning circle (between kerbs) .... 9.75 m (32.0 ft)
Steering wheel diameter:
    Except Gordini Turbo .... 381.0 mm (15.0 in)
    Gordini Turbo .... 365.8 mm (14.4 in)
Number of turns of steering wheel, lock to lock 3.7
Steering gear lubricant type .... Molykote BR2
Steering gear lubricant capacity .... 40.0 cc (2.4 cu in)

Power steering fluid type .... Dexron type ATF (Duckhams Uni-Matic or D-Matic)

Torque wrench settings

	Nm	lbf ft
Front shock absorber lower mounting bolt	79	58
Front suspension upper arm pivot bolt	88	65
Front suspension upper arm balljoint nut	34	25
Front suspension lower arm pivot bolt	98	72
Torsion bar anchor bearing bolt	117	86
Front suspension lower arm balljoint nut	49	36
Driveshaft nut:		
Except R1223 and 122B	117	86
R1223 and 122B	156	115
Rear suspension inner bearing bolt	73	54
Rear suspension outer bearing bolt	39	29
Shock absorber lower mounting bolt	79	58
Steering wheel retaining nut	44	32
Steering shaft universal joint pinch-bolt	34	25
Steering shaft flexible joint bolt	15	11
Rack end fitting pivot bolt	34	25
Power steering:		
Ram connection to steering rack	73	54
Ram spindle nuts	15	11
Roadwheel nuts or bolts	58	43

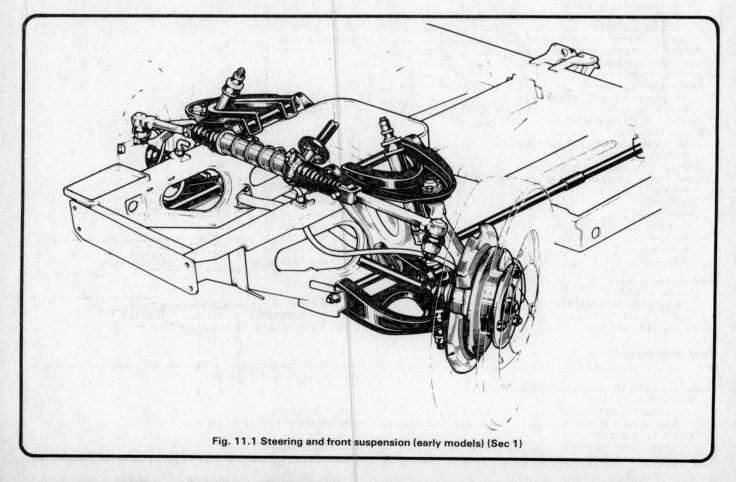

Fig. 11.1 Steering and front suspension (early models) (Sec 1)

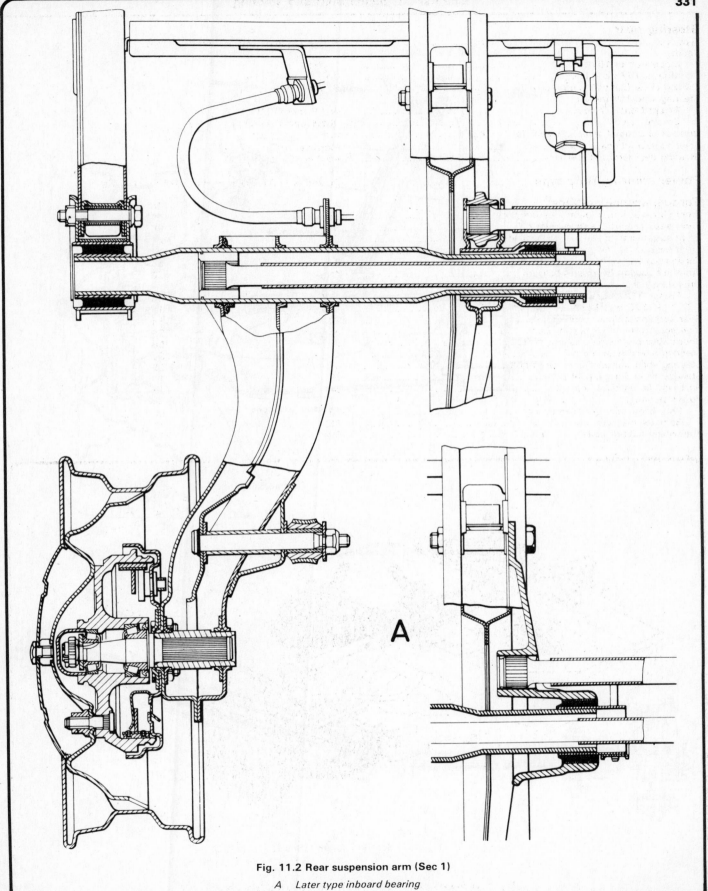

Fig. 11.2 Rear suspension arm (Sec 1)

A   Later type inboard bearing

2

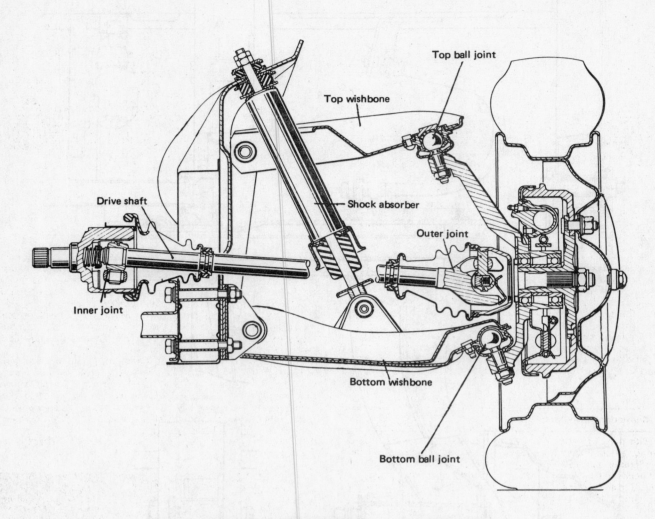

Fig. 11.3 Cutaway view of one side of the front suspension (Sec 1)

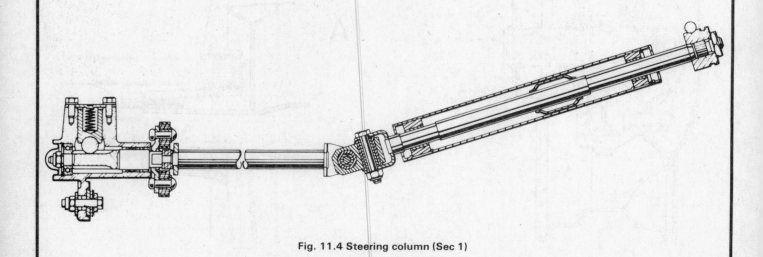

Fig. 11.4 Steering column (Sec 1)

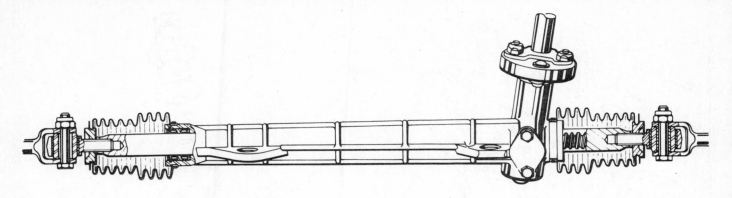

Fig. 11.5 Steering rack housing (Sec 1)

1 General description

All models have independent suspension all round.

The front suspension is of upper and lower wishbone type with longitudinal torsion bars, telescopic hydraulic shock absorbers and an anti-roll bar.

The rear suspension consists of trailing arms, transverse torsion bars, telescopic hydraulic shock absorbers and an anti-roll bar.

The steering gear is of rack-and-pinion type with a universally-jointed steering column shaft. Power-assistance is available on certain models.

2 Maintenance and inspection

1 With the elimination of lubrication points on the suspension and steering, all components must be checked regularly for wear, loose mountings or split gaiters and bellows.

2 Check the flexible bellows on the steering rack. If they are split and lubricant can be seen leaking out, the bellows must be renewed immediately, as described in Section 18.

3 Check the tie-rod flexible bushes and balljoints for wear. Do this by having an assistant move the steering wheel quickly in both directions through an arc of travel of about 60°. Any 'lost motion' at the balljoints indicates the need for their immediate renewal (Section 19).

4 Check the front wishbone flexible pivot bushes for wear.

5 At the specified intervals (see Routine Maintenance) test the shock absorbers, as described in Section 3.

6 At the specified intervals (see Routine Maintenance) check the wheel alignment and steering angles (see Section 27).

7 Refer to Chapter 8 for details of hub bearings, roadwheels and tyres.

3 Front shock absorbers – removal, testing and refitting

1 Raise the front of the car and support it securely under the underbody jacking points.

2 Jack up under the suspension lower arm and remove the roadwheel.

3 Unscrew and remove the two nuts from the top of the shock absorber spindle. The top of the shock absorber spindle is machined square so it can be still while the nuts are unscrewed.

4 Disconnect the end of the anti-roll bar, also the clamp at the points (A) shown in Fig. 11.6.

5 Unscrew the shock absorber pivot pin, remove the shock absorber (photo).

6 To test a shock absorber, grip it vertically by its lower mounting eye in the jaws of a vice. Fully extend and contract the shock absorber six times. If the movement is jerky, no resistance is evident or the unit is seized, renew it. Severe oil leakage on the outside of the casing of the shock absorber will indicate failure of the spindle seals and a new unit will have to be fitted.

7 Before fitting a new shock absorber, secure it in a vice as just described and 'pump' the unit several times to prime it. This is needed to displace the air pocket in the fluid chamber which can occur if the unit has been stored in a horizontal attitude.

8 Refit by smearing the bottom mounting pivot pin with grease and then reverse the removal operations. Leave the shock absorber bottom mounting and anti-roll bar end nuts only finger tight until the front suspension has been compressed.

9 Measure the distance from the floor of the centre of the front wheel hub H1 (Fig. 11.8) and the underside of the body side frame H2. Having subtracted one figure from the other, the difference should be 90.0 mm (3.5 in). To bring the dimension to the specified amount, compress the suspension. A special tool is made for the purpose (T. Av 605-03), but if two people carefully stand on the front bumper, this should be a good substitute.

10 With the suspension compressed, tighten the shock absorber lower mounting and anti-roll bar nuts.

3.5 Front shock absorber lower mounting

4 Front anti-roll bar – removal and refitting

1 Disconnect the nuts on the anti-roll bar end fittings.

2 Unscrew the nuts on the insulator clamps.

3 Remove the bar from the car.

4 Refitting is a reversal of removal, but on models up to 1979, only tighten the nuts after the suspension has been compressed, as described in the preceding Section.

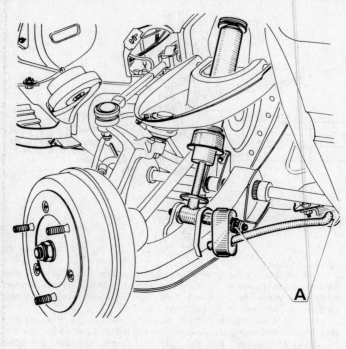

Fig. 11.6 Front shock absorber (Sec 3)
A   Anti-roll bar attachment

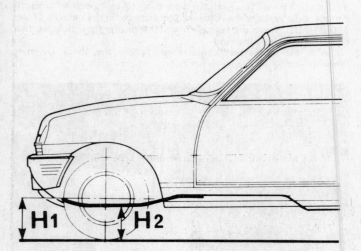

Fig. 11.8 Front suspension compressed for tightening flexible bushes (pre 1979) (Sec 3)

H1   Roadwheel hub to floor
H2   Underside of body side-member to floor

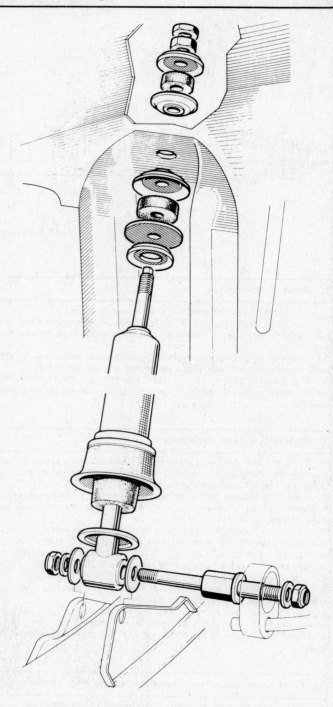

Fig. 11.7 Front shock absorber mountings (Sec 3)

5   Front suspension upper balljoint – renewal

1   Raise the car and support it securely under the sidemembers. Remove the roadwheel.
2   Unscrew the nut on the balljoint taper pin and, using a suitable balljoint separator tool, disconnect the balljoint from the upper eye of the stub axle carrier (photo).
3   Centre punch the balljoint retaining rivets and carefully drill out their heads.
4   Remove the balljoint from the suspension arm.

5   The new balljoint is attached by nuts and bolts which should be supplied with the balljoint together with a packing piece.
6   Fit the balljoint to the suspension arm, locate the packing piece and attach the nuts and bolts. Make sure that the nuts are on top of the suspension arm.
7   Reconnect the balljoint to the stub axle carrier and fit the roadwheel.
8   Provided the new balljoint is of similar pattern to the original one then the suspension and steering angles should not have altered, but it is recommended that they are checked as described in Section 27.

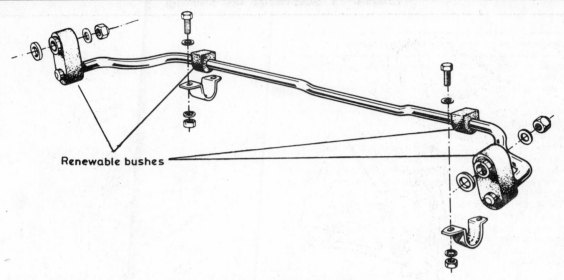

Fig. 11.9 Front anti-roll bar (Sec 4)

Renewable bushes

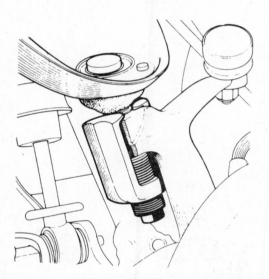

Fig. 11.10 One type of balljoint extractor (Sec 5)

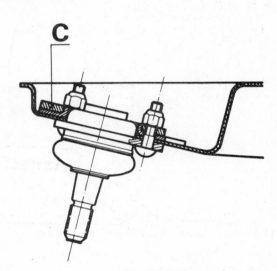

Fig. 11.11 Front suspension replacement – balljoint (Sec 5)

C Packing piece

5.2 Disconnecting front suspension upper arm balljoint

6 Front suspension upper arm – removal and refitting

1   Open the bonnet and remove the cooling system expansion bottle, the battery and the ignition coil.

2   Disconnect the upper arm balljoint as described in the preceding Section.

3   Screw a locknut onto the end of the suspension arm pivot pin which is near the front of the car.

4   Unscrew the nut from the opposite end of the pivot pin.

5   Using a socket spanner applied to the previously fitted locknut, unscrew the pivot pin and then remove the suspension arm.

6   The flexible bushes may be renewed by pressing out the old ones and pressing in the new using a piece of tubing with 25.0 mm (0.98 in) outside diameter. It is important that the bushes project by equal amounts to give the correct dimension (A), as shown in Fig. 11.14.

7   Before refitting, smear the pivot pin with grease and, once in position, screw the nuts up tight. On models up to 1979 the suspension should be compressed, as described in Section 3.

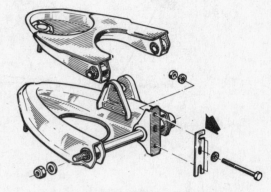

**Fig. 11.12 Front suspension wishbones
(Secs 6 and 12)**

Castor shim arrowed

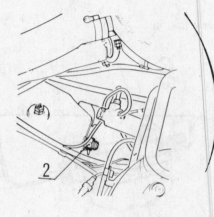

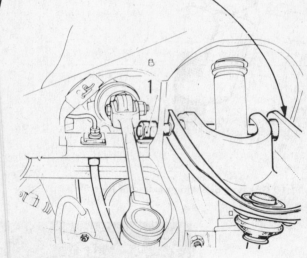

Fig. 11.13 Front suspension upper arm pivot (Sec 6)

1   *Locknut*
2   *Pivot bolt nut*

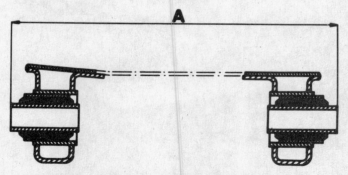

Fig. 11.14 Front suspension upper arm bush setting diagram (Sec 6)

A = 170.5 mm (6.7 in)

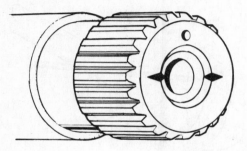

L.H. Bar

2 symbols

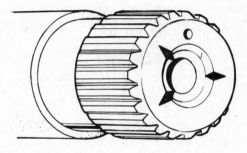

R.H. Bar

3 symbols

Fig. 11.15 Torsion bar identification (Sec 7)

7 Torsion bars – general

1 In order to remove and refit a torsion bar special tools are required to relieve the tension of the torsion bar before the anchor bolts can be unscrewed. Although it is possible to fabricate suitable tools by welding a length of bar or pipe to old torsion bar lever arms or bearings, in the absence of an adequate tool it is strongly recommended that the work is left to your Renault dealer.
2 Left-hand and right-hand torsion bars are marked on their ends, as shown in Fig. 11.15, never fit a torsion bar to the wrong side.

8 Front torsion bar (cam adjuster type) – removal and refitting

1 Early models are equipped with torsion bars having anchor bearings with cam adjusters.
2 Slide the front seat fully forward and tilt it.
3 Referring to Fig. 11.16 slacken the locknut and turn the cam towards the outside of the car to zero the adjustment.
4 Raise the car and support it securely under the side-member of the side being overhauled.
5 Working under the car, remove the cover from the adjusting lever and insert the special tool (Sus 545). Move the tool in the direction arrowed (Fig. 11.17) while an assistant working inside the car unscrews the fixing bolts.
6 Withdraw the housing cover-cam assembly, and then gently release the tension of the special tool.
7 Working at the adjusting lever end of the torsion bar, mark its relative position by scribing a line on the body crossmember.
8 Working at the suspension arm end, mark the position of the bar in relation to the lower arm anchor sleeve. Remove the bar and check that the mark made is in alignment with the punch mark on the end of the bar. If it is not, record by how many splines and in which direction it is offset.
9 On R1223 and R1224 models, the anti-roll bar end fitting must be removed.
10 To refit the torsion bar, first smear the splined ends with grease.
11 To the torsion bar fit the gasket, the housing cover-cam assembly and the adjusting lever.
12 Pass the housing cover-cam and adjusting lever end of the torsion bar inside the crossmember.
13 Now slide the bar through the hole in the body bracket and then pass the bar above the anti-roll bar.
14 Engage the bar with the suspension lower arm, aligning the marks made at dismantling, remembering to allow for any recorded offset.
15 Fit the adjusting lever on its splines, again aligning it with the line scribed on the crossmember. If a new torsion bar, or an associated unmarked component is being fitted locate the adjusting lever so that its edge is in alignment with the centre of the adjusting cam fixing hole. This will give a dimension (C) from the edge of the housing to the edge of the lever (see Fig. 11.22).
16 Tension the torsion bar, using the tool Sus 545, then align the

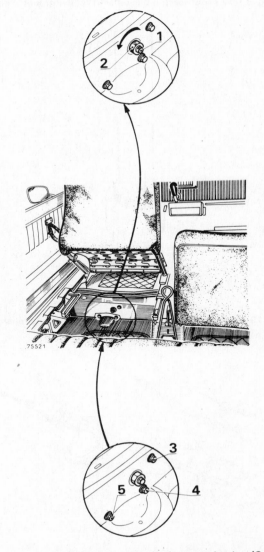

Fig. 11.16 Rear anchorage for front torsion bar (Sec 8)

1 Cam adjusting nut
2 Cam locknut
3 Adjuster lever fixing bolt
4 Adjuster lever fixing bolt
5 Adjuster lever fixing bolt

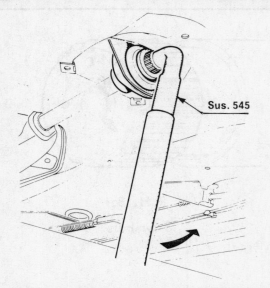

Fig. 11.17 Front torsion bar tension relieving tool (Sec 8)

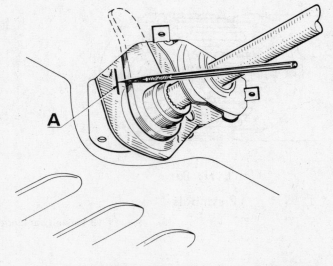

Fig. 11.18 Marking position of front torsion bar (Sec 8)
A   Scribed line at adjuster lever end

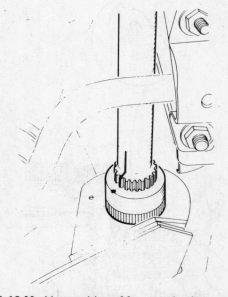

Fig. 11.19 Marking position of front torsion bar at suspension arm end (Sec 8)

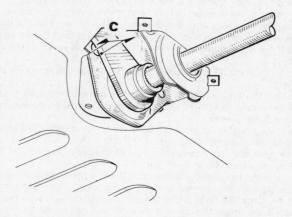

Fig. 11.20 Installing front torsion bar (Sec 8)

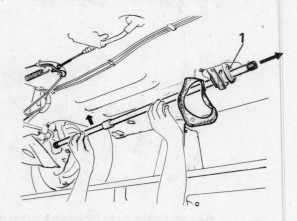

Fig. 11.21 Passing front torsion bar through body bracket (1) (Sec 8)

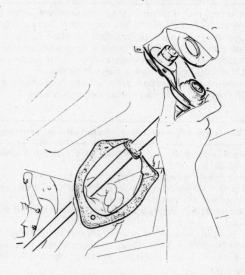

Fig. 11.22 Front torsion bar setting diagram for unmarked or new components (Sec 8)
C = 7.0 to 11.0 mm (0.28 to 0.43 in)

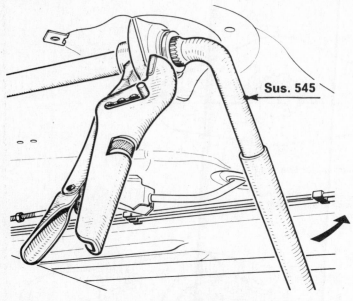

Fig. 11.23 Holding front torsion bar assembly up against body bracket (Sec 8)

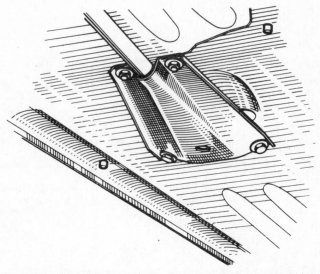

Fig. 11.24 Front torsion bar cover on R1223 models (Sec 9)

cover by locating the cam. Hold the assembly to the body bracket using a self-locking wrench. Insert the fixing bolts.

17 Lower the car to the floor and roll it backwards and forwards for a short distance to settle the suspension.

18 Check the underbody height and adjust if necessary, as described in Section 17.

19 Fit the cover to the adjusting lever housing.

9 Front torsion bar (without cam adjuster) – removal and refitting

1 Later models have torsion bars which can only be adjusted by removing the bar and turning it in either direction to vary its spline setting within the anchor plate bearings – the procedure is included in this Section.

2 Raise the car and support it under the bodyframe members so that the front suspension hangs free.

3 On R1223 models, remove the cover from the rear end of the torsion bar.

4 Slacken the nuts on the torsion bar anchor bearing, then completely remove the inboard nut and washer (photo).

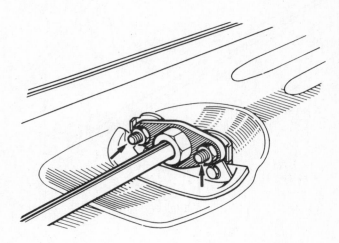

Fig. 11.25 Front torsion bar anchor bearing (Sec 9)

9.4 Front torsion bar anchor bearing

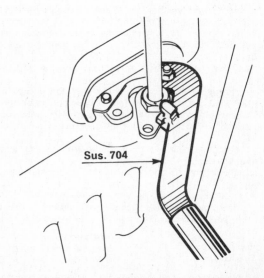

Fig. 11.26 Torsion bar tension relieving tool (Sec 9)

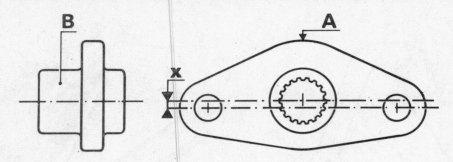

Fig. 11.27 Front torsion bar anchor bearing (Sec 9)

A   More acutely angled edge uppermost
B   Longer projecting boss towards front of car
X   Bearing offset to the top

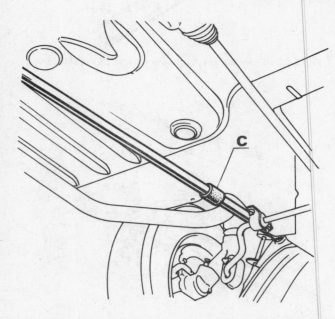

Fig. 11.28 Front torsion bar rubber sleeve (C) towards front of car
(Sec 9)

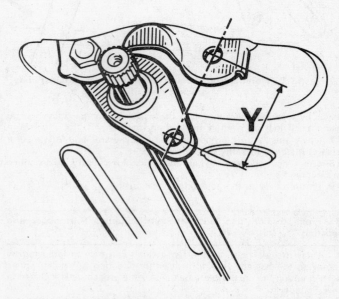

Fig. 11.29 Front torsion bar anchor bearing setting diagram
(Sec 9)

For value Y see text

5   Using the nut and washer just removed, attach the tool Sus 704 or a similar lever to the outboard bolt of the anchor bearing.
6   Apply leverage to the tool until the inboard anchor bearing bolt can be removed, then gently release the tension on the tool and torsion bar.
7   Remove the nut, tool, bolt and the torsion bar with its anchor bearing.
8   Before refitting a torsion bar, check that the anchor bearing is going to be located correctly. The longer boss should be towards the front of the car with the more acutely angled edge uppermost.
9   The torsion bar rubber sleeve should be nearest the front of the car.
10   Slip the anchor bearings onto the torsion bar so that it rests beyond the splines.
11   Attach the anchor bearing to the car using the outboard bolt (finger tight).
12   Move the anchor bearing so that dimension Y (Fig. 11.29) is as tabulated according to model. A square of cardboard having a side equal to the dimension specified will be found useful for this.

Model	Dimension Y
R1223 and 122B	38 to 42 mm (1.50 to 1.65 in)
All other models	65 to 69 mm (2.56 to 2.72 in)

13   Hold this position and tighten the previously hand tightened outboard bolt.

14   Rotate the torsion bar until a position is found where it will enter both its anchor bearing splines and the suspension arm splines simultanously.
15   Using the special tool used for removal, apply tension to the anchor bearing until the remaining bolt can be inserted in the anchor bearing. Tighten both bolts to the specified torque.
16   Roll the car forwards and backwards to settle the suspension and then check the underbody height (see Section 17).

10   Front suspension lower arm – removal and refitting

1   Remove the torsion bar as previously described (Section 8 or 9).
2   Release the driveshaft nut (refer to Chapter 8).
3   Disconnect the anti-roll bar and the shock absorber lower mounting.
4   Disconnect the steering tie-rod balljoint.
5   Release the suspension lower arm balljoint using a suitable splitter tool. The balljoint can only be released, not fully separated, until the stub axle carrier/hub assembly is withdrawn from the splined end of the driveshaft.
6   Unbolt the suspension arm pivot pin bracket from the body side-member (photo), retain the castor shims – see Fig. 11.12.
7   Force the driveshaft partially out of the hub, using a pressure tool

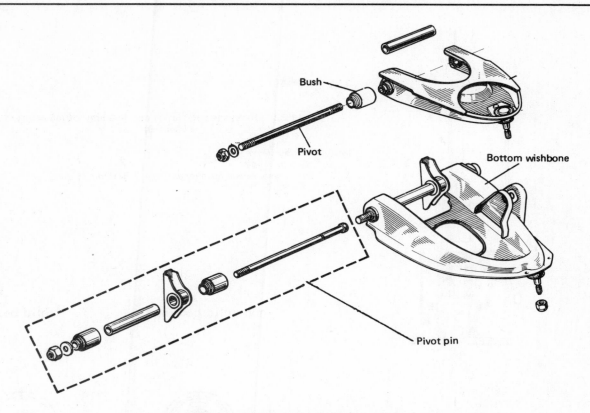

Fig. 11.30 Front suspension wishbones and bushes (Sec 10)

10.6 Front suspension lower arm pivot

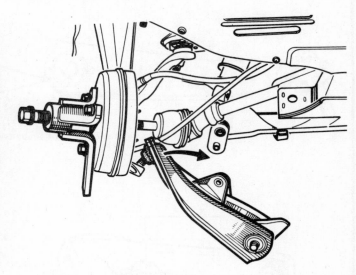

Fig. 11.31 Removing front suspension lower arm (Sec 10)

if necessary. Without separating the shaft completely from the hub withdraw it just enough to be able to disconnect the suspension arm balljoint from the stub axle carrier.

8   The suspension arm flexible bushes may be renewed once the pivot pin tube has been pressed out, using a 13.0 mm (0.51 in) drift.
9   When pressing out the old bushes and fitting the new ones, take care not to distort the arm, and make sure that the distance (V) between the inner rims of the bushes is maintained (Fig. 11.32). This operation requires the use of a special setting gauge and sleeve and is therefore best entrusted to your dealer.
10 Smear the pivot pin with grease and press in the pin with the tube and bracket. Make sure that the bracket is set in relation to the edge

of the shock absorber mounting pin hole, as shown in Fig. 11.34.
11 Should a new suspension lower arm have to be fitted to a model with a brake ventilation conduit (R1223 or 122B) then the new arm will have to be drilled to accept a special nut which is required for attaching the conduit. Refer to Fig. 11.35.
12 If the balljoint is to be renewed, refer to Section 11.
13 Refitting is a reversal of removal, make sure that the caster setting shims are returned to their original position (refer to Section 27).
14 Do not fully tighten the nuts and bolts associated with any flexible bushes until the front suspension on models up to 1979 has been compressed, as described in Section 3.

342

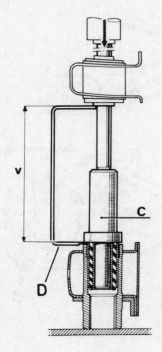

Fig. 11.32 Front suspension lower arm bushing setting diagram (Sec 10)

C Setting sleeve
D Setting gauge
V Distance between bush inner rims – 150.0 mm (5.9 in)

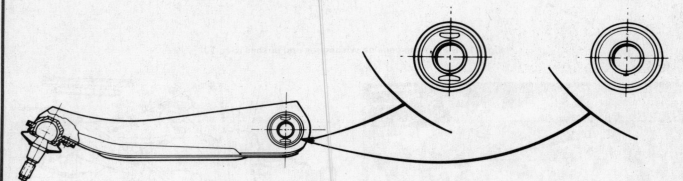

non-solid bearing   solid bearing

Fig. 11.33 Orientation of front suspension lower arm flexible bushes (Sec 10)

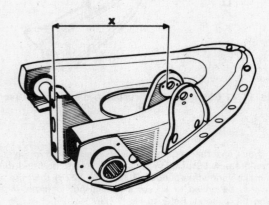

Fig. 11.34 Front suspension lower arm bracket to shock absorber lower mounting hole (Sec 10)
X = 165.0 mm (6.5 in)

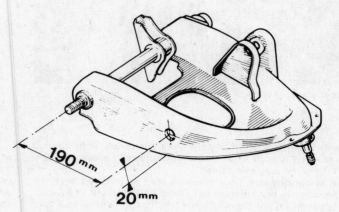

190 mm
20 mm

Fig. 11.35 Location of disc brake ventilation conduit fixing hole (R1223 and 122B) in lower suspension arm (Sec 10)

11 Front suspension lower arm balljoint – removal and refitting

1   To renew the suspension lower arm balljoint there is no need to remove the torsion bar or suspension arm from the car.
2   Raise the car on the side being worked upon, remove the roadwheel and unscrew and remove the driveshaft nut.
3   On cars with disc calipers remove the caliper and tie it up out of the way.
4   Disconnect the suspension arm balljoints from the upper and lower ends of the stub axle carrier (photo). The lower balljoint can only be freed if the driveshaft is partially pushed out of the hub assembly, as described in the preceding Section.
5   Disconnect the tie-rod end balljoint.
6   Support the hub-disc or drum assembly to prevent straining the brake hose or handbrake cable (R1221 model).
7   Renew the balljoint in a similar way to the upper balljoint (see Section 5).
8   Refitting is a reversal of removal.
9   It is recommended that the front wheel alignment and steering angles are checked on completion of the work (Section 27).

12 Rear shock absorbers – removal, testing and refitting

1   Working within the luggage compartment, disconnect the shock absorber upper mounting (photo). Note the sequence of fitting of the mounting components which differs between early and later models.
2   Unscrew the nut and disconnect the shock absorber lower mounting (photo).
3   Testing is as described in Section 3.
4   Refit by reversing the removal operations.

13 Rear anti-roll bar – removal and refitting

1   A rear anti-roll bar is only fitted to certain models.
2   Removal is simply a matter of disconnecting the end fittings and removing the bar from under the car.

11.4 Front suspension lower arm balljoint

12.1 Rear shock absorber upper mounting

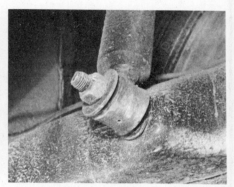
12.2 Rear shock absorber lower mounting

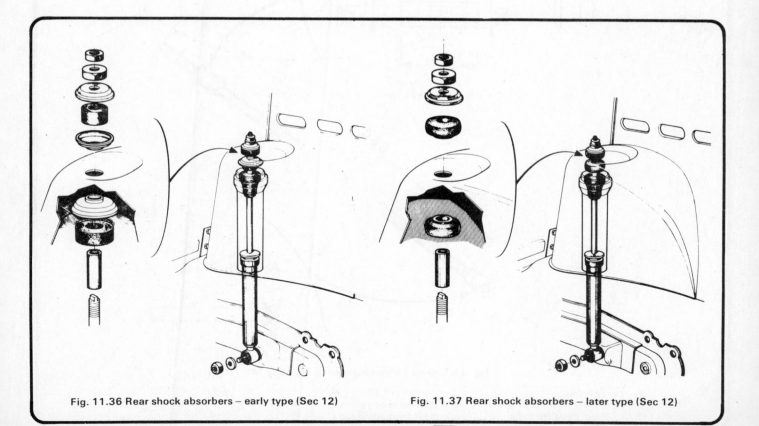
Fig. 11.36 Rear shock absorbers – early type (Sec 12)

Fig. 11.37 Rear shock absorbers – later type (Sec 12)

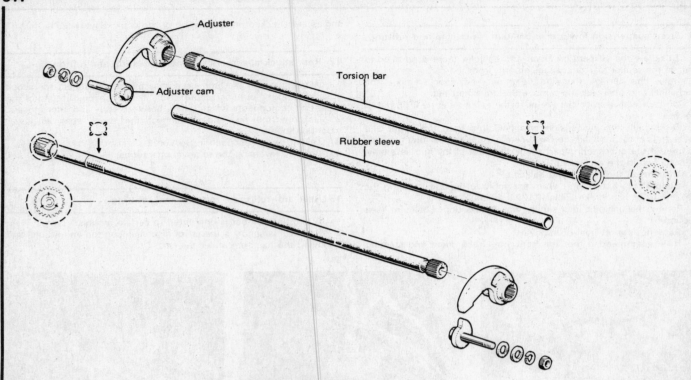

Fig. 11.38 Rear torsion bars (Sec 14)

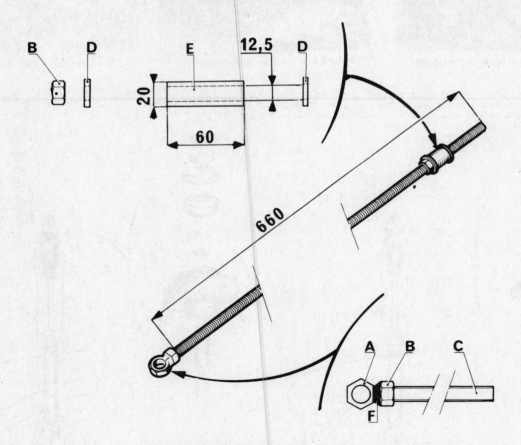

Fig. 11.39 Rear torsion bar setting tool (Sec 14)

A   14.0 mm nut
B   12.0 mm x 1.75 nut (2 off)
C   12.0 mm threaded rod
D   Washers (2 off)
E   Spacing tube (all measurements in mm)
F   Weld

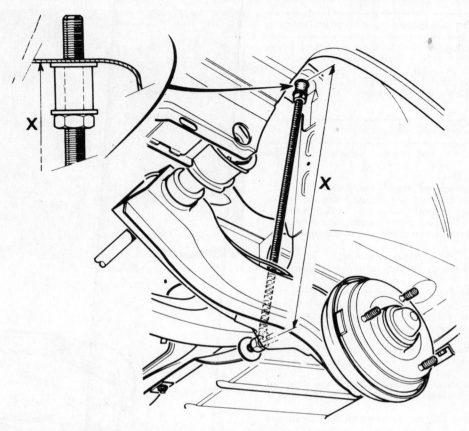

Fig. 11.40 Setting position of rear suspension arm (Sec 14)
For value of X see text

14 Rear torsion bar (cam adjuster type) – removal and refitting

1 Early models are equipped with torsion bars having anchor bearings with cam adjusters.
2 Working within the luggage compartment, disconnect the shock absorber top mounting.
3 Raise the car and support it securely under the bodyframe members.
4 Disconnect the shock absorber lower mounting and remove the unit from the car.
5 Remove the roadwheel.
6 Release the cam locking nut and turn the cam to zero.
7 Using a rod, tap out the torsion bar, so that it emerges from outside the car. If the right-hand bar is being removed, the cover will have to be removed from the brake pressure regulating valve.
8 Before the torsion bar can be refitted, a setting tool must be fabricated from a length of threaded rod, in accordance with Fig. 11.39.
9 Fit this tool instead of the shock absorber and adjust its length in accordance with the following dimensions.

All models except R1223 and 122B:
    LH suspension arm   X = 610.0 mm (24.0 in)
    RH suspension arm   X = 600.0 mm (23.6 in)
R1223:
    LH suspension arm   X = 575.0 mm (22.7 in)
    RH suspension arm   X = 565.0 mm (22.3 in)
122B:
    LH suspension arm   X = 565 mm (22.3 in)
    RH suspension arm   X = 560 mm (22.1 in)

10 Without the setting tool, it is possible to set the specified dimension by jacking up the suspension arm and using a prop between the top of the arm and the underframe member.
11 Bring the torsion bar adjusting lever into contact with the zero cam.

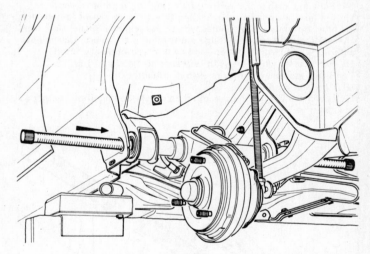

Fig. 11.41 Fitting a rear torsion bar (Sec 14)

12 Check that you are fitting the correctly marked (LH or RH) torsion bar and then smear the splines with grease. Insert the bar into both the bearing and suspension arm. The bar will require rotating in order to find the position where the torsion bar enters both sets of splines easily.
13 Tighten the cam locking nut.
14 Remove the tool and refit the shock absorber and roadwheel.
15 Lower the car and push it backwards and forwards to settle the suspension.
16 Check the underbody height and adjust if necessary, as described in Section 17.

15 Rear torsion bar (without cam adjuster) – removal and refitting

1   The operations are virtually identical to those described in the preceding Section, except that reference to the cam adjuster and lever should be ignored.
2   On certain models a cover is fitted to the end of the torsion bars which must be removed before starting operations.

16 Rear suspension arm – removal and refitting

1   Raise the rear of the car and support securely under the bodyframe.
2   Remove the roadwheels.
3   Remove the shock absorbers and anti-roll bar, if fitted (photo).
4   From the side being operated on, disconnect and plug the flexible brake hydraulic hose and the handbrake cable (not R1221 models).
5   Refer to the previous Sections and remove both rear torsion bars.
6   Unscrew the three inner and two outer suspension arm fixing bolts.
7   Withdraw the suspension arm hub/drum assembly.
8   Remove the hub/drum, if necessary, after reference to Chapters 8 and 9.
9   The suspension arm flexible bearings may be removed after saturating them in hydraulic or releasing fluid by drawing off the bearing outer sleeves with a two-legged claw type extractor. Use a hacksaw to cut through the bearing inner sleeve, but take care not to damage the suspension arm itself.
10 When fitting the new bearings to the suspension arms, carefully note the setting angles, depending upon whether the inner bearing has a pressed-steel or cast-steel housing.
11 New bearings should be pressed into the suspension arm tubular section. The outer bearing should be positioned so that edge A is at 90° to edge B (Fig. 11.46).
12 The inner bearing with pressed-steel housing should be located as shown in Fig. 11.47.
13 The cast-steel type inner bearing housings must be pressed into position so that their elongated slots are parallel with the suspension arm and the setting dimension as shown in Figs. 11.48 and 11.49.
14 Refit the suspension arm by reversing the removal operations.
15 If a new suspension arm is being fitted it is important to note that the new arm must be of similar type to the original. Suspension arms of two different camber settings are used in production. Always have both arms of identical pattern and of the type originally fitted.
16 Refit the torsion bars with reference to Section 14 or 15.
17 Bleed the brake hydraulic system (Chapter 9).
18 Refit the roadwheels.
19 Lower the car to the floor and then check the underbody height as described in Section 17.

16.3 Rear suspension trailing arm

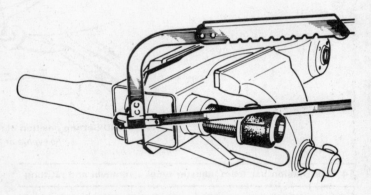

Fig. 11.43 Cutting rear suspension arm bearing inner sleeve
(Sec 16)

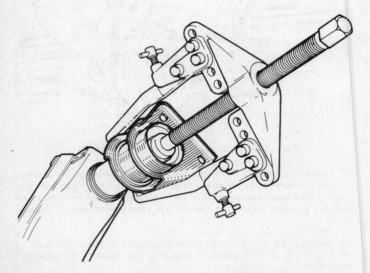

Fig. 11.42 Drawing bearing off rear suspension arm (Sec 16)

17 Underbody height – checking and adjustment

1   Have the car standing on a level floor with a full fuel tank and tyres correctly inflated.
2   At the front and rear of the car and on both sides, measure the distance between the floor and the roadwheel hub centres (H1 and H4) and then between the floor and the underside of the body side-members (H2 and H5 Fig. 11.51).
3   Record the dimensions and then calculate the differences – H1 minus H2 and H4 minus H5. Compare the results with the specified dimensions for your particular model (paragraph 12).
4   The difference between the left-hand and right-hand sides of the car must not exceed 10.0 mm (0.39 in), the driver's side being the higher.
5   Where adjustment is required carry out the following operations:

Torsion bars with cam adjusters
6   To increase underbody height at the front, unlock the cam adjuster under the front seat and turn the adjuster towards the opposite front seat. Re-lock the cam.
7   To increase underbody height at the rear, unlock the cam and turn in a clockwise direction when viewed from the roadwheel.
8   Where sufficient adjustment by cam alteration cannot be achieved then the torsion bar will have to be removed, as described in earlier Sections of this Chapter, and the setting dimension (C) of the lever altered (see Fig. 11.22).

Fig. 11.44 Rear suspension arms (Sec 16)

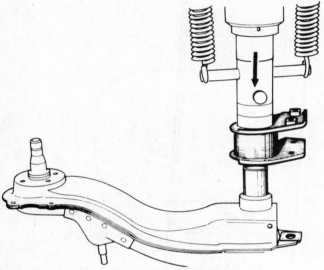

Fig. 11.45 Pressing on rear suspension arm bearing (Sec 16)

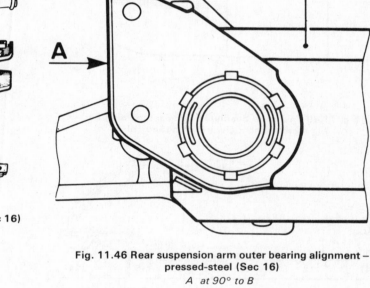

Fig. 11.46 Rear suspension arm outer bearing alignment –
pressed-steel (Sec 16)
A at 90° to B

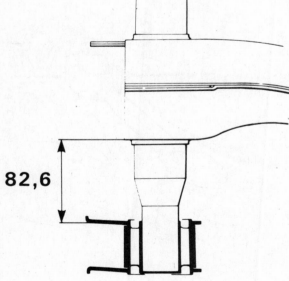

82,6

Fig. 11.47 Pressed-steel bearing housing setting diagram –
measurement given in mm (Sec 16)

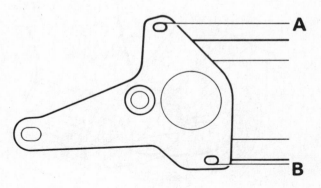

Fig. 11.48 Rear suspension arm outer bearing alignment – cast-
steel (Sec 16)
A and B Slots parallel to arm

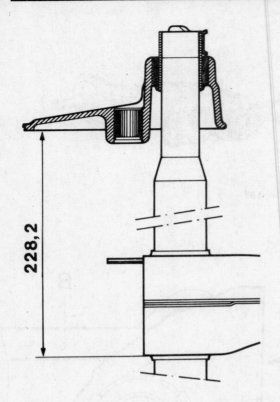

228,2

Fig. 11.49 Cast-steel bearing housing setting diagram –
measurement given in mm (Sec 16)

H_1 H_2 H_5 H_4

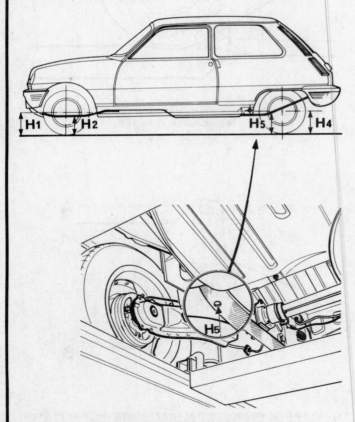

H_5

Fig. 11.51 Underbody height setting diagram (Sec 17)

For H values see text

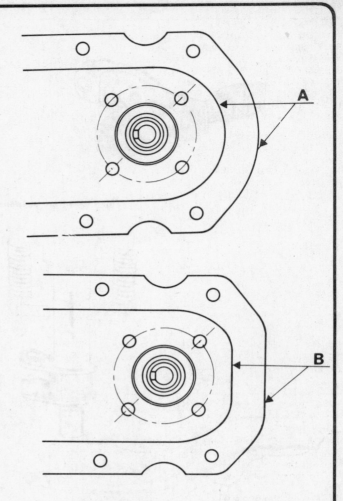

A

B

Fig. 11.50 Rear suspension arm (Sec 16)

A *Early type – rounded end for positive camber*
B *Later type – flattened end for negative camber*

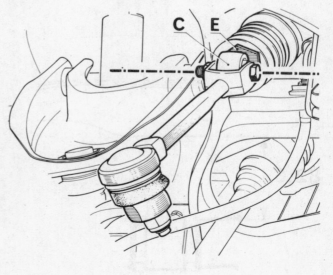

C E

Fig. 11.52 Tie-rod end fitting – early models (Sec 18)

C *Rack end fitting*   E *Locknut*

Torsion bars without cam adjusters

9 To increase underbody height at the front of the car, remove the torsion bar as described in Section 9 of this Chapter and increase dimension Y (Fig. 11.29) by 1.0 mm (0.039 in) to give 3.0 mm (0.12 in) increase in height.

10 To increase the underbody height at the rear of the car, remove the torsion bar (Section 15) and increase dimension X (Fig. 11.40) by 3.0 mm (0.12 in) to increase the underbody height by a similar amount.

General information

11 Where the underbody height must be reduced at front or rear, reverse the procedure just described for increasing it.

12 The following underbody heights should be used to set your suspension for all normal purposes:

Front (H1 minus H2)

All models except R1223, 122B, R1221, R1222, R1391, R1392	58.0 mm (2.28 in)
R1223	80.0 mm (3.15 in)
122B	100.0 mm (3.94 in)
R1221, R1222, R1391, R1392	48.0 mm (1.87 in)

Rear:

All models except R1223 and 122B	H5 to be between 11.0 mm (0.43 in) below and 10.0 mm (0.39 in) above H4
R1223 (H4 minus H5)	35.0 mm (1.38 in)
122B (H4 minus H5)	55.0 mm (2.17 in)

13 A tolerance of 10.0 mm (0.39 in) is permitted on these dimensions.

18 Steering rack bellows – renewal

Early models

1 Up until 1979 the steering rack end fittings are of flexibly-bushed eye type, using bolts to connect them to the forked ends of the steering tie-rods.

2 To renew a split bellows, remove the rack end fitting to tie-rod bolt.

3 Prevent the rack from turning by using a spanner on its flats and release the end fitting locknut.

4 Counting the number of turns, unscrew and remove the rack end fitting and locknut.

5 Withdraw the bellows.

6 If the bellows have been split for some time, wipe away the old grease from the end of the rack and apply fresh grease of the specified type.

7 Slide on the new bellows and retaining band.

8 Screw in the rack end fitting by the same number of turns as was recorded at removal. Check that the tie-rod connecting bolt will be perfectly horizontal when connecting the rack end fitting to the tie-rod before tightening the locknuts.

9 Fit and tighten the tie-rod connecting bolt.

Later models

10 After mid 1978 all models except Gordini versions are fitted with a modified steering rack and tie-rods.

11 Using a balljoint extractor, separate the tie-rod balljoint from the steering arm on the stub axle carrier.

12 Using an open-ended spanner on the flats of the tie-rod, release the locknut with a second spanner.

13 Unscrew the tie-rod end fitting from the tie-rod, counting the number of turns required to disconnect it.

14 Withdraw the bellows.

15 If the bellows have been split for some time, wipe away the old grease from the end of the rack and apply fresh grease of the specified type.

16 Slide on the new bellows and retaining band.

17 Screw on the tie-rod end fitting by the same number of turns as was recorded at removal.

18 Connect the balljoint to the steering arm and then make sure that the balljoint is held at the centre of its arc of travel while the locknut is tightened.

All models

19 Check the front wheel alignment, as described in Section 27.

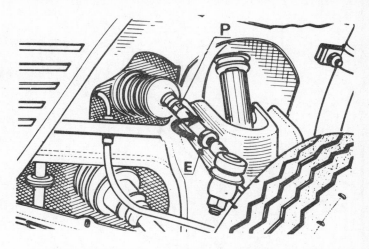

Fig. 11.53 Tie-rod and balljoint – later models (Sec 18)

E   Locknut   P   Flats on rack end

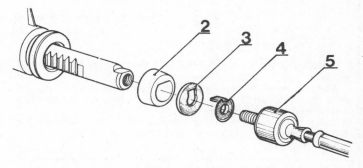

Fig. 11.54 Rack end fitting components – models 1979 and later (Sec 18)

2 Lock-stop	4 Lockplate
3 Washer	5 Balljoint

19 Tie-rod end fittings – renewal

1 The tie-rod balljoint/end fittings must be renewed should wear be observed or the dust excluding gaiter split.

2 Unscrew the nut from the balljoint taper pin and, using a suitable extractor, disconnect the balljoint from the steering arm (photo).

19.2 Tie-rod end balljoint

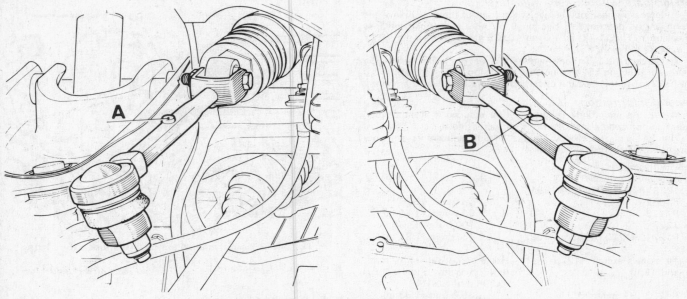

Fig. 11.55 Early type tie-rod end fitting identification (Sec 19)

A   *Single boss RH*   B   *Dual boss LH*

3   Disconnect the tie-rod end fitting as described in the preceding Section.
4   Refit by reversing the removal operations, tighten all nuts and bolts to the specified torque and then check the front wheel alignment, as described in Section 27.
5   If both early type tie-rod end fittings are being renewed, note the method of identifying LH and RH assemblies (Fig. 11.55).

20 Steering wheel – removal and refitting

1   Pull the embellisher from the centre of the wheel (photo).
2   Unscrew the steering wheel retaining nut (photo).
3   The wheel should come off its tapered splines if a moderate thump is given to both sides of the rear of the steering wheel rim.
4   If it is seized an extractor will be required.
5   Before fitting the steering wheel, set the front roadwheels in the straight-ahead position or centre the steering gear (see Section 27). Apply a little grease to the shaft splines and then push the steering wheel onto the shaft so that the spokes are correctly positioned in the lower half of the wheel circle.

21 Steering column bushes – renewal

1   Wear in these bushes can be detected by side-to-side or up-and-down movement of the shaft when the steering wheel is moved.
2   Disconnect the battery.
3   Remove the steering wheel (Section 20).
4   Remove the instrument panel (Chapter 10).
5   Remove the direction indicator switch.
6   Release the fixing screws and lower the fusebox.
7   Remove the bolts from the steering shaft universal joint.
8   Working within the engine compartment, disconnect the steering shaft flexible coupling, retaining the flexible packing piece located in the coupling.
9   Tap the end of the steering shaft downward with a plastic-faced hammer until the bottom bush frees from the column tube.
10   Extract the circlip on the top bush and ease the bush out of the column tube with a small screwdriver.
11   Before fitting the new bushes, smear them with molybdenum disulphide grease.
12   Locate the split type bottom bush on the lower end of the shaft.
13   Reduce the outside diameter of the old bottom bush by about 2.0

20.1 Removing steering wheel embellisher

20.2 Steering wheel retaining nut

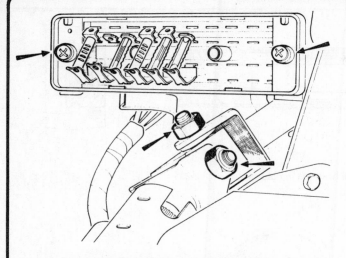

Fig. 11.56 Steering shaft universal joint bolts and fusebox retaining screws (Sec 21)

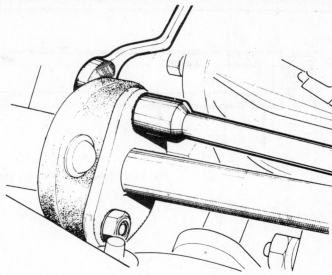

Fig. 11.57 Disconnecting steering shaft flexible coupling (Sec 21)

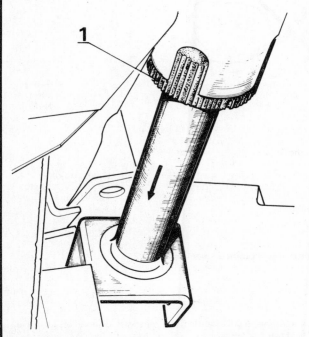

Fig. 11.58 Steering shaft bottom bush (1) (Sec 21)

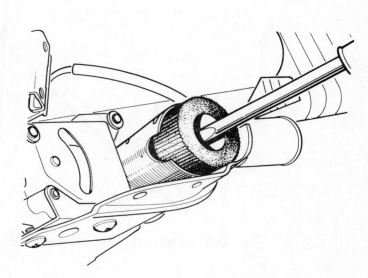

Fig. 11.59 Prising out steering shaft top bush (Sec 21)

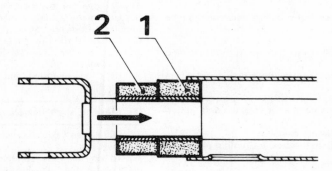

Fig. 11.60 Using old bush (2) to press in new one (1) (Sec 21)

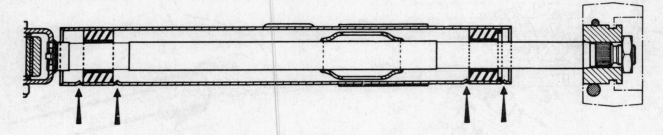

Fig. 11.61 Steering shaft bush indentations in column tube (Sec 21)

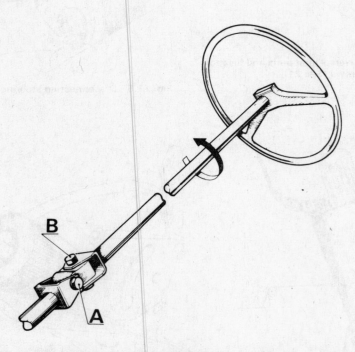

Fig. 11.62 Steering shaft universal joint pinchbolt tightening sequence – see text (Sec 21)

mm (0.079 in) and then place the bush under the new one.

14 Press the steering shaft upwards so that the old bush forces the new one up into the column tube. Remove the old bush and discard it.

15 The top bush should be fitted by tapping it into position with a piece of tubing.

16 Check that the new bushes are correctly located between the tube indents.

17 Refit the top circlip.

18 Reconnect the shaft universal joint by using the following procedure.

19 Raise the front roadwheels and centre the steering gear (see Section 24).

20 Tighten the lower pinch-bolt, A, (Fig. 11.62).

21 Turn the steering wheel through one quarter of a turn and tighten the upper pinch-bolt (B).

22 Reconnect the steering shaft flexible coupling.

23 Refit the direction indicator switch, fusebox, instrument panel and steering wheel.

22 Steering column – removal and refitting

1 Disconnect the battery.

2 If the intermediate shaft is to be removed, disconnect the steering shaft flexible coupling.

3 Remove one of the pinch-bolts from the steering shaft and release the shaft from the universal joint.

4 Remove the lower section of the steering column upper shroud.

5 Unbolt the column upper support bracket, lower the column and remove it from the car interior.

6 Before refitting the column, centre the steering rack (Section 24) and connect the universal joint when the steering wheel is in the straight-ahead position.

7 Refit the column shroud and connect the battery.

23 Steering shaft flexible coupling – renewal

1 Should the flexible coupling appear to be split or frayed, it must be renewed.

2 To do this, the steering rack housing must be removed, as described in the following Section.

3 With the gear on the bench, drill out the flexible coupling rivets.

4 Discard the old flexible disc and fit the new one with the bolts supplied (7.0 mm dia x 30.0 mm long). Make sure that the heads of the bolts are towards the steering wheel and new self-locking nuts are used.

24 Steering gear – removal and refitting

1   On R1221 models, move the coolant expansion bottle to one side, and remove the radiator mounting bolts.
2   Disconnect the steering shaft flexible coupling, retaining the flexible packing piece.
3   On early models (pre 1979) disconnect the bolts to release the tie-rods from the rack.
4   On later models, disconnect the balljoints from the steering arms on the stub axle carrier.
5   Unscrew the steering rack fixing bolts, taking particular care to retain the height setting shims located under the rack housing and noting from which side they came.
6   Withdraw the rack assembly.
7   Refitting is a reversal of removal, but remember to fit the flexible packing piece at the flexible coupling and set the early type rack end fitting connecting bolts so that they are horizontal.
8   In order to maintain the steering wheel in its correct straight-ahead position the steering gear should be centred before connecting the flexible coupling. To do this on models built before 1973, measure the dimension C, shown in Fig. 11.65. This can be done through the bellows or by slipping a thin rod under the outer end. The measurement should be taken at the pinion end of the rack and the dimensions should be 71.5 mm (2.8 in).

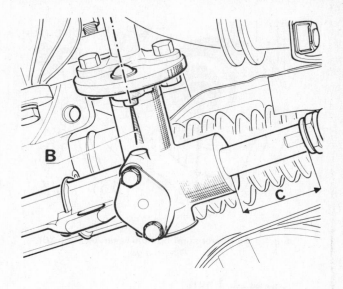

Fig. 11.65 Steering gear centred (Sec 24)

B   Models after 1973 – rivet on flexible coupling in alignment with the cast pointer
C   Models before 1973 – dimension C should be 71.5 mm (2.8 in)

9   On models built after 1973, the steering is centred when the bellows are extended equally and the rivet on the flexible coupling is in alignment with the pointer cast onto the pinion housing (see Fig. 11.65).
10 Provided the original height setting shims are refitted, the correct steering rack height setting should be maintained. It is rare to need any correction, but if the front tyres appear to wear unevenly after fitting a new or exchange rack assembly then have the height setting checked by your Renault dealer, as it is not within the scope of the home mechanic.
11 Before having this done however, check the underbody height, as described in Section 17, as this may be the cause.

25 Steering gear – overhaul

1   Provided the flexible bellows are kept in good order, it should not be necessary to lubricate the assembly or adjust the mechanism. The steering gear normally has a very long life and when obviously worn, as indicated by knocking noises, stiffness or free movement of the rack, it is recommended that a new or factory rebuilt unit is installed rather than attempt to overhaul the original assembly.

26 Power-assisted steering

1   In 1982, the TX and certain other models were equipped with power-assisted steering.
2   The pump/reservoir assembly is belt-driven from the crankshaft pulley.
3   The operations involved in the removal of the power steering gear are similar to those described for manual steering, except that the fluid flow and return pipes must be disconnected and plugged.

Maintenance

4   At the specified intervals, check the fluid level in the pump reservoir. The fluid should be up to the bottom of the strainer mesh. Top up with the specified fluid if necessary; look for leakage if frequent or heavy topping up is necessary. Maintain scrupulous cleanliness throughout.
5   Also at the specified intervals, check the tension and condition of the pump drivebelt. Adjustment is achieved in the same way as for the alternator drivebelt, by slackening the pump pivot and tensioner bolts and moving the pump as necessary.

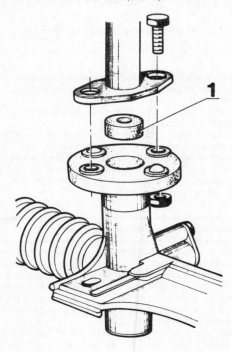

Fig. 11.63 Steering shaft flexible coupling packing piece (1) (Sec 24)

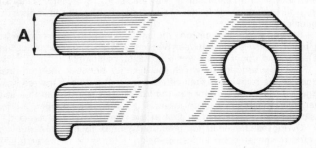

Fig. 11.64 Steering rack height setting shim (Sec 24)

Shims are available with dimension (A) in seven sizes between 8.9 mm (0.35 in) and 14.9 mm (0.587 in)

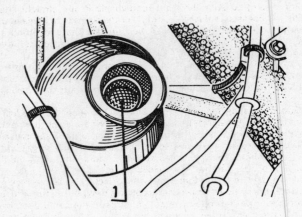

Fig. 11.66 Power steering fluid reservoir (Sec 26)

1   Filter gauge

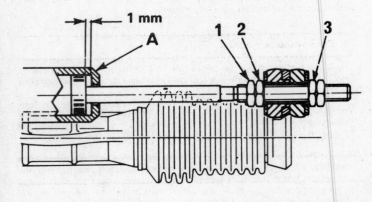

Fig. 11.68 Power steering ram setting diagram (Sec 26)

1   Locknut   3   Adjuster nut
2   Adjuster nut   A   End bearing

Overhaul

6   It is not recommended that the power steering gear or pump are overhauled. Apart from the difficulty of obtaining individual components, special tools are required to do the work satisfactorily.
7   When wear is evident or a fault occurs, obtain a new or factory rebuilt unit.
8   Removal of the steering pump is achieved by freeing the drivebelt from the pulley, disconnecting and plugging the hoses at the pump (note the hose positions for refitting), then removing the tensioner and pivot bolts. Refit in the reverse order, and refill and bleed the system as described below.
9   Removal of the steering rack is essentially as described in Section 24. Additionally, disconnect the pipes from the rack and plug them to prevent fluid leakage. Refit in the reverse order, and refill and bleed the system as described below.

Bleeding

10   If the fluid level in the system falls so low that air is introduced into the pump, or after components of the system have been disturbed, bleeding should be carried out as described below.
11   Fill the reservoir with specified fluid right to the top. Turn the steering from lock to lock, then top up.
12   Start the engine and again turn the steering from lock to lock. Top up if necessary to the bottom of the strainer mesh, then refit the reservoir cap.

Removal of the hydraulic ram

13   If the steering rack hydraulic ram is to be removed, there is no need to remove the rack housing.
14   Disconnect the fluid hoses and drain the hydraulic circuit.

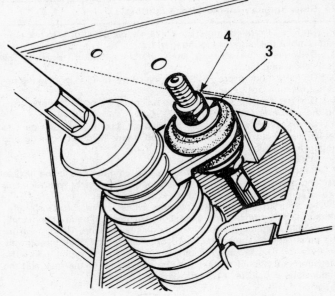

Fig. 11.67 Power steering ram (Sec 26)

3   Nut   4   Locknut

15   Unscrew and remove the nut and locknut from the end of the ram spindle, also the ram mounting bolt on the rack assembly.
16   Withdraw the ram.
17   Before refitting the ram, fully extend the steering rack on the end opposite to the pinion housing.
18   With reference to Fig. 11.68 release the locknut (1) and unscrew it, also release the adjuster nut (2) a turn or two.
19   Move the ram spindle until the piston contacts the bearing.
20   Unscrew the adjuster nut (3) to obtain a working clearance of 1.0 mm (0.039 in) between the piston and its end bearing (A).
21   Tighten all nuts to the specified torque.

27 Steering angles and front wheel alignment

1   Accurate front wheel alignment is essential to provide good steering and roadholding characteristics, and also to ensure slow and even tyre wear. Before considering the steering angles, check that the tyres are correctly inflated, that the front wheels are not buckled, the hub bearings are not worn or incorrectly adjusted and that the steering linkage is in good order, without slackness or wear at the joints. Wheel alignment consists of four factors:
2   **Camber:** the angle at which the road wheels are set from the vertical when viewed from the front or rear of the vehicle. Positive camber is the angle (in degrees) that the wheels are tilted outwards at the top from the vertical.
3   **Castor:** the angle between the steering axis and a vertical line when viewed from each side of the vehicle. Positive castor is indicated when the steering axis is inclined towards the rear of the vehicle at its upper end.
4   **Steering axis inclination:** the angle, when viewed from the front or rear of the vehicle between vertical and an imaginary line drawn between the upper and lower suspension balljoints.
5   **Toe:** the amount by which the distance between the front inside edges of the roadwheel rims differs from that between the rear inside edges. If the distance between the front edges is less than that at the rear, the wheels are said to toe-in. If the distance between the front inside edges is greater than that at the rear, the wheels toe-out.
6   Owing to the need for precision gauges to measure the small angles of the steering and suspension settings, it is preferable that adjustment of camber and castor is left to a service station having the necessary equipment.
7   For information purposes, however, adjustment of the castor angle is described here. Camber and kingpin inclination are non-adjustable and, if incorrect, this must be due to collision damage or worn

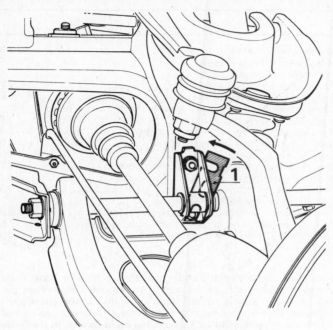

Fig. 11.69 Castor adjusting shims (1) (Sec 27)

suspension components. The castor angle is controlled by shims located behind the suspension lower arm bearing. One shim alters the castor angle by 1°. The total shim pack thickness must not exceed 3.0 mm (0.12 in).

8   To check the front wheel alignment, first make sure that the steering is centred with the front roadwheels in the straight-ahead position. If necessary adjust the lengths of the tie-rods to achieve this. On early models, remove the pivot bolt, unlock the end fitting and screw it in or out as necessary. On later models, release the tie-rod locknut and rotate the tie-rod.

9   Obtain a tracking gauge. These are available in various forms from accessory stores, or one can be fabricated from a length of steel tubing suitably cranked to clear the sump and bellhousing and having a setscrew and locknut at one end.

10 With the gauge, measure the distance between the two wheel inner rims (at hub height) at the rear of the wheel. Push the vehicle forward to rotate the wheel through 180° (half a turn) and measure the distance between the wheel inner rims, again at hub height, at the front of the wheel. This last measurement should differ from the first by the appropriate toe-out – see Specifications.

11 Where the toe-out is found to be incorrect, release the rack and fitting locknuts or tie-rod locknuts, according to type, and turn the rack end fittings or the tie-rods by equal amounts in the same direction.

12 Only turn them a quarter of a turn at a time before re-checking the alignment. Do not grip the threaded part of the track rod/balljoint during adjustment and make sure that the bellows outboard clip is eased off, otherwise the bellows will twist as the track rod is rotated.

13 On completion, tighten the end fitting or tie-rod locknuts and reconnect the pivot bolt on early models.

28 Rear wheel alignment

1   The camber angle is non-adjustable and any deviation from Specification will be due to collision damage or worn suspension components.

2   The alignment is correct when the rear roadwheels toe-in (pre 1975 models) or toe-out after that date. It is rare for the alignment to require adjustment, but should this be required it can be altered by moving the suspension arm inner bearing (refer to Section 16).

29 Fault diagnosis – suspension and steering

Before diagnosing faults from the following chart, check that any irregularities are not caused by:
1   *Binding brakes*
2   *Incorrect 'mix' of tyres*
3   *Incorrect tyre pressures*
4   *Misalignment of the bodyframe or rear suspension*

Symptom	Reason(s)
Steering wheel can be moved considerably before any sign of movement of the wheels is apparent	Wear in the steering linkage, gear and column coupling
Vehicle difficult to steer in a consistent straight line – wandering	As above Wheel alignment incorrect (indicated by excessive or uneven tyre wear) Front wheel hub bearings loose or worn Worn balljoints or suspension arms
Steering stiff and heavy	Incorrect wheel alignment (indicated by excessive or uneven tyre wear) Excessive wear or seizure in one or more of the joints in the steering linkage or suspension arm balljoints Excessive wear in the steering unit
Wheel wobble and vibration	Road wheels out of balance Road wheels buckled Wheel alignment incorrect Wear in the steering linkage, suspension arm balljoint or suspension arm inner bushes
Excessive pitching and rolling on corners and during braking	Defective shock absorbers and/or broken torsion bar, anti-roll bar broken away
Lack of steering power-assistance	Pump drivebelt slack or broken Fluid level too low Pump or regulator valve faulty Internal leak in steering rack

Chapter 12 Bodywork

Contents

1 General description

The Renault 5 is available in three-door and five-door hatchback form.

Construction is of all-steel, welded, unitary type. In the interests of economy, the front wings are replaceable, being retained by bolts and screws. Other panels are welded in position.

2 Maintenance – bodywork and underframe

1 The general condition of a vehicle's bodywork is the one thing that significantly affects its value. Maintenance is easy but needs to be regular. Neglect, particularly after minor damage, can lead quickly to further deterioration and costly repair bills. It is important also to keep watch on those parts of the vehicle not immediately visible, for instance the underside, inside all the wheel arches and the lower part of the engine compartment.

2 The basic maintenance routine for the bodywork is washing – preferably with a lot of water, from a hose. This will remove all the loose solids which may have stuck to the vehicle. It is important to flush these off in such a way as to prevent grit from scratching the finish. The wheel arches and underframe need washing in the same way to remove any accumulated mud which will retain moisture and tend to encourage rust. Paradoxically enough, the best time to clean the underframe and wheel arches is in wet weather when the mud is thoroughly wet and soft. In very wet weather the underframe is usually cleaned of large accumulations automatically and this is a good time for inspection.

3 Periodically, except on vehicles with a wax-based underbody protective coating, it is a good idea to have the whole of the underframe of the vehicle steam cleaned, engine compartment included, so that a thorough inspection can be carried out to see what minor repairs and renovations are necessary. Steam cleaning is available at many garages and is necessary for removal of the accumulation of oily grime which sometimes is allowed to become thick in certain areas. If steam cleaning facilities are not available, there are one or two excellent grease solvents available, such as Holts Engine Cleaner or Holts Foambrite, which can be brush applied. The dirt can then be simply hosed off. Note that these methods should not be used on vehicles with wax-based underbody protective coating or the coating will be removed. Such vehicles should be inspected annually, preferably just prior to winter, when the underbody should be washed down and any damage to the wax coating repaired using Holts Undershield. Ideally, a completely fresh coat should be applied. It would also be worth considering the use of such wax-based protection for injection into door panels, sills, box sections, etc, as an additional safeguard against rust damage where such protection is not provided by the vehicle manufacturer.

4 After washing paintwork, wipe off with a chamois leather to give an unspotted clear finish. A coat of clear protective wax polish, like the many excellent Turtle Wax polishes, will give added protection against chemical pollutants in the air. If the paintwork sheen has dulled

or oxidised, use a cleaner/polisher combination such as Turtle Extra to restore the brilliance of the shine. This requires a little effort, but such dulling is usually caused because regular washing has been neglected. Care needs to be taken with metallic paintwork, as special non-abrasive cleaner/polisher is required to avoid damage to the finish. Always check that the door and ventilator opening drain holes and pipes are completely clear so that water can be drained out (photos). Bright work should be treated in the same way as paint work. Windscreens and windows can be kept clear of the smeary film which often appears by the use of a proprietary glass cleaner like Holts Mixra. Never use any form of wax or other body or chromium polish on glass.

3 Maintenance – upholstery and carpets

Mats and carpets should be brushed or vacuum cleaned regularly to keep them free of grit. If they are badly stained remove them from the vehicle for scrubbing or sponging and make quite sure they are dry before refitting. Seats and interior trim panels can be kept clean by wiping with a damp cloth and Turtle Wax Carisma. If they do become stained (which can be more apparent on light coloured upholstery) use a little liquid detergent and a soft nail brush to scour the grime out of the grain of the material. Do not forget to keep the headlining clean in the same way as the upholstery. When using liquid cleaners inside the vehicle do not over-wet the surfaces being cleaned. Excessive damp could get into the seams and padded interior causing stains, offensive odours or even rot. If the inside of the vehicle gets wet accidentally it is worthwhile taking some trouble to dry it out properly, particularly where carpets are involved. *Do not leave oil or electric heaters inside the vehicle for this purpose.*

4 Minor body damage – repair

The colour bodywork repair photographic sequences between pages 32 and 33 illustrate the operations detailed in the following sub-sections.

Note: *For more detailed information about bodywork repair, the Haynes Publishing Group publish a book by Lindsay Porter called The Car Bodywork Repair Manual. This incorporates information on such aspects as rust treatment, painting and glass fibre repairs, as well as details on more ambitious repairs involving welding and panel beating.*

Repair of minor scratches in bodywork

If the scratch is very superficial, and does not penetrate to the metal of the bodywork, repair is very simple. Lightly rub the area of the scratch with a paintwork renovator like Turtle Wax New Color Back, or a very fine cutting paste like Holts Body + Plus Rubbing Compound to remove loose paint from the scratch and to clear the sur-

2.4a Checking door drain hole

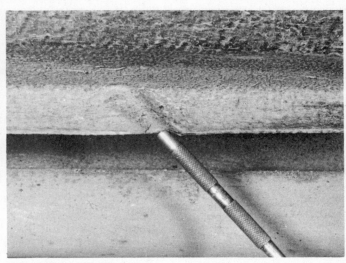

2.4b Checking sill drain hole

rounding bodywork of wax polish. Rinse the area with clean water.

Apply touch-up paint, such as Holts Dupli-Color Color Touch or a paint film like Holts Autofilm, to the scratch using a fine paint brush; continue to apply fine layers of paint until the surface of the paint in the scratch is level with the surrounding paintwork. Allow the new paint at least two weeks to harden: then blend it into the surrounding paintwork by rubbing the scratch area with a paintwork renovator or a very fine cutting paste, such as Holts Body + Plus Rubbing Compound or Turtle Wax New Color Back. Finally, apply wax polish from one of the Turtle Wax range of wax polishes.

Where the scratch has penetrated right through to the metal of the bodywork, causing the metal to rust, a different repair technique is required. Remove any loose rust from the bottom of the scratch with a penknife, then apply rust inhibiting paint, such as Turtle Wax Rust Master, to prevent the formation of rust in the future. Using a rubber or nylon applicator fill the scratch with bodystopper paste like Holts Body + Plus Knifing Putty. If required, this paste can be mixed with cellulose thinners, such as Holts Body + Plus Cellulose Thinners, to provide a very thin paste which is ideal for filling narrow scratches. Before the stopper-paste in the scratch hardens, wrap a piece of smooth cotton rag around the top of a finger. Dip the finger in cellulose thinners, such as Holts Body + Plus Cellulose Thinners, and then quickly sweep it across the surface of the stopper-paste in the scratch; this will ensure that the surface of the stopper-paste is slightly hollowed. The scratch can now be painted over as described earlier in this Section.

Repair of dents in bodywork

When deep denting of the vehicle's bodywork has taken place, the first task is to pull the dent out, until the affected bodywork almost attains its original shape. There is little point in trying to restore the original shape completely, as the metal in the damaged area will have stretched on impact and cannot be reshaped fully to its original contour. It is better to bring the level of the dent up to a point which is about $\frac{1}{8}$ in (3 mm) below the level of the surrounding bodywork. In cases where the dent is very shallow anyway, it is not worth trying to pull it out at all. If the underside of the dent is accessible, it can be hammered out gently from behind, using a mallet with a wooden or plastic head. Whilst doing this, hold a suitable block of wood firmly against the outside of the panel to absorb the impact from the hammer blows and thus prevent a large area of the bodywork from being 'belled-out'.

Should the dent be in a section of the bodywork which has a double skin or some other factor making it inaccessible from behind, a different technique is called for. Drill several small holes through the metal inside the area – particulary in the deeper section. Then screw long self-tapping screws into the holes just sufficiently for them to gain a good purchase in the metal. Now the dent can be pulled out by pulling on the protruding heads of the screws with a pair of pliers.

The next stage of the repair is the removal of the paint from the damaged area, and from an inch or so of the surrounding 'sound' bodywork. This is accomplished most easily by using a wire brush or abrasive pad on a power drill, although it can be done just as effectively by hand using sheets of abrasive paper. To complete the preparation for filling, score the surface of the bare metal with a screwdriver or the tang of a file, or alternatively, drill small holes in the affected area. This will provide a really good 'key' for the filler paste.

To complete the repair see the Section on filling and re-spraying.

Repair of rust holes or gashes in bodywork

Remove all paint from the affected area and from an inch or so of the surrounding 'sound' bodywork, using an abrasive pad or a wire brush on a power drill. If these are not available a few sheets of abrasive paper will do the job just as effectively. With the paint removed you will be able to gauge the severity of the corrosion and therefore decide whether to renew the whole panel (if this is possible) or to repair the affected area. New body panels are not as expensive as most people think and it is often quicker and more satisfactory to fit a new panel than to attempt to repair large areas of corrosion.

Remove all fittings from the affected area except those which will act as a guide to the original shape of the damaged bodywork (eg headlamp shells etc). Then, using tin snips or a hacksaw blade, remove all loose metal and any other metal badly affected by corrosion. Hammer the edges of the hole inwards in order to create a slight depression for the filler paste.

Wire brush the affected area to remove the powdery rust from the surface of the remaining metal. Paint the affected area with rust inhibiting paint like Turtle Rust Master; if the back of the rusted area is accessible treat this also.

Before filling can take place it will be necessary to block the hole in some way. This can be achieved by the use of aluminium or plastic mesh, or aluminium tape.

Aluminium or plastic mesh or glass fibre matting, such as the Holts Body + Plus Glass Fibre Matting, is probably the best material to use for a large hole. Cut a piece to the approximate size and shape of the hole to be filled, then position it in the hole so that its edges are below the level of the surrounding bodywork. It can be retained in position by several blobs of filler paste around its periphery.

Aluminium tape should be used for small or very narrow holes. Pull a piece off the roll and trim it to the approximate size and shape required, then pull off the backing paper (if used) and stick the tape over the hole; it can be overlapped if the thickness of one piece is insufficient. Burnish down the edges of the tape with the handle of a screwdriver or similar, to ensure that the tape is securely attached to the metal underneath.

Bodywork repairs – filling and re-spraying

Before using this Section, see the Sections on dent, deep scratch, rust holes and gash repairs.

Many types of bodyfiller are available, but generally speaking those proprietary kits which contain a tin of filler paste and a tube of resin hardener are best for this type of repair, like Holts Body + Plus or Holts No Mix which can be used directly from the tube. A wide, flexible plastic or nylon applicator will be found invaluable for imparting a smooth and well contoured finish to the surface of the filler.

Mix up a little filler on a clean piece of card or board – measure the hardener carefully (follow the maker's instructions on the pack) otherwise the filler will set too rapidly or too slowly. Alternatively, Holts No Mix can be used straight from the tube without mixing, but daylight is required to cure it. Using the applicator apply the filler paste to the prepared area; draw the applicator across the surface of the filler to achieve the correct contour and to level the filler surface. As soon as a contour that approximates to the correct one is achieved, stop working the paste – if you carry on too long the paste will become sticky and begin to 'pick up' on the applicator. Continue to add thin layers of filler paste at twenty-minute intervals until the level of the filler is just proud of the surrounding bodywork.

Once the filler has hardened, excess can be removed using a metal plane or file. From then on, progressively finer grades of abrasive paper should be used, starting with a 40 grade production paper and finishing with 400 grade wet-and-dry paper. Always wrap the abrasive paper around a flat rubber, cork, or wooden block – otherwise the surface of the filler will not be completely flat. During the smoothing of the filler surface the wet-and-dry paper should be periodically rinsed in water. This will ensure that a very smooth finish is imparted to the filler at the final stage.

At this stage the 'dent' should be surrounded by a ring of bare metal, which in turn should be encircled by the finely 'feathered' edge of the good paintwork. Rinse the repair area with clean water, until all of the dust produced by the rubbing-down operation has gone.

Spray the whole repair area with a light coat of primer, either Holts Body + Plus Grey or Red Oxide Primer – this will show up any imperfections in the surface of the filler. Repair these imperfections with fresh filler paste or bodystopper, and once more smooth the surface with abrasive paper. If bodystopper is used, it can be mixed with cellulose thinners to form a really thin paste which is ideal for filling small holes. Repeat this spray and repair procedure until you are satisfied that the surface of the filler, and the feathered edge of the paintwork are perfect. Clean the repair area with clean water and allow to dry fully.

The repair area is now ready for final spraying. Paint spraying must be carried out in a warm, dry, windless and dust free atmosphere. This condition can be created artificially if you have access to a large indoor working area, but if you are forced to work in the open, you will have to pick your day very carefully. If you are working indoors, dousing the floor in the work area with water will help to settle the dust which would otherwise be in the atmosphere. If the repair area is confined to one body panel, mask off the surrounding panels; this will help to minimise the effects of a slight mis-match in paint colours. Bodywork fittings (eg chrome strips, door handles etc) will also need to be masked off. Use genuine masking tape and several thicknesses of newspaper for the masking operations.

Before commencing to spray, agitate the aerosol can thoroughly, then spray a test area (an old tin, or similar) until the technique is mastered. Cover the repair area with a thick coat of primer; the thickness should be built up using several thin layers of paint rather than one thick one. Using 400 grade wet-and-dry paper, rub down the surface of the primer until it is really smooth. While doing this, the work area should be thoroughly doused with water, and the wet-and-dry paper periodically rinsed in water. Allow to dry before spraying on more paint.

Spray on the top coat using Holts Dupli-Color Autospray, again building up the thickness by using several thin layers of paint. Start spraying in the centre of the repair area and then, with a single side-to-side motion, work outwards until the whole repair area and about 2 inches of the surrounding original paintwork is covered. Remove all masking material 10 to 15 minutes after spraying on the final coat of paint.

Allow the new paint at least two weeks to harden, then, using a paintwork renovator or a very fine cutting paste such as Turtle Wax New Color Back or Holts Body + Plus Rubbing Compound, blend the edges of the paint into the existing paintwork. Finally, apply wax polish.

---

5   Major body damage – repair

1   Where this has occurred, the bodyframe will almost certainly have been distorted.
2   Leave the repair to your dealer as he will have the necessary jigs and gauges to ensure that the structure is correctly aligned. Without this there may be problems with the steering, suspension or rapid tyre wear.

---

6   Bonnet – removal and refitting

1   The help of an assistant will be required.
2   Remove the headlamps, as described in Chapter 10.
3   The nuts on the bonnet hinge mounting brackets are now accessible.
4   With your assistant supporting the bonnet in the fully open position, remove the hinge bracket nuts (photo) and lift the bonnet away. Record the position of any shims which may be located between the hinge and the crossmember and retain them for refitting.
5   Refitting is a reversal of removal. Adjust the bonnet position between the wings by moving it sideways within the limits of the elongated hinge stud holes. Raise it to be flush with the top of the wings by inserting shims between the hinge and crossmember.

---

7   Bonnet release cable – removal and refitting

1   Open the bonnet. Remove the fasteners securing the cable release control (photo).
2   Swivel the cable clevis (photo) and release it from the bonnet lock.
3   Withdraw the cable assembly into the vehicle interior.
4   Refitting is a reversal of removal.
5   If the bonnet release cable is broken, remove the hinge pivot nuts (see Fig. 12.2) and ease the hinge legs apart while lifting the bonnet. Release the bonnet catch with a section of rod.

6.4 Unscrewing bonnet hinge bracket nuts

7.1 Bonnet release handle (later models)

7.2 Bonnet lock and cable clevis (arrowed)

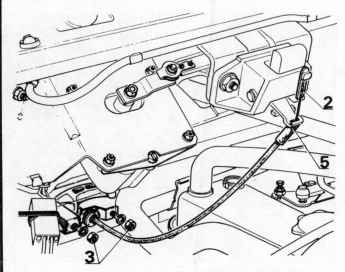

Fig. 12.1 Bonnet release cable – typical (Sec 7)

2 Cable clevis   3 Release handle nuts
5 Bonnet lock catch

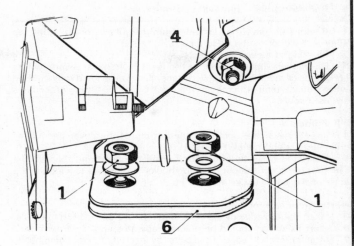

Fig. 12.2 Bonnet hinge (Sec 7)

1 Hinge bracket nuts   4 Hinge pivot nut
6 Height adjusting shim

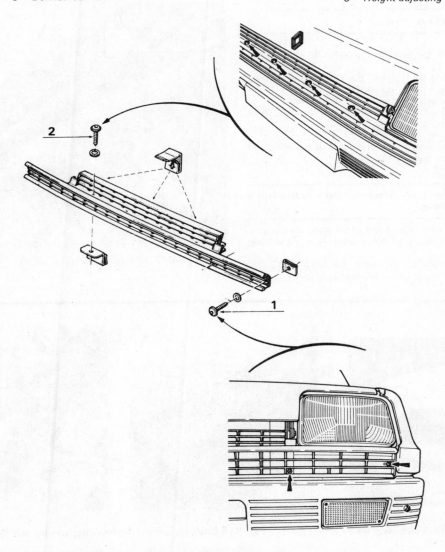

Fig. 12.3 Radiator grille securing screws (1 and 2) (Sec 8)

8 Radiator grille – removal and refitting

1   Remove the cross-head screws from the grille's front face and top edge and withdraw the grille (photo).
2   Refitting is a reversal of removal.
3   On models operating in territories which have severe winter conditions, a radiator grille cover is supplied. This should only be used when outside temperatures are below 0°C (32°F). Fitting procedures are as follows:

UK models
4   Insert one of the hooks on the bottom of the cover behind the grille vertical end panel (Fig. 12.4).
5   Insert the other bottom hook behind the grille and then do the same for the cover's upper retaining hooks, taking care to slide the top edge of the cover under the bonnet.

North American models
6   Insert the top edge of the cover between the bonnet and the grille, the short fixing rod should be pointing upwards and towards you.
7   Attach the lower edge of the cover by inserting the retaining hooks behind the vertical slats of the radiator grille.
8   Now open the bonnet and fix the ends of the short rod in the square apertures in the underside of the bonnet (Fig. 12.5).

9 Front wing – removal and refitting

1   Open the bonnet fully.
2   Unscrew and remove the top bolts from the inside edge of the wing (photo).
3   Remove the pillar bolt, the sill bolt and the headlamp mounting panel bolt from the headlamp support panel (Fig. 12.6).
4   Cut around the mastic-sealed joint and remove the wing.
5   To refit, clean away all old mastic and apply a bead of fresh material to all the wing mating surfaces on the body.
6   Bolt the wing into position.
7   Apply anti-corrosive compound to the underside of the wing and finish to match the rest of the bodywork.

10 Front bumper (excluding North American and Gordini Turbo models) – removal and refitting

1   Removal of the bumper fixing screws will necessitate the use of a special screwdriver. This may be of a Torx or other type, depending upon the date of production.
2   Remove the bumper end screws and centre screws (Fig. 12.7).
3   Disconnect the electrical leads from the sidelights and direction indicator lamps.

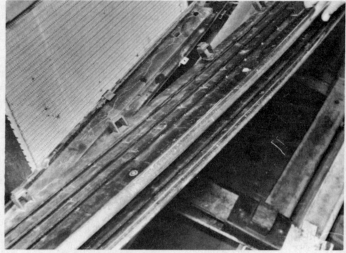

8.1 Removing radiator grille

9.2 Two front wing retaining bolts (arrowed)

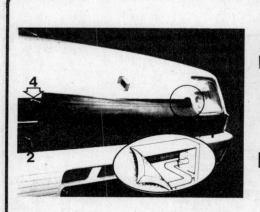

Fig. 12.4 Radiator cover from outside – UK models (Sec 8)

1 to 4 Hooks

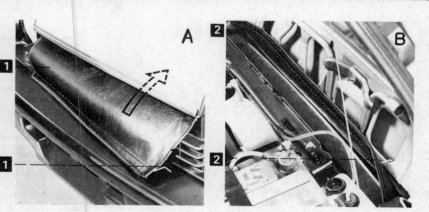

Fig. 12.5 Radiator cover – North American models (Sec 8)

A From outside   B From engine compartment

1 and 2 Hooks

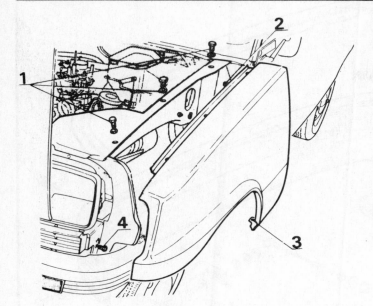

Fig. 12.6 Front wing attachment (Sec 9)

1   Top bolts   4   Headlamp support panel
2   Pillar bolt   bolt
3   Sill bolt

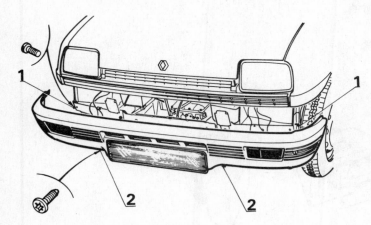

Fig. 12.7 Front bumper and fixing screws (1 and 2) (Sec 10)

4   Lift away the bumper.
5   Refitting is a reversal of removal, but make sure that the insulating pads are in good condition. Screw in the fixing screws only finger tight to start with in order to centralise the bumper before finally tightening them.

11 Rear bumper (excluding North American and Gordini Turbo models) – removal and refitting

1   Removal of the rear bumper is carried out in a similar manner to that described for the front bumper.

12 Bumpers (North America) – removal and refitting

1   The bumpers for these models are of deeper section than those on UK models, and their mountings incorporate anchor cables. Apart from these differences, removal and refitting operations are as described in Sections 10 and 11.
2   It will be easier to remove the front bumper from R1228 models if the radiator grille is removed first (Section 8).

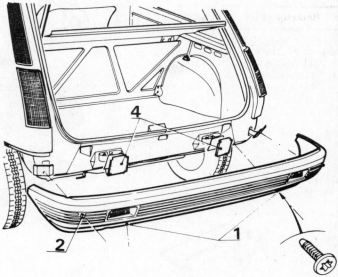

Fig. 12.8 Rear bumper (Sec 11)

1   Screw   2   Screw
        4   Insulating pads

13 Bumpers (Gordini Turbo) – removal and refitting

1   Hexagonal headed bolts are used to secure the bumpers, otherwise removal and refitting operations are as described in Sections 10 and 11.

14 Door trim panel – removal and refitting

1   Open the door and remove the screws which hold the armrest and tidy tray (photo).
2   Remove the screw which secures the lock remote control escutcheon plate (photos).
3   On early models, prise off the covering from the window winder handle. On later models, prise out the small cover plate from the handle (photo).
4   Unscrew the handle retaining nut and pull the winder handle from the regulator splines (photos).
5   Insert a flat piece of wood under the ends of the trim panel and twist it (Fig. 12.12). This will have the effect of lifting the panel out of the top and bottom retaining channels.
6   Pull the panel from the door.
7   Carefully peel away the waterproof sheet.
8   Refit by reversing the removal operations. Before fitting the waterproof sheet, make sure that it is in good condition otherwise renew it. Apply fresh sealing strip around all the door apertures if there is any doubt about a weatherproof seal.
9   Fit the window regulator handle at the same angle as the one on the opposite door with the windows wound fully up.

15 Window regulator and glass – removal and refitting

Manual regulator
1   Remove the door trim panel, as described in the preceding Section.
2   Temporarily refit the window regulator handle and wind the glass down until it is open 35.0 mm (1.4 in).
3   Remove the three fixing nuts from the window regulator (photo).
4   Push the regulator spindle inwards and then slide the regulator towards the rear of the car until the rollers come out of the window base channel (photo). Support the glass.
5   Withdraw the regulator from the aperture in the door.
6   Tilt the glass (sloping end downward)

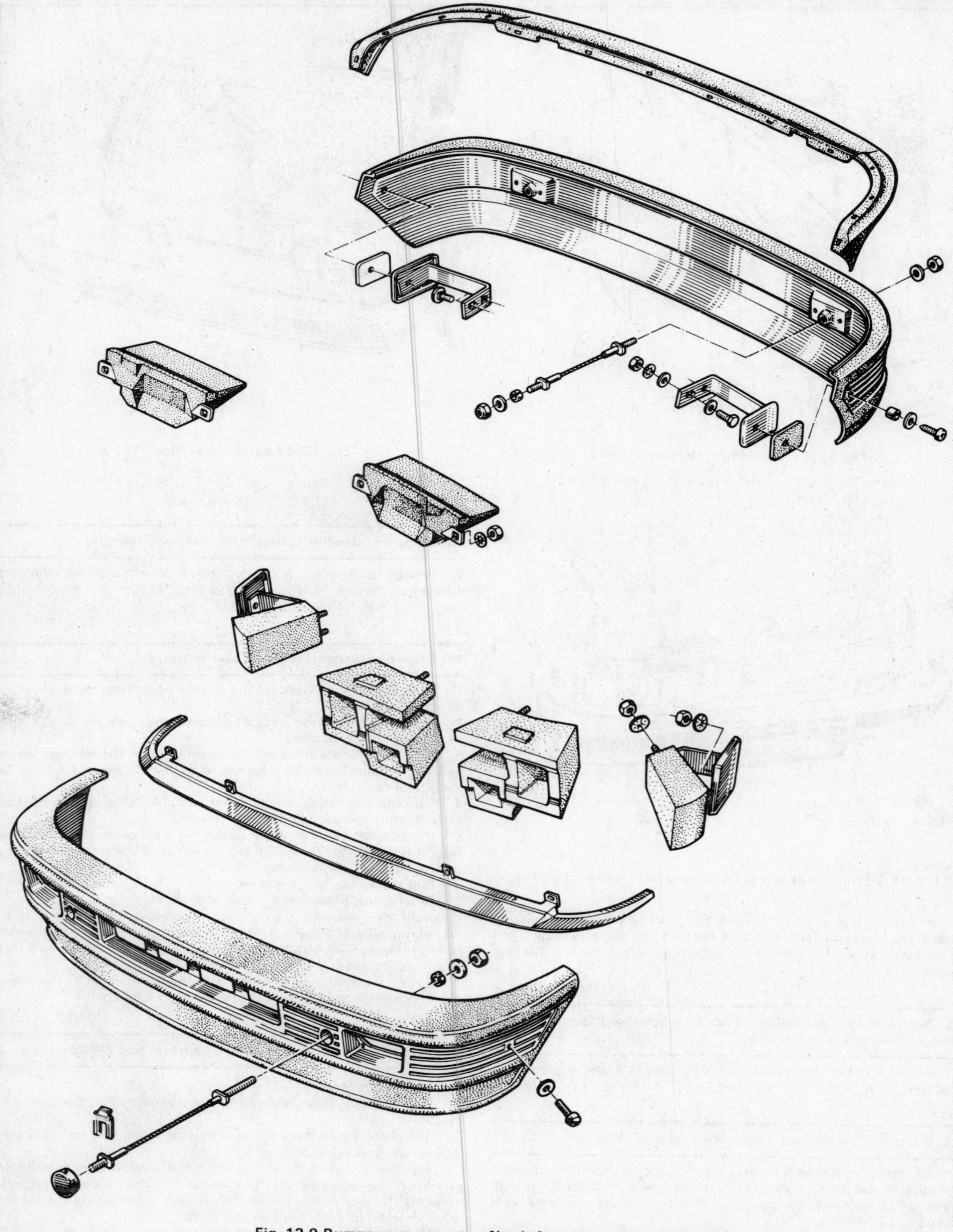

Fig. 12.9 Bumper components – North American models (Sec 12)

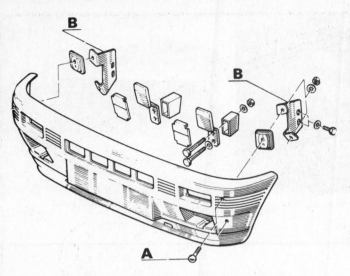

Fig. 12.10 Front bumper – Gordini Turbo (Sec 13)

A Screws   B Brackets

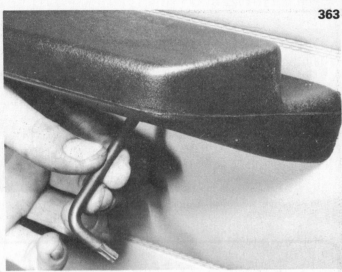

14.1 Removing door armrest screws

14.2a Extracting remote control handle escutcheon screw

14.2b Removing remote control handle escutcheon plate

14.3 Prising out window regulator handle cover plate (later models)

14.4a Unscrewing window regulator handle nut

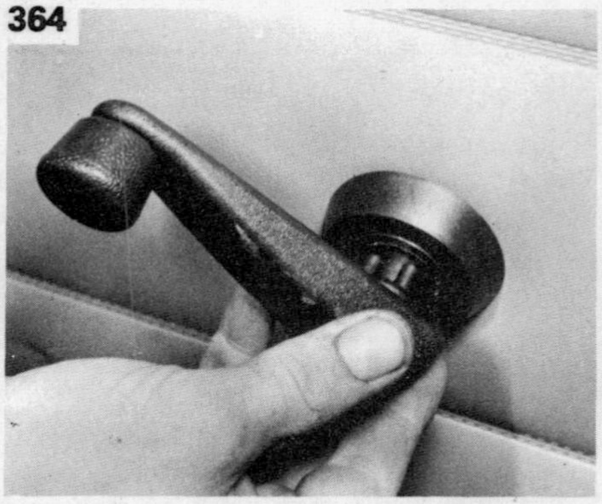

14.4b Removing window regulator handle

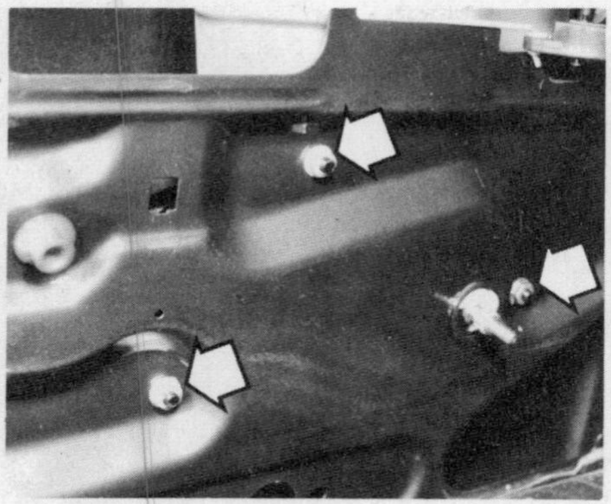

15.3 Window regulator securing nuts (arrowed)

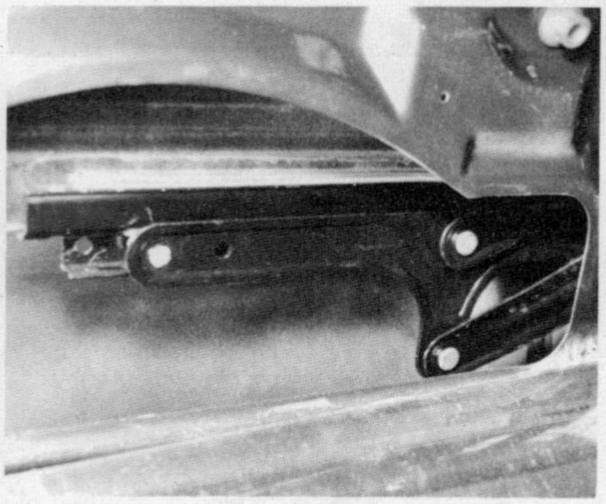

15.4 Glass slide and regulator arm

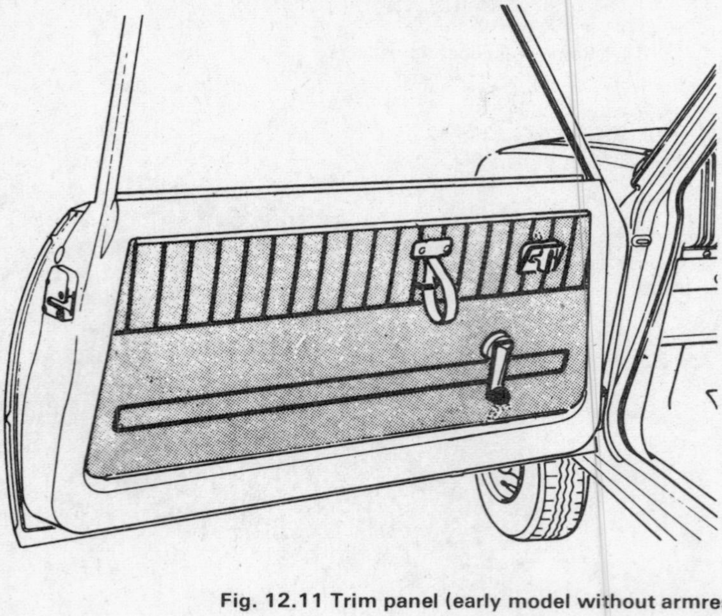

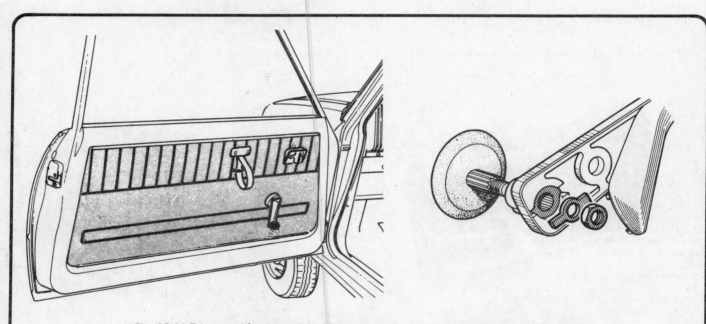

Fig. 12.11 Trim panel (early model without armrest) and window regulator handle (Sec 14)

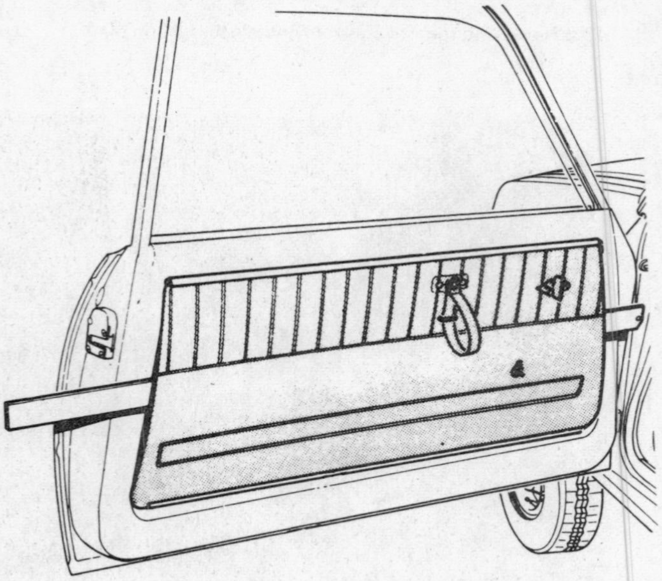

Fig. 12.12 Using piece of wood to release door trim panel (Sec 14)

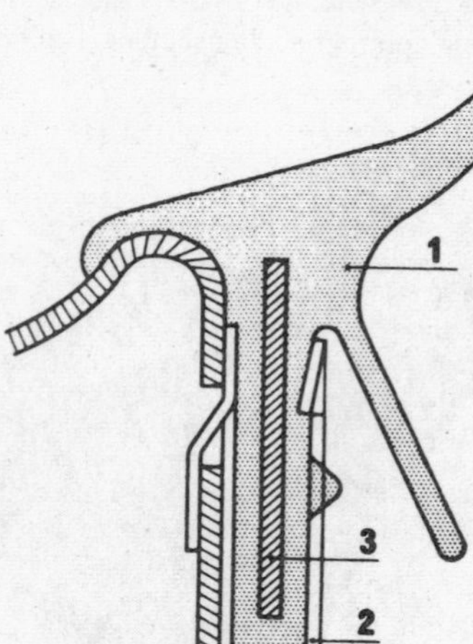

Fig. 12.13 Sectional view of glass weatherstrip (Sec 15)

1 Weatherstrip
2 Retaining clip
3 Metal strip inside weatherstrip
4 Door panel

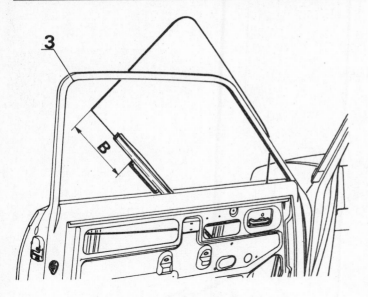

Fig. 12.14 Door glass removal (Sec 15)

3   Glass slide channel   B   222.0 mm (8.75 in)

7   Prise off the retaining clips and remove the glass weatherproof strips.
8   Pull out the glass slide channel from the door top frame.
9   Withdraw the glass from the door cavity.
10   Refitting is a reversal of removal, but observe the following points.
11   Fit the retaining clips before pushing the glass weatherproof strips into position.
12   If the glass base channel has been removed to change the glass, make sure that the channel is tapped onto the glass using a wooden or plastic hammer so that it conforms to the diagram in Fig. 12.14.

Electric regulator
13   The front windows are electrically-operated on Gordini Turbo and other later models.
14   To remove the electric motor from the door, first disconnect the battery.
15   Remove the door trim panel (Sec 14) and disconnect the electrical leads from the motor.
16   Removal of the motor/regulator and the door glass is as described earlier in this Section for the manually-operated version.

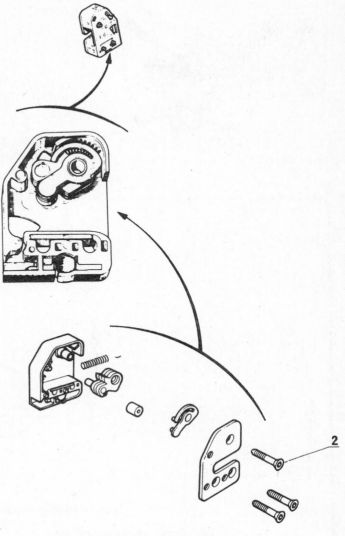

Fig. 12.15 Door lock detail (Sec 16)

2   Fixing screw

16 Door lock – removal and refitting

1   Remove the door trim panel as described in Section 14.
2   Using a special Torx screwdriver remove the three screws which hold the lock to the edge of the door.
3   Remove the retaining screw(s), pull out the lock remote control (photo) and disconnect it from the remote control rod.
4   Detach the remote control rod anti-rattle clip.
5   Push the door lock plunger inside the door and hold it vertically.
6   Pass the lock assembly around the window lower glass slide channel and remove it through the hole in the door.
7   The pushbutton lock cylinder is retained in the door by a spring clip. Where necessary, prise out the clip to remove the cylinder.
8   Refitting is a reversal of removal.
9   On some later models (1983) a central door locking system is fitted. The system employs electrically-operated solenoids to actuate the lock levers.

17 Door – removal and refitting

1   Open the door wide and support its lower edge on jacks or blocks using a pad of rags to prevent damage to the paintwork.
2   Remove the circlip from the top hinge pin and then drive the pin out in a downwards direction.

16.3 Remote control door lock handle

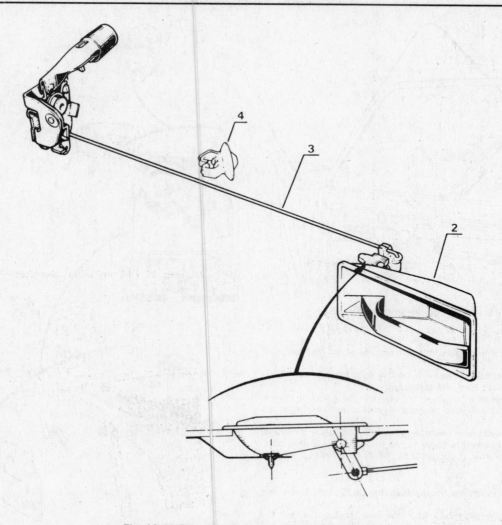

Fig. 12.16 Door lock remote control detail (Sec 16)

2   *Control and escutcheon plate*   3   *Rod*   4   *Anti-rattle clip*

3   On early models, prise out the small plastic cover panel from the base of the door pillar for access to the lower hinge bolts. On later models, the panel is not fitted and the pillar and sill trims must be removed.

4   Unscrew the hinge bolts and lift the door from the car.

5   Refit by reversing the removal operations. Any adjustments required can be carried out by placing shims between the lower hinge and the pillar, or by lifting the door within the limits of the elongated bolt holes on the pillar. Adjust the position of the lock striker if necessary to ensure smooth, positive closure (photo).

18 Tailgate – removal and refitting

1   Disconnect the battery earth lead.

2   Open the tailgate fully, and have an assistant support it.

3   Remove the supporting struts.

4   Working inside the car, prise off the hinge covers. Disconnect the washer fluid tubes.

5   Disconnect the electrical leads from the heated tailgate window and the rear number plate lamps. Disconnect the earth lead and the wiper motor leads.

6   Unscrew the four hinge nuts and with the help of your assistant lift the tailgate from the body.

7   Refitting is a reversal of removal. Adjust by moving the tailgate within the limits of the elongated hinge bolt holes. Adjust the lock striker as necessary to ensure smooth positive closure.

17.5 Door lock striker

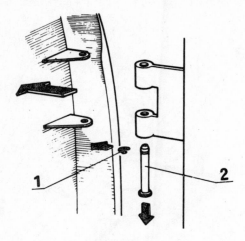

Fig. 12.17 Door hinge pin (2) and circlip (1) (Sec 17)

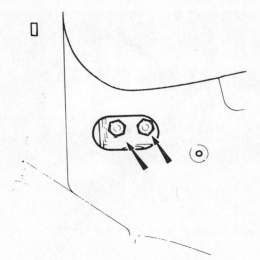

Fig. 12.18 Door hinge bolts (Sec 17)

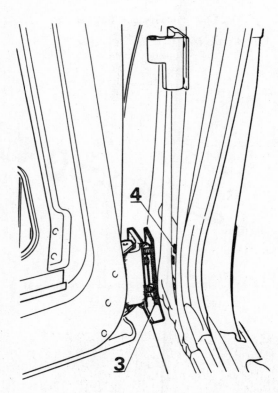

Fig. 12.19 Door hinge shim (3) and elongated bolt holes (4)
(Sec 17)

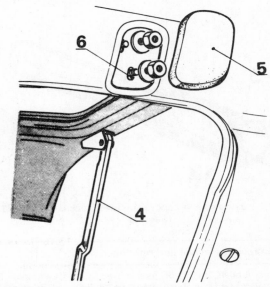

Fig. 12.20 Tailgate strut (4), hinge cover plate (5) and hinge nuts
(6) (Sec 18)

19 Tailgate lock – removal, dismantling and refitting

1   Open the tailgate fully and remove the lock cover which is held by a single screw.
2   Remove the two lock securing nuts (photo) and lift the lock from the tailgate.
3   The push-button cylinder lock assembly can be removed if the retaining lugs are depressed. This can be done without the special tool (CAR 550) by pushing a piece of tubing down the barrel to force the lugs into their recesses while the barrel assembly is withdrawn.
4   To dismantle, drive out the roll pin and remove the lock barrel (Fig. 12.23).
5   Reassembly and refitting are reversals of removal and dismantling.
6   The lock striker can be adjusted slightly to ensure smooth, positive closure (photo).

19.2 Tailgate lock

19.6 Tailgate striker

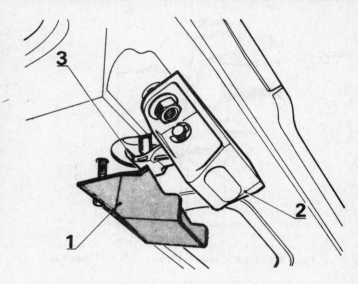

Fig. 12.21 Tailgate lock (Sec 19)

1   Cover   2   Lock
         3   Hook type catch

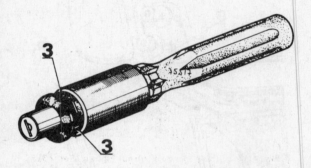

Fig. 12.22 Using special tool to compress lock barrel lugs (3)
(Sec 19)

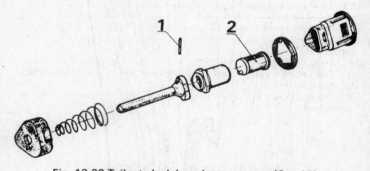

Fig. 12.23 Tailgate lock barrel components (Sec 19)

1   Roll pin   2   Barrel

20 Windscreen – removal and refitting

1   On most models, the windscreen is fixed by a conventional rubber surround. On some later North American models, the windscreen is bonded to the bodyshell.

2   While it is recommended that renewal of a windscreen is left to the specialists, the procedure for removing and refitting the type with a rubber surround is given for those who wish to carry out the work. If a bonded unit is being replaced this is definitely a job for the experts.

3   Take off the windscreen wiper arms and blades, remove the interior mirror and the vehicle tax disc, as applicable.

4   Prise out the bright trim from the rubber surround.

5   If the glass is of laminated type or is unbroken, go inside the car and pull down the lip of the rubber surround along its top edge. Hold the lip away from the headlining by inserting a length of dowel rod or similar.

6   Now sit in the front seat and place the soles of the shoes against the very top of the glass and push the glass out. Have an assistant support it as it comes out.

7   If the glass is of safety type which has broken, clean up all the glass fragments, especially from around the demister ducts. It may be necessary to remove the demister ducts or even the heater casing if a quantity of glass has entered the unit (see Chapter 2).

8   Clean away all old mastic from the grooves of the rubber surround and the body flange.

9   If the rubber surround is in good condition, fit it to the glass, if it is not, renew it.

10 The bright trim may be fitted into its groove now or left until the screen is installed. In either case, the use of a trim fitting tool will make the job easier and will avoid damage to the groove lips which can occur if a screwdriver or blade is used.

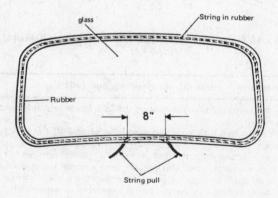

Fig. 12.24 Windscreen fitting cord (Sec 20)

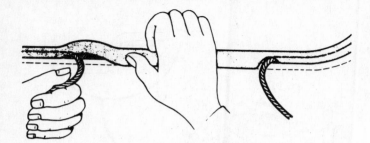

Fig. 12.25 Engaging lip of windscreen surround (Sec 20)

11 Now place a length of strong cord in the body-flange groove of the rubber surround so that the ends of the cord overlap at the centre of the base of the screen.

12 With the help of an assistant offer the lower edge of the screen rubber surround onto the body-flange. With your assistant applying firm pressure to the outside of the glass, pull the cord ends equally to bring the lip of the rubber surround over the body-flange.

13 Refit the wiper arms and blades and the interior mirror. On later models, the interior mirror is bonded to the screen, refer to Section 30.

21 Tailgate glass – removal and refitting

The operations are similar to those described in the preceding Section. Disconnect the electrical leads from the heater element.

22 Rear quarter windows – removal and refitting

1 Removal of the glass from the fixed type of window is carried out as described for the windscreen and refitting follows the same procedure.

2 From 1977 certain models have opening rear quarter windows.

3 The window catches and hinges are secured with screws which locate in weld nuts.

4 Once the screws are removed, the quarter window can be withdrawn.

23 Side protective panels – removal and refitting

1 The side protective panels fitted to some models are held at the top by spring clips engaging with welded rivets and by screws along the bottom.

2 To remove a panel, extract the screws and then slide the panel upwards off the clips. Take care not to scratch the paintwork by pushing a sheet of thin card down behind the protective panel before moving it upwards.

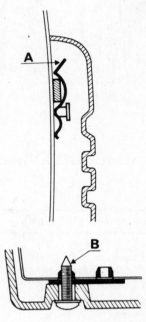

Fig. 12.27 Side protective panel fixings (Sec 23)

  A   *Spring clip*   B   *Base screws*

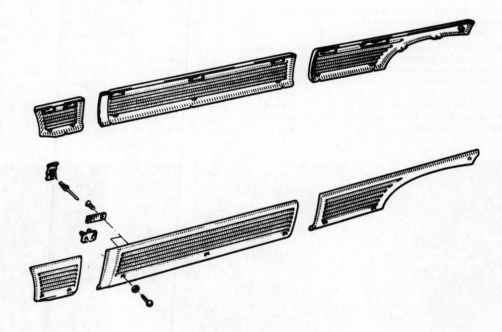

Fig. 12.26 Side protective panels (Sec 23)

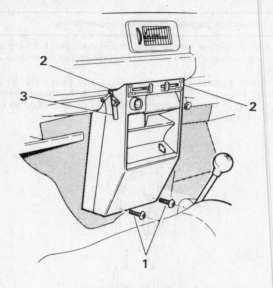

Fig. 12.28 Centre console (Sec 24)

1   *Base screws*   3   *Heater control*
2   *Upper screws*

---

24   Centre console – removal and refitting

Models up to 1980
1   Remove the two screws from the lower front edge of the console.
2   Remove the bolts which are located between the heater control panel and the facia panel. A 7.0 mm box spanner is the best tool for this job.
3   Ease the console away until the control cables and their clips can be disconnected. Withdraw the console.
4   Refitting is a reversal of removal. Set the heater control cables by means of their positioning clips to give complete movement of the valve and control flaps with just a little free movement.

Models 1980 on
5   The centre console on later models is part of the facia panel, refer to Section 28 for removal and refitting operations.

---

25   Front seat – removal and refitting

1   Move the seat to its fully forward position and then unscrew and remove the mounting screws at the rear of the frame (photo).
2   Move the seat fully to the rear and unscrew the front screws.
3   Refit by reversing the removal operations, but seal the spacer to the floorpan to prevent water seeping into the car interior.

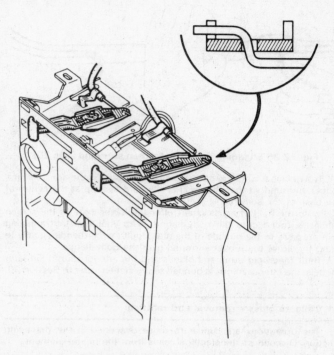

Fig. 12.29 Heater control cable clips (Sec 24)

---

26   Rear seat – removal and refitting

Bench type
1   Grip the rear edge of the seat cushion and pull it forwards. This will expose the pivots (photo).
2   Prise off the star locking washers from the pivots and remove the cushion.
3   Release the seat back levers and push the seat back forwards.
4   Remove the pivot bolts at each side of the base of the seat back (photo) and remove it.
5   Refitting is a reversal of removal, use new star locking washers, driving them into position using a piece of tubing.

Split type
6   A split type rear seat is used on some later models, including the Gordini versions. One or both seats may be folded forward to increase the luggage carrying area.
7   The spare wheel on these models is located under one of the two luggage compartment floor lids.
8   The removal procedure is similar to that for the bench type seat.

25.1 Removing front seat slide screw

26.1 Rear seat cushion pivot

26.4 Rear seat back pivot bolts

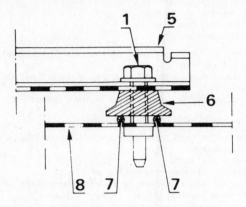

Fig. 12.30 Front seat spacer (Sec 25)

1	Bolt	7	Seal
5	Seat slide	8	Floorpan
6	Spacer		

Fig. 12.31 Lifting cover from spare wheel compartment – Gordini models (Sec 26)

27 Parcel shelf – removal and refitting

Facia shelf

1   Removal of the left-hand or right-hand parcel shelf is identical.

2   First remove the plastic kick-strips from the appropriate side.

3   Refer to Fig. 12.32 and remove the screws (C) or (F) which hold the parcel tray side panel to the body pillar.

4   Remove the screws (A) or (D) which secure the upper edge of the parcel tray to the facia panel.

5   Remove the bolt (B) which holds the base of the parcel tray to the bulkhead bracket.

6   Remove the parcel shelf.

7   Refitting is a reversal of removal.

Rear luggage compartment shelf

8   Refer to Fig. 12.33. The shelf is removed or refitted by disengaging or engaging the stud (3) with the shelf notch while the seat back is inclined slightly forward.

9   When the seat is pulled back to lock it, the shelf locks automatically.

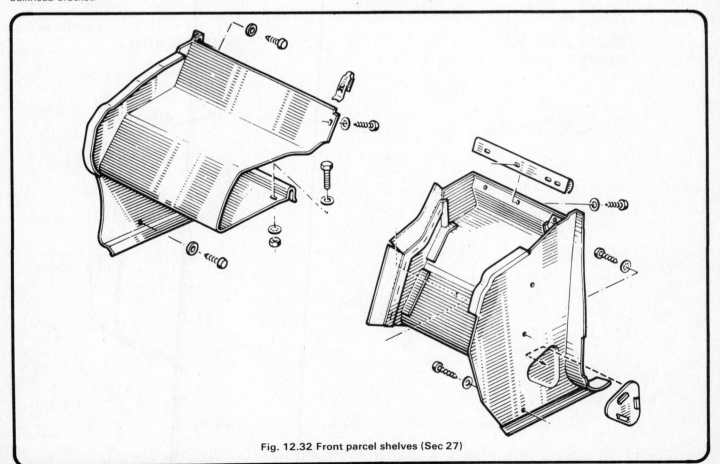

Fig. 12.32 Front parcel shelves (Sec 27)

Fig. 12.33 Rear parcel shelf and locating stud (3) (Sec 27)

28 Facia panel – removal and refitting

Models up to 1980

1   On models with an independently removable centre console, only the facia panel trim can be removed, the main facia assembly being a welded fixture.
2   Before the trim can be removed, the following items must be withdrawn:

Windscreen (see Section 20)
Instrument panel (Chapter 10)
Side trim panels

Parcel tray top mountings
Fresh air entry flap brackets
Air distribution brackets

3   Refer to Fig. 12.34 and prise off the clip (A) and peel away the lower edge of the trim.
4   Raise the trim and ease it forward so that the bead (C) clears the welded flange (B).
5   Fit the new trim by reversing the removal operations.

Models 1980 on

6   To remove the facia panel from these later models, carry out the following operations:
7   Disconnect the battery.
8   Remove the steering wheel (Chapter 11).
9   Remove the lower section of the steering column shroud after turning the twist clip (Fig. 12.35) through a quarter turn.
10   Remove the instrument panel, as described in Chapter 10.
11   Compress the retaining tab and withdraw the air duct.
12   Withdraw the heater control panel which is retained by clips.
13   Disconnect the electrical leads which run to the cigar lighter and panel lamps.
14   Disconnect and remove the radio, as described in Chapter 10.
15   Unscrew the facia panel retaining nut.
16   Release the clips from the lower edge of the facia panel.
17   Swivel the facia panel upwards to free it from the retainers and then remove it from the car.
18   Refitting is a reversal of removal.

29 Seat belts

1   Static type seat belts are fitted to models built before 1977. Inertia reel type seat belts are fitted after that date (photos).
2   On later models, anchorage points are incorporated for rear seat belts and on some models the belts are fitted as standard equipment.

CROSS SECTION
CENTRE

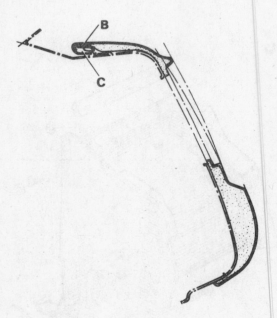

CROSS SECTION
SIDE

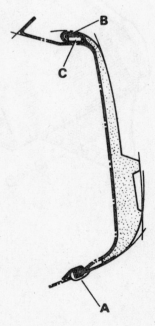

Fig. 12.34 Sectional views of facia panel trim (models up to 1980) (Sec 28)

A   Clip   B   Welded flange   C   Bead

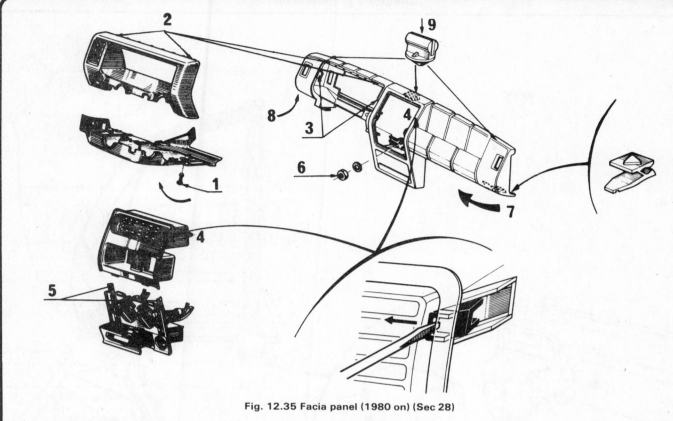

Fig. 12.35 Facia panel (1980 on) (Sec 28)

1	Twist clip	4	Air duct fixing tab	7	Clip
2	Fixing tabs	5	Control panel clips	8	Clip location
3	Fixing tabs	6	Facia panel retaining nut	9	Retainers

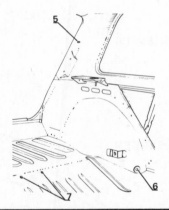

Fig. 12.36 Rear seat belt anchorage points (5 to 7) (Sec 29)

29.1a Seat belt stalk

29.1b Seat belt upper anchorage

29.1c Seat belt lower anchorage and slide

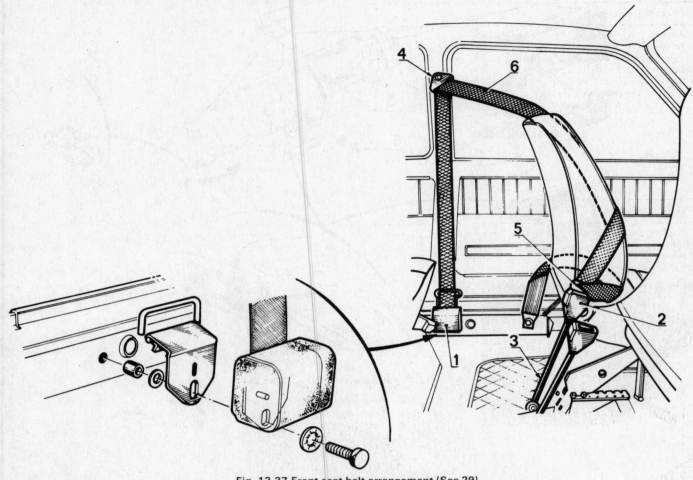

Fig. 12.37 Front seat belt arrangement (Sec 29)

1	*Inertia reel (retractor)*	3	*Centre stalk*
2	*Buckle*	4	*Pillar mounting*

5	*Clip*
6	*Strap*

3   On North American Le Car models a seat belt warning system is fitted which illuminates a warning lamp and sounds a buzzer if the front seat belts are not connected when the engine is running.
4   The seat belts should be cleaned using warm water and detergent only. Never attempt to alter the anchorage points or sequence of fitting of the fixing bolts, spacers and washers.
5   If the belts show any sign of fraying they must be renewed.

30 Interior rear view mirror (bonded type) – fitting

1   If the windscreen is changed on models which have a bonded type interior mirror then a new mirror base must be bonded to the new screen.
2   Mark the position for the mirror so that it is central and 36.0 mm (1.4 in) from the edge of the rubber surround. Masking tape is useful to mark the glass.
3   Clean the glass with methylated spirit.
4   Obtain a suitable bonding agent to fix the mirror to the windscreen. Be sure to follow the instructions carefully. Typically such a bonding agent consists of an adhesive and an activator. Each is applied in a thin layer as directed, and quickly forms a strong bond between the mirror base and the windscreen. Do not attach the mirror head until the bonding process is complete – typically in the order of ten minutes.

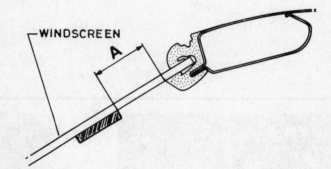

Fig. 12.38 Bonded interior mirror locating diagram (Sec 30)

A = 36.0 mm (1.4 in)

31 Front seat headrests

1   The headrest is adjustable for height simply by sliding it up or down.
2   To remove a headrest, turn the collar (Fig. 12.39) through one quarter turn.

32 Sunroof – operation

1   A folding type of sunroof is available on all models as an option.
2   To open the sunroof, disengage the rubber retainers (Fig. 12.40) at the side and pull-down on the release handle then disengage the handle from the securing latch.
3   Raise the roof covering and fold it towards the rear. Retain the cover pivot rods using the two straps (Fig. 12.41).
4   To close the roof, reverse the operations just described.

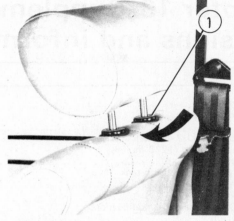

Fig. 12.39 Front seat head rest (Sec 31)

1   Collar

33 Grab handles

1   These handles are secured just above the doors by self-tapping screws.
2   Access to the screws is obtained by prising up the end covers with a small screwdriver (photo).

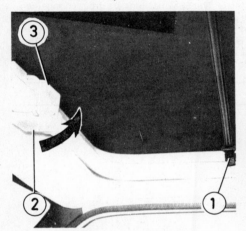

Fig. 12.40 Sunroof controls (Sec 32)

1   Rubber retainer
2   Release handle
3   Securing latch

Fig. 12.41 Sunroof folded open (Sec 32)

4   Retaining straps

33.2 Interior grab handle

Chapter 13 Supplement:
Revisions and information on later models

Contents

1 Introduction

This Supplement contains information which is additional to, or a revision of, material in the first twelve Chapters. Although most of the material relates to 1984 and later models, some items apply retrospectively to all models.

The Sections in the Supplement follow the same order as the Chapters to which they relate. The Specifications are grouped together for convenience and are in Chapter order, too.

It is recommended that before any particular operation is undertaken, reference is made to the appropriate Section of the Supplement. In this way, any changes to procedure or components can be noted before referring to the main Chapters.

2 Specifications

Engine
Oil filter

956 cc from November 1984, and all other engines from July 1984 ..	Champion F101

Fuel system
Carburettor – Solex 32 DIS

Mark	806
Float level	36.5 mm (1.44 in)
Initial throttle opening	0.75 mm (0.03 in)
Idle speed	625 to 675 rpm
CO percentage in exhaust gas at idle speed	1.5 to 2.5

Carburettor – Weber 32 DIR

	Primary	Secondary
Mark	107	
Application	122B with C6J 7-50 engine	
Settings:		
Choke tube	23	24
Main jet	117	135
Air compensating jet	175	190
Idle jet	47	–
Mixture centraliser	4R	4R
Emulsion tube	F50	F24
Fuel inlet valve	1.75	
Fuel level	7.0 mm (0.28 in)	
Accelerator pump	60	
Throttle part open setting (mechanical)	8.5 mm (0.33 in)	
Throttle part open setting (vacuum)	6.0 mm (0.24 in)	
Initial throttle valve plate opening	1.00	
Throttle valve plate angle	12°30′ (5.32 mm/0.21 in)	
Idle speed	900 to 1000 rpm	
CO percentage at idle	0.5 to 1.5	

Garrett turbocharger

Application	Model 122B
Wastegate opening pressure on full load:	
At 6000 rpm	390 to 450 mbar
Static opening pressure	555 to 615 mbar

Air cleaner element

956 cc engine models from November 1984	Champion W191

Ignition system
Ignition cut-out switch activating pressure
122B models .... 0.65 to 0.75 bar (9.4 to 10.9 lbf/in²)

AEI (Renix)
Application .... 122B models
Initial advance setting (at idle):
   Advance curve no:
      RE 009 .... 13 to 15°
      RE 036 .... 12 to 14°
      RE 046 .... 12 to 14°

Manual transmission (type NG5)
Refer also to Specifications Section in Chapter 6

Synchromesh type
1st/2nd .... Renault
3rd, 4th, 5th .... Borg Warner

Differential/final drive
Crownwheel-to-pinion backlash .... 0.12 to 0.25 mm (0.005 to 0.010 in)
Bearing preload (turning force):
   Used .... No preload, no end play
   New .... 9 to 29 Nm (6 to 21 lbf ft)

Torque wrench settings

	Nm	lbf ft
Reverse lever pivot bolt	24	18
Half casing bolts	24	18
Primary shaft nut	128	94
Secondary shaft worm nut	109	80
Crownwheel bolts	98	72
Clutch housing bolts:		
8.0 mm	24	18
10.0 mm	35	26
Differential ring nut lockbolt	24	18

Braking system
Rear disc brakes
Application .... Gordini Turbo (122B)
Disc diameter .... 227.8 mm (8.97 in)
Caliper piston diameter .... 36.1 mm (1.42 in)

---

3   Engine

Rocker cover (C6J-7 engine)
1   Whenever the rocker cover is disturbed, fit a new gasket.

Engine modification (122B models)
2   Commencing 1984, Gordini Turbo models are fitted with a type C6J7-50 engine using a Weber 32 DIR carburettor and Garrett T3 turbocharger.
3   Although the engine is essentially as described for the type C6J-7-26 in Chapter 1, refer to the Specifications Section in this Supplement and also to the Ignition and Fuel Sections which follow.

---

4   Cooling system

Modified coolant expansion tank
1   As from 1984, a 'hot' type expansion tank may be fitted which has a continuous flow of coolant through it.
2   The filling and bleeding procedures for the cooling system with this type of tank are as for other systems, as described in Chapter 2.

---

5   Fuel system

Anti-pinking device
1   On Gordini Turbo models built after May 1983, an ignition advance corrector is fitted which operates during acceleration.

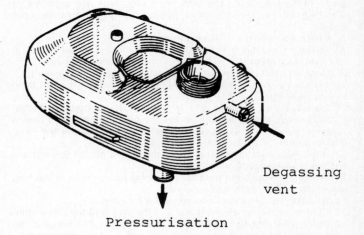

Fig. 13.1 'Hot' type expansion tank (Sec 4)

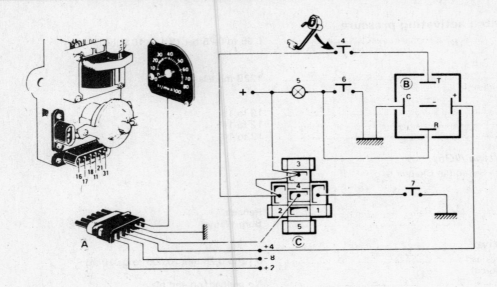

Fig. 13.2 Anti-pinking device circuit (Sec 5)

4   Throttle spindle switch
5   Choke 'ON' warning lamp
6   Choke 'ON' warning lamp switch
7   Ignition cut-off switch
11 Feed (+)

16 Advance terminal (+2°)
17 Retard terminal (−8°)
18 Advance terminal (+4°)
21 Earth

31 Rev counter
A   Module connector
B   Relay timer connector
C   Ignition cut-out relay connector

2   A switch is fitted to the carburettor which is controlled by the 1st barrel throttle spindle.

3   A relay timer under the air cleaner is activated to prevent earthing of the advance correction leads from the module for a period of 1.3 seconds.

4   The leads from terminals (16, 17 and 18) in Fig. 13.2 when earthed, correct the ignition advance by 2° advance, 8° retard and 4° advance.

5   On later models, terminal (18) is connected to the (T) terminal on the relay timer (B). The 4° advance applied to this terminal is eliminated automatically for a 1.3 second period when switch (4) is activated.

6   If pinking occurs during acceleration, check that the correct fuel grade (4-star) is being used, the spark plug type and gaps are as specified and that the vacuum capsule on the ignition module is not leaking.

7   Check also that the TDC sensor is not faulty.

8   To further investigate the problem, check that the advance is 18° at idle then disconnect the +4° terminal on connector (A).

9   Connect a test lamp between terminal +4 on (A) and battery (+).

10 Make sure that the choke knob is pushed fully in. The test lamp should illuminate.

11 Switch on the ignition and then open the carburettor throttle butterfly valves slowly. As soon as the secondary throttle valve begins to open, the switch (4) should activate the relay and the test lamp should go out for a period of 1.3 seconds.

12 If the lamp does not go out, check the switch (4), all connections and the choke warning lamp bulb.

13 Where it is found that the test lamp lights up too soon or too late, adjust the switch in the following way.

14 Remove the carburettor and take off the switch.

15 Cut the switch locating peg and refit the switch to the carburettor.

16 Insert a 6.0 mm (0.24 in) diameter rod or twist drill between the edge of the secondary throttle valve plate and the carburettor body.

17 Connect a test lamp and battery circuit between the switch leads then slowly move the throttle control rod.

18 As soon as the rod is free, the test lamp should light up. If this does not happen, adjust the position of the switch in its slots and if necessary bend the arm (1) Fig. 13.3. Make sure that the switch arm does not pass behind the lug on the carburettor which could cause the throttle to jam.

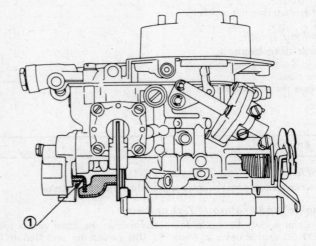

Fig. 13.3 Throttle spindle switch arm (1) and spindle lug (Sec 5)

Garrett T3 turbocharger – modified type

19 This is used in conjunction with a Weber carburettor on later Gordini Turbo models.

20 Pressure generated by the turbine (1) – Fig. 13.4 – is controlled by the wastegate valve (2). Wastegate operation is subject to both the pressure generated and the vacuum pressure at the carburettor base.

21 Simple maintenance is within the scope of the home mechanic, refer also to Chapter 3, Section 19.

22 Periodically, clean any dirt from the passages in the bleed tee union.

23 It is also important to keep the crankcase ventilation system in good condition. Check that the system hoses are clean and tight, and the calibrated jet is clean and of the correct size.

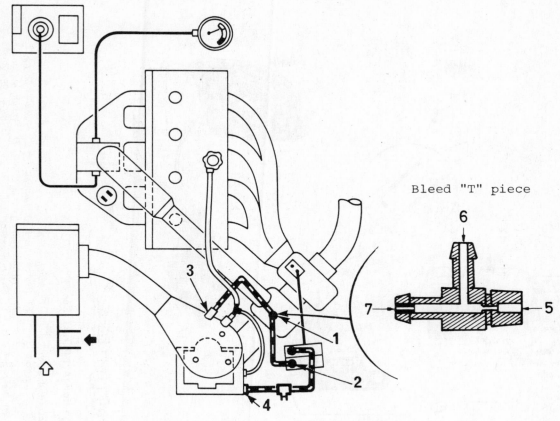

Fig. 13.4 Turbocharger layout (1984 on) (Sec 5)

1 Tee piece   3 Carburettor inlet   5 Governing pressure   7 Partial pressure from turbine
2 Wastegate valve   4 Carburettor base   6 Calibrating pressure

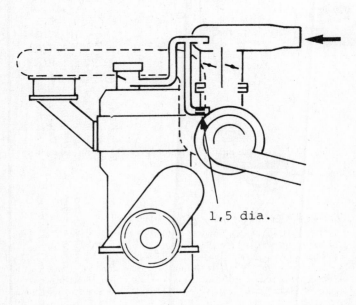

**Fig. 13.5 Location of crankcase vent calibrated jet
(Sec 5)**

6 Ignition system

Ignition cut-out

1 Commencing with 1984 Gordini Turbo (122B) models, an ignition cut-out device is fitted to prevent over-revving by limiting engine speed to 6400 rpm.
2 It is possible for misfiring to occur at maximum revs, this should be ignored.

Integral electronic ignition (AEI – Renix)

Description

3 Later 122B models are equipped with this type of ignition system in which the main functions of the distributor are replaced by a computer module.
4 The system consists of three main components, namely the computer module which incorporates an ignition coil and a vacuum advance unit, the distributor which directs the HT voltage received from the coil to the appropriate spark plug, and an angular position sensor which determines the position and speed of the crankshaft by sensing special magnetic segments in the flywheel.
5 The computer module receives information on crankshaft position relative to TDC and BDC and also engine speed from the angular

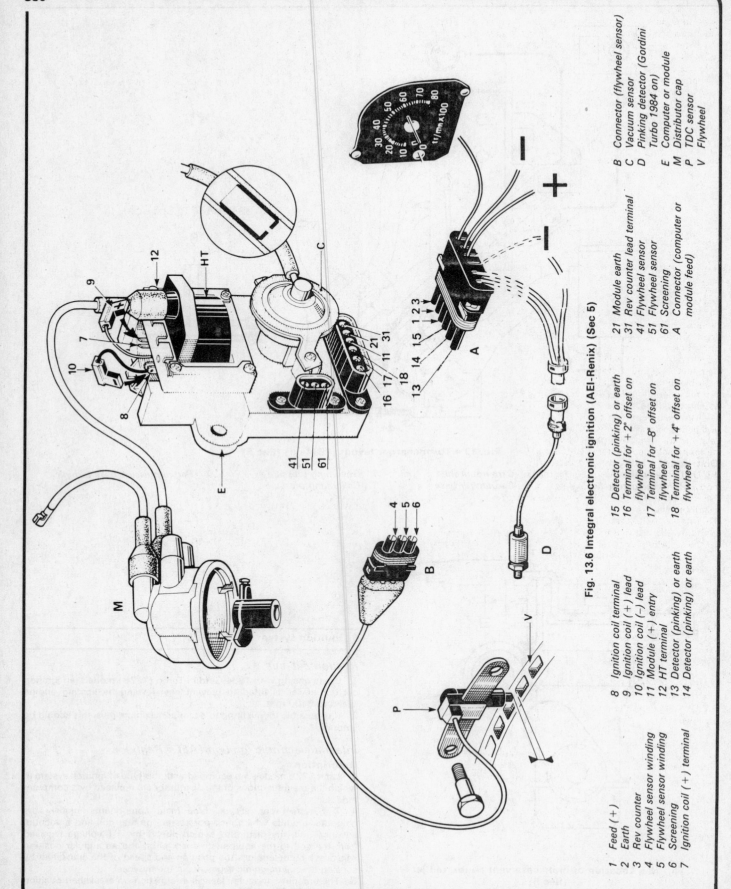

Fig. 13.6 Integral electronic ignition (AEI-Renix) (Sec 5)

1 Feed (+)
2 Earth
3 Rev counter
4 Flywheel sensor winding
5 Flywheel sensor winding
6 Screening
7 Ignition coil (+) terminal

8 Ignition coil terminal
9 Ignition coil (+) lead
10 Ignition coil (−) lead
11 Module (+) entry
12 HT terminal
13 Detector (pinking) or earth
14 Detector (pinking) or earth

15 Detector (pinking) or earth
16 Terminal for +2° offset on flywheel
17 Terminal for −8° offset on flywheel
18 Terminal for +4° offset on flywheel

21 Module earth
31 Rev counter lead terminal
41 Flywheel sensor
51 Flywheel sensor
61 Screening
A Connector (computer or module feed)

B Connector (flywheel sensor)
C Vacuum sensor
D Pinking detector (Gordini Turbo 1984 on)
E Computer or module
M Distributor cap
P TDC sensor
V Flywheel

position sensor, and receives information on engine load from the vacuum advance unit. From these constantly changing variables, the computer calculates the precise instant at which HT voltage should be supplied and triggers the coil accordingly. The voltage then passes from the coil to the appropriate spark plug, via the distributor in the conventional way. The function of the centrifugal and vacuum advance mechanisms as well as the contact breaker points normally associated with a distributor, are all catered for by the computer module, so that the sole purpose of the distributor is to direct the HT voltage from the coil to the appropriate spark plug.

AEI ignition system – precautions
Due to the sophisticated nature of the electronic ignition system the following precautions must be observed to prevent damage to the components and reduce the risk of personal injury.

6   Ensure that the ignition is switched off before disconnecting any of the ignition wiring.

7   Ensure that the ignition is switched off before connecting or disconnecting any ignition test equipment such as a timing light.

8   Do not connect a suppression condenser or test lamp to the ignition coil negative terminal.

9   Do not connect any test appliance or stroboscopic timing light requiring a 12 volt supply to the ignition coil positive terminal.

10 Do not allow an HT lead to short out or spark against the computer module body.

Maintenance
11 The only components of the electronic ignition system which require periodic maintenance are the distributor cap, HT leads and spark plugs. These should be treated in the same way as on a conventional system and reference should be made to Chapter 4.

12 On this system dwell angle and ignition timing are a function of the computer module and there is no provision for adjustment. It is possible to check the ignition timing using a stroboscopic timing light, but this should only be necessary as part of a fault finding procedure, as any deviation from the specified setting would indicate a possible fault in the computer module.If it is necessary to check the timing, it will be noted that the initial advance figures given in the Specifications relate to the serial number of the computer module. This number will be found stamped on a label attached to the side of the module body.

Distributor – removal and refitting
13 Undo the two screws securing the distributor cap to the distributor body, lift off the cap and move it to one side (photo).

14 Release the engine wiring harness from the clip at the base of the distributor.

15 Undo the bolt securing the distributor to the cylinder block, withdraw the distributor from its location and recover the seal (photo).

16 To refit the distributor, place it in position in the cylinder block and turn the rotor arm until the drive dog at the base of the distributor shaft positively engages with the driveshaft.

17 Align the hole at the base of the distributor with that in the block and refit the retaining bolt.

18 Refit the distributor cap and locate the wiring harness in the clip.

Computer module – removal and refitting
19 Disconnect the battery negative terminal.

20 Disconnect the HT lead from the ignition coil on the front of the module.

21 Detach the vacuum pipe from the vacuum advance unit and release the pipe from its support clip.

22 Disconnect the two multi-plug wiring connectors from the front of the module (photo).

23 Undo the two nuts securing the unit to the engine compartment bulkhead or inner wing panel and remove it from the car.

24 If required, the ignition coil may be removed after disconnecting the two wires and undoing the four retaining screws. Do not, however, attempt to remove the vacuum unit, as it is attached internally by a very fine wire which will break if the unit is removed.

25 Refitting the ignition coil to the module, and the module to the car is the reverse sequence to removal.

TDC sensor – removal and refitting
26 Disconnect the battery negative terminal.

27 Disconnect the smaller of the two wiring multi-plugs from the front of the computer module.

28 Undo and remove the two bolts securing the sensor to the top of the clutch bellhousing and lift off the unit. Note that the two retaining bolts are of the shouldered type and must not be replaced with ordinary bolts.

29 Refitting is the reverse sequence to removal.

6.13 Removing distributor cap

6.15 Distributor fixing bolt location (arrowed)

6.22 Ignition module connections
A   HT lead at ignition coil   C   Multi-plug connectors
B   Vacuum pipe   D   Module fixing nuts

Fault diagnosis – AEI system

Problems associated with the electronic ignition system can usually be grouped into one of two areas, those caused by the more conventional HT side of the system, such as the spark plugs, HT leads, rotor arm and distributor cap, and those caused by the LT circuitry including the computer module and its related components. For these tests a good quality 0 to 12 volt voltmeter and an ohmmeter will be required.

Engine fails to start
Note: *The figures and numbers shown in brackets refer to the multi-plug connectors and terminal locations shown in Fig. 13.6.*

Test conditions	Test	Remedy
1 Connector (A) disconnected, ignition switched on, starter cranking	Is the voltage between pin (1) in connector (A) and earth at least 9.5 volts?	Yes: Proceed to next test No: Check battery condition, check feed wire to connector (A)
2 Connector (A) disconnected, ignition switched off	Is the resistance between pin (2) in connector (A) and earth 0 ohms?	Yes: Proceed to next test No: Check module earth wire to connector (A)
3 Connector (A) disconnected, ignition switched off	Is the resistance between module pin (11) and coil feed wire (9) 0 ohms?	Yes: Proceed to next test No: Renew the computer module
4 Connector (A) plugged in, ignition switched on	Is the voltage between coil terminal (7) and earth at least 9.5 volts?	Yes: Proceed to next test No: Move connector (A) in and out, if still incorrect, renew connector
5 Connector (B) disconnected, ignition switched off	Is the resistance betweens pins (4) and (5) in connector (B) 100 to 200 ohms	Yes: Proceed to next test No: Renew the angular position sensor
6 Connector (B) disconnected, ignition switched off	Does the ohmmeter read infinity when connected between pins (4) and (6) and also between pins (5) and (6) of connector (B)	Yes: Proceed to next test No: Renew the angular position sensor
7 Connector (B) disconnected, ignition switched off	Is the distance between the angular position sensor and the flywheel 0.5 to 1.5 mm (0.02 to 0.06 in)	Yes: Proceed to next test No: Renew the angular position sensor
8 Connectors (A) and (B) plugged in, wires (9) and (10) disconnected, starter cranking	Does a test bulb connected between wires (9) and (10) flash at starter motor speed?	Yes: Proceed to next test No: Renew the computer module
9 Ignition coil HT lead disconnected, ignition switched off	Is the resistance between coil terminals (7) and (12) 2500 to 5500 ohms?	Yes: Proceed to next test No: Renew the ignition coil
10 Wires (9) and (10) disconnected, ignition switched off	Is the resistance between coil terminals (7) and (8) 0.4 to 0.8 ohms?	Yes: Proceed to next test No: Renew the ignition coil
11 Connector (A) disconnected, ignition switched off	Is the resistance between pins (2) and (3) of connector (A) greater than 20 000 ohms?	Yes: Renew computer module No: Repair wiring or renew tachometer

Engine is difficult to start, but performs satisfactorily once running

Test conditions	Test	Remedy
1 Disconnect HT lead from centre of distributor cap, hold lead 5 mm away from the cylinder block	Is there a rapid succession of blue sparks between the end of the lead and the cylinder block with the engine cranking?	Yes: Proceed to next test No: Carry out the test procedure under 'Engine fails to start' earlier in this Section
2 Stroboscopic timing light connected to No 1 cylinder, engine idling, vacuum pipe disconnected	Is the ignition timing in accordance with the specified setting?	Yes: Check carburetion and engine mechanical condition No: Renew the computer module

Engine performance unsatisfactory

Test conditions	Test	Remedy
1 Run engine at a steady 3000 rpm, disconnect vacuum pipe at computer module	Does the engine speed drop as the vacuum pipe is disconnected?	Yes: Carry out the previous tests under 'Engine difficult to start' No: Renew the computer module

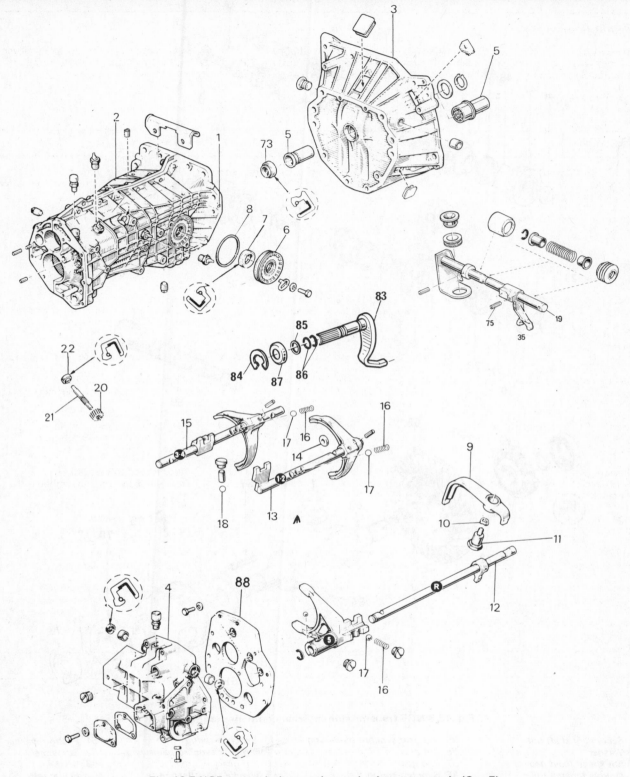

Fig. 13.7 NG5 transmission, casing and selector controls (Sec 7)

1 Half casing (RH)	8 O-ring	15 3rd/4th selector shaft/fork	22 Oil seal
2 Half casing (LH)	9 Reverse lever	16 Detent spring	75 Roll pin
3 Clutch bellhousing	10 Wave washer	17 Detent ball	83 Control shaft
4 Rear casing	11 Reverse lever bolt	18 Interlocking ball	84 Circlip
5 Release bearing guide tube	12 Reverse selector shaft	19 Selector input shaft	85 Shim
6 Differential ring nut	13 1st/2nd selector shaft/fork	20 Speedo drivegear	86 O-ring
7 Oil seal	14 Interlocking disc	21 Speedo pinion shaft	87 Plastic clip
			88 Spacer plate

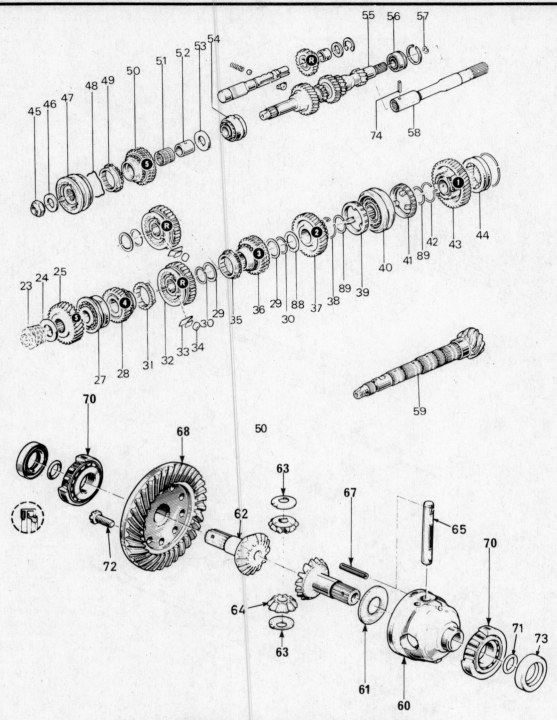

Fig. 13.8 NG5 transmission internal components (Sec 7)

23 Secondary shaft nut	35 3rd gear synchro baulk ring	48 Synchro spring	61 Friction washer
24 Washer	36 3rd gear	49 5th gear synchro baulk ring	62 Sunwheel
25 5th speed fixed gear	37 2nd gear	50 5th gear	63 Washer
27 Double tapered roller bearing	38 Synchro spring	51 Needle roller bearing	64 Planet wheel
28 4th speed idler gear	39 2nd gear synchro baulk ring	52 Bush	65 Shaft
29 Splined washer	40 1st/2nd synchro	53 Washer	67 Roll pin
30 Circlip	41 1st gear synchro baulk ring	54 Double roller ball-bearing	68 Crownwheel
31 4th gear synchro baulk ring	42 Synchro spring	55 Primary shaft	70 Bearing
32 3rd/4th synchro with reverse gear	43 1st gear	56 Roller bearing	71 O-ring
33 Spring	44 Roller bearing	57 Washer	72 Crownwheel bolt
34 Roller cage	45 Primary shaft nut	58 Clutch shaft	73 Oil seal
	46 Washer	59 Secondary shaft	74 Roll pin
	47 5th gear synchro	60 Differential case	88 Splined washer
			89 Circlip

7 Manual transmission (type NG5)

Transmission – dismantling

Casings

1 With the transmission removed from the car (see Chapter 6), clean away external dirt and then drain the oil.

2 Remove the clutch release components from inside the bellhousing (photo).

3 Unbolt the bellhousing and remove it from the transmission casing (photos).

4 Select neutral and then remove the plug (B) – Fig. 13.9. Extract 5th gear detent spring and ball.

5 Remove plug (C) and extract the plunger and interlocking ball which serves 3rd/4th and 5th gear shafts.

6 Unbolt and remove the rear casing, retrieve the 5th gear selector fork ball.

7 Select two gears simultaneously by moving two synchro sleeves. With the gearshafts locked up, relieve any staking and unscrew the nuts (23) and (45) – Fig. 13.10.

8 Use a C-spanner to release the worm nut (23).

9 Extract the circlip (D) from the end of the reverse shaft.

10 Withdraw 5th gear synchro and selector fork as an assembly from the primary shaft.

11 Remove 5th gear from the secondary shaft. A puller may be required for this.

12 Remove 5th gear from the primary shaft.

13 Remove the spacer plate, noting which side is towards the gear casing.

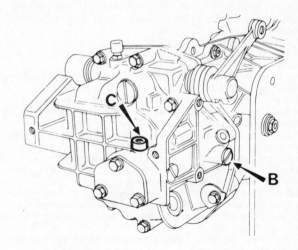

Fig. 13.9 Rear casing plugs (Sec 7)

B 5th gear detent
C 3rd/4th and 5th interlock

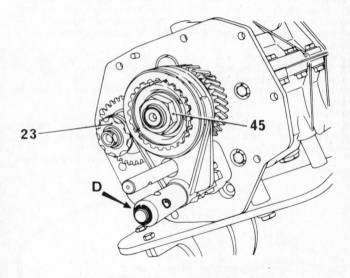

Fig. 13.10 Rear casing removed (Sec 7)

23 Worm nut   D Circlip
45 Nut

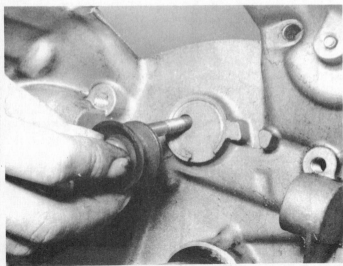

7.2 Clutch release arm pivot bolt

7.3A Clutch bellhousing interior fixing bolts

7.3B Clutch bellhousing exterior fixing bolts

7.3C Removing the clutch bellhousing

14 Mark the half casing connecting bolt heads so that they can be returned to their original positions. Unscrew and remove the bolts.

15 Separate the casing half sections.

16 Lift out the differential/final drive.

17 Lift out the primary and secondary geartrains.

Secondary shaft – overhaul

18 Grip the shaft vertically, by means of 1st gear, in the jaws of a vice fitted with jaw protectors.

19 The components can now be taken from the shaft once the gear circlips have been extracted. Keep the components strictly in their originally fitted sequence and the correct way round.

20 Note that the bearing rollers (44) – Fig. 13.8 – are not retained by an inner track or cage.

21 Inspect all components for wear and renew as necessary. If there has been a history of noisy gearchanging, or if the synchro could be easily 'beaten', renew the synchro assembly.

22 Press each baulk ring onto its gear cone using a twisting motion. It should stick on the cone leaving a good clearance between the ring and the gear teeth. If these conditions are not met, renew the baulk ring.

23 Reassembly of the secondary shaft is a reversal of dismantling, but observe the following points.

24 Use new circlips, taking care not to bend them during fitting.

25 When fitting 1st/2nd synchro, make sure that the longer chamfer on the synchro sleeve is towards the pinion – Fig. 13.12.

26 The synchro-hubs are free turning on the shaft and it may be necessary to turn them in order to find their best free sliding position.

27 When fitting 3rd/4th synchro unit, the hub-to-sleeve relationship varies according to the position of the groove on the shaft. The dimension X or Y will indicate which synchro arrangement is to be used – Fig. 13.13.

Primary shaft – overhaul

28 Drive out the roll pin and separate the clutch shaft from the primary shaft. Remove the small washer.

29 Use a puller to remove the shaft bearings, noting the adjustment shim.

Differential

30 It is rare for the pinion or crownwheel teeth to wear, but if either component has to be renewed, then the other one must be too, as they are matched in production.

31 The differential bearings may be renewed by drawing them from the differential case.

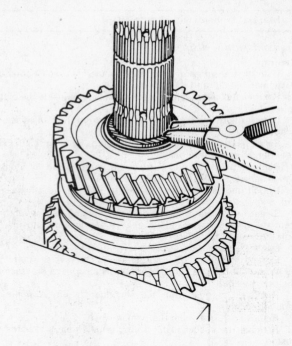

Fig. 13.11 Extracting a gear circlip (Sec 7)

32 The bearing outer tracks can be removed after first having unscrewed the ring nuts. Use a piece of tubing to drive out the tracks from the casings.

33 If new bearings or components have been fitted, then the differential/final drive will have to be adjusted in the following way to achieve the specified backlash and preload.

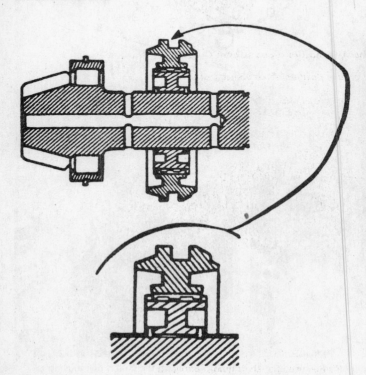

Fig. 13.12 Correctly fitted 1st/2nd synchro (Sec 7)

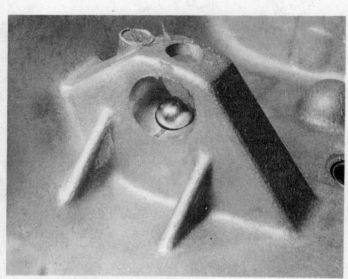

7.37 Reverse idler shaft detent ball

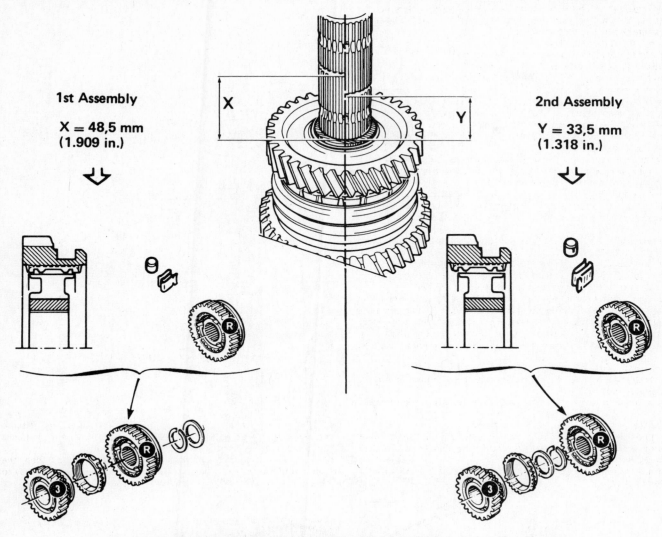

1st Assembly

**X = 48,5 mm
(1.909 in.)**

2nd Assembly

**Y = 33,5 mm
(1.318 in.)**

Fig. 13.13 3rd/4th synchro assembly. Alternative types shown (Sec 7)

Synchro assembly parts identical but shaft groove position determines construction

34 Fit the differential in the casing and tighten the crownwheel bolts to the specified torque. Make sure that the crownwheel is on the correct side, as shown by the bolt heads in Fig. 13.14. Oil seals should not be fitted at this stage.

35 Adjust the bearing preload as described in Chapter 6, Section 15, paragraphs 13 to 19.

Reverse shaft

36 Extract the circlip, then withdraw the shaft, gear, friction washer and guide. Retrieve the ball and spring.

37 To refit the reverse shaft, locate the ball and spring in the left-hand casing (photo). Enter the reverse shaft, fit the gear with its boss towards the differential then the friction washer, bronze side towards the gear.

38 Fit the guide from inside the shaft hole and then push the shaft right home. Fit a new circlip (photo).

Selector mechanism

39 Slide the reverse selector shaft fully home.

40 Drive out the roll pin from the 3rd/4th selector fork, withdraw the shaft and fork. Retrieve the detent ball and spring and the locking disc from between the shafts.

41 Remove the other forks and shafts in the same way.

42 Remove the pivot bolt from the reverse selector lever. Remove the lever and shaft.

7.38 Reverse idler shaft guide (arrowed)

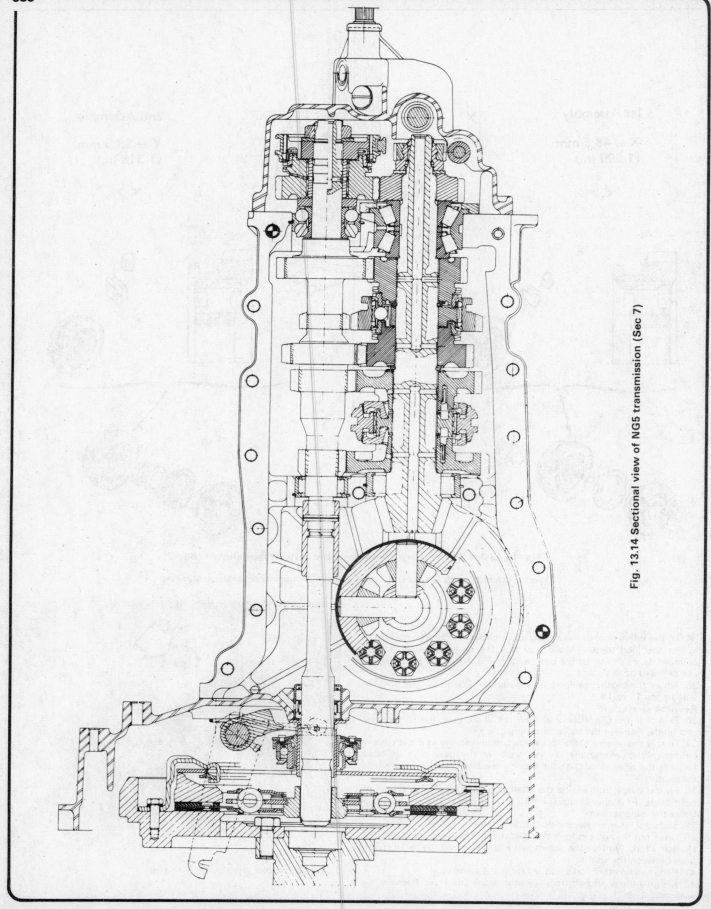

Fig. 13.14 Sectional view of NG5 transmission (Sec 7)

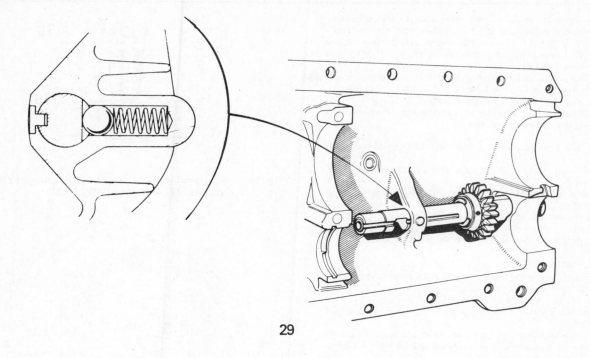

29

Fig. 13.15 Reverse shaft arrangement with detent ball and spring (Sec 7)

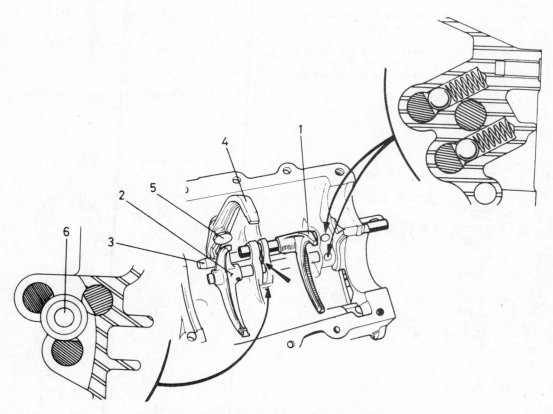

Fig. 13.16 Selector shaft arrangement (Sec 7)

1	3rd/4th selector shaft/fork	3	Reverse selector shaft	5	Reverse selector lever pivot
2	1st/2nd selector shaft/fork	4	Reverse selector lever	6	Locking disc

43 Examine the forks for wear. If they have worn to give excessive clearance in the synchro sleeve grooves then they must be renewed.

44 Reassemble by locating the end of the reverse selector lever in the slot in the shaft. Fit a new pivot pin and tighten to the specified torque, having applied thread locking fluid.

45 Locate 1st/2nd detent ball and spring, hold the fork in position and slide in the shaft. Fix the fork to the selector shaft using a new roll pin. The roll pin slit must be towards the rear casing.

46 Fit 3rd/4th selector shaft and fork in a similar way. Remember to locate the locking disc between the shafts.

Rear casing

47 From inside the casing, drive out the roll pin from the selector finger shaft.

48 Remove the plug, extract the circlip and withdraw the shaft, bushes and spring.

49 The reverse stop plunger and spring may be removed after unscrewing the plug.

50 If necessary remove the speedo drive pinion and gear.

51 Renew all worn components including the oil seals.

52 Reassembly of the rear casing is a reversal of dismantling.

Transmission – reassembly

53 Fit the gear trains and differential into the right-hand half casing.

54 Smear the casing flanges with a suitable non-hardening jointing compound. Fit the left-hand half casing, insert the bolts in their original positions and tighten in the sequence shown to their specified torque (Fig. 13.19).

55 If the differential bearings and ring nuts have not been disturbed then the original backlash and preload settings will be restored once the casings have been bolted together.

56 If new differential/final drive components have been fitted, then adjust the crownwheel and pinion backlash in the following way.

57 Bolt a dial gauge to the transmission casing so that its plunger is at right angles to the flank of one of the teeth as close as possible to the periphery of the crownwheel.

58 Move the crownwheel back and forth with the fingers. The backlash indicated on the gauge should be between 0.12 and 0.25 mm (0.005 and 0.010 in).

59 If the backlash is too small or too great, release the ring nut locktabs and unscrew one nut and tighten the other by the same amount until the correct backlash is established. Tighten the locktab bolts.

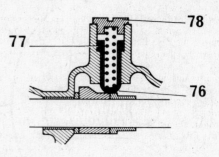

Fig. 13.17 Sectional view of reverse stop plunger (76), spring (77) and plug (78) (Sec 7)

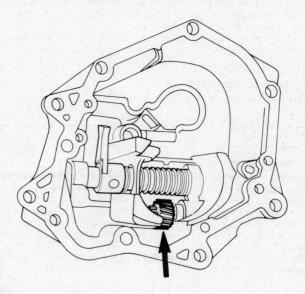

Fig. 13.18 Speedo drive pinion and gear – arrowed (Sec 7)

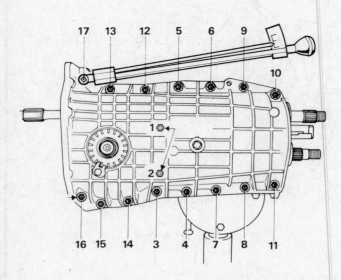

Fig. 13.19 Half casing bolt tightening sequence (Sec 7)

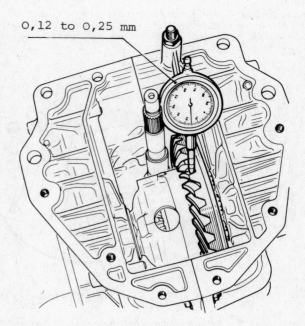

0,12 to 0,25 mm

Fig. 13.20 Checking crownwheel to pinion backlash (Sec 7)

60 Fit the spacer plate, and tighten the bolts.

61 Fit 5th gear to both shafts. Make sure that the secondary shaft 5th gear is fitted the correct way round (boss towards nut), fix it to the shaft with thread locking fluid.

62 Fit 5th gear synchro and selector fork as an assembly.

63 Fit a new circlip to the reverse shaft.

64 Engage 5th and reverse gears simultaneously by moving both synchro sleeves to lock the shafts.

65 Apply thread locking fluid to the shaft threads and screw a new nut onto the primary shaft and the worm nut to the secondary shaft. Tighten to the specified torque, then select neutral.

66 Locate the 5th gear selector fork ball and bolt on the rear casing using a new flange gasket smeared with jointing compound.

67 Fit the detent spring, ball and plug also the plunger, interlocking ball and plug to the rear casing.

68 Use a new paper gasket smeared with jointing compound and bolt on the clutch bellhousing. A new oil seal should have been fitted to the bellhousing; protect its lips from damage by taping the clutch shaft splines as the bellhousing is offered up.

69 Refit the clutch release components after reference to Chapter 5.

70 The transmission should be filled with oil after it has been installed in the car.

Gearchange mechanism

71 Refer to Section 20, Chapter 6.

8 Driveshafts

Driveshaft joints

1 Commencing with 1984 models, flat metal retaining bands are used to retain the driveshaft bellows. In order to remove the bellows, cut the bands through using a pair of side cutters.

2 Dismantling the joint and renewal of the bellows is as described in Chapter 8, but later models now incorporate a shim under the head of the thrust ball to eliminate axial clearance. This shim must be refitted at reassembly.

3 Fit new securing bands to the bellows, clinch the loop in the band to tighten them securely. A pair of pincers will do the job.

9 Electrical system

Battery

1 As from 1984, a 'no-maintenance' type battery is fitted.

2 With this type of battery, simply keep the outside of the casing clean, the leads secure and the terminal posts free from corrosion by smearing them with petroleum jelly.

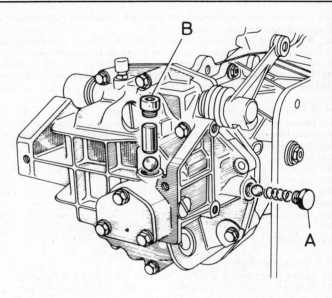

Fig. 13.21 Rear casing detent spring, ball and plug (A) and plunger, ball and plug (B) (Sec 7)

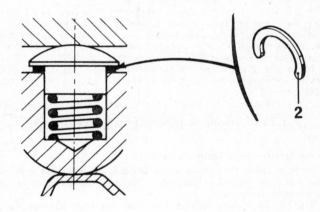

Fig. 13.22 Driveshaft thrust ball shim (2) (Sec 8)

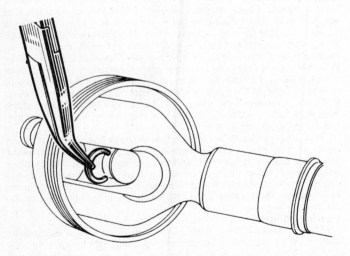

Fig. 13.23 Fitting the thrust ball shim (Sec 8)

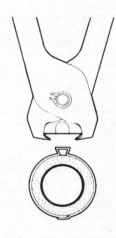

Fig. 13.24 Tightening driveshaft bellows clip (Sec 8)

3   The electrolyte level should be checked occasionally by observing it through the translucent case.

4   A low electrolyte level will indicate a leak in the casing or overcharging, in which case have the charging circuit checked.

5   Should charging be required from an external source, this is carried out in the same way as for a conventional battery; described in Chapter 10, Section 2.

Auxiliary driving lamps

6   On models fitted with a deep front spoiler, the problem of fitting auxiliary lamps has been overcome by special brackets which can be supplied under Part No 77 01 406 359.

Fig. 13.25 Driving lamp mounting bracket (Sec 9)

Radio equipment – later models

7   As from 1984, TS and Automatic models are equipped with an aerial and feeds during production to facilitate the fitting of in-car entertainment equipment.

8   The TX, TX Automatic and Turbo do not have speaker leads installed.

Mobile radio equipment – interference-free installation
Aerials – selection and fitting

The choice of aerials is now very wide. It should be realised that the quality has a profound effect on radio performance, and a poor, inefficient aerial can make suppression difficult.

A wing-mounted aerial is regarded as probably the most efficient for signal collection, but a roof aerial is usually better for suppression purposes because it is away from most interference fields. Stick-on wire aerials are available for attachment to the inside of the windscreen, but are not always free from the interference field of the engine and some accessories.

Motorised automatic aerials rise when the equipment is switched on and retract at switch-off. They require more fitting space and supply leads, and can be a source of trouble.

There is no merit in choosing a very long aerial as, for example, the type about three metres in length which hooks or clips on to the rear of the car, since part of this aerial will inevitably be located in an interference field. For VHF/FM radios the best length of aerial is about one metre. Active aerials have a transistor amplifier mounted at the base and this serves to boost the received signal. The aerial rod is sometimes rather shorter than normal passive types.

A large loss of signal can occur in the aerial feeder cable, especially over the Very High Frequency (VHF) bands. The design of feeder cable is invariably in the co-axial form, ie a centre conductor surrounded by a flexible copper braid forming the outer (earth) conductor. Between the

inner and outer conductors is an insulator material which can be in solid or stranded form. Apart from insulation, its purpose is to maintain the correct spacing and concentricity. Loss of signal occurs in this insulator, the loss usually being greater in a poor quality cable. The quality of cable used is reflected in the price of the aerial with the attached feeder cable.

The capacitance of the feeder should be within the range 65 to 75 picofarads (pF) approximately (95 to 100 pF for Japanese and American equipment), otherwise the adjustment of the car radio aerial trimmer may not be possible. An extension cable is necessary for a long run between aerial and receiver. If this adds capacitance in excess of the above limits, a connector containing a series capacitor will be required, or an extension which is labelled as 'capacity-compensated'.

Fitting the aerial will normally involve making a ⅞ in (22 mm) diameter hole in the bodywork, but read the instructions that come with the aerial kit. Once the hole position has been selected, use a centre punch to guide the drill. Use sticky masking tape around the area for this helps with marking out and drill location, and gives protection to the paintwork should the drill slip. Three methods of making the hole are in use:

(a)   Use a hole saw in the electric drill. This is, in effect, a circular hacksaw blade wrapped round a former with a centre pilot drill.

(b)   Use a tank cutter which also has cutting teeth, but is made to shear the metal by tightening with an Allen key.

(c)   The hard way of drilling out the circle is using a small drill, say ⅛ in (3 mm), so that the holes overlap. The centre metal drops out and the hole is finished with round and half-round files.

Whichever method is used, the burr is removed from the body metal and paint removed from the underside. The aerial is fitted tightly ensuring that the earth fixing, usually a serrated washer, ring or clamp, is making a solid connection. *This earth connection is important in reducing interference.* Cover any bare metal with primer paint and topcoat, and follow by underseal if desired.

Aerial feeder cable routing should avoid the engine compartment and areas where stress might occur, eg under the carpet where feet will be located. Roof aerials require that the headlining be pulled back and that a path is available down the door pillar. It is wise to check with the vehicle dealer whether roof aerial fitting is recommended.

Loudspeakers

Speakers should be matched to the output stage of the equipment, particularly as regards the recommended impedance. Power transistors used for driving speakers are sensitive to the loading placed on them.

Before choosing a mounting position for speakers, check whether the vehicle manufacturer has provided a location for them. Generally door-mounted speakers give good stereophonic reproduction, but not all doors are able to accept them. The next best position is the rear parcel shelf, and in this case speaker apertures can be cut into the shelf, or pod units may be mounted.

For door mounting, first remove the trim, which is often held on by 'poppers' or press studs, and then select a suitable gap in the inside door assembly. Check that the speaker would not obstruct glass or winder mechanism by winding the window up and down. A template is often provided for marking out the trim panel hole, and then the four fixing holes must be drilled through. Mark out with chalk and cut cleanly with a sharp knife or keyhole saw. Speaker leads are then threaded through the door and door pillar, if necessary drilling 10 mm diameter holes. Fit grommets in the holes and connect to the radio or tape unit correctly. Do not omit a waterproofing cover, usually supplied with door speakers. If the speaker has to be fixed into the metal of the door itself, use self-tapping screws, and if the fixing is to the door trim use self-tapping screws and flat spire nuts.

Rear shelf mounting is somewhat simpler but it is necessary to find gaps in the metalwork underneath the parcel shelf. However, remember that the speakers should be as far apart as possible to give a good stereo effect. Pod-mounted speakers can be screwed into position through the parcel shelf material, but it is worth testing for the best position. Sometimes good results are found by reflecting sound off the rear window.

Unit installation

Many vehicles have a dash panel aperture to take a radio/audio unit, a recognised international standard being 189.5 mm x 60 mm. Alternatively a console may be a feature of the car interior design and this, mounted below the dashboard, gives more room. If neither facility is available a unit may be mounted on the underside of the parcel shelf;

these are frequently non-metallic and an earth wire from the case to a good earth point is necessary. A three-sided cover in the form of a cradle is obtainable from car radio dealers and this gives a professional appearance to the installation; in this case choose a position where the controls can be reached by a driver with his seat belt on.

Installation of the radio/audio unit is basically the same in all cases, and consists of offering it into the aperture after removal of the knobs (*not* push buttons) and the trim plate. In some cases a special mounting plate is required to which the unit is attached. It is worthwhile supporting the rear end in cases where sag or strain may occur, and it is usually possible to use a length of perforated metal strip attached between the unit and a good support point nearby. In general it is recommended that tape equipment should be installed at or nearly horizontal.

Connections to the aerial socket are simply by the standard plug terminating the aerial downlead or its extension cable. Speakers for a stereo system must be matched and correctly connected, as outlined previously.

Note: *While all work is carried out on the power side, it is wise to disconnect the battery earth lead.* Before connection is made to the vehicle electrical system, check that the polarity of the unit is correct. Most vehicles use a negative earth system, but radio/audio units often have a reversible plug to convert the set to either + or – earth. *Incorrect connection may cause serious damage.*

The power lead is often permanently connected inside the unit and terminates with one half of an in-line fuse carrier. The other half is fitted with a suitable fuse (3 or 5 amperes) and a wire which should go to a power point in the electrical system. This may be the accessory terminal on the ignition switch, giving the advantage of power feed with ignition or with the ignition key at the 'accessory' position. Power to the unit stops when the ignition key is removed. Alternatively, the lead may be taken to a live point at the fusebox with the consequence of having to remember to switch off at the unit before leaving the vehicle.

Before switching on for initial test, be sure that the speaker connections have been made, for running without load can damage the output transistors. Switch on next and tune through the bands to ensure that all sections are working, and check the tape unit if applicable. The aerial trimmer should be adjusted to give the strongest reception on a weak signal in the medium wave band, at say 200 metres.

Interference

In general, when electric current changes abruptly, unwanted electrical noise is produced. The motor vehicle is filled with electrical devices which change electric current rapidly, the most obvious being the contact breaker.

When the spark plugs operate, the sudden pulse of spark current causes the associated wiring to radiate. Since early radio transmitters used sparks as a basis of operation, it is not surprising that the car radio will pick up ignition spark noise unless steps are taken to reduce it to acceptable levels.

Interference reaches the car radio in two ways:

(a) by conduction through the wiring.
(b) by radiation to the receiving aerial.

Initial checks presuppose that the bonnet is down and fastened, the radio unit has a good earth connection (*not* through the aerial downlead outer), no fluorescent tubes are working near the car, the aerial trimmer has been adjusted, and the vehicle is in a position to receive radio signals, ie not in a metal-clad building.

Switch on the radio and tune it to the middle of the medium wave (MW) band off-station with the volume (gain) control set fairly high. Switch on the ignition (but do not start the engine) and wait to see if irregular clicks or hash noise occurs. Tapping the facia panel may also produce the effects. If so, this will be due to the voltage stabiliser, which is an on-off thermal switch to control instrument voltage. It is located usually on the back of the instrument panel, often attached to the speedometer. Correction is by attachment of a capacitor and, if still troublesome, chokes in the supply wires.

Switch on the engine and listen for interference on the MW band. Depending on the type of interference, the indications are as follows.

A harsh crackle that drops out abruptly at low engine speed or when the headlights are switched on is probably due to a voltage regulator.

A whine varying with engine speed is due to the dynamo or alternator. Try temporarily taking off the fan belt – if the noise goes this

is confirmation.

Regular ticking or crackle that varies in rate with the engine speed is due to the ignition system. With this trouble in particular and others in general, check to see if the noise is entering the receiver from the wiring or by radiation. To do this, pull out the aerial plug, (preferably shorting out the input socket or connecting a 62 pF capacitor across it). If the noise disappears it is coming in through the aerial and is *radiation noise*. If the noise persists it is reaching the receiver through the wiring and is said to be *line-borne*.

Interference from wipers, washers, heater blowers, turn-indicators, stop lamps, etc is usually taken to the receiver by wiring, and simple treatment using capacitors and possibly chokes will solve the problem. Switch on each one in turn (wet the screen first for running wipers!) and listen for possible interference with the aerial plug in place and again when removed.

Electric petrol pumps are now finding application again and give rise to an irregular clicking, often giving a burst of clicks when the ignition is on but the engine has not yet been started. It is also possible to receive whining or crackling from the pump.

Note that if most of the vehicle accessories are found to be creating interference all together, the probability is that poor aerial earthing is to blame.

Component terminal markings

Throughout the following sub-sections reference will be found to various terminal markings. These will vary depending on the manufacturer of the relevant component. If terminal markings differ from those mentioned, reference should be made to the following table, where the most commonly encountered variations are listed.

Alternator	Alternator terminal (thick lead)	Exciting winding terminal
DIN/Bosch	B+	DF
Delco Remy	+	EXC
Ducellier	+	EXC
Ford (US)	+	DF
Lucas	+	F
Marelli	+B	F

Ignition coil	Ignition switch terminal	Contact breaker terminal
DIN/Bosch	15	1
Delco Remy	+	–
Ducellier	BAT	RUP
Ford (US)	B/+	CB/–
Lucas	SW/+	–
Marelli	BAT/+B	D

Voltage regulator	Voltage input terminal	Exciting winding terminal
DIN/Bosch	B+/D+	DF
Delco Remy	BAT/+	EXC
Ducellier	BOB/BAT	EXC
Ford (US)	BAT	DF
Lucas	+/A	F
Marelli		F

Suppression methods – ignition

Suppressed HT cables are supplied as original equipment by manufacturers and will meet regulations as far as interference to neighbouring equipment is concerned. It is illegal to remove such suppression unless an alternative is provided, and this may take the form of resistive spark plug caps in conjunction with plain copper HT cable. For VHF purposes, these and 'in-line' resistors may not be effective, and resistive HT cable is preferred. Check that suppressed cables are actually fitted by observing cable identity lettering, or measuring with an ohmmeter – the value of each plug lead should be 5000 to 10 000 ohms.

A 1 microfarad capacitor connected from the LT supply side of the ignition coil to a good nearby earth point will complete basic ignition interference treatment. *NEVER fit a capacitor to the coil terminal to the contact breaker – the result would be burnt out points in a short time.*

If ignition noise persists despite the treatment above, the following sequence should be followed:

(a) Check the earthing of the ignition coil; remove paint from fixing clamp.

(b) If this does not work, lift the bonnet. Should there be no change in interference level, this may indicate that the bonnet is not electrically connected to the car body. Use a proprietary braided strap across a bonnet hinge ensuring a first class electrical connection. If, however, lifting the bonnet increases the interference, then fit resistive HT cables of a higher ohms-per-metre value.

(c) If all these measures fail, it is probable that re-radiation from metallic components is taking place. Using a braided strap between metallic points, go round the vehicle systematically – try the following: engine to body, exhaust system to body, front suspension to engine and to body, steering column to body (especially French and Italian cars), gear lever to engine and to body (again especially French and Italian cars), Bowden cable to body, metal parcel shelf to body. When an offending component is located it should be bonded with the strap permanently.

(d) As a next step, the fitting of distributor suppressors to each lead at the distributor end may help.

(e) Beyond this point is involved the possible screening of the distributor and fitting resistive spark plugs, but such advanced treatment is not usually required for vehicles with entertainment equipment.

Electronic ignition systems have built-in suppression components, but this does not relieve the need for using suppressed HT leads. In some cases it is permitted to connect a capacitor on the low tension supply side of the ignition coil, but not in every case. Makers' instructions should be followed carefully, otherwise damage to the ignition semiconductors may result.

Suppression methods – generators

For older vehicles with dynamos a 1 microfarad capacitor from the D (larger) terminal to earth will usually cure dynamo whine. Alternators should be fitted with a 3 microfarad capacitor from the B+ main output terminal (thick cable) to earth. Additional suppression may be obtained by the use of a filter in the supply line to the radio receiver.

It is most important that:

(a) *Capacitors are never connected to the field terminals of either a dynamo or alternator.*

(b) *Alternators must not be run without connection to the battery.*

Suppression methods – voltage regulators

Voltage regulators used with DC dynamos should be suppressed by connecting a 1 microfarad capacitor from the control box D terminal to earth.

Alternator regulators come in three types:

(a) *Vibrating contact regulators separate from the alternator. Used extensively on continental vehicles.*

(b) *Electronic regulators separate from the alternator.*

(c) *Electronic regulators built-in to the alternator.*

In case (a) interference may be generated on the AM and FM (VHF) bands. For some cars a replacement suppressed regulator is available. Filter boxes may be used with non-suppressed regulators. But if not available, then for AM equipment a 2 microfarad or 3 microfarad capacitor may be mounted at the voltage terminal marked D+ or B+ of the regulator. FM bands may be treated by a feed-through capacitor of 2 or 3 microfarad.

Electronic voltage regulators are not always troublesome, but where necessary, a 1 microfarad capacitor from the regulator + terminal will help.

Integral electronic voltage regulators do not normally generate much interference, but when encountered this is in combination with alternator noise. A 1 microfarad or 2 microfarad capacitor from the warning lamp (IND) terminal to earth for Lucas ACR alternators and Femsa, Delco and Bosch equivalents should cure the problem.

Suppression methods – other equipment

Wiper motors – Connect the wiper body to earth with a bonding strap. For all motors use a 7 ampere choke assembly inserted in the leads to the motor.

Heater motors – Fit 7 ampere line chokes in both leads, assisted if necessary by a 1 microfarad capacitor to earth from both leads.

Electronic tachometer – The tachometer is a possible source of ignition noise – check by disconnecting at the ignition coil CB terminal. It usually feeds from ignition coil LT pulses at the contact breaker terminal. A 3 ampere line choke should be fitted in the tachometer lead at the coil CB terminal.

Horn – A capacitor and choke combination is effective if the horn is directly connected to the 12 volt supply. The use of a relay is an alternative remedy, as this will reduce the length of the interference-carrying leads.

Electrostatic noise – Characteristics are erratic crackling at the receiver, with disappearance of symptoms in wet weather. Often shocks may be given when touching bodywork. Part of the problem is the build-up of static electricity in non-driven wheels and the acquisition of charge on the body shell. It is possible to fit spring-loaded contacts at the wheels to give good conduction between the rotary wheel parts and the vehicle frame. Changing a tyre sometimes helps – because of tyres' varying resistances. In difficult cases a trailing flex which touches the ground will cure the problem. If this is not acceptable it is worth trying conductive paint on the tyre walls.

Fuel pump – Suppression requires a 1 microfarad capacitor between the supply wire to the pump and a nearby earth point. If this is insufficient a 7 ampere line choke connected in the supply wire near the pump is required.

Fluorescent tubes – Vehicles used for camping/caravanning frequently have fluorescent tube lighting. These tubes require a relatively high voltage for operation and this is provided by an inverter (a form of oscillator) which steps up the vehicle supply voltage. This can give rise to serious interference to radio reception, and the tubes themselves can contribute to this interference by the pulsating nature of the lamp discharge. In such situations it is important to mount the aerial as far away from a fluorescent tube as possible. The interference problem may be alleviated by screening the tube with fine wire turns spaced an inch (25 mm) apart and earthed to the chassis. Suitable chokes should be fitted in both supply wires close to the inverter.

Radio/cassette case breakthrough

Magnetic radiation from dashboard wiring may be sufficiently intense to break through the metal case of the radio/cassette player. Often this is due to a particular cable routed too close and shows up as ignition interference on AM and cassette play and/or alternator whine on cassette play.

The first point to check is that the clips and/or screws are fixing all parts of the radio/cassette case together properly. Assuming good earthing of the case, see if it is possible to re-route the offending cable – the chances of this are not good, however, in most cars.

Next release the radio/cassette player and locate it in different positions with temporary leads. If a point of low interference is found, then if possible fix the equipment in that area. This also confirms that local radiation is causing the trouble. If re-location is not feasible, fit the radio/cassette player back in the original position.

Alternator interference on cassette play is now caused by radiation from the main charging cable which goes from the battery to the output terminal of the alternator, usually via the + terminal of the starter motor relay. In some vehicles this cable is routed under the dashboard, so the solution is to provide a direct cable route. Detach the original cable from the alternator output terminal and make up a new cable of at least 6 mm² cross-sectional area to go from alternator to battery with the shortest possible route. *Remember – do not run the engine with the alternator disconnected from the battery.*

Ignition breakthrough on AM and/or cassette play can be a difficult problem. It is worth wrapping earthed foil round the offending cable run near the equipment, or making up a deflector plate well screwed down to a good earth. Another possibility is the use of a suitable relay to switch on the ignition coil. The relay should be mounted close to the ignition coil; with this arrangement the ignition coil primary current is not taken into the dashboard area and does not flow through the ignition switch. A suitable diode should be used since it is possible that at ignition switch-off the output from the warning lamp alternator terminal could hold the relay on.

Connectors for suppression components

Capacitors are usually supplied with tags on the end of the lead, while the capacitor body has a flange with a slot or hole to fit under a nut or screw with washer.

Connections to feed wires are best achieved by self-stripping connectors. These connectors employ a blade which, when squeezed down by pliers, cuts through cable insulation and makes connection to the copper conductors beneath.

Chokes sometimes come with bullet snap-in connectors fitted to the wires, and also with just bare copper wire. With connectors, suitable female cable connectors may be purchased from an auto-accessory shop together with any extra connectors required for the cable ends after being cut for the choke insertion. For chokes with bare wires, similar connectors may be employed together with insulation sleeving as required.

VHF/FM broadcasts

Reception of VHF/FM in an automobile is more prone to problems than the medium and long wavebands. Medium/long wave transmitters are capable of covering considerable distances, but VHF transmitters are restricted to line of sight, meaning ranges of 10 to 50 miles, depending upon the terrain, the effects of buildings and the transmitter power.

Because of the limited range it is necessary to retune on a long journey, and it may be better for those habitually travelling long distances or living in areas of poor provision of transmitters to use an AM radio working on medium/long wavebands.

When conditions are poor, interference can arise, and some of the suppression devices described previously fall off in performance at very high frequencies unless specifically designed for the VHF band. Available suppression devices include reactive HT cable, resistive distributor caps, screened plug caps, screened leads and resistive spark plugs.

For VHF/FM receiver installation the following points should be particularly noted:

(a) Earthing of the receiver chassis and the aerial mounting is important. Use a separate earthing wire at the radio, and scrape paint away at the aerial mounting.
(b) If possible, use a good quality roof aerial to obtain maximum height and distance from interference generating devices on the vehicle.
(c) Use of a high quality aerial downlead is important, since losses in cheap cable can be significant.
(d) The polarisation of FM transmissions may be horizontal, vertical, circular or slanted. Because of this the optimum mounting angle is at 45° to the vehicle roof.

Citizens' Band radio (CB)

In the UK, CB transmitter/receivers work within the 27 MHz and 934 MHz bands, using the FM mode. At present interest is concentrated on 27 MHz where the design and manufacture of equipment is less difficult. Maximum transmitted power is 4 watts, and 40 channels spaced 10 kHz apart within the range 27.60125 to 27.99125 MHz are available.

Aerials are the key to effective transmission and reception. Regulations limit the aerial length to 1.65 metres including the loading coil and any associated circuitry, so tuning the aerial is necessary to obtain optimum results. The choice of a CB aerial is dependent on whether it is to be permanently installed or removable, and the performance will hinge on correct tuning and the location point on the vehicle. Common practice is to clip the aerial to the roof gutter or to employ wing mounting where the aerial can be rapidly unscrewed. An alternative is to use the boot rim to render the aerial theftproof, but a popular solution is to use the 'magmount' – a type of mounting having a strong magnetic base clamping to the vehicle at any point, usually the roof.

Aerial location determines the signal distribution for both transmission and reception, but it is wise to choose a point away from the engine compartment to minimise interference from vehicle electrical equipment.

The aerial is subject to considerable wind and acceleration forces. Cheaper units will whip backwards and forwards and in so doing will alter the relationship with the metal surface of the vehicle with which it forms a ground plane aerial system. The radiation pattern will change correspondingly, giving rise to break-up of both incoming and outgoing signals.

Interference problems on the vehicle carrying CB equipment fall into two categories:

(a) Interference to nearby TV and radio receivers when transmitting.
(b) Interference to CB set reception due to electrical equipment on the vehicle.

Problems of break-through to TV and radio are not frequent, but can be difficult to solve. Mostly trouble is not detected or reported because the vehicle is moving and the symptoms rapidly disappear at the TV/radio receiver, but when the CB set is used as a base station any trouble with nearby receivers will soon result in a complaint.

It must not be assumed by the CB operator that his equipment is faultless, for much depends upon the design. Harmonics (that is, multiples) of 27 MHz may be transmitted unknowingly and these can fall into other user's bands. Where trouble of this nature occurs, low pass filters in the aerial or supply leads can help, and should be fitted in base station aerials as a matter of course. In stubborn cases it may be necessary to call for assistance from the licensing authority, or, if possible, to have the equipment checked by the manufacturers.

Interference received on the CB set from the vehicle equipment is, fortunately, not usually a severe problem. The precautions outlined previously for radio/cassette units apply, but there are some extra points worth noting.

It is common practice to use a slide-mount on CB equipment enabling the set to be easily removed for use as a base station, for example. Care must be taken that the slide mount fittings are properly earthed and that first class connection occurs between the set and slide-mount.

Vehicle manufacturers in the UK are required to provide suppression of electrical equipment to cover 40 to 250 MHz to protect TV and VHF radio bands. Such suppression appears to be adequately effective at 27 MHz, but suppression of individual items such as alternators/dynamos, clocks, stabilisers, flashers, wiper motors, etc, may still be necessary. The suppression capacitors and chokes available from auto-electrical suppliers for entertainment receivers will usually give the required results with CB equipment.

Other vehicle radio transmitters

Besides CB radio already mentioned, a considerable increase in the use of transceivers (ie combined transmitter and receiver units) has taken place in the last decade. Previously this type of equipment was fitted mainly to military, fire, ambulance and police vehicles, but a large business radio and radio telephone usage has developed.

Generally the suppression techniques described previously will suffice, with only a few difficult cases arising. Suppression is carried out to satisfy the 'receive mode', but care must be taken to use heavy duty chokes in the equipment supply cables since the loading on 'transmit' is relatively high.

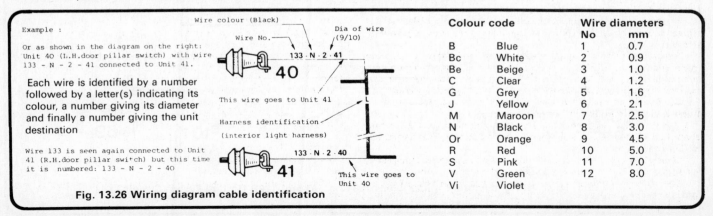

Example :

Or as shown in the diagram on the right:
Unit 40 (L.H.door pillar switch) with wire
133 - N - 2 - 41 connected to Unit 41.

Each wire is identified by a number followed by a letter(s) indicating its colour, a number giving its diameter and finally a number giving the unit destination

Wire 133 is seen again connected to Unit 41 (R.H.door pillar switch) but this time it is numbered: 133 - N - 2 - 40

Wire colour (Black)
Wire No.—
Dia of wire (9/10)
133 - N - 2 - 41
This wire goes to Unit 41
Harness identification
(interior light harness)
133 - N - 2 - 40
This wire goes to Unit 40

Colour code		Wire diameters	
		No	mm
B	Blue	1	0.7
Bc	White	2	0.9
Be	Beige	3	1.0
C	Clear	4	1.2
G	Grey	5	1.6
J	Yellow	6	2.1
M	Maroon	7	2.5
N	Black	8	3.0
Or	Orange	9	4.5
R	Red	10	5.0
S	Pink	11	7.0
V	Green	12	8.0
Vi	Violet		

Fig. 13.26 Wiring diagram cable identification

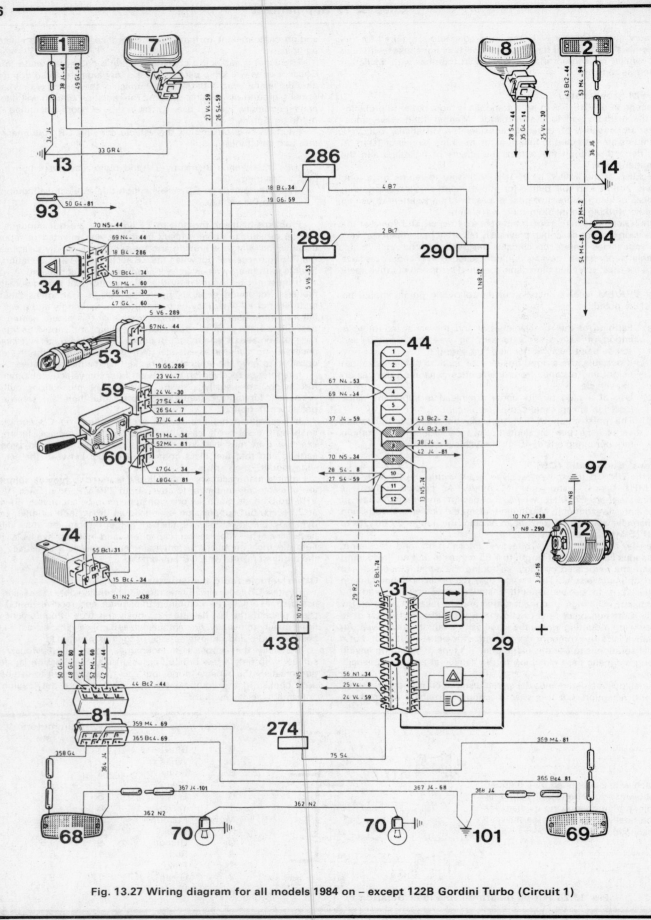

Fig. 13.27 Wiring diagram for all models 1984 on – except 122B Gordini Turbo (Circuit 1)

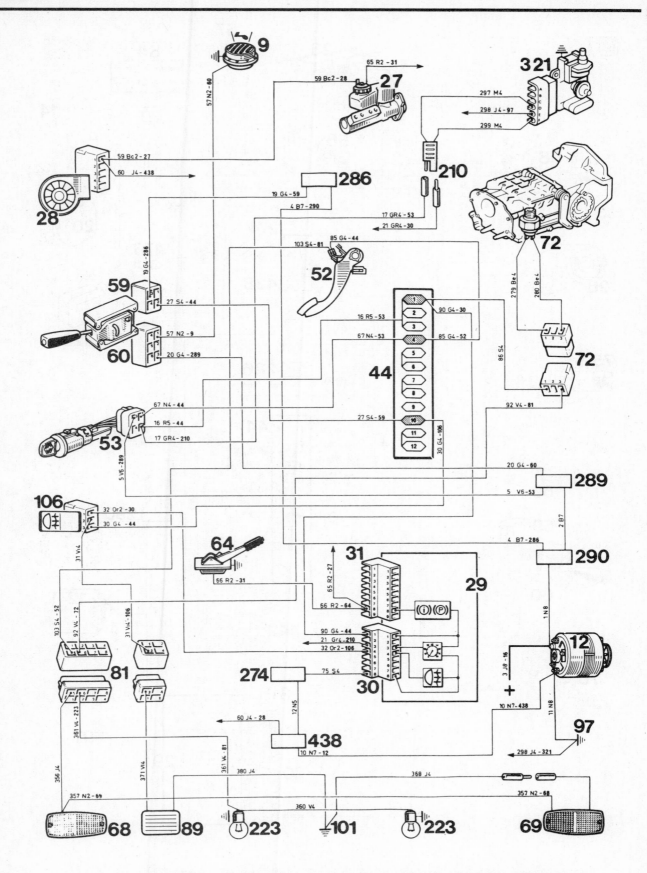

Fig. 13.27 Wiring diagram for all models 1984 on – except 122B Gordini Turbo (Circuit 2)

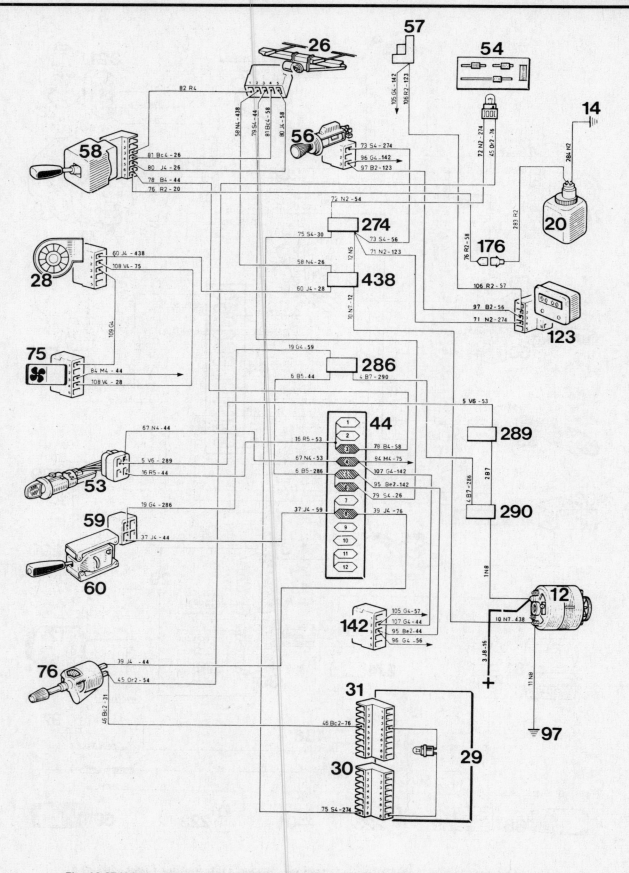

Fig. 13.27 Wiring diagram for all models 1984 on – except 122B Gordini Turbo (Circuit 3)

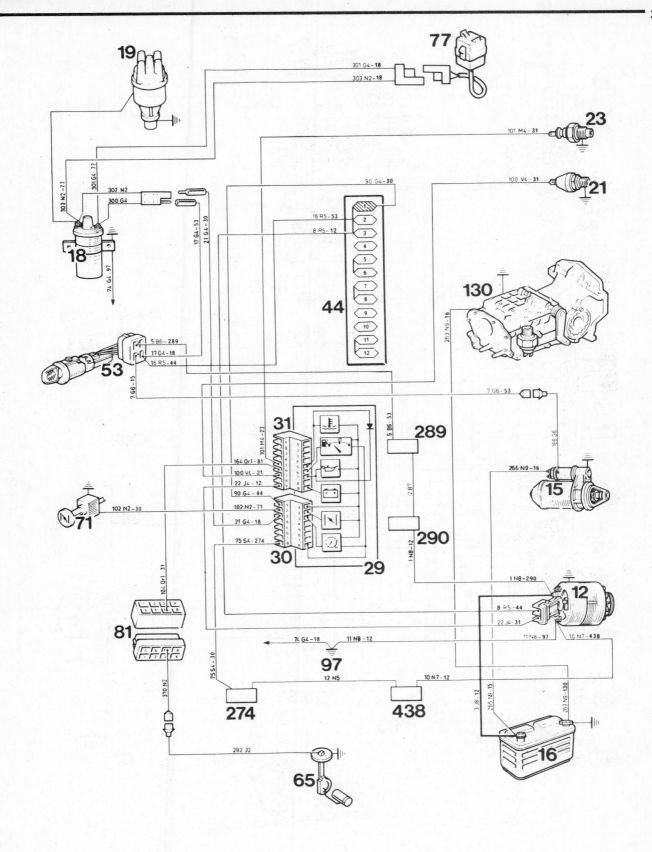

Fig. 13.27 Wiring diagram for all models 1984 on – except 122B Gordini Turbo (Circuit 4)

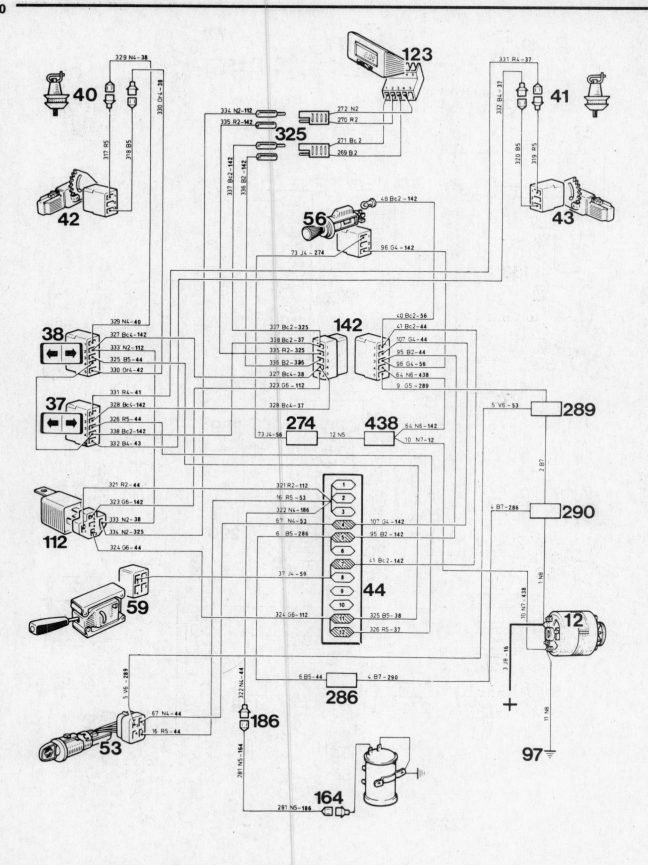

Fig. 13.27 Wiring diagram for all models 1984 on – except 122B Gordini Turbo (Circuit 5)

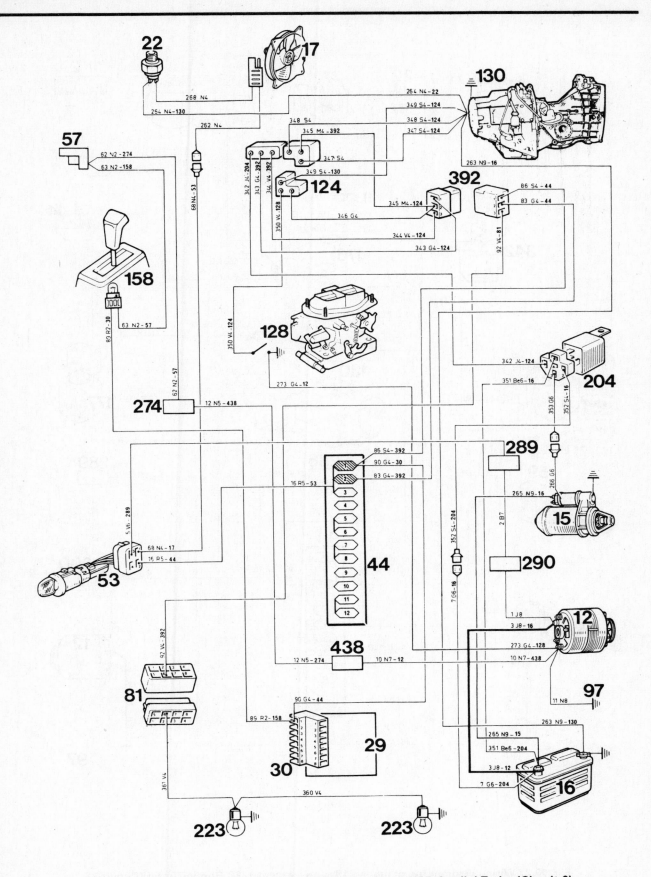

Fig. 13.27 Wiring diagram for all models 1984 on – except 122B Gordini Turbo (Circuit 6)

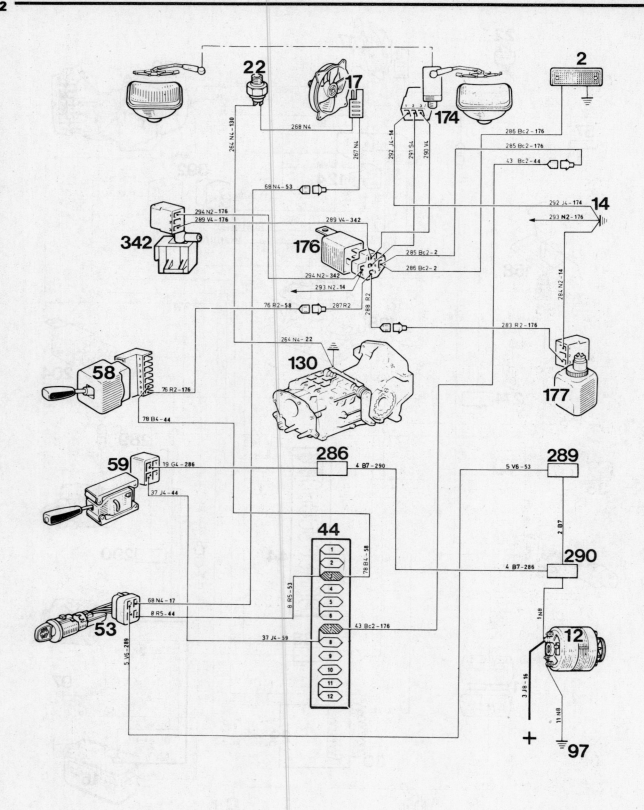

Fig. 13.27 Wiring diagram for all models 1984 on – except 122B Gordini Turbo (Circuit 7)

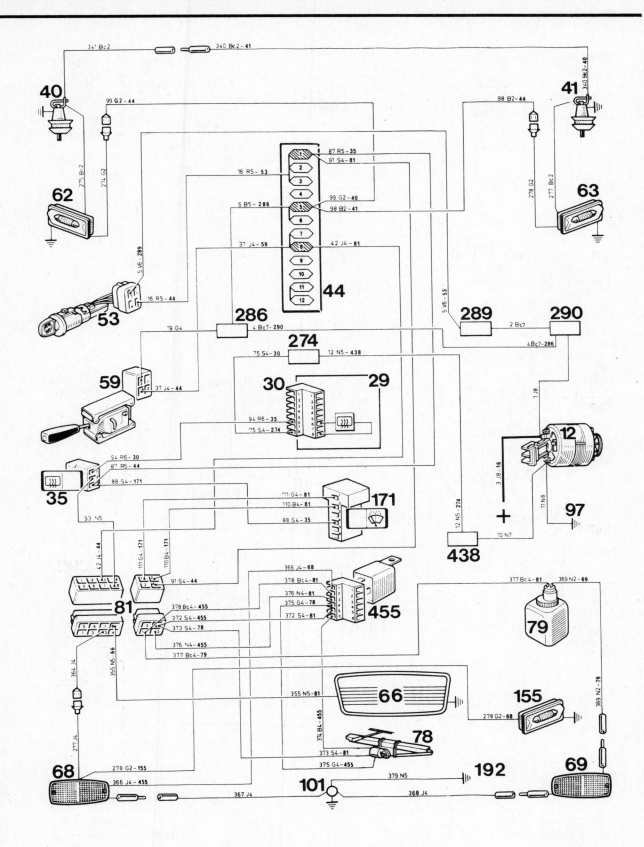

Fig. 13.27 Wiring diagram for all models 1984 on – except 122B Gordini Turbo (Circuit 8)

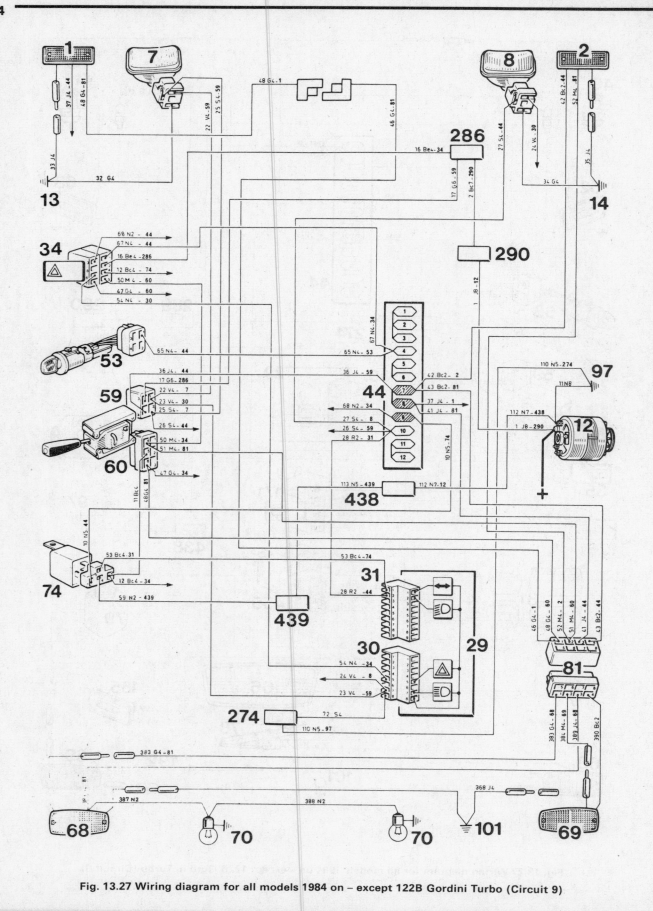

Fig. 13.27 Wiring diagram for all models 1984 on – except 122B Gordini Turbo (Circuit 9)

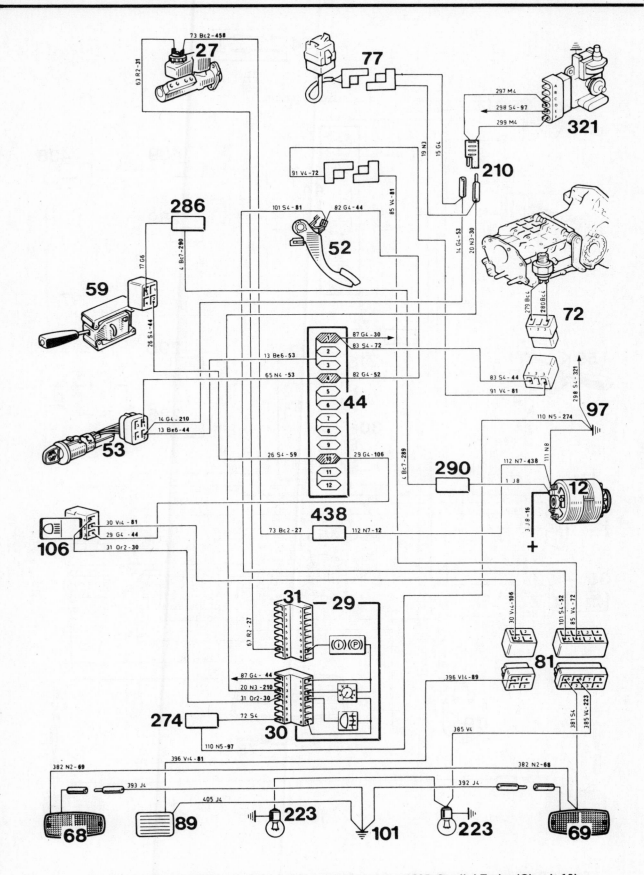

Fig. 13.27 Wiring diagram for all models 1984 on – except 122B Gordini Turbo (Circuit 10)

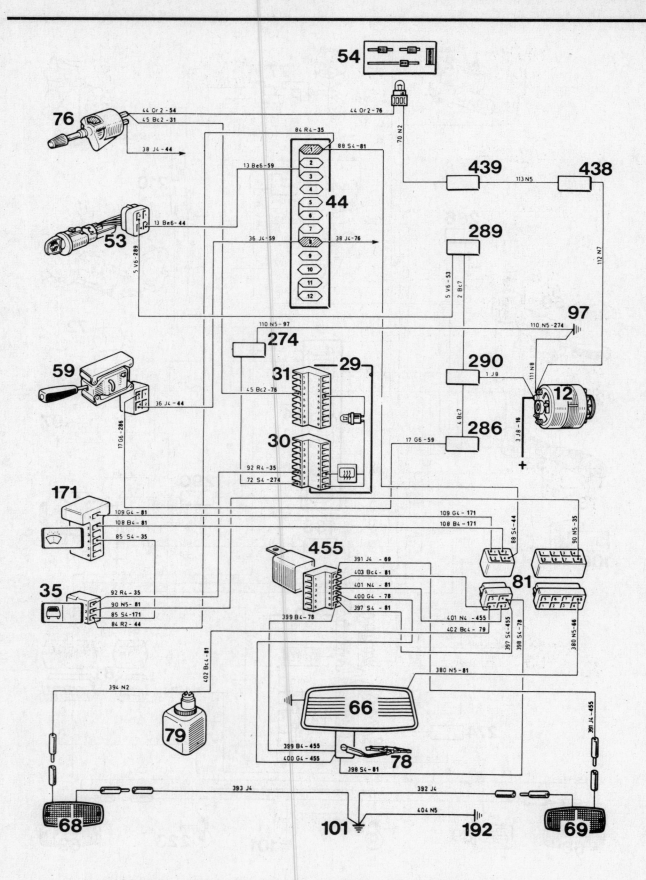

Fig. 13.27 Wiring diagram for all models 1984 on – except 122B Gordini Turbo (Circuit 11)

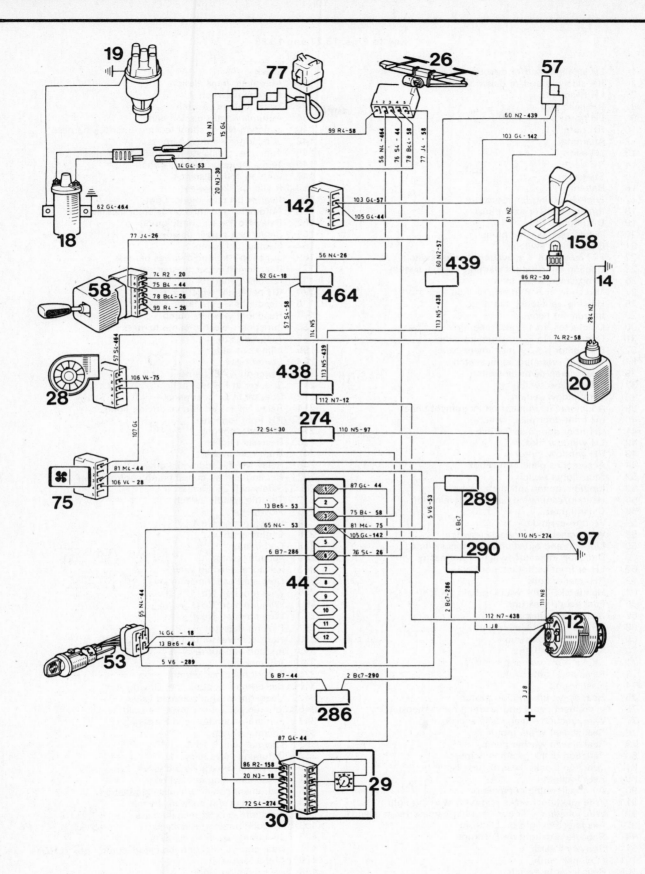

Fig. 13.27 Wiring diagram for all models 1984 on – except 122B Gordini Turbo (Circuit 12)

Key to Figs. 13.27 and 13.28

1	LH sidelight and/or direction indicator	123	Clock
2	RH sidelight and/or direction indicator	124	Automatic transmission
7	LH headlight	128	Kickdown switch
8	RH headlight	129	Front foglights switch
9	LH horn	130	Automatic transmission earth
10	RH horn	140	Junction No 1 – door locking/interlock harness
12	Alternator	142	Junction – window harness
13	LH earth	145	Junction – transistorized ignition harness
14	RH earth	146	Temperature or thermal switch
15	Starter	147	Ignition coil resistance
16	Battery	153	Radio speaker wires
17	Engine cooling fan motor	155	Rear or LH rear interior light
18	Ignition coil (or mounting)	158	Automatic transmission selector illumination
19	Distributor	162	Relay No 1 – air conditioning
20	Windscreen washer pump	163	Safety belt buzzer timer relay
21	Oil pressure switch	164	Electric fuel pump
22	Fan motor No 1 activating thermal switch	169	Junction – solenoid valves harness
23	Cooling temperature warning thermal switch	171	Rear screen wiper/washer switch
26	Windscreen wiper motor	172	Impulse generator
27	Nivocode or ICP (pressure drop indicator)	174	RH headlight wiper motor
28	Heating-ventilating fan motor	176	Headlight wipers timer relay
29	Instrument panel	177	Headlight washers pump
30	Connector No 1 – instrument panel	186	Junction – electric pump harness
31	Connector No 2 – instrument panel	192	Tailgate earth
32	Connector No 3 – instrument panel	195	Idling cut-out
34	"Hazard" warning lights switch	204	Starter relay
35	Rear screen demister switch	210	Junction – AEI harness
37	LH window switch	211	Speaker in RH rear panel
38	RH window switch	212	Speaker in LH rear panel
39	Additional instrument on instrument panel	214	Relay No 1 – additional driving lights
40	LH front door pillar switch	215	RH front foglight
41	RH front door pillar switch	216	LH front foglight
42	LH window motor	223	Reversing lights
43	RH window motor	241	Horn compressor
44	Accessories plate or fusebox	248	Relay No 2 – additional driving lights
52	Stop-lights switch	262	Heating and air conditioning control panel
53	Ignition-starter-anti-theft switch	266	Safety belt centre stalk
54	Heating/ventilating controls illumination	272	Throttle spindle switch
56	Cigar lighter	273	Flowmeter
57	Feed to car radio	274	Wire junction No 1
58	Windscreen wiper/washer switch	276	Engine earth
59	Lighting and direction indicators switch	278	Carburettor
60	Direction indicator switch or connector	280	Vacuum switch
62	LH or front centre interior light	283	Advance solenoid valve
63	RH interior light	285	Cold start enrichment relay
64	Handbrake "On" warning light switch	286	Wire junction No 2
65	Fuel gauge tank unit	289	Wire junction No 3
66	Rear screen demister	290	Wire junction No 4
68	LH rear light assembly	291	Pinking detector
69	RH rear light assembly	296	Horn compressor relay
70	Number plate lights	319	Ignition cut-out relay
71	Choke "On" warning light	321	AEI module
72	Reversing lights switch	325	Junction – clock wiring
74	Flasher unit	340	Car-borne computer for "Driving Aid"
75	Heating-ventilating fan switch	342	Headlight washer solenoid valve
76	Instrument panel and warning lights rheostat	346	Ignition coil relay ("Extreme Cold")
77	Wire junction – diagnostic socket	347	Junction – ignition coil harness
78	Rear screen wiper motor	351	Thermal switch
79	Rear screen washer pump	353	Thermal switch 15°C
80	Junction block – engine harness	358	Defuming valve relay
81	Junction block – rear harness No 1	359	Recycling valve solenoid valve
89	Rear foglight	361	Air conditioning control box
90	Air conditioning compressor	366	Instrument panel switches illumination
91	Wire junction – brake pad wear warning light	383	Ignition cut-out pressure switch
92	Wire junction – air conditioning harness (engine end)	392	Junction – starter relay harness
93	Repeater sidelight on LH front	403	Air conditioning resistances
94	Repeater sidelight on RH front	407	Junction – speakers harness
97	Bodyshell earth	411	Dual control direction indicators control box (LHD)
101	Fuel tank earth	416	Anti-knock relay
106	Rear foglight switch	438	Wire junction No 5
110	Engine cooling fan motor relay	439	Wire junction No 6
112	Windows relay	440	Wire junction No 7
114	Windscreen wiper timer relay	441	Wire junction No 8

Key to Figs. 13.27 and 13.28 (continued)

452	Solenoid valve relay		464	Wire junction No 11
455	Rear screen wiper timer relay		468	Junction – daylight side and tail lights
456	Junction – engine cooling fan harness		469	Lighting switch
459	Anti-pollution solenoid valve		470	Junction – heated seat wiring
460	Wire junction No 9		471	Driver's heated seat resistances
461	Wire junction No 10		486	Earth cut off relay (daylight side and tail lights)
463	Lighting relay			

Not all items are fitted to all models

Key to circuits in Fig. 13.27

	Circuit				Circuit	
	All models	Automatic transmission			All models	Automatic transmission
AEI (integral electronic ignition)	10			Ignition (conventional)	11	
Charging circuit	4	6		Instrument panel lights	11	3
Choke	4			Nivocode	10	
Cigar lighter	5	5		Oil pressure switch	4	4
Clock – dashboard	3			Radio feed	12	6
Clock – digital	5			Rear foglight	19	
Cooling fan motor	7	6		Rear interior light	8	
Direction indicators	9	1		Rear screen demister	11	
Fuel gauge	4			Rear screen wiper	11	
Front interior lights	8			Reversing lights	10	6
Fuel pump	5			Selector illumination	12	
Handbrake	2			Sidelights	9	
Headlight – dipped beam	9			Starter	4	6
Headlight – main beam	9			Stop-lights	10	
Headlight wipers	7			Thermal or coolant temperature switch	4	4
Headlight wipers solenoid valve	7			Window winders	5	
Heating/ventilating	12			Windscreen washer	12	
Heating/ventilating control lights	11	3		Windscreen wiper	12	
Horn	2					

Not all circuits apply to all models

Key to circuits in Fig. 13.28

	Circuit			Circuit
AEI ignition	4, 10, 12		Horn	2, 8
Charging circuit	4		Instrument panel lighting	3
Choke "On" warning light	4		Nivocode	2, 8
Cigar lighter	3, 9		Oil pressure switch	4, 11
Coolant temperature switch	4, 11		Radio feed	5
Cooling fan motor	4, 9		Rear foglight	2, 8, 11
Digital clock	3, 9		Rear number plate lights	1, 7
Direction indicators	1, 7		Rear screen demister	5
Front foglight	2, 8, 11		Rear screen wiper/washer	5
Front interior lights	6, 10		Reversing lights	2, 8
Fuel gauge	4		Sidelights	1, 7
Handbrake	2		Starter	4
Headlight – dipped beams	1, 7		Stop-lights	2, 8
Headlight – main beams	1, 7		Window winders	5
Heater control panel illumination	3		Windscreen wiper/washer	3, 9
Heating-ventilating	3, 9			

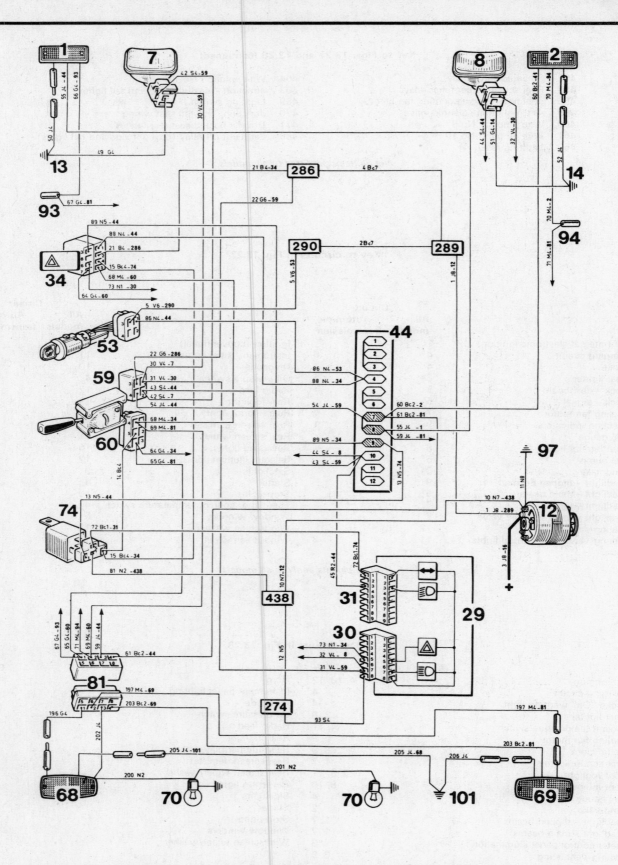

Fig. 13.28 Wiring diagram for 122B Gordini Turbo models – 1984 on (Circuit 1)

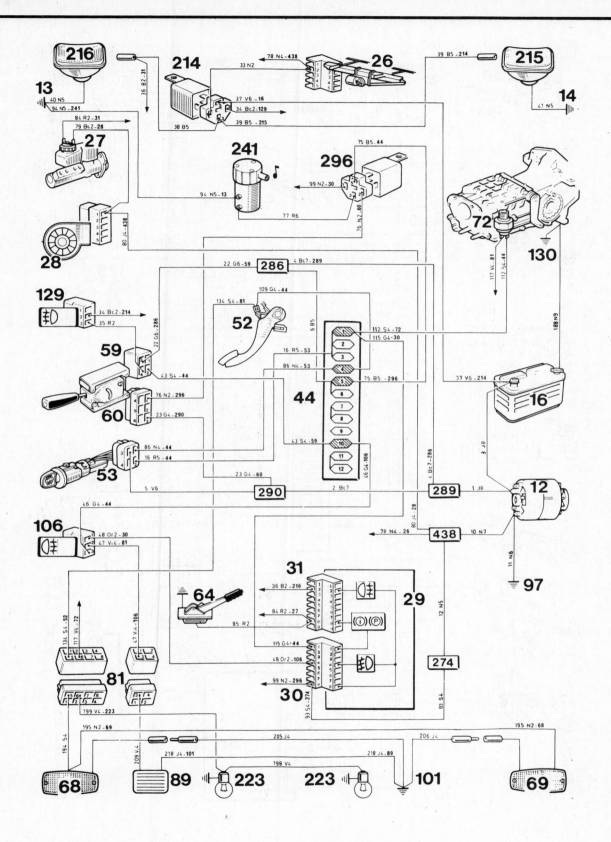

Fig. 13.28 Wiring diagram for 122B Gordini Turbo models – 1984 on (Circuit 2)

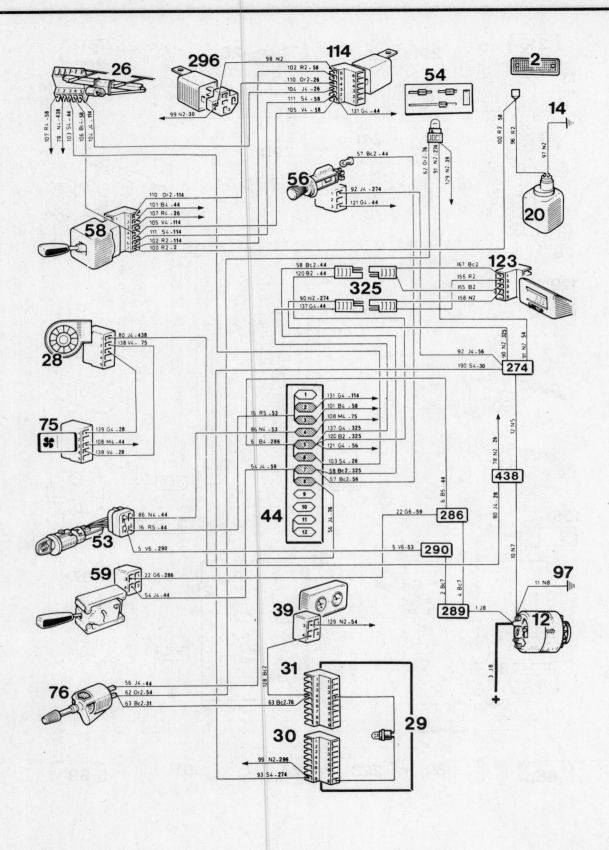

Fig. 13.28 Wiring diagram for 122B Gordini Turbo models – 1984 on (Circuit 3)

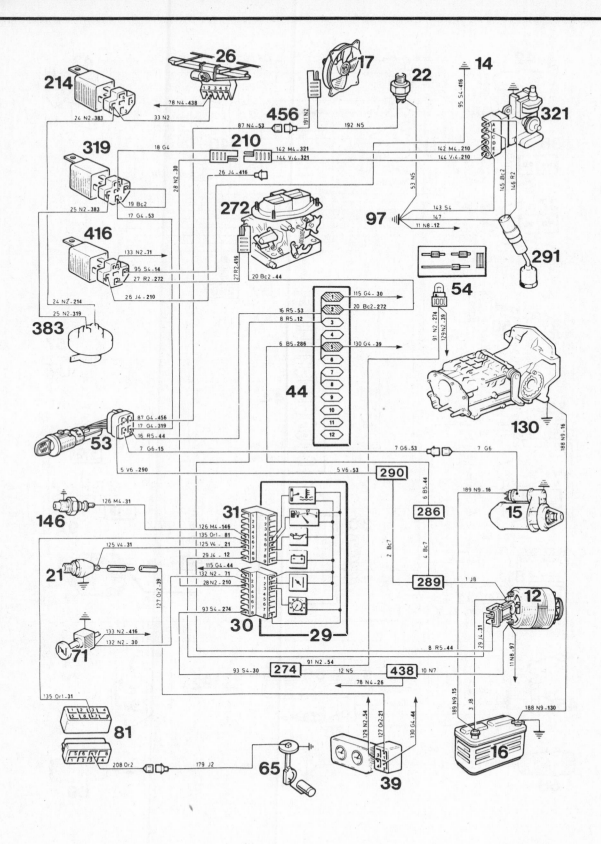

Fig. 13.28 Wiring diagram for 122B Gordini Turbo models – 1984 on (Circuit 4)

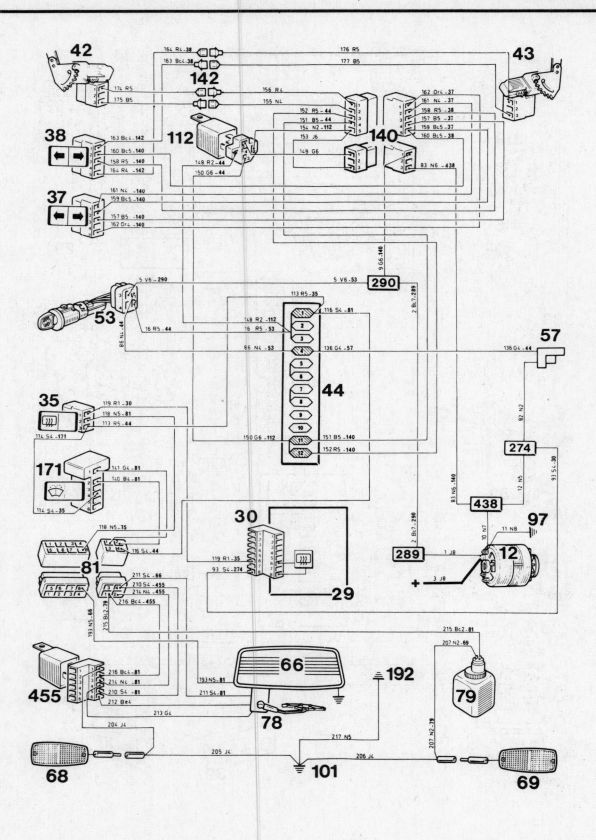

Fig. 13.28 Wiring diagram for 122B Gordini Turbo models – 1984 on (Circuit 5)

415

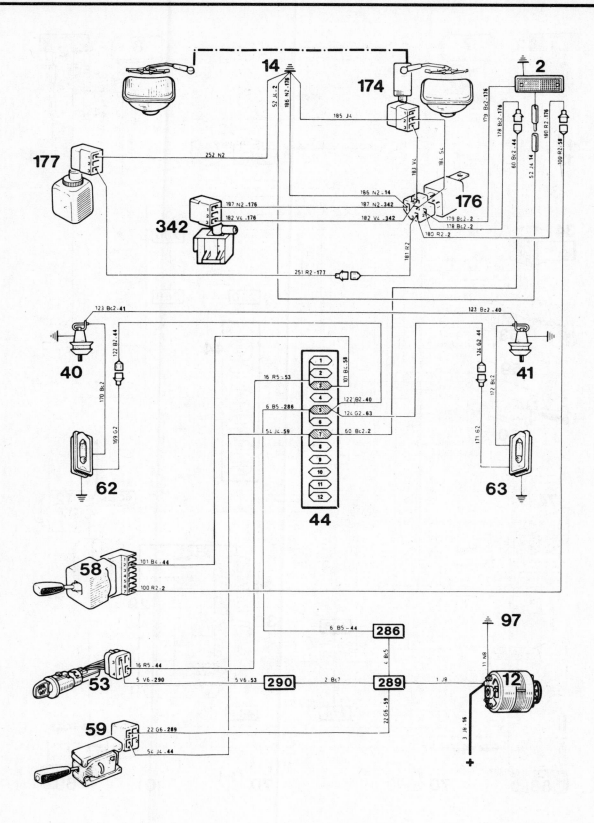

Fig. 13.28 Wiring diagram for 122B Gordini Turbo models – 1984 on (Circuit 6)

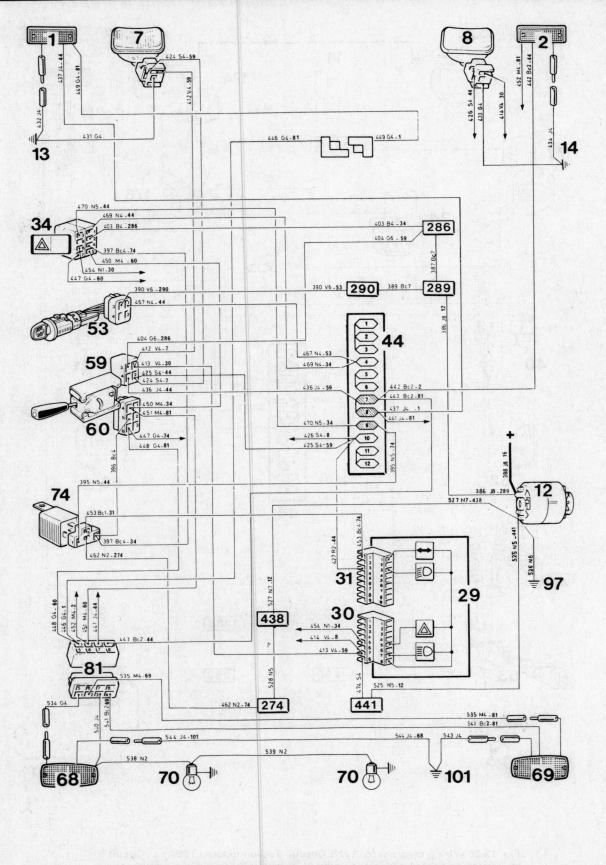

Fig. 13.28 Wiring diagram for 122B Gordini Turbo models – 1984 on (Circuit 7)

417

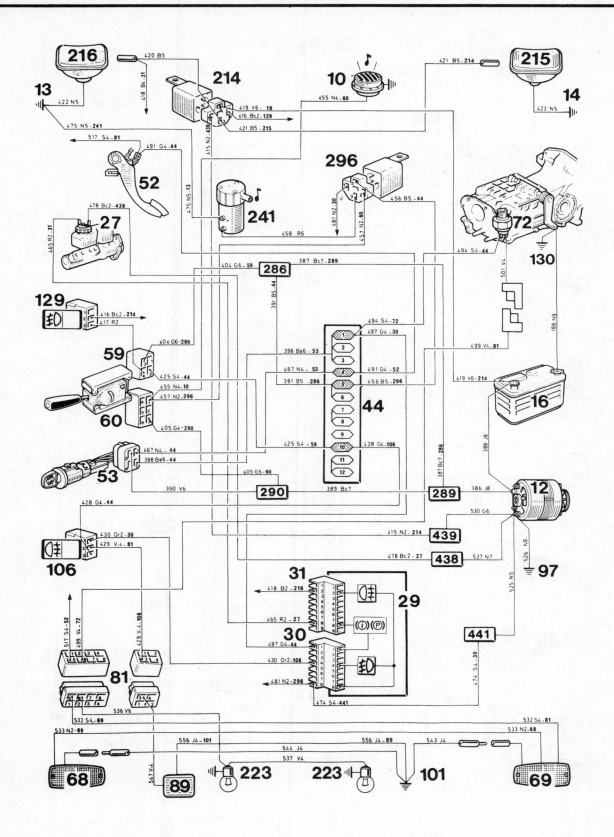

Fig. 13.28 Wiring diagram for 122B Gordini Turbo models – 1984 on (Circuit 8)

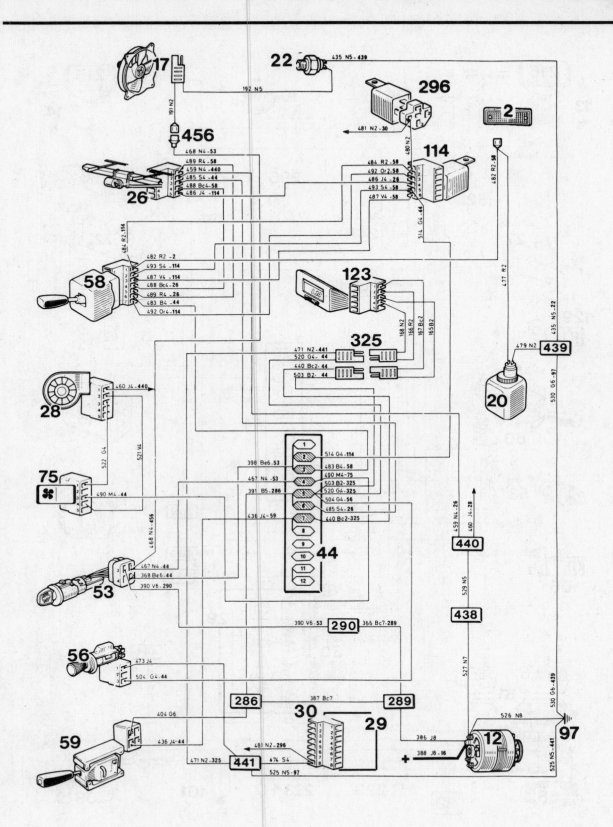

Fig. 13.28 Wiring diagram for 122B Gordini Turbo models – 1984 on (Circuit 9)

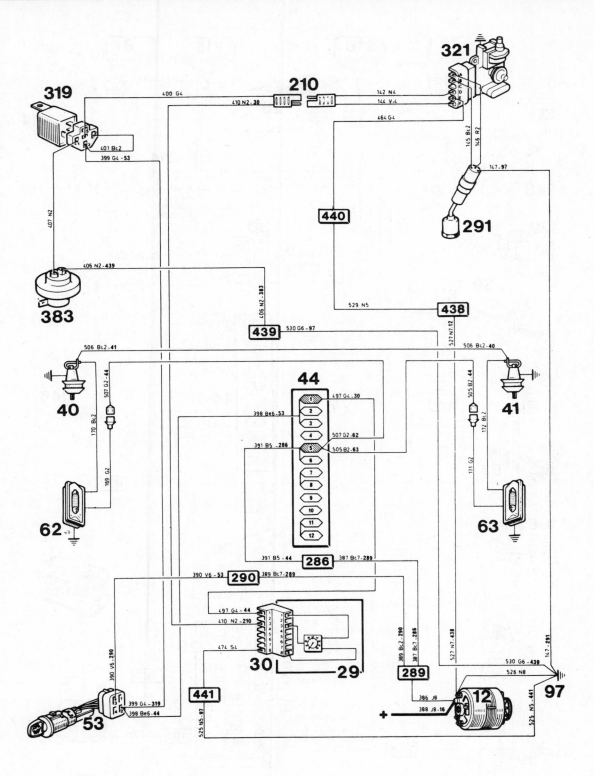

Fig. 13.28 Wiring diagram for 122B Gordini Turbo models – 1984 on (Circuit 10)

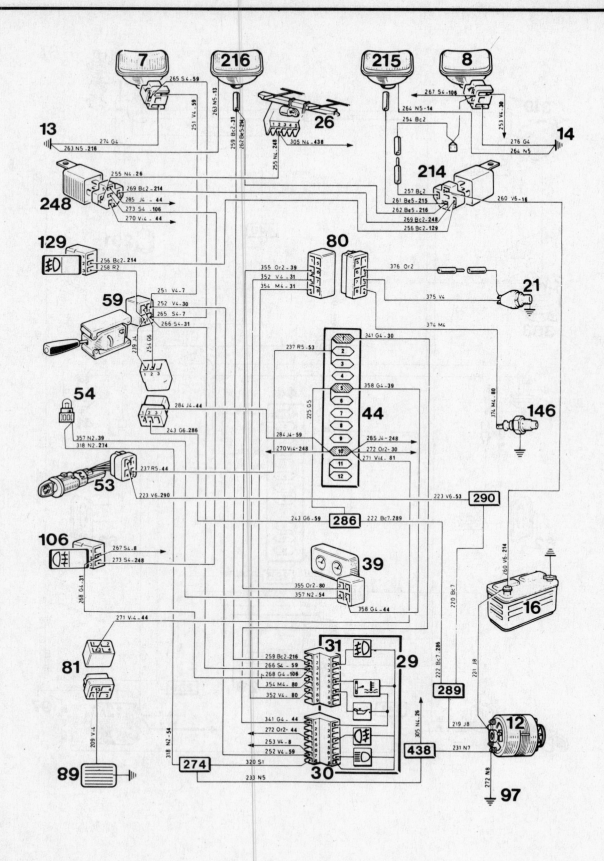

Fig. 13.28 Wiring diagram for 122B Gordini Turbo models – 1984 on (Circuit 11)

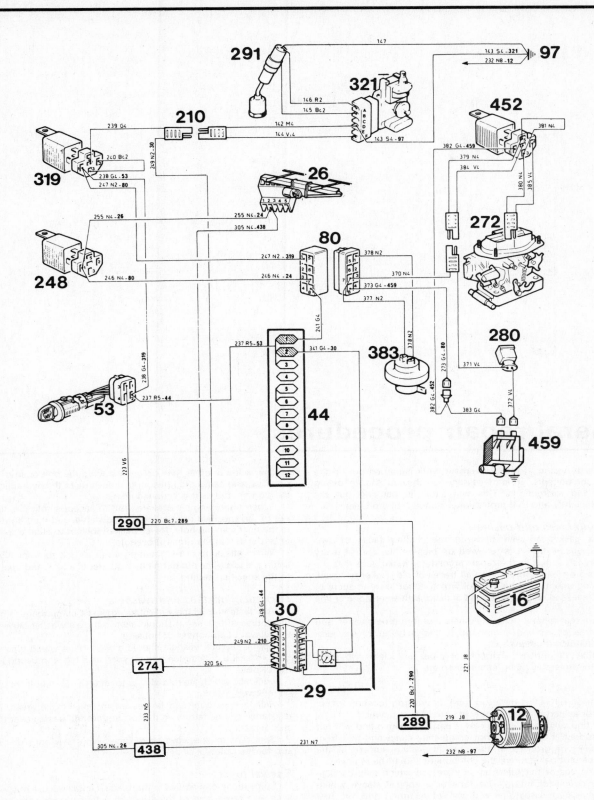

Fig. 13.28 Wiring diagram for 122B Gordini Turbo models – 1984 on (Circuit 12)

General repair procedures

Whenever servicing, repair or overhaul work is carried out on the car or its components, it is necessary to observe the following procedures and instructions. This will assist in carrying out the operation efficiently and to a professional standard of workmanship.

Joint mating faces and gaskets

Where a gasket is used between the mating faces of two components, ensure that it is renewed on reassembly, and fit it dry unless otherwise stated in the repair procedure. Make sure that the mating faces are clean and dry with all traces of old gasket removed. When cleaning a joint face, use a tool which is not likely to score or damage the face, and remove any burrs or nicks with an oilstone or fine file.

Make sure that tapped holes are cleaned with a pipe cleaner, and keep them free of jointing compound if this is being used unless specifically instructed otherwise.

Ensure that all orifices, channels or pipes are clear and blow through them, preferably using compressed air.

Oil seals

Whenever an oil seal is removed from its working location, either individually or as part of an assembly, it should be renewed.

The very fine sealing lip of the seal is easily damaged and will not seal if the surface it contacts is not completely clean and free from scratches, nicks or grooves. If the original sealing surface of the component cannot be restored, the component should be renewed.

Protect the lips of the seal from any surface which may damage them in the course of fitting. Use tape or a conical sleeve where possible. Lubricate the seal lips with oil before fitting and, on dual lipped seals, fill the space between the lips with grease.

Unless otherwise stated, oil seals must be fitted with their sealing lips toward the lubricant to be sealed.

Use a tubular drift or block of wood of the appropriate size to install the seal and, if the seal housing is shouldered, drive the seal down to the shoulder. If the seal housing is unshouldered, the seal should be fitted with its face flush with the housing top face.

Screw threads and fastenings

Always ensure that a blind tapped hole is completely free from oil,

grease, water or other fluid before installing the bolt or stud. Failure to do this could cause the housing to crack due to the hydraulic action of the bolt or stud as it is screwed in.

When tightening a castellated nut to accept a split pin, tighten the nut to the specified torque, where applicable, and then tighten further to the next split pin hole. Never slacken the nut to align a split pin hole unless stated in the repair procedure.

When checking or retightening a nut or bolt to a specified torque setting, slacken the nut or bolt by a quarter of a turn, and then retighten to the specified setting.

Locknuts, locktabs and washers

Any fastening which will rotate against a component or housing in the course of tightening should always have a washer between it and the relevant component or housing.

Spring or split washers should always be renewed when they are used to lock a critical component such as a big-end bearing retaining nut or bolt.

Locktabs which are folded over to retain a nut or bolt should always be renewed.

Self-locking nuts can be reused in non-critical areas, providing resistance can be felt when the locking portion passes over the bolt or stud thread.

Split pins must always be replaced with new ones of the correct size for the hole.

Special tools

Some repair procedures in this manual entail the use of special tools such as a press, two or three-legged pullers, spring compressors etc. Wherever possible, suitable readily available alternatives to the manufacturer's special tools are described, and are shown in use. In some instances, where no alternative is possible, it has been necessary to resort to the use of a manufacturer's tool and this has been done for reasons of safety as well as the efficient completion of the repair operation. Unless you are highly skilled and have a thorough understanding of the procedure described, never attempt to bypass the use of any special tool when the procedure described specifies its use. Not only is there a very great risk of personal injury, but expensive damage could be caused to the components involved.

Conversion factors

Length (distance)

Inches (in)	X	25.4	= Millimetres (mm)	X	0.0394	= Inches (in)
Feet (ft)	X	0.305	= Metres (m)	X	3.281	= Feet (ft)
Miles	X	1.609	= Kilometres (km)	X	0.621	= Miles

Volume (capacity)

Cubic inches (cu in; in³)	X	16.387	= Cubic centimetres (cc; cm³)	X	0.061	= Cubic inches (cu in; in³)
Imperial pints (Imp pt)	X	0.568	= Litres (l)	X	1.76	= Imperial pints (Imp pt)
Imperial quarts (Imp qt)	X	1.137	= Litres (l)	X	0.88	= Imperial quarts (Imp qt)
Imperial quarts (Imp qt)	X	1.201	= US quarts (US qt)	X	0.833	= Imperial quarts (Imp qt)
US quarts (US qt)	X	0.946	= Litres (l)	X	1.057	= US quarts (US qt)
Imperial gallons (Imp gal)	X	4.546	= Litres (l)	X	0.22	= Imperial gallons (Imp gal)
Imperial gallons (Imp gal)	X	1.201	= US gallons (US gal)	X	0.833	= Imperial gallons (Imp gal)
US gallons (US gal)	X	3.785	= Litres (l)	X	0.264	= US gallons (US gal)

Mass (weight)

Ounces (oz)	X	28.35	= Grams (g)	X	0.035	= Ounces (oz)
Pounds (lb)	X	0.454	= Kilograms (kg)	X	2.205	= Pounds (lb)

Force

Ounces-force (ozf; oz)	X	0.278	= Newtons (N)	X	3.6	= Ounces-force (ozf; oz)
Pounds-force (lbf; lb)	X	4.448	= Newtons (N)	X	0.225	= Pounds-force (lbf; lb)
Newtons (N)	X	0.1	= Kilograms-force (kgf; kg)	X	9.81	= Newtons (N)

Pressure

Pounds-force per square inch (psi; lbf/in²; lb/in²)	X	0.070	= Kilograms-force per square centimetre (kgf/cm²; kg/cm²)	X	14.223	= Pounds-force per square inch (psi; lbf/in²; lb/in²)
Pounds-force per square inch (psi; lbf/in²; lb/in²)	X	0.068	= Atmospheres (atm)	X	14.696	= Pounds-force per square inch (psi; lbf/in²; lb/in²)
Pounds-force per square inch (psi; lbf/in²; lb/in²)	X	0.069	= Bars	X	14.5	= Pounds-force per square inch (psi; lbf/in²; lb/in²)
Pounds-force per square inch (psi; lbf/in²; lb/in²)	X	6.895	= Kilopascals (kPa)	X	0.145	= Pounds-force per square inch (psi; lbf/in²; lb/in²)
Kilopascals (kPa)	X	0.01	= Kilograms-force per square centimetre (kgf/cm²; kg/cm²)	X	98.1	= Kilopascals (kPa)
Millibar (mbar)	X	100	= Pascals (Pa)	X	0.01	= Millibar (mbar)
Millibar (mbar)	X	0.0145	= Pounds-force per square inch (psi; lbf/in²; lb/in²)	X	68.947	= Millibar (mbar)
Millibar (mbar)	X	0.75	= Millimetres of mercury (mmHg)	X	1.333	= Millibar (mbar)
Millibar (mbar)	X	0.401	= Inches of water (inH₂O)	X	2.491	= Millibar (mbar)
Millimetres of mercury (mmHg)	X	0.535	= Inches of water (inH₂O)	X	1.868	= Millimetres of mercury (mmHg)
Inches of water (inH₂O)	X	0.036	= Pounds-force per square inch (psi; lbf/in²; lb/in²)	X	27.68	= Inches of water (inH₂O)

Torque (moment of force)

Pounds-force inches (lbf in; lb in)	X	1.152	= Kilograms-force centimetre (kgf cm; kg cm)	X	0.868	= Pounds-force inches (lbf in; lb in)
Pounds-force inches (lbf in; lb in)	X	0.113	= Newton metres (Nm)	X	8.85	= Pounds-force inches (lbf in; lb in)
Pounds-force inches (lbf in; lb in)	X	0.083	= Pounds-force feet (lbf ft; lb ft)	X	12	= Pounds-force inches (lbf in; lb in)
Pounds-force feet (lbf ft; lb ft)	X	0.138	= Kilograms-force metres (kgf m; kg m)	X	7.233	= Pounds-force feet (lbf ft; lb ft)
Pounds-force feet (lbf ft; lb ft)	X	1.356	= Newton metres (Nm)	X	0.738	= Pounds-force feet (lbf ft; lb ft)
Newton metres (Nm)	X	0.102	= Kilograms-force metres (kgf m; kg m)	X	9.804	= Newton metres (Nm)

Power

Horsepower (hp)	X	745.7	= Watts (W)	X	0.0013	= Horsepower (hp)

Velocity (speed)

Miles per hour (miles/hr; mph)	X	1.609	= Kilometres per hour (km/hr; kph)	X	0.621	= Miles per hour (miles/hr; mph)

Fuel consumption*

Miles per gallon, Imperial (mpg)	X	0.354	= Kilometres per litre (km/l)	X	2.825	= Miles per gallon, Imperial (mpg)
Miles per gallon, US (mpg)	X	0.425	= Kilometres per litre (km/l)	X	2.352	= Miles per gallon, US (mpg)

Temperature

Degrees Fahrenheit = (°C x 1.8) + 32

Degrees Celsius (Degrees Centigrade; °C) = (°F - 32) x 0.56

*It is common practice to convert from miles per gallon (mpg) to litres/100 kilometres (l/100km), where mpg (Imperial) x l/100 km = 282 and mpg (US) x l/100 km = 235

Index